THE
ILLUSTRATED ENCYCLOPEDIA
OF
WORLD CRICKET

THE
ILLUSTRATED ENCYCLOPEDIA
OF
WORLD CRICKET

Peter Arnold

WHSMITH

EXCLUSIVE
· BOOKS ·

David Gower

Produced exclusively for W. H. Smith & Son Limited by
Marshall Cavendish Books Limited
58 Old Compton Street
London W1V 5PA

Phototypeset in Times New Roman by Quadraset Limited
Midsomer Norton, Avon

Printed and bound in Italy by L.E.G.O.

ISBN 0 86307 597 5

FOREWORD

*E*very year, among the books I read are those published about cricket. Very few disappoint me, and I particularly enjoy the large books which attempt to put the whole history and scope of the game into perspective. I felt privileged, then, when asked to contribute a foreword to this one.

Despite the rapid growth in recent years of one-day cricket, particularly international one-day cricket with its world cups and world championships, for me, and I suppose most players, the Test matches remain the peak of cricketing endeavour. I hit my first ball in Test cricket, at Edgbaston in 1978, for four, which critics said showed my coolness, but I well remember the excitement of the occasion.

In the following winter I made my first tour of Australia, where I shared the Test batting with men like Geoff Boycott and Mike Brearley, who had been cricketing tourists when I was still a more-or-less angelic seven-year-old at school. On their *first* tour, Ken Barrington was the established star batsman. Moving backwards like this, it is not many steps before we find ourselves in the eras of such great players as Bradman and Hobbs. And of course Hobbs played at least once with W. G. Grace.

The Test match section in this book describes, in words and pictures, the matches series by series, so we can follow the arrivals and departures of the Test players on and off the stage, from the first Test of all in 1877 to the last of the 1985 season. It brings home to me, at least, that whatever one does in cricket one can only be a small part of the wide panorama of the history of the game as a whole.

The game is as strong as ever. No doubt new players will appear to challenge the feats of those of the past. Who knows what future giant might be making his debut when the likes of Ian Botham and I finally stagger from the field for the last time?

With luck, that will not be for a few years yet. Cricket is a great game. I enjoy playing it and I enjoy reading about it, and I hope that in the following pages, which range over all its aspects, you will find the same pleasure as I do.

by David Gower

The Headingley ground during the England-Australia Test in 1985.

CONTENTS

The first England touring party on board ship to America in 1859.

PART I

THE
HISTORY
OF
CRICKET

IN THE BEGINNING ...

Games like cricket are not conceived and born like the mortals who play them. They develop, and adapt to suit changing times. They have no traceable beginning, just as they will have no sudden end. It is impossible to kill them.

Indeed, when authority, whether Church or State or both, has tried to repress cricket, the game has reacted as would a plant with a well-developed root system. Instead of dying, cricket has become stronger. Games are like jokes. Thoughtful comedians tell us that their gags are all variations on familiar themes, all of them well-used. Many games belong to the 'to and fro' category; football, for example—a game invented in England, where people have always been gregarious, and subsequently exported all over the world as both a participation and a spectator activity. Hockey, although different in that the players use an implement, is comparable, and so, for that matter, are the racquet games, all

of them to-and-fro games, even those in which a wall is used to keep the ball in play.

Then there are the games in which the players hit or throw away from a mark, usually towards another. Into this category come golf, croquet and quoits. Finally, there is the group which combines the to-and-fro element of the first class with the despatch of an object, the key characteristic of the second class. In this respect cricket shows common features with baseball. Both have their roots in a game like stool-ball, still frequently played in that area of Surrey, Sussex and Hampshire widely accepted as the cradle of cricket, thanks to the effect of some of the game's earliest literature, which has proved most effective propaganda for the men of Hambledon. As Christopher Brookes has pointed out in his history, cricket's roots are to be found in the folk-games played in the villages of medieval England, and

A fashionable lady of 1785 poses with bat, ball and two-stump wicket.

A companion print dated two years later shows the third stump has reached Oxfordshire.

stool-ball is the only one to survive relatively unchanged.

These days it is fashionable to pooh-pooh the idea that it was simple human instinct that provided the impetus for the invention of these folk-games. Yet if it is instinctive for us to move, the acts of throwing or kicking are close to basic, and that of hitting a missile with a club not much further removed. Certainly the instinctive enjoyment of these physical actions is what united the earliest groups of cricketers. With no hard evidence available it is really a matter of speculation as to how cricket evolved from these early instinctive pleasures. Certainly the ready availability of useful timber was an important factor.

In medieval times only the King's business was important enough to be recorded—filed and guarded in an undisturbed state for centuries. We read that John of Leek, Chaplain to King Edward I's son, had to pay out 100 shillings, a lot of money in those days, for 'creag et alios ludos' in the Palace of Westminster on 10 March 1299, perhaps in the indoor school, the cloisters, as it was rather early in the season. Was 'creag' in fact cricket, as historians have trained us to believe? It is pleasant to think so.

Etymologically, the origins of some of cricket's trappings disappear into Anglo-Saxon times, well before Edward II, a poor king who probably did not have the steadiness of temperament required of a Test captain. Cricket, wicket, bat, crease, stump and bail are all words of great antiquity.

By 1598, nearly 300 years after the reference above, official documents were being written in English. The then Coroner of

OPPOSITE Tom Hope of an Amsterdam family of merchants painted by Francois Jean Sable in 1792.

Guildford, one John Derrick, refers to a piece of ground in the town recently turned into a timber yard as a place where he had played cricket in the 1550s, when he was a scholar of the Free School at Guildford.

It is almost certain that local variations of the game were legion until the middle of the next century, the seventeenth, the age of the great cultural leap forward as witnessed, for instance, in the art of portrait-painting. How could it be otherwise when new ideas took as long as people to move from one country to another? Rowland Bowen suggests that cricket spread but slowly, and that it was not widely played in Cornwall or Cumbria, or indeed in Herefordshire or Monmouthshire, until the nineteenth century. By that time it was already a familiar pastime in faraway places like North America and India. Indeed, Bowen has unearthed a seventeenth-century jet-setter, Samuel Filmer, who took part in the first recorded match at Coxheath in Kent in 1646, the year in which the Scots handed Charles I over to Parliament. Filmer next emerges in Virginia before returning to England at the time of the Restoration. This match was the first time a game of cricket was used as a vehicle for betting; this may help to explain why in Cromwell's time a game at Cranbrook in Kent was described by the prosecution as unlawful.

Oliver Cromwell, according to Royalist propaganda, had earned himself the 'name of royster' by establishing a reputation for enjoying football, cricket, cudgelling and wrestling as a young man. Later, poor fellow, he acquired a reputation as a killjoy, leading men into death and destruction. By 1656 he was burning cricket bats and balls in Dublin. Two years earlier the churchwardens of Eltham in Kent—near where W. G. Grace is buried—had fined seven parishioners two shillings (10p) each for playing cricket on Sunday, the Lord's Day. The Puritans were in charge. During Cromwell's rule the remaining rich and would-be courtiers scattered to the country and only returned to London with the accession of Charles II, royal protagonist of leisure and freedom—not least the freedom to gamble.

All over Europe there was war in the seventeenth century. In terms of the general duration of hostilities the British Isles suffered a comparatively short disruption. In terms of its effects on the entire population, the Civil War was nevertheless comprehensive. A great mingling took place as the old order, and with it the remnants of the feudal world of the folk-game, was displaced in the conflict and its repercussions.

As the classes mixed, as the land prospered, and as the early factories and craft workers yielded time and resources for leisure activities, cricket benefited. It was in these middle years of the seventeenth century that the game developed the basis for its claim of being England's national game.

Royal Patronage

In Charles II's time cricket—no longer creag but now indisputably cricket—was in receipt of royal patronage and therefore by extension that of the newly revived court. Officially that sexy and stylish monarch Charles II died childless, but in fact the then Earl of Sussex was his son-in-law, and from the year 1677 there survives a ledger in which the Treasurer noted that his Lordship had taken £3 from petty cash to go to the cricket match at Dicker Common. Dicker lies north of the Sussex Downs, and the nearest sporting attraction in recent years has been the Eastbourne Speedway at nearby Arlington Stadium. In those days it was the last village on the road from Lewes Market to Hailsham Market, where they made the best pottery in East Sussex.

By March 1700 (again that early start!) they were playing the best of five games on Clapham Common 'for £10 a head each game and £20 the odd one'. In 1707 a well-advertised eleven-a-side match took place in Lamb's Conduit Fields in London, and two years later county cricket was born when Surrey took on the Kentish men.

Young men playing the game as the seventeenth century became the eighteenth lived well into the newspaper era. William Bedle, who died in 1768, was at one time the most expert cricketer in England. Yet beyond the dates of his birth and death only his reputation remains. Matches were taking place in London, Kent, Surrey, Sussex and Gloucestershire before 1750. The Henfield Cricket Club, whose players now sport a white Sussex hen on a green cap, can show proof of games played in the village as long ago as 1727. Teams took county titles because by now the great patrons of the game were gathering together the best cricketers from both town and village. It was an expensive business to promote at the rate of a guinea (£1.05) to each player for home matches and a guinea and a half (£1.57½) for travelling. Yet thousands, sometimes as many as 20,000, came to watch and pay their sixpences (2½p), all we were to be charged some two hundred years later.

First Laws

After the Articles of Agreement between the Duke of Richmond and a Mr. Brodrick in 1727, the first written Laws of Cricket to survive date from 1744 and refer to the game as played on the Artillery Ground in London. We can take this date as signifying cricket's emergence from its archaeological chrysalis into the sunshine of regular recorded fact. The origins of some of cricket's curiosities have been explained by dedicated historians of the game, and some of the paths they have opened up are worth following here. Although the basic activities of cricket, throwing and hitting, are instinctive to us, there is nothing instinctive about the formation of a cricket eleven. Why not a ten or a twelve? Ten is the number on which the Romans based the metric system, while the Anglo-Saxons handed down a

haphazard numerical system in which the number twelve features strongly. Furthermore, while 'bat' and 'ball' are words which need no further explanation, from where does the word 'cricket' derive? And why do we insist on baffling Americans and occasionally even ourselves by using the word 'wicket' to describe both the pitch and the stumps?

Rowland Bowen, who published his history in 1970, draws our attention to the first conclusive reference to cricket in the *Archives de France*. In 1478 the game was being played near St Omer in the Pas de Calais, the last part of France to be surrendered up by the Kings of England. Queen Mary, you will remember, went to her grave with Calais inscribed on her heart. And it was in this area that there was a numbering system based on *eleven* inches, or *lignes*, to a foot.

As to the word 'cricket', there are those who claim it derives from the bat and those who believe it describes the mark which the cricketer defends. Harry Altham, whose first *History of Cricket* appeared in 1926, cites the old English translation of the Twenty-third Psalm ('Thy rod and staff comfort me', where *cric* was the original word for staff) as proof that cricket is derived from the bat. The outer shape of the early bats bears some similarity to that of the old shepherd's crook. On the other hand the Flemish word *krickstoel*, meaning a low stool like those used in churches for kneeling to prayer, tends to support the argument that cricket, like stool-ball, takes its name from the mark. 'Stool' is an old Sussex word for the stump of a tree, an ideal mark to aim at or defend, bearing in mind that originally bowling was

Representation of the Noble GAME of CRICKET as played in the celebrated Cricket Field near White Conduit House. 1787.

LEFT A young cricketer, engraved from a picture attributed to Gainsborough (1727-88).
RIGHT Cricket near White Conduit House, where Thomas Lord played before building his famous ground.

under-arm, and the deliveries shot along the ground.

Most who have tried to explain cricket to the uninitiated know how confusing they find the similarity between the words 'cricket' and 'wicket'. Wicket gates are traditionally associated with shepherds and the penning of their sheep. In the North Country, and indeed in North America, 'wicket', or sometimes 'wickets', was the name of the game itself. As for the bail, originally spelt beil, this was the slip-rail the shepherd moved to unlock the wicket gate.

Cricketing Measures

Cricket dimensions will always defy the metric system, that Roman legacy to Europe. Small wonder that some Englishmen resist the uniformity of measurement required in the Common Market, based appropriately on the Treaty of Rome! What hope have we when the length of our cricket pitches is the same as the width of the Saxon acre-strip, which was the basis of the great system of field-farming which survived until the eighteenth century. This was the main period of the enclosure movement when the strips were 'enclosed' to form the great estates which glorified acreage at the expense of the old rods, poles and perches. While the bailiffs were enclosing, his Lordship was often

either playing in, staging or betting on the big cricket matches.

As for the stumps and the crease in front of them, these measurements derive from the textile trade of small-town England, the Hong Kong of the Middle Ages. The cloth-yard was forty-five inches, the length of an arrow for a long-bow. The wicket was half an arrow's length in height and an eighth of it in breadth.

Under the wicket was the popping hole into which the ball had to be dropped for a run-out. Subsequently a run-out was judged on the popping crease—a ditch an inch deep and an inch wide was cut at the end of every pitch right up until the time of W. G. Grace in the 1860s, when the chalk-mark took its place.

As for the bat, its width was not regulated until thirty years after the first Laws, and only then because a man from Reigate called 'Shock' White shook his opponents by taking guard with a bat wider than the stumps. What villainy—but what invention! Later on, bats and balls were both subject to the gauge.

When cricket became a double-wicket game (and it is difficult to be certain when and how this came about) balls were bowled alternately from either end, four balls to the over. Harry Altham has advanced the theory that it was at this stage in the game's development that two umpires became essential—each would carry a bat and a run would only be completed when the batsman touched the umpire's bat with his own. This was a great help to the scorer who could rely on a crash of bats as well as sight of the game, and also explains why old prints show the umpires much closer to the wickets than they stand today.

THE MEN OF HAMBLEDON

The trend towards the aristocratic acceptance of cricket that had begun with the Restoration in 1660 and been sustained by national notables throughout the remaining years of the Stuart dynasty continued with the arrival of the Hanoverians.

The first George may not have been able to speak English, but many of the leading figures in the land had played cricket as children and so the old folk-game remained fashionable.

The devotion of George I's grandson, Frederick, who was born in 1707, represented cricket's biggest emotional capture since Edward II. In Frederick's case, there was to be no change of heart as had occurred in Oliver Cromwell. Not that everyone has regarded Frederick, Prince of Wales, as a 'good thing', to use the language of *1066 and All That*. The *Encyclopedia Britannica*, admittedly an American publication, describes the cricketing Prince of Wales as the 'absurd' father of George III, the King who lost the American Colonies. Perhaps if this Prince of Wales had lived his full span instead of dying at the age of 44, the game and the British connection might have taken deeper root in the Colonies and survived, thus saving the United States from having to suffer baseball as their national game.

It was a cricket ball in fact which determined English history

hereabouts, for it was a blow from one that lead to the death of the Prince of Wales in 1751. And there were others who were not happy with the game. Some unknown author, writing in the *British Champion* of 1743, thought it ridiculous and unseemly that lords and gentlemen, clergymen and lawyers should associate themselves with butchers and cobblers in such diversions. An opinion which has some relevance to the inception of the Gentlemen and Players match some sixty years later. This match, in which 'Gentlemen', or amateurs, played the professionals, was held regularly until 1962.

The beerage as well as the peerage were becoming involved in patronage, even at a relatively humble level. For example, 'Lumpy' Stevens, the most famous bowler of his generation, was engaged by an innkeeper with the appropriate name of Porter in Chertsey, twenty miles away from his home in Shamley Green.

Purses needed to be deep for the great occasions. In 1735 the Prince of Wales and the Earl of Middlesex, son of the Duke of Dorset, played a match at Moulsey Hurst for £1,000 a side. The Prince's side consisted of eight from the London Club and three from Middlesex, and the Kentish men played for the Earl. Kent won by three wickets. A fortnight later, the return match was

played on Bromley Common. The aristocracy certainly got their priorities right: 'I'll attend the Board of Admiralty when at leisure from cricket,' the Earl of Sandwich told his colleagues. It was another son of the Duke of Dorset, Lord John Sackville, who made the critical catch in the famous game on the Artillery Ground in 1744 between Kent and All-England. We know all about this great match because it is the subject of James Love's long poem:

Hail Cricket! Glorious, manly, British Game!
First of all Sports: the first alike in fame!

Alas, we don't write cricket reports like this any more. Love was obviously an eye-witness of the game. Kent led England by 13 runs after the first innings (53 to 40), but at their second attempt the 'Rest' had done much better, and Newland, with the best score of the match (18) already standing to his name, was going strong once more with 15 to his credit:

The champion strikes. When scarce arriving fair,
The glancing ball mounts upward in the air.
The batsman sees it, and with mournful eyes
Fixed on the ascending pellet as it flies,
Thus suppliant claims the favour of the skies.
O, mighty Jove, and all ye powers above,
Let my regarded prayer your pity move;
Grant me but this: whatever youth shall dare
Snatch at the prize descending through the air,
Lay him extended on the grassy plain,

And make his bold adventurous effort vain!
He said: the powers attending his request,
Granted one part, to winds consigned the rest.
And now illustrious Sackville where he stood,
The approaching ball with cautious pleasure viewed,
At once he sees the chief's impending doom,
And pants for mighty honours yet to come.
Swift as the falcon darting on its prey,
He springs elastic on the verdant way;
Sure of success, flies upward with a bound,
Derides the slow approach, and spurns the ground.
Prone slips the youth, yet glories in his fall,
With arm extended shows the captive ball.

James Love's real name was Dance, and his father was the architect who designed the Mansion House, still only ten minutes' walk from the ground where this match was played. Kent won, by the way, largely because Sackville caught Richard Newland at that crucial stage in the second innings.

The Prince of Wales watched this match and so did his brother the Duke of Cumberland, the son sent by King George II to sort out the Scots after the rebellion of 1745 in favour of Bonnie Prince Charlie. If 'Butcher' Cumberland was keen on cricket no wonder most Scots took to golf!

The Hambledon Club playing at Broadhalfpenny Down in 1777, when they scored 403 against All England, and Aylward batted for three days.

Cricket is still played at Broadhalfpenny Down, where in the 18th century the men of Hambledon could challenge All-England.

In the 1750s, cricket suffered a recession, perhaps because more important matters needed attention, like the Seven Years' War, a conflict about issues more serious than its predecessor Jenkins's Ear—the winning of an Empire and the capture of export markets for the game of cricket. Nevertheless the game re-established its appeal to all classes. What was now needed was a similar leap forward in technique. This improvement was to come from the men of Hambledon, who gave cricket its air of romance, a gift more precious even than that of the great patrons who had provided it with the upper crust of social standing.

The First Cricket Heroes

Dance's poem showed that cricket could inspire feats of imagination and create its own literature. Now the Hambledon men became heroes because they could match their skills against the best from anywhere in the land. John Small's boast that he would play at cricket with anyone in England was far from bombastic. As the game grew in popularity in the Midlands and the northern and western shires, so the fame of the Hambledon men spread. Perhaps we have developed a slightly idealized view of the Hambledonians because of the stories John Nyren told about his father Richard Nyren to Charles Cowden Clarke, whose works *The Young Cricketer's Tutor* and *Cricketers of my Time* are a veritable goldmine for those who want to study cricket in the years leading up to and immediately after the French Revolution.

John Nyren, cricket's earliest regular chronicler, was five years old and the Hambledon Club about nineteen when the first recorded century partnership took place in 1769 on Broadhalfpenny Down, that upturned saucer of a field across the road from the Bat and Ball Inn, kept by Richard Nyren. This century partnership was made by Tom Sueter and George Leer, wicketkeeper and long stop, tenor and counter-tenor in the Hambledon church choir, and on this occasion opening batsmen for Hampshire against Surrey. Not that all the records were falling to Hambledon men: at Wrotham, another famous ground, John Minshull, batting first wicket for the Duke of Dorset, hit the first recorded century, 107 out of a second-innings total of 236. Minshull had his reward: the Duke appointed him

his gardener afterwards for wages of eight shillings (40p) a week.

There was no greater patron than this Duke. His cricket cost him over £1,000 a year in the early 1780s. He respected the players and won their respect. He gave John Small a new fiddle, whereupon Small, proud enough not to be upstaged, sent the Duke two bats and two balls in return. Eventually the Duke of Dorset went to Paris as Ambassador, and early in 1789 he asked the Foreign Secretary, the Duke of Leeds, for a gesture of goodwill towards the French monarchy, then having what one of England's patrician Prime Ministers, Harold Macmillan, might have described as some little local difficulties over dividing Marie Antoinette's cake. 'Send a cricket team' was the request, but the Duke of Dorset, now fleeing from the guillotine, met the cricketers at Dover and wisely called off the visit. Life insurance had not been invented. This was the first but not the last tour to be called off for political reasons.

'Lumpy' Stevens was the first out-and-out cricketer whose portrait has survived. It hangs at Knole House, near Sevenoaks, and shows the face of a hard man. Stevens was a great bowler of shooters and always wanted to choose not only the end from which he would bowl but also where the wicket should be pitched on fields which were usually anything but level. What he wanted was a downward slope, because 'Honest Lumpy did allow, he ne'er could pitch but o'er a brow'.

The Third Stump

In 1775 Stevens played as the 'given' man for Kent in a five-a-side match against Hambledon on the Artillery Ground near Finsbury Circus in London, where the Honourable Artillery Company still play the game. Several times he beat the bat of John Small and the ball fizzed through the double wicket and under the bail. When Small, the last man, had walked to the wicket Hambledon had needed 14 runs, and with that sort of luck they were bound to get them. Betting must have been heavy and the laments of the losers long, for soon afterwards a third stump was added to the

HOME BLOCK.

London. Baily, Brothers, Cornhill.

Printed by C. Graf.

A stylised print of 1845: the bat, wicket and clothing are not unlike today's.

existing wicket, eliminating this element of luck.

We shall never know whether John Small was playing with a bat curved at the bottom like a hockey stick or with a straight bat with shoulders such as we use now. From Petersfield, born in 1737, seventy-five years in the choir, John Small was one of the greatest technocrats of the game.

Here lives John Small,
Makes bat and ball,
Pitch a wicket, play at cricket
With any man in England

read the sign outside his door, and it was during his playing career that the straight bat became more than just the game's chief implement. Against the length bowling of the likes of 'Lumpy' Stevens, John Small stepped towards the ball to play the off-drive and the draw, a stroke so difficult to control and therefore dangerous that none now play it, at least deliberately, for it meant purposely playing the ball between bat and leg down to long stop's left hand. Now it is regarded as a lucky stroke, described by Etonians as the 'Harrow drive' and by north-of-the-Thames men as the 'Surrey cut'.

By the time the Hambledon men like John Small were establishing their reputation in the 1770s, cricket had already suffered its first recession. The 1760s were as barren as the 1960s and the game was said to be losing its fashionable support to golf. Also, inflation was hitting cricket equipment as hard as it is now. The price of bats went up from half a crown (12½ p) for eleven—yes, eleven!—to four shillings (20p) each between 1766 and 1773! Balls were more expensive than bats in those days, William Pett of Sevenoaks charging 3s 6d (17½ p) for a couple in 1766.

On the field the men of Hambledon wore shirts with full sleeves, knee-breeches, stockings and buckled shoes. These were dangerous, and Silver Billy Beldham told how John Wells, another Hambledonian, tore off his fingernail on a buckle as he tried to pick up the ball. Top-hats were not then part of the uniform. In the Hambledon team of the 1780s and 1790s, men like Beldham, who lived until 1862 (when he was the grand old age of ninety-six), wore purpose-built cricket shoes.

The portrait of 'Lumpy' Stevens shows him wearing a stock, waistcoat and jacket. Off the field the players wore sky-blue coats with black velvet collars and the letters CC, standing for Cricketing Club, engraved on their buttons.

Richard Nyren

Richard Nyren was the key figure of this period, the go-between linking the patrons and the players, the keeper of the Bat and Ball Inn, secretary of the Hambledon Club for nigh on forty years, the King Arthur of this Round Table. He learned his cricket from his uncle Richard Newland, one of three brothers from Slindon in Sussex, the first such trio to be recorded playing in organized cricket and the forerunners of the Graces of Gloucestershire.

Nyren was a left-arm bowler of slow lobs, always to a length, although it was as a talent spotter and coach that he was to play such a prominent part in both the Hambledon teams, old and new. The art of bowling was becoming more sophisticated. The first bowlers had simply heaved the ball along the ground, hence the passion for shooters, whether on the first, second or any old bounce. But the length bowlers, who tossed the ball under-arm on to the spot, were capable of giving the ball some bias after it had pitched, usually, in the case of a right-hander, from leg to off. With the renowned Brett and Richard Nyren, right- and left-arm men respectively, Hambledon's bowlers could set some problems. Then along came the little downland farmer with a name appropriate for a shepherd—Lamborn—who was to under-arm bowling what the first leg-break bowlers were to over-arm. By flipping the ball over his wrist he could make it move from off to leg, and when his Hambledon team played All-England the men of Surrey and Kent 'tumbled out as if they had been picked off by a rifle corps!'

It was said of the 'Little Farmer' (as Lamborn was known) that 'his comprehension did not equal the speed of lightning', and Richard Nyren spent hours trying to persuade him to pitch his off-breaks outside the off-stump instead of straight as was his wont when practising with his sheep hurdles. The lesson was hard to learn, and Lamborn once missed the Duke of Dorset's leg-stump by such a hair's breadth that he let out the earliest recorded bowler's cry of anguish: 'Ah, it was tedious near you, Sir.'

Another notable member of the team was the long-fielder, Peter Stewart, whom they called Buck—a shoemaker and carpenter, and the funny man of the party. Once when the Hambledon caravan overturned, the optimistic Buck insisted on staying in it, hoping for supernatural intervention, and claiming that 'One good turn deserved another'.

Then, as now, great teams petered out, and after some poor

The bowler about to deliver, while fielders prepare and spectators loll, in a print by Pyne, 1895.

results in 1770 the Hambledonians all but fell apart. However, they came back to fame during the next ten years by playing fifty-one matches against teams labelled 'All-England' and the like, and winning a staggering twenty-nine of them. Some village! Some players! Years later John Nyren set down the names: David Harris, John Wells, Richard Purchase, William Beldham, John Small junior, Harry and Tom Walker, Robert Robinson, Noah Mann, Thomas Scott and Thomas Taylor. 'No eleven in England,' he wrote, 'could have had any chance with these men, and I think they may have beaten any two and twenty.'

Of those mentioned, David Harris was a great bowler, quick enough to draw blood from a batsman's hands though not from rustic Tom Walker's, whose skin was 'like the rind of an old oak, and as sapless!' John Nyren tells us he was an ungainly fellow who 'toiled like a tar on horseback'.

John Wells came from Farnham, where he was a baker: a useful cricketer, and whether bowling, fielding or batting 'a servant of all work'. Noah Mann kept an inn at North Chapel near Petworth in Sussex, so he had a twenty-mile ride to play or even practise cricket. On arrival he was apt to demonstrate his party piece, picking up handkerchiefs at full gallop. Swarthy as a gypsy, he was a left-handed hitter and bowler and a fine sprinter in the field: he covered Leer at long stop and sometimes would let a ball through deliberately so that he could attempt to run out the batsman. He was once credited with a hit for ten on Windmill Down—the Hambledon men had moved their field here because Broadhalfpenny was too bleak.

Noah Mann came to a sad end: one autumn night after going shooting and celebrating his successful bag, he insisted on being left to sleep in his chair by the fire. In the night he fell on to the embers and died of his burns within twenty-four hours. His son was named after Sir Horatio Mann, the boy's godfather, one of the great patrons from Kent: Richard Nyren had been the go-between in this happy relationship between landowner and publican. On another more controversial occasion, Nyren had words with Sir Horatio, who successfully enticed away a young Hambledonian, James Aylward, to be his bailiff at Bishops-bourne in Kent. Aylward held the record score for many years,

hitting 167 out of a total of 403 for Hambledon (alias Hampshire) against England in 1777; he went in at five o'clock on a Wednesday and batted until three o'clock on Friday. No wonder Horatio Mann wanted him for Kent!

William Beldham, 'Silver Billy', was a man of Farnham like John Wells. He was younger than the others and thus still a Hambledonian when the club began to fade in the early 1790s. He perfected the cut, taking the ball 'twixt wind and water', as James Burke was apt to take the House of Commons in the same period. Beldham played his last match for the Players at the ground we know today as Lord's as late as 1821. He was fifty-five years old and made 23 not out.

These, then, were the players. The atmosphere they engendered was of the Hampshire earth itself—rich and natural. John Nyren remembered it well: 'How strongly are all those scents of fifty years gone by painted in my memory! and the smell of that ale comes upon me freshly as the new May flowers.' The fifth toast at these Hambledon dinners was always to Madge, but despite considerable research no one has succeeded in discovering the identity of this damsel. No wonder, for, according to Rowland Bowen, Madge was an eighteenth-century word for the female reproductive organ. Cricket dinners have not changed!

However brilliant the Hambledonians' cricket and however romantic it became thanks to John Nyren's ability to broadcast the tradition with filial affection, there was little possibility that Hambledon would survive. London was the centre of attraction, and elsewhere there were patrons as resolved as Horatio Mann to field a team fit to take on the best, no matter how unscrupulously they had to recruit. In 1791 Richard Nyren left Hambledon. In 1796 the last minutes of the club he had fostered were taken. Eventually even the ground was returned to the plough, though the Bat and Ball retained its hold on the memory of cricketers everywhere. In 1925 a commemoration match was played on Broadhalfpenny Down, a field now looked after by Winchester College. To Harry Altham, a former president of MCC and a man whose scholarship and teaching were always at cricket's service, belongs the credit for saving the field from the plough and for the game. Now from time to time the Lord's Taverners play there, their teams always full of notables and fun. So, if the ghosts of the great cricketers of Hambledon wish to appear, they know whose fixture list to consult.

THE ALL-ENGLAND PROFESSIONALS

William Clarke, born in Nottingham soon after the lamps had dimmed for good on Hambledon, was trained as a bricklayer, his father's trade. He was an under-arm bowler, even though round-arm bowling was legal throughout his time. He was a solemn-looking fellow and bowled from under a tall hat, his arm whipping backwards and forwards at the maximum height allowed. His appearance must have become even more formidable after 1830, the year of revolutions in Europe, when Charles X of France lost a throne and William Clarke, keeper of the Bell Inn at Nottingham, lost an eye.

In 1837 he married as his second wife the widow Chapman, who kept the Trent Bridge Inn. Within a year he had not only seduced the cricketing clientele away from the Bell Inn, where they always supped, but he had also obtained a field behind the public house which became the Trent Bridge ground. At first the new ground was not entirely successful, despite the fact that there was a charge to enter. Nevertheless Clarke stayed there until 1847, by which time he had discovered another, more profitable way of earning his living. The previous year, he had selected his first all-England XI, the first of the travelling teams of professional cricketers, now regarded as the most significant games-playing development in England's sporting history, one that was to last for twenty-four years.

Why did Clarke do it? For profit. This wandering cricket show was, in today's terms, a 'service' business providing a substantial income for a small and controllable capital outlay. Were there other motives? Certainly the lot of the cricketer who wanted to play all summer long for match money was hard in Nottingham-shire. In the middle of the nineteenth century the Dukeries were great sporting estates. They still were in the 1920s, as D. H. Lawrence reminds us, but the Dukes who lived in the great houses, like Portland, were not known as patrons of county cricket in Nottinghamshire.

In 1842, for example, only one match was played, and this paltry fixture-list had grown merely to an inadequate five by 1845. Such places in the county eleven as were available were often snapped up by amateurs of minimal skill. Clarke himself was known in cricket circles as 'Old Clarke'; hardly surprisingly since he was forty-six before he played for England. His first selection for the Players in one of the great matches at Lord's came at the age of forty-eight. From then on he averaged 340 wickets a season, and although he broke an arm at the age of fifty-two he played for three more years, taking a wicket with his very last ball. How good must he have been in his prime? Being born in Nottinghamshire was to be born to blush unseen.

Whether he began his version of a cricketing circus with any wider intent than profit with enjoyment we cannot be sure. But there is evidence that he knew what would happen. A conversation with another of the game's entrepreneurs, James Dark, the manager of Lord's, has been handed down. 'It's a going to be, Sir, from one end of the land to the other, you may depend on that,' said Clarke, 'and what is more it will make good for cricket for you as well as for me. Mark my words, you'll sell cartloads of your balls where you used to sell dozens.'

There can be no doubt that the travelling teams took cricket to new towns and villages, places it would only have reached more slowly without the travellers. The interest in their matches only began to fade when conflicts about fixtures and money began to receive public airing.

Initially, there were other factors coming to the fore which prompted the independence of Clarke, Wisden and the like.

Quite apart from the evidence all the professionals could see of the MCC's preference for promoting one or other form of amateur cricket, there were technical issues of great moment over which the professionals were arguing with the amateurs, especially the diehards among the latter. Over-arm bowling was obviously a better method of launching the ball than delivering with a round arm, because a bowler could keep the ball straighter. And, by and large, the task of bowling had landed squarely on the strong legs and shoulders of the game's artisans, the professionals, while the gentlemen took up what they considered the more elegant and enjoyable pastime of batting.

Full-time Cricketers

One factor in particular was essential to the success of the new venture—railways. Without the mobility they provided the pro-gramme Old Clarke devised would have been impossible. He set himself to play between twenty and twenty-five matches every season and 'could have had three times as many if we could have found the dates'. Suddenly the possibility of cricket six days a week for five months of the year had opened up. No longer was it crucial that a man good at cricket learn a trade or find a patron, as had been the case with the players of the Hambledon era. As an added incentive, certainly in the Midlands area, where most of the men were textile workers, the industrial revolution had made working conditions far less agreeable than five months in the cricket fields of England. As for the erstwhile patrons, they were getting fewer: nor were they so necessary, for as the game spread through the schools and travelling clubs, so did the number of players skilled enough to cope with the game at its highest level increase. William Clarke, then, was hailed, at least at the begin-ning of this era, as a great benefactor. The players were paid £5 a match (sometimes £6 if the journey involved was long), but they were obliged to pay for travel and board out of their own pockets—and sometimes there was little enough left.

As time passed Clarke became more parsimonious, and eventually two of his players led the southern men into exile, where they reformed under the title the United England XI in 1852. Despite the anger of John Wisden and James Dean, who hoped for a complete break with their former colleagues, the United England XI maintained their connection with the All-England XI and for ten years the matches between the two teams were the finest in the land. This state of affairs even survived Clarke's death, when George Parr, another of the Trent Bridge greats, took over the management of the All-England XI and kept it going for a few more years.

Some of the journeys undertaken by these travelling teams were testing. Not all could be made by train. One such, from Wisbech to Sleaford, a distance of some forty miles, was com-pleted only because Martingale, one of the players, shinned up a signpost in the middle of the night, somewhere in the depths of the Fenland, after the coachdriver had lost his way. Some of the grounds were rough, too. On one occasion Fuller Pilch had to scythe the field before a start could be made, and even then one of the players put up a covey of partridges. Nor were all the hazards to be faced of the natural variety. At Hull, the ground was prepared by inmates of the local lunatic asylum. There has always been a strong connection between cricket and mental asylums (a connection on which it is not necessary to comment further!), but usually only the staff get near the action. On this occasion one lunatic took an iron bar out of the roller and hit Job Greenwood, one of the players, over the head with it.

William Clarke trained as a bricklayer, laid out the Trent Bridge cricket ground in 1838 and created the All-England Eleven in 1846, when he was already 47 years old. He played for Nottinghamshire until he was 56.

Decline of the Professional Circuit

Eventually a decline in the playing ability of the professionals, the strength of the amateur tradition sustained at Lord's, and the rise of the county clubs (which hoped to provide for the growing county towns what MCC at Lord's and Surrey at The Oval were offering the London cricketing public) all combined to throttle the great professional elevens. The arguments against them were best summed up by the Rev. James Pycroft writing in *Cricketana* in 1865. John Arlott quoted this long passage in his history of cricket published in 1953, and some would say its sentiments became relevant once more when Kerry Packer began his operations over a hundred years after these words were written.

From *Cricketana*:

The getting-up of an All-England match in a country place is very much in this wise:

The secretary of All Muggleton is an elderly gentleman—no player, but an eating or smoking member, yet ambitious to distinguish himself, and perhaps to have his photograph taken as the Father of the Muggleton Club. Whereupon, as the cheapest kind of immortality, about October he begins to talk, and goes on talking all the winter of his determination to 'book the All England Eleven' for the coming season. He soon has a subs-

cription list with his own name at the head, and does not doubt (till he tries) that George Parr will take 'the gate'—though all the parish can creep through the hedge—instead of payment for his Eleven. But soon a polite letter comes, hinting that Muggletonian enthusiasm is not so certain as to make anything less than £70 or £80 a sufficient consideration.

Then comes the question of how to raise the wind. Whereupon the gentleman goes about with his subscription-list in hand, trying to persuade every tradesman, and, above all, every innkeeper within five miles round that the All-England match will be the making of the town and trade of Muggleton and its vicinity, and they must be public-spirited and subscribe. As to asking any players to subscribe it seems very hard to take a man's money and not to put him into the Twenty-two; yet everybody wants to be in the Twenty-two, and everybody who is left out is so sure to be offended—especially if he happens not to be in Muggleton society, for then he feels doubly snubbed,—vowing the Muggleton Club is likely to come to a speedy dissolution 'all through our secretary's match'. However, money is picked up by driblets, and a ten-pound note is volunteered by the victualler, who thus knowingly secures a monopoly of all the diluted spirits, weak beer, and

Nottingham playing Leicester around 1829. The under-arm bowler might well be William Clarke.

shabby dinners, which are remembered by grumbling spectators for weeks after . . .

As to these All-England matches, you do not play against All-England or its best Eleven by any means. At present there are two All-Englands—two bests! which is rather strange, certainly. Not only so, but neither of the two can be called best in any sense. We will speak now of Parr's Eleven, 'the All-England'; for Wisden's Eleven, 'the United All-England', having six Surrey men, play comparatively few matches, for fear of spoiling the Surrey county matches. They only play when Surrey has no fixture . . .

When a travelling circus goes round the country, you are rather staggered, as you pay your money, in looking up and seeking the face, all red and white chalk, of Mr. Meryman the clown taking the cash without a smile on his countenance, unless one is painted there, and not all like the Fool, but in the most sensible and business manner possible.

In the same way the All-England Eleven—'the gate' being part of the bargain—you pay your sixpences to a creature in flannels, pads, and spiked shoes, ready at a moment's notice to start to have his innings, which innings, no doubt, he hopes will be a creditable one to himself; but as to the issue of the match he does not care a button, not he. No; he does not play for the score—he only plays for the till. And cricket is one of those games that must be played with a will to be played well. This is especially true of old and experienced players. Boys play their best for the fun and the novelty; but there can be no novelty to a professional cricketer; and the difference between concentrated energy and the mere mechanical performance makes all the difference between the finest bowling and that which is just good enough to make the batsman play his best against it. This intensified energy, this concentration of all the powers of bowlers, wicketkeepers, and fieldsmen to one point, makes a difference of half the score.

So the truth comes to this: even if you had All-England men, you cannot have All-England play when your side is not worth beating, and when not the runs but the sixpences are all they care for . . .

But the chief reason of all that men in the All-England Eleven rarely play like themselves is this: they are fagged and jaded —stale and overdone from the beginning of the season . . .

Fuller Pilch, who for much of the 1830s and 1840s was the best batsman in England. Born in Horningtoft, Norfolk, in 1804, his style was to play forward and hit the ball before it could shoot or rise.

William Lillywhite, of the famous Sussex family of cricketers, was one of those responsible for the introduction of round-arm bowling, and was one of the leading bowlers of the 1830s and 1840s.

James Cobbett, of Middlesex, Surrey and Yorkshire. Born at Frimley, Surrey, in 1804 he was one of the best all-rounders of his day, and was on the staff at Lord's for 16 seasons, dying at Marylebone in 1842.

Imagine two matches a week, and most of their rest taken in railway trains. We remember they came to play at Bath, just landed from Ireland, half of them sea-sick. The first day they were not fit to play a decent school; still our friends flattered themselves the score they made was against All-England men! about as true as if they had been drunk. Why, as to play, we are reminded of the travelling circus over again. 'I might be fond of music,' said the French horn, 'but I am not the man to blow all day to please anyone.' Sometimes the said All-England bowlers have hardly a leg to stand on—such as cricketers' legs ought to be. We could name men we have seen quite groggy—with sore feet and swollen legs—blessing Providence for the chance of going to bed . . . when the rain came . . .

The contrast between the faces of the All-England Eleven—when paid not by 'the gate' but by the job—and the faces of the rest of the field on a rainy day, is amusing to any lover of the ridiculous. Being very civil fellows, they feel bound to seem a little disappointed, as naturally as they can, when they pass some promising young players looking much bluer than the sky is likely to be. Perhaps they may also say a sympathetic word to the caterer, whose cold lamb and cucumbers is already in a state of watery solution; but if anyone could hear their private and confidential communications, he would hear something like this: 'A good chance for your bad legs, John. Another such a day as this, and I shouldn't wonder if some of Jackson's bowling would come back again.' Now this is all we get for our money—this is the delusion we practise on ourselves when we book our clubs and grounds for one of the vacant days of the All-England Eleven. We have that Eleven, it is true, but all the powder and the spirit is out of them; and one would think that no man who had ever made one of twenty-two with two bowlers given, all fresh and lively, against eleven stiff and steady ones, could ever want to do the same thing over again.

'But if we do like to amuse ourselves,' someone will say, 'what does it matter to anyone?'

Why, it matters a great deal. Is it nothing to draw the best players away from fine county matches, which are better worth seeing by far? Very commonly the members of the Surrey Club—than whom no club has ever done more to encourage county cricket—have had a difficulty in their fixtures, because All-England matches are encouraged on the same days.

We trust all true lovers of cricket will take this into consideration before they have anything to do with these 'All-England' games. For, which is better—that for three summer months the finest matches possible shall be arranged by the Marylebone and the Surrey clubs chiefly in London, but with return matches in other counties, or that these arrangements should be spoilt for so poor an apology for a match as we have already described?

It does appear at present that there is a feeling of opposition on the part of the All-England Eleven, or certain of them, to the promoters of county matches. Surely nothing can be more suicidal. Who brought forward these very men to their present positions? Who find the sinews of war? Who provide the money for matches and the labour fund? We admit that there may be one or two men so situated that they may see little personal danger in opposing their former friends and patrons; though even they may commit the fatal mistake of kicking away the ladder before they have done with it. But let us ask—Do cricketers act wisely in supporting them? Should the rest of the All-England Eleven agree to play on days when they are wanted for our leading clubs?

We trust that this will be amicably arranged; otherwise, we should say that the Marylebone and the Surrey clubs should make it a rule that men who belong to an Eleven so regardless of their fixtures should never be employed either at Lord's or at The Oval.

(Rev. James Pycroft, *Cricketana*, 1865)

THE INFLUENCE OF THE MCC

Given the increasing popularity of cricket, the Marylebone Cricket Club was to become an essential feature of the social life and topography of London. Great houses and terraces were being built by the likes of John Nash close to clubland and in the area between Hyde Park and Regent's Park. If Thomas Lord had not acted as MCC's midwife as the eighteenth century drew to a close, someone else would have established a club or a cricket team in London to rival the men of Hambledon. Indeed, it is surprising that one had not already been established.

Thomas Lord had the right name for promotion to the upper classes. But he was a worker. He had to be, for his father—once a wealthy Yorkshire landowner—had lost his estates through his support for the Jacobites during the 1745 uprising. It is hard to appreciate what a divide such events created throughout the length and breadth of England—equivalent, perhaps, to the way in which wartime France was split between Gaullists and supporters of the Vichy régime. Young Thomas Lord was obliged to sell anything and everything to make a living. In one of his ventures he sold wine to the King and, even more important as it turned out, to the Earl of Winchilsea, one of the new generation of cricket patrons. The Earl belonged to the White Conduit Club, which played in Islington, a ground not nearly exclusive enough for the Earl's taste. Encouraged by the enthusiasm of Winchilsea and his friends, Thomas Lord leased a piece of land, now Dorset Square, from the Portman family. The first game at Lord's, in 1787, was between Middlesex and Essex, then minor counties, but a few weeks later the White Conduit Club, with six men, met All-England and lost.

Lord himself liked his cricket and was able to hold his own as a bowler. He could not, however, hold back the rapid development of London, and within twenty years he was obliged to move his ground to Lisson Grove, then owned by the Eyre family. Later, in the winter of 1809-10, Lord transported the actual turf from the old ground, its value as a pitch providing remarkable evidence of the technical developments being made in the game. When Parliament bisected his field with the Regent's Canal in 1813, Lord moved the turf yet again, to the present ground. It was probably just as well that this further move had been forced upon him, as the second ground did not prove popular. The MCC played there only three times. By this time the MCC were recognized as the premier club in the land. Their laws were the scratching post for the whole country and then, as now, they were frequently revised.

The Laws of Cricket

A study of the laws reveals many surprises. The earliest, dating from 1721, delineated only two issues: that a match should be of two innings, and that the batsman should have some right to charge down an opponent trying to catch him. Clearly there were other laws, and when the matches were important enough instructions to players and umpires were recorded. By 1735 a group was meeting at the Star and Garter in Pall Mall (also the home of the Jockey Club), and here the great men of cricket produced revisions to the laws of the game, culminating in 1744 in the *New Articles of the Game of Cricket*. Sir William Draper was chairman of the group and the Duke of Dorset, Sir Horatio Mann and the Rev. Charles Pawlett, a Hambledonian, were members. As a result, the weight of the ball was fixed between five-and-a-half and five-and-three-quarter ounces, the bat's width, *pace* 'Shock' White, at four-and-a-quarter inches, the height of the three stumps at twenty-two inches, and the width of the bails at six inches. The creases and the pitch measured as they do today.

By virtue of this set of revised laws, the away team was given choice of innings and where to pitch the wicket. Batsmen could be dismissed much as they can be today, including leg-before-wicket, lbw, 'if the batsman had a design to stop the ball and actually prevented the ball from hitting his wicket'. By this time no batsmen, 'whether under pretence of running a notch or otherwise', could impede a would-be catcher.

A match between Gentlemen and Players at Lord's in 1895. The Players in the field are awaiting the arrival at the wicket of the next Gentleman to bat, none other than W. G. Grace.

The Formation of the MCC

In 1787 the Star and Garter group, which had by now become the White Conduit Club, moved to Lord's first ground and became the Marylebone Cricket Club. In 1788, they revised the laws for the first time as MCC. Henceforward changes in the laws issued by the MCC remained unchallenged. Even today the International Cricket Conference grants to MCC the right of final custodianship of the Laws of Cricket.

Because of its pre-eminence, there have been attempts to disfavour this ancient club, the Marylebone Cricket Club, the MCC, the private club with the public function. This is nothing new. In 1864, W. G. Grace noted that an attempt by certain newspapers had been made to question the authority of the MCC and to have it replaced by a parliament of the counties. The Doctor was happy to see such a notion fail.

Historians, too, while legitimately challenging the facts as presented by previous generations of chroniclers, have shown a tendency to minimize the particular flavours of the Club's history. Lord, as we have seen, gave MCC much of its early character. His training was as a wine merchant, and the aristocracy were likely to be better customers than the *hoi polloi* who played in Islington's public fields. The successive moves within the Borough of Marylebone were designed to protect the relative exclusivity the Club enjoyed, and to encourage and control the expansion of MCC as a private club.

Even in the 1860s, the structure of cricket was much less formalized than it is today, when a computer is needed to arrange fixtures. Whereas the principal games in the early days at Lord's were between teams labelled MCC or named after one or other of the counties, the advent of other fixtures began to establish in the game the principle of exclusivity which was eventually to extend even as far as county cricket. Many of these games, which grew into traditional fixtures, were arranged between schools, by pupils past and present. Sometimes they were banned because they led to trouble between the boys of these schools. Dr. Heath, the flogging headmaster of Eton, tried to prevent Eton playing Westminster, for instance. Eton and Harrow first played in 1805, and again in 1818, but their games did not become an annual fixture until 1822. It was in this event that Charles Wordsworth and Herbert Jenner, the men who were to arrange the first fixture between Oxford and Cambridge five years later, first met on the cricket field. By 1836, the University match too had become an annual fixture. Another of the traditional Lord's fixtures, the game between Gentlemen and Players, represented the ultimate exclusivity in class teams. Later it came to epitomise the distinction between unpaid (later known as amateur) players and the professionals, a distinction which was to last, albeit often cynically blurred, right up until 1962.

Betting

In the early days of the game, however, the Gentlemen were obliged to engage Players to even out the sides in order that the match might make a better vehicle for betting. Betting was the passion of MCC members, and so in order to provide the right conditions for an even wager the vagaries of selection to which Gentleman and Players were subjected included allowing the Gentlemen sixteen players, or inviting the Players, with no option, to defend wickets twice the normal size. As betting had become such an important appendage of the game, trouble was bound to follow. By the end of the eighteenth century the 'legs', the bookmakers' assistants, used to buy up players in the Green Man and Still, a pub frequented by cricketers in Oxford Street. William Lambert (the professional employed by Squire Osbaldeston, one of the great sporting figures of the early 1800s, who resigned in pique from MCC after a celebrated duel with Lord George Bentinck) was eventually barred from Lord's in 1817 after he was alleged to have sold the match between England and Nottingham played on the ground. Lambert resumed his trade as a miller, and eventually gravitated into the Fuller's Earth

The LAWS of the NO[...]
as revised by the [...]

business, making and selling material now used for filtering swimming pools.

William Ward's benefaction in purchasing the Lord's lease saved the ground from the builders and for the future of cricket. The pavilion, alas, could not be saved for, in that same year, 1825, it went up in flames; these also consumed all the earliest precious records of the game.

In 1835 the lease was passed on to J. H. Dark, a man in the Thomas Lord tradition, a proprietor for whom profit was the principal motive. Dark staged displays of all sorts—Red Indians, canaries, pigeons—but there was no groundsman to tend the field. However, cricket was his business and he was fond of it and it must have been frustrating for him that the MCC, to whom he let his ground for cricket, could not or would not buy the freehold from the heir of the estate when it came up for sale in 1860 at a price of £7,000. Six years later the club did buy it, for £18,000.

Secretaries of MCC

For all its long history, by 1985 there had been only eleven secretaries of MCC. Initially it was an honorary appointment. Benjamin Aislabie, to whom Tom bowled slow lobs in *Tom Brown's Schooldays*, was the first to hold office, from 1822 until his death in 1842, by which time he weighed about twenty-six

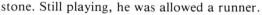

GAME of CRICKET.
at St Mary-le-bone.

LEFT The Laws of Cricket, as published in 1809, revised by the Club at St Mary-le-bone.
ABOVE Old Father Tyme removes a bail at close of play—the famous weather vane at Lord's.

stone. Still playing, he was allowed a runner.

His successor was Roger Kynaston, who served until 1858, throughout the period when the first professional circuses were in full swing. Reputed to be fussy, he had difficulty with his staff, for these were the days of change—revolution was in the air and the cities, with their factories and a new generation of wealthy men, were expanding.

After Kynaston came Alfred Baillie who remained for a five-year spell, until illness forced him to resign in 1863, whereupon Robert Alan Fitzgerald was nominated as his successor at the young age of twenty-nine. On 1 January 1868, five years after taking up the appointment, Fitzgerald became the first paid MCC secretary. He organized the first MCC tour overseas—to Paris in 1867,· when he was thirty-three and young enough to enjoy it, and to the United States and Canada five years later. He was a batsman good enough to hit the ball over the old tennis court in St John's Road on one occasion, but the lasting legacy of his term of office is the present red and yellow colours of the club, changed from the original sky-blue, although no one knows why the change was made. After Fitzgerald came Henry Perkins, 'Perkino' as he was called, whose term lasted for the next twenty-one years. He was a barrister, small in stature but with a huge beard, who walked about Lord's dressed in a grey suit with a tail-coat.

Francis Lacey

His successor, Francis Lacey, was also a barrister, a man whose manner during his period of office (1898-1926) was said to be cold and official, tending towards an over-rigid interpretation of rules and regulations; nevertheless it was during Lacey's term of office that the affairs of MCC and, indeed, of cricket the world over, were put into some sort of order. He was careful, even restrictive, about such mundane matters as club finances and facilities, especially refreshment facilities, and during his period in office the first sub-committees were formed. The Mound Stand was built a year after he took the job, and many were his other accomplishments, particularly as far as the laws and regulations of the game at the highest level were concerned.

It was to Lord's that the leading cricketers of the day automatically turned for guidance. Thus a County Cricket Council was formed in 1887 to deal with county classifications and qualifications, and in 1898 the counties asked MCC to form a Board of Control for Test matches. Three years later it was Lacey who suggested to the counties that an advisory committee should be set up to act as a forum for considering changes in the laws. By the time of the Australian season of 1903-04, MCC in England had accepted a request from the Melbourne Cricket Club (the MCC in Australia) through its secretary, Major Wardill, that future tours should always be organized from

Thomas Lord, a Yorkshireman, who built a cricket ground and was forced to move the turf around London until finally it settled at St John's Wood.

Lord's. In 1909, the Imperial Cricket Conference was established, all England delegates being nominated by the MCC.

Lacey's successor was Billy Findlay, who had been the second assistant secretary after captaining Eton and Oxford. He spent ten years in office, from 1926 to 1936, a period which included the notorious bodyline tour and its repercussions. Findlay himself, a courteous and charming man, probably did not relish all the scrapping that took place at that time between England and Australia.

His successor was Colonel R. S. Rait Kerr, a shy and efficient soldier whose daughter Diana, with encouragement from her father, created almost single-handed the Lord's library. Colonel Rait Kerr possessed an encyclopedic knowledge of the laws and increasingly complicated regulations of cricket, and in many instances was approached as a last resort for settling disputes.

Ronnie Aird, his assistant and eventual successor, was a man of great charm who succeeded to the post in 1952 and held it for ten years. It seems that MCC's decline as the guiding force in cricket either began or accelerated during his term of office. Whether or not this was due in part to his stewardship is a judgement best left to posterity.

Billy Griffith

By the time his successor, 'Billy' Griffith, took office, the game was in a state approaching ruin, in England principally but also elsewhere. Griffith was a former secretary and captain of Sussex and a Test cricketer who made his first century in his very first Test match. He then became a cricket writer on the *Sunday Times* before finding his proper niche at Lord's. The boom following the 1939-45 war had come to an end and a social revolution had taken place, and yet the attitude of the game's councils seemed too complacent and outmoded for cricket to be able to adapt and survive.

During these difficult years, matters were not improved by the onset of several formidable and insoluble cricketing conundrums such as the South African situation. Out of the agony of the 1960s came new ideas, such as the one-day competitions and Sunday cricket, which in turn led to the comparative prosperity of the 1970s, to such an extent, in fact, that cricket and cricketers became a much more attractive proposition for exploitation by commercial pirates.

When Griffith bowed out of office he handed his MCC responsibilities and those of secretary of the ICC over to Jack Bailey, another administrator with a cricketing background. Those of his duties which related to the Test and County Cricket Board, the more significant body in so far as cricket in England was concerned, were passed to another of his assistant secretaries, Donald Carr, one-time captain of Derbyshire. To suggest that relations between these two bodies (the North and South Towers in the Lord's pavilion) have been easy during the last dozen or so years would be as nonsensical as suggesting that there have been no problems between Soviet Russia and China. Suffice it to say that whereas the office of secretary of MCC is now significant chiefly in its historically important role of maintaining a club which still has custodianship of the greatest traditions in cricket (especially as keeper of the laws of the game), it was the office of secretary of the ICC which became the key appointment during the late 1970s. At that time, when tested by the likes of Kerry Packer, the Australian broadcasting

entrepreneur, the ICC's administration had been quite simply disastrous. By all accounts, Sir Francis Lacey and Colonel Rait Kerr won respect because they were always correct in their judgements.

If the office of MCC secretary has received most attention it is because that of president, the position in the public eye, has, except in war-time, been held only on an annual tenancy. Many of the figures who have held the office have been substantial influences on the development of cricket, but the office itself has usually been only incidental to that influence. Nevertheless, by studying the roles of MCC presidents, certain trends in the club's history can be traced. A love of cricket, in the majority of cases, and a facility for playing the game have been the principal qualifications for holding an office aptly described by the fifth Earl of Cardigan (then Viscount Chelsea), president in 1873, as the woolsack of cricket. Of the first nine men known to have been president, only two were titled and both of them, Lord Frederick Beauclerk and the Honourable George Ponsonby, were outstanding players, as were most of the others who held office in a decade increasingly characterized by the Duke of Wellington's civilian influence.

In the hundred years following 1834, there were only nine presidents of MCC who had no hereditary title, and one of these was a knight. From 1934 to 1964 the position changed only statistically. Beside Stanley Christopherson, who was president from 1939 until 1945, only four other commoners held the office. Since 1967 the situation has changed, with titles becoming rarer, although the Duke of Edinburgh had his second spell in 1974. By ancient tradition (and an admirable one in a private club) the president of MCC nominates his successor, and normally the secret of this man's identity is maintained until the anniversary dinner at which the appointment is announced. The time will come, no doubt, when a lady will receive the nod, but it may be a few years yet if precedent is any guide.

The tiny urn containing the Ashes, and its faded velvet bag. The Ashes remain permanently at Lord's.

FIRST-CLASS CRICKET

The concept of 'first-class cricket', from which arise, naturally, the 'first-class averages', is a comparatively new one, evolving around the 1860s.

The definition of a first-class match is a question which has exercised cricket statisticians for a long time. Not until 1947 was a first-class match officially defined. The compilation of lists of first-class averages for seasons before then was the task of the sporting press. It was only with the formation of the Association of Cricket Statisticians in 1973 that a more or less agreed list of first-class teams and matches has been retrospectively compiled, beginning with the 1864 season. This list would probably have been universally accepted among cricket statisticians, but it meant altering slightly the long-accepted career figures of a few cricketers. This was no problem in most cases, and the ACS figures have gradually superseded the older ones, but there are two notable exceptions: the cases of W. G. Grace and Jack Hobbs. In particular, Hobbs' total of 197 first-class centuries is so established in cricket lore that the addition of two extra is more than some will stand, and there are now two factions: ACS and 'Wisden-traditional'.

None of this was likely to occur to the English cricketers who first represented their counties, for whom cricket was cricket, and 'first-class' did not apply either to matches or railway carriages.

Cricket played between elevens labelled as counties (rather than as towns or clubs) began in the mid-eighteenth century, but the next century was more than a third gone before the first county cricket club, Sussex, was formally created, and it had only five years to run before the structure of a county championship was established in a form universally recognizable and recognized. It was not until 1895 that MCC was given, and willingly took upon itself, the task of officially declaring the champion county. Long before that it had been obvious to all but the blindly partisan which county had earned the title of champion in most seasons. But the method of scoring tended to be rudimentary, especially in view of the fact that counties all arranged their own fixture lists. Whereas a county like Surrey, already famous and well established at The Oval, might play as many as sixteen matches, a poor eleven like Derbyshire could arrange only six or seven matches. Derbyshire were in fact the only county ever to drop out of the Championship, albeit briefly.

Not until the publication of the 1911 edition of *Wisden Cricketers' Almanack* was a list of champion counties published, dating back to 1873. There were special reasons for choosing the year 1873, as we shall see. However, first let us trace how the nine founder members of the Championship—Derbyshire, Gloucestershire, Kent, Lancashire, Middlesex, Nottinghamshire, Surrey, Sussex and Yorkshire—developed in the formative decades of the middle of the nineteenth century. This was a period of rapid development in the country as a whole. Towns grew, funded by the profits generated by mine and mill, and the land prospered despite a population growth that terrified the economist Malthus, who had been the first to prophesy the island ant-heap we now know and sometimes love. Canals and then, rapidly, railways and better roads linked the whole together. In the midst of this expansion cricket tended to represent the good life, a feature of the game's appeal that has survived until today. Cricketers found both patrons and audiences without much difficulty in this age of penny income tax. These were the conditions in which William Clarke set up his professional troupe. When this venture failed, sufficient vested interests remained to promote the county game in all parts of the land, whether predominantly aristocratic, industrial or plain bourgeois.

We must begin with the oldest club, Sussex. Not only are they the senior county club, but following their formation, and indeed perhaps causing it, they fielded a team which could beat even Kent, then the acknowledged masters, nine times in eleven seasons. In 1847, with the greatest of Kent cricketers, Alfred Mynn, in the Sussex side, they defeated All-England. Lillywhite and Wisden were Sussex 'names', family names, later given to the

The County Championship, the basis of the English first-class game. Gloucestershire batting against Sussex in May 1973.

great chronicles of the game that began to be published towards the end of the century, the *Annual* and the *Almanack*. So were Broadbridge (he and Lillywhite formed the first pair of round-arm bowlers); Thomas Box, a wicket-keeper for no fewer than twenty-four summers; and the Eton and Cambridge batsman C. G. Taylor, a real all-rounder, an acting member of the 'old stagers' during Canterbury week, and enough of a tailor by inclination and by trade to walk down King's Parade in Cambridge wearing a pair of trousers of his own making.

The next county to be formed was Surrey—in 1845. From the very first, their home was at The Oval, where the opening match was played as the Montpelier Cricket Club against Clapton Cricket Club in that same year. It was from the Montpelier Club that Surrey sprouted, with William Ward, the saviour of Lord's,

taking the role of both midwife and gardener, as it were. In June 1846 they beat Kent by ten wickets in the first county match on the ground. In the late 1850s Surrey were a real force, as they were to be again exactly a hundred years later. Captain F. P. Miller, William Caffyn, the cricketer who was to do so much to foster the game in Australia, Julius Caesar (not a *nom de plume*), and H. H. Stephenson, the wicketkeeper who captained the first England team in Australia, were all pillars of the side.

Surrey's great bank-holiday rivals were Nottinghamshire, the next county to be founded in 1859. Nottinghamshire players really made their mark even before the redoubtable William Clarke, for the notorious Sam Redgate was a faster round-arm bowler even than Alfred Mynn. Redgate's most famous over (four balls at that time) was bowled for England at Town Malling

in Kent in 1839. The first shaved Fuller Pilch's wicket, the second bowled him out, the third knocked down Alfred Mynn's stumps, and the fourth bowled another Kent player, Shearman. It is said that the bowler downed a glass of brandy after each success. Whether this is legend or fact, drink was to be the death of poor Sam Redgate.

Clarke himself played in the side, of course, and there were no fewer than three Parrs in the original eleven, including George Parr, after whom the famous tree at Trent Bridge was named, and who subsequently went on to captain the All-England professional eleven that Clarke founded.

John Jackson was Redgate's successor as Nottinghamshire's fast bowler, but in the forty years from 1861 to 1901 this poor fellow slumped from the peak of his career as the greatest bowler in the world to a miserable death in the infirmary of a Liverpool workhouse, where even the Cricketers' Fund Friendly Society could not save him. A fifteen-stone six-footer, he was once asked if he had ever taken all ten wickets. 'No,' he replied regretfully, and then his face lit up. 'But I clean bowled nine once, and lamed John Wisden so's he couldn't bat. That'd be near enough, wouldn't it?'

Charlie Brown was the wicketkeeper in this fine team. A dyer by trade, he was apt to become so enthusiastic when talking about cricket at work that he would splash his own colour into everybody else's tub. Remarkable players tumbled out of Nottinghamshire, generation upon generation: Richard Daft, who married a Parr daughter, and built a reputation for dealing contemptuously with the most difficult balls, even shooters; his contemporary Alfred Shaw who, in a thirty-one-year career, bowled more than half his overs as maidens, so effective was his off-theory; Oscroft, who became captain of the county; and Arthur Shrewsbury who, according to W. G. Grace, was the best batsman in all the world, the first to use his pads as a second line of defence.

Gloucestershire began to play matches in 1868, and by 1870 the senior Mr. Grace, W. G.'s enthusiastic father, had enlisted support from friends and a county club was established. Naturally it was known all over the country as the county of the Graces.

For a while it seemed as if Cambridgeshire, too, would develop into a county club able to hold its own with the very best. Buttress and Tarrant, as dangerous a pair of bowlers as ever walked out on to a cricket pitch, the one a leg-breaker and the other a fast round-arm specialist, played regularly for this county. Buttress's appeal must have been interesting: a lamplighter by trade, he was also a ventriloquist, with a predilection for scaring nervous Victorian ladies in railway carriages by throwing his voice to represent a cat meowing under their seats. No batsman, he was once found under a tree when his time to walk to the wicket came. 'If I miss 'em I'm out, if I hit 'em I'm out, so what is the use—let's start the next innings,' he said. But instead of Cambridgeshire it was Derbyshire, founded in 1873, who took a place in the founding nine. William Mycroft's bowling was their great asset at this time, but despite this they were never a strong side.

Kent stood as unrivalled champions for many years in both the eighteenth and nineteenth centuries. The reason why the present county club was not founded until 1870 lies not in the poverty of that county's history, but in its very richness.

We have already seen teams under the Kent banner in action during Hambledon times and even before. In the early part of the nineteenth century, the West Kent Club was a miniature MCC, with its own professionals. The Town Malling Club, founded by Tom Selby, a businessman who turned landowner, brought Fuller Pilch from Norfolk to manage a local pub. He in turn engaged Martingell, a Surrey man, at a salary of £60 a year, for Town Malling. Even such a man as Pilch regarded 'Gentlemen as gentlemen and players as much in the same position as his head keeper may be.'

ABOVE A. E. Stoddart of Middlesex toured Australia, West Indies and North America, twice captaining sides to Australia in the 1890s. He also played rugby in the England three-quarter line.
BELOW Richard Daft of Nottinghamshire, the best professional batsman in England around 1870, led a tour to North America in 1879.

Canterbury Week, with its cricket and concert parties, began in 1842 and settled at the St Lawrence Ground five years later. In those days Kent had only one amateur, Alfred Mynn. Mynn, incidentally, missed the entire season in 1837 after taking the bowling of Redgate on his front leg for hour after hour playing in the historic North v South match at Leicester in 1836. Doctors thought he would lose the leg. Blood had run down and stained his stockings—pads were not yet in use. He was taken home to Kent strapped to the roof of a stagecoach, a journey which all but killed him.

Alfred Mynn was a splendid all-rounder, one of the round-arm men, one of the first in a long line of England all-rounders that would later comprise the incomparable Dr. W. G. Grace and Walter Hammond, and whose 1980s representative is another from a western county, Ian Botham.

In 1858 the Kent County Club was formed, and the Baker family, with Fuller Pilch as a retainer, merged their own club, the Beverley Club, with the new body so hoping to revive the fortunes of the county now that Mynn, often the only amateur in this great eleven, and Pilch had retired. On the original committee sat both Alfred Mynn and Edward Wenman, a professional. Although he later resigned, Wenman's presence on the committee reflects the Kentish tradition of former professionals assisting in administration. In recent times Les Ames, later the controller of the Hoppers, a Kent cricketing club with almost masonic characteristics, has epitomised this tradition as secretary-manager for 14 years of the county club at Canterbury. We ought to note in passing that Kent and Sussex, two counties which have been at loggerheads with the other counties in recent times, were also the leading counties in the dispute over the establishment of a parliament of cricket in 1864.

The Choosing of the Champions
The date of the first published list of champions coincides with a series of meetings held among the counties between December 1872 and June 1873, most of which took place at the Surrey County Club's behest. Their purpose was to lay down qualification rules to determine eligibility. We have already seen how, at one stage, Alfred Mynn of Kent took the field under Sussex colours. The eligibility rules eventually agreed in The Oval pavilion on 9 June 1873, stood for many years. They were:
1. No cricketer, whether amateur or professional, should play for more than one county during the same season.
2. Every cricketer born in one county and residing in another shall be free to choose at the commencement of each season for which of those counties he will play, and shall, during that season, play for the one county only.
3. A cricketer should be qualified to play for any county in which he is residing and has resided for the previous two years; or a cricketer may elect to play for the county in which his family home is, so long as it remains open to him as an occasional residence.
4. Should any question arise as to the residential qualification, the same should be left to the decision of the committee of the Marylebone Cricket Club.

When these rules were submitted to MCC for approval the latter wanted a clause inserted allowing amateurs to play for a county in which their parents had property. When this was rejected by the counties MCC attempted to stage their own championship by inviting sixteen counties to challenge for a silver cup. In the end, only Sussex and Kent offered such a challenge. They played an unhappy match on an extremely poor wicket and the scheme was abandoned.

What was not settled in 1873 was the method of deciding the Championship. This remained a knotty issue for twenty years and indeed has been the subject of debate and amendment ever since. Essentially, the method adopted was that the county with fewest matches lost should win the title. Except for one or two seasons, this method has produced results similar to

more sophisticated point-scoring schemes. Gloucestershire and Nottinghamshire, for instance, are judged to have shared first place in 1873, and Gloucestershire to have been outright winners in 1874. Thereafter, the principal rivalry was between Nottinghamshire and Surrey.

Nottinghamshire's great bowlers were Shaw and Morley. It was Morley who, in one memorable match against Surrey in 1880, bowled 19.2 overs at the opposition, who were bowled out for 16 on a treacherous wicket on which he, Morley, conceded only 9 runs for 7 wickets. That gives some idea of the intensity of rivalry of matches a century ago.

The potential for argument and the need for arbitration were particularly notable in 1886, for in that year the *Lillywhite Annual* indicated joint champions—Nottinghamshire and Surrey. Nottinghamshire were unbeaten with seven wins and seven draws; Surrey won five more matches, twelve out of sixteen, but lost three times and were therefore adjudged second in the title race. The rivalry between these counties was as intense as that between Yorkshire and Lancashire in the 1920s and 1930s.

Changes of Scoring Method
The first significant change in the Championship scoring system was the introduction of the points method: one point for a win, half a point for a draw. But with such a haphazard list of fixtures, and no real agreement as to which counties were first-class, the system was far from perfect. It was perhaps fortunate that Surrey's clear pre-eminence in the period of George Lohmann, Tom Richardson, Bill Lockwood and Bobby Abel was widely accepted by the cricketing public in the early 1890s; otherwise the arguments might have wrecked the Championship.

Despite the arguments, it was clear that Nottinghamshire and Surrey were the outstanding teams in the first twenty-two seasons of formal county cricket. Nottinghamshire were champions six times, four of them in succession, and also joint champions four times, whereas Surrey, who also won six times, shared the title only once. Gloucestershire, the team of all the Graces, judged outright winners in 1874, also won in 1876 and 1877. Yorkshire, who have now won the title more times than any other county, had to wait until 1893 to take it for the first time.

Derbyshire lost all their matches in 1887 and withdrew from the Championship, but Somerset made the number up to nine again in 1891 and three years later Derbyshire returned with Essex, Leicestershire and Warwickshire. Hampshire became an acknowledged first-class county in October of the same year. By this time yet another point system was in operation. This had been agreed in 1889 by the county secretaries, and provided that losses should be deducted from wins and no points given at all for a draw.

MCC Become Ruling Body
As the Championship entered the modern era it was fourteen counties strong. It had an agreed system for deciding the eligibility of players and a completely new scoring system: one point for a win, a point deducted for a loss and a proportion of points for games completed settled the order of merit. Above all, the County Championship now had an arbitrator. From 1894, MCC were to decide which games were first-class, and ten years later, in 1904, they set up the Advisory County Cricket Committee which was to last as the County Championship's ruling body until the formation of the Cricket Council in 1969.

Although MCC had donned the mantle of Solomon, the County Championship was still by no means an easy package to disentangle or on which to make judgements. With fourteen counties involved, the number of matches played had all but doubled from 71 to 131, but of this total Essex, for example, had some difficulty in acquiring even a minimum fixture-list of eight matches. Furthermore, draws were becoming common. This was the golden age of batting, heralded by a marked improvement in the wickets. The bowlers had to work harder for less success and so the percentage of draws crept up to a figure of over forty per cent.

In 1910, the long-established point system (one point for a win and one point deducted for a defeat, calculated as a percentage of matches played) was amended to wins as a percentage of the whole. This system lasted for one year only, for in 1911 the first-class counties adopted the idea, already implemented by the minor counties, of giving some points to a county which had a lead on the first innings. This of course was an essential feature of any two-day competition. Later, in 1911, upon Somerset's instigation, a scheme was adopted whereby five points were awarded for a win, three for a first-innings lead, and only one for a draw, a county's final score being the number of points gained expressed as a percentage of the maximum possible, with no-decision matches (those affected by rain) ignored altogether. Eventually this system was found to be statistically unsound. A county with a high rating, that is to say over three points a match, could find its total unfairly reduced because of a first-innings lead, and so a team challenging hard, for example Nottinghamshire in 1929, would deliberately throw a match into the no-decision category.

It was Tom Richardson, who walked from his home in Mitcham to The Oval and back every day—a twelve mile stretch—whose bowling won the first modern championship for Surrey. He took no fewer than 237 wickets with his great strength and pace; by August this great cricketer, described by Charles Fry as an Italian-looking bandit, must have travelled a fair distance in Surrey's service! Like many another great cricketer, unable to cope with life without the game which he loved, it is believed that Richardson eventually committed suicide.

The Rise of Yorkshire
Yorkshire ran a close race with Surrey for the Championship in the next year, and then Surrey subsequently faded away to fourth place. In the twenty years up to 1914, when cricket was suspended with the onset of the Great War, Yorkshire won the title eight times and were never below number eight in the table. In that period of total supremacy, they won 286 of their 545 matches, and only 68 were lost.

Yorkshire held the title for the first three years of the twentieth century—seasons in which they won 57 of their 99 matches. Somerset, spurred on by Sammy Woods, beat Yorkshire in Yorkshire in 1901 and 1902, these defeats making news up and down the country, as well as providing evidence that Somerset were then, as indeed they always have been, capable of surprising the cricketing world. The scores in the match at Leeds in 1901 still hold pride of place in the Taunton pavilion. Somerset were all out for 87 in the first innings and 238 adrift after Yorkshire batted. But then Lionel Palairet and Len Braund, two of the legion of greats who played for the smaller counties, put up 222 for the first Somerset wicket in the second innings, out of a total which eventually climbed to 630; whereupon Yorkshire, weary and worn, were bowled out for a mere 113.

Middlesex took the title in 1903 with a thin fixture-list compared with that of Yorkshire, the scoring system being such that a few wins and a high proportion of draws were virtually unbeatable. Incentive to win was thus reduced, and when Yorkshire managed outright success in fifty per cent of their games during this season only to be rated no higher than third, the north/south argument was again revived.

Lancashire took their second title without argument in 1904 with Yorkshire runners-up. The places were reversed in 1905, the year in which Northamptonshire entered the Championship for the first time.

In 1906, Kent won their first title. Their roll-call was as impressive as any side's, particularly as it included the names of the two great left-handers, Woolley and Blythe. Colin Blythe, or Charlie as he was known, a talented violinist, was killed near Passchendaele in 1917.

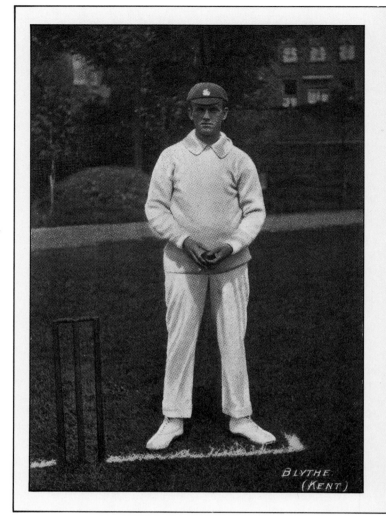

BLYTHE (KENT)

Nottinghamshire, Yorkshire, Kent for two seasons running, Warwickshire, Yorkshire, Kent again, and finally, in 1914, Surrey—these were the Champions in the years before the shells and bullets of the Western Front took out a whole generation of cricketers, some with reputations, others with promise of them. Cricket would never be the same again.

Although the Championship now took up half the English cricketing summer, most county programmes allowed sufficient blank days for country-house cricket to be played by many of the leading batsmen and bowlers, especially the amateurs—this, sadly, was a form of cricket that was never wholly re-established after the War.

The Championship after the War
Cricket began again in 1919 with two-day fixtures only. It was a dry summer, and because the Championship was decided on the old formula of percentage wins to matches played, drawn games became an epidemic and then a plague—56 out of a total of 124. Yorkshire had a new captain, D. C. F. Burton, but their players retained their old mastery, with Rhodes taking his usual 100 wickets, and the opening pair of Holmes and Sutcliffe leading the batting averages for the first time.

In the following year, first-innings points came back into the reckoning and matches were restored to three days. Thereafter, scoring methods were changed too frequently to chronicle in detail. Each change presented the captains with new challenges and new opportunities, although not all were in the best interests of the game. For example, it was decided in 1927 that all games in which it had been possible to hold less than six hours' play without a pair of innings completed be rated no-result games, and thus qualify each side for four points. This gave the captain having the worst of it every incentive to stay in the pavilion.

Three great slow left-arm bowlers at their peak when World War I arrived. LEFT Colin Blythe, of Kent, who was killed; ABOVE Wilfred Rhodes of Yorkshire; RIGHT Charlie Parker of Gloucestershire.

The season of 1920 was Plum Warner's last as captain of Middlesex, and although Yorkshire, Surrey and Kent all seemed to have a chance of winning, Middlesex took the title with Lancashire as runners-up. They won again in 1921 under Frank Mann, father of George Mann, later chairman of the Test and County Cricket Board. The great batsmen at Lord's at this time were Patsy Hendren and Jack Hearne, who in the course of this season hit thirteen centuries between them. Six of Patsy's seven were hit at Lord's, and five of 'Young Jack's', as he was known, were scored away from home. This produced as much contemporary chatter as did the home and away bowling figures of Laker and Lock when Surrey were winning so often in the 1950s. Great players get results anywhere, but runs and wickets against Yorkshire and Australia, the hardest nuts in the game, have always earned special respect from cricketers all over the world.

From 1922 to 1925, Yorkshire won consistently. Wilfred Rhodes was one of five batsmen to score 1,000 runs in 1922 for the White Rose, and four bowlers, none of them what we would now call fast, took 100 wickets. George Macaulay began life as a bowler of genuinely fast pace, but later developed into one of the earliest seam bowlers, and a very successful one. In 1923, Maurice Leyland played his first full season in the Yorkshire team, strengthening the side even more. He also made 1,000 runs.

Middlesex ran a close race with Yorkshire in 1924. War was declared between the two counties when Middlesex refused to play any more fixtures against Yorkshire because of the incessant noise made by the Sheffield crowd. The atmosphere of special hostility between these counties lingered. It was a Yorkshireman who attempted to denigrate Denis Compton by labelling him the 'the Brylcreem Boy', and at Sheffield in the 1950s, John Warr (subsequently paid a great honour by the Australians, who nominated him one of their representatives to the International Cricket Conference) was asked none too politely, after taking some stick whilst bowling, if he and his colleagues 'had come up there just to get tha' penknives sharpened'.

Not only did Yorkshire lose at Lord's that season, they also lost at Leeds in the Roses match, when Dick Tyldesley and Cecil Parkin, in one of the most famous of these closely fought encounters, bowled them out in an hour for 33 when Yorkshire needed a mere 57 to win. In 1925, Yorkshire, now captained by A. W. Lupton, were unbeaten in their thirty-two games, and during the course of this season Holmes made 2,000 runs, whilst Roy Kilner, an all-rounder whose left-arm bowling was rated superior to Rhodes' at this time, received a bumper benefit of £4,000.

After Yorkshire's run it was Lancashire's turn: for three years they took the Championship. Ted McDonald, the great Australian fast bowler, obtained 163 wickets in 1926 and Ernest Tyldesley, cousin to Dick and as thin and upright as Dick was round, batted with rare style and consistency.

In the next year Nottinghamshire looked a certainty for the Championship. All they had to do at the end of August was to beat the Rag, Tag and Bobtail Glamorgan team in their last match. Yet they lost by an innings. Glamorgan had entered the Championship in 1921, the last county to do so, and they owed much in those early days to Maurice Turnbull, who had begun to play for the county as a seventeen-year-old and who thereafter became not only a pillar of Cambridge cricket but also chief administrator of Glamorgan. He was secretary until he went off to fight in the Second World War—he was killed in Normandy in 1944. Jack Mercer, who was still scoring for Northamptonshire over 50 years later, a Sussex man by birth and during the first part of his career, took 6 for 31 for Glamorgan in this match with his off-spinners.

In May 1928, Charlie Hallows of Lancashire hit 1,000 runs. Hammond had done it in 1927, and W. G. back in 1895. With this supreme individual prizewinner in their ranks, Lancashire went through the season without defeat. Watson, Hallows' partner, was in his best form ever, and five batsmen in the team averaged over 50, while McDonald took even more wickets than usual—178. Nottinghamshire by now had their fast bowlers, Larwood and Voce, in harness, and captained by Arthur Carr, a redoubtable cricketer, they won the title in 1929. Their batting was thinner than that of their principal rivals, but with George Gunn and the young Charlie Harris following in the older players' deliciously eccentric footsteps, Nottinghamshire could never be dull.

Despite Larwood's mammoth contribution, Nottinghamshire were removed from the top by Lancashire in 1930, Eddie Paynter's first full season. Then Yorkshire, out of the limelight for five years, took the title for another three. At one stage in 1931 they were no higher than eighth place, but they won five games in a row, three of them on their southern tour, all of them by an innings, and once they arrived at the top they could not be shifted. By now Hedley Verity and Bill Bowes had joined their bowling attack and had become the chief wicket-takers, and

Jack Hobbs, 'The Master', the highest scorer in first-class cricket.

Herbert Sutcliffe was capable of averaging 97 as he did in that season. In the next year he and Percy Holmes put on 555 for the first wicket on a beautiful pitch at Leyton. It took just five minutes under seven-and-a-half hours to score this pile of runs, the largest ever accumulated by an opening pair until the record was beaten by Waheed Mirza and Mansoor Akhtar for Karachi Whites v Quetta in 1976-77.

In 1933, A. B. Sellers took over from F. E. Greenwood as captain and began to strengthen his reputation as a formidable skipper. The following season, Leonard Hutton, then eighteen, scored his first century for Yorkshire at Worcester. But it was Lancashire who took the title that year—the season that Cyril Washbrook began to make a mark for them.

In 1935 Yorkshire won again and the following year Derbyshire, captained by A. W. Richardson, took the title in what remains to this day a statistically improbable achievement. Only three of their batsmen—Worthington, Townsend and Smith—averaged over 30, and none was rated among the best in the land. But this was the year in which Bill Copson, he of the red hair and long arms, was at his fastest and most devilish. He took 140 wickets, while the leg-breaks of Tommy Mitchell, the greatest billiard-ball spinner, also claimed over 100. The next season Yorkshire were first again, and there they stayed for three years. This must have seemed a long time to all the other counties, especially Middlesex, who had been runners-up every season from 1936 to 1939—a most disheartening experience, particularly as they could boast Jim Sims bowling his leg spinners and the young Edrich and the brothers Compton coming to full maturity. Be that as it may, Yorkshire's run of seven titles in the 1930s remained the most monopolistic hold on the Championship in its long history thus far.

The Championship Resumes Again
After the Second World War, the County Championship remained, until the advent of the one-day competitions in 1963, the only tournament in which the counties played each other. And every year since 1963, at the presentation ceremonies, the county captain lucky enough to have led his team to victory in the Championship has been asked the same question: 'It's still the best competition, isn't it?' And always the same answer comes back: 'Yes.'

Many times there have been attempts to alter the structure of the Championship. Many committees have sat and much midnight oil has been consumed. Suggestions made have included abandoning the Championship altogether because of falling attendances, turning it into a smaller, four-day competition in which the counties play each other only once during a season, or, at the other extreme, increasing the number of County Championship matches. This latter alternative was actually instigated at one point, and for several years the Championship was a competition in which each county played each of its rivals twice over a three-day period—a true championship, in fact. In 1985, each county played 24 matches.

Just as the number of matches has altered over the years, so too has the method of scoring points continued to change. Indeed, at one stage the changes were so frequent as to be quite baffling to the spectators, but eventually the legislators recognized that continuous meddling with the Championship was bringing the competition into disrepute. Against this background of constant change, the system used in the 1980s, which incorporates the scoring bonus points initiated in 1968, must be judged a considerable success. For a win sixteen points are awarded (this having been increased from ten, through twelve in 1977 to sixteen in 1981), for a tie eight points (previously six and five), and for a draw (equal scores) the side batting in the fourth innings scores eight (previously six and five) points. Additionally, each county is awarded bonus points based on the first 100 overs of each side's first innings. These points are awarded for scoring each successive 50 runs once a total of 150 has been reached, and as the

shutters come down at 300 this means that there are four points available to the batting side. There are also four points available to the bowling side, who must take a minimum of three wickets before they can begin to register their bonus points. Of course, there have been attempts to manipulate the rules by declaring before the full complement of wickets has been taken and by conceding runs as part of a trade-off for a declaration, but on the whole the system has worked well.

A Limited First Innings
The experiment of a limited-over first innings in 1974 caused many older cricketers to shake their heads. They felt that this was an interference with the captain's right to plan a match, just as the system of limiting the leg-side field, introduced in 1957, was regarded by many as a catastrophic step backwards, initiating as it unquestionably did the decline in the significance of spin bowling in all forms of cricket. Another law to work to this effect is that concerning the taking of a new ball. Since the 1960s a new ball has been allowed after as few as 65 overs; at other times it has been 75 or 85 overs. With this allowance, it proved more worthwhile for captains to pack their side with economical seam-bowlers rather than include spinners in their attack, a factor which prompted a dramatic change in the composition of county teams. Whereas in the 1950s the normal pattern of a bowling attack was three spinners and two quicker bowlers, thirty years later it was almost always customary for teams to have three, if not four, seam bowlers, and often counties go into the field with but a single spin bowler. Whether this is progress or not only the crowds can tell. Certainly attendances have continued to diminish, spectators patently preferring the alternative of one-day cricket.

But despite what was to happen later, the summer of 1946 began a cricketing boom which lasted for fully five years. It represented the end of hostilities and a need on the part of everyone to return to old habits—such as watching the best cricketers in the country at play. Yorkshire won the title in 1946 with Brian Sellers still their captain. One of their outstanding bowlers that season was Arthur Booth, who had earlier been discarded because of the pre-eminence of Hedley Verity, now dead. Remarkably, Booth came back to head the national bowling averages and won his Yorkshire cap at forty-three.

Compton and Edrich's Year
In 1947, Middlesex, who had run Yorkshire close in 1946, took the title. It was a gorgeous summer, and Edrich and Compton played in masterly fashion through the season until by September hardly a day's cricket passed without a record being broken. Compton averaged 96 in that season, Edrich 77, and there were three others in the team whose average was over 40: Robertson, Thompson and Brown. Both Compton and Edrich broke the record aggregates for a summer in England, and Compton, with eighteen centuries to his credit broke the record of sixteen which Jack Hobbs had set when he was forty-two. The spinners, Jack Young, with slow left-handers, and Jim Sims, the leg-spinner, took most of the wickets, and Walter Robins, in his last season as Middlesex's captain, was as full of zest and trickery as he had been when he first began to play for his county.

The 1948 season saw Glamorgan at the head of the table, a remarkable achievement for the junior county, traditionally one of the weakest. Glamorgan bred some but not enough of its own players, and had always been obliged to recruit from elsewhere in the country. However, under the captaincy of Wilfred Wooller, who had been a distinguished rugby centre three-quarter for Wales, Glamorgan established a reputation for fearless fielding, and driven on by this tall, angular man scored enough runs and took enough wickets to beat their rivals. Perhaps the most pleasing feature of their win was that Johnnie Clay, who had played in the side which first entered the Championship in 1921, was a member of the team which beat Hampshire at

Bournemouth towards the end of August, a crucial match that clinched the Championship. He was then fifty-one and he took nine wickets in this game, following figures of 10 for 66 in the preceding game. Willie Jones, the Gloucester stand-off half and the greatest dropper of goals in post-war rugby, headed the batting averages. Emrys Davies, a veteran of the 1930s, and Gilbert Parkhouse, a young player who was later to win caps for England, fronted the batting strength. Len Muncer, an off-spinner from London, took 139 wickets, but success did not smooth his cockney tongue which could be heard around the Lord's ground, where he was one of the chief coaches, until his retirement in 1978.

In 1949, Middlesex and Yorkshire shared the title, and the following year Surrey, under Michael Barton, divided the honours similarly with Lancashire. The latter side were bringing on some magnificent new cricketers in this period, particularly bowlers—spinners like Tattersall, Hilton and Berry, and the young Brian Statham.

In 1951 Warwickshire took the title for the first time in forty years. Their splendid side, under captain Tom Dollery, lost only two matches during the season, partly because few of their team were required for Test matches. Runs came thick and fast from men like Dollery, Gardner, Hitchcock, Spooner (the wicket-keeper) and Townsend; and Eric Hollies and Tom Pritchard from New Zealand (as fast a bowler as any in England) spear-headed the bowling attack.

Surrey's Dominant Years

The following season it was Surrey who were to return to the limelight, now under the captaincy of Stuart Surridge, a member of the family famous for its bats and balls. Surridge achieved an unprecedented record: in his five years as captain he led Surrey to five consecutive Championship victories. He was a whirling dervish of a batsman and a useful away-swing bowler with the new ball, but his principal contribution to Surrey's achievements was the remarkable spirit he inspired in his team, particularly in the field (he was the forerunner of the suicidally close short-legs). Fired by his example Surrey developed into a superb all-round side, not only because their fielding was so excellent (particularly with Tony Lock, the best backward short-leg in the history of the game, in the team) but also because their batsmen and bowlers were so uniformly competent. Three of their bowlers (Lock, Alec

Bedser and Jim Laker) were automatic selections for England, all of them the outstanding practitioners of their respective styles. Bedser's combination of in-swing and cut from leg could be unplayable, and almost always entailed an early breakthrough for his county. Later he came to be supported by the fierce, whippy pace of Peter Loader. Lock was challenged as a left-arm bowler throughout this period by Yorkshire's Johnny Wardle, but there was no comparison between the two on wet wickets where Lock's action, subsequently much criticized and not least by himself, made him able to generate such pace and lift as to be virtually unplayable.

As for the County's batting strength, once the young May had become a Surrey player there was no shortage of class. Others who served the county so well in this period were players such as Bernard Constable, so difficult to dislodge even after wickets had begun to fall, David Fletcher, who promised so much but subsequently faded, reliable Tom Clark, and finally the exciting newcomers who were to go on and play many times for England: Ken Barrington and Mickey Stewart.

After Surridge's retirement Peter May took the county to two more Championships. In May's first year, 1957, the distance between Surrey and Northamptonshire, the runners-up, was huge, and they had completed their Championship win by 16 August, a very early date. Yorkshire won in 1959, a remarkable feat with their young, re-built side. But Yorkshire also had a post-war generation of outstanding merit, headed by Freddie Trueman, perhaps at the end of the day the most notorious fast bowler of all time. Irrespective of the records that he set, Trueman's contribution to a cricket side on the field was immense. He had not only pace but movement and stamina, and he was able to provide a continuous element of surprise. Add to that his fielding ability, which was second only to Lock's, and his whirlwind batting performances, and here was a figure around whom others of less character could be successfully grouped. Among the young Yorkshire tigers of this era were Close and Illingworth, then both at the peak of their capabilities and both future captains of England, and the new generation of batsmen led by Stott, Taylor and Padgett, none of whom quite developed as Yorkshiremen hoped. The captain was Ronnie Burnett, who

Shady trees, the cathedral, deckchairs, well-mown grass—the peaceful scene of cricket at Worcester.

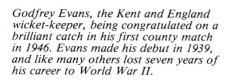

Godfrey Evans, the Kent and England wicket-keeper, being congratulated on a brilliant catch in his first county match in 1946. Evans made his debut in 1939, and like many others lost seven years of his career to World War II.

The cup which, despite the rise of the one-day game, is the most eagerly sought by the English counties—the Championship Trophy.

successfully weathered his inheritance of a troubled team in which Johnny Wardle, although a great comedian off the field, was not the easiest of dressing-room comrades. Yorkshire had lost the services of Bob Appleyard, whose career was cut short by tuberculosis just as he had established himself both in county and on tour for England as a wicket-taker of unusual skill and penetration.

Hampshire Make Their Mark

In 1960, Vic Wilson, a farmer from Malton, one of Yorkshire's veteran players, was appointed captain, and Yorkshire again won the Championship. Jimmy Binks their wicketkeeper, who could claim eventually over 400 consecutive matches for his county, took 100 victims behind the stumps in this season. Although Yorkshire had been the principal challengers to Surrey during the latter's seven-year reign as champions, their team at the beginning of the 1960s was not quite good enough to emulate Surrey's feat, and in 1961 a new name was engraved on the Championship board—that of Hampshire. Both Yorkshire and Middlesex challenged strongly, but Hampshire held top position throughout August. Colin Ingleby-Mackenzie was their captain, and a more glamorous figure has never been seen in county cricket. After Hampshire had won the title, the Ingleby-Mackenzie legend grew. He claimed his team had trained on wine, women and song, and not too much of the latter; the only rule he insisted upon was that his players should be in bed by breakfast-time. The Hampshire team on the whole were a hard-bitten lot who had had to struggle for success in cricket, but they regarded their young captain with amusement, tolerance and, in the end, almost reverence, not least because he won so many matches that year through declarations. Horton, Gray and Leo Harrison, the wicketkeeper, were steady players at the top and in the middle of the order, and among their bowlers Hampshire boasted the incomparable Derek Shackleton, whose length and movement were a phenomenon of cricket at this time. The best cricket sides require above-ordinary pace in their attack, and this was provided by the rollicking figure of 'Butch' White. Unable to establish himself in Warwickshire cricket, White came to Hampshire and eventually became as natural a Hampshireman in looks and behaviour as any in the team. So, in his cricket at least, was Roy Marshall, the most exciting batsman in the side. The first overseas player of any distinction to join the county cricket circuit after the war, Marshall joined Hampshire in 1951 and played with the greatest distinction for the county for twenty-one years. He was a rarity in his age, an opening batsman who put bat to ball from the first delivery of the innings. Between the Wars there had been many such cricketers—Charlie Barnett of Gloucestershire comes readily to mind. Roy Marshall was in the same mould, and he gave real pleasure to cricket-lovers all over the country and most especially in Hampshire. Had it not been for him the club might have suffered considerably because it was not one of the strongest counties financially.

Yorkshire Return to the Top

Vic Wilson led Yorkshire back to the Championship in 1962, his last year in the first-class game. This was an exciting season because everything hinged upon the last match, Yorkshire's game against Glamorgan. Worcestershire were ten points ahead in the table when Yorkshire put Glamorgan in to bat on a drying wicket and established a position of considerable strength on the first day. The second day was a complete wash-out, and on the third the Yorkshire spinners managed to bowl the Welshmen out cheaply yet again, whereupon Yorkshire romped home in a low-scoring match by seven wickets.

Yorkshire won again in 1963 (their centenary year), a season in which Brian Close captained them for the first time. Close was a player of outstanding natural ability and must look back over his career regretting that he did not make more runs and take more wickets than he did. It was not until he was over thirty that he began to demonstrate for the world to see the courage and the acute cricketing brain that were to make him such a respected figure in the country at large. The team he led was a strong one, with Trueman to bowl and Philip Sharpe to catch so many batsmen at slip. Above all it was the first full season of the young Geoffrey Boycott, who made three 100s in this summer, including a quite superb innings at Sheffield in one of the last Roses matches played on this great ground.

Worcestershire's Centenary Success

The 1964 season marked Worcestershire's centenary, and a few months before the actual birthday Don Kenyon led the county to their first ever Championship. Kenyon himself was a son of the county with a Brummagem accent which was almost impenetrable at times. For nigh on twenty years he was the man who had to be got out in the Worcestershire eleven, a fine opening batsman who, once established, could tear bowlers to shreds on the superb Worcestershire ground. He was joined now by Tom Graveney who had left Gloucestershire in 1961 and enjoyed one of his best seasons in this Championship year, and also by Ron Headley, son of the great George Headley, the West Indian batsman whose son's Birmingham accent rivalled that of the captain. But it was the bowlers who had a year to remember in 1964, Jack Flavell, a Black Country lad, and Len Coldwell, a Devonian, both taking over 100 wickets.

The Worcestershire centenary was actually celebrated in 1965, and appropriately the side won the Championship again. They had been well down the table in ninth position towards the end of July, but thereafter they won ten of their final eleven matches and came through to finish with one of the strongest runs in memory. Their cricket was much strengthened by the appearance for the first time of the South African Basil d'Oliveira, who had joined them the previous year. In his opening season he hit five centuries in the Championship.

From 1966 to 1968, Yorkshire won three Championships in a row. The first was a tight affair with everything depending on the last matches, in which they beat Kent, but Worcestershire, challenging again, went down against Sussex. This summer the Yorkshire bowlers were strengthened by the appearance of Tony

Nicholson, an in-swinger of high skill, and he, Trueman and Don Wilson all took over 100 wickets, while Boycott headed the batting averages. In 1967 Yorkshire needed to beat Gloucestershire to decide the Championship; they managed it in two days. A constant theme throughout the history of the Championship has been the Yorkshiremen's ability to take the title from the pack when there are very few opportunities for scoring championship points left. So many times, when confronted with a last-ditch affair, they have come out on top. Close led his county to victory for the third time in 1968, again helped by the superb batting of Boycott, with the Yorkshire spin bowlers having an especially good season.

A Second Win for Glamorgan

Glamorgan had been developing another good side during the 1960s, and in 1969 their efforts finally bore fruit when they won the Championship. They fielded a number of players who had joined the county from elsewhere. Ossie Wheatley, a fine away-swing opening bowler, who had captained them for several years, was still playing, and they now could call on the services of Majid Khan from Pakistan and Cambridge, and Brian Davis from Trinidad, as well as their Bristol-born but South African-raised all-rounder, Peter Walker. Walker had been capped for England because of his all-round skill and was accounted one of the finest short-leg fielders in the country. The team was led by Tony Lewis, who like so many of his Welsh-born predecessors was not only an outstanding cricketer but also a fine rugby player until injury ended his career.

In the following year, their centenary year, Kent won the Championship. The summer was a tribute to the quality of the Championship as a competition, because on 1 July Kent had been at the bottom of the table. Five of their players—Cowdrey, Denness, Luckhurst, Knott and Underwood—were called upon by England. It was the first triumph of a team which has seldom been out of contention in the 1970s and 1980s.

In 1971, Surrey took the title, although the issue was not decided until 13 September. Mickey Stewart, in his last season as captain of a county for which he had given so much service, led the team to triumph. John Edrich, Graham Roope, Pat Pocock, Geoff Arnold and Bob Willis (before his move to Warwickshire) were all in that Championship-winning side.

West Indian Influence

In the following season, 1972, Warwickshire, the team often unkindly called the United Nations, won the title. They had eleven Test players in the county, including no fewer than four from the West Indies—Kanhai, Kallicharran, Murray and Gibbs. Objectively examined, this was an absurd position. No one begrudged Warwickshire their Championship, but the presence in the champion county of so many players not able to play for England was plainly not in the best interests of English cricket. Bob Willis, although he was not allowed to play for Warwickshire until 1 July after leaving Surrey, nonetheless featured in the run-in to the title for the second season in succession.

The winners in 1973 were Hampshire, who had the good fortune not to lose any players to the Test side. Like Warwickshire in 1972 and Glamorgan in 1969, Hampshire came through the season unbeaten, and also took every advantage of the relatively new bonus-points system, taking 84 for batting and 81 for bowling. This gave them an overall lead over Surrey of 31 points in the final table.

Hampshire were always able to get off to a splendid start because of the batting of Barry Richards and Gordon Greenidge, an opening partnership that, when future histories come to be written, will have to be acknowledged as one of the finest in all English cricket.

Two Close Finishes

Hampshire challenged strongly in 1974. They were at the top

of the table at the end of May and stayed there for three months, but Worcestershire had narrowed the gap to two points by the middle of August and with some help from the weather were able to creep into the lead and take the Championship by the very narrow margin of two points.

This was the season in which the first-innings 100-over limit was applied. If the team batting first failed to use up their 100 overs, the remainder would be given to the side batting second. This, combined with the bonus-points system, seems to have satisfied the players with its fairness.

There was another late result in 1975. Not until 15 September were Leicestershire declared the winners, for the first time in their history. This was a great achievement for Raymond Illingworth, perhaps all the more sweet because his former county Yorkshire were runners-up. In fact the only real challengers for the title were Lancashire, who finished fourth, with Hampshire lying third and Kent fifth. The Leicestershire side had been shrewdly strengthened by their secretary-manager, Mike Turner, who was prepared to engage players of talent no matter where they came from; the Leicestershire batting averages were headed by Brian Davison from Rhodesia, and also in the team were players like Illingworth, Balderstone and Birkenshaw, all from Yorkshire, McVicker from Lincolnshire via Warwickshire, Ken Higgs from Lancashire, and Graham McKenzie from Western Australia.

Middlesex Come to the Fore

Under Mike Brearley, a young Middlesex side deserved the Championship in 1976. Not only did they win more matches than their three nearest rivals, but they also toppled the dominant West Indian tourists. Graham Barlow, a left-hander, headed the batting averages with Brearley himself second, and four of the bowlers, Titmus, Selvey, Alan Jones and Phil Edmonds, all took over 60 wickets, a big haul in the modern Championship.

In the following year, Middlesex shared the title with Kent, the first time since 1950 that there had been joint leadership. The fact that Middlesex played one more match than Kent and two more than Gloucestershire, who suffered with the weather, caused tongues to wag. Middlesex avoided the three worst days in the summer because their county fixture with Essex was re-arranged so that they could complete their Gillette Cup semi-final. Given a points scoring system whereby a team had merely to play to be certain of at least some points, this caused considerable controversy. The finale was exciting. Gloucestershire were ahead by four points as they began their final match, but Kent beat them without much difficulty. This left Middlesex needing to beat Lancashire at Blackpool to make sure of the title, with Kent virtually certain to beat Warwickshire at Edgbaston. Emburey and Edmonds, the Middlesex spinners, took 17 wickets, and their young batsman Mike Gatting scored 110 in the match which was more than Lancashire's entire first-innings total.

In 1978, Kent, joint champions in 1977, took the title almost unchallenged. They were able to do this because they had a number of fine players registered with World Series Cricket who were nevertheless eligible to play for them all through the summer. Derek Underwood enjoyed a particularly fine season. However, the presence of so many Packer players in the Kent team meant that this White Horse Championship win was less rapturously received than others had been.

Essex Break Their Duck at Last

In 1979 Essex won their first-ever Championship, and won it by a very wide margin, winning 13 matches, as many as Worcestershire and Surrey, the second and third teams, put together. Under Keith Fletcher, an astute captain who later regained an England place and led his country on tour, their assets were John Lever, who took 99 Championship wickets with his fast left-arm bowling, Graham Gooch, now a powerful and commanding opening batsman, Ken McEwan, a rapid-scoring batsman from South Africa, and an all-round side particularly

The skipper who has had much to do with the success of Essex in the 1980s, Keith Fletcher, directing his field.

strong on team spirit and humour, slow bowler Ray East being principal clown.

In 1980 Middlesex and Surrey, with ten wins each, drew away from the field, Middlesex winning on bonus points. Clive Radley averaged over 50, and Brearley and Gatting were also in the batting line-up, but it was probably the fast bowling which won the title, the county having engaged Vintcent Van der Bijl from South Africa to join Wayne Daniel as a fearsome partnership. There were other quickish bowlers, such as Hughes and Merry, to perform well in emergencies, as well as the wily slow men, Emburey and Edmonds.

With sixteen points for a win in 1981, two sides locked in a tremendous battle each passed 300 points, Nottinghamshire getting 304 and just preventing Sussex, on 302, from winning their first-ever Championship. Sussex were beating Yorkshire in their last match when news came that Notts had beaten them to the title. Both counties relied heavily on overseas bowlers. Notts, whose first Championship this was for 52 years, were indebted to South African Clive Rice and New Zealander Richard Hadlee, who took 105 Championship wickets. Rice's all-round talents were enhanced by his winning the toss in all home matches but the first. Sussex's fast bowlers were South African Garth le Roux and Pakistani Imran Khan. Derek Randall with his batting and Eddie Hemmings with his bowling were the Champions' principal 'home' performers.

It was Middlesex's turn again in season 1982, the last for

captain Mike Brearley. In a good year for them there were hopes at one time that Middlesex might take all four domestic competitions, but they could not sustain the pace. Captain-in-waiting, Mike Gatting topped the Championship batting averages, with John Emburey, Wayne Daniel and Phil Edmonds taking over 200 wickets between them. With Emburey ruled out of England consideration through having toured South Africa, and Edmonds and Gatting out of favour for one reason or another, the Middlesex side were not hampered unduly by England demands. Only one of the Championship side, the uncapped and relatively untried Norman Cowans, went to Australia in the winter.

In 1983 Essex, now one of the stronger counties, won again. Ken McEwan was easily the most successful batsman, topping 2,000 runs, with Gooch and Fletcher well behind. Lever took 98 wickets at only 16.80, and was well supported by Norbert Phillip and Neil Foster, who was the only player required by England, Gooch and Lever being South African 'rebels'.

Nottinghamshire's Disappointment
Essex retained the Championship in 1984, with the three-year ban on the South African tourists still operating in their favour. It was one of the most exciting Championship finishes, with Essex and Nottinghamshire drawing away and disputing the race right to the last over of the season. Had Nottinghamshire beaten Somerset in the last match they would have taken the title, and with their last pair together they had reduced a target of 297 to 4 from the last three balls. From the penultimate ball, Mike Bore, attempting to hit a six, was caught just inside the long off boundary and Notts, having scored 341 points, which would have

ABOVE Clive Rice turns the ball past square leg at Uxbridge in 1981, the year he led Notts to their first County Championship since 1929, and the days of Whysall, Payton, Gunn, Larwood and Voce. OPPOSITE Ken McEwan, aggressive middle-order batsman from South Africa, an Essex stalwart in three Championship seasons, played for the county from 1974–85.

won any Championship under the new scoring, had to be content with second place. Richard Hadlee had the distinction of performing the first double of 1,000 runs and 100 wickets since Fred Titmus in 1967.

Middlesex Triumph on Last Day
The 1985 season was interesting for the resurrection of Gloucestershire, who were among the leaders all season. Their last Championship win was in 1877, during the years of the Graces, and neutral observers hoped they would gain compensation for the narrow miss in 1977, but as then they could finish only third. Hampshire were again leading contenders, with Greenidge still opening for them as he had in their 1973 Championship victory, David Turner, with six appearances, being the other survivor of that side. Both these counties, and Middlesex, could win the title when the last matches began, and it was Middlesex who were the only winners and who thus recorded their ninth Championship, their fourth in ten years. Wilf Slack was easily their heaviest scorer, but Graham Barlow, Clive Radley and Roland Butcher also passed 1,000 runs. Wayne Daniel took most wickets, followed by Norman Cowans, Neil Williams and England's Phil Edmonds.

Australia

In Australia, the first reference to cricket occurs in the *Sydney Gazette* in January 1804. The first match recognised as first-class is that at Launceston in February 1851 between Tasmania and Victoria.

The domestic inter-state competition, the Sheffield Shield, was started in 1892-93. The previous season an English team, under the captaincy of W. G. Grace, had been taken to Australia by Lord Sheffield, a great patron of cricket in Sussex. Cricket had been declining in Australia, partly due perhaps to the disappointing tours of 1887-88. In that year, Lillywhite, Shaw and Shrewsbury, who had previously taken teams to Australia, took a team under the captaincy of C. Aubrey Smith, the Sussex spinner later to become famous as a Hollywood film star. However, at the request of the Melbourne Cricket Club, another side under G. F. Vernon, and captained by Lord Hawke, toured at the same time. Interests, both Australian and English, naturally clashed, the tours were disastrous financially, and no Test matches were played. Cricket might have taken many years to recover in Australia had not Lord Sheffield and his captain Grace decided to repair the damage.

During the tour Lord Sheffield donated 150 guineas (£157.50) to promote cricket in Australia. The Australian Cricket Council used the money to inaugurate the offical championship between what were then the first-class colonies in Australia, the winners to be awarded a shield—the Sheffield Shield. Only three colonies competed in the first season: Victoria, South Australia and New South Wales playing each other twice. Victoria, unbeaten, won the Shield, with New South Wales losing all four matches.

Within four seasons, each of the teams had won the Shield. The same three competitors fought for the Shield, with the exception of the war years, until 1926-27. During this time, New South Wales won 17 titles, Victoria 10 and South Australia 3.

Part of the ascendancy of New South Wales in the early days, particularly in six straight wins from 1901-02, was the greatness of the batting of Victor Trumper, the leading player of his era. He was supported by his opening partner Reggie Duff, Syd Gregory, Monty Noble and Albert Cotter. Victoria had George and Albert Trott, the great slow bowler Hugh Trumble and a young Warwick Armstrong. South Australia's heroes were George Giffen in the earliest days, then Joe Darling and Clem Hill.

In 1926-27 Queensland became the fourth side in the competition, and South Australia recorded a rare win in a very closely fought season. Victoria proved the strongest state between the wars, however. This was the era of Don Bradman, who switched from New South Wales to South Australia in 1935-36. Bradman was the greatest run-maker in cricket, but he was not the only prolific run-getter of the 1920s and '30s. Bill Ponsford of Victoria made two innings of over 400, two more of over 300, and nine others over 200. The only two innings in first-class cricket over 1,000 were both made by Victoria in the 1920s, Ponsford scoring 429 and 352 in these innings. His highest score was 437, also for Victoria, against Queensland in 1927-28. In five successive innings in this season Ponsford scored 133, 437, 202, 38 and 336. Ponsford's 437 was a world record at the time, but two years later Bradman beat it with 452 not out for New South Wales against Queensland, and went on to play 37 innings of over 200, another record. Charlie Macartney and Alan Kippax were among other heavy scorers. Some of the Australian bowlers of the inter-war years were not bad: Ted McDonald, Jack Gregory, Arthur Mailey, Clarrie Grimmett, and Bill O'Reilly among them.

After the Second World War, Western Australia joined the

OPPOSITE Sheffield Shield cricket. Kerry O'Keeffe turns one to leg for New South Wales against Queensland at Sydney in 1975-76.

FAR LEFT W. L. Murdoch (right), a Victorian who captained
Australia and played for England, poses with W. G. Grace, with
whom he played for London County.
LEFT Monty Noble, from Sydney, another Australian captain, and
their best pre-World War I all-rounder.

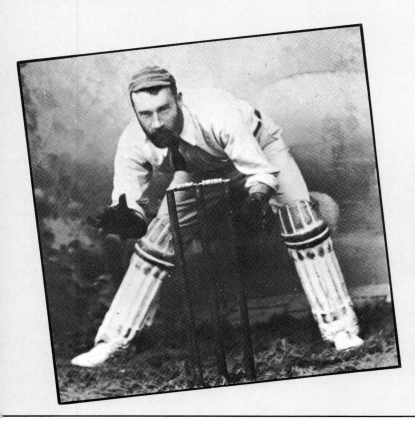

LEFT Jack Blackham, brilliant Victorian wicket-keeper who
was on the first eight Australian tours to England.
ABOVE Warren Bardsley, stylish New South Wales and
Australia left-handed batsman.

Graeme Pollock, one of two great South African batsmen of modern times (Barry Richards was the other) whose Test careers suffered because of South Africa's sporting isolation.

other four Sheffield Shield contestants in 1947-48, and won at the first attempt, though only on average—they completed four matches to the others' seven. Being so far from the other cricketing centres, Western Australia had to pay much of the expenses of visiting states. It was not until 1956-57 that Western Australia were fully integrated, playing each of the other states home and away, so that all states played eight matches. In turn, Tasmania joined the tournament in 1977-78 and were fully integrated in 1982-83, making a full programme of ten matches per state.

In 1948 Australia sent to England one of the strongest elevens ever to play cricket. This team not only defeated England comprehensively in the Tests, but went undefeated throughout the season. Of its principal players, Neil Harvey, Lindsay Hassett, Ian Johnson and Bill Johnston played for Victoria, Ray Lindwall and Keith Miller, the opening bowlers, and Sid Barnes and Arthur Morris, the opening batsmen, played for New South Wales, Bradman for South Australia and Don Tallon, the wicket-keeper, for Queensland.

From 1953-54 New South Wales started on a run of nine consecutive Sheffield Shield triumphs, a record. From 1965-66, however, New South Wales have had a very lean time and from the early 1970s Western Australia emerged to enjoy a spell as the strongest state. Dennis Lillee and Rodney Marsh were two of their strongest players. One curiosity of the Sheffield Shield is the difficulty experienced by Queensland in registering a first win. In modern times Australian captains Greg Chappell and Allan Border have played for Queensland.

South Africa

South Africa was an early convert to cricket, with a first reference appearing in the *Cape Town Gazette and African Advertizer* in 1808, although it is certain that cricket was played earlier than this. The first recognised first-class match was that between an England touring team and a South African side, played at Port Elizabeth in March 1889. The first first-class domestic match was played in December 1889 between Natal and Port Elizabeth.

In 1876 a 'Champion Bat' was presented by Port Elizabeth for competition between towns and villages. Then, in 1888-89, Sir Donald Currie presented a cup for competition and the Currie Cup has since been the major trophy in South African domestic competition. In 1951-52 the competition was divided into two sections, A and B. Since 1977-78 Section B has been called the Castle Bowl.

The Currie Cup is confined to only the leading teams, usually the four provinces, Transvaal, Natal, Eastern Province and Western Province, plus Zimbabwe (formerly Rhodesia). Transvaal and Natal have been easily the most successful teams, while Zimbabwe and Eastern Province have found it as difficult as Queensland have in Australia to win the premier competition at all. Because there are so few top-class teams, there has been much less first-class cricket in South Africa than elsewhere.

Because of the government's policies of *apartheid*, South Africa has been isolated from world competition since 1969-70. This, from the point of view of the home supporters, was a great pity, since after years of being a weaker cricketing nation, the team of 1969-70, which marked South Africa's farewell to Test cricket, was not only the best in the country's history, but probably one of the best teams of all time. Australia were beaten comprehensively in all four Test matches. Among the leading

The breathtaking setting of the ground at Port-of-Spain, Trinidad.

players were Graeme and Peter Pollock, Barry Richards, Mike Procter, Eddie Barlow, Colin Bland and Dennis Lindsay, all amongst the best post-war players in the world.

Many South African players have since played in other parts of the world, notably Garth le Roux, Vintcent van der Bijl, Ken McEwan, Clive Rice, Allan Lamb and Kepler Wessels, the last two having qualified and played for England and Australia respectively.

The West Indies

The first reference to cricket in the West Indies occurs in 1806, when St. Anne's Cricket Club held a meeting in Barbados. The first inter-colonial match was between Barbados and Demerara (now Guyana) in 1865, and this is regarded as the first first-class match in the West Indies. In 1892-93 a tournament was held in Port of Spain between Barbados, Demerara and Trinidad, and

this was repeated, being held in each colony in turn 27 times until the Second World War. In 1956-57 the tournament was revived with Jamaica competing for the first time. In 1961-62 the Combined Islands of Leeward and Windward took part. Two years later a league championship was tried, and in 1965-66 the Shell Shield for Caribbean Regional Cricket Tournament was first instituted. The competition has been held each year, with Barbados, Guyana, Jamaica, Trinidad, Leeward and Windward Islands being the competing teams, the last two playing until the 1980s as Combined Islands, and winning in 1980-81. Barbados has been the most successful side.

Whereas before the Second World War the truly great West Indian players, like George Headley and Learie Constantine, were occasional figures, a steady trickle afterwards, with Alf Valentine and Sonny Ramadhin, Basil Butcher, Frank Worrell, Everton Weekes, Clyde Walcott, Lance Gibbs, Gary Sobers and

Wes Hall, finally become a deluge as whole teams appeared at once, with the likes of Viv Richards, Gordon Greenidge, Clive Lloyd, Andy Roberts, Michael Holding and Joel Garner.

West Indian cricket, being crowded into a short domestic season, with its players and teams spread over a number of islands, is not strong financially, and often makes difficulties for itself with inter-island rivalry among the officials, but on the field of play it has become since the 1970s the strongest in the world.

New Zealand

New Zealand cricket is far from being an adjunct of Australia's —indeed it was not until 1946-47 that the first Test took place between the two countries. The first reference to the game dates back only to 1832, although cricket was certainly played many years before this. The first inter-provincial match to last for more than a day took place at Dunedin in January 1864 between Otago and Canterbury, and this is regarded as the first first-class match in New Zealand.

Very few of the first-class records date back to before the First World War, and it is only since the Second World War that New Zealand has produced cricketers of top Test standard at all regularly. Indeed it was not until the 1970s that New Zealand could contemplate Test matches without the near-certainty that they would be the underdogs.

Two left-handed batsmen whose careers spanned the Second World War, Martin Donnelly and Bert Sutcliffe, proved that New Zealand could produce players of the highest class. Since then John Reid, Glenn Turner and Richard Hadlee have been outstanding as the nation's fortunes have blossomed.

The domestic first-class competition was the Plunket Shield, presented by Lord Plunket, Governor-General of New Zealand, in 1906-07 for competition between the major cricket associations of Auckland, Wellington, Canterbury and Otago. First awarded to Canterbury, it was competed for on an annual challenge basis until 1921, being held mainly by Canterbury and Auckland, with Wellington being twice successful. From 1921-22 the winners were decided on a league basis. In 1950-51, Central Districts were admitted, and in 1956-57 Northern Districts, these being amalgamations of the smaller provinces. Each of the six competing provinces recorded at least one victory before the competition was discontinued in 1974-75, with Wellington's 14 victories just beating Auckland's 12. Since 1975 the Plunket Shield has been awarded to the winners of the match between the North and South Islands.

From 1975-76 the Plunket Shield was replaced by two first-class competitions sponsored by the Shell Oil Company, the Shell Cup and the Shell Trophy. The Shell Cup operated for only four seasons, after which the Cup was used for one-day competition. The Shell Trophy continues.

India

Cricket is a long-established game in India. A game played by English sailors at Cambay, about 30 miles from Baroda, in 1721 represents the first reference. There was a club in Calcutta in 1792, and possibly the first major match was the visit of Calcutta to Madras in 1864. In 1889-90 G. F. Vernon took a team from England to India, and in 1892-93 an All-India team played Lord Hawke's tourists. On both these tours a match was lost at Bombay to the Parsis, who had formed a club there in 1848, and remained for some time the leading Indian cricketing community. In 1886 the Parsi Gentlemen became the first Indian side to tour England, a planned tour in 1879 having been abortive.

The Parsis began to play the Bombay Europeans from 1877, the series leading in 1892 to the Bombay Presidency matches, the start of first-class domestic competition in India.

The domestic championship in India is the Ranji Trophy, established in 1934 to commemorate the great batsman K. S. Ranjitsinhji, who had died in 1933, a year after India's first Test match in 1932. India was divided into four zones—North, East,

South and West—each of which found its champion by a knock-out competition, the four champions then taking part in another knock-out to decide the winners. There have been slight changes over the years. A fifth zone, Central, was added in 1953-54, and from 1957-58 the zonal champions have been decided on a league basis, and both champions and runners-up go forward to the final knock-out rounds. The Ranji Trophy has had a variety of winners, with Bombay being the most frequent victors.

India's great cricketers are mostly from the batting and spin-bowling departments, although Lala Amarnath, Vinoo Mankad and Kapil Dev were outstanding all-rounders. Some of the best pre-1932 cricketers appeared in Tests for England, Ranjitsinhji and his nephew, K. S. Duleepsinhji, being the best known, while the Nawab of Pataudi played for both England and India, captaining India, as did his son, also the Nawab.

Among India's more recent great players are Vijay Merchant, Polly Umrigar and Sunil Gavaskar as batsmen, and Bishan Bedi and Bhagwat Chandrasekhar among the slow bowling brigade, while there is no lack of others ready to take their place as Indians retain a great love of the game.

Pakistan

The formation of the state of Pakistan as a result of the partition of India in 1947 meant a new country with a ready-made supply of cricketers, including some already of Test class. The first first-class match took place in 1948: Punjab University v Governor's XI at Lahore. However, because of the troubles caused by partition, first-class games were rare until 1953-54, the first year of the national competition, the Qaid-i-Azam Trophy. From the 1960s there have been various other first-class tournaments in Pakistan from time to time, but the Qaid-i-Azam has continued. Various systems have been used to decide the winners. From 1980-81 the basis has been a league table.

Outstanding among a host of excellent Pakistani Test players have been all-rounders Imran Khan, Majid Khan and Asif Iqbal and batsmen Hanif Mohammad, Javed Miandad and Zaheer Abbas.

Sri Lanka and Other Cricketing Countries

Sri Lanka (formerly Ceylon) became the eighth Test-playing country in the 1981-82 season. This was 150 years after the first reference to cricket in Sri Lanka in the *Colombo Journal* in 1832, when the Colombo Cricket Club was formed. G. F. Vernon's touring team of 1889-90 to India played All-Ceylon at Kandy, the first important match. Previously, the Hon Ivo Bligh's team to Australia which brought back the first Ashes in 1882-83, had played XVIII of Colombo on its way out.

First-class cricket is played in many countries which do not yet aspire to Test-match status. There are seven Foundation Members or Full Members of the International Cricket Conference. These seven are the current Test-playing countries. South Africa was a founder-member of its forerunner, the Imperial Cricket Conference, in 1909, but ceased to be a member in 1961 on withdrawing from the British Commonwealth. In 1965 the Conference was renamed to allow the election of non-Commonwealth members.

The Associate Members of the ICC might be regarded as those countries nearest to Test status. With their year of election these are: Argentina (1974), Bangladesh (1977), Bermuda (1966), Canada (1968), Denmark (1966), East Africa (1966), Fiji (1965), Gibraltar (1969), Hong Kong (1969), Israel (1974), Kenya (1981), Malaysia (1967), Netherlands (1966), Papua New Guinea (1973), Singapore (1974), USA (1975), West Africa (1976) and Zimbabwe (1981).

This list in no way exhausts the countries with cricketing traditions. Others are Belgium, Belize, Brazil, Burma, Chile, Corfu, Egypt, Ghana, Mauritius, New Caledonia, New Hebrides, Nigeria, Portugal, and Uganda. For a game often described as 'peculiarly English' cricket has spread far.

THE ONE-DAY GAME

The young swashbuckling Ian Botham.

One-day cricket began in England in 1963. The effect was comparable to that of a blood transfusion on an ailing patient, for make no mistake, cricket was dying as a national pastime in the 1960s. The decline had begun in the previous decade, following the first rush of enthusiasm for cricket after the end of the Second World War. By the late 1950s gates were declining and the appeal of the County Championship, the bulwark of first-class cricket in England, had dissipated, certainly as far as the general public were concerned, if not in the players' eyes.

It was a bad time for the game, and somehow this was reflected in a lack of zest in contemporary Test matches. Far too many Tests against Australia in the 1960s were ending in draws. Furthermore, there was a lack of new talent entering the game, which had never been the case before, and what few players of class there were (May and Dexter, for instance) seemed to be deserting cricket just as soon as they became household names.

Colin Cowdrey was one of the few members of his generation who stayed constant through good and bad times and survived to usher in a new, different and better era. For this was what was implied by the first one-day knock-out cup competition held in 1963.

Already a trial one-day competition involving four of the Midland counties—Leicestershire, Derbyshire, Nottinghamshire and Northamptonshire—had taken place in May 1962. It was an unqualified success, and plans for a full scale tournament in the following year went ahead. The main problem was the question of weather. What would happen should rain affect play, thus delaying the outcome and causing disproportionate expense to those counties whose matches were interrupted or extended by bad weather? Originally, the sponsorship of Gillette, which in its first year totalled £6,500, was designed in order to provide some insurance for the counties against the increased expenditure that might be necessary in the event of rain. However, the enormous popularity of the competition in its first year and the sell-out for the final at Lord's on the first Saturday in September ensured that the competition would be a financial success. Indeed, so enthusiastic was the crowd at that first Gillette Cup final that the atmosphere was more electric even than expected at a Test match against Australia.

Sponsorship Increases

Subsequently, therefore, sponsorship was gradually increased. It became normal for sponsors to come forward with sums well in excess of £100,000. The purpose of sponsorship, whether it be in England or any other country of the world, is now far removed from the concept of insurance against wet weather, which was the original notion of the Gillette Company, its Managing Director, Mr. Henry Garnett, and its PR expert, Gordon Ross, an experienced journalist and promoter. Often, when competitions become successful enough to be regarded as institutions, the founding fathers are forgotten as the story unfolds, for not every innovator can be as memorable as Christopher Columbus. Not so

these two: they not only helped to launch the Gillette Cup, as it quickly became known, but also gave cricket sponsorship its style of non-interference. This was a precious gift and one which could easily have been abused.

Perhaps the fact that cricket had more than its share of scandals as long ago as the 1820s, when players were accused, and justly accused, of throwing matches when large sums of money were involved, has enabled the game to remain free of such charges in this modern era. In the 1960s charges were made, and made to stick, against certain soccer players of selling games for money. Even though the funds flowing into cricket have increased to the point where the game earns over £1,000,000 from sponsorship, there have been no such suggestions made against cricketers, nor have there been many complaints by members of the cricketing public about the use of advertising boards or promotional materials by the companies involved. Certainly there have been rows about the positioning of such boards and the use of advertising by the media, but these arguments have been restricted to the various professionals involved and have seldom come to the notice of those who watch the games with evident enjoyment and in steadily increasing numbers.

Even a sustained campaign against tobacco sponsorship by the anti-smoking lobby has had little effect. Cricket has long enjoyed the best of relations with the tobacco companies, who have been loyal supporters of the game when it has needed funds most desperately. Indeed, two of the four domestic competitions in England have long been sponsored by tobacco companies, the John Player League covering the Sunday afternoon games, and Benson & Hedges taking sponsorship of the first of the full-scale knock-out competitions to be played in the season. The first tobacco company to become involved with cricket was Rothmans, who fielded a team called the Rothmans Cavaliers, playing mostly for the benefit of players at the end of their careers. Such were the relationships established at that time that Sunday cricket became a feature of the first-class scene with relative ease.

As far as the merit of the cricket played is concerned, the players themselves are in no doubt that the 60-over game is best for a one-day competition. The 40-over variety of the Sunday League, with its restrictions and its various compulsions on bowlers and batsmen, tends to debase the game to a certain extent, and yet there is no doubt that the excitement, the hilarity even, of these matches has re-established cricket's previously fast-diminishing popularity. Many are the children who have been brought up on 20-over evening cricket up and down the country, and their appreciation of cup cricket has been thankfully extended to the first-class game at a time when the greatest possible attendance has been needed, not only from the financial point of view, but also because of the opportunity afforded of influencing the younger generation.

Outstanding Performances

At first there was much scepticism as to the value of the new competitions, but one individual who was intrigued by the format, and did his utmost to understand it, was Ted Dexter. He subsequently led Sussex, who had hitherto won nothing, to success in the first two Gillette Cups. Even now Sussex remains a team which performs better in one-day cricket than in the more traditional form of the game.

There have been some memorable individual performances in one-day cricket. Outstanding in many minds is the innings played by Boycott when Yorkshire won the Gillette Cup in its third year. His 146 against Surrey that day remains among the most brilliant one-day innings ever seen. It was played on a pitch which neither the captains nor the umpires thought was fit for play, which in itself is a reminder of how cup cricket and large attendances have

The Benson and Hedges Cup. Clive Radley (left) and Mike Gatting celebrate Middlesex's victory in 1983.

Mike Denness with Kent's Gillette Cup in 1974.

forced players to get on with the game when voices of caution have said that it would be better to remain in the pavilion. It was only on the insistence of the then MCC secretary, Billy Griffith, that the above-mentioned match was started with only an hour's delay.

Another match which few people will forget is that in which Lancashire beat Gloucestershire in the dark at Old Trafford in 1971. At 8.50, when the railway station alongside the ground and the pavilion were both ablaze with lights, the match was taken live into the BBC news bulletin. Viewers saw David Hughes bring the scores level with 24 in one pulsating over from John Mortimore: 4, 6, 2, 2, 4, 6. The millions of viewers could see the ball better than the 25,000 packed into the ground, but nothing could diminish the excitement of those present at such a climax.

The success of sponsorship for those companies prepared to devote a part of their advertising budget to this end has been

ABOVE Graham Gooch, a brilliant one-day batsman, straight drives during his innings of 91 for Essex in the NatWest final of 1985. Bruce French (Notts) is the keeper.
OPPOSITE Medium-paced Max Walker of Victoria, an ideal limited-overs bowler throughout the 1970s and 1980s.

so self-evident that now sponsors have come forward for the County Championship, for Test matches, and for one-day internationals. Cricket in England has now had three insurance companies, the Cornhill, the Prudential and the Britannic Assurance, a food and drink company, Schweppes, two tobacco companies, Imperial and Gallaher, a manufacturer of what are best described as sundries, Gillette, and a bank, NatWest, as its valued sponsors. Of course it has to be part of the policy of the game's administration to ensure that there is always sufficient potential goodwill from sponsors waiting in the wings in the event of any of those currently involved deciding to drop out. The idea that sponsorship is fixed for all time is a most dangerous one to entertain in the case of an institution like cricket, or indeed any other sport.

The Role of Channel Nine
Not surprisingly, as each new development has been announced there has been anxiety lest the intrusion of yet more commercial interests should start to affect the game adversely. In fact, only when the media have taken a hand in sponsorship has the game been threatened, as witnessed by the intervention of Kerry Packer's Channel Nine in Australia. This of course was a development to be expected, but once a television station, with all its particular requirements, enters the sponsorship area, then it is

clear that the needs of the game are likely to be sacrificed for what seems to be a good gimmick for television. An example has been the installation of microphones around players and wickets which the BBC attempted to follow, then wisely abandoned. If the game is to hold any enjoyment for the players, as it must, and if they are to communicate that enjoyment to the crowds, then the players must have some element of privacy.

The example set by sponsored cricket in England has now been followed in other countries where inevitably difficulties have appeared. These are usually due to geographical factors, and the difficulty of arranging one-day matches when huge distances have to be travelled—often they tend to be tacked on to longer matches. Differences of national temperament have also dictated that certain countries should accept the one-day version of the game with greater enthusiasm than others. For example, the West Indians have always relished it, whereas it has been considered rather inferior sport in Australia until recently. The Australians shared their lack of enthusiasm with Yorkshire, but eventually cricket's hardest men have come to appreciate that the one-day game, if sufficiently extended, can be as demanding as three- or five-day matches.

Nowadays all the leading countries have their sponsored one-day competitions. Australia have their McDonald Trophy, the West Indies the Geddes Grant/Harrison Line Trophy, South Africa the Datsun Shield (formerly the Gillette Cup), India the Deodhar Trophy, New Zealand the Shell Cup. Also, one-day international cricket has flourished, culminating in the four-yearly Prudential World Cup.

One-day cricket is here to stay.

Geoffrey Boycott gets the ball away against Australia.

PART II

THE INTERNATIONAL GAME

TEST MATCH CRICKET

Like many of cricket's older fixtures and customs, Test cricket developed gradually, even haphazardly. There was never a moment when any one person stood up and announced that Test matches would start. Indeed, it was not until 1894-95 that the term 'Test' was used, and only later in the decade that a Board of Control was formed in England.

The original international matches were simply between Australia and England, who were joined later in the 19th century by South Africa. The first Test is now acknowledged to have been played at Melbourne on March 15, 16, 17 and 19, 1877—hence the venue for the centenary match—and these encounters were known merely as matches between an Australian XI and an England XI.

Grace's Tour

Not that these matches always evoked the partisanship they do now. Tours then were organized privately—official MCC tours did not start until 1903-04—and many players had little incentive to make themselves available. W. G. Grace, for example, made only one tour of Australia, though he played in Tests at home for over 20 years after they started. Some idea of the Australian outlook in those days can be gleaned from the fact that their original tour programme of 1880 did not include the representative match at the Oval in September that is now on record as the first Test played in England. And their methods of selection are cast in some doubt by the frequently told story of the second wicket-keeper who, when on the high seas bound for England, was found never to have kept wicket.

South Africa entered Test cricket in 1888-89, and became with England and Australia one of the founder members of the Imperial (now International) Cricket Conference (ICC) when it was formed, on a South African suggestion, in 1909. South Africa left the ICC in 1961, because, under the constitution, membership was restricted to countries within the Commonwealth, but they continued to play Test matches, until they were banned for political reasons. Even so, they were still included in the record books and aroused no less public interest. Strictly speaking, however, only those matches between the full members of the ICC—England, Australia, West Indies, New Zealand, India, Pakistan, and Sri Lanka—warrant the designation 'Test'.

Test cricket is only loosely controlled by the ICC, the arranging of matches and series being purely a matter for the individual governing bodies of the countries concerned. Thus South Africa never played West Indies, India, or Pakistan, and from 1960-61 to 1978 India and Pakistan did not compete for political reasons.

It was not until 1928 that the fourth Test-playing country joined the other three, West Indies playing three Test matches that year in England. Eighteen months later, they were host to the Hon. F. S. G. Calthorpe's team in the Caribbean, and that same season, 1929-30, England sent another team to New Zealand under A. H. H. Gilligan, so bringing the number of Test playing countries to five. India's first Test was played against England at Lord's in 1932, and after partition Pakistan began with a series in India in 1952-53.

From this, it can be seen that the conception of Test matches being the meeting of the strongest teams that could be put in the field is, outside the England-Australia series, relatively new. In the days when several amateurs were good enough for most England teams, many were prevented by business from touring, and only since World War II have full-strength England teams gone to West Indies, India, and Pakistan. Many of the early Test matches against South Africa, too, were played by what would have passed as 'second XIs'.

Though the series between England and Australia have overall been evenly fought, South Africa have been only fitfully successful in Test cricket. They did not win a Test until 1905-06, when they won four matches against P. F. Warner's side, and though they won again four years later it was another 21 years after that before their next rubber was won. And it was not until 1935 that, by beating England at Lord's, they won their first series overseas. Thirty years later, they won again in England, heralding in a golden era of South African cricket that included two annihilations of Australia.

West Indies' Success

West Indies cricket soon established its huge potential by drawing the first home series with Calthorpe's team, and it was not until 1960 that England, under Peter May, won a series in the West Indies. Prior to that, only Ian Johnson's Australians of 1954-55 had been successful, their 3-0 victory halting the triumphs of the Worrell-Walcott-Weekes era. The Sobers-Hall-Griffith period followed in the 1960s, when they defeated all-comers, and if the later 1960s witnessed a recession, West Indies were undoubtedly the most successful side of the 1970s and 1980s. The controlled power

BELOW The Centenary Test at Melbourne in 1977 and Derek Randall, Man of the Match, disconsolate as he is caught Marsh bowled Lillee for 174.

ABOVE Colin Cowdrey, whose 114 Test matches is a record. RIGHT Imran Khan, a genuine Test all-rounder with 2,000 runs and 200 wickets for Pakistan.

improvement with victories over West Indies and India and a series win in Pakistan. The most important signs of the development of New Zealand cricket, however, came with long-awaited victories over Australia and England. Strangely, New Zealand had played only one Test—in 1946—against neighbours Australia up to 1973-74. Then, during reciprocal tours, New Zealand notched a welcome five-wicket win at Christchurch. To this, the New Zealanders, in 1978, added a maiden triumph over England, and in 1983-84 went one better with a series victory.

India and Pakistan

India and Pakistan, hard to beat at home, initially failed to live up to the potential of much of their cricket when they toured. One of the principal reasons for this was that, for reasons of climate, diet, and physique, they found it difficult to produce the fast bowlers needed in England and Australia. India, nevertheless, have been a major attraction with their four masters of the art of spin bowling: Bedi, Chandrasekhar, Prasanna and Venkatarghavan. Between them they had taken an astonishing aggregate of 768 wickets in 192 Test matches by the end of the 1977-78 tour of Australia. Kapil Dev then emerged as a successful fast bowler. Pakistan have fielded some strong teams since the mid-seventies and recently, in Imran Khan, found a genuine fast bowler.

The latest Test-playing country, Sri Lanka, played brilliantly at Lord's in 1984, and soon came to be regarded as more than just an easy team to beat.

Influence of Television

As a result of the general tendency, encouraged by television, to concentrate on the main events of each sport and on the best players, the Test match has tended to become increasingly important in modern times at the expense of ordinary first-class cricket. In England, especially, where the county matches are the game's bread and butter, there was a danger that there could be too many Test matches. Fortunately, it has been recognized that they could lose their novelty, and that the goose that lays the golden egg could well be killing itself off. Should this happen in England, the sufferers would be the first-

FOLLOWING PAGES A Test match panorama. The main picture is of Andy Roberts (West Indies) bowling a bouncer to Graham Yallop (Australia). TOP TO BOTTOM, LEFT, are the New Zealanders who toured England in 1973, Arthur Nourse (South Africa) and Sunny Gavaskar (India). TOP TO BOTTOM, RIGHT, India and Pakistan toss and Chris Old (England) drives.

of batsmen Sobers, Lloyd, Kanhai, Greenidge, Kallicharran, Richards and Fredericks together with the fast-bowling battery of Roberts, Holding, Croft and Garner and the wily off-spin of Gibbs made West Indies in the 1970s one of the most formidable sides ever, a strength maintained in the 1980s as Haynes, Gomes, Richardson, Dujon and Marshall came to the fore.

New Zealand, on the other hand, have known repeated frustrations. With the perennial handicap of playing cricket on rugby grounds that produce poor cricket pitches, they took a long time to fulfil the promise of the early and immediate post-war years when players of the calibre of Stewart Dempster, Bert Sutcliffe, and Martin Donnelly were among the best in the world. In 1961-62 New Zealand drew in South Africa, and later in the 1960s showed marked

class counties, who share in the Test match profits. Test cricket is not, however, subsidizing county cricket, as is sometimes thought. Rather it is compensating it. Moreover the tremendous increase in popularity of limited-over cricket —with the three major competitions, the Gillette (later NatWest) Cup, the John Player League and the Benson and Hedges Cup—has deflected some of the light from the Test arena and supported county cricket.

There is not the same problem in the other countries, though. In Australia, there are fewer Test series, and the country is big enough to absorb an extension of a rubber from five matches to six, as in 1970-71. This was to allow Perth to become the latest addition to the list of Test centres, and it resulted in an aggregate gate there of nearly 90,000.

England first had six Test matches in the season of 1965, and has had them at two-yearly intervals since. The innovation of half-season visits to England, which does not involve Australia, was instituted for a number of reasons, the original inspiration being the general desire of many to see the attractive West Indians of 1963 again as soon as possible. It has numerous advantages, even though the first half of an English summer is apt to be a much less congenial and profitable time to tour. It was appreciated in South Africa, where players often had trouble in obtaining more than three months leave from their jobs. And it is especially appreciated in New Zealand, because they can now visit England every four years instead of every eight, with the result that they can tour with a good number of players with previous experience. The system was also appreciated in England because a one-sided series of three matches is much less painful to watch than one of five. There has lately been a levelling of standards.

Duration of Tests

From being a three-day fixture in the beginning, the Test match grew until, in the period between the wars, there was no time limit in Australia, but elsewhere matches of three or four days were played, with provision in certain circumstances for the final match of a series to be 'timeless'. It has since contracted again to the general norm of five days. This, like other playing conditions, however, is purely a matter for the two countries concerned.

Test match grounds vary from the colossus of Melbourne, with its increased capacity of 121,000, to the relatively small but exotic grounds of the West Indies or the

Peter Parfitt (England) falls victim to Dennis Lillee (Australia) in the fifth Test at the Oval in 1972, one of Lillee's 31 wickets in the series.

Fred Trueman (England), the first bowler to take 300 Test wickets in 1964. The record lasted 12 years but has since been passed often.

scenic splendours of Newlands in the Cape, which requires extra stands to be erected in order to accommodate 18,000. In Australia, the second biggest ground is the Sydney Cricket Ground, which holds nearly 50,000. The capacity of England's six Test grounds is now less than it once was because seating accommodation has been improved at the cost of larger crowds. Most of them, when full, rarely take as many as 30,000. In South Africa, the splendid new Wanderers Ground in Johannesburg has held over 30,000. The record attendance for a whole Test, however, was at the Eden Gardens, Calcutta on January 1-6, 1982, when more than 425,000 were reported to have watched the game between India and England.

There is only one exception to the concept of a Test series being a simple clash between two countries. In 1912, a triangular tournament was played in England between Australia, England, and South Africa, but for several reasons it was a failure. The weather was bad; South Africa, passing through a transitional period, were extremely weak; and Australia, because of domestic squabbles, were without six of their leading players. There have been occasions recently when two series were played concurrently— England v India and Pakistan in 1961-62 and Australia v England and West Indies in 1979-80—and there have been three very popular World Cups, played under limited-overs rules, in 1975, 1979 and 1983.

The biggest upset in the steady tenor of Test cricket occurred soon after the celebration of the centenary of Test cricket in March 1977. Australian media magnate Kerry Packer, denied exclusive television rights for his channel, set up his own organization by signing over 50 of the world's leading cricketers for a private series of matches in opposition to regular cricket. This organization was called World Series Cricket (WSC) or, somewhat derisively in the press, the Packer 'Circus'. There was much opposition from the establishment, and a legal battle in England between, on the one hand, WSC and three of its cricketers, England captain Tony Greig, John Snow and South African Mike Procter, and, on the other the ICC and the TCCB. The former won, and the rival form of cricket was well established.

WSC series were played in Australia and West Indies, and for a while WSC players were not selected for Test matches. Finally, on 30 May 1979, the Australian Board announced a 10-year agreement with the Packer group, by

which Packer won the exclusive right to promote, televise and merchandize 'regular' cricket in Australia. In return, the World Series matches ceased. After a time, the Packer cricketers were assimilated again into the Test scene and cricket proceeded as before.

The next big disturbance to Test cricket concerned South Africa. A party of English cricketers called, after the sponsors, the South African Breweries England XI, toured South Africa in 1982. Official tours to South Africa had been banned by all the ICC members in accordance with the Gleneagles agreement, and the TCCB acted against the 'rebels' by banning them from Test cricket for three years. Nearly all the players were Test cricketers, and would certainly have been chosen during this period, the most prominent being G. Boycott, J. E. Emburey, G. A. Gooch, A. P. E. Knott, D. L. Underwood and P. Willey. Les Taylor, who had not played Test cricket before the tour, made his debut in 1985, when the ban ran out.

Meanwhile in 1981, an England replacement on a tour of the West Indies, R. D. Jackman, was expelled from Guyana because of South African cricketing connec-

tions. The whole England party left the island and the Test was cancelled. The Guyana batsman, A. I. Kallicharran, was then banned by the West Indies for playing for Transvaal, and in 1983 a West Indian team toured South Africa, leading to the ban from Test cricket of its members, some of whom, apart from Kallicharran, were prominent Test players, notably L. G. Rowe, C. E. H. Croft, C. L. King, D. A. Murray and D. R. Parry.

In 1985 some Australian players agreed to tour South Africa and the Australian Cricket Board requested the members of the team chosen to tour England to sign a statutory declaration that they would not later tour South Africa. Three, T. M. Alderman, R. J. McCurdy and S. J. Rixon, declined and were omitted from the party. Former Test players who signed for the South African tour included the recent captain K. J. Hughes, J. Dyson, R. M. Hogg and G. N. Yallop.

So Test cricket had faced as many upsets and threats in eight years as it had in the hundred which went before. It remains, however, the pinnacle of the cricket world and will continue to be the great showcase of the sport's supreme skills.

ENGLAND v AUSTRALIA

When those players representing England and Australia took the field at Melbourne in 1877, little could they have realized they were not just playing the first match between the two countries but that they were initiating one of the great sporting institutions. Other series may be more adventurous and entertaining, but none receive the attention and generate the same feeling as that between England and Australia, which from 1883 has been a battle for the Ashes.

The very existence of the Ashes themselves is proof of the importance of the series. It was considered a national disaster when England were beaten by Australia at the Oval in 1882. A mock memorial notice appeared in the *Sporting Times* 'in remembrance of England cricket'. It was said that 'the body will be cremated and the Ashes taken to Australia'. Ivo Bligh, who was taking a touring team to Australia the following winter, promised to bring back 'the Ashes', and when his team was successful some ladies in Melbourne burnt the bails in the deciding match and presented the Ashes to Bligh in an urn. Those Ashes remain at Lord's, but are mythically played for in each series.

Australia could not hope to beat England at full strength on level terms: that was the view of English cricket followers up to the time of the first of all 'Test' matches, played at Melbourne in March 1877. Yet Australia won a notable victory by 45 runs. The English touring party was all-professional, so it was not quite fully representative, but it was a strong team, and few had doubted beforehand that it would be good enough to win.

Right from this first encounter no quarter was asked and none given. Charles Bannerman, whose hard-hitting 165 set Australia on the road to victory, had his knuckles so badly bruised by the fast rising deliveries of George Ulyett of Yorkshire that he was eventually forced to retire. The English tourists won the return, but the Australians confirmed their new status as international cricketers at Melbourne in 1879 by beating another touring English side by 10 wickets.

Those three matches introduced some of the greatest of all names to Test cricket, especially on the Australian side: the Bannermans, Charlie and Alec; W. L. Murdoch, batsman and later captain; the bearded wicket-keeper Blackham; and the legendary Spofforth, first of the great modern bowlers. All bear comparison with the illustrious names of later years. The batting on the whole was less

accomplished than England's, and the fielding at first was inferior, as was the understanding of tactics. But in this early period the strength and penetration of Australian bowling was a revelation.

Those who maintained, despite these reverses, that England at full strength on her own ground would prove invincible found confirmation of their view at the Oval in 1880, in the first Test match in England and the only one of that Australian tour. Grace's 152 in his first Test was bettered by Murdoch's 153 not out, but not before Australia had followed on. England were left with only 57 to win, yet they lost five wickets in the process, and received such a fright that complacency should have been dispelled for ever.

Another all-professional party visited Australia in 1881-82, a strong combination that included G. Ulyett, R. G. Barlow, W. Bates, Arthur Shrewsbury, W. H. Scotton, Thomas Emmett, Alfred Shaw, and E. Peate, but it lost two of the four Tests played and failed to win any. These men must have been well aware what England would be up against in 1882, but belief in invincibility at home remained.

As in 1880, only one Test was played, at the Oval, and it set the seal on Australian maturity. Needing only 85 to win in a low-

England captain Lord Harris races to cut off a boundary in the first Test on English soil—at the Oval in 1880. England won by five wickets.

OPPOSITE A composite of a Lord's 'Test' between England and Australia. The Prince of Wales, later Edward VII, and his wife stroll on the outfield as the Australians field to W. G. Grace and W. W. Read. The portraits are of Test players of the early 1880s: R. G. Barlow, W. H. Scotton, W. Barnes, A. N. Hornby, Hon. A. Lyttelton, W. G. Grace, A. G. Steel, Lord Harris, G. Ulyett, W. W. Read and A. Shrewsbury; T. W. Garrett, P. S. McDonnell, S. P. Jones, A. C. Bannerman, H. J. H. Scott, F. R. Spofforth, G. Giffen, G. E. Palmer, J. McC. Blackham, W. L. Murdoch and G. J. Bonnor.

THE AUSTRALIAN ELEVEN, 1880.

G. E. PALMER. W. H. MOULE. G. J. BONNOR. G. ALEXANDER. T. U. GROUBE.
R. SPOFFORTH. H. F. BOYLE. W. L. MURDOCH. P. S. M'DONNELL. A. C. BANNERMAN.
A. H. JARVIS. J. SLIGHT. J. M. BLACKHAM.

LEFT The Australians that toured England in 1880 and played a single Test, at the Oval. Their performance should have warned England that the Australians would soon be a strength to be reckoned with. BELOW LEFT The match in 1882 when Australia won by seven runs—England's defeat being the cause of the now-famous obituary for England cricket and the start of the Ashes. BELOW Australia's win was in no small part due to the devastating bowling of F. R. Spofforth, who was known as 'The Demon', as the caricature for Hampstead CC's annual dinner shows.

Series of the 19th century	
1876-77 in Australia	**1887-88 in Australia**
Australia 1 England 1	Australia 0 England 1
1878-79 in Australia	**1888 in England**
Australia 1 England 0	England 2 Australia 1
1880 in England	**1890 in England**
England 1 Australia 0	England 2 Australia 0
1881-82 in Australia	**1891-92 in Australia**
Australia 2 England 0 Drawn 2	Australia 2 England 1
1882 in England	**1893 in England**
England 0 Australia 1	England 1 Australia 0 Drawn 2
1882-83 in Australia	**1894-95 in Australia**
Australia 2 England 2	Australia 2 England 3
1884 in England	**1896 in England**
England 1 Australia 0 Drawn 2	England 2 Australia 1
1884-85 in Australia	**1897-98 in Australia**
Australia 2 England 3	Australia 4 England 1
1886 in England	**1899 in England**
England 3 Australia 0	England 0 Australia 1 Drawn 4
1886-87 in Australia	
Australia 0 England 2	

scoring match, England were bowled out for 77, a feat immortalized by the famous lament in the *Sporting Times* on the death of English cricket. Spofforth in this match took 14 for 90—figures that, until 1972, were not to be beaten by an Australian.

England regained the 'Ashes' somewhat luckily in 1882-83 by winning two of a rubber of three matches. Australia squared the series by winning a fourth match, but the fate of the Ashes was held to have been decided already. Following this somewhat hollow revenge, England went on to retain the Ashes for the next nine years, but they were often fortunate to

do so. Up to 1885 the Australians probably had the stronger side. Their great quartet of bowlers—Spofforth and T. W. Garrett, fast or fast-medium, and G. E. Palmer and H. F. Boyle, medium pace—were more dangerous than any English combination, the fielding had improved dramatically, and only a tendency to rashness in the batting, and disputes that affected selection, allowed English teams to prevail.

After a disappointing tour of England in 1886, when several leading Australians were absent, and with the great quartet of bowlers ageing or anyway less effective, Australian cricket went

into decline. From 1886 to 1890, 11 Tests were played and England won 10 of them, losing only once. This period coincided with the peak of the Surrey fast-medium bowler George Lohmann, and it also saw the emergence of the slow left-arm bowlers Johnny Briggs and Bobbie Peel. Yet no pair of bowlers has ever been quite so destructive on English wickets as were the Australians, C. T. B. Turner and J. J. Ferris—right arm fast-medium and left arm above-medium respectively—in 1888. Poorly supported, they often had to bowl at impossible targets because of batting that lacked the necessary skill and concentration,

and for all their effectiveness they could not triumph on their own over the great all round strength of the English teams of the period.

The recovery of Australian cricket came at last in the winter of 1891-92, when England sent a strong side, led by W. G. Grace, but lost the first two Tests of a three-match rubber. Australian batsmen had learnt to play steadily, with stonewaller Alec Bannerman the great stumbling-block, and Turner found a new bowling partner in George Giffen. Giffen's record places him, with Noble, Armstrong, and Miller, among the greatest of Australian all-rounders. Abel, A. E. Stoddart, Briggs, and Lohmann did best for England in a series that brought a timely revival of interest in Australia.

England's nine-wicket victory in the first Test at Sydney was their only win in the five-match series of 1897-98.

With several of their leading players absent and with their great bowlers less effective, the Australians of 1886 lost all three Tests that year.

England came back to win the next three series, in 1893, 1894-95, and 1896, and they owed much to their batting strength, Shrewsbury, F. S. Jackson, William Gunn, Grace, Stoddart, and Ranjitsinhji being outstanding. But the power that tipped the scales in this period was fast bowling, especially that of Tom Richardson. His tally of 88 wickets in only 14 Test matches places him still among those with the highest striking rates of wickets taken per Test match. It was not until his power began to wane that Australia won another rubber. But then, with the emergence of players of the calibre of Victor Trumper, Clem Hill, M. A. Noble, Joe Darling, Hugh Trumble, and fast bowler Ernest Jones, they finished

the 1890s strongly by winning the last two series. The Australian side of 1899, led by Darling, was by general consent the strongest seen in England since 1882 and is still considered one of the best ever.

1901-02 in Australia
Australia 4   England 1
This English tour, led by A. C. MacLaren, was the 15th and last of Australia under private management. A number of leading players were not available, but the inclusion of S. F. Barnes, plucked out of league cricket with very little first-class experience and plunged straight into the turmoil of an Australian tour, was a surprise. In the first two Tests, of which the two countries won one each, Barnes took 19 wickets, but he was over-bowled, and early in the third Test he broke down. Australia won the last three Tests and proved their superiority beyond doubt.

Without Barnes, the England

bowling lacked a spearhead, and the batting, apart from MacLaren and Tom Hayward, was disappointing though Braund proved a valuable all-rounder. For Australia, the left-handed Clem Hill was outstanding as a batsman, making 521 runs and becoming the second man to exceed 500 in a series (another left-hander, Joe Darling, was the first, in 1897-98). Medium-pacers Noble and Trumble took 60 wickets between them. The Australians had picked up the rudiments of swerve bowling in Philadelphia on their way home from previous tours, and this was the first series in which it was exploited to any degree.

1902 in England
England 1   Australia 2   Drawn 2
Victory in this unsatisfactory series probably went to the better of two great sides. But the traumatic events of Old Trafford, linked for all time with the name of Fred Tate, and the exhilarating victory at the Oval, inspired by Gilbert Jessop, have long tortured English cricket followers with what might have been. England began the series with a substantial score at Edgbaston, then shot the Australians out for 36 after heavy rain—their lowest-ever score. But the rain that had treated the tourists so unkindly returned to save them, and the second Test, too, was spoilt by rain.

Bearing the results of the fourth and fifth Tests in mind, the decisive game was the third Test at Sheffield, played against a drab background in appalling light. Here, after Australia had gained a first-innings lead of 49, Trumper and Hill decided the issue by aggressive batting, sweeping aside the combined efforts of Barnes, Hirst, Braund, Jackson, and Rhodes, and 339 to win was too much for England.

At Old Trafford, Australia, 37 ahead on the first innings, had soon lost 3 wickets for 10 runs. Then Darling was missed on the square leg boundary by Tate, and the score was advanced to 64 before another wicket fell. The runs were crucial—and Tate could still have redeemed himself, but with four runs wanted and one wicket to fall, he was clean bowled. At the Oval, England looked hopelessly placed in the fourth innings at 48-5 with 263 wanted, but Jessop arrived to complete an astonishing hundred in 75 minutes, and George Hirst and Wilfred Rhodes, coming together for the last wicket, made the 15 runs needed to win with characteristic aplomb.

1903-04 in Australia
Australia 2   England 3
After winning four consecutive series, Australia were overthrown by the extraordinary variety of the English attack, in which B. J. T. Bosanquet with his googlies, although sometimes expensive,

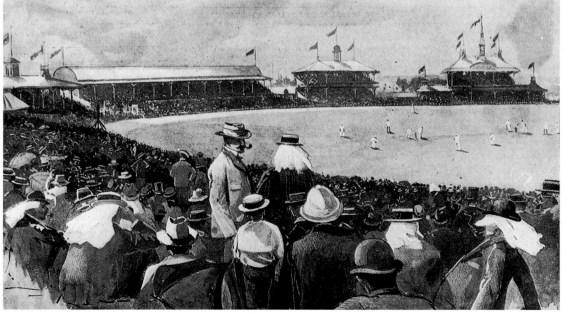

was the decisive factor. The first Test was remarkable for two of the greatest innings ever played, one of 287 by R. E. Foster that gave England a long first-innings lead, and another by Trumper of 185 not out that helped set England a sizeable fourth-innings task. This they proved equal to, and they won the next Test through getting in their first knock before the rain came. An unaccountable batting collapse then cost them the third.

Winning the toss in the vital fourth Test, England again faltered; but a fine defensive innings by A. E. Knight dominated their recovery, and the Australians, handicapped by rain that quickened the wicket, and mesmerized by Bosanquet, never got in the game. In the fifth Test England had the same wretched luck with the weather as the Australians had had in the second, and were easily beaten.

A section of the crowd demonstrated against the umpire in the

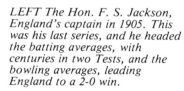

LEFT The Hon. F. S. Jackson, England's captain in 1905. This was his last series, and he headed the batting averages, with centuries in two Tests, and the bowling averages, leading England to a 2-0 win.

ABOVE Joe Darling's Australians of 1902, who won a magnificent Test series by two Tests to one. The immortal Trumper is seated at the left. Trumble and Armstrong flank the manager.

first Test at Sydney when Hill was run out, and only a personal appeal from Noble, the Australian captain, dissuaded 'Plum' Warner from withdrawing his team. The hooting and bottle-throwing were even worse in the fourth Test, when the crowd were incensed by the repeated stoppages for rain.

1905 in England
England 2   Australia 0   Drawn 3
The Australian side again looked a strong one, but it was soon apparent that the bowling, weakened by the decline of Noble, was below Test match standard, and the powerful England batting, led by Jackson, C. B. Fry, J. T. Tyldesley, and MacLaren, was rarely in difficulty. England for their part always managed to find bowlers to suit the conditions, while the Australian batting could not surmount the wretched form of Trumper and Hill. Some fast bumpers from A. Cotter gave Australia an encouraging start at Trent Bridge, but Jessop replied in kind, and the bumpers were withheld from then on. England amassed 426-5 in their second innings, and then Bosanquet (8-107) ran through the Australians, England winning by 213 runs.

The second and third Tests, although drawn, went very much in England's favour, and England won the fourth by an innings. Jackson, the England captain, got his second hundred in successive Tests, and the Australians batted recklessly when caution might have saved the day. The most even game was the last, when both sides scored heavily and when Australia

came within sight of victory on the last morning. Stubborn defence and the benefit of some hotly disputed umpiring decisions, however, enabled England to draw.

Jackson crowned a highly successful career in home Tests by topping both the batting and the bowling averages (492 runs for an average of 70.28 and 13 wickets at 15.46 each). He also won the toss in all five Tests.

1907-08 in Australia
Australia 4   England 1
The extraordinary depth and resilience of the Australian batting finally mastered an England attack that relied chiefly on pace. The England batting, weakened by withdrawals through financial disagreements, was unexpectedly stiffened by George Gunn, who happened to be wintering in Australia. His innings of 119 and 74 should have won the first Test, but England could not polish off the Australian tail. In the second match, in which Hobbs made 83 in his first Test, it was the English tail that wagged, the last pair putting on 39 for victory. But in the third Test England, after outplaying their opponents for more than three days, were demoralized in the Australian second innings by an eighth wicket stand of 243 between Hill and R. J. Hartigan.

In the fourth Test England had the worst of the wicket and they were led on the first innings by 109, but they hit back so well that the Australians slumped to 77-5. Then came another demoralizing recovery, the Australian total reached 385, and the Ashes were won. In the final Test England actually gained a lead of 144 on the first innings, but again the Australian batting, led by Trumper (166), came back to ensure victory.

J. N. Crawford, A. Fielder, and Barnes took 79 of the 93 Australian wickets that fell, heavily underlining the spin-bowling weakness that nourished Australia's powers of recovery. Four times in succession the side scored more runs at the second attempt.

1909 in England
England 1 Australia 2 Drawn 2
Australia began their tour badly and were beaten in the first Test. They had, however, brought a side of considerable all-round strength, and of the players new to England, V. S. Ransford nearly always made runs and Warren Bardsley and Charles Macartney did well. Brilliant fielding, and the astute leadership of Noble, finally saw them to victory.

The turning point came at Lord's in the second Test, when Australia won comfortably by 9 wickets. England did well to total 269 after being put in, but no fast bowler had been chosen and Australia, helped by dropped catches, gained a lead of 81, after which England collapsed. England made six changes for the third Test at Headingley, and this proved the decisive game. The wicket gave the bowlers a chance, and England began confidently, getting Australia out for 188 and reaching 137-2. Then Macartney (7-58) ran through the side. The struggle proved completely absorbing as Australia fought to set England a formidable fourth-innings target, and it was Macartney who provided the stability when Australia were in trouble at 127-7. Set 214 to win, England reached 56-2 overnight, but then collapsed before Cotter and Macartney.

One up in the series, Australia concentrated on avoiding defeat at Old Trafford and the Oval, where Bardsley scored two centuries.

1911-12 in Australia
Australia 1 England 4
This series will always be remembered for the great bowling of Frank Foster and Barnes; but a decisive battle had to be fought by the England batsmen before these two bowlers could triumph. The danger came from the Australian googly bowler H. V. Hordern, who took 12 for 175 in the first Test, which Australia won by 146

The 1911-12 MCC side that recovered the Ashes. STANDING LEFT TO RIGHT S. P. Kinneir, E. J. Smith, F. E. Woolley, S. F. Barnes, J. Iremonger, R. C. Campbell, J. Vine, H. Strudwick. SEATED W. Rhodes, J. W. H. T. Douglas, P. F. Warner, F. R. Foster, T. Pawley (manager), J. B. Hobbs, G. Gunn. FRONT J. W. Hearne, J. W. Hitch. INSET C. P. Mead.

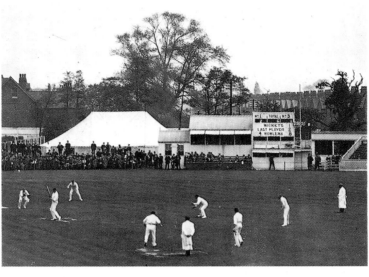

George Hirst bowling in the first Test at Edgbaston in 1906. He took nine wickets and Blythe eleven in England's win.

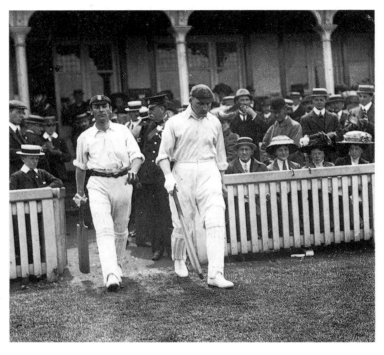

Jack Hobbs and captain Archie MacLaren open England's innings in that match. Both failed. Hayward, Fry, Warner and Spooner were also to open in this series.

runs. Only J. W. Hearne (76 and 43) played him safely, and it was Hearne (114) who played the innings of the series in the second Test, after Australia had collapsed to Barnes on the first morning. At lunch Australia were 32-4, all to Barnes, and soon afterwards they were 38-6. They fought back but never really recovered, and a century by Jack Hobbs in the England second innings helped to settle the issue.

The third and fourth Tests had many similarities. Australia batted first in each and were shot out cheaply by Foster and Barnes; in the fourth Test they were actually put in. Hobbs and Rhodes passed the Australian score each time before being parted, putting on 147 at Adelaide and 323 at Melbourne. Australia fought back magnificently at Adelaide to total 476 in their second innings, but England knocked off the runs easily, and there was no fight back at Melbourne, where England won by an innings and 225 runs.

The final Test at Sydney, although interrupted by rain, proved the most even contest. Hordern worried all the England batsmen, but a century from Frank Woolley ensured a fair total. The Australian batting again failed, but Hordern's googlies gave them a chance, and with 363 wanted they reached 193-3 on the fifth day. Then came more rain, and England won by 70 runs.

1912 in England
England 1 Australia 0 Drawn 2
The experiment of running a triangular tournament between England, Australia, and South Africa proved a failure, partly because of a disastrously wet summer. The first Test at Lord's was so curtailed by rain that each side batted only once, and at Old Trafford only the England first innings was completed. It was, therefore, decided to play the Oval Test to a finish but showers before the game and a huge storm after England had batted made Australia's task impossible. The features of the series were the batting of Rhodes, who at times outshone even Hobbs, and a great innings of 99 by Macartney at Lord's when England for a time scented victory.

Australia's supremacy in the early part of the new century had brought them level with England in number of victories in 1911, but England had reasserted themselves and now led by 40 wins to 35, with 19 matches drawn.

1920-21 in Australia
Australia 5 England 0
Australia cleared the board, the only time this has been done in a five-match series between the two countries, and were not flattered. Their victories were by 377 runs, an innings and 91 runs, 119 runs, eight wickets, and nine wickets, and only in the third match did England get the merest glimpse of

a win. The England batting, apart from Hobbs and the dour Johnny Douglas, was barely adequate, and a weak attack was quickly disheartened by dropped catches. No England bowler approached the penetration of Jack Gregory, and the Australian batsmen scored so heavily that there were always plenty of runs in hand to give Arthur Mailey a long bowl. By taking 36 wickets, Mailey beat the previous England v Australia record of 34 set up by S. F. Barnes in 1911-12.

Only twice was the Australian first innings score kept within reasonable bounds—at Sydney in the first Test, where they were dismissed for 267, and at Adelaide in the third, where they made 354 and were led for once on first innings. But each time they came back with a record second innings score— 581 at Sydney and 582 at Adelaide. England fought hard to make the 490 they needed for victory at Adelaide (Hobbs 123), but they failed.

1921 in England

England 0 Australia 3 Drawn 2
Australia extended their unbroken run of victories by winning the first three Tests, and the margins were again nearer to routs—10 wickets, 9 wickets, and 219 runs. Few England batsmen could cope with the lifting ball as propelled by Gregory, while the pace and accuracy of Ted McDonald proved the perfect foil. Hobbs, although fielding briefly at Headingley, otherwise missed the entire series through illness, and the England selectors rang the changes on 30 players in all. England had no bowler of pace and no class spinner, and the Australians made what runs they needed and then bowled England out.

In such an uneven contest it was inevitable that peripheral matters should command more than average attention. At Trent Bridge during the first Test the crowd roared their disapproval of Gregory's bumpers. At Headingley for the third Test, Douglas was replaced as captain, after seven successive defeats, by the Hon Lionel Tennyson, although he held his place in the side. He then found himself in charge again soon after the start when Tennyson injured his hand. Although severely handicapped Tennyson made his famous 99 runs in the match. And at Old Trafford, with the rubber and the Ashes safe and the Australians easing the pressure, Tennyson made his famous blunder of declaring too late after what had become the first day of a two-day match following rain. Warwick Armstrong, who bowled the last over before the argument, then bowled the first afterwards, so adding more confusion to the incident. At the Oval, Armstrong read a newspaper in the outfield to indicate his boredom. It was not one of the happiest series for England.

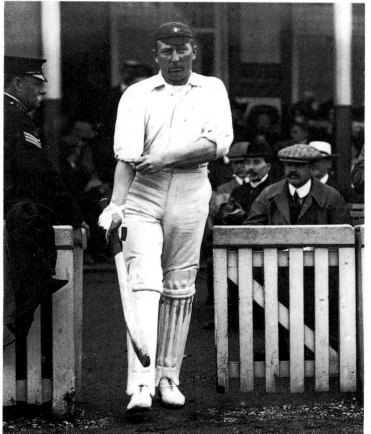

1924-25 in Australia

Australia 4 England 1
The graph of the series faithfully records England's progress. Beaten by 193 runs in the first Test and 81 in the second, they lost by only 11 runs at Adelaide and would almost certainly have won but for an injury to Maurice Tate. They went on to win the fourth Test by an innings and 29 runs. A heavy defeat in the last match rightly emphasized the solidity of the Australian batting, but the decisive factor was the introduction of a new bowler named Clarrie Grimmett.

A second-wicket partnership of 190 between Herbert Collins (114) and Bill Ponsford (110) formed the basis of Australia's first innings 450 at Sydney, and although Hobbs and Herbert Sutcliffe replied with 157 (Hobbs 115), England were all out for 298. Another century opening partnership in the England second innings and a century from Woolley still

ABOVE Warren Bardsley is caught at slip by Frank Woolley off the bowling of Johnny Douglas at Headingley in 1921. The Australians, having already won the first two Tests, won this one by 219 runs to take a 3-0 lead in the series.
LEFT Warwick Armstrong, known as 'The Big Ship', was the Australian captain in this series. The England side was constantly changed in an effort to find a winning formula, but to no avail.

left England a long way short. In the second Test, Hobbs and Sutcliffe put on 283 after Australia had amassed a record 600 (Ponsford 128, Victor Richardson 138), but the later batting failed, and a second hundred by Sutcliffe could not save England. The third Test ended after many fluctuations in a narrow Australian victory, and England won the fourth Test easily after winning the toss for the only time. Then came Grimmett, taking 5-45 and 6-37 in Australia's 307-run victory.

Sutcliffe's aggregate of 734 runs was a record, as was Tate's bag of 38 wickets.

1926 in England

England 1 Australia 0 Drawn 4
Going to the Oval after four drawn games with all to play for in a 'timeless' Test, England dropped their captain Arthur Carr for Percy Chapman. They also restored Harold Larwood and the 48-year-old Wilfred Rhodes. They won the toss but frittered the advantage away, and Australia led on the first innings by 22. Hobbs and Sutcliffe put England in front again before the close on the second day, and then came the storm.

The story of how Hobbs and Sutcliffe defied the Australian spinners on a 'sticky dog' has become legendary. The bowlers best suited to the conditions were A. J. Richardson, off-spin round the wicket, and Macartney, left-arm over, and they spun and kicked viciously from an impeccable length. But somehow Hobbs and Sutcliffe came through. Hobbs made 100 out of 172, by which time the match was virtually won; the wicket would never be 'plumb' again. Sutcliffe went on to make 161. The Australian second innings was then broken by Larwood and Rhodes.

The earlier matches in this series had underlined the frustrations of three-day Tests, and the clamour for a fourth day became insistent (Tests in Australia had been played to a finish almost from the beginning). The four drawn matches were remarkable for the aggressive batting of Macartney, who made hundreds in the three middle Tests, including a century before lunch at Leeds, and the consistency as a pair of Hobbs and Sutcliffe.

1928-29 in Australia
Australia 1   England 4
The series was dominated by the monolithic batting of Walter Hammond. After a moderate first Test (44 and 28), he made 251 in the second, 200 and 32 (run out) in the third, and 119 not out and 177 in the fourth. A disappointing final match (38 and 16) left him 95 runs short of a thousand for the series. Three other England batsmen, Patsy Hendren, Sutcliffe, and Hobbs, averaged over 50, and it was Hendren (169) who played the innings that turned the opening Test England's way. This was the match in which Chapman batted again although leading by 399 on first innings. With two players

RIGHT Tom Webster has a look at one of the problems that beset England in 1924-25.
BELOW Hobbs and Sutcliffe defy Australia at the Oval in 1926 to set England on the road to a Test victory that also won them the series.

indisposed, and with a final stab in the back from the weather, Australia were sunk without trace.

England had gone into the first Test with three bowlers plus Hammond, but they did not take this risk again. George Geary, who played in the remaining four Tests, topped the bowling averages, and 'Farmer' White, Larwood, and Tate completed the main attack. For the second Test Australia made the mistake of dropping Bradman, playing in his first series, and England crushed them with a record 636.

England won the third and fourth tests narrowly, by three wickets and 12 runs respectively. The third Test, after Hammond's 200, was remarkable for a superb stand in the second innings by Hobbs and Sutcliffe on a sticky wicket when England were set 332

to win. The fourth Test, which introduced the 19-year-old Archie Jackson (164) to Test cricket, was saved for England by a stand of 262 between Hammond and Douglas Jardine in the England second innings, but the decisive moment was the running out of Bradman by Hobbs when Australia seemed set for victory. Australia won the fifth Test by consistent batting after England had begun with 519.

1930 in England
England 1   Australia 2   Drawn 2
If the 1928-29 series was dominated by Hammond, still more will that of 1930 be remembered for England's first sight of Don Bradman. Eight and 131; 254 and 1; 334; 14; and 232—those were his scores in the five Tests, totalling 974 runs and averaging 139. It was

an avalanche that would have overwhelmed most sides, and England did well to go into the final Test all square. Hobbs at the age of 47 began the series well but faded, Hammond could not reproduce his Australian form, and only Sutcliffe, who missed the second Test through injury, batted up to his reputation. Grimmett harassed the England batsmen throughout.

England won the first Test by 93 runs, but they had the best of the conditions, and there was a point when Australia seemed likely to get the 429 they needed to win. Winning the toss again at Lord's, England made enough runs to have ensured a draw in normal circumstances; but they reckoned without the astonishing speed and certainty of Bradman's run-getting, and Australia replied to their first innings 425 with 729-6 (Bradman 254). The Headingley Test, in which a cloudburst saved England, will always be remembered for Bradman's 334, of which 309 came on the first day (105 before lunch, 115 in the afternoon, and 89 after tea). The Old Trafford Test was spoiled by rain.

R. E. S. Wyatt replaced Chapman as captain at the Oval, and, thanks largely to a sixth-wicket stand of 170 between Sutcliffe (161) and his new captain, England totalled 405. In any normal series this would have ensured a fight; but Australia now demonstrated their batting superiority beyond all doubt in a total of 695, and England lost by an innings.

1932-33 in Australia
Australia 1   England 4
Faith in fast bowling as the only form of attack likely to subdue Bradman was triumphantly vindicated in this series. But the manner in which it was deployed was bitterly resented throughout Australia. Fast leg-theory as conceived by Jardine, or bodyline as it was dubbed by the Australians, took on a different connotation when projected by bowlers of the pace and accuracy of Harold Larwood and Bill Voce, and the batsmen felt themselves under continual physical attack. Nevertheless Jardine persisted with his policy throughout an explosive series, which at one point seemed likely to be abandoned. When the full facts were known the method was generally condemned, and legislation to outlaw this type of bowling was eventually passed. What Bradman might have achieved without bodyline can never be known, but the likelihood is that England would still have won. Although outclassed in wrist-spin, they were in other respects the better side.

Australia went into the first Test without Bradman, who was unfit, and were saved on the first day by a superb innings from McCabe, whose 187 not out was the greatest innings played against bodyline. Nevertheless centuries from Sutcliffe, Hammond, and Pataudi

ABOVE England scored 405 in their first innings at the Oval in 1930, but Australia, with Don Bradman making 232, replied with 695 and won by an innings and 39 runs.
RIGHT In 1932-33 England countered Bradman with bodyline and The Don was bowled by Bill Bowes for a duck in his first Test innings.
RIGHT BELOW On the third day of that Melbourne Test, which Australia won to level the series, a record crowd of 68,188 saw the home side get on top.

gave England a long lead, and then the Australians crumpled before Larwood. In the second Test on a slow wicket, bodyline was less successful, and O'Reilly (10 for 129) and Bradman (0 and 103 not out) got Australia home in a low-scoring match. The genius of Bill O'Reilly (27 wickets in the series) ensured that England did not have matters all their own way in the remaining matches, but they won them all. Larwood broke all records for a fast bowler by taking 33 wickets, but Gubby Allen, who avoided bodyline throughout, took 21, seeming to underline what Larwood might have achieved by orthodox methods.

1934 in England
England 1   Australia 2   Drawn 2
Partly as a result of the controversy that followed the 'bodyline' series, England were without Jardine, Larwood, and Voce, and injuries to other key players continually weakened the team. A wicket that took spin helped Australia to a thrilling victory in the first Test with only 10 minutes to spare, but luck went England's

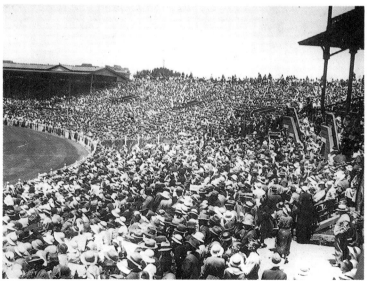

way at Lord's, where they made 440 (Ames 120, Leyland 109) and then caught Australia on a rain-affected wicket. Wyatt, the England captain, was criticized for batting on into the second afternoon, but England would never have won had he not done so. As it was, the Australians nearly saved the follow on, when England would have had to bat on the worst of the wicket. Verity took 14 wickets in a single day and 15 in the match.

At Old Trafford came the famous O'Reilly over after the ball was changed. England slumped from 68-0 to 72-3, but Hendren (132) and Maurice Leyland (153) then led a recovery and England totalled 627. The wicket was over-prepared, and Australia saved the follow-on, but the honours went to England. The pendulum swung back at Headingley, where England collapsed unaccountably. Bradman made 304, putting on a record 388 with Ponsford (181), but again a draw resulted, this time through rain. At the Oval, where Australia won the toss, Bradman (244) and Ponsford (266) broke their own record with a partnership of 451 on the first day, and England were overwhelmed.

The bowling of O'Reilly and Grimmett was also a vital factor in the Australian victory.

1936-37 in Australia
Australia 3   England 2
After a moderate start to the tour, England surprised everyone by winning the first two Tests. After being 20-3 at Brisbane they made 358, thanks chiefly to Leyland (126), and then Voce and Allen bowled them to a substantial first innings lead despite a hundred from Jack Fingleton. Australia, set 381 to win, found their task eventually made impossible by rain. The second Test brought a double century from Hammond (231 not out), and then, after rain stopped play on the second day, an overnight thunderstorm compounded England's advantage. Only a pronounced change of luck, or massive scoring by Bradman, seemed likely to save the series for Australia. As it happened both were forthcoming.

Yet the Ashes seemed almost won on the first afternoon of the third Test, when Australia had fallen to 130-6 on a good wicket. Soon afterwards came the rain, Australia declared at 200-9, and England were shot out for 76 (M. W. Sievers 5-21, O'Reilly 3-28). Bradman then changed his batting order, holding Fingleton and himself back to No. 6 and No. 7, by which time the wicket had recovered. Bradman (270) and Fingleton (136) then put on 346 together, and not even another

Herbert Sutcliffe, though not as prolific as of yore, usually managed to give the England innings a steady start in the 1934 series of Tests.

Leyland hundred could save England.

Neither side could establish a commanding first-innings position at Adelaide, but 212 from Bradman at the second attempt and fine bowling by Fleetwood-Smith and O'Reilly were instrumental in levelling the series. Bradman (169) and the two spin bowlers also dominated the final Test, and Australia came from behind to retain the Ashes.

1938 in England
England 1   Australia 1   Drawn 2
In a series of generally over-prepared wickets, it was ironic that a dusty pitch at Headingley should decide the fate of the Ashes. Taken all round England were the stronger side, but they did not help their chances by playing only one

fast bowler in the first Test and failing to reconstruct their side at Headingley when three key players reported unfit. The entire Old Trafford match was rained off.

Three England batsmen— Charles Barnett, Len Hutton, and Denis Compton—made centuries at Trent Bridge and one, Eddie Paynter, a double-century, and England totalled 658-8. Yet the innings of the match was played by McCabe. Faced with impending disaster at 194-6, McCabe put on 69 with B. A. Barnett, then dominated the strike so successfully that he made 127 out of the last 148 in 80 minutes after Barnett was out. He made 232 out of a total of 411. Australia followed on, but Brown (133) and Bradman (144 not out) saved the match. At Lord's it was England's turn to scent defeat, despite a great 240 in their first innings by Hammond, but they closed their ranks and a draw resulted. Then came the dusty wicket at Headingley, a great century by Bradman in appalling

light, and magnificent bowling by O'Reilly, who took 10 for 122 in the match.

Thus England could only square the series at the Oval, but this they proceeded to do. Hutton made a record 364, Leyland 187, and Joe Hardstaff 169 not out, and Hammond declared at 903-7. This crushing weight of runs, and injuries to Bradman and Fingleton, made the rest of the match a formality.

The position of the two countries at this stage was Australia 57, England 55, with 31 Tests drawn.

1946-47 in Australia
Australia 3   England 0   Drawn 2
The last pre-war Test had ended in England's biggest-ever victory; the first post-war Test brought a record victory for Australia. Yet England might have come much closer to recovering the Ashes but for Bradman. And even Bradman needed a slice of luck to re-establish himself in Test cricket at the age of 38. After an uncertain beg-

With Len Hutton batting in a masterly manner for a record 364 at the Oval, England were able to declare at 903-7 and won to square the 1938 series.

Denis Compton's centuries in each innings at Adelaide were brighter moments for England in the somewhat Australian-dominated series of 1946-47.

inning at Brisbane he had made 28 when he gave what seemed a perfectly clean catch to Ikin in the gully, only to be given not out. He went on to make 187 in that match and 234 in the next, both of which Australia won by an innings.

At Brisbane England had cruel luck with the weather, but they could offer no such excuse at Sydney, where Sid Barnes and Bradman put on 405 for the Australian fifth wicket. For the remainder of the series Bradman's scores were kept within reasonable limits, and with Cyril Washbrook, Hutton and Compton finding their form England put up a much

better show. The third Test was drawn after an even fight (Tests in Australia were now limited to 30 hours' playing time, as in England), England saved the fourth after Compton had made a hundred in each innings, and England were going reasonably well in the final Test when Hutton (122) had to retire with tonsilitis. England actually gained a first-innings lead, but Hutton's illness and the spin of Colin McCool redressed the balance and Australia, although pressed all the way, won by five wickets.

Hammond at 43 failed tragically, and the successes of the tour were Bill Edrich, who proved the most consistent batsman, and Norman Yardley, whose all-round form was a surprise. Alec Bedser and Doug Wright carried the bowling, but the support was

weak. Ray Lindwall and Keith Miller led a strong Australian attack.

1948 in England
England 0   Australia 4   Drawn 1
With Lindwall and Miller reaching their peak, ably backed up by Bill Johnston, with Arthur Morris emerging as a left-hander in the great Australian tradition, and with Bradman, Barnes, and Lindsay Hassett as effective as ever, this was a great Australian side, lacking only a top-class spinner. The experimental rule that allowed a new ball every 55 overs, however, enabled Bradman to shrug off this weakness. England were unlucky at Trent Bridge to bat first on a wicket enlivened by rain, and Australia led on the first innings by 344, Bradman and Hassett making centuries. England fought

back well, and not until Compton fell on his wicket after making 184 did England's chance of saving the match disappear. At Lord's England were again facing defeat at the end of the second day (Australia 350, England 207-9) and they never recovered.

England hit back at Old Trafford to total 363 after being 119-5. Compton, struck on the head by a Lindwall bouncer, returned to make 145 not out. Bedser and Dick Pollard bowled Australia out for 221 (Barnes was absent injured), and England lost a great chance of victory when the fourth day was washed out.

The Headingley Test is of particularly poignant memory for England. Centuries from Washbrook and Edrich took them to 496, Australia replied with 458 and when England declared on the last morning Australia wanted 404 in 344 minutes to win. England muffed their chances, Morris and Bradman put on 301, and Australia won by 7 wickets.

At the Oval England were dismissed for 52 (Hutton 30), and Australia never relaxed their grip on the game.

1950-51 in Australia
Australia 4   England 1
England included several young and inexperienced players, and Australia introduced a new and unorthodox spin bowler named Jack Iverson, who topped their averages. Miller, Hassett, and Harvey scored consistently for Australia, but Washbrook and Compton failed, and none of the new England batsmen prospered. Hutton was magnificent, but until

Australian 'keeper Don Tallon makes sure he has souvenirs of Australia's triumphant series under Bradman in 1948.

the last Test the next most successful batsman was Freddie Brown. Brown also took more wickets (18) than any previous England captain, but Bedser (30 wickets) was the outstanding bowler.

After dismissing Australia for 228 on the first day at Brisbane, England were caught on a rain-affected wicket and declared at 68-7. Australia in turn declared at 32-7, setting England 193 to win. They slumped to 30-6, and on the last day a great innings by Hutton (62 not out) could not save them. Fine bowling by Bedser and Trevor Bailey and a rousing 62 from Brown gave England a narrow advantage at Melbourne, but the varied Australian attack eventually achieved a narrow victory. In the third Test, Bedser, J. J. Warr, and Brown strove heroically after Bailey and Wright were hurt, but they could not prevent an Australian first innings lead of 136 (Miller 145) and England collapsed to Iverson (6-27) to lose by an innings.

A fine 206 by Arthur Morris was matched by 156 not out from Hutton at Adelaide, possibly his greatest innings, but the remaining England batsmen could muster only 95 between them, and England lost a match they should have saved. Consolation came in the final Test when England, thanks largely to Simpson (156 not out) and Hutton, won their first Test against Australia since the war.

1953 in England

England 1 Australia 0 Drawn 4
Four draws and a victory at the Oval to England, who thus regained the Ashes after losing three post-war series, was history repeating itself. But there comparisons ended. The four drawn games were packed with drama. First the Australians were dismissed for 249 at Trent Bridge (Hassett 115) and then England collapsed to Lindwall and lagged by 105. Great bowling by Alec Bedser (14 for 99 in the match) brought England right back into the game, the target needed being 229, but rain spoilt the match with England 42-1.

The Lord's Test was remarkable for the great match-saving stand between Willie Watson (109) and Bailey (71), after England had begun the final day facing almost certain defeat. Australia made 346 (Hassett 104), England replied with 372 (Hutton 145), and then Australia, helped by 109 from Miller, set England 343 to win and had them 20-3 before nightfall. There were still five hours left when Bailey joined Watson next morning, and they were not parted until 5.30.

Rain ruined the Old Trafford Test, but England got a horrible fright on the last day at Headingley, where Australia, wanting 177 in 115 minutes, set off at a gallop. The gate was closed by Bailey, bowling wide of the leg stump off a long run, but his tactics were not widely approved.

On a typical Oval wicket of the period, Australia had no answers to Jim Laker and Tony Lock in the deciding Test. But the bowler of the series was Bedser, who took a record 39 wickets.

1954-55 in Australia

Australia 1 England 3 Drawn 1
After a wretched start at Brisbane, England turned the tables and won the next three Tests. The chief destroyer was Frank Tyson, splendidly partnered by Brian Statham, but there were many significant performances in support. Bob Appleyard, Johnny Wardle, and Trevor Bailey completed a varied attack, while Peter May, Colin Cowdrey, Denis Compton, and Len Hutton all played important innings in the matches that were won. The Australian batting was vulnerable, but England always had to fight for their runs.

RIGHT Frank Tyson wraps up the Australian innings at Sydney in 1954-55 to give England a vital victory.
BELOW Peter May out to Gordon Rorke at Adelaide in 1958-59. There was controversy over Australian bowling actions.

Ray Ullyett.

Put in at Brisbane on what proved to be a lifeless wicket, Australia made 601-8 declared (Harvey 162, Morris 153). Then Lindwall and Miller demonstrated that they were still great bowlers, and England followed on and were easily beaten. In the second Test England were themselves put in, and after lagging on the first innings by 74 they were 55-3 and in an apparently hopeless position when May and Cowdrey put on 116. Australia were set 223 to win, and Tyson, despite a huge bump on the head from a Lindwall bouncer, took 6-85 and got England home.

Early life in the wicket had left England in trouble at Melbourne, but Cowdrey (102) and Bailey pulled the game round, May made 91 in the second innings, and Tyson (9-95) and Statham (7-98) did the rest, England winning by 128. At Adelaide the wicket was more suited to spin, and Australia made 323, England replied with 341, and then great bowling by Tyson and Statham after Apple-

Cartoonist Roy Ullyett sums up the Old Trafford Test of 1956, when Jim Laker took an unprecedented 19 wickets in the match: 9 for 37 in the first innings and all 10 for 53 in the second.

yard had made the breakthrough left England wanting only 94, which they got for five wickets. The first three days of the final Test were lost through rain, but there was time for a superb hundred from Tom Graveney and for some inept Australian batting that left England pressing for victory.

1956 in England
England 2   Australia 1   Drawn 2
With Hutton retired, Compton crippled, and Tyson, Statham, and Trueman injured, England had to rebuild their side for Trent Bridge. They reached a commanding position on the last day despite interruptions by rain, but could not seal their advantage. The Lord's Test saw the return of

Statham and Fred Trueman, but good Australian teamwork, highlighted by an audacious 97 from Richie Benaud in the Australian second innings and 10 for 152 in the match by Miller, left Australia the winners by 185 runs.

Only May (63 and 53) had made runs for England at Lord's, and the selectors recalled Cyril Washbrook at Headingley. Joining May when England were 17-3, he helped to add 187 for the fourth wicket, and the partnership proved decisive. The wicket began to help the spinners, and a great 69 from Harvey only delayed the end.

David Sheppard (113) was the man recalled at Old Trafford, Peter Richardson made 104, and Cowdrey 80, and as at Headingley the ball began to turn. But the Australian collapse (84 all out) was difficult to account for. Rain allowed only short periods of play on the next two days, but it deadened the wicket, and Australia put up a terrific fight. Colin McDonald and Ian Craig were together for more than four hours, but in the final session the ball turned again and Jim Laker completed his great feat of taking all 10 wickets and 19 in the match to put England one up, so retaining the Ashes. Lock in 55 overs in the second innings failed to take a wicket.

Compton was the man resurrected for the final Test, and he and May (94 and 83 not out respectively) retrieved a bad start. But the match was spoilt by rain. Laker took a record 46 wickets in the series.

1958-59 in Australia
Australia 4   England 0   Drawn 1
After a long apprenticeship, Alan Davidson and Richie Benaud had developed into great bowlers, McDonald's application brought him 520 runs, and a new batsman

The end of the England Test career of J. G. Dewes, a brilliant left-handed batsman from Cambridge University. In the second innings at Melbourne in 1950-51 he was caught Harvey, bowled Iverson.

of Test class emerged in Norman O'Neill. The England bowlers could never quite get on top, and of the batsmen only Cowdrey and May showed anything like their true form; but they had to contend with much bowling of dubious legality.

At Brisbane on a green wicket, it was not until O'Neill got going in the Australian second innings that bat was put to ball, and then Australia ran out easy winners. At Melbourne there were centuries from May (113) and Harvey (167), and the match looked evenly poised when England batted a second time. They collapsed to the jerky, erratic Meckiff (6-38), and Australia went on to win, as at Brisbane, by eight wickets.

The England batting failed again at Sydney, and although their bowlers hit back Australia recovered to lead by 138 on first innings, and the rubber seemed decided when England slid to 64-3. Then May (92) and Cowdrey (100 not out) put on 182 and the match was saved. At Adelaide Laker reported unfit, England were forced to rely on pace, and the issue was settled as McDonald and Burke put on 171 for the first wicket after being put in. England lost this time by 10 wickets.

Meckiff, whose action was generally conceded to constitute a throw, missed this match through injury, and the man who took the eye was the giant Rorke, whose drag was unprecedented. Put in to bat in the final Test, England lost by nine wickets, and Lindwall, recalled for the fourth Test, broke Grimmett's Australian record of 216 wickets in Test cricket.

1961 in England
England 1   Australia 2   Drawn 2
When the two sides went to Old Trafford for the fourth Test, they had won one match each with one game drawn. The scene was set for one of the greatest of all Test matches. Australia won the toss and thanks to fine bowling on a green wicket by Statham (5-53) they were dismissed for 190. With the wicket easier, England then made 367 (May 95, Barrington 78).

pleted Australian attack England held on for a draw.

1962-63 in Australia

Australia 1   England 1   Drawn 3
England ruined their chances by dropping too many catches, and they never mastered Davidson, who took 24 wickets in his last series. The Australian batting was always solid, with Brian Booth and Simpson the most consistent. By drawing the series Australia retained the Ashes.

At Brisbane Australia recovered from 194-6 to make 404 (Booth 112). England in turn were precariously placed at 169-4, but long defensive innings by Ken Barrington and Peter Parfitt helped them to 389. England could make no headway when Australia batted again, and on the last day they needed 378 to win at 63 an hour. That an England win still looked possible in mid-afternoon was due to Dexter (99), but the game ended with England staving off defeat. At Melbourne, Australia again recovered from a moderate start, but England gained a narrow first innings lead thanks to Cowdrey (113) and Dexter (93), and a chanceless century from Booth

LEFT An expensive miss by Colin Cowdrey in the final Test of 1962-63: Peter Burge went on to a century that helped Australia to a lead.

did not wholly counterbalance inspired bowling by Trueman. Sheppard (113) redeemed himself for two vital dropped catches and a duck in the first innings in England's seven-wicket win.

When Cowdrey (85) was out in the third Test, England were 201-4. They were all out for 279, Davidson and Simpson causing the damage. Australia were 174-1 in reply when Titmus got four wickets in 58 balls for 5 runs, and the Australian lead was kept to 40. But Davidson destroyed England's second innings and Australia won by eight wickets. More dropped catches helped Australia to 393 (Harvey 154, O'Neill 100) at Adelaide, and England survived to draw thanks largely to Barrington (63 and 132 not out) and a pulled Davidson hamstring. Barrington (101 and 94) and Burge (103 and 52) dominated the final Test, which ended, like the series, in stalemate.

1964 in England

England 0   Australia 1   Drawn 4
England could justly claim some deprivation by the weather in this series. Half the playing time was lost at Trent Bridge, but England

BELOW Burge, who at Headingley played the innings that won the 1964 series, falls leg before wicket to Titmus in the fifth Test at the Oval.

Then Bill Lawry and Bobby Simpson put on 113, and O'Neill made 67, but at 334-9 Australia were only 157 ahead. Soon afterwards Davidson suddenly hit Allen for 20 in one over, and 98 runs were made for the last wicket.

With 256 wanted at 67 an hour, the game was brought to a thrilling climax by a magnificent 76 in 84 minutes by Ted Dexter. Then Benaud went round the wicket and aimed at the bowler's footmarks, and after getting rid of Dexter he bowled May second ball. Australia won by 54 runs with 20 minutes to spare. Whatever happened at the Oval, they would retain the Ashes.

Led by 321 on the first innings at Edgbaston, England saved the game through Dexter (180) and Ramon Subba Row (112), but they lost the Lord's Test by five wickets through a faulty appreciation of the wicket. England played two spinners, whereas Australia turned the absence of the injured Benaud to fortuitous account by playing three fast bowlers plus Mackay. Lawry (130) was the rock on which victory was built. The third Test at Headingley was a triumph for Trueman (11 for 88), but in a low-scoring match on a patchy wicket England owed much to Cowdrey (93) for their eight-wicket victory. Cowdrey then missed the vital Old Trafford match through illness.

Australia did much to confirm their superiority at the Oval by scoring 494 in the best batting of the series (Peter Burge 181, O'Neill 117). But against a de-

still had a chance of victory when the rain returned on the final day. The first two days were lost at Lord's, and then Dexter put Australia in. They recovered from 88-6 to 176 all out, and John Edrich (120) was chiefly responsible for England's lead of 70. Australia batted more solidly at the second attempt, and they were safe from defeat when the rain came again.

Great catching by Australia held England to 268 at Headingley, and Australia were 187-7 when Dexter took the second new ball. Subsequent events did not endorse his decision, Burge (160) proceeded to play the innings that won the series, and Australia led by 121. England could do no better than 229 (Barrington 85), and Australia won by seven wickets. Thus fortified they went on to Old Trafford and won the toss. Lawry (106) and Simpson (311) put on 201, Booth made 98, and on the best wicket seen for many years Australia declared at 656-8. England soon lost Edrich, but Geoff Boycott and Dexter put on 111, and then came the great stand of 246 between Dexter (174) and Barrington (256), which eclipsed the partnership of Lawry and Simpson and lifted England to within 45 of the mammoth Australian total. It was a spirited reply that captured the imagination, but the inevitable draw meant that the Ashes stayed with Australia.

At the Oval England batted first in unfavourable conditions and were led on first innings by 197. But Geoff Boycott (113) and Cowdrey (93 not out) had more than restored the balance when rain washed out the final day.

1965-66 in Australia
Australia 1   England 1   Drawn 3
At Brisbane, Australia made 443-6 declared (Lawry 166, Doug Walters 155 in his first Test), and interruptions for rain left Australia only 11 hours to bowl England out twice, which they failed to do. At Melbourne, England over-hauled the Australian score of 358 and led by 200 (Edrich 109, Cowdrey 104), but a missed stumping chance let Australia off the hook and Burge (120) and Walters (115) forced a draw. England's best match was at Sydney, where Boycott (84), and Bob Barber (185) put on 234 for the first wicket and Edrich made 103. On a wicket known to favour spin after a day or so, Australia lost by an innings.

At Adelaide it was Australia's turn. Boldly changing their side, but lucky in restoring Graham McKenzie because of an injury to the man chosen to replace him, they lost the toss and in a humid atmosphere soon had England 33-3. A shout from the wicket-keeper misled Cowdrey into thinking he had been called for a run and he was run out. England did well to total 241. Simpson (225) and Lawry (119) then emulated the opening stand of Boycott and Barber at Sydney, and they actually put

Australia in front before they were parted. Australia led by 275, and despite 102 from Barrington, England were a beaten side.

For the second series in succession in Australia the two sides went into the final Test all square, but although Barrington made 115 and England totalled 485, their attack simply was not good enough to force a result and Australia passed their score with five wickets down (Bob Cowper 307, Lawry 108).

1968 in England
England 1   Australia 1   Drawn 3
After Australia had made 357 at Old Trafford and Boycott and Edrich had put on 86 for the first wicket, England collapsed unaccountably and Australia led by 192. Although England fought commendably, they never looked like saving the game. Their fielding in the series was on the whole lamentable, but they excelled

at Lord's, where they hung on to some incredible catches after declaring at 351-7, made in three rain-affected days. With conditions helping the quicker bowlers Australia were dismissed for 78, and they began the final day needing 273 to avoid an innings defeat, but the rain returned to save them. And again at Edgbaston in the third Test England dominated the game but were frustrated by the weather. After making 409 (Cowdrey 104, Graveney 96), England dismissed Australia for 222, then pressed for runs and declared. Australia needed 321 to win in six hours, but what might have been a great finish was again spoilt by rain.

Australia needed only to draw the fourth Test to retain the Ashes, and they were helped by more dropped catches and further periods of rain. England eventually needed 326 at 66 an hour, and with Australia concentrating on a draw

Colin Cowdrey reflects on the state of the Oval pitch in 1968, when it seemed that the weather would rob England of victory. It did not.

the task proved beyond them.

Few more dramatic denouements have occurred on a cricket field then the final scenes at the Oval, in the last Test. After England had made 494 (John Edrich 164, Basil d'Oliveira, dropped after the first Test and now recalled for the injured Prideaux, 158), Australia were dismissed for 324 (Lawry 135). England then went for quick runs and left Australia 352 to win at 54 an hour. Eighty-five for 5 at lunch on the final day, Australia were a beaten side when a storm flooded the playing area. With the crowd willingly helping, the deluge was mopped up just in time, and England achieved victory with six minutes to spare.

1970-71 in Australia

Australia 0   England 2   Drawn 4
Keith Stackpole's 207 at Brisbane, supported by Walter's 112, ensured a sizeable Australian score to open the series, but John Snow and Derek Underwood came back to dismiss Australia for 433. England got a first innings lead of 31, then bowled Australia into trouble, but Lawry (84) led a dour recovery and the game was drawn. The second Test at Perth saw England surrender a strong position to a great Test debut by Greg Chappell (102). Australia were 107-5 against England's 397 (Brian Luckhurst 131) when Chappell went in. Redpath made 171, and it was England who had to steer clear of defeat (Edrich 115 not out). After this match D. G. Clark, the MCC tour manager, criticized both sides for undue caution in the opening Tests.

The third Test was abandoned without a ball being bowled and replaced by another, six having been originally arranged. On a wicket of uncertain bounce England won a great victory in the fourth Test at Sydney. Gaining a first-innings lead of 96, they consolidated through 142 not out from Boycott; Snow (7-40) then blasted Australia out for 116,

TOP LEFT Alan Knott stumps Bob Cowper off Ray Illingworth at Headingley in 1968. Illingworth took 6 for 87 in the second innings.

LEFT AND RIGHT England's two stalwarts in the Ashes-winning 1970-71 tour, Geoff Boycott (left) and John Snow (right)—both injured at the end.

though Lawry carried his bat for 60. Helped by dropped catches, Australia came back to score 493 in the fifth Test at Melbourne (Ian Chappell 111), and England were in trouble at 88 for 3. But d'Oliveira (117) and Luckhurst (109) resisted, and with two cautious captains in charge a draw resulted.

The sixth Test at Adelaide began well for England. Boycott and Edrich put on 107, and Fletcher (80) played his best innings, but most memorable was the running out of Boycott. His display of petulance was forgivable; his reported refusal to apologize to the umpires, however, was inflammatory. Unmoved by criticism, he made 119 not out in the second innings, after Ray Illingworth, with good precedent, had foreborne to enforce the follow on. Stackpole (136) and Ian Chappell (104) dominated Australia's escape. Lawry was then relieved of the captaincy and dropped from the Australian side, Ian Chappell taking charge.

A great final conflict at Sydney was overshadowed by a long-threatened confrontation between Illingworth and the umpires. Jenner was hit by a Snow bouncer; Snow, as had happened several times previously in the series, was warned for intimidation; the crowd demonstrated, a spectator manhandled Snow, and Illingworth led his team off the field. England, 80 behind on the first innings, held together to make 302, and 223 to win proved beyond Australia, despite an injury to Snow. The Australians were never happy against the fast rising deliveries of this bowler, who took 31 wickets in the series.

1972 in England
England 2   Australia 2   Drawn 1
England as expected retained the Ashes, but only after a tremendous fight against Ian Chappell's unheralded side. The performances of Stackpole and Greg Chappell with the bat and Lillee and Massie with the ball contributed to a thrilling drawn series.

The fate of the Ashes was decided in controversial circumstances in the fourth Test at Headingley. Derek Underwood, who had been out of favour, was recalled to bowl on a turning pitch perfectly suited to his brisk left-arm spin. He returned match figures of 10 for 82 and England were home by nine wickets on the third day.

They had previously won the

TOP RIGHT Bob Massie goes round the wicket at Lord's in 1972. He took eight wickets in each innings of his debut Test in a brilliant display.

ABOVE Derek Underwood, the hero of the Headingley Test of 1972, claims the wicket of Doug Walters, caught prodding outside off stump by Parfitt.

first Test by 89 runs in a low-scoring match in which the Australians never recovered from being bowled out by Snow and Arnold for 142 in the first innings, Lillee's magnificent 6 for 66 never quite redressing the balance.

The series was squared at Lord's in a remarkable match dominated by the swing bowling of Bob Massie who took 8 wickets in each innings to finish with 16 for 137. Greg Chappell showed immense class in making 131 and Australia won by eight wickets.

Poor fielding cost England an early advantage in the third Test, Stackpole, who made 114, being particularly favoured. But after failing once more against Massie and Lillee and seeing Edwards make 170 not out, the England batsman competently saved the game in the fourth innings.

Appropriately it was Lillee's pace which brought the series level at the Oval. He took 10 for 181 for a final return of 31 wickets. Both Chappells got hundreds and Australia won a great victory by six wickets.

1974-75 in Australia
Australia 4   England 1   Drawn 1
With a revitalized Dennis Lillee and a new fast bowling sensation, Jeff Thomson, Australia crushed England who could not cope with a barrage of ferocious pace bowling.

Lillee, Thomson and their willing foil Walker took 81 wickets between them in the six-match series, and England, who had profited from Snow's ferocity on the preceding trip, found themselves under attack.

Australia began with convincing wins at Brisbane and Perth and retained their stranglehold of supremacy until the final Test when, on a significantly slower wicket and with Thomson absent, Denness' side achieved some consolation.

At Brisbane, Greig dodged the bouncers to make a splendid 110 and Willis counter-attacked with his pace to take seven wickets in the match, but Thomson broke the resistance in the second innings and for the rest of the series.

At Perth, Edwards (115) and Walters (103) exceeded England's first innings—Walter's century coming between tea and the close of play on the second day. Thomson reigned supreme in the second innings despite gallant resistance from Titmus and Australia won by nine wickets.

After an exciting low-scoring draw at Melbourne—Australia were eight runs short with two remaining at the close—Australia regained the Ashes by winning the fourth Test, in which Edrich led England, Denness having dropped himself because of poor form.

Second innings centuries from Redpath and Greg Chappell set England an impossible task but defeat became capitulation after a fearsome barrage from Lillee and Thomson.

England squandered a splendid

RIGHT A concerted appeal by Bob Willis and Alan Knott, with Cowdrey looking optimistic, against Ian Chappell in 1974-75. BELOW Keith Fletcher struck by Jeff Thomson in 1974-75. The Australian duo, Lillee and Thomson, dominated the series.

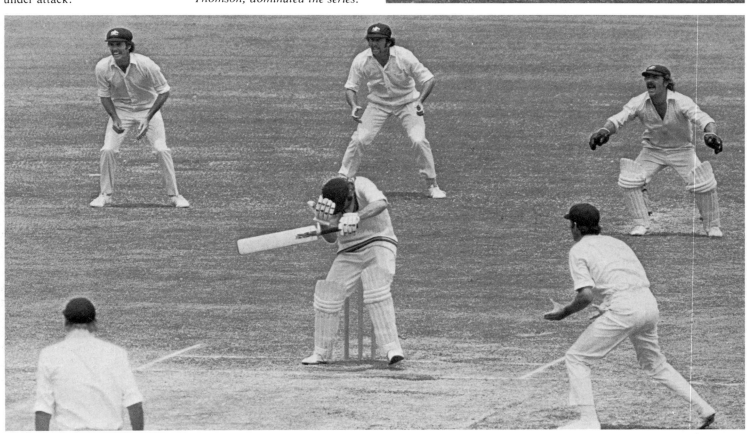

chance to win the fifth Test when Underwood, 7 for 113, helped reduce Australia to 84 for 5. But Jenner led a recovery and when Thomson, Lillee and Mallett bowled the visitors out for 172, England trailed by 134. Despite a flamboyant century from Knott in the second innings, the final margin of defeat was 163 runs.

All of which made the sixth Test the more remarkable. Lever took 6 for 38 in just 11 overs, and Denness, in the face of mounting criticism, was more at home on the slower pitch and made 188 along with Fletcher's 146.

Greg Chappell made another hundred but England won by an innings—a hollow victory at the end of a series in which a lack of quality and character in batting had been cruelly exposed by aggressive, very fast bowling.

1975 in England

England 0   Australia 1   Drawn 3
Australia retained the Ashes by winning a four-match series arranged to fill a gap in the Test Match calendar.

When the series began in July after the first World Cup, it was quite clear that England were still under the clouds of their defeat in Australia in the previous winter. Still facing a side led by Denness, Australia batted consistently and then, with the help of the weather, destroyed the England batting.

Replying to 359, England had just begun their innings when a thunderstorm drenched Edgbaston and despite a characteristic fight by Edrich they capitulated to Lillee and Walker for 101. Fletcher's half century added a little solidity in the follow on, but with Thomson now the main tormentor, England lost by an innings and 85 runs.

Denness, having made 3 and 8, resigned the captaincy and Tony Greig, leading the side for the first time at Lord's, made a flamboyant if not winning debut. Greig scored 96 and 41 but Edrich was the key figure in a much improved batting performance. His 175 was his seventh hundred against Australia. Another batting success came from 33 year old David Steele, making 50 and 45 on his first appearance. But despite gaining a first innings lead, the England attack could not penetrate consistent batting from McCosker, the Chappells and Edwards and the end product was a draw.

At Headingley the two sides fashioned a Test Match of per-

LEFT Edrich and Steele resisted Australia's pace attack in 1975 and even managed to survive this mid-wicket muddle.
BELOW LEFT At 33, David Steele made a triumphant entry into Test cricket, averaging over 60 in his first series.
BELOW Tony Greig and Ian Chappell survey the vandalism at Headingley which caused the match to be abandoned.

fect balance which had to be abandoned in unique and controversial circumstances.

On the final day Australia required a further 225 runs to win with seven wickets in hand. Yet no play was possible because, overnight, vandals dug holes in and spread oil on the wicket. It reduced to naught another revitalized England performance in which Edrich, Steele and Greig again batted manfully; another newcomer Edmonds took 5 for 28 in 20 overs as Australia were tumbled out for 135 after Gilmour, 6 for 85, had enjoyed similar success in England's first innings. Not even the rain which finally fell steadily on that last day and would probably have ruined play could reduce the disappointment at such an unsatisfactory conclusion.

With the Ashes now out of reach, England fought a stern rearguard action to earn a third draw at The Oval. After Ian Chappell, 192, and McCosker, 127, had inspired a large first innings total, Thomson, Walker and Lillee bowled out the home side for 191 and forced the follow-on. But yet again Edrich and Steele dug in aided by Roope, Knott and finally Woolmer, who occupied the crease for 499 minutes in scoring 149, the slowest century made by an Englishman against Australia. Grey haired, bespectacled David Steele enjoyed a popular triumph, averaging 60 in his first series.

ABOVE Jubilant Australia as Denness falls at Edgbaston in his last Test match as the England captain.

BELOW Denness' successor, Tony Greig, bowled by an exultant Max Walker during the Centenary Test in 1976-77.

OPPOSITE ABOVE Rodney Marsh scored a valuable century. OPPOSITE BELOW The final scoreboard of a great match.

1976-77 in Australia—Centenary Test Match

With the 100th anniversary of the first-ever Test match approaching, the authorities in Melbourne set about planning an appropriate celebration, and in March 1977 an ambitious operation costing a large fortune and supported by big business was carried through with the greatest aplomb. Every surviving cricketer who had played in England-Australia Tests in Australia was invited, expenses paid, and the eyes of the entire cricket world were on Melbourne for the grandest of birthday parties.

Midst oceans of reminiscence and celebrity-spotting, official and unofficial functions abounded; and to cap it all, the match itself was as fluctuating and thrilling as any in the long saga of England-Australia matches.

England, fresh—or perhaps more accurately a little weary —from their tour of India and Sri Lanka, excelled themselves by dismissing Australia first for 138. This was set in perspective when England crashed before Lillee and Walker for 95, the former taking 6 for 26, the latter 4 for 54. It then seemed that the match might be over in three days, and the Queen was due to visit the ground on the fifth.

Then the match settled down, Davis and Walters made sixties, and David Hookes, aged 21, stroked a delightful 56, with five consecutive fours off Greig's bowling. Finally, to ram home Australia's advantage, Marsh recorded the first Test century by a regular wicket-keeper for Australia against England, having already passed Wally Grout's record of 187 Test catches and stumpings. Marsh was assisted towards the end by McCosker, 25, who batted with a fractured jaw wired up and bandaged, the legacy of an attempted hook which cost him his wicket in the first innings.

Thus, England were set the unlikely target of 463, with plenty of time. By the fourth evening they were a promising 191 for 2, with Derek Randall, the jittery young man from Nottingham, making 87 not out in confident style.

On a memorable last day, England forged nearer and nearer to their 'impossible' requirement. Lillee, though not fully fit, bowled courageously and O'Keefe shared much of the work. Equally vital was Greg Chappell's effort: 16 overs for 29 runs and a wicket. Amiss made 64, and Greig and Knott made forties; but the star turn was Randall, who scored 174 in his first Test against the old enemy, with flashing cuts and drives and spasms of hilarious animation. While he was in, victory had to come. When he left, it was a slender hope.

Yet in defeat there was no sorrow this time. The jubilation was for the glory of the game as much as for Australia's success.

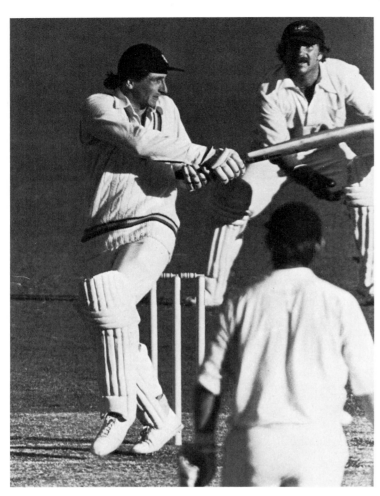

And the margin, as if arranged by the gods, was 45 runs—as it was in the first Test match, on that same ground 100 years before.

Man-of-the-Match Derek Randall, whose magnificent 174 nearly won the Centenary Test.

evening: 226 in 165 minutes. Wickets fell during the charge, with Hookes hitting 50, before the challenge was abandoned.

England's nine-wicket win at Manchester came from a fine all-round effort. The wickets were shared by a balanced attack, Underwood climaxing the victory with 6 for 66, and most of the batsmen made runs, principal scorers being Woolmer, with his third century in consecutive home Tests against Australia, Randall, 79, and Greig, 76. Walters made his highest score in Tests in England—88—in Australia's first innings of 297, but the most delightful demonstration of batting came from Chappell when Australia went in again 140 runs behind. He made 112 with elegance and dash. But the cause was lost. England needed only 79, and made them for the loss of Brearley, 44.

Another victory came at Nottingham, where Boycott returned after 3½ years of self-imposed exile, and made 107. The sensation of Australia's innings was England debutant Ian Botham's 5 for 74. Boycott then dominated the scene, though with anything but scintillating stroke-play. After three hours he had made 20, and when McCosker missed him at slip it was the turning point of the series. He went on to his century, uplifted by Knott's perky, rescuing century and putting behind him the nightmare memory of having run out local hero Randall. McCosker returned to form with 51 and 107, but Australia's second knock of 309 left England 189 to get, and

eighties by Brearley and Boycott ensured victory soon after tea on the last day.

England demolished Australia at Leeds in the fourth Test, to go three-up, to recover the Ashes, and to provide a dramatic background to Boycott's 100th hundred in first-class cricket. Long and loud was the acclamation from his Yorkshire crowd when he straight-drove Chappell to bring up his century. He was last man out for 191 as England totalled 436, and in less than 32 overs Australia were out for 103, Hendrick taking 4 for 41 and Botham, again getting movement in the air and off the pitch, 5 for 21. Following on, the tourists managed 248, thanks to a forceful 63 towards the end by Marsh.

Australia gained some crumbs of comfort from a 'first-innings win' at The Oval, when Mick Malone took 5 for 63 off 47 overs in his first Test and followed with 46 in a ninth-wicket stand of 100

OPPOSITE ABOVE Sunshine and a packed pavilion at Lord's for the Jubilee Test, but another disappointment for Amiss, bowled by Thomson.
OPPOSITE BELOW Not a relay race baton exchange but the pulling of the stumps at Headingley where, after six years, England regained the Ashes. Under the captaincy of Brearley England demolished a weak-fielding Australian side.
BELOW One wicket-keeper catches another. Alan Knott dives on the leg side to dismiss Rodney Marsh at Headingley.

1977 in England
England 3 Australia 0 Drawn 2
Australia's 3-0 drubbing, their worst in England this century, was attributed to the disturbance caused by the recent Packer signings—only a handful of the team were uninvolved—and by the poor weather. But England's greater depth in bowling and the very successful return to Test cricket of Geoff Boycott would almost certainly have guaranteed English success under any conditions, even though Lillee missed the tour.

The first Test, at Lord's, known as the Jubilee Test in honour of the Queen's 25 years on the throne, was curtailed by rain, with honours even. England's 216 owed everything to Woolmer, 79, and Randall, 53, while Jeff Thomson, carrying major responsibilities in the attack, took four wickets in each innings. Australia took a first-innings lead of 80, thanks to captain Greg Chappell's 66, Walters' 53 and newcomer Craig Serjeant's 81, though Willis returned 7 for 87. Woolmer, 120, and Brearley steadied England's second innings with 132 for the second wicket, and Greig made a valuable 91, but England were out for 305, denied the luxury of a declaration, and Australia had a target, albeit difficult, on the last

with Walker, 78 not out. But rain was the victor, and Australia's 385-214 advantage meant little against the series landslide.

1978-79 in Australia
Australia 1 England 5
Both sides were without the players who had joined Kerry Packer's World Series Cricket, Australia being the more handicapped. Yallop and Brearley were captains. This season marked the showdown between the two factions, with six Ashes Tests pitted against the WSC razzmatazz. The Tests were poorly attended, largely due to the Australian side being outclassed, while Packer registered a few big crowds, notably at Sydney for the first flood-lit match.

In the first Test at Brisbane, Australia batted and were put out for 116. England made 286, with Randall (75) being top scorer. Rodney Hogg, making his Test debut, took 6 for 74. John Maclean, Australia's other debutant, took five catches behind the wicket, equalling the record for most in an innings in Ashes matches. In the first innings, Bob Taylor, himself making his debut in an Ashes Test, had also equalled the record. Two Australians batted with determination in the second innings. Yallop (102) and Hughes (129) added 170 for the fourth wicket, over half Australia's total of 339. England needed 170, and made them for the loss of three wickets, Randall being not out 74.

At Perth, Australia put England in. Boycott scored 77 from 337

balls, without a boundary. Gower made 102 as England reached 309. Hogg took 5 for 65. Toohey (81 not out) was the only Aussie batsman to resist for long. Willis took 5 for 44 as they were shot out for 190. England made 208, with Hogg (5 for 57) taking five wickets for the third time in three completed Test innings. Australia were dismissed for 161 (Wood 64) to lose by 166 runs. There was criticism of the umpiring during this match, and Tom Brooks, the senior Australian umpire, was provoked into announcing his retirement on the last day.

Allan Border made his debut in the third Test at Melbourne. Australia won the toss on a pitch which rapidly deteriorated, and their first-innings 258 (Wood 100) proved a match-winning score. England made only 143 (Hogg 5 for 30). Australia then scored 167 and England 179 (Hogg 5 for 36), leaving Australia winners by 103. Hogg had now taken five wickets in an innings in all five completed Test innings. His total of 27 wickets in his first three Tests had been beaten for Australia only by C. T. B. Turner in 1886-87.

LEFT Geoff Boycott celebrated his return to Test cricket in 1977 in the best way possible—by scoring his 100th hundred on his home ground, Headingley.
BELOW Ian Botham grabs the ball close in at point to dismiss Ian Chappell at Sydney, 1979-80. He was Derek Underwood's 100th Australian victim.

At Sydney, England batted and were quickly out for 152 (Botham 59, Hurst 5 for 28). Australia made 294, with Darling (91) and Border (60 not out) top scorers. When England went in 142 behind and Boycott was dismissed first ball (for the first time in his 193 Test innings), it seemed Australia would level the series. But Randall came in and made the slowest century (353 balls) in Ashes Tests. He went on to 150 in stifling heat (Maclean retired with heat exhaustion and Yallop kept wicket for the end of England's innings). Brearley made 53 and England 346 (Higgs 5 for 148), setting Australia 205 to win. They collapsed for 111, and England had retained the Ashes.

At Adelaide, the first innings scores were almost level. England were put in and recovered from 27 for 5 to 169, thanks to Botham (74). Australia made more even progress to 164. Darling required heart massage when a ball from Willis struck him under the heart in the first over. Swift work by Emburey and umpire O'Connell prevented a tragedy. Darling was stretchered off but happily resumed his innings next day. The match turned when England, 132 for 6 in the second innings, managed to reach 360, Taylor making 97 and Miller 64. Australia could make only 160 and lost by 205.

In the final Test at Sydney, Yallop decided to bat and was forced to hold Australia together. He made 121 of a total of 198. England batted consistently for 308 (Gooch 74, Gower 65) and then skittled Australia for 143 (Miller 5 for 44). Yardley, coming in at 48 for 5, scored 61 not out to save the innings defeat. England needed 34 and won by nine wickets. Hogg's aggregate of wickets for the rubber was 41, an Australian Ashes record.

1979-80 in Australia
Australia 3   England 0
In 1979-80, with peace made between the Packer organization and established cricket, England and West Indies both went to Australia and each played a three-match Test series against the home country. India had been due to tour, but had been displaced as part of the agreement with Packer. The Australians picked their Packer stars, but England took only Underwood from the WSC party. England insisted beforehand that the Ashes would not be at stake in the short series, a view the Aussies did not share.

At Perth, England put Australia in and dismissed them for 244, Hughes scoring 99 and Botham taking 6 for 78. With openers Boycott and Randall both dismissed by Lillee for a duck, Eng-

land failed by 16 to reach this total, Brearley making top score with 64, batting at six. Border made 115 in Australia's second-innings 337 (Botham 5 for 98). England's 215 fell 138 runs short of the target. Boycott batted right through the innings to score 99 not out, the first such score in Test cricket. Lillee (who was in one innings caught Willey bowled Dilley) took his 100th Test wicket.

The Sydney pitch for the second Test was the subject of controversy. Soaked by rain for days beforehand, it was underprepared and, according to Greg Chappell before the match, utterly unfit for Test cricket.

However, he won the toss and asked England to bat—in effect the toss decided the match. England were 90 for 7 at the close of a short first day, and all out next day for 123. Australia reached only 145, Ian Chappell, on his return to Test cricket after his retirement in 1975-76 and subsequent Packer adventures, being top scorer with 42. England, 38 for 3 overnight, improved when night-watchman Underwood made 43, and Gower, batting at seven, then scored 98 not out. But he ran out of partners and England's 237 left Australia only 216 to make. The wicket was now improving, and Australia won comfortably by six wickets, Greg Chappell also reaching 98 not

The Centenary Test at Lord's in 1980. Kim Hughes straight drives Emburey back over his head during his century.

out, the same score as Gower.

In the final Test at Melbourne, Gooch batted excellently only to be run out for 99, attempting a single for his first Test century. Brearley, with 60 not out batting at seven, helped England to 306 (Lillee 6 for 60). All the Australian batsmen except Hughes scored well, with Greg Chappell getting 114 in a total of 477. Despite a not out 119 from Botham, Australia needed a mere 103 to win, and did so by 8 wickets.

Botham scored most runs and took most wickets for England in the series—the Chappells headed the Australian batting and Dymock and Lillee were the best bowlers.

1980 in England
Drawn 1
The second Centenary Test Match—the centenary being that of Test cricket in England—was played at Lord's in August. The weather, unfortunately, was very poor, and eight hours were lost through rain and bad light, despite an extra hour being played on each of the last two days: half-an-hour before and after the scheduled times. The match will always be

remembered not for its cricket, but for the behaviour of some MCC members when the start of play was delayed on Saturday. The England captain Botham was struck and the umpires were jostled as they returned to the pavilion from inspecting the pitch.

Greg Chappell decided to bat, and Australia reached 227 for 2 by the close. On the Friday this was increased to 278 for 4 in the 75 minutes played, and Chappell declared at 385 for 5 at tea on Saturday. Wood scored 112 on the first two days, while Hughes batted on all three and reached 117. England received only two balls before play ended again.

England were all out 205 on

England edge nearer a famous victory at Headingley in 1981. Taylor throws the ball high after catching Lawson off Willis in the second innings.

Monday (Boycott 62, Gower 45), and Chappell, helped by 59 from himself and a brisk 84 from Hughes, declared at 189 for 4 on Tuesday, setting England to score 370 runs in 350 minutes. Gooch was out attacking but Athey could not get going, and the chase was soon given up. Boycott enjoyed himself, batting out time for 128 not out, and with Gatting 50 not out, proceedings ended at 244 for 3.

Kim Hughes, who became the third man after Boycott and M. L. Jaisimha to bat on all five days of a Test match, was chosen Man of the Match.

1981 in England
England 3   Australia 1   Drawn 2
The first Test was at Trent Bridge, on a wicket and in conditions which helped seam and swing bowlers. England had Dilley, Willis, Hendrick and Botham, and

the Australians also had a battery of seamers in Lillee, Alderman and Hogg. After England had been put in, only Gatting made more than 50, and it took 34 from Dilley batting at nine to get England up to 185 all out. However, before the first day was over Australia had sunk to 33 for 4. The next day was interrupted by rain and bad light, and was distinguished by England dropping several catches. Nevertheless Australia were finally out on Saturday for 179 (Border 63). By the time play ended at 2.37pm on Saturday, England were 94 for 6. Play continued on the Sunday, for the first time in an English Test match, and at last it was a sunny day, but it was too late for England, all out 125. Australia had a few alarms reaching 132 for 6, but eventually went one up in the series. Lillee, with 8 wickets for 80 was Man of the Match, although his West Australia protégé, Alder-

man, had 9 for 130 in his first Test.

The Lord's Test always looked a draw. Hughes put England in again, but after a bright start by Gooch, the innings proceeded slowly. With an interruption for bad light, only 191 for 4 were scored on the first day, and there was more time lost on the second, when England were out for 311, Willey 82. There were scenes of crowd dissatisfaction for the second year running at Lord's when, after Australia's innings had been suspended for bad light, the sun shone brightly after the players had been 'dismissed' for the day. Next day, after Wood made 44 out of 62 in an hour, four wickets were down for 81, but Hughes, Border, Marsh, Bright and Lillee made good contributions as Australia reached 345, extras contributing an Ashes record 55, including 32 no-balls. It was now well into the fourth day,

and England's hopes of setting a target were not helped by Boycott, in his 100th Test, taking 279 minutes for 60. The England captain, Botham, was out first ball on the last morning attempting a sweep, thereby bagging a pair. He declared at 265 for 8, leaving Australia 170 minutes to make 232. But three wickets went for 17, and Australia went on the defensive, ending at 90 for 4. Lawson, who took 7 for 81 in England's first innings (Lillee 0 for 102), was announced as Man of the Match, but the real sensation came shortly afterwards, when it was announced that Botham had resigned from the captaincy just before he was to be sacked. In twelve Tests as captain, he had won none and felt that media sniping was getting to his family. Mike Brearley was appointed to resume the captaincy for the remainder of the series.

The third Test at Headingley was the most exciting of modern times, and featured the biggest reversal of fortune anyone can remember. As if to make a point, the main hero was Botham.

Australia won the toss, batted, and made 401 for 9 dec, using up

At Perth in 1982-83, Terry Alderman, attempting to disperse a pitch invasion, broke his collarbone and was carried off. The England physio, Bernard Thomas, helps.

almost all of the first two rain-interrupted days. Dyson made his first Test century, 102, skipper Hughes 89, while ex-skipper Botham took 6 for 98. On Saturday, England were shot out by Lillee, Alderman and Lawson for 174. Botham was top scorer with 50—extras came next with 34. England were forced to follow-on, and Gooch was out for the second time on the same day for a total of 2 runs. On the Monday England slid to 41 for 4. Boycott and Willey took the score to 105 for 5, when Botham came in to join Boycott. At 133, Boycott, having stayed 215 minutes for 46, was lbw, and at 135 for 7 Taylor was out. That was the nadir. Still 92 short of avoiding an innings defeat, with only three wickets left, England were quoted by the bookmakers at 500-1 to win—Lillee and Marsh, it later transpired, invested a sporting pound or two at these odds.

Dilley joined Botham, and with nothing to lose the pair attacked the bowling—they added 117 in 18 overs. Bright earned himself a special place in history by dropping a hard chance off Botham when he was 32. When Dilley was out for 56, Old continued in the same vein of sensible aggression. With a six and a flurry of fours, Botham reached 103 off 87 balls, having scored his last 64 with two singles and 62 in boundaries. When Old was out for 29 at 319, the last two wickets had taken the

score from 92 behind to 92 ahead at almost six runs an over. Willis now remained to help Botham set Australia a target (even now the relief of respectability rather than a possible win was the popular feeling). The two saw out the day at 351 for 9—the last session contained 175 runs, of which Botham had scored 106. It was one of the most thrilling sessions in Test cricket, as unexpected as it was exciting.

On the last day Willis was out for 2, having helped Botham add 37 for the last wicket. Botham was not out 149 (148 balls), England were 356, and Australia needed 130 to win. The target, and the glorious futility of all that had gone before, seemed to be put in perspective when Wood hit the first two balls from Botham for four each. But Wood was caught behind off Botham: 13 for 1. Dyson and Chappell proceeded comfortably, however. Old came on for Dilley, Willis came on (as second change) for Botham, and proceeded to bowl a number of no-balls, Willey was tried, but the batsmen took the score past 50 with no trouble. Then Willis was switched to the Kirkstall Lane end and transformed the situation. Three wickets for no runs in 11 balls, and from 56 for 1 Australia found themselves lunching at 58 for 4, with just a whiff of anxiety in the air. After lunch, with Willis inspired, the rout continued—65

for 5 (Old got this one) then 68 for 6 as Dyson (34) was out. Dilley caught an attempt at a six from Marsh—74 for 7—and Lawson was caught behind—75 for 8. Lillee and Bright then made a stand of 35 in four overs. Two more overs and all might have been in vain for England, but Lillee offered a dolly to mid-on, Gatting either slipped or misjudged it, but finally dived forward to hold it. One run later Willis yorked Bright, made a triumphant run for the pavilion and England, after following on, had won by 18 runs. Willis, in his best Test performance, had 8 for 43, enough to win any other Man of the Match award, but this was 'Botham's match'. One hundred and ninety-nine runs, seven wickets, two catches, odds of 500-1 upset—who could ask for more?

The fourth Test at Edgbaston began in Australia's favour after England batted. England were dismissed in five hours for 189, Alderman taking 5 for 42, including Botham, bowled for 26. Old had two Australians out for 14, but night-watchman Bright, Hughes, Yallop and Kent managed to get the score to 258, a lead of 69. There were 21 no-balls. Willis failed to take a wicket, his last three analyses being 0-72, 8-43, 0-63.

Brearley was out overnight, and on the Saturday England batted grimly to repair the damage. No-

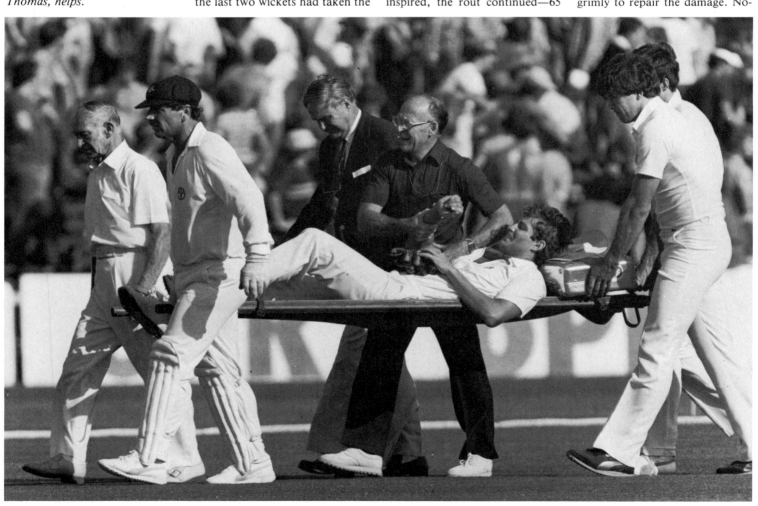

body scored more than Gatting's 39, and at 167 for 8 England were only 98 ahead. A stand of 50 between Emburey (37 not out) and Old (23) meant England totalled 219, however, and Australia were set 151 to win. Old got Wood overnight, and on Sunday (Edgbaston's first Test Sunday) 142 were needed with 9 wickets left.

Border (40) and Yallop (30) repaired the score after being 29 for 3, but both were out to Emburey. At 105 for 5, Australia needed 46, but then Brearley called on Botham. The last five wickets fell for seven runs, all to Botham, Australia were out for 121, England won by 29, Botham had 5 for 11, and was, for the second time running, Man of the Match.

The Old Trafford Test was a match of contrasts—high and low innings, fast and slow scoring. England batted, and were out for 231, 94 coming from the last two wickets, thanks to 52 not out from Allott. Tavare batted 287 minutes for 69 in his Ashes debut, and was out to Whitney, co-opted into the team because Hogg and Lawson were injured. Whitney had played only six first-class matches, and was summoned from Cheltenham when about to play for Gloucestershire. Australia were then dismissed for 130 in 30.2 overs (Kent 52). With Gooch out before tea on Friday, Boycott and Tavare then batted very slowly, adding only 72 in 156 minutes.

This was rapid compared to the pre-lunch session on Saturday,

only 29 runs being scored in 28 overs, a policy of consolidation which appeared mistaken as England also lost three wickets and then slid to 104 for 5, mainly due to Alderman.

Next Botham joined Tavare, played himself in, then launched an attack on Lillee and Alderman with the new ball, scoring 66 in eight overs, England's total increasing by 57 in five overs. Botham passed 100 in 86 balls with a six, and when he was out he had scored 118 from 149 in 123 minutes, taking 102 balls, and had hit 6 sixes (an Ashes record) and 13 fours. Many said it was a better innings than at Headingley: *Wisden* said 'its ferocious yet effortless power and dazzling cleanness of stroke, can surely never have been

The vital catch in the fourth Test at Melbourne in 1982-83. Miller catches Thomson after Tavare had failed to hold the ball and England win by 3 runs.

bettered in a Test match'. He was out to Whitney, who missed a very difficult chance when Botham was 32 (the same score at which he had been missed at Headingley).

Tavare scored the slowest 50 in an English first-class match (75 overs, 306 minutes) and went on to 78 in 423 minutes (289 balls). Knott and Emburey scored well against the tired attack and England reached 404. Australia needed 506 to win and lost two for 24. Yallop played a beautiful and gallant innings of 114, however, and Border, with a broken finger, a brave and dogged one of 123 not out in nearly seven hours. Australia had the consolation of passing 400 by 2 runs, but England won by 103, and Botham, for the third successive time since relinquishing the captaincy, was Man of the Match.

The sixth Test at the Oval could not live up to the previous three. Australia, put in mistakenly by Brearley, made 352, with Border (106 not out) top scorer. England replied with 314, Boycott being seventh out for 137 out of 293. Lillee's 7 for 89 was his best Test bowling to date. England had a chance to win on the Monday when Australia were 104 for 4 and Wellham offered an easy catch to Willis. It was dropped, however, and Wellham, making his Test debut, scored 104, the first Australian since Harry Graham in 1893 to make a debut Test hundred in England. Hughes declared at 344 for 9, leaving England the last day to make 383. Boycott was out to Lillee without a run on the board, but England survived, comfortably in the end, at 261 for 7, although Knott needed to bat 167 minutes for 70 not out to save the game. Lillee was Man of the Match in his last Test in England; Botham, of course, Man of the Series.

1982-83 in Australia
Australia 2 England 1 Drawn 2
England toured Australia without the South African 'rebels', principally Gooch, Boycott, Emburey, Underwood and Knott, and with Willis as captain. The series began at Perth on a batsman's wicket, on which England, put in, made 411 (Tavare 89, Gower 72, Randall 78). When England reached 400 there was a pitch invasion by drunken English supporters which developed into a skirmish, and Alderman, who tried to do some personal policing, dislocated a shoulder and stretched a nerve. He took no further part in the series. Australia passed England's total and declared at 424 for 9 (Chappell 117, Hughes 62, Hookes 56, Dyson 52, Lawson 50). With England at one stage 80 for 4 there was a possibility of a result, but Randall, whose 115 won the Man of the Match award, and Lamb (56), helped England to recover to 358, and the match ended in a tame draw with Australia 73 for 2.

With Lillee having bone flakes removed from his knee, Thomson and Rackemann joined the Australian attack at Brisbane. In the event, Lawson (6 for 47) was the wrecker of the England innings. Put in again, England were out for 219, only Lamb (72) passing 50. South-African born Wessels, making his debut for Australia, then scored 162, after being dropped at 15. On a pitch getting easier, Chappell and Yardley each made 53 and Australia totalled 341. Fowler (83), Miller (60) and no-balls (35) helped England to make 309 in their second knock,

Lawson taking five wickets. With Wessels dropped before he scored, Dyson retired injured, and three men out for 93, there was just a hint of a collapse like those in England in 1981, but Hughes and Hookes (66 not out) saw Australia home by seven wickets. Wessels' aggregate of 208, the highest by an Australian debutant, won him the Man of the Match award.

At Adelaide Willis erred in putting Australia in to bat (a policy he had apparently decided in advance of seeing the fast, dry pitch). Australia were always going well, and with Chappell making 115 and Hughes 88 they reached 458. Only Gower (60), Lamb (82) and Botham (35) batted well for England, and the last seven wickets crashed for 35 runs; England, at 216, followed on. This time Gower made 114 and Botham 58, but the lower order was again disappointing, the last seven wickets doing little better by adding 68. Australia made the 83 wanted for the loss of two wickets. Man of the Match was Lawson, who took nine wickets.

Needing to win the last two Tests to retain the Ashes, England played much better at Melbourne. Put in (again) they made 284, with Tavare (one run in the previous Test), batting at number three, scoring 89 in very untypical manner (5 fours in 8 balls off Yardley). With Botham making 83, the innings was cruising along at 217 for 3, but the last seven wickets again disappointed, adding 67, and 284

was fewer than hoped. Australia passed it only by three, however (Hughes 66, Hookes and Marsh 53 each). Only Fowler (65) passed 50 in England's second innings, when the later order at last came good. From 45 for 3, and 129 for 5, England reached 294, leaving Australia 292 to win. From 71 for 3, Hughes (48) and Hookes (68) added exactly 100, putting Australia on top. Six wickets then fell for 47, leaving Border and Thomson to make 74 for the last wicket. Half of these were made by the close on the fourth day, and 18,000 entered the ground free on the last day to see if they could make the other 37. They almost did. When three runs short of the England total, Thomson snicked Botham to Tavare at second slip. Tavare could only knock the ball up over his head, but Miller at first slip came round the back of him to hold the ball just above the turf. Cowans, who took 6 for 77, was Man of the Match.

Australia won the toss for the final Test at Sydney and for the first time the winning captain decided to bat. Throughout the series, television replays had highlighted some bad umpiring decisions. Now, on the sixth ball of the match, came the worst. Dyson, palpably run out by almost a yard, was allowed to stay. He stayed for over five hours for 79, and England's chance of retaining the Ashes took a severe blow. Border made 89, and Australia totalled 314. England, batting consider-

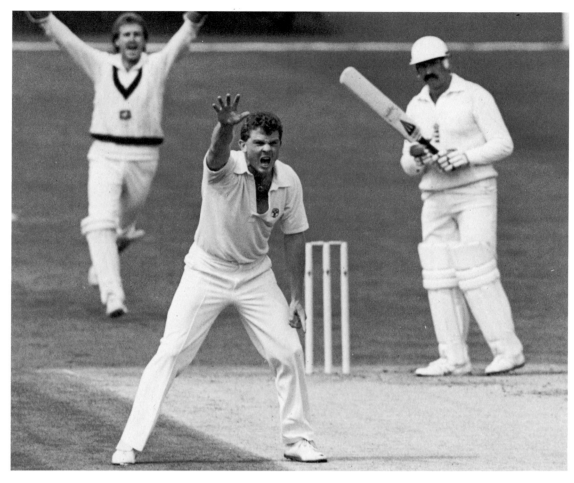

Craig McDermott appeals vehemently and successfully for lbw against Gooch at Headingley in 1985. He was Australia's best bowler.

ably faster, made 237, Gower and Randall each scoring 70. Hughes made 137, Border 83 and Wessels 53 in Australia's second innings, the side reaching 382. England lost Cook overnight and began the last day needing 452 to win. It was clearly impossible, even with night-watchman Hemmings making 95, and the day ended at 315 for 7. Hughes was Man of the Match, Lawson Man of the Series. A fan donated an urn, in which the Australians burnt a bail, to claim the 'new Ashes', or, as the Australian newspapers put it, 'Urnie'.

1985 in England
England 3 Australia 1 Drawn 2
Allan Border's Australians met an England side captained by Gower, whose place after a run of bad scores was made safe only by a century in the final Texaco Trophy match.

In the first Test at Headingley, Australia batted and overcame the early life in the pitch, passing 200 with only two men out, but they collapsed later and were all out for 331 (Hilditch 119). Gooch, Willey and Emburey returned to the England side after the lifting of the three-year ban on the players who toured South Africa with the 'rebel' XI. Gooch was soon out, but Tim Robinson, playing his

Murray Bennett is caught and bowled by Les Taylor at the Oval in 1985 and England have won the Ashes. Botham, Gooch, Downton and Gilbert watch.

first Test against Australia, was the backbone of a splendid England effort. He made 175, and supported by Gatting (53), Botham (60) and Downton (54), helped the total to 533. With intermittent rain and bad light the match became a race against time. Australia's second innings eventually closed at 324 (Hilditch 80, Wessels 64, Wayne Phillips 91, Emburey 5 for 82), leaving England 200 minutes to score 123, a target they achieved, but not without losing five wickets. There was minor controversy on the last ball, as the crowd invaded the pitch and came dangerously close to Lawson, who was attempting a difficult catch in the outfield, and must have distracted his attention.

Australia put England in at Lord's and early on the second day had them all out for 290, Gower (86) being the principal scorer and McDermott taking 6 for 70. The rest of the day was frequently interrupted by bad light, to the annoyance of spectators. Border (196) and Ritchie (94) were batting at the end of it, and they eventually added 216 for Australia's fifth wicket. A total of 425 (Botham 5 for 109) meant a lead of 135. England lost six wickets reaching 100, but a stand of 131 between

Gatting (75 not out) and Botham (85) promised recovery. Botham's dismissal by Holland (5 for 68) virtually meant the end. All out 261, England set Australia 127 to win. They made hard work of it, and a smart run out of Wessels, pushing forward, by Gower at silly point added to the tension. At 65 for 5, talk of the 1981 Headingley match was in the air. But Border and Phillips stood firm and Australia won by four wickets.

England batted on an easy wicket at Trent Bridge and scored 456, an insurance against defeat. It was nevertheless slightly disappointing, as 358 was reached with only two wickets down. Gatting was then run out by a Gower drive which Holland touched and the momentum was lost. Gower made an elegant 166, Gooch 70 and Gatting 74. Lawson returned to form with 5 for 103.

Wood asserted himself when Australia batted, making an uncharacteristically steady 172. Later Ritchie, at number seven, made a more aggressive 146, adding 161 with Wood. Australia reached 569. The pitch was too good and the weather breaks too frequent for a result. There was time only for Robinson to please local fans with 77 not out from 196 for 2.

Rain was also the victor at Old Trafford, although England were pressing for a result until the last day. Australia, put in, made only 257, with Boon (61) top scorer. England passed this total with only

three men out, and finally declared at 482 for 9. Gatting made 160 (his first Test century in England), Gooch 74 and Lamb 67, but the feature was the bowling of Mc-Dermott, who took 8 for 141 and was the only Australian to take a wicket in the match. When the last day began, England required six Australian wickets, but rain had the last laugh. Play started 1½ hours late, Border was missed in the first over, and that was that. He went on to 146 not out and Australia to a draw at 340 for 5.

England won the toss at Old Trafford and put Australia in, but when, after the first two interrupted days, Australia were apparently safe from defeat at 335 for 8, the decision seemed mistaken. However, Saturday's play turned the series and established the pattern for the rest of the season. The last two wickets fell without addition in the first over. Border (83) and Lawson (53) were the top scorers, and Ellison, recalled to the England team, took 6 for 77. Robinson and Gower then batted so well that at Saturday's close England were ahead at 355 for 1. Robinson went on to 148 and Gower to 215 (the stand was worth 331), while Gatting scored 100 not out before Gower declared on another rain-abbreviated day (Monday) at 595 for 5. Ellison then took 4 for 1 in the evening to reduce Australia to 35 for 5 at the close. On the final day rain delayed the start till 2.30 and then

again after two balls. No wickets fell before tea. The breakthrough came in controversial fashion. Phillips, batting aggressively to reach 69, slashed square, Lamb at silly point jumped, the ball hit his instep and was caught by Gower. The umpire at the bowler's end, who was unsighted, consulted with the other, and the batsman was given out, to his, and later, the Australian captain's expressed disappointment. The last three wickets went down in the first six of the statutory last 20 overs, and Australia, 142 all out, had lost by an innings and 118 runs. It was the first time in Ashes history that a side had won a match without losing more than five wickets.

Australia had to win at the Oval to square the series and retain the Ashes. This looked impossible after the first day, on which England batted. On a fast pitch, the first wicket fell at 20, whereupon Gooch (196) and Gower (157) added 351, England making 376 for 3 on the first day. A collapse to 464 all out suggested an Aussie fightback, but they in turn could do no better than 241 (Ritchie 64 not out). Gower applied the follow-on, and although rain on Saturday delayed the end, only Border (58) put up much resistance. Early on Monday (sadly, for the first time in England all seats were sold in advance for a fourth day) the innings was over for 129, and England won the series 3-1.

ENGLAND v SOUTH AFRICA

In 1970, South African cricket was at its peak, and had a series been played between England and South Africa that year, it would have been between the world's strongest countries. Unhappily, any chance of such a clash was bedevilled by political intrusions.

The early days of England-South Africa meetings were not at all significant as trials of strength between the two countries. Many of the South African players were not long out from England, and the England sides that went to South Africa were at best second XIs. Though four Test series were played in South Africa before the South African War broke out in 1899, no Test matches were played in that period whenever South African sides toured England. Indeed, although the first Test between these two countries was played in Port Elizabeth in 1889, the first in England did not take place until 1907.

Curiously, the war strengthened rather than weakened South African cricket, a great number of young Englishmen settling there after the hostilities. Almost immediately South Africa entered one of its more successful eras, with its googly quartet of R. O. Schwarz, G. A. Faulkner, G. C. White, and

A. E. Vogler. P. F. Warner's team to South Africa in 1905-06 lost four Tests, and the Springboks were not easily beaten in England in 1907. But thereafter their strength faded, and it was 1935 before H. F. Wade's team won the first Test (and with it the series) in England. Twenty years later, Jack Cheetham's team was narrowly beaten 3-2 in perhaps the best Test series ever played in England, and in 1965 Peter van der Merwe's side repeated the 1935 feat of winning one match and so the series.

In between these Springbok successes, the series had usually gone England's way, although South Africa have had their successes at home, where they have won 13 of their 18 Test victories against England. The modern tragedy of South African cricket is that, when it reached the highest pinnacle of all and was in a position to make a stimulating contribution to world cricket, it has not been able to play its oldest adversary, England.

RIGHT Barbed wire at Lord's against demonstrators who eventually caused the cancellation of the 1970 tour.
BELOW Basil d'Oliveira, whose selection for England prevented the 1968 tour to South Africa.

Series of the 19th century
(all in South Africa)
1888-89
South Africa 0   England 2
1891-92
South Africa 0   England 1
1895-96
South Africa 0   England 3
1898-99
South Africa 0   England 2

The first four England sides to South Africa were led by C. Aubrey Smith, W. W. Read, and Lord Hawke, who took the last two. Smith, many years later to be knighted as a world famous Hollywood film actor, was the captain when the first Test was played in March 1889. Bobby Abel made 46 and 23 not out in that match, and 120 in the second Test at Cape Town, where Johnny Briggs, who had taken six wickets at Port Elizabeth, had the astonishing figures of 7-17 and 8-11. Briggs hit the stumps 14 times and had one man lbw—an achievement unlikely to be equalled for individual devastation in Test cricket.

The somewhat casual rules of qualification in use at the time are illustrated by the inclusion in W. W. Read's touring side three years later of W. L. Murdoch and J. J. Ferris, who had previously played for Australia against England. F. Hearne, who opened the innings for South Africa, with J. T. Hearne in opposition, had played for Aubrey Smith's side on the first tour.

Lord Hawke's first team included C. B. Fry and S. M. J. Woods, but its most successful player was the Surrey bowler George Lohmann, who took 7-38 and 8-7 at Port Elizabeth—so redeeming himself for his 'pair' as opening batsman. At Johannesburg he took the last 9 wickets for 28 in South Africa's first innings, and in all three Tests he took 35 wickets.

The last England team before the outbreak of war also contained names that appeared in other ranks. Albert Trott had played for Australia, and Frank Mitchell, who opened the innings with 'Plum' Warner, was to captain South Africa in the triangular tournament of 1912. J. H. Sinclair, now the mainstay of South Africa's batting, made their first Test hundred, in Cape Town, but in the second innings the home side were dismissed for only 35 by Trott (4-19) and Schofield Haigh (6-11).

When war broke out several

Lord Hawke took two sides to South Africa in the 1890s. His first side of 1895-96 included (inset, left to right) C. B. Fry, and two Surrey players, George Lohmann, who captured 35 wickets in the three Tests, and Tom Hayward, who hit 122 in the Johannesburg Test. Inset below them is Albert Trott, who played in Hawke's 1898-99 side after having played for Australia in 1894-95.

weeks later, South Africa could not be said to have made much advance as a force in Test cricket. But a visit from Darling's Australians on their way home from England in 1902 did much to restore cricket and raise standards, and the next England team to South Africa had a rude shock.

1905-06 in South Africa
South Africa 4   England 1
South Africa's first ever victory, when it came in the first Test of the series in Johannesburg, was a thrilling affair by one wicket. Plum Warner's team included some famous names, J. N. Crawford, David Denton, A. E. Relf, Haigh, and Colin Blythe, but like all visiting teams up to World War II, it was well below full England strength. South Africa, needing 284 to win after being bowled out for 91 in the first innings, made the runs largely through an unbroken last-wicket stand of 48 between the left-handed Dave Nourse and his captain P. W. Sherwell.

In this series the South African selectors took the probably unique step of picking the same side for all five Tests, and their confidence was confirmed when Sherwell's side won all but the fourth Test—and most of the others by big margins. They had a highly effective opening bowler in S. J. Snooke, and the spinners Schwarz, Faulkner, and Vogler, were beginning to make a big impact. The batting was consistent and had depth.

1907 in England
England 1   South Africa 0
Drawn 2
After their success against Plum Warner's team, South Africa were accorded full Test status when they went to England a year later.

They met the full-strength England side, most of whom had helped beat Australia 2-0 two years before. Of those who played for England in the first Test, only Crawford and Blythe had been on the tour to South Africa. Rain spared South Africa in this match, in which their captain Sherwell, promoted from the depths of the order to open the innings, made a second innings of 115. In the second Test, however, England were bowled out after rain for 76, Faulkner taking 6-17. South Africa led on the first innings and needed only 129 to win in the last innings, but after more rain Blythe (7-40) had the last word, and England won by 53 runs.

The last of the three Tests was drawn, with honours even, and so South Africa had emerged with credit from their first overseas series.

1909-10 in South Africa
South Africa 3   England 2
H. D. G. Leveson Gower's English touring team was stronger in its early batting than some of its predecessors, boasting an order that went Jack Hobbs, Wilfred Rhodes, Denton, F. L. Fane, and

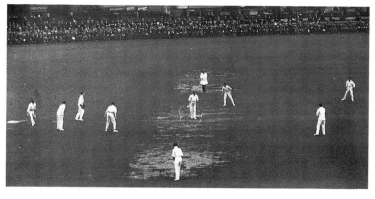

Frank Woolley. But its bowling was less menacing for South African batting, which had grown in confidence. Faulkner was now a world class all-rounder, and in the first Test, which South Africa won by 19 runs, he made 78 and 123, as well as taking 8 wickets. South Africa clinched the series in the fourth Test, and when Hobbs made 187 in the last Test it was too late for England to save the series.

1912 in England
England 3   South Africa 0
For some years South African cricket had been riding high, but now it declined with a bump and stayed down for many years. In the very wet summer of the triangular tournament, South Africa found their great spinners of other years less effective, and they lost even more easily to England than they did to Australia. In particular, they fell foul of Sydney Barnes, who took 34 wickets in the three matches and, as it proved, had worse in store for South Africa.

1913-14 in South Africa
South Africa 0   England 4
Drawn 1
If ever one man dominated a series, Sydney Barnes dominated the last Test series before World War I. He did not play in the last Test in Port Elizabeth, yet in the first four he captured 49 wickets. South Africa had a high-class opening batsman in Herbie Taylor, their captain, but an England side including Hobbs, Rhodes, Philip Mead, J. W. Hearne, and Woolley made plenty of runs, and Barnes did the rest. In the second Test at Johannesburg he took 17 wickets, a feat not exceeded until Jim Laker's historic 19 in 1956.

1922-23 in South Africa
South Africa 1   England 2
Drawn 2
Though ill health kept Hobbs out, the England team that F. T. Mann took was not far below the best, and South Africa did well to run them to a close series. Taylor, still the outstanding player in the country, made 176 in the first Test, enabling South Africa to win by 168 runs. England won the second in a thrilling match at Cape Town, but only by one wicket. A left-arm bowler, A. E. Hall took 11 wickets for South Africa, but George Mac-

L. A. Stricker is clean bowled by Sydney Barnes at the Oval during the triangular tournament of 1912, when the South Africans fell foul of Barnes and an extremely wet summer.

aulay, playing in his first Test, joined Alec Kennedy for the last wicket when England needed five runs to win, and his first scoring stroke in Test cricket won the match. Phil Mead made 181 in a rain-ruined third Test in Durban, and Frank Woolley 115 not out in another draw at Johannesburg, which left all depending on the final Test in Durban.

A hundred in each innings by England opener Jack Russell was the deciding factor. Taylor, with R. H. Catterall and Dave Nourse, were formidable opponents for the England bowling of A. E. R. Gilligan, Alec Kennedy, George Macaulay, Percy Fender, and Woolley, but though Taylor made 102 in the last innings South Africa went down by 109 runs.

1924 in England
England 3   South Africa 0
Drawn 2
Arthur Gilligan was the England captain when Herbie Taylor took the 1924 Springboks to England, and he played a major part in the

A Test win in England still eluded the South Africans in 1929, when Walter Hammond was just one England batsman they found in run-getting mood.

sensational events of the first Test at Edgbaston. Put in by Taylor, England made 438, G. M. Parker, who had been brought in from the Bradford League to strengthen the touring side's bowling, taking 6-152. South Africa were then bowled out for 30 by Gilligan (6-7) and Maurice Tate (4-12). They made 390 in the second innings, but had suffered a severe blow from which they never recovered. Catterall made 120 in the second innings at Edgbaston, and the same score in the first innings of the Lord's Test, which by another coincidence was lost by the identical margin of an innings and 18 runs. At Lord's England made a mammoth 531-2 declared, Hobbs (211) and Sutcliffe making 268 for the first wicket before Woolley (134 not out) and Patsy Hendren (50 not out) added to the agony. Catterall played another fine innings of 95 in two hours in the last Test, which was spoiled by rain, but the tour overall was a disappointment.

1927-28 in South Africa
South Africa 2   England 2
Drawn 1
When Captain R. T. Stanyforth took a reasonably strong English team to South Africa, Herbie Taylor's long tenure of captaincy had ended, though at 38 he was to play in several more Test series before he retired. Dave Nourse had gone and his son, Dudley, had not yet appeared on the first-class scene, but some promising cricketers, including the wicket-keeper-batsman H. B. Cameron, were coming to the fore.

The new captain, H. G. Deane did well to bring South Africa from being two down after two Tests to halve the series. Hundreds by Herbert Sutcliffe and Ernest Tyldesley and 12 wickets by George Geary won England the first Test, and Sutcliffe, Percy Holmes, and Tyldesley won them the second after South Africa had held a first innings lead of 117. George Geary, who had promised to be a formidable opponent on the matting, did not play after the

second Test, and after an even draw at Durban in the third Test South Africa came back boldly. The pace bowling of A. E. Hall and G. F. Bissett took 17 wickets to defeat an England side that began Holmes, Sutcliffe, Tyldesley, Hammond, Wyatt. Taylor made a hundred in this match, and that other pillar of Springbok batting, Catterall, made 119 at Durban, where Bissett took 7-29 in the second innings and England were beaten by 8 wickets.

1929 in England
England 2   South Africa 0
Drawn 3
South Africa had given an excellent performance to halve the previous series in South Africa, but once again, in 1929, they could not win a Test in England. On four occasions they led England on the first innings, without being able to press home their advantage, and England won at Leeds and Manchester, R. E. S. Wyatt and Frank Woolley making hundreds at Old Trafford, where Tich Freeman's leg-spin took 12 wickets. At the Oval, Sutcliffe made two hundreds and with Walter Hammond (101 not out) prevented South Africa from winning after they led by 234 runs on the first innings. Tests were still of three days then.

It had long been realized that the disparity between South Africa's performances at home, where they had won 10 Tests by now, and in England, where they had not won any, was largely connected with the matting pitches used in South Africa. The transformation to turf had been gradually coming, however, and the fruits of it were not long in being realized.

Ivan Siedle was opening bat on his second tour of England when South Africa won their first victory there in 1935.

1930-31 in South Africa
South Africa 1   England 0
Drawn 4
The first Test match on grass in South Africa was played in Cape Town when Percy Chapman's team went there. One of the strongest English sides to visit the country so far, they had lost the first Test in Johannesburg by 28 runs and had only narrowly avoided an innings defeat at Newlands, where Bruce Mitchell, I. J. Siedle, and the indestructible Herbie Taylor made hundreds in the South African score of 513-8. Three more draws followed, South Africa having slightly the better of them, so that their victory in the series by the first Test win, was well deserved. Against an England team including Wyatt, Hammond, Maurice Leyland, Hendren, Andy Sandham, Tate, Bill Voce, and J. C. White, it was no mean feat.

1935 in England
England 0   South Africa 1
Drawn 4
Tests were still of only three days when H. F. Wade's team went to England in 1935, though it was for the last time in a series between the two countries. In the four drawn Tests England were a shade superior, though South Africa were never near defeat in any of them. At Lord's, however, the match was finished, and South Africa won their first-ever victory in England by 157 runs. They were not to know then that it would also decide the series. England were in a period of transition—the Lord's Test was the last of Herbert Sutcliffe's 54 Tests—and the fast bowling did not mount the same menace as that of a few years before. Yet only 18 months later England were making a bold effort to recover the Ashes in Australia.

Oddly, when the great Springbok victory was at last won, only three batsmen made any big contribution to it. In the first innings a total of 228 was reached through a magnificent 90 out of 126 in 105 minutes by Jock Cameron, who was to die so sadly within a few weeks of the end of the tour. When South Africa went in a seond time with a lead of 30, Bruce Mitchell batted for 5½ hours to make 164 not out, supported by Eric Rowan, who made his second 40 of the match. England were left to make 309 to win in 4¾ hours, but were easily dismissed, the Greek leg-spin bowler Xenophon Balaskas adding four wickets to his five of the first innings.

1938-39 in South Africa
South Africa 0   England 1
Drawn 4
By now it was clear that England sides visiting South Africa must be nearly the strongest available, and the one Walter Hammond took in the last pre-war season lacked few of the best players. Numerous runs were scored on what were by now turf pitches, and England took the

series by winning the third Test, in Durban, where Eddie Paynter made 243 and Hammond 120. Seven wickets by giant fast bowler Ken Farnes helped to complete the job.

But it was the last Test, one of the four draws, that has gone down in history as the breaker of many records. Scheduled to be played to a finish, it was given up after 10 days, when the MCC team had to leave Durban to catch their ship home. They were then 42 runs short of victory with 5 wickets in hand, a remarkable state of affairs for they had needed 696 runs to win when they began their last innings late on the sixth day. South Africa opened by making 530, Peter van der Byl 125 in 7¼ hours and Dudley Nourse 103. England were bowled out for 316, but South Africa batted again with van der Byl (97) and Alan Melville

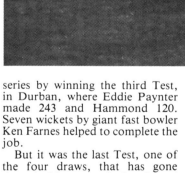

(103) making 191 together in their second opening stand of more than 100, and this time the South African score reached 481. Thereafter the pitch was frequently restored by rain, which also took away the eighth day's play, and England batted steadily on. Paul Gibb, who opened the innings with Len Hutton, made 120, Bill Edrich 219, and Walter Hammond 140. On the 10th day England needed only 200 runs, but rain further interrupted play and eventually the match was abandoned. It was the last 'timeless' Test.

1947 in England
England 3   South Africa 0
Drawn 2
When Alan Melville, the 1938-39 captain, took the Springboks to England in 1947, South African cricket was suffering from much the same post-war ailments as

brook, and Denis Compton leading the batting, and Alec Bedser, Cliff Gladwin, and the leg-spinner R. O. Jenkins taking most of the wickets, were just the better side, but not by much. Dudley Nourse had a fine series for South Africa, Eric Rowan was as obdurate as ever, and his brother Athol was by now a world-class off-spinner.

England won two narrow victories in the first and last Tests to clinch the series. The first, by two wickets, came in one of the most exciting finishes in Test history. England, needing 128 to win on an unpredictable pitch, got home when Cliff Gladwin and Alec Bedser ran a desperate leg-bye off the last ball of the match. The second Test in Johannesburg was notable for an opening stand of 359 between Hutton and Washbrook that lasted throughout the first day.

The last Test was also unusual, for England won after a declaration by Dudley Nourse, made, as it were, in desperation because his side were one down on the last day of the series. It asked for 172 runs in 95 minutes, and though there scarcely seemed time for England to be bowled out, they did in fact lose seven wickets before they won with a minute to spare. It remains a splendid example of a challenge thrown out boldly and taken up in the same spirit.

1951 in England
England 3   South Africa 1
Drawn 1
It was a younger team that Dudley Nourse took to England in 1951, and though well beaten it contained much promise for the future. Nourse and Eric Rowan were still the mainstays of the

LEFT Denis Compton scored 208 and Alan Melville (INSET) 117 at Lord's in 1947.
BELOW Len Hutton and Cyril Washbrook, who opened with 359 at Johannesburg in 1948-49.
BOTTOM Dudley Nourse made a brave 208 in 1951.

English cricket. Their players had mostly been away in the Middle East, few young ones had developed and so it was a fairly senior team, short of top-class experience, that went on tour. Especially it was short of penetrative bowling, and it coincided with a glorious English summer, splendid pitches, and Denis Compton and Bill Edrich in full spate.

The Springboks, notably Dudley Nourse, Alan Melville, and Bruce Mitchell, made a lot of runs and could take satisfaction from their contribution to a spectacular series that was a great advertisement for cricket. But they were well beaten in a series remembered for the superb batting of Compton and Edrich. Compton made 753 in the series at 94.12 and scored six hundreds against the Springboks, four in Tests. Edrich played in only four Tests but made 552 runs

and averaged 110.40. South Africa could look back with frustration on the first Test, which they only drew after leading by 325 runs on the first innings and making England follow-on. Alan Melville made a hundred in each innings, a feat Bruce Mitchell repeated in the last Test. Mitchell batted nearly 8 hours in a grim struggle against defeat, and eventually South Africa, at 423-7 finished only 28 runs short of an unconsidered victory.

1948-49 in South Africa
South Africa 0   England 2
Drawn 3
If the previous series did much to restore cricket in England after the war, the visit of George Mann's MCC side to South Africa 18 months later did the same there. In a notably happy tour, England, with Len Hutton, Cyril Wash-

batting, but Jackie McGlew, Roy McLean, John Waite, and Russell Endean were clearly on the way up. Athol Rowan was still a fine off-spinner, but Hugh Tayfield, who came during the tour as a reinforcement, was a worthy successor to him and Clive van Ryneveld was a valuable all-rounder.

This young team began by winning the first Test at Trent Bridge, where Nourse made 208 despite a broken thumb. Though Reg Simpson and Denis Compton made first innings hundreds for England, the pitch took some spin later and Athol Rowan (5-68) and N. B. F. 'Tufty' Mann (4-24) ran through the England second innings. At Lord's, however, the rain helped England, and the Lancashire off-spinner Roy Tattersall took 12 wickets for 101 to enable them to win by 10 wickets. Twelve wickets by Alec Bedser in wet conditions at Old Trafford brought England a nine-wicket victory there.

The fourth Test was drawn at Leeds, where Eric Rowan made 236 and 60 not out and Peter May scored a hundred in his first Test. England won the last, however, in three days, though only after some moments of doubts as to whether the last innings target of 163 was within their range.

1955 in England
England 3   South Africa 2
The Springbok promise of four years earlier was handsomely fulfilled when Jack Cheetham took his side to England in 1955 and played what many people consider

TOP Jubilation at Johannesburg in 1956-57. Neil Adcock hugs Hugh Tayfield after the off-spinner had bowled South Africa to a fourth Test win by taking 9-113 in England's second innings. Their 17-run victory put South Africa back into the series after they had been two Tests down.
LEFT Paceman Peter Pollock spearheaded the Springbok emergence of the 1960s.

the best post-war Test series. In mostly fine weather England won the first two Tests, South Africa the next two, and all depended on the last at the Oval. At that time, England's batting relied to an enormous extent on Peter May, and it is widely acknowledged that if a very close lbw decision at the Oval had not been given in his favour, South Africa would have won the rubber. May, in his first series as England captain, averaged 72, Denis Compton 54; no one else exceeded 25.

One of the Springboks' strengths was the combination of two fine fast bowlers, Peter Heine and Neil Adcock, but Tayfield was also at his best, taking 26 wickets in the series and Trevor Goddard, left-arm medium pace, took 25. McGlew was steady and averaged 52, but the other batting was not prolific, although some brilliant innings were played on occasions —the 142 of McLean at Lord's and the 108 of the tall, hard-driving Paul Winslow at Old Trafford. The Springboks' field-

ing was superb and they were excellently led.

The result of the first Test was deceptive, England winning by an innings. Frank Tyson, fresh from his triumphs in Australia, took 6-28 in the second innings. At Lord's, however, England were bowled out on a fast, grassy pitch for 133 on the first day, and McLean's dazzling innings helped give South Africa a 171-run lead. But May made a spectacular 112 in the second innings, and Brian Statham (7-39), helped by a deteri-

ABOVE The South Africans of 1955 featured in one of Test cricket's most exciting series and were considered unlucky not to win it. All depended on the final Test at the Oval where England won by 92 runs.
RIGHT When Eddie Barlow went to England in 1965, he was a fine opening batsman. Five years later, he would have been a valuable member of the Springboks as an all-rounder.

orating light that gave him time to rest, bowled South Africa out. Cheetham chipped a bone in the elbow in the second innings and did not play in either of the next two Tests, which South Africa won.

The Manchester victory was an especially fine one. Compton made 158 for England in the first innings and May 117 in the second, but in between, South Africa, batting with great dash, scored 521-8—McGlew 104, Waite 113, and Winslow who reached his only Test 100 with an enormous straight six over the sightscreen, 108. In the second innings they needed 145 to win in 2¼ hours against Bedser, Tyson, and Lock, and lost two wickets for 23. But McLean and McGlew added 72 in 50 minutes and the Springboks eventually won a historic match by three wickets with a few minutes to spare.

They won more easily at Leeds, where Tayfield (5-94) and Goddard (5-69) shared the wickets in the last innings, but could not quite hold Laker and Lock in the last Test on a typical Oval pitch of the day. But if Peter May had been given out lbw when on 4, instead of going on to make 89 not out, the series must have had another ending.

1956-57 in South Africa
South Africa 2 England 2
Drawn 1
Another fine series in South Africa saw the luck reversed in some ways. Peter May, though making hundreds of runs in other matches, failed in Test matches, often through brilliant catching, and South Africa won a vital toss in the last Test to help them to halve the series. The cricket was less spectacular than that of the previous

Ali Bacher was to have captained the South Africans on the cancelled tour of 1970.

series, and England began with dourly earned victories at Durban and Cape Town, the latter pressed home by Johnny Wardle (7-36) on a pitch taking some spin.

England were not far off winning the third Test and the rubber, but they stuck there. South Africa won an exciting victory by 17 runs at Johannesburg, one notable as their first win over England at home on a turf pitch. Hugh Tayfield (9-113) bowled them to success in the second innings. The last Test at Port Elizabeth was played on a pitch of impossibly low bounce. Van Ryneveld won the toss, and Endean's first-innings 70 took South Africa to 164, which was a winning score in the conditions.

1960 in England
England 3 South Africa 0
Drawn 2
The 1960 tour was one of the most disappointing ever undertaken by South Africa. McGlew's side contained many young players of less obvious promise than those of nine years before, and they met a damp and miserable English

summer that gave them no chance to settle in. The tour was further marred by the inclusion of the young fast bowler Geoff Griffin, who was frequently no-balled for throwing and did not bowl in the second half of the tour.

England, captained by Cowdrey, won the first three Tests, and though the Springboks led by 264 runs in the fifth Test at the Oval, a second innings opening stand of 290 between Geoff Pullar (175) and Colin Cowdrey (155) prevented them from coming anywhere near victory.

1964-65 in South Africa
South Africa 0 England 1
Drawn 4
When Mike Smith's team went to South Africa, the Springboks were approaching, but were not yet quite at, the stage of positive and commanding cricket they were to reach later. However, they were by the end the better side, and England were lucky to win the series.

England won the first Test at Durban, where the pitch deteriorated after hundreds by Ken

Play in the first Test at Lord's in 1965 was held up while the bowler's run-up was dug out and then relaid.

Barrington (148) and Jim Parks (108), and the England spinners Fred Titmus and David Allen bowled South Africa out twice. In the second Test England were within sight of what would have been a dashing and worthy win at the start of the last day, for Bob Barber (97) and Ted Dexter (172) had played superbly at the start. But one of many fine innings by Colin Bland (144 not out) thwarted them, and thereafter, increasingly hampered by injuries, they hung on to their lead against strengthening opposition.

1965 in England
England 0 South Africa 1
Drawn 2
The last series between England and South Africa before politics intruded was in the second half of the 1965 summer. It produced three thrilling matches; two draws with close finishes and one easier win for Peter van der Merwe's Springboks at Trent Bridge. In the first Test at Lord's, England's eighth-wicket pair were defending grimly when the end came. In the second, South Africa were always in control after Graeme Pollock had played an incredible innings of 125 in discouragingly damp, typically English conditions on the first day. He batted only 2 hours 20 minutes and in 70 minutes after lunch made 91 out of 102.

The last Test at the Oval was drawn in an atmosphere of frustration that was symbolic of the years to come. England needed 399 to win in the last innings on a pitch becoming ever easier. They reached 308-4 (Cowdrey 78 not out) and needed another 91 in 70 minutes when a thunderstorm finished the match.

The weather had prevented a tremendous climax, just as politicians and agitators were to prevent the playing of some almost certainly tremendous cricket in the series of 1968-69 and 1970 that never took place.

ENGLAND v WEST INDIES

Though West Indies have made many exciting contributions to cricket, they did not erupt suddenly and brilliantly on the Test scene. As far back as 1900 a West Indian team had toured England, and English teams had visited the Caribbean for many years before West Indies were considered strong enough to be given Test status, in 1928. In 1923, the West Indians had won 12 matches on their tour of England, which featured a stronger fixture list than previous visits, and it was on the results of this tour and that made to the Caribbean in 1925-26 by the Hon F. S. G. Calthorpe's team that the decision was made.

The 1928 tour overall was a success, but the Test rubber was disappointing, and until World War II West Indies generally failed to do themselves full justice in Test matches in England, though they built up a reputation for colourful cricket. In the same period, on their own pitches, however, they were more than good enough for the below-strength England teams that were sent out.

During World War II, cricketing careers were less disrupted in the West Indies than elsewhere, and some great players, notably the three 'Ws'—Everton Weekes, Clyde Walcott, and Frank Worrell—amassed hundreds of runs. The first England team to tour the West Indies after the war lost two Tests and failed to win any in the four-match series, but it really needed the triumphs by the 1950 side in England to establish West Indies as a cricketing nation that could hold its own with the best. There was a slight recession in the late 1950s, when England were able to recover the mastery at home. But under Frank Worrell and Gary Sobers in the 1960s, West Indies went on to even greater triumphs.

There is always the feeling in West Indian cricket that some new prodigy may burst forth dramatically from an obscure plantation. Powerful batting and the spin of Sonny Ramadhin and Alf Valentine won the 1950 successes. A decade later it was batting and the fast bowling of Wes Hall and Charlie Griffith. But as the fast bowling strength began to fade, West Indies were kept going mainly by the genius of Gary Sobers, who in an all-round capacity did the work of three or four players.

Since 1973, when they won the series in England, West Indies have been in command, and in 1984 won the series 5-0. In the 1980s their strength has been mainly the batting of Richards and Greenidge and the fast bowling of Roberts, Holding, Garner and Marshall.

During most of this time of supremacy, Clive Lloyd was an

During the 1960s, the all-round genius of Gary Sobers helped West Indies to two convincing series victories over England. His batting was often brilliant, and with his varied bowling he was able to exploit most conditions.

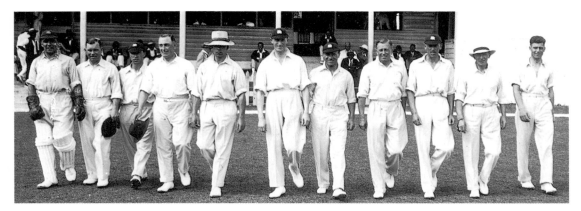

inspiring captain, welding his individuals into a team.

1928 in England

England 3   West Indies 0

For many years West Indian batting had been dependent on George Challenor, a great player when West Indies had gone to England in 1923. But by the time the first test was played at Lord's in June 1928, he was 40 and not enjoying anything like the success of former days. Disappointingly, too, the exciting all-rounder Learie Constantine, who was producing electrifying feats against the counties, did little in the Tests.

The Tests were played over three days, and England won all three by an innings. Ernest Tyldesley (122) made the first hundred in the series at Lord's. Tich Freeman took five wickets in each innings at Old Trafford, and Jack Hobbs scored 159 at the Oval.

1929-30 in West Indies

West Indies 1   England 1
Drawn 2

The first Test series in England may have been disappointing to West Indies, but the first series at home showed how difficult they would be to beat in the Caribbean. The side that the Hon F. S. G. Calthorpe led to West Indies contained some distinguished players, among them Wilfred Rhodes, George Gunn, Leslie Ames, Bill Voce, and, above all, Patsy Hendren. Hendren was 40 at the time but his record has seldom been exceeded on any tour: 223 not out, 211 not out, 80 and 36 not out in the first Test, 40 and 96, 30 and 12, 77 and 205 not out in the second Test, 254 not out, 171, 56 and 123 in the third Test, 1, 10 and 25, 61 and 55 in the fourth Test. He averaged 126 in all matches and 115 in the Tests, in which he scored 693 runs.

Tests were played over five days, but England, though they had the better of the match, could not force a win in the first Test, a second innings of 176 by the great George Headley holding them up. At Port of Spain in the second Test, however, Hendren and Ames (105) added 237 for the fourth wicket, and Voce took 7-70 to bring England victory after West Indies had led on the first innings. At Georgetown West Indies gained their first win over England. Victory was never really

Ames, Hendren and Sandham (first three from the left) enjoyed remarkable personal success in the 1929-30 series against West Indies—the first held in the Caribbean.

in doubt as long as England could be bowled out in time, which was done with 15 minutes and 289 runs to spare. George Headley made a hundred in each innings, and West Indies seized the initiative on the first day when C. A. Roach made 209 and England dropped catches.

The final Test at Kingston, though drawn, was remarkable in several ways. As the series was level it was decided to play it to a finish, but rain prevented play on the eighth and ninth days and it was given up. England began by making 849, with Andy Sandham's 325 then the highest Test score. They led by no less than 563 runs, but did not enforce the

follow-on and eventually declared, setting West Indies to make 836 to win. The score had reached 408-5 when the match was abandoned. George Headley's contribution to this was 223, and in the series he scored 703 runs, average 87.

1933 in England

England 2   West Indies 0
Drawn 1

West Indies' share in the previous colourful series in the Caribbean had roused hopes that they would show great improvement when they went to England in 1933. But it was only slight improvement.

They were blessed by a fine summer, and they had in G. C. Grant a captain who knew English cricket well. But Constantine, playing in the Lancashire League at this time, was released for only one Test, and could not form the fast bowling partnership with Martindale that might have influenced events strongly. Thus too much rested on George Headley, who averaged 55 against the 23 of the next batsman.

Of the three Tests only the second was not one-sided. England won the other two by an innings, Walter Robins taking 6-32 with leg-spin at Lord's, and Charles Marriott taking 11 wickets at the Oval. At Old Trafford West Indies led by one run on the first innings in a draw famous for the bodyline bowling of Constantine and Martindale to the England captain Douglas Jardine. Jardine met it with characteristic courage and skill and scored 127.

George Headley, run-getter extraordinary, shows other talents, leaping to catch A. H. Bakewell at the Oval in 1933.

RIGHT Emmanuel Martindale bowled some fierce bodyline to England skipper Jardine at Old Trafford in 1933.

1934-35 in West Indies

West Indies 2 England 1
Drawn 1

Though it was clear by now that England had to be near their best to win in the Caribbean, the team that R. E. S. Wyatt took was not within six or seven players of their strongest, and it was soundly beaten. Hendren, now 45, could not be expected to be the force of the previous tour, and an early injury to Ken Farnes weakened the English fast bowling. West Indies, with Constantine, Martindale, and L. G. Hylton, outgunned them in fast bowling and won two handsome victories, in the second of which Headley made 270 not out.

England's only success was at Bridgetown in a unique first Test of only 309 runs. The pitch began wet, and rain intervened later so that both sides manoeuvred to get the other in when the pitch was at its worst. England declared their first innings at 81-7, 21 runs behind. West Indies then declared their second innings at 51-6, leaving England to score 73 runs on what appeared to be an impossible pitch. But Wyatt reversed his batting order, and though England were at one time 48-6, Wyatt himself and Walter Hammond were there to steer England home by four wickets.

1939 in England

England 1 West Indies 0
Drawn 2

However convincing their cricket at home, West Indies were still immature in the Test sense overseas. They would assemble less as a team than as a group of individuals from different parts of the world, needing to be knit into a team. Not everyone was happy about the selection of the side in those days, either, although this is always a likely situation in a team representing numerous well separated islands.

In the last pre-war season, England, who with such gifted young players as Len Hutton and Denis Compton were on a rising tide of strength, won their victory at Lord's in the first of three Tests. Hutton made 196 and Compton 120, sharing in a stand of 248 in 140 minutes. For West Indies, George Headley made a hundred in each innings, by 1970 still the only time this feat had been performed in a Lord's Test. But he had little support, and West Indies did not reach 300 in either innings.

1947-48 in West Indies

West Indies 2 England 0
Drawn 2

The England team that made the first post-war visit to the West Indies was even more below strength than its predecessors. In those days, English cricket rested heavily on a few great players, notably Compton, Edrich, Hutton, Bedser, and, on overseas tours, Doug Wright. None went on this tour, though when the side was beset by injuries Len Hutton was sent out as a reinforcement.

England succeeded in drawing the first two Tests. In the second, wicket-keeper Billy Griffith was brought in as a deputy opening batsman and, playing in his first Test, made his maiden first-class hundred. Generally, however, the cricket was unexceptional, and West Indies comfortably won the last two Tests, Frank Worrell making 131 not out in one and Everton Weekes 141 in the other.

1950 in England

England 1 West Indies 3

The 1947-48 tour, easily though it had been won by West Indies, had not given any idea of how they would, for the first time, dominate a series in England. They themselves were surprised, for the completeness of the victory owed much to the success of unknown players —of London club cricketer Alan Rae, who proved a wonderfully consistent opening partner for Jeff Stollmeyer, and of Sonny Ramadhin and Alf Valentine, two untried 20-year-old spin bowlers. The three 'Ws' made a lot of runs, but that had been expected, and so talented a player as Roy Marshall was not required in a Test.

The series did not have an especially promising start for John Goddard's side. At Old Trafford

A defiant 104 from Godfrey Evans gave England their only victory of the 1950 Test series against West Indies.

they met a bad pitch for which England, with the advantage of winning the toss, were better equipped. But from the second Test at Lord's, which West Indies won by 326 runs to record their first win in England, there was only one side in it. England were without Denis Compton for most of that season, and when he was fit again and able to play in the fourth and last Test he was needlessly run out for 44 in England's first innings, through which Len Hutton played undefeated for 202 out of 344, a magnificent effort.

Peter May's 285 not out at Edgbaston in 1957 brought an end to a period of dominance by West Indies spinners.

ABOVE The Headingley Test of 1963, and Ken Barrington sets off from second slip to try to keep the runs down. West Indies ran out convincing winners by a margin of 221 runs.
RIGHT It had been a different story on the same ground six years earlier when England won by an innings. Clyde Walcott is caught at slip by Cowdrey off Laker.

The number of sparkling innings on the other side was ever growing—Clyde Walcott's 168 not out in the second innings at Lord's, the memorable 261 of Frank Worrell and the 129 of Everton Weekes at Trent Bridge, and Worrell's 138 that accompanied Alan Rae's second hundred of the series, at the Oval.

In the field, though the side had no great strength in fast bowling, it did not need it. Valentine, slow left arm, took 33 wickets and Ramadhin, with off-breaks and well disguised leg-breaks, 26. West Indies had arrived.

1953-54 in West Indies

West Indies 2 England 2 Drawn 1
When Len Hutton went to the Caribbean early in 1954, he had with him a team that could at last be considered representative of the best of English cricket. The English weakness, though, was that too much was apt to depend on the first few batsmen, on Hutton and Compton and on Peter May, who was about to take on the burden, and consequently the batting could not conquer the West Indian bowling, especially that of Ramadhin, in the first two Tests. But in the third England for the first time batted first. Len Hutton made 169, West Indies followed on, and were beaten. A match of huge scores was drawn after all three 'Ws' had made hundreds for West Indies, and May and Compton had replied for England. But in Kingston England won a remarkable victory in the last Test to square the series. Catching West Indies on a lively pitch on the first day, Trevor Bailey took 7-34 and bowled them out for 139. Hutton then made 205 of an England score of 414, and West Indies were eventually bowled out in time for England to win by nine wickets.

1957 in England

England 3 West Indies 0 Drawn 2
The post-war hey-day of West Indian cricket was over by the time John Goddard took his second side to England in 1957. There were some brilliant young players, such as Gary Sobers and Collie Smith, in the making. Wes Hall was still only a boy with a lovely action, and though Gilchrist was very fast, he was erratic. But there was still Ramadhin, whom English batsmen had never really sorted out, and it was the wearing down of him by the England captain Peter May, supported by Colin Cowdrey, that, in the first Test at Edgbaston, turned the series conclusively to England.

In the first innings of this match England were bowled out for 186, Ramadhin taking 7-49. To this West Indies replied with 474, Collie Smith 161. When England lost Peter Richardson, Brian Close, and Doug Insole for 113 by early morning of the fourth day, they seemed certain to lose. But Peter May stood firm, for nearly 10 hours in all, to make 285 not out. Cowdrey made 154 in a record-breaking stand of 411, and England were eventually able to declare. West Indies, weary and disillusioned, then lost 7-68 and it needed a desperate stand by Goddard and D. Atkinson to halt the slide to defeat. Ramadhin in the second innings had bowled 98 overs for 179 runs and only two early wickets. He was never the same force again, and England went on to win three Tests by an innings. Cowdrey made 152 at Lord's, and Peter Richardson 107 and Tom Graveney 164 on a pinkish-coloured pitch at the Oval, where West Indies subsequently were bowled out for 89 and 86 by Lock and Laker.

1959-60 in West Indies

West Indies 0 England 1 Drawn 4
The last series in England, for all its ultimate one-sidedness, had left no doubts about the potential of some of West Indies' young players, and by the time Peter May's team arrived early in 1960 Wes Hall headed a formidable battery of fast bowlers. May, fighting against an illness that caused his return home before the last Test, was inevitably not at his best, but Cowdrey, opening the innings, was in fine form and Ted Dexter fulfilled the highest hopes of him on hard pitches.

The series was decided in a dramatic second Test in Trinidad. Ken Barrington (121) and Mike Smith (108) made hundreds in England's first innings of 382, and on the third day the West Indies batting broke down against the accurate fast bowling of Trueman (5-35) and Statham (3-42). The match had been tensely fought with much hostile fast bowling by both sides, and there was great tension elsewhere. The crowd, for the varying reasons that cause a West Indian crowd to riot, stopped the match with a storm of bottle-throwing and an invasion of the playing area. The last three days of the match were peaceful, however, and England went on to win by 256 runs. They held their lead without much difficulty in the last three matches.

1963 in England

England 1 West Indies 3 Drawn 1
The West Indies tour of 1963 had much in common with that of 1950. Though it was acknowledged at the outset that West Indian strength had been growing, nobody quite expected the scintillating victory that was won. England were unlucky to lose Colin Cowdrey with a broken arm in the famous second Test at Lord's, but their batting at this time could not cope with the formidable fast bowling of Hall, Griffith, and Sobers. And Frank Worrell could also call on a high class off-spinner in Lance Gibbs to support them. Though Fred Trueman took 34 wickets, England's bowling was ageing, and batsmen of the class of Sobers, Conrad Hunte, Rohan Kanhai, Seymour Nurse, and Basil Butcher could make plenty of runs.

Worrell won the toss on a deteriorating Old Trafford pitch and West Indies, making England follow on, spun them out a second time and won the first Test by 10 wickets. At Lord's, after an even first innings, England were thwarted of victory by Basil Butcher (133), the rain, the injury to Cowdrey, and the fast bowling marathon of Hall and Griffith that led to one of the most pulsating finishes in Test cricket. In the end Cowdrey, with broken arm, had to return to partner the last man for

In 1963, and again to some extent in 1966, big, fearsome Charlie Griffith tore into the England batting.

the last two balls when England were only six runs short of victory.

England levelled the series by winning the third Test at Edgbaston on a pitch that retained moisture throughout and gave the seam bowling of Trueman, Derek Shackleton, and Dexter skilfully exploited assistance. However, West Indies won the last two Tests with an exhibition that warmed the heart of a public already stimulated by the excitement of the Lord's finish.

1966 in England
England 1 West Indies 3 Drawn 1
The West Indies team under Gary Sobers three years later showed marked signs of decline and inevitably had a difficult job matching the exhilarating feats of 1963. That it triumphed again was due to Sobers himself who made 722 runs, took 20 wickets, and held the weakening giant together

The off-spin bowling of Lance Gibbs was a major factor in the test victories of the great West Indies side of the 1960s. Against England in 1963 he took 26 wickets—only Griffith took more—and in 1966 headed the list with 21.

well enough to beat a troubled England side captained by Mike Smith at the start, Colin Cowdrey in the middle, and Brian Close at the end.

Like Worrell, Sobers was fortunate in winning the toss at Old Trafford on a pitch that took spin increasingly. This time the victory was by an innings. At Lord's West Indies were within sight of defeat on the fourth day, but an unbroken sixth wicket stand of 274 between cousins Sobers and David Holford saved them. They won the next two Tests, and the series was settled by the time England, against relatively light-hearted opposition, won at the Oval.

1967-68 in West Indies
West Indies 0 England 1 Drawn 4
Though there had been signs of cracks in West Indies' citadel in 1966, few expected England to beat them two years later on their own hard pitches. But under Colin Cowdrey, who batted superbly himself, England did it by winning the fourth Test. John Snow, who did not play in the first Test, which England were near to winning, developed as a menacing fast bowler at least as formidable as the ageing Hall and Griffith.

England nearly won the second Test as well, when a riot interrupted them in Jamaica. When they did win, it was through a remarkable declaration by Sobers, who set England to make 215 in 2¾ hours. Cowdrey followed up his first innings 148 with 71, Boycott acted as the anchor man with 80 not out, and with three minutes to spare England won by seven wickets. They were perilously near losing the last Test in Georgetown, but a four-hour stand between Cowdrey and Alan Knott held West Indies up, and England's last pair earned the vital draw.

1969 in England
England 2 West Indies 0 Drawn 1
A much weakened and less experienced West Indies, whom not even Gary Sobers could hold together, were beaten in a short half-season series early in 1969. This time England, captained by Ray Illingworth, won the toss and the match at Old Trafford. An even second Test was drawn, and England clinched the rubber with an exciting win by 30 runs in the third Test at Leeds. They batted slowly in a low-scoring match, but the pitch eased on the last two days and at one time West Indies, needing 303 to win, were 219-3 with Sobers to come. But when a brilliant innings of 91 by Basil Butcher ended, Sobers played on for 0 and the effort died away.

1973 in England
England 0 West Indies 2 Drawn 1
Without a Test victory since 1969 and a win over England since 1966, West Indies put an end to their losing streak in the first Test at the Oval and never looked back during the entire series.

They owed much of their success to the captain, Rohan Kanhai, and to the late recall of Sobers to the Test arena. After Lloyd had made 132, England suffered at the Oval from a virtuoso performance from Boyce. Coming in at number 9, he slammed 72 and then took 5 for 70 and 6 for 77. For England, Boycott made 97 and Hayes, on his debut, made 106 but West Indies won by 158 runs.

A draw in the second Test at Edgbaston had its controversial moments. Umpire Arthur Fagg threatened to withdraw after he had been intimidated by West Indian fielders after turning down an appeal for a catch behind the wicket against Boycott. He later received an apology. Fredericks made 150 but the innings of the match came from Sobers who revived many memories with an exquisite 74. England easily batted out time to save the match.

There was more drama at Lord's in the final Test when the ground was evacuated because of a 'bomb scare'; the players took their sanctuary in the middle of the pitch.

The only blast came from the West Indian batting, from Kanhai

157, Sobers 150 not out and Julien 121. England capitulated to Boyce, Holder, Julien and Gibbs and lost by an innings and 226 runs.

1973-74 in West Indies
West Indies 1 England 1 Drawn 3
After losing the first Test and being largely outplayed in the series, England surprisingly squared the rubber in the final game.

With Denness out of form with the bat and under fire as leader, it was not a happy tour and there were moments of embarassment—notably in the first Test when Greig, England's outstanding performer, ran out Kallicharran as the West Indies batsman was walking off after the last ball of the day had been bowled. Greig's appeal was later withdrawn and Kallicharran reinstated.

West Indies won by seven wickets after bowling out England for 131 and, thanks to Kallicharran extending his innings to 158, earned, not for the last time in the series, a huge first innings lead. Amiss' second innings 174 was in vain.

Amiss did perform a rescue miracle in Kingston when England again trailed against batting in depth highlighted by a century from Rowe. But the Warwickshire opener resisted in heroic vein for nine and a half hours for 262 not out to save the game.

At Bridgetown it was Fletcher's turn to mastermind the escape. Although Greig, 148, and Knott, 87, pulled the first innings together, there was still a massive deficit after Rowe made the highest ever score by a West Indian against England. His 302 took only 140 overs and he was supported by another century from Kallicharran. But Fletcher, 129 not out, held firm after four wickets had gone very cheaply in the second innings.

Rain ruined the fourth Test at Georgetown after Amiss and Greig had each made centuries—a more convincing performance but one which did little to anticipate the surprising events at Port-of-Spain.

Though Rowe made another century and finished the series with 616 runs, England found superb performances from two individuals. Boycott, making 99 and 112, held the side together while Greig, in his recently acquired off-spinning style, took thirteen wickets. Set to get 226 to win, no West Indian could make

more than 36 and England, winning by 26 runs, had climaxed a series of near-defeats by escaping with a drawn rubber.

1976 in England
England 0 West Indies 3 Drawn 2
After managing to draw the first two matches in the series, England were finally outplayed by a side which batted extravagantly and bowled at a pace against which no batsman could provide an adequate counter-attack.

Vivian Richards dominated with the bat making 232, 63, 4, 135, 66, 38 and 291—he missed the second Test through illness. Holding, splendidly athletic, and Roberts each took 28 wickets, and Daniel and Holder the same number between them. Although West Indies lacked a class spinner, the

poor balance of their attack was irrelevant so devastating were the pacemen.

Under Greig, England began in a defensive vein with an elderly side which included the return to Test cricket of Close at the age of 45. At Nottingham, Steele made a patient hundred, Snow bowled with penetration and two elder statesmen, Edrich and Close, played out the draw.

England might even have won at Lord's after Close made a gallant 60 and Snow and Underwood had earned a first innings lead. But set to make 332 West Indies, and Fredericks in particular with a fine century, resisted on a lasting wicket.

The rout began at Old Trafford, ironically after a good England start. Selvey in his first Test made

an immediate breakthrough and West Indies dropped to 26 for 4. Even though Greenidge led a recovery with a brilliant 134, they finished 211 all out. But England collapsed to Roberts, Holding and Daniel—71 all out was their lowest total against West Indies—and they scarcely improved after Greenidge and Richards had made further hundreds; the margin of defeat was a stunning 425 runs.

Greenidge made his third successive Test century at Headingley alongside another from Fredericks. But England, 169 for 5, battled back into the game with scores of 116 apiece from Greig and Knott, two men previously disastrously short of form. Willis, back after injury, then took 5 for 42 to give his side a fighting chance but, although Greig was again

defiant, England, needing 260, fell 55 runs short.

Richards was at his most punishing at the Oval—his 291 being the highest ever score for West Indies in England. Amiss, recalled after his anxieties in Australia, made a marvellous comeback with 203, but then England's resistance collapsed. Greenidge and Fredericks set up a declaration by slamming 182 off just 32 overs. Then Holding, who had claimed 8 for 92 in the first innings, sustained his assault with 6 for 57 to become the first West Indies bowler to take 14 wickets in a Test. It was an appropriate finale to the series.

1980 in England
England 0 West Indies 1 Drawn 4
Ian Botham was the new England captain as the West Indies series began at Trent Bridge. He played the best knock when he chose to bat, making 57 of England's total of 263. With fast bowlers Roberts, Holding, Marshall and Garner bowling all but one of the overs, 91.5 overs took 395 minutes, a rate of only 14 overs per hour which continued throughout the match. West Indies scored 308 in reply, Greenidge (53), Richards and Murray (64 each) passing the half-century. Boycott batted obstinately in England's second turn, scoring 75 in 345 minutes, but he was not supported by the middle order, four wickets falling between 174 and 183, Boycott's being the last of these. A small recovery took the score to 252, the odd 52 of which were extras, an England-West Indies record. West Indies were left 208 to win, and reached 109 for 2 by close on Monday. However, a small crowd saw them have to fight hard on the last day. At 180 for 7 the match could still go either way, but the match had been one of missed catches, and more on the last day proved crucial as West Indies inched home at 209 for 8 (Haynes 62). Roberts, who scored 22 not out at the end, to add to 21 in the first innings and eight wickets, was Man of the Match.

At Lord's, England decided to bat again, and Gooch made a brilliant 123, being one of the few batsmen who could hit the West Indian fast bowling in front of the wicket. When he was second out the score had reached 169, but England collapsed to be all out 269 (Holding 6 for 76). Richards then played a brilliant innings of 145 for West Indies, which won the Man of the Match award. He added 223 for the second wicket with Haynes, who went on to 184, and with Lloyd adding 56 batting number seven, West Indies made 518. Rain cut short England's knock, which started on Saturday. By Tuesday, they had reached 133 for 2 when the match was drawn.

Rain severely affected the third Test at Old Trafford. Lloyd put England in—and out again for 150. Newcomer Brian Rose was responsible for the total not being

far worse—he scored 70. However, by the close on the first day Greenidge, Haynes and Bacchus had been dismissed for one run between them—West Indies 38 for 3, Richards not out 32. Rain meant that the West Indian innings did not finish until the morning of the fourth day—Lloyd 101, Richards 64 in a total of 260. England still had the match to save, but the top seven, headed by Boycott (86), Gatting (56) and Willey (62 not out), all made useful scores, and at 391 for 7 at the close England had made the highest score of the match. Lloyd, for his century, was Man of the Match.

Botham decided to bat again at the Oval, and after Boycott had retired hurt at 9, Gooch (83) and Rose (50) took the score to 155 before a wicket fell. Boycott then returned to make 53, and England prospered to 370. West Indies were reduced to 105 for 5, with Lloyd unable to bat, but Bacchus made 61, and Marshall, Garner and Holding helped raise the score to 265. By now it was the fourth day, the Saturday having been washed out, and with England reduced to 20 for 4 overnight there was a chance of a shock win for West Indies. This improved on the last

ABOVE Viv Richards on his way to 291 at the Oval in 1976, the great year in which he finished with 829 runs, despite missing one Test through illness.

BELOW Alan Knott raised his hands in hope or expectation as England captain Tony Greig dives at point in an unsuccessful effort to catch Lawrence Rowe.

day as England slumped to 92 for 9. Willis now joined Willey, who had gone in at number eight, and was dropped with England at 111 —West Indies would probably have won easily had this been held. Willey, however, went on to 100 not out, shielding Willis, who nevertheless managed 24 not out by the end, Botham declaring at 209 for 9 when Man of the Match Willey reached 100.

England needed to win at Headingley to tie the series, but the dreadful summer continued and with the first and fourth days washed out they had little chance. Put in eventually by West Indies, they were dismissed by the West Indian fast bowlers for 143. West Indies scored 245. Gooch became the only batsman to reach 50 in the match when making 55 of 227 for 6 declared in England's second knock. That ended the action. Haynes, who made 42, was adjudged Man of the Match, Garner, with 26 wickets, Man of the Series.

1980-81 in West Indies
West Indies 2 England 0 Drawn 2
England went to the West Indies after losing 1-0 to them in the summer. The first Test at Port-of-Spain began late because rain had left wet patches on the pitch, both covers and pitch having been sabotaged by locals protesting at the omission of Deryck Murray from the West Indian team. As the damage looked on a fast bowler's length, Botham chose to field. England played an ill-balanced team, with three off-spinners Emburey, Miller and Willey. West Indies made 144 for 0 on the shortened first day, and eventually 426 for 9 declared. Greenidge (84), Haynes (96), Lloyd (64), Roberts (50 not out) and new wicketkeeper David Murray (46) were the main scorers. Emburey took five wickets. England, beginning their innings on the third day, made a

bright start but were later destroyed by Croft (5-40), losing the
last eight wickets for 68 runs.
After further rain, England followed on with less than nine hours
remaining, but only Boycott made
a determined effort to save the
match, batting 315 minutes for 70.
As it happened, rain again inter-
ferred, but England were dis-

missed with an hour or so to spare
for 169, a defeat by an innings and
79.

   The second Test at Guyana was
cancelled, the first ever to be cancelled for political reasons days
before its scheduled start. Willis
and Rose had been forced to leave
the party, Willis for a knee
operation, Rose because of eye

trouble. Robin Jackman replaced
Willis, and, belatedly, Athey
replaced Rose. Jackman arrived in
Guyana by air on 23 February.
Three days later he was served with
a deportation order. Jackman,
married to a South African, had
played in South Africa for the
previous 11 winters, and was un-
acceptable to the Guyana auth-

*Graham Gooch watches the ball
but it has already broken his
wicket as he is bowled by Joel
Garner in the third Test at
Barbados in 1980-81.*

orities. The England party declined to play the Test without
Jackman, and the party left early
for Barbados.

The third Test at Bridgetown was marred by the sudden death through a heart attack of Ken Barrington, the assistant manager and coach of the England team, on the evening of the second day.

England won the toss, and Botham again asked West Indies to bat. Roland Butcher, a Barbados-born black batsmen who played for Middlesex, made his Test debut for England. On a lively pitch, West Indies were 65 for 4, Jackman taking a wicket with his fifth ball in Test cricket. Lloyd (100) and Gomes (58) righted the ship, but all out 265 was an encouraging score for England. Holding bowled a devastating over to Boycott, however, which ended with him bowling England's mainstay for a duck. Gatting soon followed: 11 for 2. England were rapidly shot

RIGHT Robin Jackman boards the plane at Georgetown Airport after being banned from Guyana in 1980-81. The second Test was thereby abandoned.
BELOW Jackman obtained his first Test wicket with his fifth ball when eventually making his debut at Bridgetown, Barbados: Greenidge caught by Gooch.

out for 122, but got Greenidge for a duck before the close. Next day, after the players, officials and capacity crowd had stood in tribute to Barrington, England bowled with sad hearts. Night-watchman Croft made 33, Richards eventually went on to 182 not out, and Lloyd scored 66. When he declared at 379 for 7, England needed 523 to win. Boycott fell to Holding again, for 1, but Gooch showed once more how to play fast bowling with 116 and Gower made an encouraging 54. England's other batting failed, however, and at 224 they had lost by 298 runs.

Botham decided to bat in the fourth Test in Antigua. Boycott and Gooch put on 60, but there-after wickets fell steadily on a good batting pitch until Peter Willey, batting at number seven, made 102 not out from 133 added for the last five wickets. England were all out 271. Richards, in his home island, then made 114, and with backing from Greenidge (63), Mattis (71), Lloyd (58) and Holding (58 not out), helped West Indies to 468 for 9 declared, adding 172 from the fall of the seventh wicket. The fourth day was washed out with Antigua's first rain of the year, and on the fifth England easily saved the game with 234 for 3, Boycott

making 104 not out and Gooch 83.

In the fifth Test at Kingston, Jamaica, Lloyd put England in. Gooch again batted brilliantly for most of the first day, and made 153, but at the fall of his wicket England were only 249 for 5. They then tumbled from 277 for 6 over-night to 285 all out, Holding taking 5 for 56. After Greenidge (62) and Haynes (84) had given West Indies a good start, Lloyd (95) and Gomes (90 not out) batted well later and the innings totalled 442. On a rain-shortened fourth day England were in trouble at 32 for 3, but Gower and Willey made a stand which took the score, on the last day, to 168 before Willey was out

for 67. Gower went on batting and found a useful partner in Downton —between them they batted out time at 302 for 6, Gower 154 not out. Gooch was Man of the Match for his first-day century, and Lloyd Man of the Series. Richards, Lloyd, Gooch and Gower were the best batsmen of the series, while the West Indian fast bowlers, par-ticularly Holding and Croft, won the series for the home team.

1984 in England
England 0 West Indies 5
David Gower was England's new skipper when West Indies toured in 1984. He decided to bat in the first Test at Edgbaston, and dis-aster followed rapidly. On a lively pitch Fowler was caught and Randall played on, each from lifters from Garner for ducks, and new opening batsman Andy Lloyd was struck on the head by a Marshall bouncer and went to hospital for eight days. When Gower and Lamb were out before lunch England were 49 for 4, effectively for 5. A belligerent Botham scored 64, but England were all out for 191. When Gomes (143) and Richards (117) shared a third wicket stand of 206, the match was as good as decided. Lloyd followed with 71, and Baptiste (87 not out) and Holding (69) flogged a tired attack for a ninth-wicket 150 stand. West Indies were 606 all out. On the third day Marshall was warned for intimidatory bowling, at which Lloyd showed dissent. England's lesser batsmen (particularly Downton, who opened in Lloyd's place, with 56 in 275 minutes) showed determination in delaying the inevitable, but soon after lunch on the fourth day the innings closed on 235, with West Indies victors by an innings and 180. Gomes was Man of the Match.

At Lord's Lloyd put England in, but the innings started in very different fashion from Edgbaston. Fowler (106) and newcomer Chris Broad (55) had 100 on the board without loss. Nobody else did much, however, and a total of 286 was disappointing. Botham quickly had three men back in the pavilion for 35 in reply, and main-tained the pressure. Despite Richards' 72, the West Indies were all out for 245, with Botham taking 8 for 103. Botham was required to perform with the bat in the second innings, coming in at 88 for 4. He made 81, and with Lamb (110) added 128 for the fifth wicket. Lamb and Pringle went off for bad light on Monday evening with England 328 ahead and think-ing of victory—it was probably a mistake, and Gower erred in not being on the balcony to make a decision. England went on to 300 for 9 declared on the last day, setting West Indies 342 to win.

The players grab the stumps and run (umpire Constant just runs) as the West Indies complete a 'blackwash' at the Oval in 1984.

Richard Ellison's first Test wicket. A brilliant catch by Botham at second slip dismisses Gomes at the Oval in the fifth Test, 1984.

Whatever England's hopes, a magnificent innings by Greenidge (214 not out), supported by Gomes (92 not out) had the match safe by the middle of the day. At 344 for 1, West Indies ran out comfortable 9-wicket winners. Greenidge and Botham shared the Man of the Match award.

The third Test, at Headingley, was another overwhelming victory for West Indies. England won the toss, batted, and needed a second successive 100 from Lamb to reach 270. Marshall fractured his left thumb early in the innings when fielding at slip. West Indies were reduced on the second day to 206 for 7, but Gomes (104 not out) and Holding (59, with 5 sixes off Willis) helped them to 302 and a lead of 32. Marshall helped Gomes to his century by coming in at number eleven and scoring 4 in a stand of 12, batting one-handed.

Fowler scored 50 in the second innings but England collapsed, losing the last eight wickets for 55. Marshall, with his left hand in plaster, had his best Test analysis of 7 for 53. All out 159, England set West Indies only 128 to win. Half-way through the fourth day this was achieved for the loss of two wickets. Gomes was Man of the Match.

At Old Trafford, West Indies won the toss and batted. At 70 for 4 (three to Allott) England were prospering, but Greenidge, with his second double century of the series (223) and Dujon (101) added 197. Then fast bowler Winston Davis, in for Marshall, hit a rapid 77, and West Indies reached exactly 500. England were away to a good start, 90 being hoisted for the first wicket, but injury struck again when Davis, in a spell in which he consistently hit the batsmen, broke Terry's left arm. Like Marshall at Headingley, Terry came in last to bat one-handed, his left arm in a sling, and again like Marshall, he stayed while his partner completed a

century. Lamb's 100 not out was his third century in successive matches. There was confusion about the object of Terry's effort. Lamb prepared to leave on scoring his 100, but Terry stayed to try to avoid the follow-on—a second example of lack of communication between Lamb and Gower in this series. England, at 280, followed on, and on a pitch now taking spin Harper took 6 for 57, while Gower, with 57 not out, was the only batsman to look confident. The side was out for 156 on the fifth morning, West Indies winning by an innings and 64, with Greenidge Man of the Match.

At the Oval, England had only the vestiges of pride to play for. Bowlers Ellison and Agnew were brought in for Test debuts and, after the injuries to early batsmen, Tavare was recalled. West Indies won the toss and batted, and not for the first time in the series England soon got on top. At 70 for 6 West Indies were reeling. It took 60 not out from Lloyd to reach the comparative respectability of 190. Botham took 5 for 72, including

his 300th Test wicket. The second day contained the worst aspects of West Indian cricket, a ludicrously slow over rate as the fast bowlers alternated, and, of the minimum number of balls bowled, a maximum of bouncers, particularly from Marshall, who forced Fowler to retire with a bruised arm, West Indies' third 'victim' of the series. Umpires Constant and Meyer did nothing, a strange contrast to the previous season, when slow bowler Edmonds had been no-balled for excessive bouncers. Fowler returned, but nobody could score freely and England were out for 162, 28 behind. In the second innings, Haynes, the only West Indian to fail so far in the series, scored 125 to become Man of the Match. West Indies made 346, setting England to score 375 to win, but they could manage only 202, despite Botham's defiant 54 in 51 balls and Tavare's contrasting 49 in 202 minutes. West Indies had achieved what they called a 5-0 'blackwash'. With two double centuries Greenidge was Man of the Series.

ENGLAND v NEW ZEALAND

Though it was not until 1929-30 that New Zealand played their first Test match, there has always been an especially close relationship between English and New Zealand cricket, with a special feeling of responsibility on the English side. This has been accentuated by the relative lack of interest shown by Australia in New Zealand cricket, but it also has deep roots, going back perhaps to the first visit of an English team in 1864, when George Parr's side moved on to New Zealand from Australia.

One thorny problem since New Zealand entered the Test arena has been whether or not it was a good thing for England teams to visit New Zealand only on brief visits at the end of a long Australian tour. The England players are by then tired and the extra month is an anti-climax. On the other hand, it costs little to take the team on to New Zealand, and a series there at that time has the advantage of months of advance publicity while MCC tour Australia.

There has, however, been a significant change in the arrangements for New Zealand visits to England. Whereas the period between visits of New Zealand teams once ranged from six to nine years, under the half-season touring system now employed by England there is a visit roughly every four years. This gives New Zealand greater continuity, and so more players can use the experience of one tour on another. As a result, there was a noticeable improvement in New Zealand cricket as England were tested in 1973 and eventually beaten in 1978, with a series win coming in New Zealand in 1983-84.

1929-30 in New Zealand
New Zealand 0 England 1
Drawn 3
When they played their very first Test against New Zealand, England had another team currently playing a series in West Indies, so they were by no means at full strength. A. H. H. Gilligan had taken over the captaincy when his brother Arthur was taken ill, and he had under him a side that was approximately half-amateur and

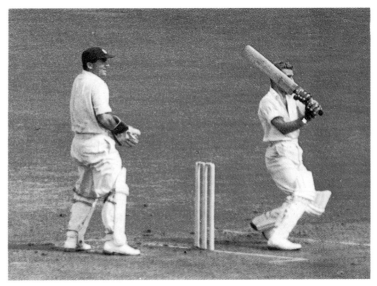

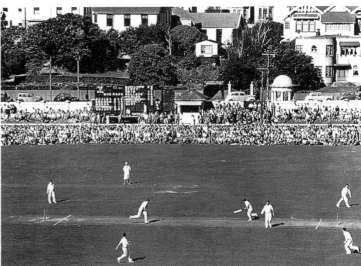

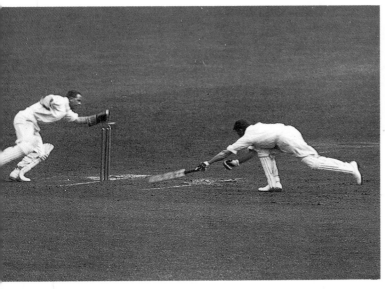

LEFT Wally Hammond just scrapes home as wicket-keeper Ken James whips off the bails at the Oval in 1931. Hammond went on to a century.
LEFT BELOW A general view of the ground. Notice the hats.

TOP Bert Sutcliffe batted well for New Zealand in the 1949 series, in which all the three-day Tests were drawn.
ABOVE A contrast to the Oval: Sunny Wellington in 1950-51, where England won.

had Duleepsinhji and Frank Woolley as its stars. England won the first match at Christchurch by eight wickets when Maurice Allom took 5-38 as part of a destructive opening fast bowling partnership with Maurice Nichols.

But they could only draw the other three matches. At that time C. S. Dempster, who opened the innings for New Zealand, was one of the most prolific scorers in the world, and he made 136 and 80 not out in a drawn second Test, sharing in an opening stand of 276 with J. W. E. Mills (117). New Zealand had the better of this match, but as on other occasions in later years, when they were in a good position they were not vigorous enough to press home their advantage.

1931 in England
England 1 New Zealand 0
Drawn 2
When Tom Lowry took the first Test-playing New Zealand side to England in 1931—another had done well on a visit in 1927 but had not played Tests—it was intended that the only Test should be at Lord's. But in a wet summer the New Zealanders did so well in the preliminary matches, and in the Test, that two other Tests were arranged at Old Trafford and the Oval.

At Lord's, they were thwarted in the first innings by an eighth-wicket stand of 246 between Leslie Ames (137) and Gubby Allen (122) —in 1985 still a record—but made 469-9 in their second innings, Dempster 120, M. L. 'Curly' Page 104. They were not out of the reckoning when the match was left drawn. England, needing 240 to win, were then 146-5. At the Oval, Herbert Sutcliffe, Duleepsinhji, and Walter Hammond made hundreds for England in a score of 416-4, and after some rain New Zealand were beaten by an innings, Allen taking 5-14 in the first innings. Rain almost completely washed out the Manchester Test.

1932-33 in New Zealand
New Zealand 0   England 0
Drawn 2
The two matches played at the end of the 'Bodyline' tour produced two scores of over 500 by England, but no result. Rain affected both matches, which were notable mainly for two enormous innings by Walter Hammond—227 in Christchurch after being missed in the slips early on, and 336 not out in Auckland out of a total of 548-7 declared. This innings lasted 5¼ hours, a historic piece of hitting including 10 sixes and 33 fours, and by passing Bradman's 334 made at Leeds in 1930, it became the highest Test innings to date.

1937 in England
England 1   New Zealand 0
Drawn 2
The three-match Test series in 1937 introduced Len Hutton to Test cricket in the first Test and Denis Compton in the third. Hutton was out for 0 and 1 in the first, which was drawn with England comfortably on top, but made 100 in the second Test at Manchester, which England won by 130 runs after Tom Goddard had taken 6-29 in the second innings. One significant feature of this match was the isolated resistance in the last innings of 19-year-old Martin Donnelly. Test matches played by New Zealand in this era were of only three days, and the third was also drawn. Joe Hardstaff made his second hundred of the series, and Compton scored 65 before being run out by a deflection off the bowler.

1946-47 in New Zealand
New Zealand 0   England 0
Drawn 1
Only one Test, at Christchurch, was played by Walter Hammond's team immediately after the war, and it was drawn after Walter Hadlee had made 116 for New Zealand and Hammond, in his last Test, had made 79. The match suffered badly from the weather, and for the first time in history an extra day was added when rain prevented play on the third day.

1949 in England
England 0   New Zealand 0
Drawn 4
The visit of Walter Hadlee's team to England in 1949 was both a success and a failure. It was a success from the New Zealand point of view because they had a strong side, especially rich in batting, and in a glorious summer of hard pitches made many runs. But the Test matches, still of only three days, were all drawn and are remembered as monuments of stalemate and frustration.

New Zealand shared the honours in the first Test at Headingley, and led by 171 runs on the first innings at Lord's, where Martin

Donnelly made 206. Donnelly made 75 and 80 at Old Trafford, where Bert Sutcliffe scored 101 in the second innings, and though Reg Simpson's 103 helped England to a first innings lead of 147, there was still no sign of a result.

In the last Test, at the Oval, New Zealand were at one time within sight of defeat, for though they made 345 in the first innings, England replied with 482, Len Hutton 206 and Bill Edrich 100, and took five wickets for 188 in the second innings. But two resolute innings by W. M. Wallace and John Reid steered New Zealand safely out of danger, and the series ended on the same note of batting mastery as had existed throughout.

1950-51 in New Zealand
New Zealand 0   England 1
Drawn 1
The note was maintained at Christchurch 19 months later when Sutcliffe made 116 for New Zealand and Trevor Bailey 134 not out for England in another high-scoring draw. But England won the other Test by six wickets, after being made to work hard on a deteriorating pitch. New Zealand were still a formidable batting side in this era, though Donnelly had settled in Australia and was no longer available.

1954-55 in New Zealand
New Zealand 0   England 2
When Len Hutton's team went to New Zealand after retaining the

Ashes in Australia, New Zealand standards had declined. The first match was interrupted by rain and the third and fourth days of what, unusually, was a five-day match were lost through rain. However, the English bowlers finished off the earlier work of Tyson and Statham, and England won by eight wickets.

The second, which England won by an innings with a score of only

BELOW John Reid being caught by Jim Parks off John Snow at Lord's in 1965. His was a vital wicket in the 1950s and 1960s. BOTTOM Fieldsmen crowd the bat of Brian Hastings at Lord's in 1969 as he pushes forward. Underwood won the Test.

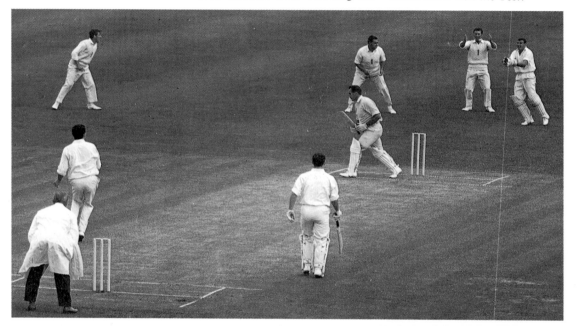

In 1965 John Edrich took a triple century off the New Zealanders at Headingley as England amassed 546-4.

1962-63 in New Zealand
New Zealand 0   England 3
Three years later Ted Dexter's England side won all three Tests, Ken Barrington (126), Peter Parfitt (131), and Barry Knight (125) making hundreds in the first, which was won by an innings, as was the second. A hundred by John Reid kept the margin in the third to seven wickets.

1965 in England
England 3   New Zealand 0
Throughout the lean years, John Reid was often fighting a lone battle, supported by players of considerably less ability and experience than himself. When he took the 1965 side to England for the first half-season tour, the weaknesses in batting and spin still remained, and wet weather and bad pitches did not help. England, captained by Mike Smith, made big scores, culminating in the 546-4 at Leeds where John Edrich (310 not out) and Ken Barrington (163) put on 369 for the second wicket.

1965-66 in New Zealand
New Zealand 0   England 0
Drawn 3
Although the run of defeats ended in this series, New Zealand were within a fraction of defeat in the first two matches and their failings, as well as one cause of them, were painfully obvious. The low bounce of pitches prepared on rugby grounds discouraged stroke-play and this, plus the long years of struggle, especially against England, produced a negative approach to the game. Such negativity robbed New Zealand of the elusive first victory when they had England in difficulties in the final Test. With a first innings lead of 74, they took six hours to make 129 in the second innings, and then they bowled defensively in the last innings. It seemed a sadly significant performance.

1969 in England
England 2   New Zealand 0
Drawn 1
Though the 2-0 defeat does not suggest it, there was heartening improvement in New Zealand's performance on the 1969 tour. A promising left-arm spinner, Hedley Howarth was an encouraging find, and there were more signs of belligerence in the batting. They were unlucky to play the first Test on a bad pitch at Lord's, where John Edrich made the first of two hundreds, and to play the last amid showers at the Oval, where Derek Underwood took 12 wickets for 101.

1970-71 in New Zealand
New Zealand 0   England 1
Drawn 1
New Zealand's rising standards

246 and a first innings lead of only 46, was remarkable for New Zealand's melancholy achievement of the lowest score in Test history. On a pitch of varying bounce that took some spin, Frank Tyson (2-10) and Brian Statham (3-9) made the initial breakthrough and Bob Appleyard (4-7) and Johnny Wardle (1-0) carried on. The innings of 26 lasted only 27 overs.

1958 in England
England 4   New Zealand 0
Drawn 1
If the collapse of March 1955 had been a bitter moment in New Zealand's cricket history, there was not much to relieve the memory in the next tour of England in 1958. The summer was extremely wet, which always tends to give England an extra advantage, and though New Zealand had capable fast bowlers in Bob Blair, John Hayes, and Tony MacGibbon, they were short of orthodox spin and experienced batting. Reid had a good all-round tour, but Bert Sutcliffe, past his best perhaps, was haunted by injury.

England, with Peter May playing some magnificent innings, were far too good. They began by bowling New Zealand out for 94 at Edgbaston, Trueman 5-31, and in a calamitous match at Lord's, which was over by 3.30 p.m. on the third day, New Zealand made 47 and 74. England made only 269, but after heavy rain the pitch gave a lot of help to the redoubtable Laker and Lock, who took 4-13 and 5-17 respectively. In the second innings, these two, with Trueman, Peter Loader, and Bailey, were almost as devastating.

New Zealand's torment at the hands of Laker and Lock continued at Headingley, where they were bowled out for 67, and England needed to make only 267-2, Arthur Milton 104 not out and Peter May 113 not out, to win easily by an innings. They won by an innings again in Manchester, where May made another 100, but the almost incessant rain came to New Zealand's aid in the last Test. The New Zealanders were still a long way short of equality.

1958-59 in New Zealand
New Zealand 0   England 1
Drawn 1
Another innings defeat followed in Christchurch seven months later when Lock took 11 wickets and Ted Dexter made 141. But rain interrupted the second Test when May (124 not out) had taken England to a big lead.

were confirmed 18 months later when Ray Illingworth's side arrived after winning in Australia. England won the first Test in Christchurch after bowling New Zealand out for 65 on a damp pitch on the first day. But New Zealand came back remarkably well later as the pitch dried. In the second Test, on a splendid pitch in Auckland, they came as near to winning as they had done in the long history of the series. After some rousing batting by Mark Burgess and Mike Shrimpton had enlarged on a sticky start and enabled Graham Dowling to declare only a few runs behind, England lost four cheap wickets and had Cowdrey and d'Oliveira injured. However, Cowdrey, with a runner, batted well and Alan Knott followed up a dashing first-innings century with a dogged 96 in the second to delay New Zealand's first win for yet another series.

1973 in England

England 2 N. Zealand 0 Drawn 1
Bevan Congdon's New Zealand team twice had chances to record their first win in England, but narrowly failed to make use of either opportunity.

Illingworth was preferred to Lewis as England's leader, and in the first Test the home country struggled to make 250 in the first innings. The pace trio of Snow, Arnold and Greig shot New Zealand out for 97. After Greig had followed that with 139 to add to Amiss's 138, England looked set for a massive win as they set the visitors a target of 479.

Four wickets fell for 130, then Congdon, 176, and Pollard, 116, masterminded such a recovery that they fell only 38 short of turning

LEFT The middle-order batting of Vic Pollard proved a considerable thorn in England's side in 1973. His 116 at Trent Bridge was followed by 105 not out at Lord's and 62 at Headingley.

TOP Bev Congdon played two big innings in 1973, his 176 at Trent Bridge almost enabling New Zealand to get the 479 required in the fourth innings. He made 175 at Lord's, where New Zealand led by 302.

ABOVE Congdon was twice caught Knott bowled Arnold at Leeds.

defeat into victory.

New Zealand should have won the second Test at Lord's, after Congdon, 175, Pollard, 105 not out, and Burgess, 105, had given them a first innings lead of 302. But a dropped catch behind the wicket at a vital stage on the last day saved England for whom Fletcher played a match-saving innings of 178.

The third Test went more to form. Boycott made an excellent 115 and England led by 143 runs on the first innings. New Zealand failed in the face of some immacu-late outswing bowling by Arnold, England's most impressive performer with the ball throughout the series. Though Turner, whose Test form had not equalled that which had brought him 1,000 runs in May, was last out, New Zealand were still easily beaten by an innings.

1974-75 in New Zealand

New Zealand 0 England 1 Drawn 1
A comprehensive victory by England in the first Test was marred by a fearful accident to Ewen Chatfield, the New Zealand last man. Chatfield's heart actually stopped beating for several seconds after he was struck on the temple by a lifting delivery from Lever. Only swift action by the England physiotherapist, Bernard Thomas, saved Chatfield.

For England, Denness and Fletcher continued in good vein making 181 and 216 respectively. While the New Zealand batting could not hold out against Greig who took ten wickets in the match, they drew comfort from the promise of a century by Parker, two fifties from Morrison and an impressive debut from Geoff Howarth.

Turner made 98 in the rain-ruined second Test, and Amiss,

after his personal disaster in Australia, took the opportunity to fashion a return to form with 164 not out.

1977-78 in New Zealand

New Zealand 1 England 1 Drawn 1
Crossing from Pakistan to New Zealand, England met their destiny in the first Test, at Wellington, where New Zealand beat them for the first time, after 48 years and 47 previous attempts. On a worsening pitch and midst much short, aggressive bowling by both sides, the innings totals were successively smaller. New Zealand made 228, John Wright 55 on debut, Old 6 for 54; England 215, Boycott 77; New Zealand 123, Willis 5 for 32; and England, wanting 137 for victory, all out 64, only Botham and Edmonds reaching double figures. Hadlee and Collinge bowled every over bar one, the former taking 6 for 26, the latter 3 for 35. Local delight deafened most ears to criticism of the pitch, to umpires' leniency in the matter of short-pitched bowling and to the extreme caution of England's batsmen while the pitch still played reasonably well. Congdon was allowed to bowl 17.4 overs for 14 runs, and Boycott took 7 hours 20 minutes over his 77 in the first innings.

England gained revenge at Christchurch, where Botham scored his first Test century, Miller made 89, and Roope and Edmonds 50 apiece in a total of 418. All-rounder Botham then took 5 for 73 and Edmonds 4 for 38 as New Zealand foundered for 235 on a decent pitch which was to last throughout the match. Anderson and Parker alone passed 50.

England declared their second innings at 96 for 4, Randall having been run out by bowler Chatfield while backing up, and spearheaded by Willis, the England bowlers made short work of New Zealand's second innings, which ended at 105, a loss by 174 runs.

With all to play for in the third Test at Auckland, England anaesthetised the game. New Zealand made 315, Geoff Howarth 122, Burgess and Edwards fifties, Botham yet another five-wicket haul, and then England plodded to 429 off 156 overs, Clive Radley reaching 158 after getting to within a minute of Peter Richardson's 488-minute slowest Test century for England. Boycott, Roope and Botham all made half-centuries, but the theory that the New Zealanders would be hopelessly fatigued by the fifth afternoon of this six-day match misfired. Geoff Howarth made another century, Edwards and Anderson fifties, and the draw came with New Zealand 382 for 8 and well satisfied with a shared series.

1978 in England

England 3   New Zealand 0
The first Test was at the Oval, New Zealand batting and reaching 234 (Howarth 94, Wright 62). England took a lead of 45 thanks to 111 from Gower, his maiden Test century. New Zealand could muster only 182 in their second effort, Edmonds bowling 34.1 overs for only 20 runs and four wickets. Rain washed out the fourth day, but, led by Gooch (91 not out), England made the 138 needed with seven wickets and nearly an hour to spare.

At Trent Bridge, England batted first and the major batsmen

ABOVE Jubilation and stump and ball souvenirs for Warren Lees and Geoff Howarth as New Zealand beat England for the first time in 1977-78.
BELOW Despair for Lever, whose bouncer hit Chatfield and caused a fracture of the skull in 1974-75.

scored well, with Boycott (131), Radley (59), Gooch (55) and Brearley (50) leading the way to a total of 429. New Zealand were skittled for 120, largely by Botham (6 for 34), who was continuing a very successful summer, and following on, did a little better with 190 (Edgar 60), but were defeated by an innings and 119.

The final Test was at Lord's, and New Zealand began as if to put all disappointments behind them, scoring 339, with 123 from Howarth and 68 from captain Burgess. Botham took 6 for 101. It ensured a lead of 50 as England were put out for 289 (Radley 77, Gower 71). Hadlee took 5 for 84. Botham, however, excelled himself as a bowler in the second innings for the second time at Lord's that season, taking 5 for 39. With Willis supporting well, New Zealand were hurried out for just 67, leaving England to get only 118. This was duly achieved on the fourth day for the loss of three wickets, England's fifth Test victory of the season.

1983 in England

England 3   New Zealand 1
England and New Zealand were meeting for the first time for five years during the 1983 tour. New Zealand registered their first-ever victory on English soil. It was their 29th try.

Willis won the toss for England in the first Test at the Oval and batted on a fast, bouncy pitch. Richard Hadlee took full advantage of its help by taking 6 for 53, only Randall, with 75 not out, playing with confidence. England made a modest 209. New Zealand played brothers, Jeff and Martin Crowe. Unfortunately, Willis got both of them, plus Wright, for a duck, and New Zealand found themselves 41 for 5. Then Hadlee led a revival with an aggressive 84 in 79 balls and New Zealand finished only 13 behind on 196. Edmonds was no-balled for over-doing the bouncers. In their second effort England began with a 223 opening stand, and ground their way slowly to 446 for 6 declared (Fowler 105, Tavare 109, Lamb 102 not out). Wright made 88 and captain Howarth 67, but New Zealand could reach only

270, and lost by 189 runs. Hadlee's all-round performance, however, won him the Man of the Match award.

New Zealand put England in at Leeds and on a wicket initially dampish, bowled them out for 225, Cairns doing the damage with 7 for 74. This time New Zealand did not throw the good start away. After Edgar had retired hurt, and Howarth been run out, New Zea-land plummetted from 168 for 1 to 169 for 4, then 218 for 5, but Edgar (84) and Hadlee (75) were principal scorers in New Zealand's 377. When England batted again, Chatfield bowled excellently, taking 5 for 95, while Gower tried to farm the bowling and keep

England in the game. When he ran out of partners he had 112 not out, and England were 252. New Zealand needed only 101 to win. There were alarms as Willis pounded in with 5 for 35—could he have bowled at both ends it might have been different. But New Zealand eased home at 103 for 5. Cairns was Man of the Match. Hadlee, remarkably, had not taken a wicket in 47 overs. It was an excellent team performance and champagne flowed freely as New Zealand opened their account in England after 52 years.

It was down to earth with a bump at Lord's. Howarth won the toss and for the eighth successive time in Tests put his opponents in.

Cook, Foster and C. L. Smith made debuts for England, Gray for New Zealand. Smith was out to Hadlee to his first ball in Test cricket, and New Zealand might have progressed further had Cairns held a dolly catch from Gower. Gower went on to 108 and the Man of the Match award, Tavare (51) helped him add 149 for the second wicket and New Zealand's morale slumped. Gatting scored 81 and England totalled 326. Cook was the most

Jeremy Coney celebrates after hitting the run which gave New Zealand their first victory on English soil at Headingley, in the second Test of 1983.

impressive of England's debutants, taking 5 for 35. New Zealand were out for 191, Edgar, with 70, providing most resistance. England were dismissed for 211 (Botham 61) but New Zealand never looked like making 347, and lost by 127, Coney's 68 being best in their 219.

England chose to bat in the fourth Test at Trent Bridge. Gower was hit on the head by a delivery from Hadlee, and bravely

After New Zealand scored 496 for 9 declared at Auckland in 1984 Richard Hadlee claimed Graeme Fowler, caught by Ian Smith, with his first ball.

batted on after attention, still helmet-less, and made an attractive 72. At 169 for 5, Botham (103) and Randall (83) shared a brilliant stand of 186—164 glorious runs coming in 32 overs after tea. England totalled 420. Cook bowled beautifully again for England, taking 5 for 63, and New Zealand were out for 207, Edgar, with 62, again being top scorer. There was no rest day in this match, play continuing on Sunday, so Willis did not enforce the follow-on. Only Lamb passed 33, and he made 137 not out, nearly half England's score of 297. Hadlee took his 200th Test wicket. New Zealand needed 511 in nearly two

days. Edgar made 76 in 73 overs, and Coney made 68 even more slowly. Cook bowled 22 maidens in 50 overs, and Hadlee made a typical rapid 92 not out, helping the last four wickets add 161. But, at 345, New Zealand lost by 165 runs. Cook, with nine wickets, was Man of the Match, and Hadlee Man of a most successful Series.

1983-84 in New Zealand
New Zealand 1 England 0 Drawn 2
Five months after their last meeting, New Zealand were playing England in a new series at home. At Wellington Howarth won the toss, for the ninth time in Tests, and for the first time decided to

bat. While most batsmen made a start, only Jeff Crowe (52) passed 30, and New Zealand were all out 219, with Botham taking 5 for 59. The England innings, at 115 for 5, was following the same pattern (New Zealand had been 114 for 5), but then Botham and Randall got together and showed the Basin Reserve crowd what had delighted the Trent Bridge crowd a few months before. They added 232 this time, Botham making a spectacular 138, while Randall, after sticking for 50 minutes at 99, including a drinks interval, went on to 164. England made 463. The pitch had eased, and the home batsmen did much better. Martin Crowe scored 100, his first in Tests. For most of the innings England had a chance to win: 302 for 6, 334 for 7, 402 for 8. But Coney batted on and on, past his first Test century, and his first in any cricket for seven years. Cairns hit 64 out of 118 for the ninth wicket, and when the innings closed at 537 (Coney 174 not out) the match was saved. England made 69 for 0. Botham, with a century and five wickets in an innings for the fifth time in Tests (three more than anybody else) was Man of the Match.

Play in the second Test lasted only 12 hours on a controversial wicket. Howarth won the toss and batted again, a match-winning choice. Tony Pigott of Sussex and Wellington was co-opted into the England side because Foster and Dilley were injured. New Zealand batted adequately, Hadlee brilliantly. He raced to 99 in 81 balls and was then caught behind the wicket. New Zealand's 307 was a reasonable score on a suspect Christchurch pitch. Play began late on the next day after rain. The wicket, full of cracks, was also now spongy, and England ended the day at 53 for 7. All out for 82 they followed on and did little better—all out 93. Hadlee took 5 for 28, eight wickets in all, which with his 99 won him the Man of the Match award.

England had to win the last Test at Auckland to avoid a series defeat by New Zealand for the first time. This became difficult when Howarth again won the toss and batted on an easy pitch, and almost impossible when rain interrupted play on the first three days. Three players dominated New Zealand's effort: Wright (130), Jeff Crowe (128) and Man of the Match Ian Smith (113 not out). The innings was declared closed at 496 for 9, and, with little more than two days left, the match was virtually already drawn. Randall made 104, Chris Smith 91 and Botham a swashbuckling 70 before being run out. England closed on 439. There was just time for five overs and 16 runs in New Zealand's second innings before the celebrations began: New Zealand's first series victory over England following six months after their first win in England.

ENGLAND v INDIA

Though Test matches between England and India date from only 1932, cricketing relations between the two countries can be traced back to the 19th century. G. F. Vernon took an English side to India in 1888-89, and another side, under Lord Hawke, went there in 1892-93. Since 1932, England have dominated the series, although from the 1950s India have shown themselves much stronger opposition, especially on their own wickets.

1932 in England
England 1   India 0
The batting of Duleepsinhji in the county championship was still to the fore of English cricket, perhaps promising great things from his countrymen when they toured England in 1932 and played the first Test match between the two countries. In the event, England won without too much trouble, although they lost Percy Holmes, Herbert Sutcliffe, and Frank Woolley for 19 runs in the first 20 minutes. Douglas Jardine and Les Ames led a recovery to 259, but India were unable to consolidate their advantage and found the task of scoring 346 to win in the second innings too much.

1933-34 in India
India 0   England 2   Drawn 1
England sent a comparatively strong team for the first series in India, and proved too good all round. India found the bowling of Nobby Clark, Morris Nichols, Hedley Verity and James Langridge a difficult proposition, and were unable to total more than 258. England, on the other hand, twice made over 400. At Bombay Bryan Valentine in making 136 helped England to 438, and despite 118 by Lala Amarnath in India's second innings, England won by nine wickets. India followed on at Calcutta, only to save the match, but England clinched the series in the last Test, winning by 202 runs. Amar Singh took 7-86 in England's first innings, and Verity replied with 7-49 when the Indians batted.

1936 in England
England 2   India 0   Drawn 1
India's chances of winning their first Test were upset when Amarnath, their leading all-rounder, was sent home for disciplinary reasons before the Lord's Test. England won two of the matches handsomely, but India had their moment of glory in the drawn second Test at Old Trafford. Facing a first-innings deficit of 368, India were given a great start by Vijay Merchant (114) and Mushtaq Ali (112) who shared a stand of 203. For England, Walter Hammond made 167 in a total of 571-8 declared.

England won the first Test at Lord's by 9 wickets, Gubby Allen taking 5-35 and 5-43 in the match. Hammond was again in fine form at the Oval, where England once more won by 9 wickets. He scored 217 and with Stan Worthington (128) put on 266 for the fourth wicket. India, following on 249 behind, scored 312 with Allen taking 7-80.

1946 in England
England 1   India 0   Drawn 2
In the only match finished, England won at Lord's by 10 wickets, but later India only just escaped defeat at Old Trafford. The Oval Test was ruined by the weather. The series was notable for the introduction to Test cricket of Alec Bedser, who took 11 wickets in each of the first two games. He claimed 7-49 and 4-96 at Lord's where Joe Hardstaff hit a magnificent 205 not out in a total of 428. At Old Trafford, India, facing England's first innings of 294, began with an opening stand of 124 from Merchant and Mushtaq Ali, but were out for another 46. They saved the game when their last pair, Sohoni and Hindlekar stayed together for the last 13 minutes. Bedser's figures were 4-41 and 7-52. Merchant scored 128 at the Oval where India totalled 331, but England managed only 95-3 before the game was abandoned.

1951-52 in India
India 1   England 1   Drawn 3
India made history by recording their first victory over England,

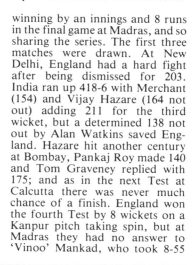

Vijay Hazare, a useful medium-pace bowler, though it was as batsman that he shone, and he captained India on the 1952 tour.

winning by an innings and 8 runs in the final game at Madras, and so sharing the series. The first three matches were drawn. At New Delhi, England had a hard fight after being dismissed for 203. India ran up 418-6 with Merchant (154) and Vijay Hazare (164 not out) adding 211 for the third wicket, but a determined 138 not out by Alan Watkins saved England. Hazare hit another century at Bombay, Pankaj Roy made 140 and Tom Graveney replied with 175; and as in the next Test at Calcutta there was never much chance of a finish. England won the fourth Test by 8 wickets on a Kanpur pitch taking spin, but at Madras they had no answer to 'Vinoo' Mankad, who took 8-55

and 4-53. Roy (111) and 'Polly' Umrigar (130) led the Indian batting.

1952 in England
England 3   India 0   Drawn 1
After their promising performances in the previous series, India went to England minus Merchant, Mankad (who later played in three Tests), Amarnath, and Mushtaq Ali, played defensively too often, and were outclassed. Only rain saved them from overwhelming defeat in all four games. The first match, at Headingley, was notable for the worst start to an innings in Test history. Facing arrears of 41, India lost their first four second-innings wickets without a run being scored and England won by 7 wickets.

A magnificent all-round effort by Mankad made the Lord's match. He scored 72 and 184, and bowled 73 overs for 5-196 in England's first innings. Despite this, England won easily by 8 wickets, Len Hutton making 150 and Godfrey Evans 104 in a total of 537. Fred Trueman demoralized India at Old Trafford, taking 8-31 in a first innings total of 58. They did little better when they followed on, being out for 82 and so were dismissed twice in a day. Hutton made 104 in the England innings of 347-9 declared.

1959 in England
England 5   India 0
For the first time ever England won all five Tests in a series, India's contribution to this feat being a somewhat dubious distinction. The negativity that had beset the 1952 side seemed amplified, and few of the batsmen seemed prepared to take advantage of one of England's finest summers.

Three of England's victories came with an innings to spare, and the other two were won with plenty in hand. Brian Statham and Fred Trueman consistently upset the Indian batting, and the bowlers

Ted Dexter captained England in 1961-62, when India won their first-ever series over England by two Tests to none.

encountered Peter May, Colin Cowdrey, Ken Barrington, and Geoff Pullar full of runs.

Only the fourth Test provided any real interest, and it was the only one that went into the fifth day. Geoff Pullar (131) and Mike Smith (100) scored centuries for England, and when India batted a second time wanting 548 to win A. A. Baig, an Oxford freshman recruited during the tour, made 112 and Umrigar 118 before they went down by 171 runs.

1961-62 in India

India 2   England 0   Drawn 3

For the first time India won a series against England, their success being well deserved. The England batting was unreliable and the bowling lacking in penetration, and the absence of players such as Cowdrey, Statham, and Trueman should not detract from the Indian victory.

At Bombay, England reached 500-8, Barrington 151 not out, but India saved the game comfortably. England were made to follow on for the first time against India at Kanpur, but with Pullar (119), Barrington (172), and Ted Dexter (126 not out) showing a return of form they reached 497-5 without inviting India to bat again.

After rain had washed out the last two days at New Delhi, the teams met in Calcutta, where India

ABOVE Salim Durani batting. In 1961-62 in Calcutta he did well with both bat and ball.

BELOW The Nawab of Pataudi, India's captain in 1967, bowled after scoring 148 at Headingley.

won by 187 runs, C. G. Borde and S. Durani doing most damage. Durani (6-105 and 4-72) was again a problem for the England batsmen at Madras, and with the Nawab of Pataudi scoring 103 in their first innings India took the match by 128 runs and the series by two Tests.

1963-64 in India

India 0   England 0   Drawn 5

Though five draws in a five-Test series was not a novel experience for India, who had achieved it twice before with Pakistan, it was for England. Not that it affected attendances, for the grounds were packed to capacity for the run-glut encouraged by the easy pitches. England suffered heavily from injury and sickness, and Cowdrey and Peter Parfitt were flown out. Cowdrey had been originally chosen as captain but was injured, M. J. K. Smith taking his place.

Cowdrey's arrival brought England their first century in the series, when he scored 107 in the third Test at Calcutta. B. K. Kunderan (192) and Manjrekar (108) had opened India's century account in the first Test at Madras. Cowdrey followed with 151 at New Delhi, but Hanumant Singh (105), Kunderan (100), and Pataudi (203 not out) gave India a century advantage of six to two. M. L. Jaisimha had scored 129 at Calcutta.

With Barry Knight (127) and Parfitt (121) to the fore, England made 559-8 at Kanpur, and Fred Titmus then took 6-73 to make India follow on. But a century by R. G. Nadkarni (122 not out) ensured the stalemate would not be broken.

1967 in England

England 3   India 0

Upset by terrible weather and injuries, India gave a dismal display in the first half of a shared tour with Pakistan. Only in the second innings of the first Test at Headingley, where they followed on and made 510, did they distinguish themselves. Pataudi's 148 proved to be their only Test century. Not even that score could stop England winning by 6 wickets, and Close's men found less resistance in the other two Tests.

1971 in England

England 0   India 1   Drawn 2

In the third match of this short series, an England batting collapse in the second innings at the Oval gave India their first win on English soil. Such a collapse came hardly as a surprise, because in all the Tests the home players had shown distinct vulnerability against a three-pronged spin attack of Chandrasekhar, Bishan Bedi and Venkataraghavan.

The first Test at Lord's had been left ruined by rain with India 38 runs short of a target of 183 runs with two wickets in hand. England had been grateful for John Snow's highest Test score of 73 in the first innings, after being 71-5 to Chandrasekhar and Bedi. Captain Wadekar, Viswanath and Solkar all made solid contributions for India, while Gavaskar's second innings 53 seemed to create a certain win, until Gifford pegged them back.

Rain saved India at Old Trafford when they were 65 for 3, needing 420 to win. Illingworth and Luckhurst made hundreds, and Peter Lever, at number 9, hit 88 not out.

But at the Oval, the visitors needed only 173 for victory, which they accomplished with six wickets down. After England had led by 71 on the first innings, they crumbled in the face of Chandrasekhar

Tony Greig (left) and Dennis Amiss, who both hit maiden Test centuries on the tour of India and Pakistan in 1972-73.

whose bounce and turn proved mesmeric. He finished with 6 for 38, a performance to win both the match and the series.

1972-73 in India

India 2   England 1   Drawn 2

Not until the end of the series did a weakened England come to grips with the spin of Chandrasekhar and Bedi, who had plagued their batsmen so much in England in 1971. Only three England wickets fell to pace in the five Tests. The visiting spinners were, however, less effective.

Nevertheless England won the first Test by six wickets, a remarkable start for captain Tony Lewis playing his first Test. Though Chandrasekhar had 8 for 79 in the first innings, Greig, 68

not out and 70 not out saw England home.

The Indian spinners held sway in Calcutta and Madras, earning wins by 28 runs and 4 wickets. But Lewis steadied his ship in the fourth Test with a fine 125 which ensured his side would not lose.

The bat was always in command at Bombay and England could not square the series. Engineer and Viswanath made hundreds for India while Fletcher and Greig hit their first three-figure scores for England.

Chandrasekhar finished with 35 wickets, Bedi with just 10 less. On wickets so suited to spinners, England's failure could be deduced from the fact that the top three in their bowling averages were Arnold, Greig and Old, all at

LEFT The Nawab of Pataudi pulls a short ball to leg at Edgbaston in 1967, causing the England fielders to take evasive action. He had only one good eye after a car accident in 1960.
RIGHT The middle stump remains while the leg and off stumps are knocked out of the ground. Madan Lal is the unlucky batsman at Old Trafford in 1974, Mike Hendrick the clever bowler.
BELOW John Edrich was twice out caught Farokh Engineer bowled Bishan Bedi in the 1971 series in England.

about medium to fast-medium.

1974 in England
England 3 India 0
In damp, cold weather, England took full advantage of conditions to their liking and comprehensively defeated India in all three Test Matches of the series.

Despite the industry of Abid Ali, the visitors with their reliance on spin could not compete in a contest of seam bowling. At Old Trafford in the first Test, rain fell on the first four days and England and particularly Fletcher, 123 not out, found few problems emerging from the cold fingers of Bedi, Chandrasekhar and Venkataraghavan. Seven Indian wickets tumbled for 143 until Gavaskar found staunch support from Abid

ABOVE David Lloyd in only his second Test at Edgbaston in 1974, on his way to 214 not out against India.

Ali and completed a gallant hundred. But after Edrich, on his return to international cricket after two years, reached three figures, India were bowled out on the last day and lost by 113 runs.

At Lord's the margin was even wider—a massive win for England by an innings and 285 runs. Omitting Boycott, England amassed 629—Amiss 188, Denness 118, Greig 106, Edrich 96. Although Gavaskar and Engineer put on 131 for the first wicket in reply, the follow-on was inevitably forced. Then India crumbled in 77 minutes and 17 overs to 42 all out, the lowest score in Test history at Lord's. Arnold, 4 for 19, and Old, 5 for 21, administered the slaughter.

India had little taste for the fight in the third Test and conceded defeat again by an innings. Bowled out for 164 and 216 by the England seam attack, they took only two wickets in reply as England declared at 459. Lloyd, in only his second Test, made 214 not out, and he put on 207 for the second wicket with his captain, Denness, reaching his second century of a one-sided series.

1976-77 in India
India 1 England 3 Drawn 1
After the hardships of the preceding three years, England came back strongly to overwhelm India by three Tests to one, their first series victory in India in five rubbers since the war. Inspiringly led by Tony Greig, England played with flair and determination against a side which had had some

Bhagwat Chandrasekhar, whose leg-breaks took many England wickets in the 1970s.

pronounced successes during the 1970s.

The first Test, at New Delhi, was won by an innings and 25 runs after Amiss had weathered an ominous start which saw England 65 for 4 and 125 for 5. His 179 was the backbone of an innings of 381 to which Knott had contributed 75 and John Lever, in his first Test, 53. Lever, though, was to make his debut memorable for his 10 wickets, seven of them for 46 in the first innings, which realised only 122. The Essex left-armer swung the ball prodigiously. In the follow-on India reached 234, only Gavaskar with 71 surviving for long.

England's victory at Calcutta was almost as overwhelming: 10 wickets. The aggressor this time was Willis, whose fast bowling brought him 5 for 27 as India crashed for 155. Batting was not easy for England either, but a protracted and punishing century by Greig, the second-slowest ever for England at that time (415 minutes), aided by Tolchard's 67, a masterpiece of self-denial, plus a vigorous 52 from Old, saw England to 321. The lead of 166 was adequate, India falling for only 181 at the second attempt.

England won the series at Madras with their third win in a row, this time by 200 runs; but controversy surrounded the game after India's captain accused Lever of having used the vaseline on his forehead to shine the ball. The bowler was officially cleared of the charge, but the stigma caused lasting ill-feeling. On a deteriorating pitch runs became harder to find as the match progressed, and England's 262 and 185 for 9 declared eclipsed India's 164 and 83. Brearley and Greig made the only half-centuries of the match, and the damage done by India's

spinners was more than offset by Lever's 5 for 59 in the first innings and Underwood's 4 for 28 in the second.

India came back with a win by 140 runs in the fourth Test, at Bangalore, Chandrasekhar taking nine wickets, Bedi seven, and Prasanna three. They were well served by the close-in fielders, who perched like vultures, and Yajurvindra took a record-equalling seven catches. The unquestioned ability of some of India's top batsmen, such as Gavaskar, Gaekwad, Surinder Amarnath and Viswanath, was demonstrated, at last, even though the rate of scoring continued to be funereal. The only

LEFT A jubilant Tony Greig is chaired off the field by Old and Lever after winning the series in 1976-77.
ABOVE Amarnath is caught in the leg trap by Woolmer off Underwood in the third Test.
BELOW LEFT A packed Calcutta for the second Test in 1976-77.
RIGHT A contrasting scene at Lord's in 1977. Heavy floods in front of the Taverner's Bar.

England batsmen to prosper were Amiss, 82, and Knott, whose 81 not out in the last innings was in a forlorn cause.

The fifth Test, though drawn, had periods of excitement. Gavaskar's century and Patel's brisk 83 set up an Indian total of 338, to which England replied with 317, Brearley making 91, Greig 76, and the consistent Amiss 50. Underwood took his bag of wickets for the series to 29 when India went in again, his 5 for 84 restricting them to 192. This left England to make 214 in four hours, and both sides had some nervous moments before the close at 152 for 7, Ghavri taking 5 for 33.

1979 in England

England 1   India 0   Drawn 3
Venkataraghavan led the tourists against Brearley's successful side. He lost the first toss at Edgbaston, and England amassed 633 for 5 declared, their highest post-war total. Gower, with 200 not out, led the way. Boycott made 155, Gooch 83 and Miller 63 not out. Remarkably, Kapil Dev took all the wickets (5 for 146). India made 297 (Gavaskar 61, Viswanath 78) and 253 (Gavaskar 68, Chauhan 56, Viswanath 51, Botham 5 for 70), England winning in four days by an innings and 83 runs.

Rain helped India save the

Sunil Gavaskar cover-drives off the back foot at the Oval in 1979, during his marathon double century on the last day.

second Test at Lord's. They scored only 96 in the first innings, Botham taking 5 for 35. England scored 419 for 9 declared (Gower 82, Randall 57, Miller 62, Taylor 64). When Botham dismissed Gavaskar for 59 in the second innings, he took his 100th Test wicket in a record time (2 years, 9 days), although he was not quickest in terms of Tests played. Vengsarkar (103) and Viswanath (113) turned the tide for India, adding 210 for the third wicket, and at 318 for 4, India forced the draw.

At Headingley, Botham hit a rapid 137, including 99 before lunch (9 to 108), but this was the fourth day, half the first day and all of the next two being lost to rain. England made 270, India 223 for 6 (Gavaskar 78, Vengsarkar 65 not out) in a hopeless draw.

The fourth and final Test at the Oval provided one of the best finishes of recent years. England batted and made 305 (Gooch 78, Willey 52), India replying with 202 (Viswanath 62). Boycott made 125 when England went in again, and debutant Bairstow 59, allowing England to declare at 334 for 8, setting India a target of 438 with over eight hours to get them. They made an impressive start, Gavaskar and Chauhan (80) putting on 213 for the first wicket, a record for England v India tests. When the last hour began, India had still lost only the one wicket in over a day's play—at 328 for 1 they needed 110 from the last 20 overs. Vengsarkar was out for 52, closely followed by Kapil Dev—and then a tired Gavaskar was out for a magnificent 221, one of Test cricket's best innings. India lost a little momentum and wickets fell —at 429 for 8 at the close they were just eight runs short of a great victory. Perhaps India took a few too many overs avoiding defeat, but it was a memorable draw. Botham completed 1,000 Test runs during the match, and became the quickest to a Test double of 1,000 runs and 100 wickets, achieved in only 21 matches.

1979-80 in India
India 0   England 1
The Test match played at the Wankhede Stadium, Bombay, in February 1980 to celebrate India's Golden Jubilee was a triumph for Ian Botham, and, to a lesser extent, Bob Taylor. England were on their way home from the tour of Australia.

Viswanath won the toss for India and batted, and Gavaskar and Binny had 56 on the board in 50 minutes before Binny was run out. Gavaskar's 49 proved to be India's top score, Botham taking 6 for 58 and Taylor taking seven catches behind the stumps. India's 242 looked a better score when

BELOW The first Test in Bombay was the only one not drawn in 1981-82. Azad was caught by the substitute (Gatting) off Underwood, but India won.

England were 58 for 5, but Botham (114) and Taylor (43) added 171. Early in the stand Viswanath sportingly withdrew an appeal for a catch at the wicket against Taylor. England were all out 296 (Ghavri 5 for 52), 54 ahead. Botham then skittled India even more dramatically than in the first innings, taking 7 for 48 as the Indians were all out 149. Gooch and Boycott made 98 without loss and England won by 10 wickets. Botham became the first player to score a century and take 10 wickets in a Test match.

1981-82 in India

India 1 England 0 Drawn 5

Keith Fletcher's team in India in 1981-82 played the first Test at the Wankhede Stadium, Bombay. During the match the England team were unhappy about several umpiring decisions. Gavaskar won the toss and batted. He made 55 himself on a pitch of variable bounce, but India's total of 179 appeared inadequate. Boycott (60) and Tavare (56) batted slowly and carefully and took the score to 95 before England's second wicket fell, but 71 runs later the innings was over for 166, with English batsmen unhappy at some dismissal decisions given against the sweep shot. India, 13 ahead, struggled to 157 for 8, but 46 from 51 balls from Kapil Dev took the score to 227 (Botham 5 for 61), setting England 241 to win. Only Botham could get any satisfaction at all from England's second innings, his 29 making him the third player to reach 2,000 runs and 200 wickets in Tests. Kapil Dev took 5 for 70 and Madan Lal 5 for 23 as England crashed for 102, of which the last-wicket stand of 27 was the highest of the innings. Kapil Dev was Man of the Match.

At Bangalore, England batted first and made 400 on a benign pitch, but as it took 158 overs, and the overs took two days, the match was destined to be a draw from the start. Gooch (58), Gower (82), Botham (55) and Dilley (52) were the principal scorers. Fletcher, given out caught behind as he swept, hit the stumps in petulant disagreement, for which he later apologised. Gavaskar was determined there would be no mishaps, and despite confident lbw appeals, and a 20-minute wait on 99, he eventually went on to 172, batting through the last day and being at one end for all but 14 minutes of India's 11-hour innings of 428. It earned him the Man of the Match award. Lever took 5-100. England made 174 for 3 in the time left.

Umpire Ghouse was replaced before the start of the third Test at Delhi after an English objection. The match followed the same pattern as the previous one. England chose to bat and made 476 for 9 declared, but the innings took 156 overs, which lasted into the third

day. Boycott made 105, over-taking Garfield Sobers as the leading run-getter in Test history. Tavare made 149 and was Man of the Match. Botham made a quick 66 and Fletcher 51. England's strongest hope of winning came when three men, including Gavaskar, were out for 89, but the previously out of form Viswanath, who had shaved his beard and given up smoking, made 107 and closed the door. Later Shastri made 93 and Kirmani 67, the last three wickets adding 233. England made 68 without loss to end the match.

Fletcher won the toss and batted at Calcutta, in a match watched by an estimated 425,000, a world record for any match. Fletcher (69) and Botham (58), with 93 for the fifth wicket, provided the backbone of England's 248. Kapil Dev took 6 for 91. India were removed for 208 (Vengsarkar 70) although it took until near the end of the third day, putting England in with their best chance to level the series for some time. Comparatively quick batting allowed England to declare at 265 for 5 (Gooch 63, Gower 74, Fletcher 60 not out), giving themselves just over a day to bowl out India for 306. However, the last day started 70 minutes late because of bad light, and Gavaskar, with 83 not out from 170 for 3, was not going to give in. Fletcher was Man of the Match. Boycott, who had not

fielded on the last day because of ill-health, played golf instead, and then left for home 'by mutual agreement'.

Fletcher gambled for the fifth Test at Madras, packing his side with fast bowling and asking India to bat. The plan misfired. After 51 for 2, the next wicket added 415. Vengsarkar and Viswanath added 99 when Vengsarkar (71) retired hurt, then Viswanath (222) and Yashpal Sharma (140) added a further 316. India declared at 481 for 4, and England's task was to avoid the follow-on rather than play for a win. The first wicket put on 155, Gooch scored 127, Tavare stayed 332 minutes for 35, Gower made 64 and Botham 52, and despite the last seven wickets falling for 49, the total of 328 saved the match. India made a further 160 for 3 declared (Roy 60 not out). Viswanath was Man of the Match.

The sixth Test at Kanpur was a victim of mist and rain, and there was time for only 237 overs, not enough to finish two innings on a lifeless pitch.

England chose to bat, and with century stands between Gower (85) and Botham (142) for the fourth wicket and Botham and Gatting for the fifth England reached 349 before the fifth wicket fell, and declared at 378 for 9. Earlier Gooch made 58. Gavaskar (52), Viswanath (74) and Yashpal Sharma (55 not out) helped India avoid the follow-on, and on the

last day Kapil Dev scored an entertaining 116, passing his century off 83 balls, one of the quickest in Test history. India finished on 377 for 7.

1982 in England
England 1   India 0   Drawn 2
Six months after meeting in Kanpur, the two sides met again in the first Test at Lord's. Willis was England's new captain. Before the match, India objected to umpire Constant, who had officiated in the Prudential Trophy, and he was withdrawn from the Test panel.

Willis won his first toss, batted, and Kapil Dev took the first four wickets, with England having only 96 on the board. Botham made 67, but at 166 for 6 England needed an innings from Randall, and as usual he obliged. Edmonds (64) joined in a stand of 125. Taylor helped Randall (126) add another 72, then Allott and Willis added 70 for the last wicket. England were all out 433. India made a desperate start, Botham, who finished with 5 for 46, Willis and Pringle reducing them to 45 for 5. Gavaskar (48) and Kapil Dev (41) added 67 for the sixth wicket but this proved more than half the total of 128, the next highest individual score being 6. At 24 for 2 India appeared to be going the same way when they followed on, but Vengsarkar played a masterly innings of 157. At 275 for 8, however, it looked like an innings defeat, but Kapil

Dev, missed at 5, smashed 89 in 55 balls and India reached 369. Needing 65, England faced eight overs on the fourth evening, during which Kapil Dev grabbed three wickets while 18 were scored, but next day the target was reached without further loss. Kapil Dev, with two good innings and eight wickets, was Man of the Match.

In the second Test at Old Trafford, Cook and Tavare put on 106 for the first wicket when England decided to bat, but this good start slid to 161 for 5. Botham then made a typical quick 128, and Miller, with 98, helped in a stand of 169. There was no play after lunch on the second day, and with interruptions on all days it was late on the third day before the innings was completed at 425. The top three Indian batsmen were out for 25 before the close, and the follow-on was a possibility. But on the Sunday Viswanath made 54, night-watchman Kirmani a stubborn 58 and Patil a brilliant 129 not out, which included six fours in an over (one no-ball) from Willis. Kapil Dev hit 65 from 55 balls and India ended the day at 379 for 8. The last day was washed out. Patil was Man of the Match.

England batted again at the Oval, and provided some brilliant

Sandeep Patil cuts at the Oval in 1982. Allan Lamb at silly point jumps in alarm. Botham is slip and Taylor is the keeper.

attacking batting. The top six batsmen all scored runs, but the highlight was, as so often, the innings of Botham, and it was one of his best. He hit 208, his highest Test score, from 226 balls, probably the quickest Test 200 in terms of balls bowled, though not in time taken. He hit 4 sixes and 19 fours, and one shot broke the ankle of Gavaskar, fielding at silly point. He was, of course, Man of the Match. Lamb made a brilliant 107, Randall 95, Cook 50, and England ended at 594. The Indian batsmen, without Gavaskar, made a spirited reply, only Vengsarkar of the top seven failing. Shastri made 66, Viswanath 56 and Patil 62, but at 248 for 5 (effectively 6) the follow-on target was still 147 ahead. Kapil Dev, who won the Man of the Series award, soon settled this, hitting 97 in 93 balls, including 2 sixes and 14 fours. India reached 410. Willis was not inclined to give India a chance to draw the series with a generous declaration. At 191 for 3 declared (Tavare 75 not out) he set India 376 in an impossible time, to the disgruntlement of the spectators. They reached 111 for 3 (Viswanath 75 not out).

1984-85 in India

India 1   England 2   Drawn 2

Tragedy accompanied this series. Three hours after the English tourists arrived in India, the Prime Minister, Mrs Gandhi, was assassinated. The rioting and unrest which followed, and the period of mourning, led to the tourists retreating to Sri Lanka for a while. The tour itinerary was revised. Then, on the eve of the first Test, the British Deputy High Commissioner to Western India was murdered. The last engagement he had fulfilled the previous evening was to entertain the tourists to cocktails.

It was decided that the Test should go ahead as planned, and Gower, the England captain, won the toss at the Wankhede Stadium and batted. On a comparatively placid pitch the batting collapsed feebly. The highest stand of the innings was 61 for the eighth wicket between Downton and Edmonds. England were all out 195, the main destroyer being an 18-year-old wrist spinner, Laxman Sivaramakrishnan, with 6 for 64. All India's early batsmen scored a few, then Shastri (142) added 62 for the sixth wicket with Kapil Dev (42), and 235 for the seventh with Kirmani (102). India declared at 465 for 8. Sivaramakrishnan took 6 for 117 in England's second knock, but this time Gatting, with his first Test century in his 54th innings, played him easily and scored 136. Fowler (55) and Downton (62) helped Gatting raise England's total to 317. But India needed only 48, and got them for the loss of two wickets. It was India's first win for 32 Tests.

England were attempting to halt a losing sequence of 13 at Delhi,

Mohinder Amarnath turns the ball to leg in the second Test at Delhi in 1984-85. Paul Downton and David Gower watch.
England won and, led by Gower, went on to take the series.

where Gavaskar won the toss and batted. India's performance was adequate, a total of 307 being satisfactory after they were 140 for 6. Kapil Dev (60) was the only player to pass 50, but the last four batsmen all passed 25, and the last wicket added 49. England's reply was built round Tim Robinson, playing in his second Test. He batted for 8½ hours, spread over three days, for 160. Lamb (52) and Downton (74) were his main allies as England (418) took a lead of 109. Sivaramakrishnan again took 6 wickets (mostly tail-enders) for 99. India, in their second innings, played most uncharacteristically and many got themselves out with rash shots, even Gavaskar (65). Amarnath made 64, but when the last six wickets fell for 28, England, surprisingly, had two hours to make 125, and made no mistake, winning by 8 wickets.

The third Test at Calcutta was a disappointment. The Indian crowd was angry with Gavaskar to start with, as Kapil Dev had been dropped for 'cavalier play' (he had hit Pocock for six off the fifth ball he faced at Delhi, and 'holed out' the next). As Botham was resting at home this winter, neither of the great all-rounders played at Calcutta. It would have been better if they had, for the Indian innings was a protracted, strokeless affair of 437 for 7 declared off 200 overs.

Only newcomer Mohammad Azharuddin could feel happy—he made 110 in his first Test. Shastri made 111. As there was also plenty of rain, the irritated crowd bombarded the field with oranges. Gavaskar was actually advised by the local police to declare to prevent a disturbance. England made 276 (Lamb 67), and there was time only for India to make 29 for 1 by the end of a pointless match.

Records fell in the fourth Test at Madras. India decided to bat, and on a fast pitch with bounce, went for their shots. Amarnath made 78, Kapil Dev, restored, a quick 53 (hitting his first ball defiantly for four). But 272 (Foster 6 for 104) was not a match-winning score. Fowler and Robinson, England's openers, were both dropped—very expensive misses—before Robinson was out for 74 at 178. At 293 for 1 at the end of the second day England were already ahead. On the third day the second wicket stand reached 241 before Fowler (201) was out. Lamb hit 62, and then Gatting was out for 207. This was the first occasion two England batsmen had passed 200 in the same Test match. Gower batted on into the fourth day (begun at 611 for 5) and declared at 652 for 7. On a still good wicket, Foster again bowled beautifully, dismissing the top three Indian batsmen with only 22 on the board, but Amarnath (95) and Azharuddin (105) made their second century stand, this time of 190, before Foster returned to remove Amarnath. Azharuddin became the fourth player to score a century in his first two Tests. At 246 for 4 at

the close of the fourth day, the match still looked to be a draw, but on the last day two more wickets went at 259. Kapil Dev and Kirmani added 82 before Kapil Dev was out for 49—a few more overs and he might have made it safe. Kirmani went on to 72, helping the last wicket to add 51, but India were eventually all out 412, and England had plenty of time to make 35 for 1 to win. Foster took 11 wickets in the match. For the first time a visiting side in India had come from a match down to lead in the series, and now all England required was a draw at Kanpur.

India batted first again, and again Gavaskar (who averaged only 17.5 in the series) was out cheaply. India needed to score quickly and Srikkanth (84) and Azharuddin (122) did, in a second-wicket stand of 150, but then lost their way a little. Vengsarkar made 137, Shastri a quick 59 and Kapil Dev 42 in 33 balls, enabling Gavaskar to declare at 533 for 8, but the rate of under 3½ per over was not quite quick enough. Fowler (69) and Robinson (96) put on 156 for the first wicket, Gatting made 62 and Gower 78, but for England there was no hurry, and their 417 at 2.2 per over lasted into the final day. Gavaskar made the gesture of declaring at 97 for 1 (Azharuddin 54 not out) asking England to attempt 234 in 46 overs. The offer was declined and 91 without loss was the closing score. Azharuddin became the first player to score a century in each of his first three Tests, and he ended with an average of 109.75.

ENGLAND v PAKISTAN

Pakistan achieved the unexpected and the unprecedented on their first tour of England by winning one Test and so drawing the series. No other touring side had managed to win a Test on their first visit, but as they embarked on a half-tour in 1982 it was still their only success on English soil. Although they had produced a number of good individual efforts, too often their sides have lacked depth in English conditions. On their own pitches, however, they have proved much sterner opposition, and they registered their first series victory over England in 1983-84.

1954 in England
England 1   Pakistan 1   Drawn 2
A series that was to have such a satisfying climax for the tourists began in a depressing manner, rain preventing play until mid-afternoon on the fourth day of the first Test. Further frustration followed at Trent Bridge, this time in the batting of Denis Compton (278) and Reg Simpson (101), and England won by an innings and 129 runs. Rain proved their saviour at Old Trafford, when they were 25-4 in the second innings, having made only 90 in reply to England's 359-8.

Then came the thrilling last Test at the Oval, where Pakistan won by 24 runs. England, needing 168 to win, were 109-2 at one stage, but collapsed completely and were out for 143. Fazal Mahmood took 6-53 and 6-46 to offset Johnny Wardle's 7-56 in Pakistan's second innings.

1961-62 in Pakistan
Pakistan 0   England 1   Drawn 2
England's first-Test victory at Lahore by 5 wickets with 35 minutes to spare proved decisive. Pakistan began strongly, but slumped from 315-3 to 387-9, Javed Burki 138, and 139 from Ken Barrington kept England within striking distance. MCC then went on to India, where they played five Tests, before the second and third Tests were played at Dacca and Karachi. Hanif Mohammad scored a century in each innings of a dull draw at Dacca, and Dexter's double century (205) and Parfitt's 111 in England's 507 in the last Test gave Pakistan no hope of squaring the series.

1962 in England
England 4   Pakistan 0   Drawn 1
Hopes that the Pakistanis would do well again in England were not fulfilled, and only the weather saved them from defeat in all five Tests. Their leading batsman Hanif Mohammad was far from fit and never struck form, although his younger brother Mushtaq was a success. Bowling was the tourist's main weakness,

and only once could they dismiss England for less than 400. Both Parfitt and Graveney enjoyed averages of a hundred or more, and no Pakistan bowler averaged less than 30 in the Tests.

This was a young, inexperienced touring side, and it found the English conditions vastly different from those at home. Pakistan had only recently been changing from matting wickets to lifeless turf that allowed little movement of the pitch. Consequently, they were at a loss against the seam bowling of Len Coldwell, Statham, and Trueman.

1967 in England
England 2   Pakistan 0   Drawn 1
As on the previous tour, Pakistan's main problem was their bowling, for although they had a capable spin attack, there was no penetrating fast bowling. The batting had more depth, but, like the Indians earlier in the season, the Pakistanis seemed reluctant to throw caution to the winds. Only when Asif Iqbal launched his unexpected attack at the Oval was there any indication of what might have been.

Solid batting from Hanif (187 not out) and Asif enabled the tourists to open the series with a draw. Barrington scored 148 in England's first innings. Rain interfered with the second Test at Trent Bridge, where England won by 10 wickets after Pakistan had been

dismissed for 140, and England, with Barrington batting nearly seven hours for his 109 not out, led by 112. The conditions were tailor-made for Derek Underwood when the tourists batted again, and he finished with 5-52.

Geoff Arnold (5-58) was mainly responsible for Pakistan's dismissal for 216 at the Oval, and after Barrington had hit his third century in three games, Pakistan batted again 224 in arrears. At 65-8 they looked doomed to an innings defeat. Then Asif came to the wicket, and with Intikhab Alam increased the Test record for the 9th wicket to 190. Unprecedented scenes greeted his century in 2 hours 19 minutes. Hundreds of Pakistanis raced on to the field and hoisted him shoulder high until the police rescued him. Revived with a drink from the team manager, he then continued the entertainment until stumped by Alan Knott for 146. Barrington fittingly hit the winning runs for England, whose 8-wicket victory with a day to spare was something of an anticlimax.

1968-69 in Pakistan
Pakistan 0   England 0   Drawn 3
Internal political riots ruined the series and finally caused the abandonment of the third Test. The unrest was apparent from the first Test, in which Cowdrey scored 100 and Asif (70) and Majid Jahangir (68) batted well and entertainingly for Pakistan. D'Oliveira's unbeaten 114 was the outstanding innings of a dull game at Dacca. At Karachi, Colin Milburn enlivened

ABOVE Asif Iqbal, who made a magnificent 146 in the last Test of the 1967 series at the Oval. With Intikhab Alam he added 190 for the ninth wicket, a record. LEFT Alan Knott batting for Kent against the Pakistanis in 1971, when he made 116 against them in the Edgbaston Test.

the proceedings with a quick-fire 139, Graveney scored 105, and Alan Knott was within four runs of his maiden Test century when rioting stopped play.

1971 in England
England 1   Pakistan 0   Drawn 2
An England side still flushed from success in Australia found themselves brought back to reality in the first Test as Pakistan kept them in the field for more than two days as they amassed 608-7. Young Zaheer Abbas batted just over 9 hours for a magnificent 274 and shared a stand of 291 with Mushtaq Mohammad (100). Asif Iqbal also reached his century, and it needed a fighting 73 by D'Oliveira and 116 from Knott to give the England innings respectability after Asif Masood had shown the England bowlers up. England followed on 255 behind, but rain on the final day cost Pakistan almost certain victory.

Luckhurst scored 108 not out in England's 229-5 and Asif Masood finished with match figures of 8 for 147.

Rain for most of the second Test meant that all depended on Headingley, where England won an exciting victory by 25 runs. Boycott followed his second-Test 121 not out with 112, but Pakistan passed England's 316 by 34 and then dismissed England for 264, Salim Altaf taking 4-11. The tourists needed 231 for victory with more than a day to play, but on the final day Illingworth made the initial breakthrough on a wicket that had threatened to take spin throughout, and though the youngest Mohammad, Sadiq, scored 91, the series, somewhat unjustly, eluded Pakistan.

1972-73 in Pakistan
Pakistan 0   England 0   Drawn 3
Both teams arrived in Pakistan following a gruelling programme of Test cricket—Pakistan from their sojourn in Australia and New Zealand; England from the five keenly fought Tests in India.

This weariness undoubtedly contributed to three rather stagnant Tests in which the Pakistan batting held the upper hand. The England batting coped marginally more successfully than they had in India and always made enough runs to survive.

Pakistan had already sprung one bombshell in New Zealand by announcing that Intikhab Alam had been relieved of the captaincy while play was actually in progress during the final Test.

Majid Khan, his replacement, was not an immediate success as the new skipper, nor did he show the same flair with the bat that he had shown in Australia.

Amiss became the fourth player on the tour to make his maiden Test century when he compiled 112 on the opening day of the first Test at Lahore. But largely through the efforts of Sadiq Mohammad, 119, and Asif Iqbal, 102, Pakistan gained a first innings lead. England batted consistently in the second innings to earn a draw.

At Hyderabad, Amiss led the way with 158 as England amassed 487. Pakistan replied with 569 for nine declared—Mushtaq Mohammad 157, Intikhab 138—and looked to be on the way to victory as England slumped to 77 for 5. But Greig and Knott added 112 and staved off the impending defeat.

The last match provided, if nothing else, a remarkable statistic in that three batsmen were dismissed for 99. That fate befell both Majid and Mushtaq in Pakistan's first innings of 445 for six declared. And Amiss, seeking his third hundred in successive Tests, fell at the same score as England totalled 386, Lewis making 88.

As on the previous tour, student unrest caused stoppages, both in Karachi and Hyderabad. Particu-

larly in Karachi, where more than an hour's play was lost on one day, the play and the players were inhibited by impending invasions of the playing area.

1974 in England
England 0   Pakistan 0   Drawn 3
Pakistan brought perhaps their strongest-ever side to England and returned home undefeated, but all three Tests ended as draws.

At Headingley and Lord's, rain robbed England of victory. In the first Test, they required 44 runs with just four wickets remaining to win a memorable contest when no cricket could be played on the final day. More than a hundred behind on the first innings, England needed 282 for victory, and after both openers had failed, Edrich, Denness and Fletcher had edged their side towards the target in the face of some penetrating seam bowling by Sarfraz.

The second Test was steeped in controversy and the weather conditions which stopped a certain England win probably prevented a loud outcry from Pakistan. The complaint was of inadequate covering of the wicket, and each time the rain fell it was Pakistan who suffered. The first downpour

Zaheer Abbas made a mammoth 274 at Edgbaston in 1971, his country's first double century against England.

reduced their innings from 71 for no wicket to 130 for 9 declared, Underwood 5 for 20. And the visitors were similarly affected in the second innings when Underwood collected a further eight wickets. Needing 87 to win England had made 27 without loss when the rain finally won the day.

The final Test on the paceless wicket at the Oval produced a high scoring, but boring draw. For Pakistan, Zaheer constructed a marvellous 240, while England in slower vein responded with 183 from Amiss and 122 from Fletcher. Nevertheless it was a frustrating end to a contest between two evenly-matched sides.

1977-78 in Pakistan
Pakistan 0   England 0   Drawn 3
Three Tests were played by England in Pakistan in 1977-78 and three more draws were added to the long list of that country's uncompleted matches. Dead pitches, slack over rates and persistent delays and interruptions cast a shadow of futility over the entire operation.

The first Test, at Lahore, was remarkable for Mudassar Nazar's 557-minute century, the slowest ever in any Test, and more attractive innings by Haroon, 122, and Miandad, 71. For England, who made 288 in reply to Pakistan's 407 for 9, Boycott stayed 5¾ for 63 and Geoff Miller made his

ABOVE In the 1977-78 series some dull cricket was reflected in dust-bag fights in the crowd at Karachi.

RIGHT Majid Khan and Shafiq Ahmed are the slips allowing Keith Fletcher to escape with a life at Headingley in 1974.

highest first-class score, 98 not out, to see his side to safety. Pakistan were 106 for 3 when play ended prematurely after the second crowd disturbance.

England had some anxious moments before the second Test, at Hyderabad, was drawn. Haroon, with another century, and Miandad, 88 not out, took Pakistan to 275, and the little leg-spinner Abdul Qadir confused the England batsmen, taking 6 for 44. Boycott made 79, but only three others reached double figures. Bari probably let Pakistan bat too long in their second innings. They declared at 259 for 4, and England allayed all anxiety by batting through most of the final day without losing a wicket, Brearley making 74 and Boycott 100 not out.

The Karachi Test, pointless in its palsied play, was overshadowed by events off the field. When there seemed a possibility that Pakistan might call up their Packer players it was revealed that some of the England team would refuse to take the field against them. After telephone calls to Lord's and statements by all and sundry, the danger receded, and fundamentally the same Pakistan as before did its bit to put spectators and radio listeners to sleep. England scored at hardly above two runs per 8-ball over in making 266, Roope 56, and Pakistan went on to a lead of 15, Mudassar top-scoring with 76 and Phil Edmonds taking 7 for 66. Boycott, replacing the injured Brearley as captain, and

Randall made fifties as England batted out the match for 222 for 5.

1978 in England

England 2   Pakistan 0   Drawn 1
This was the series in which Cornhill Insurance first sponsored Test matches and Ian Botham really established himself as a Test all-rounder. In the first Test at Edgbaston Pakistan were dismissed for 164, Old taking 7 for 50, including 4 in 5 balls. After Radley (106) and Gower (58) had established an England lead, Botham hit 100, and England declared at 452 for 8 wickets. Pakistan failed to avoid the innings defeat, being dismissed for 231 (Sadiq 79). In the second innings Willis controversially felled tail-ender Iqbal Qasim with a bouncer after Iqbal had resisted for 42 minutes as a night-watchman.

At Lord's England batted first when play began 45 minutes late on the second day. Gooch (54), Gower (56), Roope (69) and Botham (108) took the total to 364. Pakistan were rapidly dismissed for 105 (Willis 5 for 47, Edmonds 4 for 6), and following on were out for 139 after reaching 100 for 2. The damage was done on a fourth morning which favoured swing by Botham, whose 8 for 34 was the best Test analysis recorded at Lord's.

Rain ruined the final Test at Headingley, the Pakistan first innings of 201 (Sadiq 97) not finishing until the fourth afternoon. England made 119 for 7 (Sarfraz 5 for 39).

ABOVE Ian Botham makes Javed Miandad hop out of the way at Lord's in 1978. RIGHT Four years later leg-spinner and googly merchant Abdul Qadir was at Lord's. Botham was given not out.

1982 in England
England 2   Pakistan 1

In 1982 Pakistan followed India as tourists in England. Willis and Imran were the captains. Willis won the toss at Edgbaston for the first Test and batted. Randall and Lamb were soon out, and then a stand of 127 between Tavare (54) and Gower (74) provided the backbone of England's moderate 272 all out. Gower led a charmed life, and even played on without disturbing a bail. Imran's 7 for 52 was a reward for pace and control. Mudassar was out second ball when Pakistan batted, and although all the batsmen got started, only Mansoor Akhtar (58) passed 50, and Pakistan, at 251, ended 21 behind on first innings. Ian Greig claimed 4 for 53 in his first Test. England's second innings depended heavily on Randall, who hit 105 when all the other batsmen failed. At 212 for 9 it looked as if Pakistan were on top, but Taylor (54) and Willis (28 not out) then batted for over two hours to add 79 for the last wicket. Tahir Naqqash took 5 for 40, and Pakistan needed 313 to win. For the second time Mudassar was lbw to Botham on the second ball, and when the promoted Mansoor was out in the same over Pakistan were 0 for 2. When at 38 Javed was run out by Gatting at short leg as the momentum of his stroke took him out of his ground, Pakistan had little chance. Imran scored a

defiant 65, which, added to his bowling, won the Man of the Match award, but at 199 all out, Pakistan were beaten by 113.

At Lord's Gower captained England as Willis was injured. Pakistan chose to bat on an easy batting pitch and Mohsin, dropped twice, scored 159 not out on the first day, Pakistan at the close being 295 for 3. They built steadily on this base, Mohsin, the Man of the Match, going on to 200 and kissing the ground, after having had to wait through a four-hour rain stoppage on 199. Mansoor (57) and Zaheer (75) helped Pakistan to 428 for 8 declared. England began their innings on Saturday, but excellent bowling, mainly by leg-breaker Abdul Qadir (4 for 39) dismissed them for 227, the top scorer being extras with 46. England thus failed by two runs to avoid the follow-on and worse was to follow. On the first Sunday Test play at Lord's, Mudassar, hardly regarded even as a change bowler (he bowled four overs in the first innings) came on in the tenth over and captured Randall, Lamb and Gower in six balls without a run conceded: 9 for 3. It was a situation for Tavare, who batted 407 minutes for 82. Botham scored 69 (even he batted 202 minutes). With Mudassar coming back to claim more wickets (he finished with 6 for 32), England's last effort to avoid defeat was a last-wicket stand of 41 between Taylor and Jackman. It nearly succeeded. When England were all out 276 there were only 18 overs left. Pakistan needed 77 and Mohsin and Javed scored them without loss with nearly five overs to spare. It was Pakistan's second victory in England, 28 years after the first.

The final Test, the decider,

was played at Headingley, and was fought evenly throughout. Graeme Fowler and Vic Marks made England debuts; injuries to bowlers forced Pakistan to bring in Ehtesham-ud-Din from Daisy Hill, a Bolton Association side. Imran chose to bat, and after two wickets had gone for 19, Mudassar (65) and Javed (54) added exactly 100. Later Imran scored 67 not out and Pakistan finished on 275. The England batting did not get going until Botham entered at 77 for 4 and scored 57 out of 69 in 59 balls before being caught in the deep. Gower alone survived and scored 74, as in the first Test, but again, as in the first Test, he survived a confident appeal for a catch—Imran, after the match, was to complain about the umpiring. At 209 for 8, England were in trouble, but Jackman stubbornly stayed with Gower while 46 were added, and at 256 all out, England trailed by 19. Willis made the best possible start by dismissing both Pakistani openers for ducks in the second innings. Mansoor (39), Javed (a flashing 52) and Imran (46) brought some respectability to the batting, but overall it was not impressive, and a total of 199 left England to get 219 to win the series. Fowler and Tavare began with a stand of 103, and then the score proceeded to 168 without alarms when Mudassar got Fowler for 86. With Mudassar quickly getting three more wickets, England nearly lost the game from this strong position, six wickets going for 31 runs. At 199 for 7 Pakistan had the chance of effecting a sensational comeback, but Marks and Taylor, in the next 30 minutes, scored the 20 runs required for a three-wicket victory. Imran was Man of both Match and Series.

1983-84 in Pakistan

Pakistan 1   England 0   Drawn 2
England arrived for a three-match series in Pakistan after losing in New Zealand. The Tests were threatened by student disruption, and went ahead under heavy security precautions. In the first Test at Karachi Willis beat Zaheer in the toss and decided to bat. On a slow pitch no batsman mastered Qadir, and after Gower had made 58 the innings sank from mediocrity at 154 for 5 to paucity at 182 all out. Quadir took 5 for 74. Pakistan, after Mohsin scored 54, fared even worse for a while, and at one time stood at 138 for 6. Salim Malik then made 74, and Qadir (40) helped him add 75 for the seventh wicket. With the last wicket pair adding 37, Pakistan, at 277, had got 95 ahead. Nick Cook took 6 for 65. England's second-innings performance was worse than the first, Qadir again mesmerizing the batsmen. His figures of 3 for 59 did him less than justice —the England total of 159 all out did. Gower (57) was again the only batsman to score many. Needing only 65 for their first home win

against England, Pakistan batted nervously in face of another excellent spell from Cook, who took 5 for 18. Wickets fell regularly—at 40 for 6 it was anybody's match. Amil Dalpat, the debutant wicket-keeper, remained cool for 16 not out, however, and at 66 for 7 Pakistan had scraped home by three wickets.

Botham, who had played 65 consecutive Tests to equal Alan Knott's England record, missed the rest of the tour through an injured knee. Dilley, through injury, and captain Willis, through illness, did likewise, and all three returned home early. Before the second Test at Karachi, stories were being freely circulated in some English papers of some England players being involved with drugs during the earlier New Zealand tour. The stories were all denied. Gower led the weakened team in the second Test, which, unlike the first, was a batting feast. Pakistan went in first, and declared at 449 for 8, Salim Malik (116), Wasim Raja (112), Zaheer Abbas (65) and Abdul Qadir (50) being the principal scorers. England replied powerfully, Gower (152), Marks (83), Gatting (75), Chris Smith (66), Randall (65) and Fowler (57) allowing England to declare in turn at 546 for 8. The match was clearly drawn, Pakistan's second innings 137 for 4 being academic.

The final Test was exciting. Zaheer put England in at Lahore on a dampish pitch, and soon reduced them to 83 for 5. Fowler (58) and Marks (74) then fought back with a stand of 120 which took England to a final total of 241. Qadir had 5 for 84. Pakistan also started badly at 13 for 2 and despite 73 from Qasim Omar looked like being in arrears at 181 for 8. Sarfraz Nawaz played an astonishing innings of 90, although England thought he was caught behind early on. There were many disputed decisions in this match. Captain Zaheer (82 not out) stayed with Sarfraz in a ninth-wicket stand of 161, and Pakistan, at 343, were 102 ahead. Foster (5 for 67) was the most successful bowler. England were not disheartened and Gower played a captain's innings of 173 not out. With Gatting making 53 and Marks 55, England were able to declare at 344 for 9 (Qadir 5 for 110). Pakistan were set 243 to win in a generous 59 overs—but of course they did not have to chase the runs. Mohsin (104) and Shoaib Mohammad (80) batted easily in an opening stand of 173 in just over 3½ hours—in fact Pakistan needed only 99 from the last 20 overs with all wickets in hand. But Cowans (5 for 42) was recalled to bowl beautifully, six wickets crashed for 26 runs, and eventually Sarfraz (the Man of the Match) and Rameez put up the shutters, batting out the last half hour. At 217 for 6, the match was drawn, and Pakistan took the series.

ENGLAND v SRI LANKA

1981-82 in Sri Lanka

Sri Lanka 0   England 1
Elevated to full membership of the International Cricket Conference, Sri Lanka played their first Test match at the Saravanamuttu Oval, Colombo, on 17-21 February, 1982, against the England team which had recently toured India.

Geoff Cook made his Test debut. Warnapura won the toss and batted on a damp pitch, and was himself one of four batsmen dismissed while the score crept to 34. Madugalle (65) and Ranatunga (54) then added 99 in the biggest stand of the innings. Sri Lanka reached 218 (Underwood 5 for 28). England in turn lost three wickets reaching 40, and it took an innings of 89 from Gower, supported by Fletcher and Taylor, to enable England to pass the Sri Lanka total with their last pair together. The first innings lead was only five. At 160 for 3 on the fourth morning Sri Lanka seemed to have prospects of a shock win, thanks mainly to Dias (77). But then Emburey produced a spell of 5 for 5, and Sri Lanka lost their last seven wickets while adding eight runs. Emburey's final figures were 6 for 33 as Sri Lanka crashed to 175 all out, leaving England to score 171 to win. Tavare scored 85 and the target was reached with few alarms as England won by 7 wickets.

1984 in England

Drawn 1
Sri Lanka were expected to be the side which received the backlash of England's whitewash by the West Indies in 1984, but they provided a great surprise in the single Test.

Gower put Sri Lanka in, and Wettimuny played the longest innings in a Test match at Lord's —642 minutes. He batted into the third day as rain and bad light interrupted the first two. He made 190, while at the other end Ranatunga made 84 and then captain Mendis made 111. Sri Lanka finally declared at 491 for 7, the batting, if a little slow (just under 3 an over), being for the most part elegant, as all the batsmen showed a liking for the drive. When England saved the follow-on with five men out, the match was destined to be drawn. Broad (86), Gower (55) and Lamb (117) were the main scorers in a total of 370 (at just over 2½ per over). Sri Lanka batted out time, offering England no consolation, scoring 294 for 7 declared, with wicketkeeper and opener Amil Silva being 102 not out (his first first-class century), and Mendis scoring 94 from 97 balls. Botham took 6 for 90.

Mendis, who made over 200 runs in the match, hooks for four at Lord's in 1984. Tavare watches.

AUSTRALIA v SOUTH AFRICA

In a series of much excitement and memorable cricket, the pendulum has swung noticeably from one country to the other. In the first 50 years of Australia-South Africa encounters, South Africa won only one Test, but then in the next 20 years they won 13 to Australia's 8. There were two extraordinary series, in 1952-53 and again 11 years later, when South Africa, against all expectations, earned a draw. The Test ban on South Africa has prevented any series since 1969-70.

1902-03 in South Africa
South Africa 0   Australia 2
Drawn 1
The outbreak of war in South Africa in 1899 could scarcely have been expected to raise standards, but though hostilities dragged on into 1902, there was plenty of evidence of the keenness of the English-speaking population to restart and improve their cricket. It was then that the South African cricket authorities issued an invitation of great boldness and farsightedness. They invited Joe Darling's Australian side, then touring England, to return home by way of South Africa. The invitation was accepted, South African cricket surged forward from that time, and though well beaten in two of the three Test matches, the home side had their moments.

Australia, transplanted to matting from the turf pitches of England, where they had won the series, found themselves fielding while South Africa made 454 in the first Test in Johannesburg. L. J. Tancred made 97 and C. B.

Australia batting against South Africa at Old Trafford in the first match of the Triangular Tournament in 1912.

Llewellyn followed up an innings of 90 by taking 6-92. Australia, amazingly, had to follow on, but they had no trouble in saving the three-day match, and twice in the other two Tests bowled South Africa out for 85. South Africa's defeat in the last Test was delayed by a spectacular innings of 104 in 80 minutes by J. H. Sinclair, which included six sixes, but Australia won by 10 wickets and Darling took his side home having made a lasting contribution to South African cricket.

1910-11 in Australia
Australia 4   South Africa 1
When P. W. Sherwell took the first South African side to Australia in 1910, South Africa had enjoyed some years of success founded largely on the googly bowling of Ernest Vogler, Reginald Schwarz, and Aubrey Faulkner. But they proved less effective on Australian turf than at home on matting and in England. In addition, there was no genuine fast bowler, and the others could not stop Australia making hundreds of runs. In the first Test Warren Bardsley made 132 and Clem Hill 191. In the second Victor Trumper made 159, in the third 214 not out. Hill (100) and Warwick Armstrong (132) made hundreds in the fourth Test, and Macartney 137 in the fifth.

South Africa were not entirely eclipsed, for an innings of 204 by Faulkner kept the losing margin to 89 runs in the second Test (South Africa's innings were 506 and 80!) and they actually won the third in Adelaide. J. W. Zulch (105) and S. J. Snooke (103) made hundreds in the first innings, Faulkner made 115 in the second and on a deteriorating pitch on the sixth day Australia went down by 38 runs. It was

the last time for nearly 42 years that South Africa were to win a Test match against Australia.

1912 in England
Australia 2   South Africa 0
Drawn 1
The Triangular Tournament of 1912 has gone down in cricket history as a major disaster, but no one had a more disastrous season on the playing side than the South Africans, who lost all three Tests to England and the first two to Australia. They were still passing through a recession after the decline of the googly bowlers, and Australia outplayed them in the first Test at Old Trafford, winning by an innings. C. Kelleway (114) and Bardsley (121) made hundreds, and though Faulkner scored 122 not out for South Africa, T. J. Matthews performed the feat, by 1971 achieved only four times in first-class cricket history, of taking a hat-trick in each innings. Oddly he took no other wickets in the match.

In the second Test at Lord's, Kelleway (102) and Bardsley (164) again made hundreds and South Africa lost by 10 wickets. It was only in the third at Nottingham that they had any relief. The match was drawn after they had led by 110 runs on first innings.

1921-22 in South Africa
South Africa 0   Australia 1
Drawn 2
Once again South Africa was visited after a war by an Australian side that helped boost its cricket. But the Australian Imperial Forces side led by H. L. Collins did not, of course, play official Tests on its way home from England. Two years later, however, the triumphant Australians of 1921 also called on their way home and played three Tests. Warwick Armstrong had sustained an injury on the sea voyage, and so the side was again captained by Collins, who

made 203 in the second Test in Johannesburg.

The first two matches were drawn in Australia's favour, though C. N. Frank made 152 and the left-handed Dave Nourse 111 after South Africa had followed on in the second. Australia won the third in Cape Town by 10 wickets, Arthur Mailey taking 4-40 in the first innings and Charlie Macartney 5-44 in the second. Previously much of the damage had been done, as in England, by Jack Gregory and Ted McDonald.

1931-32 in Australia
Australia 5   South Africa 0
The 1930s were not an easy decade for South African cricket, which was slowly negotiating the change from matting to turf pitches at home. When they went to Australia in 1931, under the dashing wicket-keeper-batsman Jock Cameron, they were in no state to resist the genius of Don Bradman in his prime, and lost all five Tests by big margins—three by an innings, one by 10 wickets, and one by 169 runs.

Having begun by being caught on a bad pitch at Brisbane, a fate wont to befall weak sides, they finished on the worst of Melbourne sticky pitches, which reports say had been turned into a 'surface of treacle'. On the first day at Melbourne, South Africa were bowled out for 36 in less than 90 minutes, the slow left-arm bowler Bert Ironmonger taking 5-6. In fact, 10 batsmen contributed 17 runs between them, for Cameron made 11 and extras came to 8. Australia made only 153, but it was easily enough to give them victory by an innings. After a blank second day and a late start on the third, Ironmonger (6-18) and Bill O'Reilly (3-19) bowled South Africa out again in less than 90 minutes for 45. The whole match was over in 109 overs.

Bradman, injured in the field,

CLOCKWISE FROM ABOVE
Arthur Morris still has a long way to go as John Waite runs him out in 1952-53.
Mike Procter plays to leg in 1969-70, when he took a prominent part in Australia's 4-0 defeat.
Barry Richards was South Africa's opening batsman in that victorious series.
Eddie Barlow and Graeme Pollock, who made a third-wicket stand of 341 at Adelaide in 1963-64.
Richie Benaud bowling in his last Test match, that against South Africa at Sydney in 1963-64.
Keith Stackpole hooks and Ali Bacher, South Africa's captain in their last Test, ducks in 1969-70.
Dennis Lindsay, the South African wicket-keeper, enjoyed a successful series behind the stumps and with the bat in 1969-70. Australia's Doug Walters is driving.
Keeper Grout and bowler Benaud (joining forces here to dismiss Adcock) were Aussie successes in 1957-58.

did not bat in this match, but his previous scores—226, 112, 2 and 167, and 299 not out—gave him an average of 201.50.

1935-36 in South Africa
South Africa 0   Australia 4
Drawn 1
When the next Australian team went to South Africa, under Vic Richardson, the Springboks had every reason to hope they would do better, for they had just returned from winning their first series in England. But within a few days 'Jock' Cameron, a tower of strength in England, had died suddenly, and this melancholy event seemed to set the tone for what followed. Had it not rained during the second Test in Johannesburg, South Africa would have lost all five Tests. As it was, they lost three by an innings and one by nine wickets.

Australia seemed, by now, to have some jinx over South African cricket, which they had done much to foster. In particular, Australian spinners feasted on the South African batsmen—in this series Clarrie Grimmett took 44 wickets at 14 apiece and O'Reilly 27 at 17 each. With the bat Stan McCabe averaged 84 and Jack Fingleton 79. Dudley Nourse played a fine innings of 231 in the second innings of the drawn Test, but otherwise the encounter was a bitter disappointment for South Africans.

1949-50 in South Africa
South Africa 0   Australia 4
Drawn 1
The immediate post-war period was not the time to expect the balance to change, and Lindsay Hassett's Australian team had almost as easy a passage as its predecessor. The South African bowling was exceptionally thin,

Lee Irvine scored his only Test 100 in his country's last Test.

and the Australian batsmen Arthur Morris, Neil Harvey, Hassett, and others made hundreds of easy runs. In the drawn Test in Johannesburg J. A. R. Moroney made a hundred in each innings.

There was only one rough patch in Australia's triumphant passage —when they found themselves in danger of following on 236 runs behind in the third Test at Durban. After making 311 themselves, Eric Rowan 143, the Springboks had incredibly removed Australia for 75, thanks to a magnificent piece of off-spin bowling by Hugh Tayfield (7-23 in 8.4 overs). Dudley Nourse, the Springbok captain, had the weekend to decide whether to enforce the follow-on, and eventually he decided against it. South Africa were then bowled out for 99 by Bill Johnston (4-39) and Ian Johnson (5-34). Australia, needing 336 on a pitch not entirely reliable, made them with 25 minutes and five wickets to spare, Neil Harvey playing a superb innings of 151 not out. The Springboks must have wondered then if they would ever beat Australia again.

1952-53 in Australia
Australia 2   South Africa 2
Drawn 1
A defeat in England in 1951 did little to raise South African spirits, although there were promising young cricketers in Jackie McGlew, Roy McLean, John Waite, and Russell Endean. Yet they actually won two Tests and squared the series in Australia. Under the inspiring captaincy of Jack Cheetham, the young and athletic Springboks achieved a standard of fielding seldom seen before or since. They caught everything, and Hugh Tayfield emerged as a great off-spinner in Australian conditions.

The first Test went to Australia, though the Springboks, who had

not won a state match and had lost to New South Wales, did better than most people expected, and lost by only 96 runs. They then staggered the cricket world by winning the second Test, in Melbourne, their first victory over Australia for 42 years. They were slightly behind on the first innings, but Endean made 162 not out in the second innings and Tayfield (7-81) completed the triumph. Within a fortnight Australia had won the third Test by an innings, Neil Harvey (190) making the third of his four hundreds in the series, and when Australia had much the better of a draw in Adelaide, there was inevitably a tendency to write off South Africa's second-Test success as a flash in the pan.

But back at Melbourne they won one of the most glorious victories in Test history, for it was achieved after Australia, batting first, had made 520 in their first innings, Harvey 205. The Springboks scored consistently to reach 435, and then the fast bowler Eddie Fuller, with help from Tayfield and P. N. F. Mansell, dismissed Australia for 209. The Springboks still had to score 295 to win, and at 191-4 the match was in the balance. Then Roy McLean came in to make 76 out of 106 in 80 minutes, the match was won, and the rubber magnificently halved.

1957-58 in South Africa
South Africa 0   Australia 3
Drawn 2
When Ian Craig, aged only 22, took Australia's next team to South Africa, there was roughly the same cause for hope among South Africans as there had been in the 1930s, for South Africa had met with more success in England in 1955 than Australia had in 1956. But the bogey of Australian spin was not laid. Richie Benaud took 30 wickets and Lindsey Kline 15, and with Alan Davidson's 25 this was quite enough to defeat some

over-defensive South African batting. Mackay, who averaged 125, and Benaud easily covered up the moderate form of Craig and Neil Harvey.

Though South Africa began the first Test by making 470-9, they lost the second, could not press home a promising position in the third, when Neil Adcock and Peter Heine bowled Australia out in the first innings for 163, and easily lost the last two.

1963-64 in Australia
Australia 1   South Africa 1
Drawn 3
Once again South Africa's chances in Australia seemed hopeless and once again they amazed everybody by sharing the honours, this time through the fast bowling of Peter Pollock, the swing bowling of J. T. Partridge, and the exciting batting of their young stars, Eddie Barlow, Graeme Pollock, and Colin Bland. Only their fielding was below par.

The series began with a draw at Brisbane in a match made memorable by the calling of Ian Meckiff for throwing. Though Eddie Barlow made 109 and 54 in the second Test, Bill Lawry's 157 helped Australia win it comfortably by eight wickets. South Africa were by no means out of the running in the drawn third Test, and they followed with a magnificent 10-wicket victory won mainly by a historic third-wicket stand of 341 in 283 minutes between Barlow (201) and Graeme Pollock (175). With more enterprising captaincy by Trevor Goddard in the last Test, South Africa might have won the series, for they had much the better of the draw.

1966-67 in South Africa
South Africa 3   Australia 1
Drawn 1
So often had South Africa failed at home against Australia that when Bobby Simpson's team went there

AUSTRALIA v WEST INDIES

in 1966 many people envisaged another disappointment. But this time they picked the right teams, they were well led by Peter van der Merwe, their young batsmen destroyed the Australian spin, and Trevor Goddard, free of the captaincy, bowled magnificently to take 26 wickets.

Before the start of the Test series, excitement was kindled by Transvaal's victory over the Australians, the first ever over an Australian side in South Africa, and a series of much magnificent cricket was followed with intense enthusiasm. South Africa won a sensational first-Test victory in Johannesburg after Australia had passed their first innings total of 199 with only one wicket down. In the second innings the Springbok wicketkeeper Denis Lindsay played the first of three swashbuckling hundreds that tipped the scales at vital times—he was to score 606 runs in the series and take 24 catches. Australia won the second Test in Cape Town with 25 minutes and seven wickets to spare, in spite of Graeme Pollock's second innings 209. Of the last three, South Africa won two and would have won the other by the biggest margin of all but for rain. The scales had at last been tipped.

1969-70 in South Africa
South Africa 4   Australia 0
When Bill Lawry's team went to South Africa early in 1970 after a two-month tour of India, there were some who thought they would be more successful than their immediate predecessors, and that the Springboks, not having played Test cricket for three years, would be at a disadvantage. But to the heroes who had won the last series South Africa could now add Barry Richards and Mike Procter in their prime, and though Trevor Goddard was not the force of other days they won even more easily.

Australia's best chance was in the first Test at Newlands, where the pitches that season had been taking spin. But Ali Bacher won the toss, Eddie Barlow made 127, and South Africa, with more maturity of judgement than they had shown in the previous series, never lost their grip on a match they won by 170 runs. After that there seemed little hope for Australia on the other pitches, and their defeats were even more conclusive.

None was more devastating than that in the second Test in Durban. Richards, while making a superb 140, almost reached 100 before lunch on the first day, and Graeme Pollock made 274, the highest Test score by a South African. Australia were routed, and the cricket world was left regretting more than ever the factors outside cricket that prevented South Africa playing against all the other main cricketing countries in this golden era.

A ticker-tape farewell to a cricket team sounds like something out of sporting fiction. But that is what was given to Frank Worrell's West Indians in Melbourne after they had played—and lost—one of the most colourful series in Test history, in 1960-61. Australia v West Indies matches usually had an above-average share of incident and eventful cricket. The first series was in 1930-31, less than three years after West Indies had been accorded Test status, and they were still in a largely disorganized state of development. The various islands were several days' journey apart, and many

The farewell given to Frank Worrell's West Indian tourists at Melbourne after the exciting series in 1961-62.

members of the first side to Australia met each other for the first time on the voyage out.

1930-31 in Australia
Australia 4   West Indies 1
In spite of their inexperience and the renown of Bradman, just back from his first tour of England, the West Indians were far from apprehensive. They had three formidable fast bowlers in G. N. Francis, H. C. Griffith, and Learie Con-

stantine, who was also a spectacular all-rounder, and a great batsman in George Headley. They hoped for fast pitches, improvement from their lesser known players, and that their fallible slip-catching, one of the failings of their 1928 tour of England, had been repaired.

But like their equally hopeful successors 21 years later they were in for a disappointment. Their captain, G. C. Grant, a former Cambridge blue, made 50 not out in each innings, but the fast pitches they had been expecting were not forthcoming and the leg-spin of Clarrie Grimmett proved the decisive factor in the first Test. West Indies were caught on a wet pitch at Sydney in the second Test and beaten by an innings. A second-wicket stand of 229 and an innings of 223 by Bradman started them on the road to another innings defeat at Brisbane, though Headley made 102 not out in a total of 193. At Melbourne, Bradman made 152 after Bert Ironmonger (7-23) and Grimmett had bowled West Indies out for 99 and they lost by an innings again.

At the end of this gloomy first tour there was, however, one ray of light. In the last Test, at Sydney, West Indies found a faster pitch that was affected by rain more than once. They batted first, scoring 350-6 through 123 not out by F. R. Martin and 105 by Headley. Grant was able to declare twice when it suited him, and with his fast bowlers enjoying a damp, lively pitch, West Indies won their first victory over Australia by 30 runs.

1951-52 in Australia
Australia 4   West Indies 1
In the 21 years between the first and second series West Indian cricket had made big advances to the era of the three 'Ws' and of Ramadhin and Valentine. Australia were still strong, retaining the bulk of the great 1948 side, but Bradman had retired, and West Indies, still fresh from their English triumphs of 1950, travelled with some confidence. Nevertheless, the result was the same, a 4-1 defeat and a grievous disappointment. Mostly the damage was done by the Australian fast bowlers, Ray Lindwall, Keith Miller, and Bill Johnston, who were too much for the main West Indian batsmen. Sonny Ramadhin was not a force on Australian pitches, though the left-arm spinner Alf Valentine took 24 Test wickets at 28 apiece. The downfall of the three 'Ws' was complete, for Frank Worrell averaged only 33, Everton Weekes 24, and Clyde Walcott 14. Their performance was typical of the general inability of John Goddard's side to adapt themselves.

Australia won the first Test only by three wickets, but Lindsay Hassett and Miller made hundreds in the second, which was won by seven wickets. By now the West

Indian batsmen were in some trouble against the bumpers of Lindwall and Miller, but their luck changed temporarily over Christmas at Adelaide. The third Test there began on a wet pitch, and Gerry Gomez, Worrell (6-38), and Goddard bowled Australia out for 82. Before the end of the first day West Indies had themselves been bowled out for 105 and Australia had lost two second innings wickets. On the third day, Christmas Day, West Indies needed 233 to win, and with Australia not holding their chances, they won by six wickets.

Australia clinched the rubber with a thrilling win by one wicket at Melbourne. No innings total exceeded 300, and Australia needed 260 to win in the last innings on a pitch taking some spin. A brilliant innings of 102 by Hassett, the Australian captain, took Australia a long way towards victory, and though the odds always seemed to be slightly on West Indies, a last-wicket stand of 38 between Doug Ring and Bill Johnston, who took advantage of questionable field-placing, won the match. After their narrow

escape, Australia won the last Test easily.

1954-55 in West Indies
West Indies 0   Australia 3
Drawn 2

Australia's first visit to the Caribbean was made immediately after they had lost a home series against Len Hutton's England team. The tour came unusually late in the West Indian season, from March to June, and the Australians were highly popular. They also made a lot of runs, Neil Harvey and Keith Miller making three Test hundreds each. For West Indies Clyde Walcott made no less than five, including one in each innings of the second and fifth Tests. But the spin of Richie Benaud and Ian Johnson, plus the fast bowling of Lindwall and Miller, was too much for the other West Indian batsmen.

Australia easily won the first, third and fifth Tests and had the better of two draws in between. Injury prevented Jeff Stollmeyer

LEFT Conrad Hunte, West Indies' leading opening batsman of the 1960s, the chief scorer in his country's first victory over Australia at home.

TOP Guillen runs out Hassett at Melbourne in 1951-52. Australia won by one wicket.
ABOVE It was a tie in 1960-61 when Meckiff was run out.

from captaining West Indies for more than two Tests, a serious loss, though his deputy Dennis Atkinson shared in a remarkable world record for the seventh wicket, adding 347 with C. Depeiza (122) at Bridgetown in the fourth Test. They batted more than a day together, and Atkinson scored 219.

1960-61 in Australia
Australia 2   West Indies 1
Tie 1   Drawn 1

There was little in the early stages of the West Indies tour of 1960-61 to suggest that one of the great Test series of cricket history was about to take place. Australia, under Richie Benaud, were on the crest of a wave and West Indies were climbing back after the failure of 1957 in England. Frank Worrell had taken over the captaincy from Gerry Alexander.

The tour began with a defeat by Western Australia, and though Victoria were beaten mainly by spin, New South Wales beat the tourists by an innings, and no one

rated their chances highly in Brisbane. They began well, however, making 453, Sobers 132, but Normal O'Neill scored 181 and Australia led by 52 on the first innings. Alan Davidson, then in his prime as an all-rounder, bowled well in West Indies' second innings, and Australia eventually needed 233 to win at 45 an hour. When they were 92-6, they looked beaten but a rousing partnership developed between Davidson (80) and Benaud (52). When it had added 134 and only 7 runs were needed, the match seemed over, and in fact many people left to catch their trains or aircraft for home.

Wes Hall, with his long run, had slowed up the advance by taking the new ball when 27 were needed in 30 minutes, and with this in mind Benaud was encouraged to call for a quick single. Davidson became the first of three batsmen run out—by a throw from Joe Solomon at mid-wicket. As it proved, there was time for only one more over, and in the seven

balls Hall bowled, three wickets fell.

Six runs were needed at the start of the over and Wally Grout acquired a leg-bye off the first. Off the second Benaud was caught at the wicket for 52, and off the fourth Ian Meckiff and Grout ran a bye to the wicket-keeper. Off the fifth Grout survived a high chance to the bowler and a run resulted. The sixth saw a remarkable piece of cricket. Meckiff hit the ball hard and high towards the leg boundary and was starting the third run, which would give victory to Australia, when the nimble Conrad Hunte threw in from the boundary. The throw was perfect and Grout was just run out. Lindsay Kline, the last man, came in with the scores level and two balls to go. He hit the first towards square-leg and Meckiff, who had been backing up fast, seemed certain to get home. But Solomon again threw down the wicket, this time with only one stump in view, and the match went into history as the first tied Test.

This set the tone for all that followed. Public interest had been won to an unparalleled degree, and most of the cricket did not disappoint the big crowds. West Indies, not at their best in the second Test, also had the worst of the wicket, and Australia won by seven wickets. The third Test in Sydney, however, produced a complete change, for after Gary Sobers had played a brilliant innings of 168 on the first day, Lance Gibbs took the first three of his eight wickets in the match and West Indies won a substantial first innings lead. This was soon extended, thanks to wicket-keeper Gerry Alexander's 108. Gibbs, Valentine, and Sobers bowled Australia out in the last innings on a pitch taking spin and West Indies won by 222 runs.

In the breathless later stages of the fourth Test in Adelaide, West Indies seemed certain to take the lead in the series. They had made a good start, Rohan Kanhai scoring the first of his two hundreds in the match, and when Australia batted Lance Gibbs performed the first hat-trick recorded against Australia in the 20th century. Worrell declared the second innings leaving Australia to make 460 in 6½ hours and when they soon lost 3 wickets for 31 their chances seemed slim. By tea they were slimmer still, and the ninth wicket fell with 110 minutes left. But with runs of no importance, Ken Mackay and Kline played out time and Australia earned a draw.

So, with the series level, all depended on the last Test at Melbourne. On the first day, Benaud put West Indies in, and when, on the second day, Bobby Simpson and Colin McDonald made 146 before a world record crowd of over 90,000 all appeared to be going to Australian plans. But Gibbs and Sobers worked through the batting to restore a balance

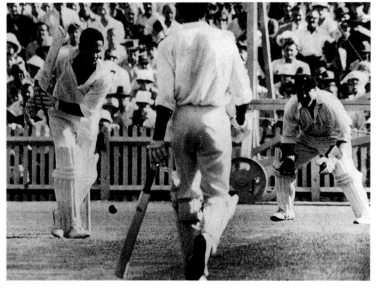

LEFT Doug Walters finally bowled by Gibbs for 242 at Sydney in 1968-69.
BELOW Skipper Gary Sobers batting on the 1968-69 tour.

ABOVE Lance Gibbs' hat-trick at Adelaide in 1960-61 was the first against Australia this century. Gibbs went on to a record total of 309 Test wickets.

fascinatingly maintained almost throughout the match, until Australia, needing 258, got home by two wickets and won.

1964-65 in West Indies
West Indies 2 Australia 1
Drawn 2

After 1960-61 there was bound to be anticlimax, and the next series was a disappointment. West Indies, at the pinnacle of a golden era, were clearly the better side, winning two of the first three Tests. But the series was marred by Australian criticism of the dubious bowling action of Charlie Griffith. In the fourth Test in Barbados, Australia made 650-6, Bill Lawry (210) and Bobby Simpson (201) beginning the match with a stand of 382 that did not end until well into the second day. But they could not win the match, and it was in vastly different conditions that they won at Port-of-Spain by 10 wickets with three days to spare. Though West Indies batted first, Australia adapted themselves better by far to a pitch of eccentric bounce.

1968-69 in Australia
Australia 3 West Indies 1
Drawn 1

The next visit of West Indies to Australia had been eagerly awaited, but when it came their fortunes were fading. Hall and Griffith were on the wane, and history shows that ageing fast bowlers have little success in Australia. West Indies began by winning the first Test on a pitch that deteriorated, but thereafter the batting of Lawry (667 runs), Ian Chappell (548), and Doug Walters (699) was too powerful.

Australia won comfortable victories in the second and third Tests and made a bold effort to score 360 in 5¾ hours on the last day of the fourth Test. When they were 304-3 they seemed likely to do it but four run-outs upset them and they eventually survived with their last pair at the crease 21 runs short. They easily won the last Test, when their batting and fielding were even more superior to West Indies' than before, and they acquired a reputation that took a rout in South Africa and a narrower defeat at home by England to deflate.

1972-73 in West Indies
West Indies 0 Australia 2
Drawn 3

Australia, playing positive and aggressive cricket, generally batted with more consistency than the home country. Their win in the series was some consolation for losing their main bowling weapon, Dennis Lillee, with a serious back injury after the first Test.

In that match Doug Walters recaptured some of the form that had totally deserted him in England in 1972, making 72 in 100 minutes. Foster replied with 125 and then Stackpole hit 142 in Australia's second innings—the match

ABOVE Lance Gibbs bowling at Melbourne during the 1975-76 series where he broke Fred Trueman's record of 307 Test wickets.

BELOW Greenidge falls to Thomson at Melbourne in the crucial third Test. Australia won by eight wickets and took a firm grip on the series.

was by then a certain draw.

West Indies were led by Rohan Kanhai in place of the injured Gary Sobers who missed his first Test since 1955. Kanhai hit 105 in the drawn second Test in which both Chappells and Doug Walters all reached their centuries.

Walters also made a century in the next match, which was the West Indies' for the taking when, chasing 334, they had reached 268 for 4. But the last five wickets fell for only 21 to put Australia one up.

The fourth Test was theirs also when fast bowlers Hammond and the tall Max Walker skittled West Indies for 109 after an even first innings in which Lloyd and Ian Chappell had made hundreds. Australia won this Test by 10 wickets.

Chappell understandably played safe in Port-of-Spain in the fifth Test, in which Walker had five more victims in the first innings, finishing with 26 wickets in a tremendous personal series.

1975-76 in Australia
Australia 5 West Indies 1

Under their new captain Greg Chappell, Australia, in the final analysis, routed West Indies in a contest between the two most successful cricketing sides in the world at the time.

In fact, at one game all the series was finely balanced, but once the West Indies lost the initiative their surrender in the face of some hostile bowling from Lillee, Thomson and Gilmour was total.

Chappell began his new responsibilities in classic style with two match-winning centuries at Brisbane. Although Rowe and Kalli-

charran both made hundreds in an attempt to restore the balance, Australia won by eight wickets.

At Perth, West Indies exacted immediate revenge thanks to Roberts' destructive 7 for 54 which bowled Australia out for 169 in their second innings. Ian Chappell had begun the game with a fine 156, but 169 from Fredericks and 149 from Lloyd created the situation which Roberts successfully exploited.

After being bowled out on the first day of the third Test by Thomson and Lillee for a mere 224, West Indies never regained the initiative. An old stager, Redpath and a debutant, Cosier, scored centuries in reply, and although Lloyd, batting ridiculously low at number six, also reached three figures, Australia were home by 8 wickets.

The West Indian batsmen failed again in the fourth Test at Sydney. Greg Chappell had rallied his side to a lead with a supreme innings of 182 not out. Then Thomson, 6 for 50, bowled West Indies out for a mere 128 and this time the Australian margin of victory was seven wickets.

Technically the series was decided at Adelaide, where Australia won by 190 runs after West Indies marred their own chances with uncharacteristic sloppy fielding. Substantial batting by Redpath, Turner and Gilmour set their opponents 489 to win. Although Richards again reached three figures and Boyce resisted for the second time in the match, Australia won convincingly.

The only consolation for the demoralized West Indies in the sixth Test came when Lance Gibbs dismissed Redpath for 101 and so beat Trueman's record of 307 Test wickets. Lillee and Gilmour destroyed their first innings and Lillee and Thomson their second after McCosker had made 109 not out for Australia. When Marsh ended the match by catching Gibbs, he equalled the Test record of 26 victims in a series.

1977-78 in West Indies
West Indies 3 Australia 1 Drawn 1
It was widely feared that the West Indian pace battery and mighty batting line-up would be too much for Simpson's coltish Australian XI, and so it turned out—until the withdrawal of World Series players from the third-Test team.

The first Test was a disaster for Australia. Put in by Lloyd, they crashed for 90 against Roberts, Croft and Garner on a deplorable Port-of-Spain pitch. West Indies made 405 after a robust start by newcomer Desmond Haynes, who made 61. Kallicharran scored 127 and Lloyd, who himself seemed to think he was caught behind for 26, went on to 86. Australia fell second time round for 209, Yallop making 81 and Roberts taking 5 for 56, having put Toohey out of the match in the first innings by first cutting his brow then following up by fracturing a thumb.

At Bridgetown the beleaguered Australians again lost inside three days, managing only 250 and 178 against 288 and 141 for 1. Wood, the promising left-hander, made 69 and 56, and Yardley thrashed 74, but the fast bowlers held command, Roberts, Croft and Garner taking 18 wickets. Haynes entertained again with 66 and 55, and for Australia Thomson bowled valiantly to take 6 for 77, but Greenidge wafted his side to comfortable victory with an attractive 80 not out.

The dropping of Haynes and Austin for the third Test prompted a suspicious Clive Lloyd and five other World Series players to pull out of the side. The upheaval tended soon to be forgotten as youngsters from both sides proceeded to cover themselves in glory in a sterling contest. West Indies led off with 205, to which Australia replied with 286. In their second innings, both Basil Williams, in his first Test, and Larry Gomes made maiden Test centuries, and Shivnarine his second half-century, as the home side amassed 439. This left Australia 359 for victory, a task they accomplished after losing their first three wickets for 22. Wood and Serjeant added a record 251, both making their first Test hundreds, and the runs were gathered with three wickets to spare.

The inexperienced West Indies side, now led by Kallicharran, fought back in its turn. In Trinidad the first three innings were even: West Indies 292 and 290, Australia 290, with Kallicharran, 92, Williams, 87, Alvin Greenidge, 69, Parry, 65, and Yallop, 75, all prospering. But on the fourth day Australia fell apart for 94 against the spin of Jumadeen and Parry, who took 5 for 15. The Sir Frank Worrell Trophy was

Clive Lloyd's century at Melbourne in 1975-76 could not save his side from defeat.

thus regained by West Indies.

Australia were on the verge of pulling a game back in the last Test, but the Kingston crowd, or a section of it, demonstrated violently on the last afternoon after Holder had shown disagreement at his dismissal, and the match was abandoned with Australia one wicket from victory. Toohey took the batting honours with 122 and 97, and Wood made 90. For West Indies, Gomes and Kallicharran scored hundreds, while Laughlin took 5 for 101.

1979-80 in Australia
Australia 0 West Indies 2 Drawn 1
Australia entertained both England and West Indies in 1979-80, playing three Tests alternately against each country, beginning with West Indies. It was the first

series in which the Australians selected their World Series players after the peace with Kerry Packer. Eight WSC players were in Australia's twelve for the first Test at Brisbane, with Greg Chappell resuming as captain. West Indies had injury problems. Captain Lloyd was unable to play and Richards and Greenidge played with injuries. Deryck Murray assumed the captaincy, won the toss and put Australia in. Bruce Laird, making his Test debut, opened and made top score of 92. Greg Chappell, who made 74 and shared a third-wicket stand with Laird of 130, was the only other batsman to pass 50 as Australia reached only 268 against the West Indian fast bowlers. When West Indies replied, Richards, batting with an injured hip and offering two return chances to Hogg,

soon after passing 50, eventually reached 140. He was well supported by the other batsmen in the top five, especially Rowe (50), and West Indies passed Australia's total with only three men out, and went on to 441, including 56 for the last wicket, nearly all scored by Garner (60), who hit four sixes and three fours after giving a first ball caught-and-bowled chance to Bright. Australia batted much better in their second innings, with Laird making 75 and sharing another century stand with Chappell, who went on to 124. Hughes made 130 not out and Chappell declared at 448 for 6, giving West Indies a token hour's batting, during which they made 40 for 3. Richards was Man of the Match.

Lloyd returned as West Indies captain for the second Test at Melbourne. Both he and Chappell

complained of the grassless pitch, expected to crumble and help spinners. Nevertheless Lloyd stuck to his pace battery, and Chappell decided to bat. After getting to lunch at 68 for 1, Australia collapsed badly and could reach only 156 all out. The West Indies knocked off 103 of these in 84 minutes by the close, and next day reached Australia's score before the second wicket fell. Richards, made Man of the Match for the second successive time, scored 96, and with runs coming from all the first nine batsmen (Roberts 54), West Indies totalled 397. The lead of 241 was too much for Australia. Laird stayed 4½ hours for 69 after being hit on the hand, and Hughes made 70, but the score of 259 left West Indies only 19 to get, which they did without loss.

Chappell, having led his side

twice to victories over England, was attempting at Adelaide to prevent the West Indies first series victory in Australia. Ian Chappell and Mallett returned to strengthen the side. Chappell put West Indies in, but only one early wicket fell. Richards hit 76 from 72 balls. At 126 for 4 the match had swung back to Australia, but Lloyd, in what was announced as his last Test in Australia (it was not), played a forcing innings of 121 which won him the Man of the Match award, and West Indies reached 328 (Lillee 5 for 78). Roberts got the Chappells with successive balls to reduce Australia to 26 for 3, and although Laird and Border showed their usual courage in scoring 52 and 54 respectively, Australia were dismissed for 203. With plenty of time left, West Indies built up their

Little Christmas spirit was shown the Australians by Holding, who quickly grabbed three wickets, including Chappell's for 0, and Australia were 26 for 4. Hughes then played a courageous innings which made him Man of the Match. Despite being hit by the fast bowlers and giving two difficult chances, he scored 100 not out, the last 29 coming in a last-wicket stand which added 43. He scored over half of Australia's meagre 198 (Holding 5 for 45). But before stumps Lillee, with three wickets, had reduced West Indies to 10 for 4. One was the night-watchman, but another was Richards. Gomes (55) led a recovery next day, but at 201 all out, the West Indies led by only three. Lillee's 7 for 83 was his best in Test cricket. Laird (64) and Wood (46) put on 82 for Australia's first wicket, and Border returned to form with 64, allowing Australia to reach 222. Holding took 6 for 62 to claim 11 for the match. Asked to score 220 to win, West Indies made another bad start, Alderman having two men out for 4, including Richards for a duck. On a wicket of unpredictable bounce, their last chance went when 150 for 6 became 154 for 9, and at 161 all out Australia had won by 58 runs.

At Sydney, Lloyd decided to bat on a better wicket, and the scoreboard soon assumed a more familiar state. Only Haynes of the top six batsmen failed to reach 40, Greenidge getting 66 and Gomes 126. West Indies reached a respectable 584. After Wood scored 63, Australia went from 108 for 1 to 172 for 7, before Border (53 not out) helped by Yardley (45)

hoisted the score to 267. Yardley made a brilliant catch to dismiss Greenidge when West Indies batted again, and helped by more good catching then returned his best career figures of 7 for 98, which won him the Man of the Match award. Haynes (51) and Lloyd (57) passed the half-century in West Indies' 255. With 104 on the board for the first wicket, there was a possibility that Australia would go for the 373 needed to win, but Chappell's dismissal for a duck stopped those ideas. Dyson made 127 not out as Australia drew at 200 for 4.

The third Test, at Adelaide, was an exciting battle as West Indies fought hard to level the series. They put Australia in and achieved the first objective when Holding and Roberts had the home side reeling at 17 for 4. Chappell (61) then played a good innings at last and put on 105 with Border, who made a courageous 78. Marsh weighed in with 39, but the Australian's 238 was disappointing. Holding took 5 for 72. The West Indies' reply depended on three stands involving Gomes (124 not out): 102 for the fifth wicket with Lloyd (53), 89 for the seventh with Dujon (51) and 82 for the eighth with Roberts (42). Yardley took 5 for 132 as West Indies took a lead of 151 at 389 all out. Australia made a spirited reply. After two wickets had gone for 35, Laird (78) and Border (126, and Man of the Match) added 166 and took Australia ahead. With Hughes scoring 84 and Marsh 38, Australia reached a lead on the last day of over 200 with six wickets standing, and began to think not only of a draw but a possible win, but then

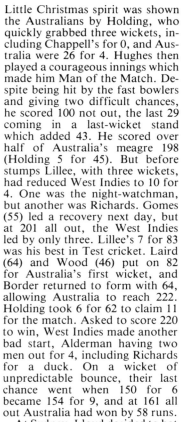

Graham Yallop was the first batsman to wear a helmet in a Test—at Bridgetown, 1977-78.

Garner (5 for 56) struck and the last six wickets went for 24 runs. West Indies needed 236 in 255 minutes, and although Haynes left early, Greenidge (52) and Richards (50) put them on course, and appropriately captain Lloyd saw them home on 239 for 5 wickets with an innings of 77 not out.

1983-84 in West Indies
West Indies 3   Australia 0
Drawn 2
Australia arrived in the West Indies without Greg Chappell, Lillee and Marsh, the first two having retired after the visit of Pakistan, and Marsh first announcing his unavailability for the West Indies, then his own decision to retire. Hughes captained Australia, and the indestructible Lloyd the West Indies.

In the first Test at Georgetown, Hughes won the toss, batted, but in an innings that spread over most of two days Australia struggled before Garner (6 for 75). Only Ritchie (78) played him well until the score reached 182 for 9, whereupon Hogan (42 not out) and Hogg (52) added 97—the highest 10th wicket stand in matches between the countries. West Indies batted slightly better throughout, with Haynes getting 60, but without a last-wicket stand like Australia's were all out 230—49 behind. Lawson was fined for dissent following a brush with an umpire. On the fourth morning Garner and Daniel ripped out five Australians for 60, but another fight back by Border (54), Wayne

Alvin Kallicharan is caught by Rodney Marsh in the third Test at Trinidad in 1972-73, one of the tall Max Walker's 26 victims in the series which Australia won by two matches to nil.

lead. Greenidge (76), Richards (74) and Kallicharran (106) piled on the runs until the side was out for 448 (Dymock 5 for 104). Australia were left to get 574 in a day and a half, but, thoroughly demoralised, were all out early on the fifth day for 165, the four fast bowlers sharing the wickets.

1981-82 in Australia
Australia 1   West Indies 1
Drawn 1
Lloyd and Chappell were captains again in 1981-82, when the first Test began on Boxing Day at Melbourne. Chappell decided to bat.

Greg Chappell made 106 in the Bridgetown Test of 1972-73.

Phillips (76) and Lawson (35 not out) allowed Hughes to declare on the last day at 273 for 9, setting West Indies 323 in 200 minutes plus 20 overs. Greenidge and Haynes now asserted their authority, scoring 120 not out and 103 not out, but Australia bowled only 45 overs in the 200 minutes and the chase was called off at 250 for 0. It was poetic justice for West Indies, whose fast bowlers had annoyed world cricket watchers for years with their slow over rate, and whose officials had rejected a 90-overs minimum for a day's play.

Allan Border was emphatically Man of the Match at Port-of-Spain. As in the first Test, Garner struck early on a rain-shortened first day. Australia, put in, were 16 for 3 and 85 for 5, and they only reached 255 on the second day thanks to Border, who ran out of partners on 98 not out. Dean Jones, in his first Test, was his main helper with 48. Garner took 6 for 60, including the first five. With Haynes getting 53 and Richards (captain in Lloyd's absence) 76, West Indies passed this total with five wickets standing, and made the most of them when Logie (97) and Dujon (130) raised the score to 468 for 8 declared. When three men were out for 55 overnight, Australia's chances of a draw looked small, and although night-watchman Hogan got 38, and Garner and Daniel were absent ill, their chances looked to have vanished at 196 for 8, still 17 behind with half a day to play. But Border was still there, and with Hogg he added 42 in 55 minutes. Then Alderman scored 21 not out in 105 minutes, Border reached 100 not out, and the game was drawn at 299 for 9. West Indies got

ABOVE Gordon Greenidge hits Yardley for six at Bridgetown in 1977-78, before the Packer West Indians withdrew.

only one of the last two wickets in nearly three hours' play while 103 were added. Border scored 198 in the match without being out.

The third Test at Bridgetown saw a reversal of fortunes. Australia, put in by Lloyd, batted down the order for 10 hours to get 429. Wood (68) and Ritchie (57) put on 103 for the second wicket, but the star was wicket-keeper Wayne Phillips, last out with 120, batting at number eight and virtually monopolising the scoring as 99 was added for the last two wickets. However, Haynes (145) and Greenidge (64) put on 132 for the first wicket, then Richardson (132 not out) helped Haynes add 145 for the second. Lloyd (76) helped Richardson take the score past the Australian total with a sixth-wicket stand of 131, and West Indies totalled 509 (Hogg 6 for 77), a lead of 80. The match looked a draw, but West Indies got four Australians for 65 before the close, with Smith and Wood forced to have X-rays afterwards —Wood had a broken finger. On the last day, on a pitch now untrustworthy, Holding and Marshall ran through the rest of the Australians, who were all out 97. Marshall (5 for 42) was Man of the Match. West Indies needed only 18, and scored them without loss.

At St John's, Antigua, Aus-

tralia batted weakly after winning the toss, and were all out 262 (Border 98, Hookes 51). Lawson dismissed the West Indian openers for 42, but then Richardson (154) and Richards (178) added 308. Both batsmen are Antiguans. Richardson was dropped at 38. West Indies made 498, and Australia needed 236 to avoid an innings defeat. After an opening stand of 50, they could reach only 200 all out, top scorer being extras. Richards was Man of the Match.

The final Test, at Kingston, was little better for the Aussies. Put in, they made 199. Haynes (60) and Man of the Match Greenidge (127) opened with a stand of 162, but at least Richards (run out) and Richardson were dismissed for 2 between them (330 fewer than in the previous innings). West Indies were restricted to 305, but only Border (60 not out) played the fast bowling battery with confidence in the second innings. Smith, like Wood in an earlier match, had had his finger broken by the short-pitched bowling in the first innings and could not bat in the second. Australia totalled only 160 and Greenidge and Haynes knocked them off without loss. Indeed, West Indies had not lost a second-innings wicket throughout the series. Garner, with 31 wickets, was Man of the Series.

ABOVE Vivian Richards drives in the third Test at Adelaide in 1979-80. West Indies took the series 2-0, and Richards scored nearly 400 runs in his four innings.
OPPOSITE Clive Lloyd after the third Test at Adelaide in 1979-80, with the Frank Worrell Trophy, for which Australia and West Indies compete.

1984-85 in Australia
Australia 1   West Indies 3
Drawn 1
Having demolished England 5-0 in 1984 to run up a string of eight successive Test victories, West Indies were back in Australia. Lloyd was still captain.

Put in by Hughes in the first Test at Perth, they reached 83 safely (Haynes 56). Then Alderman took 4 for 5 as they slumped to 104 for 5. Gomes (127) and Dujon (139) advanced the score to 335 in a good stand, although a wicket fell at 186, during a spell when Dujon had temporarily retired hurt. West Indies were eventually 416 all out (Alderman 6 for 128). Australia, on Saturday night and Sunday morning, crashed to 76 all out, with Holding being chosen Man of the Match for his

6 for 21 destruction. Australia followed on, and batted a little better, reaching 228 (Wood 56). West Indies did not need to bat again, and had now not lost a second-innings wicket to Australia for six Tests.

Brisbane was the scene of the second Test and Kim Hughes' resignation. Australia were put in and out in short order, the West Indian quickies dismissing them for 175. West Indies stood at 184 for 5 early on the second day but Richardson (138) and Lloyd (a rapid 114) added 152. Marshall got 57, and with 424 West Indies were 249 ahead. Australia passed this total with eight wickets down. Wessels (61), Boon (51 in his first Test) and Phillips (54) were the main scorers. Lawson twice trod on his stumps during his innings and each time was given not out. West Indies needed to make 23, but their sequence of not losing a second-innings wicket ended, as Haynes and Richardson were out. Haynes and Lawson had exchanged words throughout Haynes' 34-minute innings, and when bowled by Lawson Haynes made a rude gesture. Lloyd, Man of the Match, deprecated the incident in his post-match speech,

but his rival captain, Hughes, provided the sensation. He resigned the captaincy on the grounds of lacking the support of officials, selectors and team, breaking down in tears in the middle of reading his prepared statement before the television cameras. It appeared that cricketing politics had made his position impossible.

Hughes was in the team for the third Test at Adelaide, where Allan Border took over as captain. West Indies batted and their innings was a strange mixture. Four players, Greenidge (95), Gomes (60), Lloyd (78) and Dujon (77) scored 310 runs between them— the remainder, 34. With 12 extras, West Indies made 356. Lawson took 8 for 112, his best Test performance and was Man of the Match. Having dropped Greenidge twice and Dujon before he'd scored, Australia missed an opportunity to take the initiative. Their batting was also patchy. Wessels, having retired hurt earlier, went on to 98, but five players failed to reach double figures, and the final total of 284 was helped by 36 extras (including 26 no-balls). Haynes scored 50 in West Indies' second knock and Gomes 120 not out. Lloyd declared at 292 for 7,

leaving Australia to get 365 to win. Wessels top-scored for the second time with 70, and Marshall took 5 wickets for the second time (his first instance of 10 in a Test match). Australia were dismissed for 173, losers by 191 runs. There was again bad feeling between some of the rival players.

Melbourne is not a successful ground for West Indies, and put in by Border they were not too happy at 154 for 5, with Craig McDermott getting three of them on his debut, including Richardson (51) and Gomes (68). But Richards remained, and he found support in Marshall (55). Between them they added 139 for the seventh wicket. Richards had scored 208 when he was last out. West Indies were 479. Hilditch, recalled by Australia after five years, made 70 and with Wessels (90) added 123 for the second wicket, but extras, with 35, equalled Border as next highest scorer. The last pair, newcomer Murray Bennett and Hogg, did, however, add 43 and save the follow-on.

Beginning 183 ahead, West Indies lost Greenidge, lbw to Lawson, at 2, which sparked off more trouble. Greenidge later spoke privately to Lawson and the West

Allan Border cover-drives. Border took over the Australian captaincy in mid-series when Kim Hughes resigned after the second Test of 1984-85.

Indies management made an official protest about Lawson's behaviour and language, both to Greenidge and an umpire. Lawson was later fined. Lloyd misjudged his declaration in this match, batting on for 15 minutes on the last day before declaring at 186 for 5, leaving Australia to get an impossible 370 to win. Garner dismissed Wood, Wessels and Hughes, all at 17. Hughes lasted three balls in this match for 0 runs —since his resignation as captain he had scored 2 in four innings, and was dropped. Hilditch and Border batted grittily, however, Hilditch for 339 minutes, scoring 113, which won him selection as Man of the Match. Lloyd took the new ball for the last two overs, but Australia held out at 198 for 8. The 25 minutes wasted at the beginning of the day might well have meant the difference between victory and the stretching of a record 11-match winning sequence, and the draw which ended it.

At Sydney Border was persuaded to bat by his New South Wales colleagues, particularly spinners Bennett and Holland. It was probably the decisive move in the match. Wood and Wessels got Australia off to a good start with a second wicket stand of 114, although both were missed. The score was 338 before the third wicket fell, an addition of 212, but Ritchie had retired injured (struck in the face) at 30 during this session, and it was Border (69) who completed the stand with Wessels. Wessels was struck repeatedly on the body but stuck doggedly to the crease until he had scored 173. On the third day Border declared at 471 for 9. McDermott got two wickets, but then the spinners, Holland and Bennett, who had been instrumental in New South Wales' earlier defeat of West Indies, ran through the side: all out 163 (Holland 6 for 54) and following on. It was a similar story in the second innings. Richards (58) and Lloyd (72) offered some resistance for the sake of pride, but seven wickets shared by the spinners saw West Indies out for 253 and victory for Australia by an innings and 55. Holland, a 38-year-old who had retired once and been recalled, was Man of the Match, in which he'd taken 10 wickets. Marshall was chosen Player of the Series. There was more acrimony. Border, Rixon and Richards were reported by the umpires for abusive language following a decision given in Richards' favour. Later both sides claimed the other as the sinners. West Indies' unbeaten 27-match sequence had ended as Lloyd retired (finally?) from Test cricket. It was all very unedifying.

AUSTRALIA v NEW ZEALAND

1945-46 in New Zealand
New Zealand 0   Australia 1
It is hard to credit that Australia and New Zealand, separated by just 1,400 miles of ocean, had, until the 1970s, met in only one Test match. Finally, plans were agreed for an exchange of tours in 1973-74 involving three Tests in each country, but until then the match played at Wellington in March 1946 remained the only one played between the sides.

It was the first Test anywhere after World War II, and it was unfortunately played on a bad pitch that tipped the scales even more heavily in favour of the more experienced Australians. Captained by W. A. Brown, they were at full strength except for Bradman, whose health and cricket future were still uncertain. New Zealand could ill afford the absence in England of the brilliant Martin Donnelly. They were bowled out for 42 and 54, Bill O'Reilly in his farewell Test taking 5-14 and 3-19. Australia, who had declared at 199-8, won in two days.

1973-74 in Australia
Australia 2   New Zealand 0
Drawn 1
Under-prepared and handicapped by injuries, New Zealand's first ever tour to Australia proved something of a disappointment, although bad weather in the second match robbed them of a likely victory.

At Melbourne, Stackpole, dropped in the first over, went on to reach his seventh Test century as Australia batted with a consistency the New Zealanders could not match in either innings. Wadsworth's gallant 80 could not avoid the follow-on and Mallett and Walters bowled Australia to an innings victory.

The loss of two days' play at Sydney proved fatal to New Zealand's hopes of their first win over Australia—particularly the final day when the home side needed 425 to win with two wickets already lost. Centuries from Parker and Morrison against a weakened attack and penetrating pace bowling from Richard and Dayle Hadlee had worked New Zealand into their winning position.

But the last Test was a replica of the first. Marsh made 132 and Walters 94, and although Congdon batted gallantly in the second innings, O'Keeffe and Dymock bowled Australia to an innings victory.

1973-74 in New Zealand
New Zealand 1   Australia 1
Drawn 1
On March 13 1974, New Zealand finally achieved their first win over their closest rivals.

The outstanding performance in that second Test at Christchurch came from Glenn Turner who scored two centuries, the second of which steered New Zealand to their final target. Although Redpath made 71 and 58, Australia never mastered the home attack and the Hadlee brothers took twelve wickets between them to give New Zealand a convincing victory by 5 wickets.

The first Test had been drawn at Wellington in a plethora of high scoring. The Chappell brothers participated in a remarkable family double—Ian scoring 145 and 121, Greg 247 and 133. The New Zealand batsmen were equally dominant and Congdon and Hastings both reached three figures.

But at Auckland, in conditions that always suited the bowlers, New Zealand lost their chance of an outright series win. Australia were 64 for 5 until Walters, with an undefeated 104, took the total to 221 all out. Gilmour and Mallett bowled New Zealand out for a mere 112, and Redpath's 159 helped set the home side an impossible task. Despite Turner's 72, Walker's probing accuracy always ensured the Australian win that squared the series.

1976-77 in New Zealand
New Zealand 0   Australia 1
Drawn 1
Three years after their last series, the two countries competed again, making up for the lost years. This time the Australians saw through a tour of New Zealand with none of the rancour on or off the field which had developed on the previous tour.

Only two Tests were played, the first, at Christchurch, being drawn, the second, at Auckland, going to Australia by 10 wickets.

Walters was in devastating form in the first, hitting 250, his highest score, in 6½ hours. Displaying the strokeplay that had him dubbed a 'new Bradman' 10 years earlier, he added 217 for the seventh wicket (an Australian Test record) with Gilmour, who struck his first Test century. Faced with making 353 to avoid the follow-on, New Zealand scraped by with their last pair, Burgess and Hedley Howarth, both earlier having passed 60, and O'Keeffe taking the bowling honours with 5 for 101. A quick 154 for 4, McCosker 77 not out, left New Zealand 6½ hours to bat and 350 to win, and to their credit they finished 293 for 8, with Congdon making his seventh Test century.

Dropped catches cost New Zealand dearly in the second Test. They made 229, with half-centuries by Geoff Howarth and Edwards, and then allowed Australia to reach 377, McCosker 84, Gilmour 64 and Chappell 58. Furious fast bowling by Lillee then sent them back for 175, with only a spectacular 81 by Richard Hadlee putting some respectability to it. Lillee's figures were 5 for 51 and 6 for 72, underlining that he was not as yet a spent force.

ABOVE Bevan Congdon, who was captain in both series against Australia in 1973-74, scoring 132 at Wellington. In 1976-77, he helped save the Test at Christchurch with 107 not out in the second innings.
RIGHT Glenn Turner, one of the most successful of New Zealand batsmen in the 1970s, was instrumental in his country's first victory over Australia in 1973-74, scoring a century in each innings at Christchurch.

New Zealand play Australia at Basin Reserve, Wellington. Once a lake, and then a swamp, the land was reclaimed to become a glorious stadium.

1980-81 in Australia
Australia 2   New Zealand 0
Drawn 1

After winning a series against the West Indies in 1979-80, New Zealand were optimistic about their chances in Australia the following season. The first Test at Brisbane was a great disappointment, however.

Put in by Greg Chappell, they were dismissed for 225, of which 117 had come in a fourth-wicket stand between captain Howarth (65) and Parker (52). They stayed in the match, however, by getting Australia out for 305, despite Wood making 111. Cairns took 5 for 87. This flattered, because they collapsed dreadfully against Lillee in the second innings, with the exception of Edgar and Hadlee. Opener Edgar (51) was still there when New Zealand were 61 for 7. Hadlee (51 not out) then joined him and they added 53, while Hadlee was also instrumental in adding 28 for the last wicket. All out 142 (Lillee 6 for 53) New Zealand set Australia to get only 63 to win, which Wood (Man of the Match) and Dyson accomplished without loss. The match was over on the third day, with two days to spare.

The second Test at Perth had similarities and differences. New Zealand were put in and made 196 (Lillee 5 for 63), with Coney,

returned to the side, making 71. Australia made 265 (Walters 55, Marsh 91, Hadlee 5 for 87) to lead by 69. New Zealand, as at Brisbane, collapsed in the second innings, but this time mainly to spinner Higgs. They were all out 121. Edgar and Hadlee again registered the same score, but this time it was 0 (Edgar got a pair). Australia, needing only 53, made them for the loss of two wickets, but Wood, Man of the Match at Brisbane, this time also made a pair. Marsh was Man of the Match. Again, two days were left blank.

The grassless Melbourne pitch for the third Test was again under fire from both captains. Chappell, in fact, threatened not to play on it again. He claimed there was no bounce after 1½ days. The veteran Walters was the mainstay of the Australian innings after they had been put in. He made 107, only Hughes (51) joining him in passing the half-century. Australia's 321 was helped by a stand of 60 for the last wicket, during which Walters reached his century and there was controversy over a decision given in favour of Higgs. Caught behind, he was saved by a late call of 'no-ball' from umpire Bailhache, on the grounds that the short ball was intimidatory. New Zealand reached 247 before the fifth wicket fell, but finally fell four short of Australia's total with 317. Howarth (65), Parker (56) and Coney (55 not out) were the principal scorers. Hadlee (6 for 57) won the Man of the Match award for his second-innings bowling which helped dismiss Australia for

188 after they had made a reasonable start, Chappell getting 78. He was also Man of the Series. New Zealand had a chance for some revenge when chasing 193 in 2 hours and 20 overs, and looked to be taking it at 95 for 1. But 4 wickets fell for 6 runs, 3 lbw, at least one of which the New Zealanders were unhappy about, and they ended by grimly batting out time at 128 for 6.

1981-82 in New Zealand
New Zealand 1   Australia 1
Drawn 1

After beating Pakistan and drawing a series with West Indies, Australia went to New Zealand. The two sides had fought a close one-day series and expectancy was high.

The first Test was spoiled by Wellington's rain. Less than ten hours' play was possible. Chappell put New Zealand in when play began on the second morning, but the home side were unable to complete their innings till the fifth day, when Howarth declared at 266 for 7 (Edgar 55, Howarth 58 not out). Australia made 55 for 1.

In the second Test at Auckland, Howarth put Australia in on a slow wicket. No batsman played well, Hughes was out for a duck to a disputed decision, and Chappell and Border were run out from successive balls, Border also for a duck. Australia were out for 210 on the first day. New Zealand lost two quick wickets, but Man of the Match Edgar (161) stayed, adding 87 with Howarth (another run-out victim) and 154 with Coney (73). A

total of 387 was reached—a lead of 177, but there was more dissension with umpiring decisions. Wood made 100 in Australia's second innings, and the deficit was cleared with two wickets down, but with Hadlee claiming 5 for 63 Australia could not build a substantial lead. At 280 New Zealand were left with only 104 to get. There was slight anxiety at 44 for 3, but Cairns came in to smash 34 runs from 21 balls, and when Hadlee entered with the scores level he finished it with a six off Yardley.

At Christchurch, Howarth put Australia in again, but this time with less success. Wickets fell fairly regularly at one end, mostly to Hadlee (6 for 100); but New Zealand missed their chance by twice missing Greg Chappell. On the second day he scored 100 before lunch and his 176 made him the Man of the Match and took Australia to 353. New Zealand collapsed before Lillee, who broke down with figures of 3 for 13, and before the end of the second day were 87 for 8. Hadlee, despite being knocked out, and Snedden then added 62 before both were out on 149—five runs short of avoiding a follow-on. Only Wright, with 141, provided strong resistance in the second innings. When Howarth was out to another decision debated afterwards after helping him raise the score to 129 for 3, the innings folded up. It took 106 runs from the last three wickets to hoist the score to 272. Australia scored the 69 required to win by eight wickets and tie the series.

AUSTRALIA v INDIA

Having maintained a high standard of first-class cricket throughout World War II, India went to Australia in 1947-48 for the first series between the two countries. Thus they were present during the last home season of Sir Donald Bradman, then preparing for his swansong in England in 1948. It was a tough time for them to go, and they were well beaten by powerful opposition, as they were by lesser opposition on their next visit to Australia 20 years later. Between then, however, they won two matches at home against visiting Australian sides, in 1959-60 and 1964-65. In 1979-80 India had their first series win against Australia, by 2-0, and they drew the next series in Australia.

1947-48 in Australia
Australia 4   India 0   Drawn 1
There were several players of high reputation and achievement in the team Lala Amarnath captained on the first visit to Australia. But even with 'Vinoo' Mankad, Vijay Hazare, and Gul Mahomed among them, the Indians could not prove a decisive influence in alien conditions, and unfortunately the captain himself did little in the Tests. The Indians beat an Australian XI at Sydney by 47 runs before the first Test, but they were caught on a wet pitch at Brisbane. Bradman made 185, and he was able to declare at the right moment, for Ernie Toshack, left-arm medium pace, to bowl the Indians out for 58 and 98. Toshack

Australian skipper Benaud is brilliantly caught by C. G. Borde in the Calcutta Test of the 1959-60 series, in which India won their first Test victory over Australia.

took 5-2 in 19 balls in the first innings, and 6-29 in the second.

The weather was so bad in Sydney during the second Test that only 10 hours' play was possible in six days, and on this occasion D. G. Phadkar and Hazare caught Australia on an evil pitch, bowling them out for 107. But no play was possible on the last day, which would have started with India in the intriguing position of 142 runs on with three second-innings wickets standing.

This low-scoring match was the only one in which Bradman failed. His other scores in the series were 185, 132 and 127 not out, 201 and 57 retired hurt—in all 715 runs at 178.75. Though Mankad made two Test hundreds and Hazare two in the same match in Adelaide, where Denis Compton and Arthur Morris had performed the same feat a year before, Australia won two of the last three Tests by an innings.

1956-57 in India
India 0   Australia 2   Drawn 1
On the way home from England, Ian Johnson's Australian side played and lost the only Test in Pakistan before stopping in India for a three-match series. Lindwall took 7-43 in the second innings of the first Test in Madras, which Australia won, but though Jim Burke made 161 and Neil Harvey 140 in the second, India earned a draw with a long defensive action.

The third Test in Calcutta was played on a pitch that took spin, conditions that put India on a more even footing. Though short of pace as always, they had two fine spinners in Mankad and Ghulam Ahmed. 'Polly' Umrigar put Australia in on the first day, but later Richie Benaud's leg-spin,

Jaisimha hooks towards his century at Brisbane in 1968.

which accounted for 11 wickets, gave Australia the slight edge throughout and when India tried to make 231 to win in the last innings, they lost by 94 runs.

1959-60 in India
India 1   Australia 2   Drawn 2
Australian standards had risen again and the Ashes had been recovered when Richie Benaud took his side to India for a full series three years later. But the visitors were bedevilled by illness, and after India's off-spinner J. S. Patel (9-69 and 5-55) had used a new turf pitch in Kanpur with such success that Australia lost the second Test by 119 runs, they had to work hard to clinch the series. They had won the first Test by an innings.

Neil Harvey, who with Norman O'Neill was one of the successes of the series, made a second hundred in the third Test, but the only other Australian win was in the fourth at Madras, where Les Favell made his only Test hundred and Benaud took eight wickets.

1964-65 in India
India 1   Australia 1   Drawn 1
The next Australian visit was by Bobby Simpson's side on its way back from England in 1964, and for the first time India halved the series. After a holiday in Europe, Australia acclimatized themselves well to win by 139 runs at Madras, although the young Nawab of Pataudi, the Indian captain, made 128 not out. In Bombay however, India made 256 in the last innings and won by two wickets. Pataudi made 86 and 53, but Australia

were handicapped by the illness that prevented Norman O'Neill from batting in either innings. The series ended in anticlimax at Calcutta, for after India had led by 61 runs in a low-scoring first innings and Australia were fighting back with 143-1 in the second, rain set in and prevented any play on the last two days.

1967-68 in Australia
Australia 4   India 0
The Nawab of Pataudi led the second Indian tour to Australia, where his father had toured with the England team in 1932-33. India's usual lack of class fast bowling prevented them from doing themselves justice, and they were also found wanting in close catching. Nor was their later batting as obdurate as it can be in their own country.

Simpson (103) and Bob Cowper (108) made hundreds in the first Test, which Australia won by 146 runs, though India's form was an improvement on what they had shown against the states. The hundreds in the second Test at Melbourne came from Simpson (109), Bill Lawry (100), and Ian Chappell (151) and though India made 352 in the second innings, A. L. Wadekar 99, they lost by an innings. After two Tests Simpson relinquished the captaincy to Lawry, who was to take the side to England later that year on Simpson's retirement, and India gave one of their best performances

Feet in the air is Indian wicket-keeper Engineer, making a vain attempt to stump Doug Walters in 1967-68. Walters, on leave from the army, celebrated his return to the Australian side with 93 and 62 not out at Brisbane. India made a great attempt to score 395 to win but failed by 39.

1977-78 in Australia

Australia 3   India 2   Drawn 0

Cricket stood at the crossroads late in 1977 as Kerry Packer's outlawed cricketers prepared for the first series of 'Super Tests' while a weakened Australian Test team faced the Indian touring side. It transpired that many more Australians preferred to watch the Test matches, 'live' and on television, than the 'World Series' which clashed with them. The simple, age-old formula of one nation versus another proved stronger than the 'circus' concept, at least during this first season.

The Australian selectors made an inspired choice of replacement captain in persuading Bob Simpson to emerge from a 10-year retirement from the first-class game, and several of the new Test caps lost no time in establishing themselves.

The first Test, at Brisbane, was a thriller, Australia winning by 16 runs after India's gallant attempt at scoring 341, with Gavaskar scoring 113 and Kirmani 55. The first innings had been even: Australia 166, Peter Toohey 82, Bedi 5 for 55; India 153, Vengsarkar 48. Australia got into stride at the second attempt, making 327, with Simpson justifying his comeback with 89 and Toohey further distinguishing his debut with 57. At the nailbiting finish, Thomson had seven wickets in the match and Wayne Clark eight.

The second Test was also gripping throughout, Australia squeezing home at Perth by two wickets. In a high-scoring match centuries were made by Simpson, Gavaskar, Mohinder Amarnath (90 and 100), and Tony Mann (played for his spin bowling), with 88 by Chauhan and 83 by Toohey. Bedi took 10 for 194 in the match, and had the satisfaction of seeing his side become the first from India to pass 400 against Australia. Yet they were now two down with three to play.

The fightback began in Melbourne, where yet another century by Gavaskar set up a stiff target for Australia. Needing 387 for victory, they crashed before Chandrasekhar (6 for 52 in both innings) to lose by 222 runs. For India, M. Amarnath made 72 and Viswanath two fifties, and Australia's leading scorers were Serjeant, 85, and Cosier, 67.

India took a firm grip on matters at Sydney in the fourth Test, winning by an innings and two runs. Bedi, Chandrasekhar and Prasanna wove their spell, only Toohey, 85, and Cosier, 68, making real scores. In contrast

of the tour. Their off-spinner Erapalli Prasanna took 6-104 on a good pitch in Australia's second innings, after which India made a wonderful attempt to score 395 to win and lost by only 39 runs, M. L. Jaisimha scoring 101, the tourists' only hundred of the series. The last of the four-Test series was lost more easily when Simpson, playing in his last Test for 10 years, took 5-59.

1969-70 in India

India 1   Australia 3   Drawn 1

By the time Bill Lawry took the Australians to India for the last

two months of 1969, as the first half of a tour that would also take in South Africa, the spinning skill of Prasanna and B. S. Bedi was such that India were as well equipped with spin as any country in the world. But their batting collapsed in the second innings of the first Test against Alan Connolly (3-20) and Johnny Gleeson (4-56). They shared an even draw in Kanpur before winning by seven wickets in New Delhi, where Bedi (5-37) and Prasanna (5-42) bowled Australia out for 107 in their second innings, and Wadekar's 91 not out ensured

India reached 181 to win in the last innings.

Excitement was intense with the series thus levelled and two Tests to play, but Australia won them both, through the fast bowling of Graham McKenzie, Eric Freeman, and Connolly in Calcutta, and perhaps through winning the toss in Madras. In the final match, the two off-spinners Prasanna and Ashley Mallett took 10 wickets each, but Australia batted first and, though at one time they were 24-6 in their second innings, Redpath's staunch 63 restored their position.

six of India's batsmen passed 40 as they advanced to 396 for 8 declared. Australia's 131 and 263 left them underdogs for the fifth and deciding Test.

Australia turned to youth, choosing Graeme Wood, 21, and Rick Darling, 20, to open the innings. They made 89, and centuries by Graham Yallop and Simpson and 60 by Toohey took Australia to a daunting 505. Only Viswanath, 89, prospered in India's reply of 269, and when Australia added 256 second-innings runs, Darling a second half-century and Simpson 51, India's target of 493 seemed purely academic. Yet by the sixth afternoon, when their final wicket fell, they were a mere 48 runs short, having made the highest losing fourth-innings total in Test history. M. Amarnath made 86, Vengsarkar 78, Viswanath 73, and Kirmani 51, and both sides finished with the full and unstinted admiration of cricket-lovers throughout the world.

1979-80 in India
India 2   Australia 0   Drawn 4
After the exciting series in Australia, when no Test was drawn, much was expected from the series in India.

At Madras, where Hughes won the toss and batted, each side compiled a big score, but in very different ways. After two wickets had gone for 75, Border (162) and Hughes (100) added 222 for Australia. Border was dropped before he had scored, a very expensive miss, and Hughes was dropped at 65. Border was eventually run out backing up when Doshi deflected Yallop's drive on to the stumps. Dilip Doshi, playing his first Test aged 32, subdued the remaining batsmen, finishing with 6 for 103 as Australia totalled 390. India, with no centuries and no century stands, batted solidly all down the order, and when they were out on the fourth day had passed Australia's total and reached 425. The principal scorers were Gavaskar, now captain (50), Kirmani (57), Vengsarkar (65), Sharma (52) and Kapil Dev (83 in 73 balls). Leg-spinner Higgs took 7 for 143. A draw was the obvious outcome, made more certain when rain interrupted the last two days. Australia made 212 for 7 (Hilditch 55, Border 50).

The second Test at Bangalore also featured heavy scoring, and with rain interrupting the play from the first day onwards, another draw was inevitable. Australia batted again, this time with more consistency though no big scorers—Hilditch (62) and Hughes (86) were highest. They totalled 333, this time passed by India comfortably, with two centurions: Vengsarkar got 112 and Viswanath 161 not out, and Gavaskar declared at 457 for 5. Hogg kicked the stumps in anger after being consistently no-balled, but good-will all round soothed the situa-

tion. Australia made 77 for 3, all falling to off-spinning newcomer Shivlal Yadav, giving him seven for the match, before the rain came back.

India won the toss and batted for the first time in this series at Kanpur, and took the lead. On a lively pitch they scratched around but had all the luck until Gavaskar (76) was out at 114. Chauhan (58) and Vengsarkar (52) took the score past 200 before another wicket fell, but in the last half-hour of the day the luck ran out and wickets began to tumble. Only Viswanath got many next day and India were out for 271 (Dymock 5 for 99). Hughes (50) and Yallop (89) took Australia's score from 75 to 168

Kim Hughes plays off the back foot through gully. Hughes' first series as Australian captain was in India in 1979-80, a series India won 2-0.

for the fourth wicket but India's total was not passed until eight wickets were down. Opener Darling, forced to bat at number eight because of a fielding injury to his shoulder, made 59 to steer Australia to 304 and a lead of 33. Chauhan, dropped early in both innings, batted 368 minutes for 84 in his second knock, and Viswanath made 52. Even so, at 177 for 5, only 144 ahead, their opponents were well in the match. Kirmani (45) helped Chauhan add 79, and when India were out for 311 (Dymock 7 for 67, twelve in the match), Australia required 279 to win. But the pitch, a new one, wore quickly late in the match and the ball kept low. Australia were never in with a chance of even a draw and were skittled for 125, victory for India by 153.

New Delhi also had a relaid pitch, which gave the Australian bowlers some help when India

decided to bat. But they fielded badly. Gavaskar escaped three times as he made 115. Later Viswanath made a sparkling 131, Sharma a scratchy 100 not out, which eventually played him back into form and Gavaskar was able to declare at 510. Australia struggled throughout. Whatmore (77) added 65 for the sixth wicket with Yallop—the next highest was the last as Higgs helped Wright (55 not out) to add 52. At 298 all out, however, Australia were 13 short of saving the follow-on, and were put in again. Kapil Dev took 5 for 82. Australia batted with more determination in the second innings. Only Darling failed, and Hilditch made 85. The last alarm was at 242 for 5, but Whatmore (54) and Sleep (65) put up the shutters, and when Australia were all out at the close for 413, it was the Indian batsmen who had come on to bowl.

Kapil Dev hands a garland to umpire Ramaswamy. In two series against Australia he has been on the losing side only once.

On a slow pitch at Calcutta, Australia batted and, after Hilditch was out without a run on the board, set about piling up a big score, looking for the pitch to turn on the fifth day. Border made 54 in a second-wicket stand of 97, then Yallop (167) and Hughes (92) added 206 for the third wicket. Yardley made 61 not out later on, and Australia reached 442 (Kapil Dev 5 for 74). India, after losing Gavaskar, themselves decided on steady progress with the result that after three days' play only 12 wickets had fallen. However, on the fourth day the ball did begin to turn, and after Vengsarkar (89) and Viswanath (86) had gone, India subsided for 347, the last 7 wickets going for 91. Australia themselves were 81 for 5 at close of play, 176 ahead. On the last day Hughes batted on, taking his own score to 64 not out, eventually declaring at 151 for 6, leaving India to get 247 in as many minutes. While Chauhan made 50, India were not sure whether to go for the runs or not, and suffered a stop-go policy. Near the end Yashpal Sharma attacked the bowling and made 85 not out, but India ended at 200 for 4, 47 short. Had they sent in Kapil Dev, they might have clinched the series.

So the sixth Test at Bombay began with Australia needing a win to tie the series. India made this as

difficult as possible by winning the toss and batting on a slow pitch. Gavaskar (123) and Chauhan (73) then stayed put for over four hours. India were only 231 for 3 overnight. On the second day night-watchman Kirmani (missed the previous evening) scored 101 not out. Hogg reacted badly when an lbw appeal against Kapil Dev was turned down and Hughes later stated that this decision, the worst he'd seen, turned the game. Nevertheless it was Ghavri (86), not Dev, who added 127 with Kirmani for the eighth wicket, soon after which Gavaskar declared at 458 for 8, giving Australia a few minutes batting at the end of the second day. Australia, some of whose players had stomach troubles, batted as if tired and dispirited after a long tour. Yallop made 60, but Doshi took 5 for 43, including Hughes, disgusted to be given out caught 'off his sleeve'. All out 160, Australia followed on. Hughes batted well for 80, and with Border (61) added 132 for the third wicket, but all the other batsmen went quietly, the last eight wickets going for 49 runs. All out 198, Australia lost by an innings and exactly 100, and India took the series 2-0.

1980-81 in Australia
Australia 1   India 1   Drawn 1
The short series in Australia in 1980-81 was eagerly awaited. Greg Chappell was back as Australia's captain, but Gavaskar won the first toss in Sydney, and batted on a good wicket. He himself lasted

only five balls and India never recovered against Australia's three fast bowlers, Lillee, Pascoe (who each took four wickets) and Hogg. Patil was the only batsman to master the attack, but he was hit by a Pascoe bouncer when 65 and retired to hospital. India were all out 201, a score soon to be surpassed by Chappell himself. He batted superbly, giving one chance, at 100, before going on to 204, made in twice as many minutes. He shared a fifth-wicket stand of 172 with Walters (67) and scored just over half Australia's total of 406. He was naturally Man of the Match. Kapil Dev (5 for 97) and Ghavri (5 for 107) shared the wickets. India again batted poorly second time round, the ninth-wicket stand of 57 being the biggest of the innings, and repeated their first-innings score of 201. Australia won by an innings and four.

India showed much more fight in the second Test at Adelaide, despite a huge Australian first-innings score removing their chances of victory. In fact Gavaskar set out for a draw, and surprisingly put Australia in on a perfect pitch. Wood, missed in the first over, made 125, and Hughes built on a solid start by batting brilliantly, adding 82 with Wood and 129 with Border (57). He went on to 213, the second Australian double century of the series, and Australia reached 528. At 130 for 4 India were in some trouble on the third day, but Chauhan battled for 97 and added 108 with Patil, who

was dropped twice but made a brilliant 174. Sharma (47) helped him add 147 for the sixth wicket, and India achieved respectability at 419. Australia went for quick runs on the fourth afternoon but found Doshi, who opened the bowling with Dev, difficult to score from. Chappell made 52 and Hughes 53 but it was not until the last morning that the declaration came at 271 for 5, leaving India to get 331. It was a cautious declaration on a wearing wicket, and India batted out time at 135 for 8, with Gavaskar, after a couple of dubious decisions, sarcastically calling Australian umpires as good as Indian.

The last Test at Melbourne was extraordinary. Chappell put India in on the notoriously unpredictable Melbourne wicket and soon claimed successes. Lillee and Pascoe bowled well, and all the Indian batsmen failed except Viswanath, the Man of the Match. He made 114 and was largely responsible for doubling the score from 115 for 6 to 237. Australia started moderately but improved. Border (124) added 108 with Chappell (76) and 131 with Walters (78), so that at 320 for 5 Australia appeared to have the series won. There was another incident when Border, bowled by Yadav, was not given out until after the umpires conferred, while Gavaskar fumed. The last six wickets added only 99, but at 419, Australia led by 182. India fought back, and Gavaskar (70) and Chauhan put on 165 for the first wicket, when came the worst in the controversies about umpiring between the teams. Given out lbw, Gavaskar angrily indicated the ball had hit his bat, and, after beginning to leave, came back and led Chauhan off with him, aiming to forfeit the match. The manager, Nadkarni, met Chauhan near the gate and persuaded him to continue. This wicket allowed Lillee to equal Benaud's Australian record aggregate for Tests, and soon after, that of a disturbed Chauhan allowed him to pass it. The rest of the batsmen did enough to set Australia a target, but the innings closed at 324. Yadav, hit on the toe in the first innings, had bowled but could not bat and took no further part. With Kapil Dev also suffering from a suspected torn thigh muscle, which from half-way through Australia's first innings had prevented him bowling, it seemed the target of 143 to win would be a formality for Australia. However, three wickets went down quickly and at stumps on the fourth day Australia were 24 for 3. This encouraged Kapil Dev not only to appear on the fifth day after all, but to bowl, and he was inspired. He took 5 for 28 and in 48.4 overs Australia were out for 83, their lowest total against India. So India squared the series in a match which only two days earlier their captain had tried to concede.

AUSTRALIA v PAKISTAN

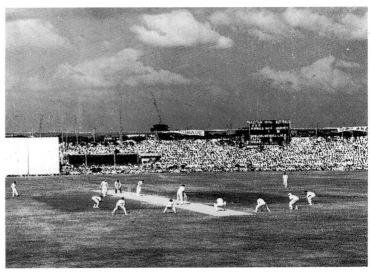

The first Test match ever played between Australia and Pakistan was historic in various ways. It was the slowest match on record by most reckoning, and its first day produced only 95 runs—still the record low for a day's play. By 1985, Australia had won nine matches and Pakistan eight in the series between the two countries.

1956-57 in Pakistan
Pakistan 1   Australia 0
In October 1956 Ian Johnson's Australian side was on its way back from an unsuccessful tour of England when, after a short holiday in Europe, they flew from Rome to Karachi. There they found a matting pitch and Fazal Mahmood, the greatest bowler in the world in these conditions. From the first the Australian batsmen, suddenly switched from the turf pitches of England and short of practice, were struggling against Fazal, who took the first 6 wickets for 26. At the end of the first day Australia had been bowled out for 80 and Pakistan had made 15-2, but it was said by those participating to be one of the most fascinating day's play they had ever known, such was Fazal's artistry.

The run output on subsequent days was not much higher—184, 138, and 112. Fazal took seven

wickets in the second innings and 13 for 114 in the match, which ended in no less bizarre fashion than it had begun. In the last 2 hours and 40 minutes of the fourth day, Pakistan, needing 69 to win, batted so slowly that with nine wickets standing they were six runs short at the end. As the next day was one of mourning on the anniversary of the death of former Prime Minister Liaquat Ali Khan, they had to wait until the day after to finish the match early in its fifth day.

1959-60 in Pakistan
Pakistan 0   Australia 2   Drawn 1
The Australians' next visit to Pakistan preceded a tour of India. They arrived fresher for it, and though rain prevented a grass pitch from being used in the first match at Dacca as had been intended, Australia, under Richie Benaud, were not undone by Fazal this time. Benaud (4-69) and Alan Davidson (4-42) bowled Pakistan out in the first innings, Benaud (4-42) and Mackay (6-42) in the second, and Australia won by eight wickets.

These were five-day Tests, and Australia won the second by seven wickets with 12 minutes to spare after Norman O'Neill had made 134 in their first innings and Saeed Ahmed had long delayed Paki-

stan's defeat with an innings of 166. The third Test was notable mainly for the presence of the President of the United States, Dwight D. Eisenhower.

1964-65 in Pakistan
Pakistan 0   Australia 0   Drawn 1
The third Australian visit to Pakistan was paid, like the first, after a tour of England, Bobby Simpson's side playing in Karachi after three Tests in India. Pakistan made a wonderful start, with 'Billy' Ibadulla, playing in his first Test, making 166 and putting on 249 for the first wicket with Abdul Kadir (95). But Simpson made a

Fazal Mahmood bowls to McDonald at Dacca in 1959-60. On an earlier meeting in 1956, Fazal had bowled the Pakistanis to a surprise win.

hundred in each innings and Australia had no difficulty in earning a draw.

1964-65 in Australia
Australia 0   Pakistan 0   Drawn 1
Within a month of the match in Karachi, Pakistan, captained by Hanif Mohammad, had begun a tour of Australia and New Zealand. The Australian section comprised three state matches, against Queensland, New South Wales, and South Australia, and one Test match at Melbourne. In this, Pakistan gave a good account of themselves and were never in serious danger of defeat, thanks mainly to the brilliant batting of their captain, who made 104 and 93.

1972-73 in Australia
Australia 3   Pakistan 0
Disturbed by off-the-field conflicts that resulted in two players being sent home, Pakistan twice played their way into winning positions only to fail badly under pressure.

A thrashing in the first Test by an innings and 114 runs—Mallett taking 8 for 59 in their second innings—led to an improvement at Melbourne. But set to make 293 on a perfect batting wicket they fell 92 short. In the third Test, their fourth innings target was only 158, but their lack of character showed when Walker (6 for 15) bowled them out for 106.

Mushtaq Mohammad, Majid Khan, and Sadiq Mohammad all made centuries but not when the pressure was really on, and the bowlers lacked penetration.

1976-77 in Australia
Australia 1   Pakistan 1   Drawn 1
Pakistan's first-ever victory on

Billy Ibadulla returned home in 1964-65 to score 166 in his first Test, at Karachi.

Australian soil came against all the odds, after they had conceded a massive first innings deficit in the drawn first Test and been crushed by 348 runs in the second.

At Adelaide, where Jeff Thomson suffered a severe shoulder injury after collision with one of his fieldsmen, Pakistan added a second-innings 466 (Zaheer 101, Asif Iqbal 152 not out) to their dismal 272. Australia had chalked up a lead of 182 after Ian Davis had made his first Test century and Walters had returned to form with 107. After Pakistan had come back into the match against a reduced Australian attack— Thomson was missing and Lillee and Gilmour both carried injuries—the home side needed 285 in 5½ hours. Greg Chappell set up a winning position, but, to the vociferous disappointment of the crowd, Cosier and Marsh put safety before daring in the last 15 overs, when 56 were needed, and Australia, six wickets down, finished 24 short.

Australia came into their own at Melbourne with totals of 517 and 315, both declared. Chappell scored his 13th Test hundred and Cosier went on to 168, while McCosker made a second-innings century. Turner and Davis made eighties in the run-glut, and. for Pakistan, Imran Khan gave evidence of his development with a return of 5 for 122. However, Pakistan were never really in the match, making 333 almost entirely from the bats of Sadiq, 105, Zaheer, 90, and Majid, 76, but collapsing for 151 in the fourth innings when Lillee and O'Keeffe took four wickets apiece.

It came as a surprise, therefore, when Pakistan bounced back at Sydney to win by eight wickets. Imran, 6 for 102, and Sarfraz used the seam skilfully in sending Australia back for 211, and Asif Iqbal's fine 120 was well supported by 57 from Haroon Rashid in his first Test and 64 from Miandad. The advantage of a 149-run lead was rammed home by Imran with another six wickets, this time for only 63, as Australia were bundled out for 180, and the 32 runs for victory were made for the loss of two wickets. This performance by Pakistan was in stark contrast to that just over a year later when, without the players who signed for Kerry Packer—Majid, Zaheer, Mushtaq, Asif, and Imran—they were annihilated by England.

1978-79 in Australia
Australia 1   Pakistan 1
After their crushing 5-1 defeat by England, Australia took on Pakistan in this Packer-influenced season. The first Test at Melbourne had an extraordinary finish. Pakistan, put in by Yallop, made 196, nobody passing 50. It was enough for a lead, however, as Australia were put out for 168. Hogg, given run out when he left his crease before the ball was dead, wrecked the wicket in disgust.

Mushtaq, the Pakistan captain, had asked the umpire if the appeal could be withdrawn but without success. Pakistan declared their second innings at 353 for 9, after Majid had made 108 and Zaheer 59. Australia needed 382 to win, and with Hilditch making 62, Border 105 and Hughes 84, they passed 300 with only three men out, and appeared almost sure winners. But the last seven wickets fell for five runs in 65 balls, and Pakistan won by 71 runs. It was a triumph for Sarfraz, with the best analysis in a Test in Australia—9 for 86. The other batsman was run out.

At Perth, Hughes captained Australia as Yallop was injured, and put Pakistan in. Javed Miandad made 129 not out but was poorly supported, the side being out for 277. Australia got off to a good start, and with Darling making 79 and Border 85, reached 327, a lead of 50. Pakistan's second-innings 285 was built around an innings of 134 not out by Asif. Hurst took 5 for 94 and ran out Sikander Bakht, who was backing up. It was a bad-tempered series, and Australia's first wicket fell for 236 to win when Hilditch was given out 'handled the ball', having, as non-striker, handed the

ball to the bowler, Sarfraz, who appealed. Darling (79) and Border (66 not out) ensured Australia got the runs for a 7-wicket win to tie the short series.

1979-80 in Pakistan
Pakistan 1   Australia 0   Drawn 2
Having tied their last series in Australia but lost in India, Pakistan were seeking a win when the Aussies began their visit.

Chappell won the toss at Karachi and batted. The wicket took spin from the start, and only Hughes (85) batted with confidence. A young debutante spinner, Tauseef Ahmed, and the more experienced Iqbal Qasim, took four wickets each as Australia were tumbled for 225. Pakistan used seven bowlers. Pakistan needed a lead, as the wicket would progressively take more spin, but at 134 for 5, with Taslim Arif and the young captain Javed Miandad out for 58 and 40 respectively, they needed somebody to stay. Majid Khan (89) did, long enough for Pakistan to get 292 and lead by 67. Bright was the main threat, taking 7 for 87. Iqbal Qasim also took 7 wickets, for only 49, when Australia batted again. Border, 58 not out, ran out of partners in a way to become familiar to him, and Pakistan, having dismissed Australia

ABOVE LEFT Haroon Rashid batting. At Sydney, in the 1976-77 series, he did much on his Test debut to help Pakistan win by eight wickets to square the series.

for 140, needed only 74 to win. Bright bowled three batsmen, but Pakistan won by seven wickets.

The match at Faisalabad was of an opposite character. Play could not start until the second day after rain had got to the pitch, an easy batting strip. Australia, after 21 for 2, cashed in. Chappell (235), Hughes (88) and Yallop (172) added nearly 400 for the third and fourth wickets. Marsh hit out for 71 and Australia reached 617, but not until well into the fourth day. Their request to play on the rest day in lieu of the blank first day was rejected. Pakistan played out time. Wicket-keeper/opener Taslim Arif made 210 not out, Javed Miandad 106 not out, and they had added 223 for the third wicket when the match ended at 382 for 2.

On another batsmen's paradise at Lahore, Australia won the toss and batted for the third time, and after Wiener had made 93 and Chappell 56, Border made 150 not out before Chappell declared at 407 for 7. Pakistan used nine bowlers. When they batted they

A press-box view of the ground at Lahore (now the Gaddafi stadium). The first Test played there was the second against Australia in 1959-60. It is a ground with volatile spectators.

were not going to forfeit the series. Mudassar (59), Wasim Raja (55), Majid Khan (110 not out) and Imran Khan (56) took them past Australia's score, and Javed declared at 420 for 9. Bright took 5 for 172, and Lillee his first wicket in the series. Australia lost two wickets for 7, but were in no danger of defeat, and had no prospect of setting a target. They batted out time at 391 for 8. Border made 153—the first batsman to pass 150 in both innings of a Test. Laird made 63 and Chappell 57. Pakistan used ten bowlers, including the keeper. Only Azmat Rana did not bowl.

1981-82 in Australia
Australia 2   Pakistan 1
In a sensational first Test at Perth, Pakistan's batting was humiliated and Dennis Lillee perpetrated perhaps the worst of his lapses into bad behaviour on the field.

Australia, put in, batted badly to be all out for 180, which took until the second day. Pakistan then collapsed to 26 for 8 before Lillee (5 for 18) and Alderman. Only Sarfraz reached double figures as they scrambled to 62 all out. Australia then batted more reasonably, declaring at 424 for 8. Laird (85) and Hughes (106) were the chief scorers. Hughes had been relieved of the captaincy in favour of Chappell after the defeat in England. Pakistan had no chance of avoiding defeat and were dismissed for 256 (Yardley 6 for 84), but Miandad made 79, during which came the incident with Lillee. Having pushed a ball from Lillee to square leg, he was impeded by the bowler as he took a strolled single. As he turned away, Lillee aimed a kick at his rear, catching him behind the knee. Miandad turned and raised his bat threateningly as Lillee prepared to defend himself with fists and the umpire came between them. Lillee was fined 200 dollars by his teammates, and suspended for two matches by the board, which neutral observers considered a ludicrously lenient punishment.

At Brisbane, Australia put Pakistan in and dismissed them for 291 (Zaheer 80, Lillee 5 for 81). After Laird and Wood (72) had got Australia off to a good start, Chappell took over with his fourth Test double-century, his 201 coming from 296 balls, and

earning him the Man of the Match award. Australia declared at 512 for 8. Pakistan's 223 obliged Australia to score 3 for 0 to win.

The wicket at Melbourne was slow, and once again drew protests from the captains. Pakistan, nevertheless, made 500 for 8 declared after being lucky enough to win the toss. Mudassar (95), Majid (74), Javed Miandad (62), Zaheer (90), Wasim Raja (50) and Imran (70 not out) all contributed. Yardley (7 for 187) bowled well and was Man of the Match. Wood scored 100 for Australia, but the fourth day was a dismal one for them. The last six wickets went for 61 as they crashed for 293, eight short of avoiding the follow-on. Then, despite 52 from Laird, the first six wickets went for 78 in the second innings, and on the last morning the rest went as quickly. Pakistan won by an innings and 82 runs, and Imran Khan was Man of the Series.

1982-83 in Pakistan
Pakistan 3   Australia 0
After the bad-tempered series in Australia, the sides met in Pakistan the following season. Hughes and Imran were by now the two skippers.

Australia batted at Karachi, and after losing Wood before a run

was on the board, passed 200 with only three wickets down, only then to collapse and be out for 284. Dyson (87), Hughes (54) and Border (55 not out) were the main scorers. When Pakistan batted, the crowd pelted Australia's outfielders with bricks and stones after Lawson had kicked up a fuss on being denied an appeal for caught behind against Mohsin. At the close of the second day Mohsin blocked Lawson's last ball and brushed it away from the wicket with his gloves. The Australians appealed and Mohsin became the third Test batsman to be given out 'handled the ball'. He made 58, and on the following day there were further crowd disturbances (mainly due to politics) which led Hughes twice to take the Australians from the field. Catches were dropped as Haroon Rashid (82), Zaheer (91) and Mudassar (52 not out) gave Pakistan a good lead at 419 for 9 declared. Australia fell in the second innings to Man of the Match Qadir (5 for 76) for 179 and at 47 for 1 Pakistan won by nine wickets.

On a good batting pitch at Faisalabad, Pakistan made full use of winning the toss. Mohsin (76), Mudassar (79), Mansoor Akhtar (111), Zaheer (126) and Haroon (51) allowed the home side to declare at 501 for 6 at the end of the second day. Abdul Qadir then won the Man of the Match award again by spinning out Australia twice for 168 and 330, taking 4 for 76 and 7 for 142. Only Laird (60) and Ritchie (106 not out in his second Test) passed 50, both in the second innings, and Pakistan won by an innings and three runs.

In the third Test at Lahore, Imran put Australia in on a fast wicket, and after Wood scored 85, Australia's middle batting failed. Lawson (57 not out) was needed to hoist the score to 316, helping to add 113 for the last three wickets. Australia dropped catches again, in particular missing Javed Miandad on 9. He went on to 138 and shared century stands for the fourth and fifth wickets with Mohsin (135) and Zaheer (52). Thomson kicked over the stumps when no-balled. Pakistan declared at 467 for 7, and were well on the way to a clean sweep when Australia were out for 214, only Dyson (51) and Hughes (39 in three hours) offering much resistance. Pakistan scored the 64 required for the loss of one wicket.

1983-84 in Australia
Australia 2   Pakistan 0   Drawn 3
On a fast wicket at Perth, Zaheer, captaining Pakistan and fearing the home side's pace attack, put Australia in to bat, and Wayne Phillips, opening in his first Test, scored 159. With Yallop (141) he added 259 for the second wicket. Without an unfit Imran, there was little threat to the Australian batsmen, who reached 436 for 9 before Hughes declared. With a battery of four fast bowlers, Australia

soon shot out Pakistan for 129. There was more resistance in the follow-on, mainly from Qasim Omar (65), but the side were out for 298 on the fourth day, leaving Australia winners by an innings and 9 runs. Man of the Match Rackemann was the principal destroyer with 5 for 32 and 6 for 86.

Rain saved Pakistan from a similar humiliation in the second Test at Brisbane. This time Zaheer decided to bat, but Lawson, picked as Man of the Match, took 5 for 49 and the visitors were dismissed for only 156 (Zaheer 56). Pakistan, without a fast bowler, could not trouble the Aussie batsmen, all of whom scored a few, Hughes (53), Border (118) and Chappell (150 not out) being the heaviest scorers in a total of 509 for 7 declared. Rain came after lunch on the fourth day with Pakistan 82 for 3. It was announced that Sarfraz was to join the tourists for the third Test.

At Adelaide, the Australian batting was more impressive than ever, 376 for 5 coming on the first day, despite Sarfraz. Wessels, dropped at 7, made 179 and Yallop, dropped at 0, made 68. Later Border made 117 not out, but on the second day Pakistan stemmed the rush and Australia

totalled 465. Pakistan then made a good start, and themselves reached 184 for 1 by the close. Mudassar was dropped from the third ball. An incident contrary to previous sporting behaviour between these countries was the disclaiming of a catch by Wessels when Qasim Omar was 52, the umpire being prepared to allow it. Omar shook Wessels' hand when next day he completed his century. He went on to 113, while Mohsin (149), Javed Miandad (131) and Salim Malik (77) also scored heavily as Pakistan reached 624, the highest against Australia since 1938. Hughes scored 106 in Australia's second innings, winning the Man of the Match award as, supported by Phillips (54) and Border (66), he ensured Australia batted out time at 310 for 7.

Imran played and resumed the captaincy in the fourth Test at Melbourne, but was unable to bowl. Pakistan batted and continued in good form, particularly Mohsin, who scored 152 from a total of 470. Imran made 83. That Australia passed this total was mainly due to Man of the Match Yallop, who scored 268. He batted 716 minutes, the sixth-longest innings ever. Hughes made 94 and debutant Greg Matthews 75 (in

252 minutes). Australia made 555 (Qadir 5 for 166). At 81 for 5 on the last day there was danger for Pakistan but Zaheer (50) and Imran (72 not out) saw them to safety at 238 for 7. Imran became the fifth player to score 2,000 runs and take 200 wickets in Tests.

During the fifth Test at Sydney, Chappell and Lillee each announced it would be their last, and later it appeared likely that the same could be said of Marsh. Man of the Match Chappell scored 182 and passed Bradman's record Test aggregate for Australia; Lillee took four wickets in each innings, ending with a record Test haul of wickets, while Marsh took six catches, ending with the record number of Test dismissals by a wicket-keeper. Australia put Pakistan in after tea on the first day, after a helicopter had helped dry the pitch. They were dismissed for 278 (Mudassar 84, Zaheer 61, Salim Malik 54, Lawson 5 for 59). Helped by Chappell, Hughes (76) and Border (64), Australia reached 454 for 6 declared. Wickets fell regularly throughout Pakistan's second innings. Javed Miandad made 60 but the side totalled only 210, Australia getting the 35 needed without loss to win the series by 2-0.

AUSTRALIA v SRI LANKA

1982-83 in Sri Lanka
Sri Lanka 0   Australia 1
Sri Lanka's eighth Test match was their first against Australia. At the Asgiriya Stadium, Kandy, Australia won the toss and batted. Only Wood missed out, Wessels (141), Yallop (98), Chappell (66) and Hookes (143 not out) building up a total of 514 for 4 declared. New keeper Woolley then caught both Sri Lanka openers for ducks. Mendis (74) and Ranatunga (90) could not prevent the follow-on, and in the second innings Wettimuny (86) could not prevent the innings defeat. All out 271 (Yardley 5 for 88) and 205 (Hogan 5 for 66), Sri Lanka were beaten by an innings and 38 runs.

Majid Khan hooks Dennis Lillee at Melbourne in the third Test of 1981-82. He scored 74 out of 500 for 8 declared and Pakistan won by an innings. Majid scored an all-run 7 off Lillee with a drive to long-off—four plus three more for an overthrow.

SOUTH AFRICA v NEW ZEALAND

South Africa and New Zealand first met on the Test field in 1931-32. South Africa had been playing Australia since 1902-03, and in 1931-32, after their second tour of Australia, the South Africans moved on to New Zealand to play two Tests. In the first of these, H. W. Taylor, one of South Africa's greatest players, ended a Test career begun in 1912.

Matches between the countries did not resume until 1952-53, again in New Zealand after a South African tour of Australia. Indeed South Africa never visited New Zealand except as an extension of a tour of Australia, and never played more than three Tests in a series there.

Only two full five-match series were played, both in South Africa. The first, in the 1950s, was one-sided, but the second, in 1961-62, was an exciting series which resulted in two wins each.

1931-32 in New Zealand
New Zealand 0   South Africa 2
South Africa arrived in New Zealand after a demoralizing tour of Australia in which they had lost the rubber 5-0. However, at Christchurch, they made 451, thanks to an opening stand of 196 between J. A. J. Christy (103) and Bruce Mitchell (113), and won the three-day match by an innings. New Zealand batted better to make 364 in the first innings of the second Test in Wellington, Giff Vivian making 100, but South Africa led them on the first innings, largely through Xeno-

phon Balaskas's only Test century —122 not out—and bowled them out cheaply in the second innings to win by eight wickets.

1952-53 in New Zealand
New Zealand 0   South Africa 1
Drawn 1
It was 21 years before the next series, which came after Jack Cheetham's unheralded South Africans had amazed the cricket world by drawing 2-2 with Australia. This time the Tests were of four days' duration, and in the first, which South Africa won by an innings and 180 runs, Jackie McGlew made 255 not out, then the highest by a South African in

Test cricket. South Africa won the toss and batted for a long time in both Tests, and in the second could not bowl New Zealand out. It ended in a dull draw.

1953-54 in South Africa
South Africa 4   New Zealand 0
Drawn 1
The result of this series was a somewhat harsh reflection on the performance of a New Zealand side that was unbeaten outside Tests and was not outplayed in any Test after the first, which they lost by an innings. They had a chance in the second Test until they lost their last seven wickets for 25 runs; they made 505, John Reid 135, in the drawn third Test, and they were in with a chance in the fifth until late in the fourth and last day. But they were often in tangles against Neil Adcock's fast bowling and the brilliant off-spin of Hugh

Tayfield, then approaching his prime.

1961-62 in South Africa
South Africa 2   New Zealand 2
Drawn 1
South Africa were in a period of transition, but New Zealand had John Reid at the peak of his powers and he made 546 runs in the series, averaging 60. New Zealand lost the first Test in Durban by 30 runs, largely because Jackie McGlew, an old enemy, carried his bat through the first innings and Peter Pollock in his first Test took 6-38 when New Zealand batted again. The second Test was drawn, but New Zealand won the third by 72 runs, batting first to make 385 and never quite surrendering the advantage.

South Africa won the fourth Test by an innings, but New Zealand were not done yet. At Port

ABOVE Jack Cheetham, catching Matt Poore off Tayfield's bowling, led South Africa to victory over New Zealand in the 1953-54 series. LEFT On his Springbok debut Peter Pollock took 6-38 in New Zealand's second innings of the first Test of the drawn series of 1961-62.

Elizabeth Reid totalled 95 runs over the two innings and took six wickets, and in an exciting match New Zealand just held on to win by 40 runs.

1963-64 in New Zealand
New Zealand 0   South Africa 0
Drawn 3
Hopes were high for an exciting series after Trevor Goddard's South Africans had emulated their predecessors in Australia by drawing a rubber there—and with most dashing batting. But the New Zealand tour was an anti-climax, and all three Tests were drawn. South Africa might have won the second Test, but could not make 65 to win in 27 minutes, and New Zealand's ninth-wicket pair thwarted them in the third.

WEST INDIES v NEW ZEALAND

Though matches between West Indies and New Zealand have been few and far between, and not until 1971-72 did a New Zealand side visit the Caribbean, the series between the two countries will always have a special significance for New Zealanders. In 1956 at Auckland, West Indies became their first ever Test victims. The 1955-56 series was notable in two other respects: it was the only full tour of New Zealand by West Indies, the others following Australian visits, and the New Zealand side included S. C. Guillen, who had played for West Indies on their first tour, in 1951-52.

1951-52 in New Zealand
New Zealand 0   West Indies 1   Drawn 1
Despite quite a respectable performance by New Zealand when the series between the two countries began at Christchurch in February 1952, West Indies were stronger in all departments and won by five wickets. Sonny Ramadhin found something akin to his English form and took nine wickets. Bert Sutcliffe, thinking that what life there would be in the pitch would be there on the first day, put West Indies in first at Auckland. But Alan Rae made 99, Jeff Stollmeyer 152, Everton Weekes 51, Frank Worrell 100, and Clyde Walcott 115, and West Indies declared at 546-6. New Zealand followed on and had lost a second-innings wicket when bad light intervened late on the third day. Rain on the fourth day prevented any play and the match was drawn.

1955-56 in New Zealand
New Zealand 1   West Indies 3
West Indies played four Tests on their two-month tour early in 1956 and one of them gave New Zealand their first Test victory. They had been playing Test cricket since 1930. First omens were unpropitious, for on the first day in Dunedin they were bowled out for 74, Ramadhin 6-23, and after Everton Weekes had made 123, West Indies went on to win by an innings. Weekes made 103 in Christchurch, and West Indies again won by an innings. John Goddard, the former captain who came now as player-manager, made 83 not out. When Weekes made 156 in the third Test—he made 904 on the tour, averaging 104 in first-class matches—and

The batting of Seymour Nurse dominated the series between West Indies and New Zealand in 1968-69. In the three Tests he totalled 558 runs at an average of 111.60, and almost swung the series West Indies' way with 258 at Christchurch.

West Indies won by nine wickets, the fourth Test in Auckland seemed a foregone conclusion. But the luck turned.

New Zealand had mustered 203-6 with some difficulty on the first day when the light failed and a tropical cyclone broke. Next day the faster bowlers had a lively pitch and Tony MacGibbon (4-44) and Harry Cave (4-22) bowled out West Indies to give their side a lead of 110. An innings of 41 by the expatriate Guillen enabled New Zealand to set West Indies to make 268 in four hours, and Cave (4-21), Don Beard, and the leg-spinner Jack Alabaster gave them no chance of recovering from a start of 22-6. Amidst great enthusiasm New Zealand won by 190 runs.

1968-69 in New Zealand
New Zealand 1   West Indies 1   Drawn 1
After the historic Australian tour of 1960-61, West Indies did not go on to New Zealand, but the next team, under Gary Sobers, did, and once again New Zealand won a Test. They played with much distinction in the first, which they lost by five wickets, Bruce Taylor's 124 in 110 minutes including five sixes. Though Joey Carew made 109 and Seymour Nurse 95, West Indies were 47 behind on the first innings. New Zealand declared their second innings with eight wickets down, setting West Indies to make 345 in 5¼ hours, and largely

The first Test of the 1968-69 series was memorable for Bruce Taylor's 124 in 110 minutes—the fifth-fastest Test century.

through some magnificent batting by Seymour Nurse (168), the runs were made for the loss of five wickets.

A week later in Wellington New Zealand had their revenge. Again the winners were led on first innings, but on a lifting pitch West Indies were bowled out for 148 in the second innings. At 39-3 New Zealand were unpromisingly placed, but a priceless innings of 62 not out by Brian Hastings won them by six wickets what was now their fifth Test victory. Another mighty innings of 258 by Seymour Nurse put them in some danger of losing the last Test, but after they had followed on, a hundred by Hastings (117) easily warded off defeat. After this series, it was hoped that New Zealand would soon visit the West Indies.

1971-72 in West Indies
West Indies 0   New Zealand 0   Drawn 5
The series of five drawn Tests represented a triumph for the New Zealanders, so often the poor relations at the highest level. But though no result was achieved, it was an exciting rubber.

The tenacity of the visitors was visible from the start as they extricated themselves from trouble to save the first two Tests. At Kingston, Lawrence Rowe made 214 and 100 not out on his Test debut, but Turner, 223, and Wadsworth, 78, saved the day with a sixth-wicket stand of 220. Bevan Congdon, the skipper, turned a score of 99 for 6 into 348 all out at Port of Spain, making 166 not out.

Dropped catches cost the New Zealanders the third Test, while the stand of 387 between Turner, 259, and Jarvis, 182, only contributed to the dullness of the fourth Test. In the final match, rain and some brave late batting from Taylor and Wadsworth ensured a draw.

As a series New Zealand had more to be proud of than their hosts, especially Turner's 672 runs at 96.00 and Taylor's 27 wickets at under 18 apiece.

1979-80 in New Zealand
New Zealand 1   West Indies 0
Drawn 2
New Zealand won a series against the West Indies for the first time, deservedly beating a very strong side. At Dunedin, Lloyd won the toss and batted, but West Indies were rapidly reduced by Hadlee to 4 for 3. Haynes (55) tried to lead a recovery, but the side were all out on the first day for 140 (Hadlee 5 for 34). New Zealand, thanks to Edgar (51) passed 100 with one wicket down but collapsed to 168 for 7. Hadlee (51) and Cairns raised the score to 249, a lead of 109. This was almost cancelled out by Haynes himself, who scored 105 and batted through to the last day after rain had washed out most of the third. But he was not well supported, and when the last wicket fell at 212 (Hadlee 6 for 68), New Zealand needed 104 to win. Holding, Croft and Garner then made a big effort, and at 44 for 6 they were favourites. When Hadlee (17) was out at 73 for 8, that seemed the end, but Cairns (19) and Troup added 27 for the ninth wicket before Cairns was out: 100 for 9. A scrambled leg-bye finally saw New Zealand winners by one wicket. During the match Holding kicked over the stumps when an appeal was disallowed, and several times the West Indians showed dissent. There were a Test record 12 lbw decisions, seven for New Zealand (all for Hadlee). Only Haynes of the West Indians attended the post-match presentations.

The West Indies were put in at Christchurch and, apart from Greenidge (91) and Kallicharran (70), batted disappointingly to be all out 228 (Cairns 6 for 85). New Zealand did not get off to a good start, but Howarth (147), Coney (80) and Hadlee (103) scored well to hoist 460, a lead of 232. When Howarth was 68 he was given not out to a caught-behind appeal, and the West Indians unsuccessfully tried to have the 'offending' umpire removed. After tea, they refused to resume for 10 minutes. Later Croft, who had already knocked off the bails after being warned for excessive bumpers and no-balled, almost knocked over the umpire when he barged into him during his run-up. The West Indies saved the match with 447 for 5 after an opening stand of 225 and big scores from Greenidge (97), Haynes (122), Rowe (100) and King (100 not out).

West Indies needed to save the series at Auckland, and once again batted first. Put in on a green pitch, they were out for 220 (Rowe 50). Again New Zealand got a lead, scoring 305, thanks largely to

a seven-hour 127 by Edgar. When rain ruled out play on Sunday, the umpires declared this as a rest day, rather than the Monday designated. West Indies declared on the last day at 264 for 9 (Troup 6 for 95), but New Zealand easily batted out the remaining 2½ hours at 73 for 4, to win only their second Test series. The West Indians, not used to defeat, had given an exhibition of bad behaviour.

1984-85 in West Indies
West Indies 2   New Zealand 0
Drawn 2
It was five years before West Indies had the chance to avenge their New Zealand defeat. With Richards now captain, West Indies batted in the first Test at Port-of-Spain and made 307. Greenidge (100), Richardson (78) and Richards (57) ensured a reasonable score after Hadlee had sent back two men with 9 on the board. Rain having cut short the third day, New Zealand batted until the fourth, reaching 262 (Jeff Crowe 64). West Indies declared at 261 for 8 (Haynes 78, Richards 78, Chatfield 6 for 73). New Zealand had to survive five hours, which seemed unlikely at 83 for 5, but they eventually reached 187 for 6. Richard Hadlee's 39 not out

allowed him to become the sixth player to score 2,000 runs and take 200 wickets in Tests.

There was a high-scoring match at Georgetown, where Richards batted on an easy pitch. Over the first two days, both of which were interrupted by rain, West Indies amassed 511 for 6, and declared (Haynes 90, Richardson 187, Gomes 53, Logie 52, Dujon 60 not out). At 98 for 4 New Zealand were struggling, but Martin Crowe scored 188, and Coney (73) and Ian Smith (53) helped him post a reasonable reply of 440. West Indies made 268 for 6 declared (Greenidge 69, Richardson 60) in the remaining time.

The match at Bridgetown was quite different. Rain delayed the start, and the wicket under the covers was found to be green. With four fast bowlers in his side, Richards invited New Zealand to bat, and they were soon 1 for 3. Rain stopped play for the day at 18, but it merely put off the inevitable, and New Zealand were out for 94. The West Indian reply was patchy, but Haynes (62), Richards (105) and Marshall (63), especially in an eighth-wicket stand of 83 with Garner, took the total to 336, a lead of 242. The intermittent rain did not save New

Zealand, although by making 248 (Wright 64, Coney 83, Marshall 7 for 80) they forced Greenidge and Haynes to bat again for 10 balls.

In an effort to draw the series at Kingston, Howarth put West Indies in to bat. Although only Haynes (76) and Dujon (70) passed 50, the other batsmen were solid and the total reached 363. When New Zealand batted, Marshall and Garner, after rain had freshened the pitch and lengthened the tea interval, let loose an uninterrupted barrage of bouncers at the batsmen, eventually breaking the arm of Coney. Despite 53 from Wright, New Zealand were out for 138 and followed on. Howarth (84) and Jeff Crowe (112) added 210 for the second wicket, but without Coney the side managed only 283. Greenidge and Haynes scored the 59 required. West Indies won 2-0, and manager Wes Hall justified the intimidatory bowling by claiming that Hadlee had begun it by bowling bouncers to Garner.

WEST INDIES v INDIA

Whereas Pakistan had had several successes against West Indies, India did not beat them until March 1971. That victory eventually brought them the series, and it was perhaps the greatest achievement in their cricketing history to that time.

1948-49 in India
India 0   West Indies 1   Drawn 4
John Goddard's side contained many of those players who were to triumph in England just over a year later, though Frank Worrell, for non-cricketing reasons, did not tour. This was also the last tour of the great George Headley, but he was then 39 and seldom fit enough to do himself justice. Travel in post-war India was still uncomfortable, the pitches generally defied the bowlers of both sides, and West Indies had a hard job to win against an Indian side that included Lala Amarnath and Mushtaq Ali, as well as the up-and-coming Vijay Hazare, 'Vinoo' Mankad, D. G. Phadkar, and Rusi Modi.

Everton Weekes, averaging 111 with four Test centuries, dominated the batting, and in the first innings of the first Test four West Indians—Clyde Walcott, Gerry Gomez, and R. J. Christiani being the others—made centuries. But the only match finished was the fourth, at Madras, which West Indies won by an innings after an opening stand of 239 between Alan Rae (109) and Jeff Stollmeyer (160).

1952-53 in West Indies
West Indies 1   India 0   Drawn 4
There was a similar result when Vijay Hazare took the first Indian team to the West Indies. Both sides indulged in an orgy of run-making —Weekes this time averaging 102 —and the only match finished was in Barbados, where there had been rain before the start. In a fairly low-scoring match, West Indies won by 142 runs. Subhash 'Fergie' Gupte, a leg-spinner who took 27 wickets in the series, served India well, but in the last innings Ramadhin (5-26) proved too much for India.

1958-59 in India
India 0   West Indies 3   Drawn 2
'Gerry' Alexander's West Indian team won an easy victory, the decisive factor being the fast bowling of Wes Hall and Roy Gilchrist who together took 56 wickets in the series. The new young batsmen such as Rohan Kanhai, Gary Sobers, and Basil Butcher made hundreds of runs, but it was not the happiest of tours. Gilchrist was prone to bowl both bumper and 'beamer' and was eventually sent home for disciplinary reasons. Without him West Indies lost their subsequent three-match rubber in Pakistan.

1961-62 in West Indies
West Indies 5   India 0
A year before, India had defeated Ted Dexter's England side, but they had an unhappy tour of West Indies in which almost everything went wrong. They lost their captain Nari Contractor, who suffered a serious injury from a Charlie Griffith bumper; Hall, Lance Gibbs, and Sobers bowled them out; Kanhai, Sobers, Worrell, and Easton McMorris made a lot of runs; and West Indies won all five Tests easily.

1966-67 in India
India 0   West Indies 2   Drawn 1
Fresh from their second triumphant tour of England in the 1960s, West Indies had little difficulty winning in India. Sobers had one of his best series, averaging 114 and taking 14 wickets. Gibbs' off-spin was another major reason for West Indies' success and only in the last Test, where it needed stern defence by Sobers and Griffith to save the match, were India on level terms.

1970-71 in West Indies
West Indies 0   India 1   Drawn 4
When India's new captain A. L. Wadekar took his side to the Caribbean early in 1971, West Indies, over-reliant on Sobers, were not the force of other days and India, in Eparalli Prasanna, B. S. Bedi, and S. Venkataraghavan, had an unusually strong hand of spinners. But the memory of previous failures in West Indies, the shortage of fast bowling, and a lack of class batting led most people to discount an Indian victory. Yet though Sobers scored 594 at an average of 87, and Charlie Davis, Rohan Kanhai, and others made runs, West Indies could not bowl out India. Sunil Gavaskar, a little known 21-year-old Bombay University student, made 774 runs at an average of 154.80, and the older Dilip Sardesai averaged 80.

Despite the fact that Prasanna was not always fit, the other spinners and the medium-paced Abid Ali brought India victory in the second Test in Trinidad. India had looked like winning the first in Jamaica, but they had to fight a defensive action to save the fourth and an even longer one in the fifth when West Indies led them by 166 runs. But Gavaskar's 220, following his 124 in the first innings, warded off defeat, and in the end it was West Indies who were saving the match.

1974-75 in India
India 2   West Indies 3
In a remarkable series in which each Test achieved a positive result, West Indies won the rubber with a resounding success in the final game.

Such a thrilling finale seemed

Nariman Contractor facing Hall in 1961-62, his last Test series.

improbable when the visitors won the first two Tests by vast margins. At Bangalore, Greenidge on his debut made 93 and 107, Kallicharran a splendid 124 and Lloyd a flamboyant but critical 163 in the second innings. India's batsmen could not muster similar form and collapsed in their second innings in the face of some aggressive pace bowling from Roberts, Boyce and Holder.

The pattern was similar at Delhi with Richards, in only his third Test innings, amassing 192 not out. Gibbs tormented India in the second innings with 6 for 76 in 40.5 overs and West Indies won convincingly by an innings and 17 runs.

But at Calcutta and Madras, India struck back in defiant fashion. In the third Test India again struggled initially against Roberts—5 for 20 in the opening innings, but despite Fredericks' 100 in reply, West Indies led by only seven runs. Engineer and Viswanath, 139, masterminded a winning position and the spinners did the rest. The victory, by 85 runs, was India's first against the West Indies at home.

On a difficult pitch in Madras India batted with more resolution although Roberts took 12 for 121 in the match. Viswanath again showed great responsibility, making 97 not out and 46, and Gaekwad's 80 in the second innings proved critical. Set to make 255 to win, West Indies again batted indifferently in the face of Prasanna's off-spin. He took his match figures to 9 for 111 and

India won by 100 runs.

But with the final Test at Bombay extended to six days, West Indies virtually took the series when Lloyd won the toss for the first time. The captain himself made 242 not out with Fredericks 104, Kallicharran, 98, and Murray, 91, playing in supporting roles.

Only a crowd disturbance which held up play for 90 minutes hindered the West Indian strokeplay. In reply, Solkar battled to a maiden Test century with Viswanath again prolific in support.

However, set 404 to win, India subsided in the face of some spirited pace bowling from Holder.

1976 in West Indies
West Indies 2   India 1   Drawn 1
The series was decided in remarkable circumstances at Kingston in the fourth Test. India were 97 for 5 in their second innings, just 12 runs to the good, when it appeared that Bishan Bedi, India's captain, declared thereby virtually conceding the match.

At first sight it appeared that Bedi was making a strong gesture against the persistent short-pitched fast bowling of Holding. But Bedi later stated that five of his team—Gaekwad, Viswanath, Patel, Bedi himself and Chandrasekhar—were not fit to bat. West Indies, in this bizarre situation, won the match and the rubber by 10 wickets.

Returning in some disarray from their disasters in Australia, West Indies had begun with a win at Bridgetown. The unlikely hero was Holford, returning to the Test scene after an absence of five

ABOVE Gary Sobers and Charlie Davis airborne between the wickets. Both took hundreds off the Indians at Port-of-Spain in 1970-71 in a losing series.
LEFT No matter what the bowling, runs flowed from the bat of Sunil Gavaskar when India won in 1970-71.

Malcolm Marshall made his debut.

At Calcutta, Gavaskar (107) and Kapil Dev (61, batting number nine) helped India to 300. With Basil Williams scoring 111 and Kallicharran 55, West Indies scored 327 for a lead. After losing a wicket at 17, India then declared at 361 for 1, the stand between Gavaskar (182 not out, his second century of the match) and Vengsarkar (157 not out) of 344 becoming India's record second-wicket partnership. West Indies avoided defeat at 197 for 9 (David Murray 66) when play ended 11 balls early through bad light.

On a fast wicket at Madras, West Indies were put out for 228, despite 98 from Kallicharran in only 155 balls. Viswanath made 124 in nearly six hours as India replied with 255, a lead of 27. Gomes replied to this with 91 in 4½ hours, but West Indies made only 151, and India needed just 125 to win. The runs were made with three wickets to spare.

Needing only two draws to win the series, India made 566 for 8 declared at Delhi. Gavaskar made 120, Vengsarkar 109, Kapil Dev 126 not out from 124 balls—his first Test century completed with a six—and Chauhan 60. The Indian bowlers then shot out West Indies for 172, enforcing the follow-on. West Indies made 179 for 3 (Bacchus 61).

India guaranteed the series victory by winning the toss on a lifeless pitch at Kanpur. With Viswanath making 179, Gaekwad 102, Amarnath 101 not out, Chauhan 79 and Kapil Dev 62, they made 644 for 7 declared. Because of bad light and rain, which washed out the whole of the fifth day, West Indies opener Bacchus batted over a period of five days (8½ hours at the crease), making 250. Jumadeen (56) was the best of his supporters, and when play ended West Indies were 452 for 8. It was India's rubber.

1982-83 in West Indies
West Indies 2   India 0   Drawn 3
The first Test was at an overcast Kingston, Lloyd winning the toss and putting the Indians in. They were soon in trouble against the four fast bowlers, and needed Yashpal Sharma (63) and Sandhu (68) to add 107 for the eighth wicket and post a respectable score of 251. The West Indies, led by Greenidge (70), made better progress, but nobody else passed 30, and the first-innings lead was only three. The match looked a certain draw when the fourth day was abandoned and play began late on the fifth, especially when India were 167 for 6 at tea. But Roberts (5 for 39) quickly grabbed the last four wickets while only seven runs were added and West Indies had 30 minutes plus 20 overs to get 172 to win. Greenidge and Haynes scored quickly, Richards struck 61 in 36 balls, and West Indies won by four wickets with four balls left.

After such a disappointment,

years, whose 5 for 23 in just 8.1 overs reduced India to first-innings tatters. 142 from Richards and 102 from Lloyd paved the way for an innings win. Although Richards made a masterly 130 at Port-of-Spain, West Indies only just avoided defeat after Gavaskar and Patel made centuries.

When the third Test was switched from Guyana to the same ground, India managed to square the series in magnificent fashion, fighting back from near defeat to score the largest winning fourth innings total in Test Match history. Richards again provided

the early domination with a supreme 177, even though Chandrasekhar took 6 for 120. India had no answer to the pace of Holding, 6 for 65, and when Kallicharran added to that lead with another hundred, India were left 403 to win and defeat for them seemed a formality. Gavaskar and Viswanath made centuries with magnificent support from Amarnath and Patel and India raced home by six wickets. With such a psychological boost, it seemed that the series was theirs for the taking until those strange events during the last Test at Kingston.

1978-79 in India
India 1   West Indies 0   Drawn 5
Having lost a short series in Pakistan, India, led by Gavaskar, took on West Indies, captained by Kallicharran, in a six-match series.

At the Wankhede Stadium, Bombay, Kallicharran surprisingly put in India, after the match had been delayed by four hours. Gavaskar made 205, Chauhan and Viswanath 52 each, and at 424 India had ensured at least a draw. Not a lead, however, as West Indies replied with 493 (Kallicharran 187, David Murray 84, Gomes 63, Parry 55, Chandrasekhar 5 for 116) after both openers scored ducks. India made 224 for 2 (Gavaskar 73, Chauhan 84).

At Bangalore, the match was drawn after the last day had been cancelled on police advice after rioting the night before (following the expulsion from government and arrest of Mrs Gandhi). There might have been a close finish. West Indies made 437 (Bacchus 96, Gomes 51, Kallicharran 71, Shivnarine 62), and India 371 (Gaekwad 87, Vengsarkar 73, Viswanath 70, Clarke 5 for 126). West Indies were 200 for 8 (Gomes 82, Ghavri 5 for 51) at the closure.

India needed to boost morale when the second Test began at Port-of-Spain, but, put in by Lloyd, they began badly. A courageous 58 by Amarnath eased them to 175, which looked much better when Haynes, Greenidge and Richards were out with only one run on the board. Gomes (123) and Lloyd (143) then put on 237, and West Indies reached 394. Facing a 219 deficit, India needed to bat with resolution to avoid defeat, and did. Amarnath scored a much deserved 117, Yashpal Sharma 50, and, with the match almost saved, Kapil Dev came in to make 100 not out from 95 balls.

There was even more rain in the third Test at Georgetown, with no play possible on the second and fourth days. West Indies batted and made 470 (Greenidge 70, Richards 109, Lloyd 81). India made 284 for 3, Gavaskar returning to form with 147 not out.

At Bridgetown, Lloyd put India in. Only 30 minutes were possible during the first-day rains, and India scored 13 for 2. Amarnath (91) scored well, before India were out for 209. Greenidge (57), Haynes (92) and Richards (80) saw West Indies well past 200 with only one wicket down, then Logie (130) and Lloyd (50) took the score to 486. Amarnath (80, after being hit in the face and retiring) and Gaekwad (50) allowed India to reach 277, meaning West Indies had to score one run to win. Wicket-keeper Kirmani bowled a no-ball, to have a peculiar Test career bowling record of 0-0-0-0.

At St John's Laxman Sivaramakrishnan made his Test debut aged 16 years 118 days, the second youngest Test player. Lloyd put India in again, and Amarnath made 54 after again having to retire, this time with nausea. Vengsarkar made 94, and Shastri (102) and Kapil Dev (98) added 156 for the fifth wicket. India made 457. West Indies passed this total, thanks to two partnerships. Greenidge (154) and Haynes (136)

put on 296 for the first wicket. Then, after five wickets had fallen for 38, Dujon (110) and Lloyd (106) added 207 for the sixth. These four players scored over 500 of the 550 total. There was another double-century partnership when India batted again, Gaekwad (72) and Amarnath (116) putting on 200 for the second wicket. India made 247 for 5 declared.

1983-84 in India
India 0   West Indies 3   Drawn 3
The strength of the West Indian fast bowling was overwhelming in the first Test at Kanpur, as they destroyed the new World Cup holders. West Indies batted and reached 454 in fits and starts, Greenidge (194) being the sheet anchor, with Dujon (81) and Marshall (92) helping him add 152 and 130 for the sixth and seventh wickets. Marshall (4 for 19) then rapidly wrecked India's innings. An all-out total of 207 was reached only by Binny and Madan Lal (63 not out) adding 117 for the ninth wicket. The second innings was worse. Vengsarkar made 65, but at 164 all out India were beaten by an innings and 83 runs.

The second Test at New Delhi was more of a match. This time India batted first, and reached 299 for 3 on the first day, thanks to Gavaskar (121) and Vengsarkar (159). Binny made 52 next day but India subsided a little to 464 all out. Captain Kapil Dev (6 for 77) then bowled well for India, but Richards (67), Lloyd (103) and Logie (63) batted long enough to make an Indian win unlikely. Indeed at 166 for 8 (246 ahead) on the last day India were in danger themselves, but they reached 233 (Vengsarkar 63) and there was time only for West Indies to make 120 for 2 (Greenidge 72 not out).

The third Test was the first to be held at Ahmedabad, where the new stadium seated 60,000. The pitch was unpredictable, unfortunately for India, who lost in four days again. However, India did

win the toss and put West Indies in. Lloyd (68) and Dujon (98) were responsible for hoisting the total to 281, which seemed unlikely at 190 for 8. Gavaskar (90) gave India the better start, and they reached 174 with only two wickets down, but at 241 all out (Daniel 5 for 39), they faced a deficit of 40. When he reached 83, Gavaskar became the highest scorer in Test history, passing the record set by Geoff Boycott in 1981. Kapil Dev bowled magnificently throughout West Indies' second innings, taking 9 for 83. West Indies were 114 for 7 but Holding then came in and made 58, helping the total to 201. On a wicket wearing rapidly, India were soon 39 for 7 before the West Indies' fast battery, needing a last-wicket stand of 40 to reach 103 and defeat by 138 runs.

Vengsarkar, who missed the third Test through illness, was back for the fourth at Bombay, and emphasised his worth with 100 when India, this time, decided to bat. Supported by Shastri (77) and Binny (65), he helped India to 463. Holding took 5 for 102, but there were 57 extras, including 26 no-balls. The West Indian innings was full of incident; Haynes (55) became the fourth Test batsman to be out 'handled the ball' when he stopped the ball rolling on to his wicket with his hand, after it had hit his pad. Richardson, in his first Test, was given out lbw for a duck to a ball he insisted by pantomime that he had played first with his bat. His fellow Antiguan, Richards, as if in revenge, struck a brilliant 120 and later Dujon (84) and Lloyd (67) carried West Indies to 393 (Yadav 5 for 131). With Malhotra making 72 not out, India declared at 173 for 5, but West Indies did not attempt the target of 244 in 156 minutes and played out time at 104 for 4.

India batted first at Calcutta and struggled to 241. Kapil Dev (69), supported by Binny and Kirmani, achieved this score after India had faced disaster at 63 for

Viswanath (left) and Gavaskar scored 112 and 102 respectively in India's fourth-innings 406 for 4 which won the third Test at Port-of-Spain, 1975-76.

6. At 42 for 4, when Lloyd entered, West Indies were doing as badly, but Lloyd hit a brilliant 161 not out. Marshall (54) and Roberts (68), who helped Lloyd add 161 for the ninth wicket, supported well, and West Indies eventually reached 377. India collapsed again, principally before Marshall (6 for 37) and this time there was no recovery, the innings closing at 90, for a defeat by an innings and 46. Mohinder Amarnath's record was extraordinary. Having scored 1,000 Test runs already in the year, and being Man of the Match in the World Cup final, he had played six completed innings in the series for one run. After the match the Indian players needed protection from the public. Malhotra and manager Abbas Ali Baig were injured when the team bus was attacked. Before the last Test there were repeated calls for changes, with even Gavaskar, because of the casualness of his approach and support for his captain, threatened with closure of his Test career.

In the event Gavaskar played triumphantly in the sixth Test at Madras. After rain had washed out play on the first day, West Indies batted solidly. Only Dujon (62) passed 50, but the side managed 313. Gavaskar batted at number four, and entered with the score 0 for 2. When India declared at 451 for 8, he had made 236 not out, the highest by an Indian in Test cricket. Shastri made 72 in a stand of 170 and Karmani 63 not out in an unfinished stand of 143. There was a half-hour stoppage on the third day when Davis was struck by a stone when fielding, and Lloyd led his men off the field. With time lost to weather also on the fourth day, the Indian declaration was a gesture and West Indies made only 64 for 1.

WEST INDIES v PAKISTAN

Matches between Pakistan and the West Indies have always been full of incident and well fought, with West Indies just ahead in victories.

1957-58 in West Indies
West Indies 3 Pakistan 1 Drawn 1
In the first Test in Barbados, West Indies scored 579-9, then dismissed Pakistan for 106. In the second innings, however, Hanif Mohammad batted for 16 hours to make 337 and save the match. More prodigious scoring followed in the third Test at Kingston; Gary Sobers made his first Test hundred and extended it to the world Test record score of 365 not out, and in the same innings of 790-3 Conrad Hunte scored 260. In the fourth Test Sobers, then only 21, made a hundred in each innings, and after that match West Indies led 3-0. But in the last Test Pakistan gave an excellent performance, bowling out West Indies through the pace of Fazal Mahmood and Khan Mohammad in the first innings and through the spin of Nasim-ul-Ghani in the second to win by an innings.

1958-59 in Pakistan
Pakistan 2 West Indies 1
Going on to Karachi after a three-month tour of India where they won 3-0, West Indies found the brilliant Fazal too much for them on matting and lost the first Test by 10 wickets. In Dacca, too, Fazal took 12 wickets for 100, and Pakistan won a low-scoring match by 41 runs. This match witnessed one of the most remarkable collapses in Test history—in West Indies' first innings the last six batsmen failed to score and 65-3 became 76 all out. But in the last Test at Lahore Rohan Kanhai made a brilliant 217, rain interfered with both Pakistan innings, and West Indies won by an innings and 156 runs.

1974-75 in Pakistan
Pakistan 0 West Indies 0 Drawn 2
In a short series, Pakistan held their own against a West Indian side that was beginning to show signs of fatigue following their long tour of India.

Roberts showed little indication of decline taking nine wickets in the first Test at Lahore. But his performance was matched by Sarfraz who claimed 6 for 89 to ensure that West Indies led by only 15 runs on the first innings. Mushtaq paved the way for a declaration with a steady 123, but West Indies declined the challenge, although Baichan took the opportunity to make 105 not out in his maiden Test.

Sobers clips another four to leg against Pakistan in 1957-58, and Sabina Park, Kingston, watches as Len Hutton's world record is attacked and broken.

Both sides batted with more purpose at Karachi. Although Majid made 100 and Wasim Raja 107 not out, West Indies responded with centuries from Kallicharran and Julien to lead by 87. At 90 for 5, Pakistan seemed on the brink of defeat even though Asif fought on to score 77. But Sadiq, hit on the face while fielding, rescued his country in gallant fashion by staying to make 98 not out. Even then Pakistan might not have survived had not two and a half hours play been lost earlier in the match through crowd trouble.

1976-77 in West Indies
West Indies 2 Pakistan 1 Drawn 2
In winning a closely contested series, West Indies, as in 1976 against England, owed much to their fast bowlers. This time, however, Holding and Daniel took no part: Roberts was teamed with two new and equally hostile bowlers in Colin Croft, from Guyana, and Joel Garner, from Barbados. Croft took 33 wickets in the five Tests and Garner 25.

West Indies struggled to save the first Test, at Bridgetown, collapsing on the final afternoon before the last pair, Roberts and Croft, held out for a draw. Majid's 88 preceded a Pakistan middle-order wobble before Wasim Raja, with a brave century, and the tailenders took the total to 435. West Indies just failed to match this, though Lloyd struck a powerful 157 and added a vital 151 with Deryck Murray for the sixth wicket. West Indies' pace attack then reduced Pakistan to 158 for 9 before Raja and Wasim Bari put on a record 133 in an amazing stand for the last wicket. Dropped catches helped their cause, and the number of extras for the innings—68—was a world Test record. Richards, 92, and Fredericks, 52, gave West Indies a good start with 130 for the second wicket, but the target of 306 gradually slipped into oblivion as Pakistan's seam bowlers took West Indies to the brink of defeat.

In the second Test, at Trinidad, Pakistan never recovered from Croft's phenomenal first-day performance of 8 for 29. Their 180 was easily overtaken by West Indies, 316, with Fredericks 120, and though they came back with 340 in their second innings, Wasim Raja top-scoring again with 84, Sadiq making 81, and Majid 54, the home side were left with only 205 to make, and did so for four wickets, Greenidge scoring 70, Fredericks 57.

More trouble awaited Pakistan at Georgetown. Put in by Lloyd, they fell for 194, the fast attack again doing the damage. West Indies then piled up 448, Greenidge making 91, Richards 50, Kallicharran 72, and Irvine Shillingford 120. Now, though, the tourists displayed courage and determination in making 540 and averting defeat. With no established spinner, West Indies offered no variety of bowling on a good pitch, and Majid, 167, Zaheer, 80, Haroon, 60, and Sadiq, 48, cashed in. West Indies' target was eventually too tall, though Greenidge had time to make his second ninety of the match.

The series came to life at Trinidad, where Pakistan drew level with a heavy victory—by 266 runs. Mushtaq, the captain, with innings of 121 and 56 and bowling figures of 5 for 28 and 3 for 69, made the match his own, although Majid's first innings of 92 and Raja's 70 were precious contributions. Pakistan's totals of 341 and 301 for 9 were answered with a mere 154 and 222. The stage was set for a deciding fifth Test.

At Kingston, Greenidge, with another stylish display, gave his side the edge with innings of 100 and 82, but Imran, with 6 for 90, kept West Indies to 280 on the first day. Only Haroon, 72, made a score as Pakistan replied with 198, and West Indies forged ahead with an opening stand of 182 in their second innings, Fredericks making 83. The total of 359—Bari having made his 100th wicket-keeping dismissal in Tests—left Pakistan the formidable target of 442, and Croft and Garner saw to it that there was never a real prospect. As the ship went down, Asif treated onlookers to a glorious exhibition of strokeplay in scoring 135, but West Indies took the series and looked as invincible as any side in the world.

1980-81 in Pakistan
Pakistan 0 West Indies 1 Drawn 3
Pakistan, under Javed Miandad, had a strong side to test the 'world champions' in 1980-81, and made this clear in the first Test at Lahore. After batting first and struggling to 99 for 5, Pakistan reached 359, Imran making his first Test century (123). Wasim Raja (76) and Sarfraz (55) helped in the recovery. Richards made 75 and wicket-keeper David Murray

50 as West Indies replied with 297, but rain had washed out the third day, and Pakistan had to be content to bat out time at 156 for 7 for a draw.

The second Test at Faisalabad saw victory for the West Indian pace battery. None of the West Indian wickets was taken by a fast bowler. West Indies won the toss and batted, reaching 235. Richards made 72, after being dropped at 5, a miss which proved vital. Nazir Junior, previously known as Mohammad Nazir, took 5 for 44. Clarke had Pakistan at 2 for 2, and despite Javed making 50, the side totalled only 176, a deficit of 59. Richards (67) was again the leading batsman in West Indies' second effort. Clarke scored 35 not out batting at number eleven, including three successive sixes off Nazir, equalling a Test record. West Indies made 242, Iqbal Qasim taking 6 for 89. Pakistan had little chance of scoring 302 to win, and were all out for 145 soon after lunch on the fourth day.

Because of rain the third Test at Karachi lost its first 1½ days, and the drying pitch was awkward when Miandad decided to bat. At 14 for 4, plus Zaheer retired hurt having been hit on the head, he must have wondered if he had made the blunder of the series, but he scored 60 himself as his side struggled to 128. West Indies did little better, but at 44 for 5 Murray and Gomes (61) made the highest stand of the match, 99, and their total reached 169. Pakistan were in danger at 85 for 5 in the second innings, but Wasim Raja made 77 not out, and the match ended with Pakistan 204 for 9. Had there been another day, the match might have had a good finish.

Rain also spoiled the final Test at Multan, allowing only 40 minutes play on the last two days, but bad behaviour by the West Indians (following the unpleasantness in New Zealand the previous season) spoiled the match still further. West Indies batted and made 249, mainly due to Richards, who, with a leg strain, made 120 not out. Imran took 5 for 62. Clarke again got Pakistan off to a bad start, dismissing both openers with only 4 on the board. Majid and Miandad (57) added 100, but Pakistan were out for 166. During the innings Clarke, annoyed by oranges thrown from the crowd, picked up a brick by the boundary and threw it back, hitting a student, who was taken to hospital. The game resumed after 20 minutes after Kallicharran had calmed the crowd. Later Richards and Croft were warned by the umpires for abusive language. Before the close on the third day, West Indies lost four wickets for one run as they slumped to 85 for 5, but when they had raised their score to 116 on the fourth morning rain ended the series. It was Lloyd's 42nd Test as captain, passing May's record, but it was not one his team could be proud of.

NEW ZEALAND v INDIA

In the first match played by India and New Zealand, at Hyderabad in 1955-56, 'Polly' Umrigar scored 223 and India amassed 498-4 declared.

As so many touring sides have discovered, India are notoriously hard to beat on their own pitches, and it is no surprise, therefore, that New Zealand did not win a Test there until 1970. It was their third visit to India, the first being in 1955-56, and prior to 1970 New Zealand rarely had the spin bowlers needed for victory on Indian pitches. It was significant that when they did win, at Nagpur, it was largely through the nine wickets of Hedley Howarth, whose left-arm spin bowling had been one of the successes of the tour of England from which they were returning. New Zealand first won a series in 1980-81, in New Zealand.

1955-56 in India
India 2   New Zealand 0
Drawn 3
The first series between the countries has been the only one of five Tests, New Zealand, under H. B. Cave, making a full 5½-month tour of Pakistan and India. Having lost 2-0 in Pakistan, they went on to India, drawing the first Test at Hyderabad. 'Polly' Umrigar (223), Vijay Manjrekar (118) and A. G. Kripal Singh (100) made hundreds for India and John Guy (102) and Bert Sutcliffe (137 not out) for New Zealand. 'Vinoo' Mankad made 223 at the start of the second Test in Bombay, and New Zealand were bowled out twice, largely by 'Fergie' Gupte, at this time one of the best leg-break bowlers in the world. In another prolific draw in New Delhi, Sutcliffe made 230 not out and John Reid 119 not out for New Zealand and Manjrekar 177 for India.

At one time during the fourth Test, New Zealand, 204 ahead on first innings, were within distant sight of victory, but in the end they had to stave off defeat after hundreds by Pankaj Roy (100) and G. D. Ramchand (106 not out) and 90 by Manjrekar had revived India. India finished with a resounding victory at Madras, where they declared at 537 for 3 after Mankad (231) and Roy (173) had put on 413 for the first wicket. Spin once again finished the match, Gupte taking nine wickets and J. S. Patel and Mankad four each.

1964-65 in India
India 1   New Zealand 0
Drawn 3
Nine years passed before John

Reid's team stopped in India on its way to England. The first three Tests were drawn, with New Zealand usually slightly better placed. In the second, the left-handed Bruce Taylor made his maiden first-class 100 in fast time and then took 5-86 and in the third Dilip Sardesai (200 not out) and Borde (109) revived India after Taylor (5-26) had played a big part in bowling them out for 88. But in the last Test, another hundred by Sardesai (106) and 113 by India's captain, the Nawab of Pataudi, combined with the offspin of S. Venkataraghavan, who took 12 wickets, to bring them down.

1967-68 in New Zealand
New Zealand 1   India 3
The first rubber in New Zealand between the two countries was played when Pataudi's team went there after touring Australia. They were delighted to find pitches that took spin, and with such bowlers as Eripalli Prasanna, B. S. Bedi and R. G. Nadkarni they were greatly superior to New Zealand in this department. Consequently, they won comfortably. New Zealand did, however, have the satisfaction of winning their first ever Test against India. Batting first at Christchurch they made 502, their captain Graham Dowling scoring 239, and their fast bowlers, notably Gary Bartlett (6-38), eventually brought victory by six wickets.

1969-70 in India
India 1   New Zealand 1
Drawn 1
The visit of Dowling's team to India confirmed the improvement in New Zealand cricket. India won the first Test by 60 runs, Prasanna and Bedi taking 16 wickets on a sympathetic Bombay pitch. The match had been transferred there from Ahmedabad at a late hour because of riots. New Zealand's victory at Nagpur followed, Howarth taking 4-66 and 5-34, and the tourists were desperately un-

At Christchurch in 1967-68 Graham Dowling made 239 and led New Zealand to her first ever victory over India.

New Zealand century-makers at Calcutta in 1964-65: Bert Sutcliffe, tucking Nadkarni away to leg, scored 151 not out and Bruce Taylor made his maiden first-class hundred.

lucky not to win the drawn third Test at Hyderabad. Only 521 runs were scored in five days amid rain and riots, and eventually when India were being bowled out in the last innings, more rain and a marked lack of urgency to dry the ground caused a final abandonment.

1975-76 in New Zealand
New Zealand 1   India 1
Drawn 1
A magnificent spell of pace bowling by Richard Hadlee—7 for 23—brought New Zealand an innings victory in the third Test and so squared a very close series.

Hadlee's burst came at Wellington after fine batting by Burgess and Turner had given the home side a first innings lead of 114. India had some excuse in the absence of the injured Gavaskar but the remainder capitulated to Hadlee who bowled just 8.3 overs. Forty-six for one became 81 all out.

India had begun the series in convincing fashion. Chandrasekhar with 6 for 94 in the first innings and Prasanna with 8 for 76 in the second bowled with too much guile for New Zealand although Congdon twice reached fifty. Gavaskar and S. Amarnath both made centuries during a partnership of 204 and though Congdon added 5 first-innings wickets to his haul with the bat, India won by 8 wickets.

Rain intervened at Christchurch after Collinge had begun well for New Zealand with 6 for 63 as India were bowled out for 270. Turner made 117 in a positive reply until rain washed out the third day and New Zealand's hopes. But at Wellington they were not to be denied.

1976-77 in India
India 2   New Zealand 0
Drawn 1
In the wake of their two-nil defeat in Pakistan, New Zealand suffered further hardships in India, falling prey time and again to the spin wiles of Bedi and Chandrasekhar.

At Bombay, India's runs came from Gavaskar, 119, wicket-keeper Kirmani, 88, and Patel, 82. Turner responded with a patient 65 and Parker with a stubborn century but a well-timed second-innings declaration by Bedi led to victory in the final hour as New Zealand were bowled out for 141, 162 runs short and smarting at what they considered several cruel umpiring decisions.

At Kanpur, all of India's batsmen reached double figures as they amassed 524 for 9 declared, including six half-centuries. New Zealand managed 350, with Turner making 113, Roberts 84 not out, and Burgess 54, but a brilliant unfinished stand of 163 by Gaekwad and Viswanath, who recorded his fifth Test century, enabled Bedi to declare again, and only a stout eighth-wicket stand of almost two hours by Lees and O'Sullivan forced the draw.

On an underprepared pitch at Madras, New Zealand, losing the toss for the third time, went down by 216 runs despite the loss of almost 11 hours through rain. Viswanath, 87, and Venkataraghavan, 64, were India's main scorers, with Cairns taking 5 for 55. But the modest total of 298 was more than double that managed by New Zealand, who collapsed for 140 to Bedi, 5 for 48, and Chandrasekhar, 3 for 28. Yet again Bedi was able to declare in a victory attempt, this time at 201 for 5. The dispirited visitors sank for 143, the spinners again wreaking havoc.

1980-81 in New Zealand
New Zealand 1   India 0
Drawn 2
After both countries had taken part in the Australian season, India played a three-match series in New Zealand in 1980-81.

In the first Test, in Wellington, India asked New Zealand to bat, and after the home side had made a solid start, captain Howarth consolidated with 137 not out. A total of 375 looked excellent as India, with only Patil (64) passing 50, were dismissed for 223, largely due to the swing bowling of Cairns, who took 5 for 33. However, the Indian bowlers quickly worked their way through the New Zealand second innings, which ended on the third day for exactly 100, leaving India to get 253 to win. The quick Hadlee and his medium-pace support did not let any batsman settle and wickets tumbled steadily until India were all out 190, losers by 62 runs.

Rain destroyed any chance India might have had of levelling the series at Christchurch. After reaching 200 with only two wickets down (Gavaskar 53, Chauhan 78, Vengsarkar 61), they reached only 255 (Hadlee 5 for 47), but by then it was already the fourth day, only 79 overs being allowed by the weather in the first three. Reid made 123 not out as New Zealand replied with 286 for 5.

Gavaskar decided to bat in the final Test at Auckland, but India started badly, and only reached 238 thanks to a ninth-wicket stand of 105 by Kirmani (78) and Yadav. Wright made 110 for New Zealand, sharing in stands of 148 with Reid (74) and 99 with Coney (65), as his side scored 366, a lead of 128. Shastri took 5 for 125. Just before lunch on the last day India were out a second time for 284 (Vengsarkar 52 not out, Patil 57), leaving New Zealand to get 157 to win in four hours. Drizzle hampered their progress and at 95 for 5 in 60 overs they settled for the 1-0 series win with four overs left. By then the crowd had invaded the pitch and demonstrated against the New Zealander's lack of effort. It was Gavaskar's first series defeat as captain.

Jeremy Coney and Geoff Howarth, two New Zealand stalwarts of the 1980s, dismiss Botham.

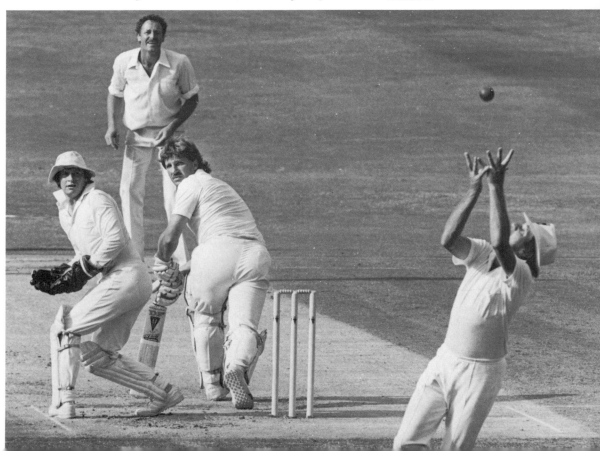

NEW ZEALAND v PAKISTAN

Four of New Zealand's six series with Pakistan to 1976-77 took place in conjunction with visits to India. The exceptions were the Pakistan tours to New Zealand. The pattern of results was similar too, for it was not until 1969-70 that New Zealand won their first Test match against Pakistan, and the rubber it gave them was, in fact, the first they had ever won against any opponents.

1955-56 in Pakistan
Pakistan 2   New Zealand 0
Drawn 1
The first Test played between the two countries was at Karachi in October 1955, at the start of the lengthy tour of the Indian subcontinent by H. B. Cave's team. It was only the second match for New Zealand tourists, and they were well beaten on the matting, the off-spinner Zulfiqar Ahmed taking 11 wickets. But they did better on turf at Lahore and twice exceeded 300, Noel McGregor 111 in the first innings, only for Pakistan to muster 561—a remarkable total considering they were 111-6 at one time. A seventh-wicket stand of 308 between Waqar Hassan (189) and Imtiaz Ahmed (209) restored them, and eventually, needing 116 to win in the last innings, they won an exciting victory by four wickets. New Zealand were lucky to escape with a draw after being dismissed for 70 in the Dacca Test, which was played in a heavy atmosphere and on wet matting.

1964-65 in New Zealand
New Zealand 0   Pakistan 0
Drawn 3
The eight-week tour of New Zealand by Hanif Mohammad's Pakistan side of 1964-65 followed a few preliminary matches and one Test in Australia. Hanif made 100 not out in the last Test, but New Zealand, with better fast bowlers in Frank Cameron, Dick Motz, and Richard Collinge, had the best of three dull, unadventurous draws.

1964-65 in Pakistan
Pakistan 2   New Zealand 0
Drawn 1
Within six weeks hostilities were resumed in Pakistan. This time Pakistan won easily, beginning with a victory by an innings in the first Test at Rawalpindi, which lasted only 12 hours 40 minutes. In their second innings, New Zealand were removed for 79, the left-arm spinner Pervez Sajjad taking four wickets in each innings. In a high-scoring draw at Lahore, Hanif made 203 not out and Barry Sinclair 130, but Pakistan gave a purposeful performance in the last Test to win by eight wickets. Reid's 128 started New Zealand off well, but Saeed Ahmad made 172 in Pakistan's first innings and, when they batted again to score 202 to win, a rousing 126 by Mohammad Ilyas quickly finished the match off.

Pervez Sajjad's 7 for 74 could not save Pakistan at Lahore in the second Test of 1969-70.

1969-70 in Pakistan
Pakistan 0   New Zealand 1
Drawn 2
It was a stronger New Zealand team, captained by Graham Dowling, that visited Pakistan on its way back from an unlucky tour of England. They drew at Karachi on a pitch that took spin throughout and then won their long-awaited first victory at Lahore in the second Test. On the first day the spinners Vic Pollard and Hedley Howarth took six wickets when Pakistan were bowled out for 114. New Zealand never relaxed their grip on the match, and won comfortably with five wickets to spare.

Earlier in 1969, England's series in Pakistan had been interrupted by public disorder, and the last Test played by the New Zealanders in Dacca had its ugly moments. A long innings of 110 by Glenn Turner set New Zealand off well, but a brilliant 92 by Asif Iqbal gave Pakistan a first-innings lead, and when New Zealand declined to 101-8 in their second innings before the spin of Intikhab Alam and Pervez, it looked as if Pakistan might save the series. But the last two wickets added 99, Mark Burgess making a magnificent 119 not out, and in the end it was a Pakistan batting collapse that the final riot interrupted.

1973 in New Zealand
New Zealand 0   Pakistan 1
Drawn 2
Pakistan gained some consolation for their disappointments in Australia by winning the second Test and with it the rubber.

Mushtaq Mohammad was the

Glenn Turner scored 110 at Dacca in 1969-70.

key figure in their win. He made a majestic 201, putting on 350 with Asif Iqbal, who scored 175. Then he and his captain, Intikhab Alam, spun New Zealand out with their leg-breaks and googlies for an innings victory.

The first Test had been drawn, after Sadiq Mohammad had begun the match with an excellent 166. But perhaps the most remarkable event of the series occurred in the last match, after Pakistan had batted first and made a promising 402.

New Zealand had slumped in their reply to 251 for 9 when last man Richard Collinge joined Brian Hastings. The pair added 151 to beat the world record for the last wicket partnership which

had stood for almost 70 years. The stand, together with 107, from Rodney Redmond in his first Test match was enough to save the game and provide some consolation for the New Zealanders in a series they had been hopeful of winning on their home soil.

1976-77 in Pakistan
Pakistan 2   New Zealand 0
Drawn 1
Pakistan comprehensively beat New Zealand in the first two Tests of the three-match series, making full use of the advantage of batting first, but New Zealand achieved some consolation by drawing the third match.

At Lahore, Pakistan owed much to a fifth-wicket stand of 281 between Javed Miandad, who made 163 on his Test debut, and Asif Iqbal who reached 166. Another notable beginning in Test cricket came from the New Zealand off-spinner, Petherick, who did the hat-trick.

In reply to a final total of 417, New Zealand were bowled out for 157, and although Burgess, 111, and Anderson, 92, saved the innings defeat, Pakistan won comfortably by six wickets.

It was a similar story and a ten-wicket win at Hyderabad. Sadiq and Mushtaq both made first-innings centuries and Majid Khan 98. New Zealand fell to the pace of Imran and Sarfraz for 219 in the first innings and to the spin of Intikhab and Miandad for 254 when they followed-on. Parker's 82 provided the only substantial resistance.

At Karachi, the third Test took the same course but New Zealand at last batted with more resolution. Pakistan's opening bursts produced a massive 565 for 9 declared—Miandad 206, Majid 112 and Mushtaq 107. New Zealand found surprising batting heroes in their wicket-keeper, Warren Lees, and pace bowler, Richard Hadlee. Lees contributed 152 and Hadlee 86.

Pakistan again batted flamboyantly and Miandad finished a magnificent series by scoring 85 in the second innings, but set 388 to win, New Zealand played out the draw.

1978-79 in New Zealand
Pakistan 1   New Zealand 0
Drawn 2
Four of Pakistan's key players were engaged in WSC matches when the first Test began at Christchurch. Burgess won the toss and asked the visitors to bat. Javed Miandad (81) was the leading contributor to a total of 271, Hadlee taking 5 for 62. Edgar batted well for New Zealand, making 129, but at 290 New Zealand led by only 19. Miandad made 160 not out in the second knock, and with Talat Ali making 61, Pakistan declared at 323 for 6. It was too many for New Zealand, who were bowled out for 176, with Mushtaq taking 5 for 59 (9 for 119

Javed Miandad was the youngest to make 200 in a Test—at Karachi in 1976-77.

in the match).

The Pakistani 'rebels' were back for the second Test at Napier, and Asif made 104 when his side elected to bat. With Wasim Raja getting 74, Pakistan reached 360. Again, New Zealand passed them, thanks to Howarth (114), Wright (88) and Coney (69). Imran took 5 for 106, but New Zealand totalled 402. The match continued on the rest day when the third day was washed out, but there was not time for a finish, Pakistan batting out the match at 234 for 3 declared (Talat not out 119).

Mushtaq put New Zealand in in the final Test at Auckland, and keeper Wasim Bari caught seven of the first eight batsmen—a Test record. Coney (82) and Hadlee (53 not out) were top scorers in New Zealand's 254. Zaheer's 135 was the backbone of Pakistan's 359 (Hadlee 5 for 104). New Zealand declared at 281 for 8 (Burgess 71) and Pakistan made 8 for 0 at the end, winning the series 1-0.

1984-85 in Pakistan
Pakistan 2   New Zealand 0
Drawn 1
Zaheer and Jeremy Coney were captains for this series, Coney winning the first toss at Lahore and batting on a slow wicket. Imran was injured and publicity-seeking Sarfraz (he was embarking on a political career) announced his retirement two days before the Test.

The stand-in opening bowler, Mudassar, soon had two wickets, and they continued to tumble, New Zealand being out for 157, despite Martin Crowe's 55. Pakistan batted with more resolution, although Mohsin Khan (58) was the only player to pass 50. A total of 221 gave a lead of 64. New Zealand batted better the second time, but after passing 200 with only four men out, mainly due to Wright (65), they totalled only 241, leaving Pakistan 179 to win. They reached 181 for 4 wickets, all batsmen contributing a little, to take a series lead.

The second Test, at Hyderabad, was the 1,000th Test match. It was a good well-fought match, with the emphasis on spin bowling. New Zealand made 267, of which Reid made 106. Abdul Qadir took 5 for 108 with his wrist-spin. Boock then bowled excellently for New Zealand, taking 7 for 87, and Pakistan needed a good innings from Miandad (104) to reach 230, 37 behind. Jeff Crowe reached 57 in New Zealand's second knock, but the other batsmen made little against Qadir and Iqbal Qasim (5 for 79) and a total of only 189 left Pakistan to get 227. At 14 for 2, it looked as if New Zealand might level the series, but the match then took another turn as Mudassar (106) and Miandad (103 not out) mastered the bowling and Pakistan won by seven wickets. Javed Miandad became the second Pakistani to score a century in each innings of a Test.

Pakistan recovered in the final Test at Karachi from 124 for 5, reaching 328 thanks to Salim Malik (50), Wasim Raja (51), Anil Dalpat (52) and Iqbal Qasim (45 not out). New Zealand then made a determined effort to win, with Wright (107), Reid (97) and Jeff Crowe (62) being top scorers in a total of 426, 98 ahead. When Pakistan batted again there came the worst of a few New Zealand disagreements with the umpires when an appeal for caught behind against Javed Miandad was turned down. Coney made as if to lead his team from the field. Miandad went on to 58, and New Zealand's last chance arrived with the score 130 for 5 with over two sessions to play. But Salim Malik (119 not out) and Wasim Raja (60 not out) held out and the match finished an hour early as a draw.

1984-85 in New Zealand
New Zealand 2   Pakistan 0
Drawn 1
New Zealand were looking for revenge when the series began in New Zealand only a month after the third Test in Pakistan. Both sides had new captains, Howarth returning for New Zealand and Javed Miandad taking over from Zaheer Abbas. In the first Test at Wellington, Reid made 148 and then Hadlee (89) and Smith (65) added 145 for the sixth wicket. New Zealand totalled 492 (Azeem Hafeez 5 for 127) and with Pakistan at 223 for 7 had every chance of enforcing the follow-on. But Pakistan reached 322 (Salim Malik 66, Abdul Qadir 54, Boock 5 for 117) and rain confirmed the likely draw by washing out the last day's play with New Zealand on 103 for 4.

At Auckland Howarth put Pakistan in on a green wicket and his seam attack shot the visitors out for 169. The New Zealand batsmen fared better against the Pakistani attack. Reid (158 not out) made his second century of the series, and Wright (66) and Martin Crowe (84) backed him up well, so that Howarth declared at 451 for 9. Only Mudassar (89) withstood the speed and seam in the Pakistan second innings. Before tea on the fourth day they were out for 183 and defeated by an innings and 99 runs.

The third Test at Dunedin was one of the most exciting of all. Howarth put Pakistan in, but with Qasim Omar making 86 and Javed Miandad 79, the total reached 241 for 2. New Zealand then hit back to such effect that Pakistan were all out 274 (Hadlee 6 for 51). Despite most New Zealand batsmen getting started, only Martin Crowe (57) passed 50, and with Wasim Akram taking 5 for 56 in his second Test, New Zealand were out for 220. With the bounce becoming unpredictable, Qasim Omar again batted well for Pakistan, making 89, and a total of 223 meant New Zealand needed to score the highest innings of the match, 278, to win. At 23 for 4 it seemed certain Pakistan would level the series, but Martin Crowe (84) and Coney (111 not out) hoisted the score to 180. There was then another collapse to 228 for 8, with Cairns retired hurt with concussion, so New Zealand needed exactly 50 when the last fit batsman, Chatfield, joined Coney. Despite Wasim Akram's 5 for 72 (10 in the match), these two added the 50 and at 278 for 8 New Zealand had won the series 2-0.

NEW ZEALAND v SRI LANKA

1982-83 in New Zealand
New Zealand 2   Sri Lanka 0
D. S. de Silva won the toss in Sri Lanka's first-ever Test against New Zealand, and put the home side in. Coney (84) and Lees (89) were principal scorers in New Zealand's 344, a recovery from 171 for 7. Sidath Wettimuny carried his bat through Sri Lanka's innings, scoring 63 not out of a total of 144, exactly 200 behind. Following on, Sri Lanka were out for 175 to lose by an innings and 25. Skipper de Silva made 52, and allowed himself to be bowled at the end of the third day to avoid the need for a fourth day. Two brothers, Sidath and Mithra Wettimuny, opened for Sri Lanka.

Put in by Howarth in the second Test at Wellington, Sri Lanka did much better. Madugalle (79) and de Silva (61) helped the score to 240, and with John then taking 5 for 60 New Zealand were dismissed for 201, giving Sri Lanka a lead of 39. Alas, Sri Lanka collapsed in their second innings against the seam attack for 93, and New Zealand needed only 133 to win. These were obtained for the loss of four wickets and a 2-0 series win.

1983-84 in Sri Lanka
New Zealand 2   Sri Lanka   0
Drawn 1
Play did not begin until after lunch on the second day of the first Test at Kandy, when New Zealand made a steady 276, the first eight batsmen passing 20, but only captain Howarth (62) going on to a half-century. John took 5 for 82. Sri Lanka replied with 215, the biggest stand being of 60 for the last wicket between John and Amerasinghe, ending in a run-out. Howarth (60) again led New Zealand's batting in the second innings, New Zealand declaring at 201 for 8. Sri Lanka then collapsed before Hadlee (4 for 8) and Boock (5 for 28), being at one time 18 for

6. Only 51 from Ranatunga saved them from complete rout, but 97 all out meant a 165-run defeat. After the match when rioters hurled abuse and missiles at the Sri Lankan players and dressing room, armed police were necessary to get the players from the ground.

Both teams were guarded by police before the second Test in Colombo. Howarth followed his usual tactic and put Sri Lanka in, and New Zealand's five bowlers shared the wickets as the home side were put out for 174. Jeff Crowe made 50 for New Zealand, but Ravi Ratnayeke took 5 for 42 and at 198 restricted the New Zealand lead to 24. S. Wettimuny (65) and Dias (108), each benefitting from being dropped, put on 163 for Sri Lanka's third wicket in their second knock. Mendis declared at 289 for 9, allowing New Zealand over a day to get 266 to win. Regrettably, they made no attempt to score the runs, ending at 123 for 4, scoring the lowest-ever total on a full last day of a Test (117 off 81 overs). In all the innings lasted 86 overs, exactly half of which were maidens. Martin Crowe batted 221 minutes, hitting two fours in the last over to raise his score to 19. Not surprisingly, it was New Zealand at whom the crowd directed another outburst of booing.

In the third Test, again in Colombo, Sri Lanka batted and made 256. Madugalle made 89 not out and Hadlee (5 for 73) and Chatfield (5 for 63) shared the wickets. New Zealand again batted very slowly, as if content with a draw. Reid made 180 and Coney 98 as the total reached 459—it was well into the fourth day and there was no prospect of defeat. In fact, Sri Lanka once again batted poorly in their second innings. Ranatunga made 50, but Dias was absent, injured while fielding. Hadlee took 5 for 29 and Sri Lanka were out for 142, losers by an innings and 61 runs.

INDIA v PAKISTAN

After three series played between 1952-53 and 1960-61 Pakistan and India did not meet for over 17 years. The political and religious differences that led to the partition of India were never far from the surface. The cricket played was wretchedly cautious, for both sides were fully aware of the damage defeat might allegedly cause to national prestige. Eventually, after 12 successive draws, the series lapsed, and the outbreak of war between the two countries in 1965 did not help to heal the breach. When Test cricket resumed in 1978-79, Pakistan won at home, and the following season India won at home, the two countries being closely matched.

1952-53 in India
India 2   Pakistan 1   Drawn 2
India were Pakistan's first opponents after they entered Test cricket, and it was a promising side that A. H. Kardar took to India in October 1952. Fazal Mahmood and Mahmood Hussain were the backbone of their fast-medium bowling, and they would have been an even stronger force if a third fast bowler Khan Mohammad had not been injured early in the tour. The batting was not as productive as it was to become later, however, for Hanif Mohammad was only 17 and the best of Imtiaz Ahmed was also yet to come. But what gave India the upper hand was the lack of spin on the Pakistan side. The left-arm spin of 'Vinoo' Mankad with Ghulam Ahmed in support was invaluable to India—they took 25 and 12 wickets respectively—and the batting of Vijay Hazare and 'Polly' Umrigar ensured India plenty of runs.

Mankad took 13 wickets in the first Test at New Delhi, when Pakistan followed on and lost by an innings. But at Lucknow, they themselves won by an innings. Hazare and Mankad were unable

to play and Fazal was in his element on matting, taking 12 wickets for 94. For Pakistan, Nazar Mohammad carried his bat through the innings of 331, making 124 not out in over 8½ hours. The veteran Lala Amarnath was too much for Pakistan on a fresh pitch on the first morning in Bombay, and India won the third Test by 10 wickets. The last two Tests in this series began the long history of draws.

1954-55 in Pakistan
Pakistan 0   India 0   Drawn 5
India's first visit to Pakistan was a two-month tour two years later. The pattern was much the same. The same three Pakistan fast bowlers gave their side an advantage when the pitches helped fast bowling, and India had the leg-spin of 'Fergie' Gupte, who took 21 Test wickets, as an important weapon on their side. Mankad, the Indian captain, also played a useful part in the attack though out of form with the bat. Pakistan's first official Test match at home was played at Dacca, and it set the defensive tone. The matches were of four days' duration, but it would have needed many more for them to be finished. The sides, evenly matched, were content to leave the issue undecided.

1960-61 in India
India 0   Pakistan 0   Drawn 5
Pakistan's second visit to India must have established in most people's minds the feeling that the meetings between the two countries were doing no good to cricket and no particular good to political relations. It is hard to apportion the blame for the deadlock other than evenly, but Pakistan, captained by Fazal, did win the toss and bat first in the first four Tests. With Hanif, Saeed, Ahmed, Javed Burki, and Imtiaz in their prime, they were rich in batting, but the great Fazal was past his best and the bowling was weaker. Nevertheless, Fazal did take 5-26 in the third Test at Calcutta, where India were bowled out for 180—the only time in the series when they made less than 400. But rain and the dead-slow tempo of the game prevented a result, even though Tests in this series were played over five days. The nearest either side came to victory was in the last Test, in New Delhi. Pakistan, following on, would have been bowled out in

*LEFT The draw between India and Pakistan at Madras in 1960-61 was the 11th in a series of 13 lasting for 26 years. The Pakistan government declared a national holiday when the sequence was broken.
RIGHT Zaheer Abbas made 235 not out at Lahore in 1978-79 to break the deadlock.*

the second innings in time for India to win but for a last-wicket stand of 38 between Mahmood Hussain and Mohammad Farooq.

1978-79 in Pakistan
Pakistan 2   India 0   Drawn 1
After the war between the countries, Test cricket resumed in 1978-79, when India made only their second tour to Pakistan, 24 years after the first.

The first Test was played on a new Test ground, Faisalabad. Mushtaq captained Pakistan and Bedi India, for whom Kapil Dev made his debut. Pakistan batted first and Zaheer (176) and Javed Miandad (154 not out) put on 255 for the fourth wicket, helping Pakistan to reach 503 for 8 declared. Viswanath made 145, Gavaskar 89 and Vengsarkar 83 in India's reply of 462 for 9 declared. In a high-scoring match, Asif made a second-innings 104 and

Zaheer another 96 before Pakistan declared at 264 for 4, allowing India time to score 43 without loss. The umpires staged a mini-strike which caused the last day to begin late; they were complaining about Gavaskar's language.

At Lahore, India were put in and dismissed for only 199 (Vengsarkar 76). Pakistan passed this total with three wickets down and eventually declared at 539 for 6, Zaheer making 235 not out. Wasim Bari made 85 and Mushtaq 67. India batted better in the second innings, causing Pakistan to use eight bowlers in an effort to shift them. They finally succeeded just in time. India made 465 (Gavaskar 97, Chauhan 93, Amarnath 60, Viswanath 83) leaving Pakistan about 29 overs to score 126. This was achieved for the loss of two wickets with 8.2 overs to spare. Bedi claimed his 250th Test wicket, and also be-

came India's most-capped cricketer. It was the first result after 13 draws between the countries, and the Pakistan government declared a national holiday.

In the final Test at Karachi, Gavaskar made 111 and Kapil Dev 59 in what was to become a typical late flurry as India reached 344. From 187 for 5 Pakistan recovered to gain a useful lead at 481 for 9 declared, thanks mainly to Javed Miandad (100) and Mushtaq (78), who added 154 for the sixth wicket. Gavaskar (137) completed his second century of the match and, supported by Amarnath (53), took India to 300 (Sarfraz 5 for 70), setting Pakistan 164 to win in 26 overs. Javed Miandad (62 not out) was the principal scorer as the target was reached with seven balls to spare for a second successive 8-wicket win. Zaheer scored 583 in the three-match series, a record, and averaged 194.33.

1979-80 in India
India 2   Pakistan 0   Drawn 4
India were looking to avenge the series defeat of the previous season. It looked as if it would be hard work as Pakistan built a big score in the first Test at Bangalore. Mudassar (126), Miandad (76) and skipper Asif (55) scored enough for a declaration at 431 for 9 late on the second day. India then scored as steadily and reached 416, with captain Gavaskar (88), Viswanath (73) and Yashpal (62) leading the way. However, during this innings rain washed out most of the fourth day, and made a draw certain. Pakistan made 108 for 2 by the close.

The second Test at New Delhi was also drawn—but it was a magnificent match. Pakistan batted first again, on a moist pitch favouring seam, and were all out for 273. Wasim Raja (97) and Asif (64) made nearly half of these in a fifth-wicket stand of 130. When India batted, Imran was forced to retire from bowling with a back injury, and Asif was unwell, but nevertheless India were shot out for 126, Sikander Bakht bowling throughout to get 8 for 69. Pakistan made 242 in their second innings (Zaheer 50, Wasim Raja 61). India then made a determined effort to score the 390 required against Pakistan's depleted bowling. They began the last day at 117 for 2, but did not press on quite quickly enough. Vengsarkar made 146 not out, but before lunch was slow. Yashpal Sharma speeded it up with 60, but at the close India were 364 for 6, still 26 short.

Gavaskar won the toss and India batted first at Bombay on a pitch which would obviously take spin. At 154 for 6 it appeared the toss advantage had been lost, but Kapil Dev made a typical rapid 69 and he was well supported by the lower order. The total reached 334. Vengsarkar had earlier made 58. After Binny had made an early breakthrough with three wickets, India's spinners took over and Pakistan were out for 173 after looking in danger of following on. India could only make 160 on a pitch increasingly taking spin (Iqbal Qasim 6 for 40), setting Pakistan 322 to win. It was never on, and despite Miandad's defiant 64 the innings ended at 190. It was India's first victory over Pakistan for 27 years.

On a green wicket at Kanpur, Gavaskar again batted, and India were rapidly 69 for 8. That they reached 162 was due to the last three in the order, particularly Ghavri, who made 45 not out. Seamers Sikander Bakht (5 for 56) and, in Imran's absence injured, Ehteshamuddin (5 for 47) shared the wickets. Pakistan's reply was similar. At 132 for 7 it seemed they would not lead, but Wasim Raja made 94 not out and the total reached 249 (Kapil Dev 6 for 63). The pitch then eased, and India reached 193 for 2 (Gavaskar 81, Chauhan 61) by the end of the

fourth day. Sikander Bakht was guilty of very unsportsmanlike behaviour when refused an appeal against Vengsarkar, walking to the batsman's end and kicking a stump from the ground. Heavy rain on the last day prevented any further play.

Pakistan batted first at Madras, and although five batsmen passed 30, only Majid Khan (56) passed 50 before he was run out. Gavaskar then made the match safe by batting for 593 minutes for 166. With Kapil Dev scoring 84 India reached 430. Imran took 5 for 114 on his return to Tests. Kapil Dev then made sure Pakistan would not save the match by taking 7 for 56. Miandad (52) and Wasim Raja (57) lifted the score to 233, forcing India to bat again. They made 78 without loss to win the series.

Viswanath was made captain of India for the sixth Test, Gavaskar having declared himself unavailable for the tour of the West Indies. India batted first and solid batting down the order, mainly by Patil and Yashpal Sharma (each 62), helped by missed catches,

allowed them to reach 331. Pakistan bravely declared behind, at 272 for 4 (Taslim Arif 90, Majid 54, Miandad 50, Wasim Raja 50 not out) in an effort to force a win, and then dismissed India for 205 (Imran 5 for 63). Pakistan went for the 265 needed but a couple of run-outs when they began to accelerate caused them to give up the chase and play out time on 179 for 6.

1982-83 in Pakistan

Pakistan 3   India 0   Drawn 3

Pakistan had recently defeated both England and Australia when India visited in 1982-83. Imran and Gavaskar were captains. Gavaskar won the toss at Lahore and put Pakistan in to bat, mistakenly as Pakistan reached 485. Mohsin made 94 and Mudassar 50 before Zaheer became the second batsman to make his 100th century in a Test match. He went on to 215. Doshi took 5 for 91. India, too, got a good start from Gavaskar (83) and Arun Lal (51) and Amarnath, returning to Tests, capitalised with 109 not out. Patil made 68 and India totalled 379.

The match was drawn, but not before Pakistan made 135 for 1, of which Mohsin scored 101 not out and became the first Pakistani to score 1,000 Test runs in a calendar year.

In Karachi, India were put in on a green wicket, and it worked, India being out for 169 despite 73 from Kapil Dev. Zaheer (186) and Mudassar (119) then added 213 for Pakistan's fifth wicket, transforming the match. All out 452 (Kapil Dev 5 for 102), Pakistan followed up with devastating bowling from Imran (8 for 60) and India could reach only 197 despite 79 from Vengsarkar and a late 52 not out from Madan Lal. Pakistan won by an innings and 86.

There was heavy scoring in the third Test at Faisalabad. Put in, India reached 372 (Viswanath 53, Patil 84, Kirmani 66, Madan Lal 54). Imran Khan got 6 for 98. Pakistan then made 652, with four century-makers, Miandad (126), Zaheer (168), Salim Malik (105) and Imran (117). Kapil Dev had the astonishing figures of 7 for 220. After Imran's great performance, his opposite number,

Javed Miandad and Zaheer Abbas between them scored 940 runs, average 188, against India in 1978-79. Javed (above) is bowled by Amarnath at Lahore for 35, the only time he was dismissed for less than 100.

Gavaskar, carried his bat through the innings (the first Indian Test player to do so), scoring 127 not out. Amarnath (78) stayed with him long enough to enable India to reach 286 and make Pakistan bat again. Imran took 5 for 82 to register a century and 11 wickets in a great personal triumph. Pakistan won by 10 wickets.

The fourth Test at Hyderabad saw even more startling batting. Pakistan batted and declared at 581 for 3 which included a third-wicket stand of 451 between Mudassar (231) and Javed Miandad (280 not out). This equalled the biggest-ever stand in Test cricket, that for the second wicket between Bradman and Ponsford at the Oval in 1934. India were disheartened and dismissed for 189 (Amarnath 61, Sandhu 71, Imran 6 for 35) and

uncommon occurrence at Karachi.

There were some remarkable Pakistan averages in this series —Zaheer 130, Mudassar 126, Miandad 118, while Imran took 40 wickets at 14.00 each.

1983-84 in India
Drawn 3

The first Test at Bangalore was marred by bad weather and bad feelings. Over seven hours were lost to the weather, some of them surprisingly—there was nearly a riot when play was stopped an hour early on the first day with the sun shining. Play later restarted. This was the first Test in which wides and no-balls were debited to bowlers' figures. India batted and made 275. Binny (83 not out) and Madan Lal (74) added 155 of these for the seventh wicket. Tahir Naqqash took 5 for 76. Pakistan replied with 288 (Miandad 99, Wasim Bari 64). Captain Kapil Dev took 5 for 58. Miandad was spoken to by the umpires after provocative behaviour. India were 176 for 0 before the end, Gavaskar making 103 not out and Gaekwad 66 not out. Gavaskar's century was completed after Zaheer had led his players off with six overs left and Gavaskar on 87. Zaheer claimed that the required 77 overs had been bowled, but after 30 minutes' argument, during which the umpires and batsmen remained on the field, he was forced to return and play out the 20 overs required in the final hour.

In the second Test at Jullunder, Zaheer was the centre of more controversy when, on the third day, during which no play was possible due to rain, he refused to consider that day as the rest day, rather than the following day. As Pakistan, at the time, were on top, it appeared that he was only seeking the draw. This view was given credence by Sarfraz, who was not in the touring party and who claimed his omission from the party later to tour Australia was because he refused to play for three draws in India. Pakistan, put in by Kapil Dev, made 337 (Miandad 66, Wasim Raja 125), and had dismissed Gavaskar and Amarnath cheaply when Zaheer refused the 'extra' day. On the fourth and fifth days, Gaekwad, assisted by missed chances, amassed 201 in 652 minutes, the slowest 200 in first-class cricket. Binny made 54 and India, at 374, led by 37. Pakistan made 16 without loss.

India batted first in the third Test at Nagpur and made 245 (Gavaskar 50, Shastri 52). With Miandad making 60, Zaheer 85 and Mudassar 78, Pakistan scored 322 (Shastri 5 for 75) and achieved a lead of 77. They did not press for a win, however, although when India were 207 for 8 on the last day they might, had they got the last two wickets cheaply, have been forced to decide whether to attempt a small target. But India reached 262 for 8 and declared,

asking Pakistan to face eight overs; they scored 42 for 1.

1984-85 in Pakistan
Drawn 2

Pakistan, looking to confirm their recent superiority over India, batted first at Lahore, but after early shocks (18-year-old Chetan Sharma took a wicket with his fifth ball in Test cricket) batted too slowly to force a result. Captain Zaheer Abbas made 168 not out, and with Ashraf Ali making 65, declared at 428 for 9, made in two days. Accurate bowling by Azeem Hafeez (6 for 46) bundled India out for 156 on the third day, but a dogged rearguard action in the second innings saved the day. Mohinder Amarnath ended a very bad sequence of scores with 101 not out, and he was supported by Gaekwad (60) and Shastri (71) as India reached 371 for 6. Gaekwad

and Kapil Dev argued with their dismissals, and Gavaskar, reinstated as captain in his 100th Test match, was critical of the umpiring.

At Faisalabad in the two-Test series, India batted first, and on a very easy pitch at the Iqbal Stadium, where New Zealand had earlier refused to play, amassed exactly 500. The backbone of the innings was a fifth-wicket stand of 200 between Patil (127) and Shastri (139), after a slow opening 74 by Gaekwad. With Kapil Dev soon breaking down, Pakistan continued batting to the end of the match, making their highest total against India, 674 for 6. After Mohsin Khan (59) and Mudassar (199) had put on 141 for the first wicket, Mudassar and Qasim Omar (210) added 250 for the second. Salim Malik (102 not out) was a third century-maker.

INDIA v SRI LANKA

1982-83 in India
Drawn 1

Sri Lanka played their first Test against India at Madras in September 1982. Batting first after Warnapura won the toss, they made 346 (Dias 60, Mendis 105, Doshi 5 for 85). After time lost on the third day, India declared at 566 for 6 (Gavaskar 155, Arun Lal 63, Vengsarkar 90, Patil 114 not out). The Sri Lankans were not

overawed and made 394 (Dias 97, Mendis 105, Ranasinghe 77, Kapil Dev 5 for 110). Mendis thus became the first Sri Lankan to score a century in each innings of a Test. India were asked to get 175 in 53 minutes plus 20 overs and made a good attempt, only giving up when Patil was run out. India finished at 135 for 7 (de Mel 5 for 68) and honours were even in the countries' first meeting.

PAKISTAN v SRI LANKA

1981-82 in Pakistan
Pakistan 2 Sri Lanka 0 Drawn 1

The two youngest Test-playing countries began their series in 1981-82 in Pakistan, Sri Lanka playing their first Test match overseas.

The Sri Lankans began very well in the first Test at Karachi, against a Pakistan side missing most of the players who had toured Australia, and who had refused to play under Javed Miandad's captaincy. Pakistan were 126 for 6, but Haroon Raschid (153) rescued them in two century stands with Tahir Naqqash (57) and Rashid Khan (59), both making their Test debuts. Pakistan reached 396, but Sri Lanka batted very consistently to score 344, only 52 behind. S. Wettimuny (71), Dias (53) and Mendes (54) were the main scorers. Pakistan declared their second innings at 301 for 4 (Salim Malik, another debutant, 100 not out, Miandad 92, Iqbal Qasim 56). At just under 19 years old, Salim Malik became the youngest batsman to score 100 in his first Test. Sri Lanka collapsed badly in their second knock and were all out for 149, Pakistan winning with two hours to spare.

At Faisalabad, Sri Lanka won

the toss, batted, and had much the best of the match. Wettimuny made 157, Dias 98 and Madugalle 91 not out as they totalled 454, despite Qasim's 6 for 141. The Sri Lankans then steadily worked their way through the Pakistan batting, only Ashraf Ali (another debutant) passing 50 as they were dismissed for 270. Sri Lanka again batted poorly in the second innings, but Goonatillake made 56 and they were able to declare at 154 for 8, setting Pakistan 339 in 330 minutes. D. S. de Silva then became the first Sri Lankan to get five wickets in an innings (5 for 59), but thanks largely to Mohsin Khan (74), Pakistan batted out time at 186 for 7.

Pakistan were at full strength at Lahore, and Sri Lanka found their opponents a different proposition. Put in, they totalled 240, with Dias making 109, but could never master Imran Khan, who took 8 for 58. Mohsin Khan (129) and Zaheer Abbas (134) then made centuries, and with other batsmen, notably Majid (63) contributing, Pakistan declared at 500 for 7. Imran (6 for 58) then wrapped up the match and series by dismissing the Sri Lankans for 158, taking his match haul to 14 wickets.

could not save the match in the second innings, being out for 273 (Gavaskar 60, Amarnath 64, Vengsarkar 58 not out).

During the match, both sides had expressed their confidence in the umpiring, although it was clear that the umpiring was causing dissatisfaction, particularly to India, who were, however, being outplayed.

Rain spoiled the fifth Test at Lahore before the first innings had been completed. Pakistan made 323 (Madussar 152 not out, Miandad 85, Kapil Dev 8 for 85). Mudassar carried his bat, a feat performed by his father, Nazar Mohammad, also against India, in 1952-53. India made 235 for 3 (Amarnath 120, Yashpal Sharma 63 not out).

The sixth Test at Karachi was another high-scoring draw. India made 393 (Shastri 128, Vengsarkar 89) and Pakistan replied with 420 for 6 declared (Mohsin 91, the amazing Mudassar 152). India made 224 for 2 (Amarnath 103 not out) before play ended. Half the fourth day was lost through invasions by rioting students, a not

THE WORLD CUP

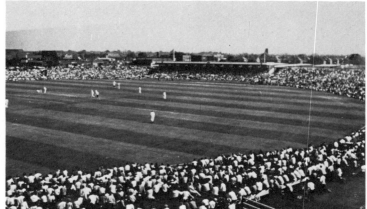

'It might not be termed first-class cricket, but the game has never produced better entertainment in one-day'. So the 1976 *Wisden Cricketers' Almanack* recorded the Prudential World Cup Final of 1975—a tribute from such an established and purist source which amply testifies to the success and acceptance of a new type of limited-over international competition.

A recent phenomenon, it has been a logical extension of the immense popularity of the shortened game in domestic cricket. From the time when the 1970-71 Australia-England Test at Melbourne was washed out and replaced with a well-attended one-day game, a one-day World Cup was never too far away.

The Prudential Cup, 60 overs a side, finally took place between 7 and 21 June 1975 in England. Eight nations took part divided into two groups—Group A included England, New Zealand, India and East Africa; Group B, West Indies, Australia, Pakistan and Sri Lanka. If the inclusion of the smaller nations produced an occasional one-sided contest, the battles of the giants offered more than adequate compensation. Moreover, the entire fortnight was blessed with perfect weather.

The attendances on the opening day of the tournament were very impressive—almost 20,000 at Lord's for England versus India, and a full house at Headingley for the first time in nine years to watch Australia take on Pakistan.

The Headingley crowds were richly entertained. At the end of their 60 overs, Australia had scored 278 for 7, with some fine mid-innings batting from Ross Edwards who made 80 not out. Although Lillee and Thomson had made an early breakthrough, Pakistan recovered as Majid and Asif hustled the score along. Majid made 65, Asif 53—and after 40 overs Pakistan had reached 172 for 4 as compared to Australia's 148 for 4 at the same point.

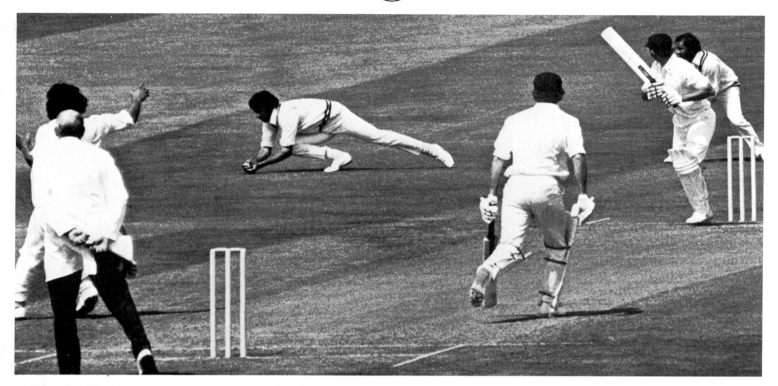

OPPOSITE TOP One-day cricket soon attracted huge audiences and the World Cup in 1975 increased its popularity.
OPPOSITE CENTRE Fredericks lbw to Sarfraz in the Group B match between West Indies and Pakistan at Edgbaston.
OPPOSITE BELOW Jeff Thomson in full cry against Pakistan at Headingley.

TOP A brilliant catch by Sarfraz Nawaz to dismiss Doug Walters off Naseer Malik, but Australia beat Pakistan by 73 runs in the Group B match.
ABOVE Geoff Arnold celebrates as he claims Solkar in the first match in Group A—England began a depressing run by India, beating them by 202 runs after making 334 in 60 overs.

But at this point Lillee returned and brought an abrupt end to the innings. His hostility earned him figures of 5 for 34 in his maximum 12 overs and the accolade of Man of the Match. 205 all out, Pakistan were beaten by 73 runs.

Elsewhere the matches were not so closely fought. At Lord's, England annihilated India by 202 runs. The home side ran up a total of 334 for 4 in the 60 overs. Amiss hit 137, Fletcher 68 and Old, who received just 28 deliveries, struck 51 not out with two sixes and four fours in an innings lasting just 35 minutes.

India made no attempt to attack such a total and Gavaskar batted through the 60 overs for 36 not out, complaining that the pitch was slow and that he had taken the opportunity to get some batting practice.

West Indies and New Zealand encountered no difficulty in overcoming the two outsiders in the field. Julien, Boyce, Roberts and Holder bowled Sri Lanka out for 86 in 37.2 overs with the top score coming from de Silva, the number ten. Only the wicket of Fredericks was lost in reply. Batting first, New Zealand, 309 for 6, were far too powerful for East Africa, with their captain Glenn Turner dominating the batting with 171 not out. Parker with 66 added commendable support, while Nana, slow left-arm, bowled with supreme accuracy in the face of such slaughter. His 12 overs brought him the fine return of 1 for 34. In reply East Africa struggled to 128 for 8.

Last Wicket Stand

The second series of contests on 11 June produced one of the competition's most fascinating encounters—the Group B game, Pakistan against West Indies.

Pakistan again batted well—Majid, Mushtaq and Wasim Raja all passing fifty. Their final total of 266 for 7 set West Indies an awkward target.

A penetrating opening spell from Sarfraz emphasized the difficulty of the task. He removed Greenidge, Fredericks and Kallicharran with the score at just 36. Kanhai and Lloyd established a minor recovery, but West Indies slumped to 166 for 8, and then 203 for 9—at which point Roberts joined Murray.

With 64 runs needed for victory and only 14 overs left, the last pair inched the score along. Murray, neat and determined, played some remarkable strokes while Roberts hung on in support. The two survived some perilous moments to the immense frustration of Pakistan and scrambled home with two balls left.

Also in Group B, Australia overcame Sri Lanka by 52 runs. For the winners it was not a satisfactory day. They batted consistently—Turner 101, McCosker 73, Greg Chappell 50, Walters 59 —to make 328 for 5. But Sri Lanka gallantly accepted the challenge, until some unnecessarily hostile bowling brought a painful end to their effort. Wettimuny, who scored 53, was struck twice in succession and after the second blow, as he swayed in agony, Thomson threw down the stumps in an effort to run him out; the appeal was disallowed. Mendis was struck on the head and retired. Nevertheless Sri Lanka finished with 276 for 4, Tissera adding a half-century.

In the other Group, England ensured their place in the semi-finals by beating New Zealand. Put into bat, England lost both openers for 28, until Fletcher came to the rescue with a splendid 131 out of a final total of 266 for 6. New Zealand batted their full 60 overs in reply but finished 80 runs short despite Morrison's skilful 55. Greig was the most successful bowler with 4 for 45.

At Headingley, India totally out-classed East Africa—bowling them out for 120. Madan Lal took 3 for 15, and Gavaskar, 65 not out, and Engineer, 54 not out, ensured a ten-wicket victory.

On Saturday 14 June, the Group matches were completed. In Group A, England finished with maximum points after their expected rout of East Africa. Wood 77, Amiss 88, and Hayes 52 were the batsmen to capitalise against a steady but never threatening attack. Snow proved to be too fast in reply; he took 4 for 11 and Lever 3 for 32 and East Africa, friendly competitors, took their leave of the World Cup bowled out for 94.

New Zealand earned the second place in the Group in their key match with India. India's final total of 230 owed much to Abid Ali who came in at 94 for 5 and fashioned a spirited 70. Turner produced a marvellous 114 not out with relatively little help, apart from 34 from Hastings. New Zealand won by 4 wickets with just seven balls remaining.

In Group B, West Indies and Australia were both certain to qualify but this did nothing to distract from the appeal of their meeting at The Oval. The capacity crowd was not disappointed.

Lloyd won the toss and asked Australia to bat. Julien dismissed McCosker in the first over and Boyce had both Chappells caught behind the wicket. Australia collapsed to 61 for 5 until the sensible Edwards and the aggressive Marsh rallied their cause. But after making a vital 58, Edwards threw away his wicket and Marsh, 52 not out, was left stranded.

The massive West Indian batting line-up needed 193 to win. They required only 46 overs thanks to the patient Fredericks and a devastating innings from Kallicharran. He settled on Lillee as his victim and, with a savage series of hooks and pulls, struck 35 in ten balls before Lillee finally got him out for 78. West Indies won the match, and the psychological battle, by 7 wickets.

The two semi-finals took place on 18 June—England versus Australia at Headingly and West Indies versus New Zealand at The Oval.

The Headingley wicket has had its share of controversy in recent years and there followed more criticism after Australia beat England in a match in which 16 wickets fell for only 187 runs.

The wicket looked green and over-watered and when Ian Chappell won the toss he put England in to bat. The conditions were perfect for the left-arm pace bowling of Gilmour who had been brought into the side at the expense of Mallett. Swinging the ball very late, he dismissed six of

the first seven in the batting order and finished with the remarkable figures of 6 for 14 in 12 overs. Denness made 27 but England were all out for 93 in 36.2 overs.

Arnold, Snow and Old ensured that the contest was not over by taking six Australian wickets as they struggled to reach 39 but with an even greater sensation in the offing, Gilmour completed a personal triumph by staying with Walters until victory had been achieved and making the top score of the match, 28 not out.

In the other semi-final, the pace of the West Indies' attack proved

too strong for New Zealand. Put in to bat, New Zealand quickly lost Morrison but Turner and Howarth counter-attacked to a lunch-time position of 92 for 1 off 29 overs. But once the impressive Howarth was dismissed for 51 the innings fell apart. Julien finished with 4 for 27 and Holder, 3 for 30, mopped up the tail.

A partnership of 128 between Greenidge and Kallicharran ensured a comfortable West Indies win, though the left-arm pace bowling of Collinge always posed problems and he fully merited his excellent figures of 3 for 28.

BELOW The West Indies keeper, Deryck Murray, attempts to run out Alan Turner in a first World Cup final which featured many run-outs.

RIGHT Alan Turner in more control as he punishes the Sri Lanka attack in the Group B match at the Oval, where he made 100 before lunch.

ABOVE A brilliant catch by Rodney Marsh at Headingley in the semi-final against England. Tony Greig was one of Gary Gilmour's six victims in his match-winning effort.

BELOW Tension in the same match as Frank Hayes just fails to run out Gary Gilmour, whose 28 not out was the top score on either side, making him the Man of the Match.

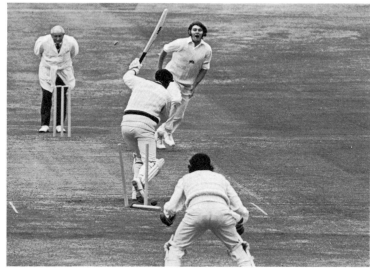

ABOVE Chris Old bowls Ross Edwards for a duck in the England-Australia semi-final.

BELOW Geoff Howarth hits his way to 51 for New Zealand in the other semi-final.

Lloyd's Century in Exciting Final

If the preliminaries had been stimulating, then the final at Lord's on 21 June surpassed everything else. The match began at 11.00 am and its last wicket fell at 8.43 pm. Twenty-six thousand people paid record receipts of almost £67,000 for the privilege of sharing in a great spectacle.

The toss went to Ian Chappell who invited West Indies to bat. With the score at 12, Lillee induced Fredericks to tread on his wicket while hooking. Kallicharran was caught behind off Gilmour and an out of touch Greenidge finally succumbed to Thomson. West Indies were 50 for 3 when Lloyd joined Kanhai.

The captain's response to the crisis was characteristic. He produced a breathtaking counter-attack that swung the whole balance of the match. Kanhai, sensing Lloyd's mood, was content to pass over the strike—one of the game's most vivid performers he spent one period of 11 overs without scoring. Lloyd, hooking Lillee for six, batted for just 108 minutes for his 102 which came off 82 balls. His partnership with Kanhai added 149 in that time. When he left the arena to tumultuous applause, Boyce and Julien wielded their bats to further good effect. Kanhai whose role had been critical finished with 55. Australia needed 292 to win the World Cup.

They might just have done it had not a combination of indifferent running and high-class fielding shattered each attempt to build up a position of strength. McCosker was an early victim of Boyce, but Turner and Ian Chappell took the score to 81 before Turner was run out by Richards. The same player combined to run out both Chappells, Ian having made 62, and although Walters and Edwards both batted responsibly, Lillee, the last man, joined Thomson at 233 for 9. But by throwing their bats in practical style and sprinting between the wickets they kept Australia in the match. Kallicharran 'caught' Thomson from a no-ball, shied at the wicket, and the ball was lost as the crowd, thinking the match was over, invaded the pitch.

But as the light began to fade and the overs run out, the task became overwhelming. Finally, with eight balls remaining, Thomson was another run-out victim with Australia 17 runs short.

There could be no more appropriate recipient of the World Cup then Clive Lloyd, whose cavalier style had dominated the final. Prince Philip presented the trophy to him as thousands of captivated supporters thronged the Lord's pavilion. A memorable finale to a competition of outstanding merit, and the next World Cup, to be held in 1979 was eagerly awaited, although much had changed in the cricket world by then.

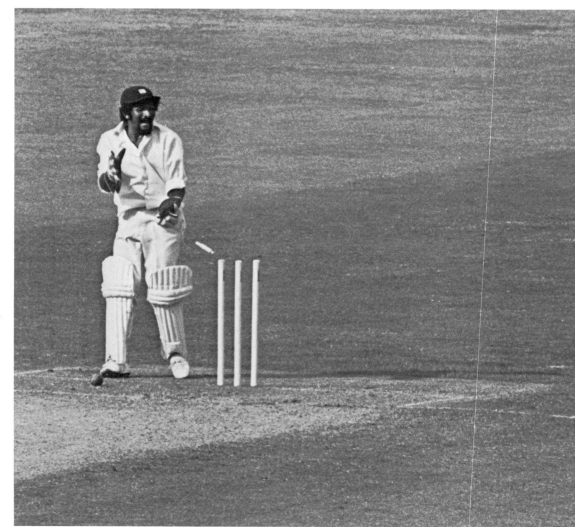

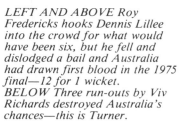

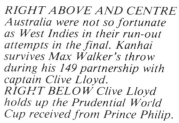

LEFT AND ABOVE Roy Fredericks hooks Dennis Lillee into the crowd for what would have been six, but he fell and dislodged a bail and Australia had drawn first blood in the 1975 final—12 for 1 wicket.
BELOW Three run-outs by Viv Richards destroyed Australia's chances—this is Turner.

RIGHT ABOVE AND CENTRE Australia were not so fortunate as West Indies in their run-out attempts in the final. Kanhai survives Max Walker's throw during his 149 partnership with captain Clive Lloyd.
RIGHT BELOW Clive Lloyd holds up the Prudential World Cup received from Prince Philip.

1979

The rules for participation in the 1979 World Cup were slightly changed. The six Test-playing countries (England, Australia, West Indies, India, New Zealand and Pakistan) were allocated places while the final two places were reserved for the two finalists in the ICC Trophy, the semi-finals of which were contested in England just before the World Cup. Sri Lanka defeated Denmark in one semi-final and joined India, New Zealand and West Indies in Group A of the World Cup, while Canada beat Bermuda and joined Australia, England and Pakistan in Group B.

The first series of matches took place on 9 June, and both Sri Lanka and Canada were comfortably beaten.

At Trent Bridge Sri Lanka scored 189 against New Zealand in 56.5 overs, the captain Tennekson being top scorer with 59. New Zealand knocked off the runs for the loss of one wicket, Turner 83 and Howarth 63 (the Man of the Match) being the not-out batsmen.

Canada won the toss and batted —the only side to do so in the whole competition. They made

OPPOSITE ABOVE Greenidge run out by Randall (left) in the 1979 final. Old, Taylor, Brearley applaud the first wicket.
OPPOSITE BELOW Sri Lanka entered the World Cup 1979 via the ICC Trophy. Warnapurra batting against USA.
ABOVE Richards and King, the match-winners, in mid-wicket.

only 139 for 9 in their 60 overs against Pakistan at Headingley. They got Majid Khan for a single, but Pakistan scored 140 for 2 in 40.1 overs for an easy win. Sadiq's 57 not out earned him the award for Man of the Match.

The West Indies battery of four fast bowlers (Roberts, Holding, Garner and Croft) and one medium-pacer (King) shared the wickets in putting India out for 190 at Edgbaston, only Viswanath playing an innings of quality. He made 75, with Extras on 16 being the next highest scorer. The Indian bowlers fared no better than the batsmen, Greenidge and Haynes putting on 134 for the first wicket. No other wickets fell before West Indies won, Greenidge scoring an unbeaten 106 out of 194 for 1 and being Man of the Match.

The match at Lord's between England and Australia promised to be most closely fought, and was. England put Australia in, and Darling 25, Hilditch 47 and Border 34 got the side off to a reasonably solid start, 100 being passed with two wickets down. But the scoring was slow against accurate bowling by Willis, Hendrick, Old and Edmonds. Yallop, Cosier, Laughlin and later Hogg were all run out attempting to increase the rate, Australia reaching only 159 for 9 in their 60 overs. Botham and Boycott shared the duties of England's fifth bowler, Boycott taking 2 for 15 in six overs.

Boycott actually took more wickets than he scored runs, for when England batted he was lbw to Hogg for 1. Randall was dismissed for the same score, and at 5 for 2 Australia were flourishing. The innings was righted when Gooch joined the captain Brearley. The pair put on 108 runs before Laughlin dismissed them both, Brearley for 44 and Gooch for 53. Gower and Botham knocked off the remaining runs to give England a six-wicket victory with over 12 overs to spare. Gooch's innings won him the Man of the Match award.

Rain Intervenes

Rain played a prominent part in the next series of games, only one finishing in the day. This was the match at Headingley between India and New Zealand. India were put in and struggled to 182. Gavaskar made 55, but wickets fell steadily and the innings lasted only 55.5 overs. Wright and Edgar put on exactly 100 for the first wicket for New Zealand, who lost only one more wicket in passing the Indian score with three overs in hand.

Edgar went on to 84 not out to be Man of the Match. This defeat effectively ended India's interest in the World Cup after two matches in which they captured only three wickets.

The match between Pakistan and Australia was spread over two days. Pakistan, put in, had 99 on the board before a wicket fell, but then Sadiq and Majid Khan were both dismissed, Majid for 61. Asif, the captain, also scored 61, and with Javed scoring 46 Pakistan reached an excellent 286 for 7 in their 60 overs. Although on the following day opener Hilditch made 72, the Australian innings never got under way and was well behind the clock when the last wicket fell at 197. Asif Iqbal was Man of the Match. As England needed only 13.5 overs to pass Canada's total of 45 on the same day, Australia's interest in the World Cup also disappeared after two matches.

The match between West Indies and Sri Lanka could not even be started on the three days allocated, each side taking two points.

Avoiding West Indies

The last Group matches were therefore irrelevant in deciding the semi-finalists: West Indies, New Zealand, England and Pakistan were already assured of their places. The main interest in the England-Pakistan match lay in avoiding a semi-final against the West Indies. Each Group winner would play the second team in the other Group, so assuming West Indies won Group A, England and Pakistan both wanted to win Group B to avoid them.

Pakistan put England in at Headingley, and Imran dismissed Brearley before a run was on the board. When Randall was also out, the score was.4 for 2. Only Gooch passed 30, and at 118 for 8 England were in a very bad way. The unlikely pair of Taylor and Willis raised the score to 161, but England were only 165 for 9 after their 60 overs.

This poor total looked more than adequate after a brilliant spell by Hendrick, which won him the Man of the Match award. He took four wickets in eight balls (4 for 15 in his 12 overs), and Pakistan were reduced from 27 without loss to 35 for 6. Asif, the Pakistan captain, then led an excellent recovery, which raised the score to 151 before Boycott took two wickets for a second time in the competition to finish the fightback.

Meanwhile the West Indies at Trent Bridge made a respectable 244 for 7 against New Zealand, although it required some hitting in the last five overs from Lloyd, Man of the Match with 73 not out, to reach this total. New Zealand made a brave reply, but were always just behind the clock, although while Hadlee (42) was batting they might have made it. They ended at 212 for 9, 32 runs behind.

In the 'dead' matches, there was great excitement initially at Edgbaston, when Rodney Hogg was despatched for 26 runs in his

Kallicharran bowled round his legs by Hendrick in the 1979 final. Richards watches, Taylor and Brearley appeal. At 55 for 3 England were on top at this stage.

first two overs by the Canadian openers, and was taken off. However, it could not last. Hurst, the Man of the Match, took 5 for 21 at the other end as Canada subsided to 105 all out in 33.2 overs. The Australians made the runs for the loss of three wickets in 26 overs.

The match at Old Trafford between Sri Lanka and India was spread over two days. Sri Lanka, put in, batted sensibly to score 238 for 5 in their 60 overs, with Wettimuny 67, Dias 50 and Mendis (Man of the Match) 64 being the principal scorers. Next day India, despite scoring half the runs, 119, before the third wicket fell, did not approach this total and were all out for 191. It was an ignominious defeat for India, who thus lost all three World Cup games.

The Semi-finals
The semi-finals were both excellent matches, each of which could have gone either way.

At Old Trafford New Zealand put England in and had Boycott and Larkins out for 38. Brearley and Gooch repaired the damage, but at 96 Brearley was out for 53 and two runs later Gower was run out for 1. Gooch went on to 71 and Randall made a quick 42 not out, but 221 for 8 was just the sort of target to give New Zealand a chance.

They began reasonably enough and Wright batted well to score 69. But they never quite achieved the acceleration in run rate required. Wright and Burgess were both run out, and Hadlee and Cairns were both dismissed, for 15 and 14, just when two or three boundaries from either could have put New Zealand in control. As it was, at the end of 60 overs New Zealand were 212 for 9, nine runs short. The fifth bowling place, shared by Gooch and Boycott, conceded only 32 runs in 12 overs and Boycott, who bowled nine overs for 24, claimed another wicket, the vital one of Howarth. Gooch was Man of the Match.

The other match for a time was even more exciting. Greenidge 73 and Haynes 65·had 132 on the board for West Indies before the first wicket fell, and with Richards 42, Lloyd 37 and King 34 weighing in with brisk knocks, West Indies scored the almost unbeatable 293 for 6 in 60 overs. Sadiq fell at 10 when Pakistan replied, but Majid Khan and Zaheer then batted so fluently that after 40 overs they had carried the score to 176 and Pakistan looked slight favourites. Then Zaheer was caught behind for 93, Majid Khan went for 81, and the other batsmen perished in attempting to keep the run rate up

to target. Pakistan were all out for 250 after 56.2 overs. Greenidge was named Man of the Match, but this might have been influenced by the convention of usually awarding it to a player of the winning side. Majid and Zaheer scored more runs and Majid was also the most economical bowler in the match, bowling 12 overs for only 26 runs, so he was entitled to feel particularly aggrieved.

Richards Triumphant
The final, on another glorious day at Lord's, lived up to expectations, from the time Brearley put West Indies in and a brilliant piece of fielding ran out Greenidge at 22. Haynes was soon caught off

Old, and Hendrick bowled Kallicharran round his legs. Much was expected again of Lloyd, but Old took a brilliant caught and bowled, and at 99 for 4 the balance was with England. Collis King then joined Richards, who had begun sketchily, and immediately set about the bowling. It was a partnership which was to win the match.

England had Gooch, Boycott and Larkins to share the 'fifth' bowler's 12 overs. Richards hit Gooch for six, King twice hit Larkins for six in an over costing 16, and then hit Boycott (bowling with his cap on) for six in an over costing 15. West Indies had been 100 for 4 at the half-way stage of

30 overs— 20 overs later King and Richards had taken the score to 236. When King was out in the next over, caught Randall bowled Edmonds, he had smashed a glorious 86 in only 55 balls, and the match was transformed. Fifty more runs, nearly all to Richards, came in the final ten overs. When Richards swung the last ball of the innings from his middle stump over long leg for six, he took his score to 138 not out, and West Indies closed at 286 for 9, a formidable total.

Openers too Slow
England began their innings at 3.35pm, and for a long time all went well enough, if slowly.

By the time of the 1983 World Cup, there were seven Test-playing countries, Sri Lanka having joined England, Australia, West Indies, India, New Zealand and Pakistan. The eighth country invited to make up the eight for the World Cup was Zimbabwe, winners of the ICC Trophy in 1982.

England, Pakistan, New Zealand and Sri Lanka comprised Group A, while Australia, West Indies, India and Zimbabwe comprised Group B. Each team would play the others in their group twice each, playing six matches in all.

The opening matches in Group A were notable for some huge scores. At the Oval, where England played New Zealand in a repeat of the 1979 semi-final, there was also a new giant television screen, to show action all round the ground.

England Begin Well
England won the toss and reversed 1979 standard procedure by electing to bat. They made 322 for 6, thanks largely to Lamb, who capitalised on a sound start by hammering 102 in 103 balls. Dilley helped at the end as 90 runs were taken from the last 10 overs, and Snedden became the first World Cup bowler to concede over 100 runs (2 for 105 in his 12 overs). Requiring nearly 5½ runs an over, New Zealand lost quick wickets and were always well behind the clock, and the main interest centred on the innings of Martin Crowe, who reached 97. New Zealand were all out for 216, with one over of their allocation left. Allan Lamb's controlled hitting won him the Man of the Match prize.

At Swansea, Pakistan were scoring even quicker than England in their match against Sri Lanka. Mudassar Nazar, Mohsin Khan, Zaheer Abbas, Javed Miandad and Imran Khan all scored heavily, the stands for the first four wickets being 88, 68, 73 and 96, the last being of only nine overs. At the close Pakistan were 338 for 5, a record for the World Cup. Sri Lanka were not disgraced when batting, however. Kuruppu scored 72 and de Alwis, who scored 59 not out, partnered Ratnayake in a record eighth-wicket stand for the competition of 54. Sri Lanka were not dismissed, finishing their 60 overs at 288 for 9, a score which would win many 60-over matches, but here meant defeat by 50 runs. Nevertheless, it was the highest second-innings score in the World Cup so far, and the match aggregate was naturally a record. Mohsin Khan and Zaheer each scored 82, the former taking the Man of the Match award.

In Group B, where the two opening matches looked to be one-sided, there were two great shocks.

Brearley was twice missed, but after 20 overs he and Boycott had 57 on the board without loss. West Indies had been 71 for 3, so the rate was not altogether impossible. At tea, after 25 overs, the score was 79 for 0—West Indies had been 84 for 3, so the match could still be won. West Indies' 100 had come up in the 30th over, with four men out, England's in the 32nd with nobody out. But West Indies had spurted at this point, while Boycott and Brearley were quite unable to do so. Boycott, on 37, drove Richards to mid on and Lloyd dropped a comparatively easy catch—cynics suggested on purpose. England did not lose a wicket until 6.07pm when

Brearley, on 64, desperately trying to increase the rate, uncharacteristically hooked Holding and was caught by King at deep square leg. This wicket fell in the 38th over, and in the 40th Boycott fell for 57. At the two-thirds mark England were 136 for 2, against West Indies 163 for 4—the gap was now too great. Whereas Gooch, Boycott and Larkins had conceded 86 runs to West Indies, their own fifth bowler, Richards, had already bowled 10 overs for only 35, and there were no easy runs to be scored later from the fast-bowling battery.

The rate now required was 7.5 per over. Randall and Gooch actually all but kept pace for the

seven overs of their partnership, adding 48 runs. They kept the match alive until 6.43pm, when Randall was bowled by Croft for 15. Twenty-three minutes later it was all over. England slid from 183 for 2 to 194 all out as Garner took 5 for 4 in 11 balls. The margin of 92 runs did not reflect how exciting, and for nearly seven hours, how close the match had been. Richards was chosen as Man of the Match for his great innings; King must have been close behind.

The World Cup competition grossed £359,700, and the ICC agreed to hold the tournament every four years, and nominated England as the venue again in 1983.

At Trent Bridge, Zimbabwe were put in by Australia, and batted very sensibly, gradually increasing their rate. Their captain, Duncan Fletcher, missed twice, went on to 69 not out, adding an unbeaten 75 for the seventh wicket with Butchart. A total of 239 for 6 was a very respectable score. Wessels and Wood opened with a stand of 61 for Australia, and Wessels added 51 for the third wicket with Hookes, taking his own score to 76, but the batting had fallen behind the clock. Marsh scored a rapid 50 not out but could not get Australia in front. Zimbabwe fielded well, held their catches and at the close Australia were still 13 runs short at 226 for 7. Fletcher took 4 for 42 to add to his batting performance and was an obvious Man of the Match. It was one of the big shocks of modern cricket.

India Beat West Indies

Meanwhile at Old Trafford, West Indies put India in in difficult conditions and found the Indians playing with much more resolution than in 1979. Yashpal was the star batsman, making 79 after the first three batsmen had gone for 76. Helped by the middle order, he took India's score to 262 for 8, only the second time they had passed 200 in the World Cup and easily their highest-ever score. West Indies' openers were out before play ended for the day at 67 for 2 off 22 overs, leaving the match nicely poised. The following day, however, West Indies collapsed to 157 for 9, making an Indian victory almost certain. Garner and Roberts then put together a last-wicket stand which passed the previous World Cup record (the unbeaten 64 of Murray and Roberts which beat Pakistan in 1973). When they had added 71, and the score was 228, only 35 more were needed in six overs, but Garner was then stumped for 37, leaving Roberts not out with the same score and India with their second World Cup victory. After beating East Africa in 1975, India had waited eight years for another win—but what a win, with the double World Cup winners the victims. Binny and Shastri each took three wickets but Man of the Match was Yashpal Sharma after his aggressive batting.

Back in Group A England began the second series of matches by following their new policy of batting when winning the toss. Against Sri Lanka at Taunton, with its short boundaries, Gower played a scintillating knock of 130, which included five sixes and 12 fours and won him the Man of the Match award. Sri Lanka had now conceded 671 runs in two innings, but once again their batting demonstrated that at least they were not outclassed in this com-

pany. R. G. de Alwis, at 58 not out, once again registered an undefeated 50, and coincidentally equalled, this time with de Mel, the World Cup eight-wicket record stand of 54 which he'd helped to establish two days earlier. Sri Lanka, all out 286, made a large total for the second time, but were beaten by 47 runs.

At Edgbaston, the New Zealand v Pakistan match began late through rain. New Zealand, put in, reached 68 for 1, but the introduction of Abdul Qadir reduced them to 120 for 5. Only 56 overs were possible on the first day, during which New Zealand reached 211 for 8; next day the last four overs added 28 and the innings closed at 238 for 9. Qadir took 4 for 21 and Edgar was top scorer with 44. Pakistan began disastrously against Hadlee and Cairns and lost three wickets before scoring a run. The later batsmen restored some respectability, and the innings closed at

186 after 55.2 overs, but it was a win for New Zealand by 52 runs. Abdul Qadir made top score for Pakistan with 41 not out, and this, allied to his bowling, ensured him the Man of the Match award, one of the few given to a player on the losing side.

In Group B, the two winners of the first round, India and Zimbabwe, met each other at Leicester. India put Zimbabwe in, but this time the batsmen could not repeat their successes against Australia. All the Indian bowlers performed well on a helpful wicket, Madan Lal's 3 for 27 gaining him the Man of the Match selection. In only 51.4 overs the innings was over for 155. There was a hint of a fight-back when Rawson dismissed Gavaskar and Srikkanth cheaply, but he then hurt his back, and Amanarth (44) and Patil (50) saw India home by five wickets in only the 38th over. The Indian defeat of the West Indies led to enthusiastic support

in Birmingham, and there was the unprecedented sound on an English ground of public address announcements in Indian.

The West Indians met the Australians at Headingley with both sides looking for their first win. Australia put the West Indies in, and were proceeding well when four wickets were down for 78. Two of the less illustrious West Indian batsmen, Gomes (78) and Bacchus (47), then repaired the damage by doubling the score. The play ended at 160 for 5 off 42 overs, a fairly balanced position taking the drizzle and bad light into account. Next day the West Indies took the score to 252 for 9 after 60 overs, Holding and Daniel launching a typical late assault by scoring 41 in the last four overs. When Australia batted, Wood was carried off unconscious after being struck in the face by a ball from Holding. Australia fought back through Hughes and Hookes, but then Winston Davis came on to

Kapil Dev hooks during his magnificent 175 not out which turned the match for India against Zimbabwe in 1983.

bowl. Davis and Daniel were in the side because Garner and Marshall were unfit, and met vastly different fortunes. Daniel was hit for 35 in three overs; Davis produced the best-ever World Cup analysis of 7 for 51 as Australia collapsed from 114 for 3 to 151 all out in only 30.3 overs (at least they were up with the clock). Davis' performance made him Man of the Match, but both captains were critical of the Headingley wicket, which they considered dangerous with the fast bowlers operating.

In the third round of matches, Pakistan won the toss against England and followed England's recent lead by deciding to bat before a capacity crowd at Lord's. Only Zaheer was comfortable against the English bowlers on a pitch with plenty of early life. Imran was struck on the foot, forcing him to have a runner, with whose help he was soon run out—more important, perhaps, he was later unable to field. After 40 overs Pakistan were only 87, and it was only thanks to Man-of-the-Match Zaheer's 83 not out that they eventually reached 193 for 8. Against a weakened attack, England had plenty of time to make the runs. Gower and Lamb each made 48 (Lamb not out) in their best masterly fashion, while Fowler made 78 not out in his own manner, looking at once dashing and vulnerable but nonetheless accumulating steadily. England coasted home at 199 for 2 after 50.4 overs, to maintain an unbeaten record.

At Bristol New Zealand put Sri Lanka in. Mendis (43) and Madugalle (60) batted well, but without a huge total to chase Sri Lanka were not as impressive as usual. However, it was Hadlee's bowling which was responsible; he dismissed both top-scoring batsmen in his second spell and later cleaned up the tail. His 5 for 25 was enough to win the Man of the Match award and to put Sri Lanka out for 206 in 56.1 overs. New Zealand were not troubled after Turner (50) and Wright (45) had opened with a fast-scoring stand of 89. Although three wickets had fallen by 110, 76 from Howarth helped New Zealand to 209 for 5 after only 39.2 overs.

In Group B, Australia, without a win, badly needed a result against the unbeaten India at Trent Bridge. They won the toss, batted, and after Wessels had been dismissed in the third over, Trevor Chappell, deputising for the injured Wood, and Hughes scored 144 in 29 overs to put Australia well on the way. Only Kapil Dev, with 5 for 43, troubled the batsmen as Chappell (110), Hughes (52) and then Yallop (66 not out) took Australia to the winning total of 320 for 9. When India went in, MacLeay, one of the lesser known of the Australian party, took 6 for 39 with his medium pacers. Srikkanth, with 39, scored well early on, and Kapil

Dev played a captain's part by following up his bowling with a top score of 40, but the other batsmen failed and India, all out for 158 after 37.5 overs, were beaten by a mammoth 162 runs. Chappell's century earned him the Man of the Match award.

At Worcester, Zimbabwe were put in by West Indies and recovered well from being 65 for 4 with over half the overs gone. Houghton (54) and another splendid unbeaten innings from captain Fletcher (71 not out) took them to 217 for 7 after 60 overs. By capturing two West Indian wickets for only 23, Zimbabwe raised their supporters' hopes, but 217 is not usually a winning score against the West Indian batting might and after only 48.3 overs Zimbabwe found themselves defeated by eight wickets, Greenidge (105 not out) and Gomes (75 not out) having added 195, a record for any wicket in the World Cup. Greenidge was Man of the Match.

The Return Matches

The teams began the return matches with England, the only unbeaten side, comfortably leading Group A and needing only one more win to be sure of a semi-final place, while West Indies and India led Group B.

England sought their win against New Zealand at Edgbaston in what turned out to be the most exciting match so far. Winning the toss, they batted and Tavare and Fowler put on 63 in 19 overs, Fowler going on to 69, but the middle order, with the exception of Gower, failed to capitalise. Gower hit four sixes and six fours in an elegant and powerful 92 not out, including 52 of the last 72, but only Marks and Dilley supported him and he was stranded when the innings closed at 234 all out, still with four overs and four balls remaining. The misjudgement proved vital as New Zealand, for whom Hadlee and Cairns each took three wickets, built their reply. At 75 for 4 New Zealand seemed to be lagging, but Howarth (60) and Coney (66 not out) put on 71, and then Coney and Hadlee (31) added a further 70. Two wickets for Willis, giving him 4 for 42, then swung the match back in England's favour. New Zealand brought the scores level in the final over, from the fifth ball of which Bracewell hit Allott for four to bring a two-wicket victory at 238 for 8. Coney's patient innings made him the Man of the Match, and New Zealand tied England at the top of Group A.

Sri Lanka put Pakistan in at Headingley, and with the ball swinging under a cover of cloud, reduced them to 43 for 5. Unfortunately for Sri Lanka, however, hard chances from Imran and Shahid were not accepted, and these two proceeded to put together a record sixth-wicket stand for the World Cup of 144 at exactly four an over. Shahid was

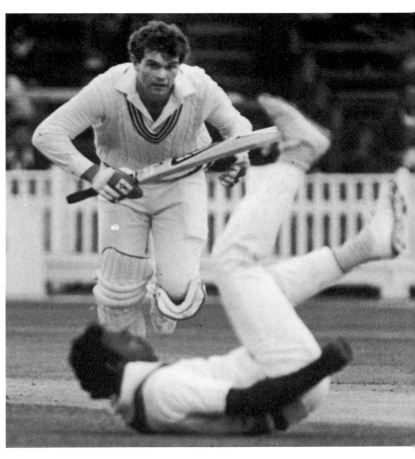

out for 77, but captain Imran went on to 102 not out and the innings reached 235 for 7 at the close, with de Mel taking an excellent 5 for 39. At last Sri Lanka had a target which was attainable, and they looked almost to have attained it after Wettimuny (50), Diaz (47) and Mendis (33) had taken them to 162 for 2 after 47 overs. Abul Qadir then took four wickets in four overs to cause a collapse to 199 for 9. A last-wicket stand of 25 was not enough and Sri Lanka finished 11 runs short after promising to win. Qadir, whose final analysis was 5 for 44, was Man of the Match again.

West Indies were all out for revenge against India at the Oval, particularly as the two were joint leaders of Group B. They decided to bat, but began slowly, a century stand by Haynes and Richards setting a foundation. When Haynes was out for 38, Lloyd scored 41 more quickly, while Richards eased himself back to form and went on to 119. West Indies' total of 282 for 9 was one which had not been overtaken in the second innings in World Cup matches so far. India, however, were well in the match at 89 for 2 in the 21st over when Vensarkar was struck on the chin by a ball from Marshall. He retired at 36 not out and took no further part. Amarnath was also hit several times but showed his courage in going on to 80. Kapil Dev made 36, but the Indians lost wickets in their attempts to keep the score moving against fast and often short bowling and were all out for 216

Martin Crowe off-drives past Mudassar Nazar at Edgbaston, where New Zealand beat Pakistan by 52 runs.

after 53.1 overs. Richards was Man of the Match.

Australia also had opportunities for revenge against Zimbabwe. They, too, decided to bat, and Wood, recovered from his head injury, got them off to a steady start with 73. A rapid 35 not out from Marsh at the end of the innings saw them reach 272 for 7, a difficult target for Zimbabwe. They began shakily, but 84 from Houghton, for which he was chosen Man of the Match, and a sixth-wicket stand with Curran which took the score to 212 for 6, gave them a little hope. But they were always behind the clock, and there was only one ball left when the side was all out for 240, leaving Australia winners by 32 and now level on points with India, behind the West Indies.

Back in Group A, England next met Pakistan before a large crowd at Old Trafford. Pakistan won the toss and batted, but Mohsin Khan, with 32 in 30 overs, was slow, and with 101 for 3 on the board after 33 overs they needed to inject some pace into the scoring. This led to the downfall of the middle order, even Javed Miandad, who was top scorer with 67, being run out. Ejaz Fakir, with 42 not out, led a late rush, but Pakistan's score of 232 for 8 set England not too daunting a task. When Fowler and Tavare had 115 on the board at the halfway stage, it looked easy, and so it proved to be, with none of England's batsmen failing. Fowler (69) was Man of the Match, but Tavare (58), Gower (31) and Lamb (38 not out) also contributed. At 233 for 3 after 57.2 overs, England booked a semi-final place.

Sri Lanka Win

Victory for New Zealand over Sri Lanka at Derby would gain them, too, a semi-final place. In cloudy conditions Sri Lanka put them in, hoping that their swing bowlers would repeat their successes of the Pakistan match. They did, particularly de Mel, who dismissed Turner and Wright in his second over. D. S. de Silva produced a spell of leg-break bowling in the middle of the innings which gave him figures of 12-5-11-2, and when de Mel returned to claim Hadlee and Cairns New Zealand were reduced to 116 for 9. Snedden (40) and Chatfield added 65 for the last wicket, but 181 in 58.2 overs gave Sri Lanka another excellent chance of a first 1983 victory. After two wickets had fallen for 49, Kuruppu (62) and Dias (64 not out) added 80, but then five wickets fell quickly, and visions of the Pakistan defeat arose again. But Dias was not one of the five, and he steered Sri Lanka to 184 for 7 in the 53rd over. Sri Lanka's win meant that all eight participating countries had now won at least once. The Man of the Match was de Mel, whose 5 for 32 was his second successive five-wicket haul.

In Group B it was Australia's turn to face the West Indies, now running into form. At Lord's Australia decided to bat. After Wood and Chappell were out with 37 on the board, Hughes (69) and Hookes (56) added 101 in good time by attacking strokes. Yallop continued his successful run with 52 not out and Marsh also fulfilled his role with a bright 37 near the end, including two sixes off Holding. When the closure came at 273 for 6, West Indies were being asked to score more than any side had scored in the second innings to win a World Cup match, and Australian hopes were high. West Indies started well, Haynes and Greenidge putting on 79 before Haynes (33) was out, but then an in-form Richards and Greenidge added 124 with little fuss or alarms. Hogg, whose 12 overs cost only 25, was the only bowler to slow them. Greenidge was out for 90, but Richards (Man of the Match again) proceeded serenely to 95 not out and after 57.5 overs West Indies arrived at 276 for 3. The seven-wicket win meant a semi-final place.

At Tunbridge Wells, India had an obvious chance to get back on the winning path against Zimbabwe. India elected to bat on a green pitch and disaster struck. Rawson and Curran bowled so well that India were soon 17 for 5. The Indian captain Kapil Dev had come in when the score was 9 for

4, and he began to play one of the great innings of all one-day cricket. For three hours he assaulted the Zimbabwe attack to the tune of six sixes and 17 fours. With Binny he added 60, with Madan Lal 62 and with Kirmani an unbeaten 126 for the ninth wicket, a World Cup record. After 60 overs India were 266 for 8, and Kapil Dev had made 175 not out, a World Cup record, all the more astonishing when it is recalled that he came in at number six. To their credit, Zimbabwe did not give in but batted resolutely in their turn. Brown made 35, Curran, who had taken three wickets, 73, and in 57 overs Zimbabwe made a respectable 235, to lose by only 31. The Man of the Match was, of course, Kapil Dev.

When the last round of matches began, England and West Indies were already semi-finalists, but New Zealand, Pakistan, Australia and India were all fighting for a place, and all had their fate in their own hands.

England began their match against Sri Lanka at Headingley needing to win to ensure avoiding West Indies, who would presumably head Group B, in the semi-final. They won the toss, put Sri Lanka in, and bowled tightly. Sri Lanka were reduced to 54 for 6 before recovering to 136 with the help of a last wicket stand of 33. England were not troubled in making 137 for 1 in 24.1 overs. Fowler (81 not out) played his fourth successive innings of 69 or more, but the Man of the Match award went to Willis, not for his good bowling (9-4-9-1) but for his skilful captaincy.

New Zealand Out

The important match was at Trent Bridge. By losing to Sri Lanka (and scoring so few runs), New Zealand had put their semi-final place in jeopardy. At four points for a win, they had 12 points to Pakistan's 8, but a win for Pakistan in the last match would mean that runs per over scored throughout the competition would decide (a side dismissed was reckoned to have used the 60 overs). New Zealand's run-rate was fractionally better, but defeat by Pakistan would be likely to tip it the other way. Pakistan decided to bat, but with Javed batting 19 overs for 25, a lunch score of 126 for 3 after 42 overs (exactly 3 an over) was not promising. However, Imran and Zaheer, who had come together after 33 overs, punished the bowling after lunch, adding a further 135 in the 18 overs remaining. Zaheer finished with 103 not out and Imran 79 not out in the total of 261 for 3.

For New Zealand, for whom the run-rate equation now meant that they had to win, the innings never quite got on terms with the clock after Turner, Wright and Howarth (39) had gone for 88. Martin Crowe made 43, then Coney 51. Lees and Bracewell (34) helped in

good stands near the end of the innings. With 26 coming from two overs, only 22 were required from the last three. Half of these were got, but New Zealand were all out for 250 with five balls left, leaving Pakistan winners by 11 runs. The two sides had 12 points each, but Pakistan's run rate was now 4.01 per over, with New Zealand's 3.93, almost exactly the opposite of what they had been before the game. Had New Zealand scored 30 or 40 more runs against Sri Lanka they would have been semi-finalists, but Pakistan took the place instead.

In Group B, West Indies comprehensively despatched Zimbabwe at Edgbaston. Curran scored an excellent 62 to rescue Zimbabwe, who had decided to bat, from 42 for 5 to 171, but Haynes (88 not out) and Bacchus (80 not out) knocked off the runs in 45.1 overs for a 10-wicket win. Bacchus was Man of the Match.

The situation in the match at Chelmsford was that, although India had 12 points to Australia's 8, Australia had a better run rate. In effect, this meant that whoever won would go through to the semi-final. India won the toss and

decided to bat, and with only Gavaskar and Sandhu failing to reach double figures they made 247 all out in 55.5 overs. Sharma (40) and Patil (30) were top scorers, with Hogg and Thomson each taking three wickets. When Australia batted, Trevor Chappell was dismissed for 2 and vented his anger on some beer glasses in the pavilion, but Australia reached 46 without further loss and seemed in control. Binny then claimed Wood, Hookes and Yallop for five runs in three overs, while Madan Lal disposed of Marsh, leaving the innings wrecked at 52 for 5. Border (36) offered resistance but the side was out for 129 in 38.2 overs, leaving India victors by 118 runs. Binny (4 for 29) was Man of the Match, while Madan Lal took 4 for 20.

So India faced England in a semi-final at Old Trafford, while West Indies played Pakistan at the Oval.

England won the toss in Manchester and batted, Fowler (33) and Tavare (32) getting them off to a good start with a stand of 69 in 16 overs. Binny then got both out and when Gower (17) went at 107 for 3 the match was evenly

poised. Lamb and Gatting looked impressive until the score reached 141, when Lamb (29) was run out by Yashpal. Thereafter wickets fell steadily until the score stood at 177 for 8. A not-out 20 by Dilley restored a little respectability but 213 all out in the full 60 overs was a target well within India's reach, although India had never beaten a Test-playing country in the World Cup when batting second. Gavaskar and Srikkanth began as if they meant business, with a stand of 46, but at 50 both were out. Amarnath (46) and Yashpal (61) set about righting the ship with care, only beginning to score freely in the 32nd over. Amarnath was run out at 142, with 20 overs left to get 72 runs. Patil (51 not out) then came in to make the final assault. Yashpal stayed till the score was 205, allowing captain Kapil Dev to enter and make a not-out single. At 217 for 4 India won with five overs to spare. Amarnath, who in addition to his fine innings dismissed Gower and Gatting, was Man of the Match, and India, until 1983 easy one-day

victims, had booked a surprise place in the final at Lord's.

In the other semi-final at the Oval, West Indies put Pakistan in to bat. Mudassar Nazar and Ejaz Fakir, playing for the injured Javed Miandad, were out for 34, and a promising knock by Zaheer (30) ended at 88. Imran and Mohsin Khan raised the score laboriously to 139, when Marshall removed Imran and went on to snatch two other wickets in 14 balls. Mohsin went on to score 70 but it took him to the 57th over. Pakistan just could not force the pace against the West Indian fast battery on a wicket which gave them plenty of lift, and the innings closed at a poor 184 for 8 after 60 overs. Imran had been unable to bowl throughout the series because of injury, and although the Pakistan attack removed both openers by 56, there were no more successes. Before the end Mohsin was allowed an over and Zaheer was bowling when Richards (80 not out) and Gomes (50 not out) passed the required total with over 11 overs in hand. Richards was Man of the Match.

Upset in the Final

So the stage was set for a David v Goliath final at Lord's. West Indies won the toss, and put India in to bat. With the score at 2, Gavaskar was out, but Srikkanth

played in his usual dashing manner and with Amarnath had hoisted the score to 59 before he was out for 38. Thereafter the going was slow. Only 90 was on the board at the half-way stage of 30 overs, then Amarnath was out and Yashpal followed two runs later, so Patil and Kapil Dev were forced to begin again. Kapil Dev attacked and hit three fours in the eight balls he faced, but he was out for 15, Kirti Azad lasted two balls, and India were 111 for 6, then 130 for 7. The match seemed lost, but the last three men, Madan Lal (17), Kirmani (14) and Sandhu (11 not out) at least raised the score to 183. India had used 54.4 overs, and general opinion (not to mention expert opinion in the betting tent) was that the West Indian batting would not require so many overs to cruise past that total.

For once West Indies did not make an impressive start. At 5, Greenidge left a ball from Sandhu which came back to hit the off stump. Richards began so confidently, however, hitting Madan Lal for three fours in four balls that 50 was on the board by the time Haynes holed out to cover for 13. Lloyd came in and began to limp badly—he was allowed a runner. Richards, having hit seven fours and scored 33 in only 28 balls, lazily hoisted Madan Lal towards the boundary only to find

Kapil Dev running 30 yards to hold the catch. At 66, Gomes flashed outside the off stump and the ball went straight into Gavaskar's stomach at slip. In the next over Lloyd, who had been in over half an hour for 8, tried to hit Binny over the fielders and Kapil Dev at mid-off held another catch. Bacchus and Dujon slowly took the score to 76 for 5 at tea after 25 overs, but on the third ball after tea Bacchus was caught, leaving West Indies 76 for 6. Dujon and Marshall then batted with determination for 16 overs, adding 43, but not daring to attack Amarnath, whom they had supposed before the match that they might be able to punish. Finally Dujon (25) played on to Amarnath, and five runs later Marshall (18) also fell to Amarnath. Roberts left, and Garner and Holding bravely held out for nearly half-an-hour before Amarnath claimed Holding. At 140 all out after 52 overs, West Indies, the World Cup kings, had lost by 43 runs to India, the rabbits of previous years. Amarnath, who played the longest, if not the highest innings, and took 3 for 12, was Man of the Match. He, captain Kapil Dev, the whole team, the whole Indian population in Britain, in or out of Lord's, and many around radios in India, celebrated into the night—or morning.

ONE-DAY INTERNATIONALS

The boom in one-day international cricket, so strong in Australia that it has resulted in no less than 31 internationals in one season (1984-85), was inspired not by the success of the one-day domestic game in England but by an unscheduled match played for a disappointed public when a Test match was rained off.

This was the third Test between Australia and England at Melbourne in 1970-71, which was abandoned on the third day through rain without a ball being bowled. A seventh Test was arranged to take its place at the end of the season, and meanwhile, on what would have been the fifth and final day, a 40 overs (eight balls) match was arranged.

This match proved to be a great success, attracting 46,000 spectators, who turned up despite the aggravations caused by the ground authorities, who had constantly promised play during the aborted Test match.

Australia won that match by

BELOW Australia beating West Indies at the Adelaide Oval in 1975-76.

five wickets, and John Edrich's 82 won him the first man-of-the-match award.

1972
When Australia visited England in 1972, the first Prudential series was played: a three-match rubber played at the end of the usual five-match Test series. England won the series 2-1, the outstanding performance being the 103 scored by Dennis Amiss at Old Trafford, the first international one-day century.

The following winter, the Pakistan tourists in New Zealand played a one-day international on the Sunday following the second Test. Having lost the Test by an innings and plenty, New Zealand won the limited-overs match by 22 runs.

1973
In 1973 there were two touring sides to England, New Zealand and West Indies, and two Prudential Trophy matches were played

LEFT Ian Chappell's 63 helped Australia gain revenge for the World Cup defeat.

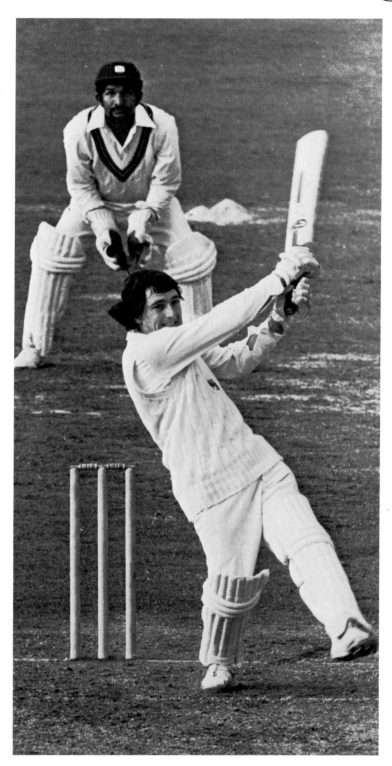

LEFT Derek Randall hitting out against the West Indies in the 1976 Prudential Trophy, in which he batted well.

BELOW Clive Lloyd bowled by Tony Greig for 79 at Edgbaston in 1976, when he led West Indies to a 3-0 win over England.

against each, at the conclusion of the three-match Test series. England beat New Zealand 1-0, the second match being washed out. Amiss, at St Helen's, Swansea, scored the second one-day century. England and West Indies shared their series 1-1, with West Indies winning the Trophy on runrate. The first match, at Headingley, was the closest yet, England winning by one wicket with three balls left. At the Oval, Roy Fredericks broke the Amiss monopoly of centuries with 105. The Headingley match was notable for being the only one-day international played by Garfield Sobers. He scored a duck and was

bowling the final over during which England's last pair won the match.

New Zealand and Australia played a two-match series in 1973-74, Australia winning both games, despite Ken Wadsworth's century at Christchurch. Ian Chappell made over 80 in each match.

1974
The two-match Prudential Trophy series resumed in England in 1974 against India and Pakistan. England beat India in both games, the second being the first 'one-day' match to need a second day, because of the weather. Pakistan

beat England in both matches of their series, although David Lloyd batted throughout England's innings at Trent Bridge for 116 not out. Majid Khan's 109 matched it. The second match, at Edgbaston, was the first to be reduced by the weather—it became a 35-overs match.

In 1974-75 England beat Australia in a single one-day match, but both matches they played in New Zealand were washed out.

1975
The first Prudential World Cup was held in England in 1975. The 15 matches are described in detail elsewhere. Glenn Turner, playing

for New Zealand against East Africa, scored 171 not out, a record score which stood till 1983, and Gary Gilmour, with 6 for 14 for Australia against England in the semi-final, became the first bowler to take five wickets or more. With 5 for 48 against West Indies in the final, he also became the second.

Australia beat World Cup winners West Indies in a single match at Adelaide in 1975-76, while New Zealand beat India 2-0 in a home series, Collinge, with 5 for 23 at Christchurch, joining Gilmour as the second man to take five wickets in one-day international cricket.

1976

England played West Indies in a three-match Prudential Trophy series in 1976, still played after the normal Test series. West Indies won all three games, in one of which Alan Knott captained England for the only time. Richards made the only century and Holder took five wickets at Edgbaston.

Pakistan staged their first one-day international in 1976-77, losing to New Zealand by one run, with their last pair together—the first one-run margin. In the same season the first one-day international was played in the West Indies, the home side beating Pakistan for the Guinness Trophy.

1977

England beat Australia 2-1 in the 1977 Prudential Trophy. At the Oval, Amiss's 108 was passed by Greg Chappell's 125 not out. For the first time the Prudential Trophy matches were played before the Test series, a tradition maintained since.

In 1977-78 England beat Pakistan 2-1 in a series played alternatively with the Test matches, and West Indies drew 1-1 with Australia in the Guinness Trophy. These were the first one-day series affected by the advent of Kerry Packer and World Series Cricket. This was particularly striking in the West Indies, where Australia were without WSC players, while West Indies played them in the match which they won, but were without them in the other match.

1978

England won all four Prudential Trophy matches in 1978, winning 2-0 against both Pakistan and New Zealand. David Gower scored 114 not out in his second one-day international, against Pakistan at the Oval, while Clive Radley scored 117 not out in the last of his four, against New Zealand at Old Trafford. Lance Cairns joined the five-wicket men at Scarborough.

Pakistan beat India 2-1 in a series in Pakistan—but only by India conceding the deciding match. Cruising to success at 183 for 2, with 23 runs wanted in four overs, the Indian batsmen were called from the field by Bishan Bedi in protest when the first four balls from the next over from Sarfraz were bouncers.

Australia played England in 1978-79 in the Benson and Hedges Cup, a four-match series with two matches played between the fourth and fifth, and then the fifth and sixth Tests. This was the season in which the England tour was competing with the second season of World Series Cricket. Australia,

Australia's Richie Robinson collides with England's Dennis Amiss—Prudential Trophy, 1977.

easily beaten in the Tests, won the Benson and Hedges Cup 2-1, the first match being abandoned.

1979

The second Prudential World Cup was held in England in 1979, and was retained by the West Indies, Joel Garner getting five wickets in the final against England. The 15-match series is described in detail in the previous chapter.

A new competition, the Benson and Hedges World Series Cup, played in Australia in 1979-80, heralded the proliferation of one-day internationals in that country. Under the agreement which ended the 'war' between the Australian Board and the Kerry Packer

A narrow escape for David Gower as he dives home before Yashpal Sharma at the Oval in 1978. Gower, Yashpal Sharma and Kirmani end in a heap.

second with five, India last with three, the final Australia v New Zealand match being abandoned. Greg Chappell made the highest score, 138 not out v New Zealand, and returned the best analysis, 5 for 15 v India.

Australia won the best-of-five final by 3-1, after New Zealand had easily won the first match. Australia's second win came at Melbourne and sparked a furore over sportsmanship. New Zealand required six to win off the final ball, which Greg Chappell instructed his brother, Trevor, to bowl underarm along the ground, thus ensuring Australia's win. One of the most notorious incidents of modern cricket, it outraged the New Zealand Prime Minister, who called it 'an act of cowardice' and aroused criticism all round the world. It was, however, in Australia at that time, legal.

England, in the West Indies, lost a series 2-0, with Colin Croft taking 6 for 15 at St Vincent, just short of Gilmour's 6 for 14 mentioned earlier. New Zealand beat India 2-0 in New Zealand after the World Series Cup disappointments.

1981
Australia came from behind to beat England 2-1 in the 1981 Prudential Trophy, with Graeme Wood making 108 at Headingley in the decisive match.

Pakistan and the West Indies then went to Australia for the 1981-82 Benson and Hedges World Series. West Indies scored seven wins, Pakistan and Australia four each. Each country had a century-maker: Greenidge, Zaheer and Bruce Laird. Pakistan were desperately unlucky not to qualify. They lost their final match to West Indies when West Indies' target had been reduced because of rain from 178 to 107 in 30 overs—they won by one wicket with one ball to spare. Australia then had to beat West Indies, and did so in another rain-affected match by virtue of Border hitting the first ball of an over from Holding for four before the players came off. Australia thus won the match on run-rate and qualified for the finals similarly. West Indies won the final series 3-1, incidentally registering their first win over Australia under floodlights, after six defeats.

The popularity of one-day internationals in Australia was shown by the attendance at Melbourne for one of the Australia v West Indies matches: 78,142.

England, meanwhile, were touring India, and took part in a three-match Wills series, which India won 2-1 after losing the first match. It was the first one-day series in India. England then went on to Sri Lanka for that country's

empire, both the West Indies and England toured Australia in 1979-80, each playing a three-match Test series against the home side. The three countries took part in a one-day competition involving first of all a league, in which each country played each other four times, followed by a three-match final between the two top teams. England won the league part easily, with five wins from seven matches (one abandoned), with West Indies finishing second with three wins from seven, and Australia last with three wins. The best performances were 153 not out by Viv Richards against Australia at Melbourne and 5 for 22 by Andy Roberts against England at Adelaide. Richards and Dennis Lillee were chosen for series awards for batting and bowling.

West Indies won the final 2-0, Richards winning more dollars as

player of the series, and Gordon Greenidge cashing in as player of the finals.

A development which had effects on the rules of future one-day internationals came in a match in which West Indies needed three runs off the final ball to beat England. Brearley placed all his fielders, including the wicket-keeper, on the boundary. In the event, Botham bowled Croft, but restrictions on field placings were not far off. Some of the matches in this series were floodlit.

West Indies played a single match in New Zealand after their success, and were beaten by one wicket.

1980
West Indies were tourists in England in 1980 and played a two-match Prudential Trophy series. Each side won one match, West

Indies taking the Trophy on scoring rate. Remarkably the two player awards were won by Chris Tavare and Geoff Boycott, neither famous for rapid scoring.

England also played a single Prudential Trophy match in 1980 against Australia, who were in England for the Centenary Test. England won after scoring 320 for 8 in 55 overs, Roland Butcher, in his debut, reaching 50 in 35 balls.

Three matches in Pakistan in 1980-81 were all won by the West Indies, while in Australia, New Zealand and India were the two visitors in the Benson and Hedges World Series Cup. This grew this year: each country played each other five times in the league. India began well in the league but lost the last five matches, while New Zealand began badly and finished well. Australia finished top with six wins, New Zealand

OPPOSITE Norman Cowans about to run out John Wright in the Benson and Hedges World Series Cup, Melbourne, 1982-83.

ABOVE The Texaco Trophy match at Lord's, 1984. Richards and Bairstow grab stumps at the end.

first Test match, and played two one-day matches, winning the first by five runs and losing the second by three runs after a collapse.

After the Benson and Hedges Cup, Australia went to New Zealand to publicize another tobacco product by taking part in the Rothmans Cup. New Zealand won the first match, despite a century from Greg Chappell, but Australia took the next two with Terry Alderman getting 5 for 17 at Wellington.

Sri Lanka, after their surprise victory in a match against England, went to Pakistan to lose a Wills series 2-1, but registered another match win, this one on run rate in a reduced match, but they were on the way to victory anyway, scoring 227 for 4 at nearly seven per over.

1982
England's Prudential Trophy series against India and Pakistan in 1982 were both won 2-0, Allan

Lamb making his debut and averaging 93 in the four matches. Derek Pringle, who made his debut against Pakistan, was born in Kenya and is the son of Donald Pringle, who played for East Africa in the World Cup of 1975.

Sri Lanka were unable to score a win in India in 1982-83, losing 3-0, but Roy Dias distinguished himself with 102 and 121 in successive matches, Sri Lanka's first one-day centuries.

Australia played a Wills series in Pakistan, losing 2-0, with one match abandoned. Mohsin and Zaheer each made centuries. Then Pakistan beat India 3-1 in another Wills series, due to more big scoring, Javed Miandad (2), Zaheer (3) and Mohsin Khan all scoring centuries. Zaheer thus scored his sixth one-day international century, passing the record of Amiss, and becoming the first to score three successive hundreds.

England and New Zealand went

to Australia for the 1982-83 Benson and Hedges World Series Cup. New Zealand won the league competition with six wins to Australia's five and England's four. England were unlucky to have their vital last match reduced to 23 overs when they had already batted for 17.3 overs, and lost. All four centuries in the series were scored by Englishmen, however, three by Gower, who was player of the series. One Australia v England match at Melbourne was watched by a new record one-day crowd of 84,153.

The final series was won 2-0 by Australia, who won the first match after having their target reduced by rain. The finals were marred by bad sportsmanship, there clearly being ill-feeling between the sides from the 'underarm' ball of the final two years earlier. The Australian side seemed to be the main offenders. On a happier note, Stephen Smith, in his third match for Australia, made 117.

New Zealand were a different proposition in a Rothmans Cup series against England, comfortably winning 3-0, a margin repeated afterwards against Sri

Lanka, with Glenn Turner making 140 in one match.

West Indies entertained India, and won 2-1, while Australia went to Sri Lanka, losing a four-match series 2-0, with two matches abandoned.

1983
In 1983 the third Prudential World Cup took place in England, and was surprisingly won by India, as described in the previous chapter. There was another instance of a 5-wicket bowler: Vic Marks for England against Sri Lanka, in which match Gower scored his sixth century to equal Zaheer's record. For West Indies against Australia, Winston Davis took 7 for 51, the only instance of a bowler taking seven wickets in a one-day international. Later Ken Macleay, for Australia against India, took 6 for 38, and in the Pakistan v Sri Lanka match at Headingley, Ashantha De Mel took 5 for 39 for Sri Lanka and Abdul Qadir 5 for 44 for Pakistan. De Mel repeated his feat with 5 for 32 against New Zealand, and Zaheer edged ahead of Gower again with his seventh century.

India confirmed their World Cup win with a 2-0 victory over Pakistan in 1983-84, but were then beaten 5-0 by West Indies in the Charminar Challenge Cup. The West Indies batting was triumphant, scoring 333 in their 45 overs at Jamshedpur.

The 1983-84 Benson and Hedges World Series Cup featured West Indies and Pakistan as Australia's visitors. West Indies easily won the league table series, with eight wins, and Australia were comfortably second. Carl Rackemann, 5 for 16 against Pakistan, and Abdul Qadir, 5 for 53 against Australia, were five-wicket men. Melbourne once again hoisted a new total for the record crowd: 86,133 watched West Indies beat Australia.

West Indies easily won the first final against Australia, but controversy surrounded the second. West Indies scored 222 for 5, Australia 222 for 9. West Indies thought they'd won by losing fewer wickets, but it was decreed that the match was a tie, and a third match was required. Although the rules suggested that even if Australia won the third match the cup would still be West Indies' on the countback of victories in the qualifying round, it was also agreed that should Australia win the cup would be shared. The whole set-up suggested manipulation. Clive Lloyd and Viv Richards found they were unfit for the deciding match and it seemed some West Indians were lacking in total commitment but, captained by Holding, West Indies dispelled any doubts by winning again, Garner taking 5 for 31.

England, meanwhile, improved on some recent performances by beating New Zealand 2-1 in a Rothmans Cup series. Richard Hadlee (5 for 32) and Vic Marks (5 for 20) each took five wickets, Marks being the first Englishman to achieve the feat twice.

Australia, after losing the World Series Cup final to West Indies, toured there, and lost a series 3-1. Desmond Haynes was man-of-the-match with not out centuries in all three wins—his series average (once out) was 340!

Sri Lanka entertained New Zealand and lost 2-1, but a player making his debut, Uvaisul Karnain, took 5 for 26 in Sri Lanka's win. England visited Pakistan, and shared a Wills series 1-1, each side recording a six-wicket victory.

The final 1983-84 series took place at Sharjah, in the United Arab Emirates, when businessman A. R. Bukhatir organised a Rothmans Asia Cup, in which Pakistan, India and Sri Lanka played each other once. India won with two wins to Sri Lanka's one.

1984

In England in 1984 a new competition, the Texaco Trophy, replaced the Prudential Trophy. West Indies beat England 2-1, England's one win being the only time in eight matches they avoided

defeat by West Indies that season. In the first match, at Old Trafford, Viv Richards scored 189 not out, the highest score in one-day internationals, sharing an unfinished partnership of 106 with Holding for the tenth wicket. Richards became the first player to pass 3,000 runs in one-day internationals.

Australia toured India in 1984-85, winning a four-match series 3-0, with one abandoned. Kepler Wessels and Ravi Shastri made centuries. India went to Pakistan for a Wills series and lost 1-0, the second match being cancelled when Mrs Gandhi's assassination was announced. Sri Lanka, at home, drew a series 1-1 with New Zealand, who then went to play Pakistan in a Wills series, Pakistan winning 3-1, although the margins were close. England,

touring India, won a five-match series 4-1. Dilip Vengsarkar, Ravi Shastri and Mike Gatting made hundreds.

Sri Lanka took part in the 1984-85 Benson and Hedges World Series Cup, and West Indies returned for a second successive year. West Indies won all ten of their matches in the qualifying series. Sri Lanka managed one victory against Australia. Four West Indians made hundreds: Haynes, Richards, Greenidge and Larry Gomes, while two Australians did: Graeme Wood and David Boon. Richards' century was his eighth in international one-day matches, passing Zaheer's mark of seven. There was a surprise when Australia won the first final, Allan Border getting 127 not out, but West Indies won the second match by four wickets, al-

ABOVE The World Championship of Cricket, Melbourne, 1984-85. New Zealand's Reid plays to the covers against Sri Lanka. OPPOSITE India do a lap of honour in a car won by Shastri in the 1984-85 Benson and Hedges World Championship.

though needing 272, and easily took the decider, Holding claiming 5 for 26.

A Rothmans Cup series in New Zealand was won by the home country who beat Pakistan 3-0, with one match rained off.

A new series in Australia was the Benson and Hedges World Championship. There were two mini-leagues. In Group A, consisting of India, Pakistan, Australia and England, India won all three games, Pakistan lost only to India,

Australia beat only England, and England lost all three games. In Group B, the match between New Zealand and West Indies was abandoned, while both beat Sri Lanka. Two semi-finalists thus emerged from each group: New Zealand were to play India and Pakistan the West Indies. India were the most impressive in the Group matches, although Pakistan's Wasim Akram had a good match against Australia, with 5 for 21.

India beat New Zealand comfortably in the first semi-final by seven wickets. Pakistan, more surprisingly, beat West Indies by the same margin. Mudassar Nazar took 5 for 28 for Pakistan, and

Ramiz Raja scored an aggressive 60 against the West Indian pace to win the man-of-the-match award. West Indies won the 'plate' final, but the real final was won convincingly by India, by eight wickets. Krishna Srikkanth, the dashing opener, was man-of-the-match with 67 of a first-wicket stand of 103.

New Zealand departed for the West Indies and lost a five-match series 5-0. Haynes had another excellent series with two centuries, taking his total in one-day internationals to eight, equalling Richards' record. Haynes' average (3 dismissals) was 135. Richards, however, took his aggregate past 4,000, remaining the leading run-

getter in one-day internationals.

There was another series at the Sharjah Stadium, UAE, called the Rothmans Four Nations Trophy. It began at the semi-final stage, India beating Pakistan by 38 runs in the first. As Imran Khan took 6 for 14 he hardly deserved to be on the losing side. In the other semi-final Australia beat England by two wickets off the last ball. Pakistan won the 'plate' match by 43 runs, and India won the trophy by beating Australia by three wickets.

India thus added this trophy to the World Cup and the World Championship, and had transformed themselves from limited-overs 'rabbits' to undeniable,

if rather surprising, champions.

1985
The 1985 Texaco Trophy in England was won 2-1 by Australia. Graham Gooch, returning to the England team after his exile due to his playing in South Africa, scored two of the four centuries, and was unlucky not to be man-of-the-match in any of the games—his average was 144.50. Gower and Wood made the other centuries, Gower's being his seventh, equalling Zaheer, and being one behind Richards and Haynes. Ian Botham registered a mark in the final match, becoming the first to the double of 1,000 runs and 100 wickets in one-day internationals.

Ian Botham hits fast-bowler Craig McDermott for six at Edgbaston, 1985.

PART III

A
GALLERY
OF
GREAT
PLAYERS

THE ALL-TIME GREATS

In the following pages are biographies, with career figures, of 67 great cricketers, from England, Australia, South Africa, the West Indies, New Zealand, India and Pakistan. The selection procedure was quite arbitrary: players were included solely by virtue of the compilers of this book considering them among the best and most interesting. It must be admitted that there is a bias towards the modern. It is no doubt true that any reasonable modern side would easily beat the best of the Golden Age, could such a contest be arranged in heaven. But that is a poor way of judging greatness. Will the immortal Paavo Nurmi be any the less great an athlete when his times are beaten by women?

Figures are a poor criterion for judging between the eras. There are so many Test matches these days that Imran Khan can take 88 Test wickets in a year (22 March 1982 to 4 February 1983), while the feared Spofforth, the 'demon bowler', could manage only six more in an entire career. But Spofforth played in only 18 Test matches—Imran played in 13 in that one hectic year alone.

No—the reason for the bias towards the modern is the thought that readers are more interested in the players they know, i.e. the current ones or those of recent memory. Thus, the only 'pioneer' included is W. G. Grace, the most famous cricketer of all time. There are four whose reputations were made wholly or mainly before the Second World War: Bradman, Hammond, Hobbs and Larwood. The other 62 are players of the last 40 years.

To redress the balance, this introduction outlines the careers of many who would be judged 'great' in the books of most cricket-lovers.

The first Test match was played when James Lillywhite, from a famous Sussex family of cricketers, took an England team to Australia in 1876-77. The first ball in Test cricket was bowled by Alfred Shaw of England to Charles Bannerman of Australia. Shaw (born 1842) was one of the outstanding English bowlers of his day. He was undoubtedly the most economical. In an era of four-ball overs he actually bowled more overs than he conceded runs. He played 33 seasons, mostly for Nottinghamshire (10 matches for Sussex) and took 2,021 wickets at only 12.12 each.

Charles Bannerman, who received that first Test ball, was actually born in Kent in 1851. He played for New South Wales from 1870-71 to 1887-88: eighteen years in which he played 44 first-class matches. He toured England in 1878, but there were no Tests. He played in only three Tests, and in the first made 165 not out, retired hurt. He retains a splendid Test average of 59.75. That first-ever Test hundred was remarkable—it remains the highest by an Australian on his debut, and it was 67.3 per cent of Australia's total of 245, a percentage still unbeaten in over 1,000 succeeding Tests.

Lillywhite later managed four more tours of Australia in partnership with Shaw and Arthur Shrewsbury. Shrewsbury (born 1856) was a Nottinghamshire colleague of Shaw, and was the best professional batsman in England throughout the 1880s and early 1890s, when most leading batsmen were amateurs. Shrewsbury topped the averages six times. In all he made 26,505 runs, average 36.65, in 498 matches. In 23 Tests he scored 1,277, highest 164, average 35.47. His highest score was 267, which he made twice. He was a methodical opening batsman, of whom W. G. Grace said 'Give me Arthur' when asked whom he would prefer to open with. He shot himself in 1908 when worried that ill-health was threatening his career—he had topped the averages the previous year.

England had some particularly strong bowlers towards the end of the 19th century. An interesting character was Bobby Peel (born 1857), the Yorkshire slow left-arm bowler. He was dismissed by Lord Hawke, the county captain, because he was occasionally drunk. But he was the best bowler of his type in the world, and went on four tours to Australia. He took 102 wickets in 20 Tests, average 16.81. In a career of 16 years he took 1,754 wickets, average 16.21. He was no great batsman, but hit 210 not out in 1896, the only year he did the double. His best bowling season was the previous year, 1895, with 180 wickets, average 14.97. Since he was sacked in 1898, Yorkshire and England probably lost some of his best years.

A great slow left-arm bowling rival of Peel was Johnnie Briggs (born 1862), of Lancashire, who began his career as a batsman and outstanding fielder. He began his bowling in 1885, his seventh season, and was so successful that he captured 2,221 wickets, average 15.93. He went on six tours of Australia and one to South Africa, where he took 7 for 17 and 8 for 11 in South Africa's second Test. In all he took 118 Test wickets, average 17.74. He developed epilepsy and had a bad seizure during the Leeds Test in 1899. He recovered to bowl well next year, but died a year or two later in Cheadle Asylum, aged only 39.

A faster man, who died even younger, was Surrey's George Lohmann (born 1865). He was a prolific wicket taker, averaging over six a match throughout his career. In 13 seasons he took 1,805 wickets at the extremely low average of 13.91. His Test average was even better. He took 112 wickets in only 18 matches, average 10.75. This is easily the best average of any bowler with over 25 Test wickets let alone 100. Because of consumption he emigrated to South Africa, but three years after his last first-class match he died there in 1901, aged 36.

Australia had some marvellous bowlers at the time, including the afore-mentioned F. R. Spofforth (born 1853), known as the 'Demon'. He came to England five times, and played in 18 Tests, taking 94 wickets, average 18.41. His destruction of England in 1882, England's first home defeat, led to the famous 'Ashes' notice. Spofforth took 7 for 46 and 7 for 44 in a match Australia won by seven runs. Most of his wickets were taken in England, and in 1889 he emigrated and played for Derbyshire.

Hugh Trumble (born 1867) was another Australian who took over half his wickets in England. He made five visits, and in 32 Tests took 141 wickets, average 21.78. He was a medium pace off-break bowler, who also averaged nearly 20 with the bat.

Australia's great all-rounder of the period was George Giffen, regarded as Australia's W. G. Grace. He was one of the hardest-hitting of batsmen and a medium-slow bowler. His best match was South Australia v Victoria in 1891-82, when he hit his highest score, 271, and took 16 wickets, a unique performance. On three of his five trips to England he performed the double. In 31 Tests he scored 1,238 runs, average 23.35, and took 103 wickets, average 27.09.

Two English fast bowlers vied for greatness as cricket approached its Golden Age. Tom Richardson (born 1870) was a gallant strong man who would bowl fast all day for Surrey or England—he exceeded 200 wickets

Arthur Shrewsbury, professional batsman, bat-maker, and organizer of tours to Australia.

ABOVE George Hirst, who in 1906 took 200 wickets and scored 2,000 runs—a double achieved by nobody else.

BELOW Sydney Barnes, thought by many to be the greatest bowler of all time, whose 189 Test wickets was a record.

ABOVE Trevor Bailey, the last all-rounder of nine to achieve 20,000 runs and 2,000 wickets, with Doug Insole.

BELOW Colin Blythe, a slow left-arm bowler, contemporary of Wilfred Rhodes and with a similar bowling average.

V TRUMPER

W ARMSTRONG

in a season three times, reaching 290 in 1895. His 88 Test wickets in 14 matches cost 25.22 each. C. J. Kortright (born 1871) was an Essex amateur who never played in a Test and took only 489 wickets, average 21.05, in a career of 150 matches. But he was the fastest bowler of his day and some claim the fastest ever.

The Golden Age of cricket is generally regarded as reaching its peak around 1902, in which year the England side is often said to be the best ever. The side for the first Test was A. C. MacLaren, C. B. Fry, K. S. Ranjitsinhji, Hon F. S. Jackson, J. T. Tyldesley, A. F. A. Lilley, G. H. Hirst, G. L. Jessop, L. C. Braund, W. H. Lockwood, W. Rhodes—giants all.

Of these, C. B. Fry (born 1872) was a legendary sportsman: captain of England at cricket, soccer international and cup finalist, and joint holder of the world long jump record. Among his cricketing feats was being the first of only three players to score centuries in six successive innings. His Sussex colleague, Prince Ranjitsinhji (born in India in 1872) hit over 3,000 runs in both 1899 and 1900. His career batting average was 56.37. His eye was amazing and he made the leg glance famous, his bat being regarded as a magician's wand by his contemporaries.

Honest John Tyldesley (born 1873) of Lancashire was the only professional batsman who could hold a place in the England team of this era. In a long career which lasted to 1923 he made 37,897 runs, average 40.66. Arthur Lilley (born 1866) of Warwickshire was the leading wicket-keeper in England for about ten years. George Hirst (born 1871) was a left-arm medium pace bowler and aggressive batsman who performed prodigies for Yorkshire, and performed the double 14 times. In a career lasting 39 years he scored 36,323 runs and took 2,739 wickets. As a batsman, he could score 341 against Leicestershire, as a bowler he took 9 for 23 against Lancashire. In 1906 he scored over 2,000 runs (2,385) and took over 200 wickets (208), a feat unique in cricket.

Gilbert Jessop (born 1874) was the most consistent of all fast scoring batsman, whose name recurs in the quick-scoring lists— his fastest 50 came in 15 minutes, 100 in 40 minutes, 200 in 120 minutes (still the fastest). His most famous innings was 104 in 77 minutes which won the last Test in 1902 against all odds.

Wilfred Rhodes (born 1877) was a slow left-arm bowler and right-hand batsman who actually surpassed Hirst as an all-rounder. Both were born in Kirkheaton in Yorkshire. Rhodes took over from Peel (see above) in the Yorkshire side in 1898 and played for 33 years. He took 100 wickets in a season 23 times, easily a record, and took 4,187 first-class wickets, the only man to top 4,000. In 1902 he went in last for England, but he then developed his batting to such an extent that he exceeded 1,000 runs in a season 20 times, per-forming the double 16 times, another record. Eventually he opened for England, and shares with Hobbs the highest opening stand in the Ashes series: 323 in 1911-12. Rhodes is the oldest player to appear in Tests, being over 52 when playing against West Indies in 1929-30. His Test career lasted nearly 32 years, another record.

One of the most enigmatic bowlers of all time was Sydney Barnes (born 1873). He was an aloof, unsociable character who played a few games for Warwickshire and Lancashire but did not care for county cricket. Mainly he played for Staffordshire and in league cricket, producing astonishing figures: nearly 1,500 wickets for Staffordshire in 22 seasons at only 8 each, nearly 3,000 league wickets at less than 7 each. MacLaren took him to Australia in 1901-02, and eventually he played in 27 Tests, mostly abroad because the Lord's authorities were wary of him. He took 189 Test wickets at an average of 16.43. A bowler whose pace varied on the fast and slow sides of medium, he could make the ball turn in either direction. He was still bowling in his 60s, and in his biography claimed to have taken 6,229 wickets at 8.33 each. Many good judges think he was the best bowler ever.

Great bowlers who did not make the side in 1902 were B. J. T. Bosanquet (born 1877), the perfecter of the googly, and Colin Blythe (born 1879), Rhodes' rival

LEFT The immortal Victor Trumper, a legendary figure in Australian cricket.
CENTRE Warwick Armstrong, who led Australia to eight wins in succession over England.
ABOVE Patsy Hendren, whose aggregate of runs was beaten only by Hobbs and Woolley.

as a left-arm spinner. Ranjitsinhji thought Blythe the better, and his Test average was much better: 100 wickets at 18.63. He had 2,506 career wickets at 16.81 (Rhodes 16.72) but he was killed at the height of his career, at Passchendaele in the Great War.

Yet the England of 1902 lost the Ashes to Australia, who also had their giants: V. T. Trumper, R. A. Duff, C. Hill, S. E. Gregory, J. Darling, M. A. Noble, W. W. Armstrong, A. J. Y. Hopkins, J. J. Kelly, H. Trumble, J. V. Saunders.

The greatest of these was Victor Trumper, no man ever having a more appropriate name. If Englishmen in the 1930s liked to claim that Hobbs was a better batsman than Bradman, there were older Australians who insisted that Trumper was the best of all. He was born in 1877, and made his Australian debut in 1899 in England. He toured England four times. A brilliant opening batsman, at Old Trafford in 1902 he hit 100 before lunch on the first day—the first of only four batsmen to do this. His figures do not support his legend—an average of 39.09 in 48 Tests, and 44.07 in

ABOVE Herbert Sutcliffe playing forward in the nets. A neat player in all senses, he had an impressive Test average of over 60.
RIGHT Frank Woolley (right), whose aggregates of runs, wickets and catches made him an outstanding all-rounder.

his career. But he scorned run-accumulation. What impressed were his artistry, his mastery when it was needed, and his charm and modesty at all times. It is safe to say there was no more admired or better loved cricketer. He died in 1915 of Bright's disease.

Clem Hill (born 1877) played 49 times for Australia as a middle-order left-hand batsman, scoring 3,412 runs, average 39.21, and taking a famous miraculous catch at Old Trafford in 1902 which virtually won Australia the match.

Syd Gregory, Joe Darling, Monty Noble and Warwick Armstrong all captained Australia. Gregory (born 1870) toured England no fewer than eight times, and he played 58 times for Australia, a lot in those days, scoring 2,282 runs, average 24.53. Darling (born 1870) was captain in 1902, and averaged 28.56 in 34 Tests. Noble (born 1873) was an all-rounder who was captain in 15 of his 42 Tests. He scored 1,997, average 30.24, and took 121 wickets, average 25.00. The giant Armstrong (born 1879)—over 6ft and on his last tour 20 stone—was known as 'The Big Ship'. He was an all-rounder with impressive

figures on his tours to England—three times he achieved the double. His figures from 50 Tests—2,863 runs, average 38.68, and 87 wickets, average 33.59—do not do him justice, because he was at his best on sticky wickets. He was Australian captain in eight successive wins over England, in 1920-21 and 1921.

Jim Kelly (born 1867) was Australia's leading wicket-keeper, and toured England four times, but injury received on the tour of 1905 ended his career. He and Trumper married sisters.

After the First World War some prolific batsmen appeared on the English scene. Elias 'Patsy' Hendren (born 1889) went to Australia three times in the 1920s. In 51 Tests he scored 3,525 runs, average 47.63. Only Hobbs of his contemporaries scored more, and only Hobbs and Woolley exceeded his 57,611 career runs, average 50.80. Herbert Sutcliffe (born 1894) formed with Hobbs the most famous opening partnership in Test cricket. Sutcliffe, known for his smartness of dress and his imperturbability, rarely failed even on the most difficult wickets. Every season between the wars, from 1919 to 1939, he completed 1,000 runs, becoming one of the few to exceed 50,000 (50,138, average 51.95). His temperament is shown by the fact that his Test average is higher. In 54 Tests he scored 4,555 runs, average 60.73. Only Bradman has scored over 2,500 runs at a higher average.

Frank Woolley (born 1887) had

a career for Kent which lasted 33 years (1906-38). Of nine cricketers who have scored 20,000 runs and taken 2,000 wickets, he scored easily the most runs, 58,969, average 40.75—only Grace of the nine approached this. His 2,068 wickets averaged 19.85. As Woolley is the only player other than a wicket-keeper to take 1,000 catches, his all-round record is unique. In 64 Tests he scored 3,283, average 36.07, and took 83 wickets, average 33.91. Even these impressive figures meant little to Woolley's admirers, who claimed that the tall left-hander's batting was the epitome of grace and artistry.

Maurice Tate (born 1895) was an all-rounder whose main asset was his medium pace bowling. He perfected the use of the seam and took 2,784 career wickets at only 18.16, and scored 21,717 runs, average 25.01. He played in 39 Tests, taking 155 wickets, average 26.16, and averaged over 25 with the bat. It was said of Tate that the ball actually increased in pace as it left the pitch after bouncing.

Two great Australian batsmen whose careers spanned the First World War were Warren Bardsley and Charlie Macartney. Bardsley (born 1882) was very successful on four trips to England, three times passing 2,000 runs. A very correct opener, he became on his first trip the first batsman to score a century in each innings of a Test, 136 and 130. His next century against England was on his last trip, in 1926, when he carried his bat for 193 not

out, the highest Test score then made at Lord's. In all he made 2,469 Test runs, average 40.47.

Charlie Macartney (born 1886) was quite different, an attacking middle-order right-hand batsman, who began as more of a slow left-arm bowler. Always ready to annihilate the bowling, his 345 against Notts at Trent Bridge in 1921 remains the highest individual score made in a day. He scored 2,131 runs, average 41.78, in 35 Tests, and also took 45 wickets, average 27.55.

Two opening fast bowlers who struck terror into English batsmen in 1921 were J. M. Gregory and E. A. McDonald. Jack Gregory (born 1895) took 116 wickets on that tour and performed the double. His 85 wickets in 24 Tests cost 31.15 each. He was his country's leading all-rounder, averaging 36.96 in Tests with the bat. Ted McDonald (born 1891), of the smooth action, took 138 wickets on the same tour. He played only 11 Tests, taking 43 wickets at 33.27 each. He returned to England and played for Lancashire from 1924 and in 1925 took 205 wickets.

Bill Woodfull and Bill Ponsford opened many an Australian innings in the 1920s and 1930s, including those in the 'bodyline' tour. Woodfull (born 1897) was by then captain of Australia. Indeed he captained them in 25 of his 35 Tests, during which he made 2,300 runs, average 46.00. His career average, for 13,388 runs, was an impressive 64.99. Bill Ponsford

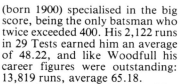

(born 1900) specialised in the big score, being the only batsman who twice exceeded 400. His 2,122 runs in 29 Tests earned him an average of 48.22, and like Woodfull his career figures were outstanding: 13,819 runs, average 65.18.

The batsman who impressed for style, however, was Alan Kippax (born 1897), unlucky because of illness and odd selection methods to play in only 22 Tests. He scored 1,192 runs at an average of 36.12. Archie Jackson (born 1909, in Scotland) was thought to have a great career ahead when in his Test debut at Adelaide in 1928-29 he scored 164 against England. He was only 19, and younger than Bradman, who made his debut in the same series (and less impress-ively). But Jackson suffered from tuberculosis and played only five seasons and in eight Tests (474 runs, average 47.40). He died in 1933, aged 23.

Australia's wicket-keeper from 1920-21 to 1936-37 was Bert Old-field (born 1894) was the best keeper of his era, who caught 78 and stumped 52 Test victims in 54 matches. He was the only pre-Second World War wicket-keeper to claim over 100 Test victims.

South Africa produced two batsmen to challenge the best each side of the First World War. Aubrey Faulkner (born 1881) was actually an all-rounder. In 25 Tests

ABOVE Charlie Macartney, known as 'The Governor', was a man who could destroy attacks with powerful batting.
ABOVE RIGHT Bert Oldfield, the Australian first choice as wicket-keeper for 15 years and the first to 100 victims.
RIGHT Stan McCabe, the talented Australian batsman who is remembered for great innings in Australia and England.

he scored 1,754 runs, average 40.79, and took 82 wickets, average 26.58. During the war he moved to London and opened a famous cricket school. Herbert Taylor (born 1889) was an opener, who played for South Africa from 1912 to 1931-32, and was captain in 18 of his 42 Tests. He scored 2,936 runs, average 40.77.

In the 1930s England had a re-markable captain: Douglas Jar-dine. Because of the bodyline tour, Jardine (born 1900) was much analysed and greatly disliked by some, but he was a winning cap-tain, and no mean batsman, with 1,296 runs, average 48.00, in his 22 Tests.

Two vastly different batsmen were K. S. Duleepsinhji and Eddie Paynter. Duleep (born 1905 in India) was the nephew of Ranji. Impressive form for Sussex won him a Test place for England in 1929-30. At Lord's against Aus-

tralia in 1930 he made 173, his highest Test score, but he was forced to retire two years later through ill-health. He made 995 runs in 12 Tests, at the high average of 58.52.

If Duleep had some of his uncle's artistry, Eddie Paynter (born 1901), a Lancashire left-hander, was strong on grit and character. He played only 20 Tests, being a victim of cricket's ever-present snobbery, all sorts of lesser players being given pref-erence. Yet he scored 1,540 runs, average 59.23, an average bettered by only half-a-dozen players or so in all Test cricket, and his average in Ashes Tests was a remarkable 84.42, higher than any batsman with over 500 runs except Brad-man.

A wicket-keeper/batsman of the 1930s was L. E. G. Ames (born 1905), first of three great Kent keepers. He played for Kent for

26 years, claiming 1,121 career victims and scoring 37,248 runs, average 43.51. In 47 Tests he caught 74 and stumped 23, and scored 2,434 runs, average 40.56. The best slow left-arm bowler of the time was Hedley Verity, born in 1905 at Headingley, Leeds, another in the Yorkshire tradition. He had a remarkable analysis of 10 for 10 for Yorkshire against Notts in 1931, the best ever recorded in first-class cricket. Almost unplay-able on a sticky wicket, he took 14 wickets in a day for England against Australia at Lord's in 1934, six in an hour, including his best Test analysis of 8 for 43. His 144 wickets in 40 Tests averaged 24.37—in his career he took 1,956 at only 14.90 each. He was killed in Italy in the Second World War, while still first choice for England.

Australia had a pair of great spinners in the 1930s, Clarrie Grimmett and Bill O'Reilly. The

ABOVE LEFT Bill O'Reilly, known as 'Tiger', an aggressive leg-break and googly bowler whose Test wickets were cheap. LEFT Three Lancashire-born Test men, batsmen Eddie Paynter and Ernest Tyldesley and wicket-keeper George Duckworth. ABOVE Bill Ponsford, the only basman to have twice exceeded 400 runs in a first-class innings, both for Victoria.

career of Grimmett (born 1891) began in 1911, and his Test career in 1924, but the last of his 37 Tests was not until 1935-36. A brilliant leg-break and googly bowler, he was the first player to take over 200 Test wickets. He ended with 216, average 24.21, and did not retire until he was 50 years old. In 1931-32 he was joined in the Australian Test side by 'Tiger' O'Reilly (born 1905), another leg-break and googly bowler, but quite different in style, being much faster and having a higher bounce. They were feared as a pair. O'Reilly played in 27 Tests, the last in 1945-46 against New Zealand, a match not granted Test status until two years later. In all he took 144 Test wickets, average 22.59.

Australia's outstanding batsman of the 1930s, after Bradman, was Stan McCabe (born 1910). He was a brilliant batsman, who

batted in cavalier fashion and played his best in adversity. Thus he is remembered for two of the greatest Test innings: his 187 not out at Sydney in 1931-32, acknowledged as the best innings against bodyline, and his 232 at Trent Bridge which rescued Australia in 1938, described by Bradman as the greatest innings he'd seen. In his 39 Tests he scored 2,748 runs, average 48.21. He also took 36 wickets.

The West Indies found two great players in the 1930s. Learie Constantine (born 1901) was an exciting all-rounder: fast-scoring batsman, fast bowler and electrifying fielder. He played 18 Tests between 1928 and 1939. He scored only 635 runs, average 19.24, and took 58 wickets, average 30.10, but, like Botham later on, his mere presence was an asset.

George Headley (born 1909) was called the 'Black Bradman' and

was not only the best pre-war West Indian batsman, but one of the best the world has ever seen. He twice made not out double centuries against England. At a time when England and Australia were easily the strongest cricket nations, and the West Indies comparatively weak, he made 2,190 runs in 22 tests, at the excellent average of 60.83, beaten by only four others in cricket history, two of those with comparatively small aggregates.

India produced an excellent batsman in Vijay Merchant (born 1911), whose Test career began in 1933-34 and lasted until 1951-52, when a shoulder injury ended it. In that time he played only 10 Tests, scoring 859 runs, average 47.72. But in his career he made 12,876 runs at the high average of 72.74.

New Zealand, too, owned a world-class batsman or two. C. S. Dempster (born 1903) played

10 Tests between 1929-30 and 1932-33, mostly against England, including New Zealand's first-ever. He made 723 runs, average 65.72, second in the list of Test averages to Bradman. He then came to England to play for Leicestershire, captaining them from 1936 to 1938. Martin Donnelly (born 1917) was a brilliant left-hand batsman whose Test career began in 1938, and was spoiled by the war. In only seven Tests he scored 582 runs, average 52.90, including 206 against England at Lord's in 1949, the only New Zealander to score over 200 against England. He played for Warwickshire in 1948-50, after attending Oxford University, but then took up a business appointment in Australia, and was lost to cricket.

Post-war players who do not appear in full in the following pages include a few who regularly comment on television or radio. Among them are Trevor Bailey (born 1923), a brilliant all-rounder known as 'The Barnacle' because of the defensive qualities of his Test batting—he could not be shifted. An excellent fast-medium bowler, he often opened the England bowling with Alec Bedser. A freer scorer in county matches, he is one of the few players to score 20,000 runs and take 2,000 wickets in a career:

28,642, average 33.42, and 2,082, average 23.13. In Tests he scored 2,290 runs, average 29.74, and took 132 wickets, average 29.21. He saved England more than once with his dogged qualities.

Batsmen of the 1940s and 1950s included Cyril Washbrook (born 1914), whose Test career began in 1937 and ended in 1956, when he was a selector and was brought back after six years—he scored 98. He was Hutton's regular Test opening partner, and scored 2,569 runs in 37 Tests, average 42.81. Tom Graveney (born 1927) played in 79 Tests as a middle-order batsman, one of the great stylists of modern times. He scored 4,882 runs, average 44.38. No batsman still alive had, in 1985, more than his 47,793 first-class runs (Boycott approached).

Brian Close (born 1931) was, in 1949, the youngest player to be capped by Yorkshire, the youngest to do the double and the youngest to play for England. Nobody could fulfil what was expected of him, but he had a distinguished career which included captaining Yorkshire and England. In his 22 Tests he scored 887 runs, average 25.34, and took 18 wickets with his off-breaks, average 29.55.

Tony Lock and John Wardle disputed England's slow left-arm bowling place in the 1950s. Wardle (born 1923) was an extrovert, a humorist on the field, but outspoken off it, which led to a curtailed career after a dispute with Yorkshire. In 28 Tests, he took 102 wickets at 20.39 each.

He also scored 633 runs, average 19.78. Lock (born 1929) was faster, but his action attracted criticism over its legitimacy. He was Laker's partner both for Surrey and England. He played in 49 Tests, and took 174 wickets, average 25.58, and also scored tail-end runs, 742, average 13.75. Late in his career he captained Leicestershire and Western Australia with great success. He was an outstanding close fielder.

A fast bowler who virtually won a Test series in Australia was Frank Tyson (born 1930). In 1954-55 he demoralised Australia with his speed, grabbing 28 wickets at 20.82 each. In 17 Tests he took 76 wickets, average 18.56. He emigrated to Australia and became a sports commentator.

Two post-war Australian batsmen whose Test careers began in 1938 were Lindsay Hassett and Sid Barnes. Hassett (born 1913) succeeded Bradman as captain, and was a popular leader in 24 of his 43 Tests. He scored 3,075 runs, average 46.56. A small man, he batted elegantly, and when fielding had a great rapport with the crowd. Sid Barnes (born 1916) opened for Australia in 13 Tests, scoring 1,032 runs at the high average of 63.05, third in the all-time list. He did not play in Tests after 1948 when he fell out with the Australian authorities.

Bill Johnston (born 1922), like Hassett and Barnes, was in Bradman's unbeaten 1948 touring team to England, when he took 102 wickets. A number eleven bats-

man, he found his batting average was 102 in the 1953 tour, by virtue of being out only once in 17 innings. He was one of Australia's best fast-medium left-arm bowlers, and in 40 Tests took 160 wickets, average 23.91.

West Indies had two outstanding slow bowlers on their visit to England in 1950—'those little pals of mine, Ramadhin and Valentine.' Sonny Ramadhin (born 1929) was an off-break bowler who for a while completely baffled England batsmen, heading the first-class averages with 135 wickets, average 14.88. In the Tests he took 26 wickets. He played 43 Tests in all, never quite being as successful again, ending with 158 wickets at 28.98 each. His partner, Alf Valentine (born 1930) was even younger and more successful in the 1950 Tests. A 20-year-old bespectacled left-arm spinner, he took 33 Test wickets, average 20.42. He, too, could never recapture the mastery of his first Test series, playing 36 Tests in his career, taking 139 wickets, average 30.32.

South Africa had an outstanding spinner in the 1950s. Hugh Tayfield (born 1928) was regarded by Jim Laker as the most accurate off-spinner he ever saw. Tayfield, a brilliant fielder off his own bowling, took 170 wickets in 35 Tests, average 25.91, including 9 for 113 against England at Johannesburg in 1956-57.

There were also some outstanding South African batsmen. Dudley Nourse (born 1910), son of

the 'Grand Old Man' of South African cricket, captained his country and scored 2,960 Test runs, average 53.81. At Trent Bridge in 1951 he made 208 against England, batting with a broken thumb. The captaincy was taken over for the rest of the match by opener Eric Rowan (born 1909), who himself made 236 at Headingley, South Africa's highest score against England. His 1,965 runs in 26 Tests between 1935 and 1951, averaged 43.66. Another opener was Derrick 'Sticky' McGlew (born 1929), who batted with extreme stubbornness. He made 2,440 runs in 34 Tests, averaging 42.06. One of his opening partners was Trevor Goddard (born 1931), left-hand batsman and fast-medium bowler. He captained South Africa in 13 of his 41 Tests. He made 2,516 runs, average 34.46, and took 123 wickets, average 26.22.

India's great all-rounder of the 1950s was Vinoo Mankad (born 1917). Against New Zealand in 1955-56 he scored two double centuries, against England at Lord's in 1952 he scored 72 and 184 and took five wickets. He was a right-hand opener and left-arm slow bowler. In 44 Tests he scored 2,109 runs, average 31.47, and took 162 wickets, average 32.32. He scored 1,000 Test runs and took 100 Test wickets in 23 matches, the fastest until beaten by Ian Botham.

India's best batsmen of the period were Vijay Hazare, from a famous cricket family, and 'Polly' Umrigar. Hazare (born 1915)

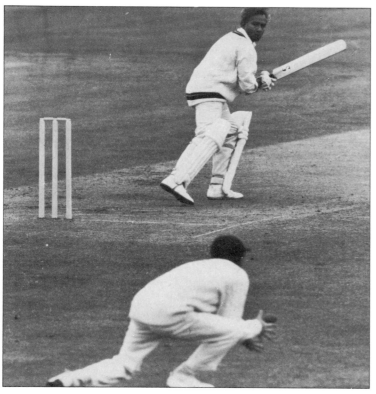

ABOVE Rohan Kanhai, the dashing West Indian batsman and captain. Only Sobers and Lloyd, also captains, scored more Test runs for West Indies.

RIGHT Bob Taylor watching Sandeep Patil hit a ball for six. Taylor, in a long career, made more first-class dismissals than any other keeper.

average 37.66, and claiming 59 dismissals. Eddie Barlow (born 1940) was one of South Africa's great Test all-rounders. A bespectacled opening bat and pace bowler, he played in 30 Tests, and scored 2,516 runs, average 45.74, and took 40 wickets, average 34.05. He played for the Rest of the World against England in 1970, and at Headingley took four wickets in five balls. An inspiring player, he later captained Derbyshire.

India's strength has been in spin bowlers in recent years. Bhagwat Chandrasekhar (born 1945) had a right bowling arm slightly affected by polio, but bowled leg-breaks at a quickish pace, and could produce devastating performances. Rarely sure of his Test place, he nevertheless appeared in 58, and took 242 wickets, average 29.74. Srinivasaraghavan Venkataraghavan (born 1945), known as Venkat, was an off-break bowler, who took 155 wickets in 55 Tests, average 35.67, and captained India in England.

Pakistan have been blessed recently with batsmen who could bowl and vice-versa. Intikhab Alam (born 1941) was captain in 17 Tests. A leg-break and googly bowler, he took 125 wickets in 47 Tests, average 35.95, and also scored nearly 1,500 runs. He played 232 matches for Surrey. Asif Iqbal (born 1943), who also captained his country, was a genuine all-rounder who appeared in 58 Tests, making 3,575 runs, average 38.85, and taking 53 wickets, average 28.33. He also captained Kent, and led them to many triumphs in the 1970s. Majid Khan (born 1946) was another genuine all-rounder who also played County cricket for Glamorgan. His batting was stronger, and he scored 3,931 Test runs, average 38.92, in 63 Tests. This beat Hanif's record aggregate, since passed by Javed and Zaheer. He also took 27 Test wickets. Sarfraz Nawaz (born 1948) was an opening swing bowler who could bat a little when necessary. In 55 Tests he took 117 wickets, average 32.75, and scored just over 1,000 runs. He appeared in 151 matches for Northamptonshire.

Batsmen still playing in England in the mid-1980s who have already produced outstanding Test form include Derek Randall, Graham Gooch, Mike Gatting, Allan Lamb and Tim Robinson. Desmond Haynes and Larry Gomes have impressed for West Indies, while Jeffrey Dujon could join the best wicket-keeper/batsmen and Malcolm Marshall has destroyed sides with as quick a pace as anybody in the world.

India's young players, batsman Mohammad Azharuddin and leg-break bowler Laxman Sivaramakrishnan have made magnificent debuts, and Pakistan's brilliant batsman Javed Miandad has already scored over 5,000 Test runs. All belong already in a gallery of great players.

Two modern Test captains. Mike Brearley (England) drives and Kim Hughes (Australia) jumps at the Oval in 1981.

played in 30 Tests, captaining India in England in 1952. His 2,192 runs were scored at an average of 47.65. Umrigar (born 1926), also captained his country. He scored 3,631 runs in 59 Tests, average 42.22, and also took 35 wickets with his off-breaks.

New Zealand's best batsman for about 20 years was left-handed opener Bert Sutcliffe (born 1923). For Otago he scored 385 and 355. In England in 1949 he hit 2,627 runs, averaging around 60 in both Tests and first-class games. The 42 Tests in his career yielded 2,727 runs, average 40.10.

Pakistan's first Test hero was Fazal Mahmoud (born 1927), a right-arm fast-medium opening bowler, who took 139 wickets in 34 Tests, average 24.70. At the Oval in 1954 his bowling won Pakistan's first victory over England and tied the series. He took 6 for 53 and 6 for 46, and dismissed Hutton, May and Compton in each innings.

The best Pakistani batsman was Hanif Mohammad (born 1934), who made the world record score of 499 for Karachi against Bahawalpur in 1958-59. He also played the longest innings (16 hours, 10 minutes) for 337,

Pakistan v West Indies at Bridgetown in 1957-58. An opening batsman whose defence was perfect, he captained Pakistan, and three of his brothers also played for their country: Wazir, Mushtaq and Sadiq, as did his son, Shoaib. He appeared in 55 Tests in all, making a century against each country he played against. He scored 3,915 runs, average 43.98.

In the last 25 years, players who have featured in the headlines include such as Basil d'Oliveira (born 1931), a Cape Coloured who came to England for first-class cricket and appeared in 44 Tests, averaging 40.06 with the bat and taking 47 wickets, usually at vital times. Mike Brearley (born 1942) was famous for his captaincy, leading England in 31 of his 39 Tests. Bob Taylor (born 1941) was a brilliant wicket-keeper who gained an England place only when Alan Knott was banned, and he himself was 29. Nevertheless he appeared in 51 Tests, and made more first-class dismissals than any keeper in history: 1,656.

Australian batsmen have performed in different styles. Norman O'Neill (born 1937) excited with his brilliant attacking play, scoring 2,779 runs in 42 Tests, average 45.55. Doug Walters (born 1945) was also an attacking batsman, the hero of the hill at Sydney, who curiously rarely

succeeded on his four visits to England, but scored 5,357 runs in 74 Tests, an aggregate beaten by only Bradman, Greg Chappell and Harvey. He averaged 48.26. Bill Lawry (born 1937) was only just behind in aggregate and average with 5,234, average 47.15, but his methods were very different. He was a left-handed opener who made stubbornness and soundness his virtues. He captained Australia in 25 Tests.

West Indies' sound opener was Conrad Hunte (born 1932), 3,245 runs, average 45.06, in 44 Tests, while the brilliant middle-order man was Rohan Kanhai (born 1935), whose exciting hooking often ended with him tumbling over. He captained West Indies in 13 Tests. His aggregate of 6,227 Test runs has been exceeded for West Indies only by Sobers and Lloyd. He played in England for Warwickshire, and with Jameson set a world-record second-wicket stand of 465 unfinished against Gloucestershire.

Derryck Murray (born 1943) was West Indies' wicket-keeper in 62 Tests, claiming 189 victims, and scoring nearly 2,000 runs.

South Africa, too, had a brilliant wicket-keeper/batsman in Dennis Lindsay (born 1939). He played in 19 Tests before South Africa ceased to be a Test-playing country, scoring 1,130 runs,

BARRINGTON
Kenneth Frank
b 1930–d 1981

Ken Barrington was one of the most prolific post-war batsmen in world cricket, until a heart attack in October 1968 ended his first-class career shortly before his 39th birthday. Over the years he had worked out a method of playing which could never be called graceful but which was highly effective, especially in conditions outside his native England. Early in his career for Surrey he had a strong off-side style, but this became less pronounced, and by the time of his test recall, in 1959, he had changed his stance to face more towards the bowler. Thus he was mainly an on-side player and a fine cutter, but could hit the ball off the front foot on the off-side if required.

His technique, though not strictly from the text-book, was less controversial than his approach to batting. It was generally thought that for a player of his run-making capacity, he scored too slowly. He was too good a batsman, it was felt, to submit to a bowler as readily as he sometimes appeared to do, and the fact that he had periods of fluency in most innings strengthened this belief. He would often come in and make 30 runs in reasonable time before slowing down. Several times in Test matches he suddenly emerged from a period of inactivity to reach his hundred with a perfectly struck six. On one famous occasion in Melbourne he made the fastest Test hundred of the year by an Englishman—in 122 balls—and played as boldly and as well as anyone could have asked. But though he was a saver of matches rather than a winner of them, he was a rare comfort to

any captain as a reliable, remarkably consistent backbone to the innings. He was one player whom many Australians of his day have said they would have liked on their side, a batsman of immense patience, determination, and application.

A very competent fielder either in the slips or, in later years, away from the bat, he was also a leg-break bowler who was only just beginning to be fully appreciated when he retired. His control was good and he spun the ball more than many modern leg-spinners. And if the MCC tour of South Africa had taken place in 1968-69 and his health had been maintained, he would have been played as an all-rounder, certainly for the minor matches. In the 1964-65 tour of South Africa, his Test figures were only 3 for 33, but he took 24 wickets in all first-class matches at an average of 7.25.

It was as a leg-spinner that Barrington was recommended to Surrey in 1947. Born in Reading, he had become assistant groundsman to the Reading club, for which he was taking many wickets, when at the age of 16 he was invited to play for the Surrey Colts. He became a professional in 1948 but had to do military service, and it was 1951 before his promise as a batsman became obvious. Under the coaching of Andrew Sandham, he soon began to make runs in the Minor Counties competition. He first played for Surrey in a first-class match in 1953, and developed so fast in 1954 that he played in his first Test match the following year.

Perhaps he had come up too swiftly. For though by then he was 24, the normal peak of the average slow-developing English batsman is around 30. After his two Tests at Lord's and Leeds against South Africa in 1955, he did not play

Test cricket for four years—but 80 Tests were to follow.

Though he had poor seasons in 1956 and 1957, he had the advantage of playing in a strong, confident side—this was Surrey's seven-year reign as champions—and especially of watching at close quarters Peter May, considered the best batsman in the world at that time. By 1959, which he began by making a hundred in each innings against Warwickshire, he was a welcome sight for selectors looking for new blood after England's 4-0 defeat in Australia the previous winter.

Thus was resumed a Test career in which he made 20 hundreds, including at least two against each of England's opponents, and 6,806 runs, a number surpassed at the time of his retirement only by Hammond, Cowdrey, Bradman, and Hutton. His first two hundreds were made in the 1959-60 tour of West Indies, and for some years he made most runs on overseas wickets in India, Pakistan and

Australia. Strangely, too, he developed a humorous presence on the field which communicated itself more easily to overseas crowds than it ever did in England.

It was not until 1964 that he made his first Test hundred in England, but characteristically, when it came, it was extended to 256 in the marathon innings at Old Trafford with which England answered Australia's 656 and Bobby Simpson's 311. He was dropped by the England selectors in 1965 after taking what was considered an excessive time to score 137 against New Zealand, but this was a passing interlude in a career for Surrey and England which, though seldom spectacular, was immensely productive.

When he retired, he was a popular manager or coach on England tours, and he was assistant manager on the tour of the West Indies in 1980-81 when he suffered a second heart attack and died during the Test match at Bridgetown, Barbados.

BARRINGTON Kenneth Frank

Teams: Surrey and England

Test series		Tests	Runs	100s	Average
1955	v South Africa	2	52	—	17.33
1959	v India	5	357	—	59.50
1959-60	in West Indies	5	420	2	46.66
1960	v South Africa	4	227	—	37.83
1961	v Australia	5	364	1	45.50
1961-62	in India	5	594	3	99.00
1961-62	in Pakistan	2	229	1	76.33
1962	v Pakistan	4	60	—	20.00
1962-63	in Australia	5	582	2	72.75
1962-63	in New Zealand	3	294	1	73.50
1963	v West Indies	5	275	—	27.50
1963-64	in India	1	80	—	80.00
1964	v Australia	5	531	1	75.85
1964-65	in South Africa	5	508	2	101.60
1965	v New Zealand	2	300	2	150.00
1965	v South Africa	3	202	—	33.66
1965-66	in Australia	5	464	2	66.28
1966	v West Indies	2	59	—	14.75
1967	v India	3	324	—	64.80
1967	v Pakistan	3	426	3	142.00
1967-68	in West Indies	5	288	1	41.14
1968	v Australia	3	170	—	56.66
Totals		82	6,806	20	58.67

Career runs: 31,714 *Average:* 45.63
Highest Test and career score: 256 v Australia, Old Trafford, 1964
Career wickets: 273 *Average:* 32.62

BEDI
Bishansingh Giansingh
b 1946-

Recognised everywhere in the cricket world by his colourful patkas (turbans) and his relaxed gait, Bishan Bedi took a record number of wickets for India. From his Test debut in 1966-67, he was a popular figure on the cricket grounds wherever he played.

His gentle philosophy occasionally gave way to demonstrations of pique and indignation, as when he protested at John Lever's alleged use of Vaseline to polish the ball during England's visit to India in 1976-77. He was criticised, too, for allowing India's innings to close at 97 for 5 at Kingston in 1976 after West Indies' fast bowlers had inflicted several injuries on his batsmen by short-pitched bowling. Then, in 1978, after being sacked by Northamptonshire, for whom he had played since 1972, he took the matter to an industrial tribunal only to lose his claim for unfair dismissal.

As a slow left-arm bowler possessed of every known kind of variation and deception, he took 266 Test wickets and over 1500 in first-class cricket. Like many who have practised his craft, he looked quite innocent from afar, but the world's top batsmen for over a decade found that it was almost impossible to secure any lasting mastery over him. As with the early master of slow left-arm bowling, Wilfred Rhodes, he was

at least as great a threat immediately after being hit for six as before. He could hurry the ball on, 'hold it back', curl it in the air, spin it marginally or almost at right-angles; and with his effortless approach to the bowling crease he was never seen to be tired.

He made his first-class debut at the tender age of 15½, for Northern Punjab in the 1961-62 Ranji Trophy, and later transferred to Delhi. At 20 he played his first Test match, at Calcutta against West

LEFT Bishan Bedi wearing over his patka a sun-hat adorned by the signatures of cricketers of the world.

ABOVE Bedi's action required no great physical effort but it was far from soft, as nearly 300 Test batsmen will testify.

Indies, and by the early 1970s it was clear that India had a richer pool of spin bowlers from which to draw than any side in history. By the end of their careers the quartet of Bedi (266), Chandrasekhar, leg-spin/googly (242), Prasanna, off-spin (189), and Venkataraghavan, off-spin (156) had taken a phenomenal total of 853 Test wickets between them in a combined number of 231 appearances, around

threequarters of the wickets taken by India in those matches. It coincided with India's most successful period in 45 years of Test cricket, and contributed vitally to series victories against England, West Indies and New Zealand, and a closely-fought series against Australia.

In his six seasons with Northamptonshire he took 434 County Championship wickets, finishing top of the county's bowling averages in 1973 and 1974, and taking most first-class wickets (105) in the 1973 English season. Quite as remarkably, against established custom, he was often also a force in limited-overs cricket, where slow bowling is seldom seen as being worthwhile.

His batting was something of a self-confessed joke, though he has been known to strike occasional useful blows, as in the 1976 Gillette Cup semi-final against Hampshire, when he smashed the second-last ball to the long-on boundary to steal a two-wicket victory. And he always moved too comfortably to occupy a vital position in the field, having to be hidden in a non-chasing position.

But as a purveyor of cunning left-arm slows he made for himself an imperishable mark on the game. Since his retirement in 1981 he has been active in Indian cricket politics, waging a crusade against the poor organization of the Delhi and Districts Cricket Association, and remains a popular figure in Indian cricket.

BEDI Bishansingh Giansingh

Teams: Northern Punjab, Delhi, Northamptonshire and India

Test series		Tests	Wkts	Average
1966-67	v West Indies	2	7	32.57
1967	in England	3	7	33.71
1967-68	in Australia	2	4	55.75
1967-68	in New Zealand	4	16	23.18
1969-70	v New Zealand	3	15	20.53
1969-70	v Australia	5	21	20.57
1970-71	in West Indies	5	15	43.73
1971	in England	3	11	29.54
1972-73	v England	5	25	25.28
1974	in England	3	10	52.30
1974-75	v West Indies	4	15	33.26
1975-76	v New Zealand†	2	4	30.50
1975-76	in West Indies†	4	18	25.33
1976-77	v New Zealand†	3	22	13.18
1976-77	v England	5	25	22.96
1977-78	in Australia	5	31	23.87
1978-79	in Pakistan†	3	6	74.83
1978-79	v West Indies	3	7	46.28
1979	in England	3	7	37.57
Totals		**67**	**266**	**28.71**

Career wickets: 1,560 *Average:* 21.69
Best Test bowling: 7-98 v Australia, Calcutta, 1969-70
Best career bowling: 7-5, Delhi v Jammu and Kashmir, New Delhi, 1974-75
Highest Test score: 50* v New Zealand, Kanpur, 1976-77
Highest career score: 61, Delhi v Jammu and Kashmir, Srinagar, 1970-71
61, Northants v Glos., Northampton, 1974

*Not out †Captain

BEDSER
Alec Victor b 1918-

Alex Bedser was a model bowler and, in an age when the successful professional cricketer was often touched by controversy, had an exemplary career as a player. After his retirement, he gave cricket the same service off the field as he did on it, and he was awarded the OBE in 1964.

Tall and powerfully built, Bedser had a bowling action that was a marvel of economy. He took a relatively short run-up, but the swing of his massive body dragged the maximum bounce from the pitch while allowing him to sustain life and accuracy at a fast-medium pace over long periods.

Bedser's main delivery was the inswinger with which, during his career, he had many of his great opponents, from Don Bradman downwards, caught at backward short leg. He also bowled a slightly slower leg-cutter, which on a wet pitch could be akin to a fast, high-bouncing leg-break.

The leading English bowler of the early post-war years and an automatic selection for England until 1954-55, Bedser was unlucky that the war cut into his early career. He was born in Reading, and with his twin brother, Eric, joined the Surrey staff in 1938 after a period in a firm of solicitors. He made his first-class debut the following year against Oxford University, but it was not until 1946 that he took his first first-class wicket. He was then 28, and the intervening years had been spent in the RAF.

It was not long before English cricket realised that it possessed a potentially great fast-medium bowler. Bedser was selected to play against India in the 1946 series, and he took 7-49 and 4-96 against them in the first post-war Test at Lord's. In the next decade, he took 236 Test wickets to surpass Clarrie Grimmett's 216 wickets—the most taken by a bowler in Test cricket to that date.

England's bowling was weak during the early part of Bedser's career, and he had to carry much of the burden on his own shoulders. Yet he carried the burden so lightly that in 1953, when England's fortunes were about to turn, he took 39 wickets in the series against Australia. In the first Test at Trent Bridge, he took 7-55 and 7-44.

He decided not to go on the 1953-54 tour of West Indies, and played in only two of the four Tests in the following summer against Pakistan. But the real turning point in his international career came in December 1954, on

Alec Bedser as administrator, pictured on his appointment as chairman of the England Test selectors, a post he held from 1969 to 1982.

his third tour of Australia.

He had toiled through Australia's massive winning total of 601-8 dec in the First Test of the series. But on a grassy, damp wicket, which seemed tailor-made for his swing and cut, he was left out at Sydney for the Second Test. In that match Frank Tyson and Brian Statham bowled England to a 38-run win and, although Bedser was once again within a whisker of being picked for the Third Test, he did not return to the side again on that tour. Until the Sydney match he had played in every post-war England-Australia Test. Indeed, he played in only one more Test, against South Africa at Old Trafford in 1955—a match the Springboks won by three wickets with minutes to spare.

He was then 37, but he continued playing for Surrey through their championship-winning years and then two more years during their gradual decline. In 1960, he took on the captaincy of the county while Peter May was ill, and at the end of that season, aged 42, he retired.

A successful businessman, he still made time after his retirement as a player to serve on committees and to become an England selector from 1962. He has been manager and assistant manager on Test tours abroad, and in 1969 began a record term as chairman of selectors, which lasted until 1982, when he was succeeded by Peter May.

Alec Bedser as opening bowler. Power and control combined to produce a fine bowler respected by all who faced him. Don Bradman reckoned that in certain conditions he was the most difficult bowler in the world to play. Yet he was no mean batsman—sent in as a nightwatchman against Australia at Leeds in 1948 he hit 79—and he held 290 catches during his first-class career.

BEDSER Alec Victor

Teams: Surrey and England

Test series		Tests	Wkts	Average
1946	v India	3	24	12.41
1946-47	in Australia	5	16	54.75
1946-47	in New Zealand	1	4	23.75
1947	v South Africa	2	4	58.25
1948	v Australia	5	18	38.22
1948-49	in South Africa	5	16	34.62
1949	v New Zealand	2	7	30.71
1950	v West Indies	3	11	34.27
1950-51	in Australia	5	30	16.06
1950-51	in New Zealand	2	2	69.00
1951	v South Africa	5	30	17.23
1952	v India	4	20	13.95
1953	v Australia	5	39	17.48
1954	v Pakistan	2	10	15.80
1954-55	in Australia	1	1	131.00
1955	v South Africa	1	4	38.25
Totals		51	236	24.89

Career wickets: 1,924 *Average:* 20.41
Best Test bowling: 7-44 v Australia, Trent Bridge, 1953
Best career bowling: 8-18, Surrey v Nottingham, Oval, 1952
8-18, Surrey v Warwickshire, Oval, 1953
Highest Test score: 79 v Australia, Leeds, 1948
Highest career score: 126, Surrey v Somerset, Taunton, 1947

BENAUD
Richard (Richie) b 1930-

Captain of Australia from 1958 to 1963, Richie Benaud was the first player to score 2,000 runs and take 200 wickets in Test cricket. Yet for all his brilliance as an all-rounder, it is as a captain that his reputation stands highest of all.

An astute competitor, he had a flair for putting over his side's performance in the best possible light. He took more risks than most captains and was greatly respected by his own players and many others. The completeness of Australia's 4-0 victory to regain the Ashes from England in 1958-59 was a tribute to his aggressive leadership.

In one way, Benaud had an advantage over previous Australian Test captains in England. As a professional journalist, he was a frequent visitor to England,

reporting tours other than those in which he was playing, and he knew English cricket unusually well.

Benaud was born in Penrith, near Sydney, the son of a successful Sydney grade-cricketer and schoolmaster. At 18, he played for New South Wales, primarily as a batsman, and his Test career began at 21 against the visiting West Indians in 1951-52. He toured England for the first time in 1953.

Few visiting leg-break bowlers have prospered in England on limited experience, and talented though Benaud was, he might not have survived the tours of 1953 and 1956 as a bowler alone.

In 1953, he took two Test wickets and 57 tour wickets. He was left out, perhaps injudiciously, of the side that lost the Ashes at the Oval. On the 1956 tour, he took 60 wickets including eight in the Tests.

He was, however, an ideal batsman to have at No. 7 or 8 in a Test side, confident and full of attacking strokes. In 1953, he played an extraordinary innings of 135 at Scarborough in which he hit 11 sixes. In the Lord's Test match that same year, he made a vigorous 97. (It was in this Test that he took a brilliant catch in the gully off Cowdrey. The catch, taken from a well-timed square drive, lives in the memory of all who saw it.) He hit 100 in 78 minutes against the West Indies at Kingston in 1954-55, the third fastest hundred in Test history.

Between his visits to England, Benaud was highly successful on the harder pitches in Australia, South Africa, India, and Pakistan. He had an outstanding tour of South Africa, taking 106 wickets—a record for a visiting bowler—and scoring four centuries, including two in Test matches. His aggressive and

positive play in South Africa helped the Australian selectors choose him for the captaincy against England in 1958-59. In that series, he claimed 31 wickets, and on the 1959-60 tour of India and Pakistan took another 47 in the Tests. In all, he bagged 248 Test wickets, a number exceeded at that time only by Fred Trueman and Brian Statham of England.

The spectacular series with the West Indies in 1960-61, beginning with the famous tie at Brisbane, set the seal on Benaud's captaincy. Not only had he regained the Ashes from England, but his policy of attacking cricket recaptured much of the waning enthusiasm for cricket in Australia.

His most memorable bowling feat followed in July 1961 when, in the fourth Test at Old Trafford, England needed 256 runs to win. Benaud, troubled with a persistent shoulder condition since the initial first-class match of the tour, had

Richie Benaud, an astute leg-breaker and student of the game.

bowled himself sparingly. But with England advancing to 150 for one, he bowled round the wicket into the rough and suddenly broke the back of the England innings. He had Dexter caught at the wicket, bowled May round his legs, had Close caught at square leg, and bowled Subba Row. Australia won the match by 54 runs with 20 minutes to spare, and kept the Ashes. In 32 overs, Benaud had taken 6 for 70.

In 1962, Benaud was awarded the OBE. His reign as captain lasted through a halved series with Ted Dexter's England team in 1962-63 until a year later when he handed over the captaincy to Bobby Simpson during the series with South Africa.

After his retirement, he reported Australian tours in the West Indies, South Africa, and England, where he became a regular television commentator every summer. In 1977, when Kerry Packer set up his World Series company, Benaud became one of his principal consultants.

BENAUD Richard

Teams: New South Wales and Australia

Test series		Tests	Runs	100s	Average	Wkts	Average
1951-52	v West Indies	1	22	–	11.00	1	14.00
1952-53	v South Africa	4	124	–	20.66	10	30.60
1953	in England	3	15	–	3.00	2	87.00
1954-55	v England	5	148	–	16.44	10	37.70
1954-55	in West Indies	5	246	1	41.00	18	27.00
1956	in England	5	200	–	25.00	8	41.25
1956-57	in Pakistan	1	60	–	30.00	1	36.00
1956-57	in India	3	53	–	13.25	23	16.86
1957-58	in South Africa	5	329	2	54.83	30	21.93
1958-59	v England	5*	132	–	26.40	31	18.83
1959-60	in Pakistan	3*	84	–	28.00	18	21.16
1959-60	in India	5*	91	–	15.16	29	19.58
1960-61	v West Indies	5*	194	–	21.55	23	33.86
1961	in England	4*	45	–	9.00	15	32.53
1962-63	v England	5*	227	–	32.42	17	40.47
1963-64	v South Africa	4*†	231	–	33.00	12	37.41
Totals		63	2,201	3	24.45	248	27.04

Career runs: 11,719 *Average:* 36.50
Highest Test score: 122 v South Africa, Johannesburg, 1957-58
Highest career score: 187, Australians v Natal, Pietermaritzburg, 1957-58
Career wickets: 945 *Average:* 24.73
Best Test bowling: 7-72 v India, Madras, 1956-57
Best career bowling: 7-18, New South Wales v MCC, Sydney, 1962-63

*Captain †After the first Test of this series, Benaud handed the captaincy over to Bobby Simpson

BORDER
Allan Robert b 1955-

Allan Border came into the Australian side during the World Series Cricket problems, when Australia were forced to look for almost a complete new side. He began as a left-handed number six batsman whose slow bowling could prove useful. He had moved up to number three by the time the giants of WSC, led by Greg Chappell, returned, but he retained his place, albeit moving down to number five or six again. As the seasons progressed, so Border's bowling became less used, and his batting developed, a sound defensive technique and an array of attacking strokes being polished, while he lost none of the competitiveness and determination which marked his early play. As others retired or fell by the wayside he found himself, in 1985, occupying the place Greg Chappell had filled five years earlier: not only captain of Australia, but clearly his country's best batsman.

Border was born in Cremorne, a suburb of Sydney, New South Wales, in 1955. He played schoolboy and junior cricket, and took a job in the film library of an oil company. He made his first-class debut for New South Wales in the 1976-77 season, and at the end of the season went to England to broaden his experience in league and county second eleven cricket in Gloucestershire, playing one match for the county against Oxford University.

Back in Australia, he made a century against Western Australia in 1978-79, and soon afterwards was introduced into the Test side which had lost the first two Tests against England. Australia promptly won—their only win a series lost 5-1—but Border's contribution was modest. He did better in the next Test with 60 not out and 45 not out, batting number six and running out of partners, which was to become not uncommon in his career. He also took his first Test wicket: Mike Brearley, bowled.

However, by the sixth Test he was left out, only to return for the two-match series with Pakistan. This time he batted number three, and made 20 and 105, thus establishing another tendency, to do well in the second innings when the chips were down. With 85 and 66 not out in the next match, average for the series 92, he had staked a claim to be Australia's number three batsman. He did not enhance his reputation in the 1979 World Cup in England, and in the 1979-80 concurrent home series against West Indies and England, he did noticeably better against England, displaying a weakness against the West Indian pace attack, particularly outside off stump. In Pakistan later that season, however, he scored 150

not out and 153, becoming the first batsman to score 150 in each innings of a Test match.

For the following season he accepted an offer to move to Queensland, captained by Greg Chappell, and against whom he had recently scored a double century. He himself assumed the captaincy in 1983-84.

Border's Test status improved considerably on the tour to England in 1981, when Australia crumbled before the onslaughts of Botham and Willis. At Old Trafford, despite Australia losing by 103, Border made 123 not out with a fractured finger, taking Australia's fourth-innings score to over 400, but inevitably running out of partners. It was an innings full of grit. After his friend Botham's match-winning century in 86 balls, Border's century in an attempt to save the match took 337 minutes, the slowest by an Australian in Tests. At the Oval he made 106 not out, again running out of partners although batting number five, and 84, ending with

an average of 59.22 in a losing series. He scored most runs for Australia in both the Tests and the tour as a whole (807, av 50.43).

At home against the West Indies in 1981-82, Border averaged 67.20, making 126 at Adelaide against Holding, Roberts, Croft and Garner to prove that he could now handle the fastest bowlers.

A lean period followed, but against England at Melbourne in 1982-83 he did nearly win a match for Australia with 62 not out in the fourth innings—he and Jeff Thomson added 70 for the last wicket before Thomson was out four short of victory.

In 1983-84 he really came into his own. Against Pakistan he scored 188 at Brisbane and 117 not out at Adelaide, and in a series in the West Indies in which Australia were well beaten, he scored over 500 runs, including two courageous innings at Port-of-Spain of 98 not out and 100 not out, batting in all 634 minutes without being beaten and saving the match.

When the West Indies visited Australia in 1984-85 Kim Hughes resigned the Australian captaincy in tears after two Tests, protesting at the political factions in Australian officialdom and the lack of support given him. Border was the natural successor.

He led Australia in England in 1985 in a series which was evenly fought for three or four matches but in which England overwhelmed Australia in the last two. Border, however, had a triumphant tour personally, and scored 597 runs in Tests, average 66.33, and in the season as a whole he was third in the averages behind Richards and Boycott with 1,355 runs, average 71.32, having scored eight centuries. A feature of the tour was the sporting atmosphere, making Border a popular as well as inspiring Test captain.

BORDER Allan Robert

Teams: New South Wales, Gloucestershire (1 match), Queensland, Australia

Test series		Tests	Runs	100s	Average
1978-79	v England	3	146	—	36.50
1978-79	v Pakistan	2	276	1	92.00
1979-80	in India	6	521	1	43.41
1979-80	v West Indies	3	118	—	19.66
1979-80	v England	3	199	1	49.75
1979-80	in Pakistan	3	395	2	131.66
1980	in England	1	77	—	—
1980-81	v New Zealand	3	100	—	25.00
1980-81	v India	3	228	1	45.60
1981	in England	6	533	2	59.22
1981-82	v Pakistan	3	84	—	16.80
1981-82	v West Indies	3	336	1	67.20
1981-82	in New Zealand	3	44	—	14.66
1982-83	in Pakistan	3	118	—	23.60
1982-83	v England	5	317	—	45.28
1982-83	in Sri Lanka	1	47	—	—
1983-84	v Pakistan	5	429	2	85.80
1983-84	in West Indies	5	521	1	74.42
1984-85	v West Indies‡	5	246	—	27.33
1985	in England†	6	597	2	66.33
Totals		**72**	**5,332**	**14**	**50.78**

Career runs: 11,821 *Average:* 52.30
Highest Test score: 196 v England, Lord's, 1985
Highest career score: 200, New South Wales v Queensland, Brisbane, 1979-80
Test bowling: 15 wickets *Average:* 41.66

†Captain ‡Captain in last 3 Tests   Career figures correct to end of 1985 season

BOTHAM
Ian Terence b 1955-

It is possible to claim that Ian Botham is the greatest cricketer the world has seen. Throughout his career he has passed milestones so rapidly that from quite early it appeared certain that he would not only become the first player to score 3,000 Test runs and take 300 Test wickets but that he would no doubt eventually pass 4,000 and 400, and possibly 5,000 and 500. It is a measure of his stature that although he is on the brink of becoming the most prolific Test wicket-taker in history, he is likely to be remembered most for his batting.

Botham has not been free of criticism during his career. He has been involved in court cases and has frequently offended the cricketing authorities. He has been accused at times of a carefree attitude, at others for being domineering and too 'greedy' (i.e. demanding to bowl). He has been blamed for allowing himself to get too fat. He lost the England captaincy, and there have been those who have suggested that at times he should have lost his England place altogether.

However, he remains the man who can turn Test matches on his own, the man whose entry to bat is enough to excite crowds to expectancy, the most charismatic cricketeter of the 1980s.

Ian Botham might have been a Yorkshireman, like his father, but he was born prematurely at Heswall, in Cheshire. A Yorkshireman by temperament, he was thus unqualified to play for that county, which still insists on playing only local born players. His cricketing allegiance was settled when the family moved to Yeovil when he was three years old.

He made his debut for Somerset in 1974 and after four first-class appearances, really showed his mettle in a Benson and Hedges match against Hampshire at Taunton. With Somerset facing a total of 182, the 18-year-old Botham entered at 113 for 7, which was soon 113 for 8, with 70 needed in 15 overs. When the score had been edged to 131, Andy Roberts, the West Indian fast bowler, came on and a fast short ball struck Botham on the face, half felling him. In those pre-helmet days, Botham suffered severe pain as blood oozed from his gums and mouth—he was to lose four teeth. With apparent foolhardiness he batted on, even hitting a second six and a few fours. Roberts, on his second-last over, claimed Ian's partner lbw—seven more to get and the last man in. Botham finished it with a four—the youngster had 45 not out, and the 6,500 crowd had seen the first instance of the power of a new star.

In 1977 came the Test call-up, in the third Test against the touring Australians. Botham's first wicket was Greg Chappell—he finished the first innings with 5 for 74. In the winter he scored his first Test century against New Zealand (and took eight wickets in the match). By the end of 1978, during which he hit Pakistan with two centuries and his best Test analysis, 8 for 34, and New Zealand with 24 wickets, he was the hottest property in cricket—the new golden all-rounder at only 22 years old. There was also the first public indication of his off-the-field newsworthiness —he went to Australia with his arm in a sling, having put it through a glass door during a farewell party in Doncaster.

In 1979 Botham passed 1,000 runs and 100 Test wickets in his 21st Test, two quicker than the previous record of Vinoo Mankad. In February 1980, in Bombay, in India's Golden Jubilee Test, he scored 114 and took thirteen wickets—the first player to score a century and take 10 or more wickets in a Test.

With the retirement from the England captaincy of Brearley, Botham took over for the visit of the West Indies in 1980. By his standards, he had a poor series, followed by a poor Centenary Test against Australia at Lord's, and then a bad tour of the West Indies, where he was not helped by the sad death of assistant manager Barrington, with whom he shared a birthday and mutual respect, and

A bearded Botham bowling in the third Test against West Indies at Old Trafford in 1980.

the political troubles over Jackman. A campaign began to relieve him of the England captaincy, on the grounds that his form was affected by the responsibility.

The climax to this campaign, and a big turning point in Botham's career, came during the second Test with Australia in 1981. Having lost the first Test, England could only draw the second. Skipper Botham was bowled first ball in the second innings for a pair, and returned to the pavilion in a frosty atmosphere. After the match he resigned the captaincy, claiming that excessive media attention to his difficulties was making life impossible for his family. It transpired that the selectors were about to reinstate Brearley as captain for three Tests anyway. Botham had been captain for 12 matches, of which four were drawn and eight lost.

The next Test, with Botham reduced to the ranks, was one of the most amazing in Test history, with Botham's all-round performance being one of the greatest ever seen. With the ball he took 6 for 95 and 1 for 14, and with the bat he scored 50 and the match-winning 149 not out, which allowed England to become only the second side in all Test cricket to win after following on. The series continued with Botham in similar form, taking a match-winning 5 for 11 at Edgbaston, and hitting a superb 118 at Old Trafford.

Botham resumed, after these heights, his former role of outstanding Test all-rounder. In the first Test of the winter tour of India, he became the third player, after Benaud and Sobers, to score 2,000 Test runs and take 200 Test wickets. He did it in the fewest matches (42), the shortest time (4 years, 126 days) and he was the youngest of the three at 26 years and 7 days.

Season 1983-84 provided more crises for Botham. First, a damaged left knee caused him problems on the tour of New Zealand, and then a Sunday newspaper made allegations of the England tourists as a whole indulging in riotous living, including drug-taking. Being a senior member of the side, and its most newsworthy, naturally Botham could not escape being associated with these charges. Nothing came of these strenuously denied insinuations.

The knee, however, proved more of a problem. After one Test in Pakistan Botham was forced to return home, thus ending a run of 65 consecutive Tests for England, which equalled a record set by Alan Knott. Later, in hospital, he made a jokey but disparaging remark about touring Pakistan for which he was obliged to apologize.

In 1984, in the series lost 5-0 to West Indies, Botham played extremely well at Lord's, taking 8 for 103 and scoring 30 and 81. Botham completed 4,000 Test runs in this match—in the last Test he became

Ian Botham on his walk from John o'Groats to Land's End in November 1985. With him is John Border, brother of Allan.

the first player to complete the double of 3,000 Test runs and 300 Test wickets.

Botham took a rest from cricket during the winter of 1984-85, deciding not to tour India. On New Year's Eve, he was arrested in connection with drugs charges, and in February was fined £100 for possession of cannibis. This was not Botham's first court appearance, there having been an assault charge in 1981, which was dismissed. Neither Somerset not the TCCB considered the drugs conviction serious enough to affect his career.

It is, of course, inevitable that a man of Botham's temperament and ability and with his preference for physical and often dangerous pursuits is going to attract headlines. He shoots, has flown with the Red Devils aerobatic team, crashed Saab cars and played League football with Scunthorpe United (he transferred in 1984-85 to Yeovil Town).

Because of his England commitments, his figures for Somerset were naturally less impressive than might be hoped. He was made captain for the 1984 season, but lost the job at the end of the 1985 season. Strangely, this was one of his most successful batting seasons for the county. He hit 80 sixes in the season, a record, passing the 50-year-old total of 66 set by Arthur Wellard, also a Somerset player. By now Botham had an agent, had put blonder streaks into his hair, was modelling flashy clothes and considering (or his agent was for him) a Hollywood career.

The Ashes series of 1985 was another triumph, especially with the ball, his 31 wickets raising his total to 343. He was again before the TCCB disciplinary sub-committee for showing dissent during the Trent Bridge Test, and was reprimanded.

Botham is a cricketer who is always in the game, making runs, taking wickets or making catches. Some of his catches have been bewilderingly spectacular. His favourite position is second slip, where he usually stands a metre or so closer to the bat than the line of slips. Frequently he has his hands on his knees as the ball is delivered, and the critics have chided him for it, but he is a cricketer who makes his own rules and, with his record, who can say he is wrong?

There being a few weeks between the end of the 1985 season and the tour to the West Indies, Botham completed a sponsored walk from John O'Groats to Land's End for charity—always active, always in the news. Somewhere along the way he was described as 'the last working class hero'.

BOTHAM Ian Terence

Teams: Somerset and England

Test series		Tests	Runs	100s	Average	Wkts	Average
1977	v Australia	2	25	—	12.50	10	20.20
1977-78	in New Zealand	3	212	1	53.00	17	18.29
1978	v Pakistan	3	212	2	70.66	13	16.07
1978	v New Zealand	3	51	—	17.00	24	14.04
1978-79	in Australia	6	291	—	29.10	23	24.65
1979	v India	4	244	1	48.80	20	23.60
1979-80	in Australia	3	187	1	37.40	19	19.36
1979-80	in India	1	114	1	114.00	13	8.15
1980	v West Indies†	5	169	—	18.55	13	29.61
1980	v Australia†	1	0	—	—	1	132.00
1980-81	in West Indies†	4	73	—	10.42	15	32.60
1981	v Australia‡	6	399	2	36.27	34	20.58
1981-82	in India	6	440	1	55.00	17	35.76
1981-82	in Sri Lanka	1	13	—	13.00	3	21.66
1982	v India	3	403	2	134.33	9	35.55
1982	v Pakistan	3	163	—	27.16	18	26.55
1982-83	in Australia	5	270	—	27.00	18	40.50
1983	v New Zealand	4	282	1	35.25	10	34.10
1983-84	in New Zealand	3	226	1	56.50	7	50.57
1983-84	in Pakistan	1	32	—	16.00	2	45.00
1984	v West Indies	5	347	—	34.70	19	35.10
1984	v Sri Lanka	1	6	—	6.00	7	29.14
1985	v Australia	6	250	—	31.25	31	27.25
Totals		**79**	**4,409**	**13**	**36.13**	**343**	**26.37**

Career runs: 13,437 *Average:* 35.08
Highest Test score: 208 v India, Oval, 1982
Highest career score: 228 v Gloucestershire, Taunton, 1980
Career wickets: 896 *Average:* 25.62
Best Test and career bowling: 8-34 v Pakistan, Lord's, 1978

†Captain ‡Captain in first two Tests   Career figures correct to end of 1985 season

BOYCOTT
Geoffrey b 1940-

Geoffrey Boycott is one of the most controversial cricketers of modern times. No batsman ever compiled runs in a more single-minded, dedicated manner. Few batsmen have been as successful. Until Sunil Gavaskar passed his aggregate in November 1983, he had scored more runs in Test matches than any other cricketer. By then Boycott had lost his Test place by participating in a 'rebel' tour of South Africa.

Boycott's dealings with Yorkshire brought him even more into the news. Sacked as captain, he took on the whole Committee and forced their resignation, becoming a Committee member himself. Idolised by some, who called him 'Sir' Geoffrey, he is denigrated by as many, who blame him for most of the ills of Yorkshire during the 1970s and 1980s.

Born in 1940 in Fitzwilliam, near Pontefract, Boycott made his debut in 1962 and established a regular place a year later.

Just 23 in his first full season, Boycott made 1,778 runs, and in 1964 he made 2,110. At first sight he was not obviously a batsman of the highest class, but his performances allowed no argument. On further analysis the observer would note his watchfulness, the way in which he moved into position, the fluency of his off-side strokes, especially against the ball just short of a length, and above all, his intense concentration. Although not possessing the natural gifts that many great batsmen have, he had worked out an effective method of playing, and he had the necessary application and temperament.

After his leap to fame, however, he had some difficult periods, and at the end of the 1969 season it seemed his later career was not quite fulfilling its immense early promise.

In some ways his concentration has not always been an unqualified asset to him. For at times when he has been below form, Boycott has fought on grimly, apparently oblivious to everything happening around him, playing a long, slow innings that may not have been in the best interests of the side and certainly was no pleasure to spectators. In 1967 he made 246 not out against India at Leeds but spent nearly six hours over the first 100. The selectors had previously called for a positive approach to batting, and this flagrant disregard for their requirements and the fact that it was not warranted by the state of the match caused Boycott to be dropped for the next Test as a disciplinary measure. In 1969 he played another painfully slow innings at Lord's against the West Indies.

At that time he had just begun playing in contact lenses instead of in his customary spectacles.

Season 1970-71 in Australia, however, was a personal triumph. His 657 Test runs at an average of 93.85 were instrumental in helping England to regain the Ashes.

In 1974 he voluntarily withdrew from Test cricket. Mike Denness had been appointed captain of England for the 1973-74 tour of the West Indies, at a time when many thought Boycott, or Greig, had the better claims. In the third Test, Boycott was asked to bat at number four for England for the only time. Whether or not these events had any bearing, he declined to tour Australia in 1974-75, and did not return to Test cricket until the summer of 1977.

Having recovered his personal poise—and having rejected an offer to sign a Packer contract— Boycott announced that he was available for England again. The selectors called him up for the third Test at Nottingham.

His comeback was dour, nerve-wracking, but triumphant, for he

ABOVE A young Boycott attempts to play the ball through the gully. His stroke appears to lack the certainty which rapidly developed in his batting after he changed to contact lenses.
LEFT A classic shot which became Boycott's chief scoring weapon. With the bat perfectly straight he drives the ball square on the off-side, or in an arc ranging from just forward to just backward of point.

made 107 and 80 not out. He had luck. If he had been held at slip after batting for three hours for 20 the outcome would probably have been entirely different. But with confidence high, he made an even more emotional century in the next Test, before his home crowd at Leeds, and his 191 happened to be his 100th first-class century.

More ups and downs lay ahead. During the winter tour he succeeded to the England captaincy when Brearley suffered a broken forearm, but after averaging 82.25 against Pakistan he had the galling experience of leading England in their first defeat by New Zealand. The reversal was compensated with victory in the second Test, but in the spring of 1978 he became a casualty himself when fielding a hard drive, and found himself unable immediately to regain his place in the England XI. He also, not for the first time, found himself the centre of controversy over the way he captained and batted for Yorkshire.

Yet both for country and county the responsibility on his shoulders had been frequently so great that his ability to play one long innings after another was desperately needed—particularly for the weak-batting Yorkshire side whose captaincy he took over in 1971. It was no coincidence that in his first year in charge he averaged over

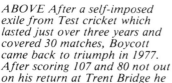

ABOVE After a self-imposed exile from Test cricket which lasted just over three years and covered 30 matches, Boycott came back to triumph in 1977. After scoring 107 and 80 not out on his return at Trent Bridge he went better (above) by scoring his 100th first-class century at his home ground of Headingley—the first player to achieve this feat in a Test match.
RIGHT His numerous fans welcome him back to the fold.

100, though his side made no sort of show in any of the competitions. He felt he had to do everything himself.

This attitude was regarded by enemies as selfishness, however, and in 1977 a campaign was begun to remove him from the captaincy. In 1978 two Yorkshire batsmen, Hampshire and Johnson, batted so slowly in the final 10 overs of Yorkshire's innings against Northamptonshire (prior to the enforced closure at 100 overs) that they were assumed to be protesting about a slow century by the skipper. The Yorkshire Committee relieved Boycott of the captaincy and gave it to Hampshire. A pro-Boycott Reform Group was formed and challenged the Committee, at first unsuccessfully. Boycott was forced to play under Hampshire.

In 1983 came a further blow to his pride. After being granted a benefit in 1984, the Committee in fact sacked Boycott altogether after the 1983 season to end the 'rancour and controversy of recent years'. This time the pro-Boycott group, at a special meeting, won votes of no-confidence in the Committee, who resigned, and at the new elections Boycott himself stood for, and was elected to, the Committee. Boycott has continued since to play for Yorkshire, but the Yorkshire 'situation' remains volatile, and far from free of rancour and controversy.

Meanwhile more headlines sur-

rounded Boycott in 1981. Picked to tour India in the winter, he was accepted by the Indian authorities only after the Prime Minister, Mrs Gandhi, had intervened and he had made a statement condemning *apartheid*. Boycott had played in South Africa the previous winter.

There was more controversy when he left India early, it being reported that he had played golf while taking a day off from fielding during the fourth Test, when suffering from ill-health. It was during this tour that Boycott passed Sobers' record aggregate of runs in Test cricket.

Soon after his return to England, Boycott announced that he was take part in a 'rebel' tour of South Africa in 1981-82. Together with the other England Test players who took part on this tour, he was banned from Tests for three years. When the ban was lifted in 1985, Boycott found that competition for places as opening batsmen in the England side against Australia was now fierce, and he was not selected.

Boycott remains a batsman who insists his figures speak for him. Approaching 50,000 runs, over 8,000 in Tests, twice averaging over 100 in a season, his achievements are impressive. His technique at the crease is faultless. Critics claim that figures are meaningless without their context, and that cricket is more than just the accumulation of runs. Boycott's career will be controversial to the end.

BOYCOTT, Geoffrey

Teams: Yorkshire, Northern Transvaal, and England

Test series		Tests	Runs	100s	Average
1964	v Australia	4	291	1	48.50
1964-65	in South Africa	5	298	1	49.66
1965	v New Zealand	2	157	—	52.33
1965	v South Africa	2	75	—	18.75
1965-66	in Australia	5	300	—	42.85
1965-66	in New Zealand	2	13	—	4.33
1966	v West Indies	4	186	—	26.57
1967	v India	2	277	1	138.50
1967	v Pakistan	1	16	—	16.00
1967-68	in West Indies	5	463	1	66.14
1968	v Australia	3	162	—	32.40
1969	v West Indies	3	270	2	54.00
1969	v New Zealand	3	101	—	20.20
1970-71	in Australia	5	657	2	93.85
1971	v Pakistan	2	246	2	123.00
1971	v India	1	36	—	18.00
1972	v Australia	2	72	—	18.00
1973	v New Zealand	3	320	1	64.00
1973	v West Indies	3	202	—	50.50
1973-74	in West Indies	5	421	1	46.77
1974	v India	1	16	—	8.00
1977	v Australia	3	422	2	147.33
1977-78	in Pakistan‡	3	329	1	82.25
1977-78	in New Zealand†	3	166	—	33.20
1978	v New Zealand	2	159	1	53.00
1978-79	in Australia	6	263	—	21.91
1979	v India	4	378	2	75.60
1979-80	in Australia	3	176	—	35.20
1979-80	in India	1	65	—	65.00
1980	v West Indies	5	368	—	40.88
1980	v Australia	1	190	1	190.00
1980-81	in West Indies	4	295	1	42.14
1981	v Australia	6	392	1	32.66
1981-82	in India	4	312	1	44.57
Totals		**108**	**8,114**	**22**	**47.72**

Career runs: 47,434 *Average:* 56.94
Highest Test score: 246* v India, Leeds, 1967
Highest career score: 261*, MCC v President's XI, Bridgetown, 1973-74

*Not out   †Captain   ‡Captain in 1 Test   Career figures correct to end of 1985 season

BRADMAN
Sir Donald George
b 1908-

If a batsman had to be named as the greatest ever, the choice of many people would certainly be Australian cricketer Don Bradman. His record is unsurpassed, indeed unapproached, even though World War II and poor health took six years out of his career. Between 1927 and 1948 Bradman averaged 95.14 against the 56.10 of Walter Hammond, who had the next best record. In Test matches he averaged 99.94. This is nearly double the figure of the next most successful Australian batsman, Greg Chappell, with 53.86, who is followed by Bobby Simpson, Neil Harvey, and Bradman's two great contemporaries Bill Ponsford and Stan McCabe, all of whom averaged just over 48. In his 52 Test matches he made 29 centuries, a record later passed by Sunil Gavaskar, who required twice as many matches.

These figures give an idea of Bradman's pre-eminence amongst batsmen of all times. Yet it was not only his consistency and freedom from error that made men marvel, but also the swiftness and facility with which he made his runs.

He undoubtedly saw the ball in flight as early as it can be seen by the human eye, but it was the speed of his reflexes that was at the heart of his genius. Quick-footed and perfectly balanced, he always seemed in position to play the stroke that the length of the ball required. And often the speed of his footwork would make the ball the length *he* wanted. He had all the strokes and a rare gift of improvisation. He was a wonderfully quick cutter and hooker, but if one stroke more than any other impressed itself on the memory of cricket fans, it was his hitting of the ball through mid-wicket, especially off the back foot. He seldom hit the ball in the air and always—it seemed—placed it wide of a fielder. His placing was a miracle of precision.

It has been said that on bad pitches he was but a shadow of the great batsman he was on hard, true pitches. But his record shows that he was a formidable figure even in adversity—in the 'bodyline' series of 1932-33 he still averaged 56. It was also a significant tribute to his greatness that he was able to play again so successfully after the war. In 1948 he was nearly 40 and, to those who had watched him in his youth, was less spectacular and less imbued with the old quicksilver magic. But he still averaged 72 in the Test series and made 2,428 runs in first-class matches on the tour at an average of 89.92.

One of the first inklings the outside world had that a new

cricket prodigy had arrived was a report early in 1927 that a certain Don Bradman of Bowral, New South Wales, had made 320 in a grade final. He had also exceeded 300 in the previous year's final.

Born in Cootamundra, New South Wales, on August 27, 1908, Bradman spent his boyhood in Bowral, some 80 miles from Sydney. He was only 19 when, in his first Sheffield Shield match, he made 118 for New South Wales against South Australia at Adelaide.

His first Test match, in the following season, was a grim experience for a young Australian for England won at Brisbane by 675 runs. Bradman was only twelfth man in the second Test. But he made 79 and 112 in the

ABOVE Bradman during a practice session at Lord's in 1948, when he captained a great unbeaten touring team.
LEFT Bradman off-drives during an innings of 187 in 125 minutes against Essex.

third and soon the idea of an Australian team without him became absurd. In the vital Sheffield Shield match that season he made 340 not out against Victoria, the first of his big scores, and by the time he went to England in 1930 his reputation was enormous. Yet his achievements there were even greater. Beginning with 236, the first of three successive double centuries at Worcester, he made 2,960 runs, averaging 98.66. In Test matches he made four centuries and 974 runs, averaging 139.14.

At Lord's, Bradman's 254 was an innings that made watchers think, perhaps correctly, that they would never again see such dominating batting in this class of cricket. At Leeds he made 309 not out on the first day of the third Test, increasing it to 334 the next day. In a single day, Bradman had beaten a Test record that had stood since 1903 when R. E. Foster made 287 for England at Sydney. At the Oval he made 232.

From his overwhelming mastery

of English bowling and the subsequent series at home, when he made two centuries against the West Indies and four against South Africa, there developed 'bodyline' with which England, under Douglas Jardine, countered Bradman and other successful batsmen in 1932-33. But Bradman was back in England in 1934, no less devastating than four years before, and he returned as captain in 1938. Between these tours he had moved from New South Wales to South Australia.

It was a stroke of irony that his pre-war career of almost uninterrupted triumph should end with one of his few reverses. The

last Test of 1938 was due to be played to a finish and England, batting first at the Oval, made 903 for 7 declared. Len Hutton's 364 in this innings took from Bradman one of the few records he surrendered in his playing career. In his younger days he had been a useful leg-break bowler and, as the England score mounted and his bowlers tired, he put himself on. But in bowling, he trod on a worn footmark and badly injured an ankle. He was carried from the field and took no further part in the match. England subsequently won the match by an innings and 579 runs, squaring the rubber.

When the war ended, it was not certain if Bradman's health would let him play again. But he made 76 and 106 in his first two matches against the MCC touring side of 1946-47, and 187 and 234 in the first and second Tests. He carried on at a level of brilliance only just below that of his pre-war days.

The physical attributes and the astonishing co-ordination that produced his peerless batting were supported by a temperament combining great application, an intense sense of purpose, and a streak of ruthlessness. These qualities served him well as a captain and he never lost a rubber. The unbeaten record of the great

1948 Australians was a suitable climax, though his own Test career finished at the Oval on a note of anti-climax. Coming in to play his last Test innings to a great ovation, he was bowled second ball by Eric Hollies. He had needed only four runs from that innings to average exactly 100 throughout his Test career.

It is now usual in Australia for great players to become active administrators, but Bradman, knighted in 1949, became almost as commanding a figure in Australian cricket off the field as he had been on it. He has been an immensely influential figure in the game in Australia, both as a selector and a member and chairman of the Board of Control. It was typical that when in the early 1960s he became convinced of the dangers to the game of illegal bowling and the growing number of 'throwers', the menace was stamped out more quickly and more thoroughly in Australia than anywhere else in the world.

LEFT One of Bradman's more prolific and unorthodox strokes—the pull through mid-wicket of a ball not necessarily on the leg side.
BELOW Bradman sweeping against Leicestershire. Again the shot is unorthodox, and needs a perfect eye.

BRADMAN Sir Donald George

Teams: New South Wales, South Australia, and Australia

Test series	Tests	Runs	100s	Average
1928-29 v England	4	468	2	66.85
1930 in England	5	974	4	139.14
1930-31 v West Indies	5	447	2	74.50
1931-32 v South Africa	5	806	4	201.50
1932-33 v England	4	396	1	56.57
1934 in England	5	758	2	94.75
1936-37 v England†	5	810	3	90.00
1938 in England†	4	434	3	108.50
1946-47 v England†	5	680	2	97.14
1947-48 v India†	5	715	4	178.75
1948 in England†	5	508	2	72.57
Totals	52	6,996	29	99.94

Career runs: 28,067 *Average:* 95.14
Highest Test score: 334 v England, Leeds, 1930
Highest career score: 452* New South Wales v Queensland, Sydney, 1929-30

*Not out †Captain

CHAPPELL
Gregory Stephen b 1948-

Greg Chappell's career began satisfactorily in the shadow of his five-years-older brother Ian, blossomed into brilliance on his Test debut, settled down into consistent excellence, stuttered once or twice when World Series Cricket and an unsporting incident in a limited-overs game tarnished his popularity, and ended in a blaze of glory with the captaincy of Australia and a record number of Test runs for an Australian.

Chappell was born in Unley, South Australia in 1948. Older brother Ian and younger brother Trevor were both to become Test cricketers, and grandfather Vic Richardson, also born in Unley, was a captain of Australia in the 1930s. Greg made his debut for South Australia in 1966-67.

In his first season in the Sheffield Shield as an 18-year-old he made a century against Queensland, later his adopted state.

Australia called on the younger brother of their captain, Ian Chappell, in a state of some crisis. A series in South Africa had been lost in disastrous circumstances and Illingworth's England were the visitors as Australia's batting wore a brittle look.

Greg Chappell answered the call by making 108 in his first innings, batting at number seven. From that moment he became anything but an overshadowed younger brother.

In 1971-72 he really showed his class, batting brilliantly for Australia against the strong Rest of the World side which toured Australia and played a series of unofficial Tests. He made 115 not out at Sydney, 197 not out at Melbourne and 85 at Adelaide.

In 1975 he succeeded his brother as captain of his country, not surprisingly the only instance of brothers captaining Australia.

He responded to that office with the authority which had established him as one of the world's master batsmen. In his first match as captain he scored 123 and 109 not out against West Indies and led his side to the devastating series win of five matches to one, including a personal contribution of 702 runs (average 117.00).

Stangely this voluminous triumph followed the only really unproductive spell of his career—a mere 106 runs from seven innings against England in 1975; a rare drought in a first-class career which began in 1966 for South Australia. Later he moved with considerable success to Queensland where he earned his spurs as a captain before leading his country. He spent two seasons in county cricket with Somerset, which helped develop his all-round stroke play after a leg-side bias in his early days. His all-round qualities were also developed as a

The classic style and skill of Greg Chappell are evident in this leg glance. With his neatness, straight back and serious countenance, there was an Edwardian touch about his play. His aggregate of Test runs is an Aussie record.

useful medium-pace bowler with a high action after he had toyed with leg-spin. In 1968 he scored 1,108 Championship runs for Somerset and took 26 wickets. He also became an outstanding fielder. His sharp reflexes close to the wicket made him a valuable member of Australia's close catching ring.

But it was his effortless upright stroke play which made his real mark on the game. He struck a masterly 131 in 'Massie's Test' at Lords in 1972 and in partnership with Ian reached three figures again at The Oval. In statistical

terms his best Test performance came at Wellington in 1974 when he recorded an extravagant 247 not out and 133 in the same match.

More than that, he had played a leading role in Australia's growth from the uncertainty at the time of his Test debut into the most powerful side in the world, as the overwhelming defeat of the West Indies in his first series as captain proved.

A successful series against Pakistan (av. 57.16) and a tour of New Zealand during which he tried to restore Australia's bruised reputation preceded a tour of England in 1977 which was to provide the saddest of temporary farewells to Test cricket. Having signed for Kerry Packer, Chappell captained a side whose morale sank further with every match. The series was lost three-nil, and apart from a glorious hundred at Manchester,

he was a shadow of his former self, victim of increasing and unique strain. Yet to the end he maintained characteristic dignity.

Chappell was thought to be one of the prime supporters of Kerry Packer and his World Series Cricket. He captained the WSC Australia side.

When WSC ended, Greg Chappell resumed his position as captain of Australia, and was back in his best form, quickly revenging his defeat in England in 1977 with a 3-0 win in Australia in 1979-80. Later in the season in Faisalabad he scored 235 against Pakistan, but lost the series. He captained Australia in the 1980 Centenary Test at Lord's, having also been captain in the pre-Packer 1977 Centenary Test at Melbourne.

Under his brother's captaincy, Australia had earned a reputation as being one of the toughest sides

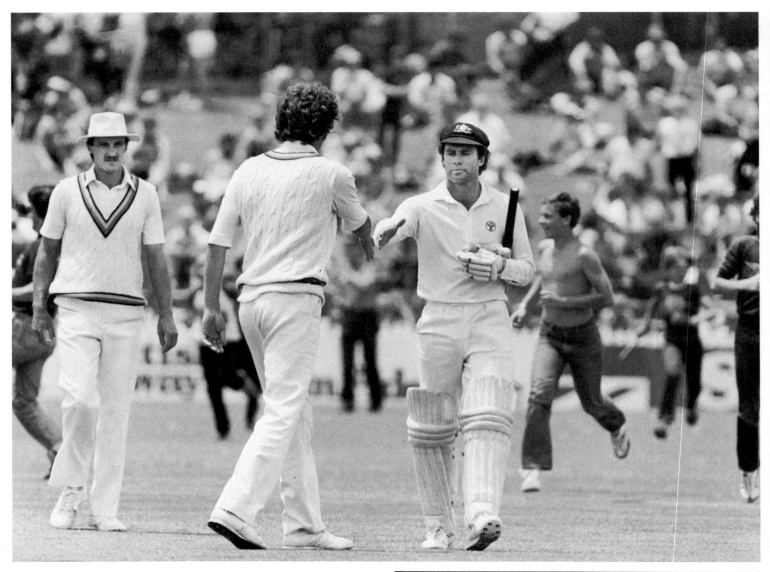

Greg Chappell shakes hands with England skipper Bob Willis at the end of the third Test at Adelaide in 1982-83, won by Australia.

in Test history, making a cult of aggression and intimidation and developing the practice of 'sledging'—verbal abuse of the batsmen. Greg was generally aloof from this, but in the 1980-81 season he attracted criticism from all round the world for his action in a limited-overs match against New Zealand. With New Zealand requiring six runs to win off the last ball Chappell instructed his brother Trevor to bowl it underarm along the ground, making the batsman's task impossible.

Showing a liking for Pakistan, Chappell made 201 against them in 1981-82 in a winning series. He continued a tendency for occasional big innings later in the season with 176 against New Zealand.

For his last series against Pakistan in 1983-84 Chappell relinquished the captaincy to Kim Hughes. When he announced his retirement during the fifth Test he was on the brink of two records. Having caught Mudassar in the first innings he had equalled

Cowdrey's record (excluding wicket-keepers) of 120 Test match catches, needing another in the second innings to beat it. He also needed 69 runs to pass the record Test aggregate for an Australian, a record held by the great Don Bradman.

Chappell scored the runs and went on to make 182, thus not only beating the record but joining fellow-Australians R. A. Duff and W. H. Ponsford in scoring centuries in their first and last Tests. When Pakistan batted again Chappell quickly caught Mohsin Khan to beat Cowdrey's record—later he also caught Salim Malik to end with 122 Test catches.

Chappell was not the most astute of captains tactically. He led by example. He was the best Australian batsman of his era, both in figures and in style, and he held his catches, mostly at slip. Of 48 Tests in which he was captain, he won 21, drew 14 and lost 13. On retirement, he said that there were a couple of things he would have liked to have done differently, presumably referring to the underarm delivery. It would be better to remember his upright stance, and his elegant, classic driving, particularly to the on-side.

CHAPPELL Gregory Stephen

Teams: South Australia, Queensland, Somerset and Australia

Test series		Tests	Runs	100s	Average	Wkts	Average
1970-71	v England	5	243	1	34.71	5	51.00
1972	in England	5	437	2	48.55	2	62.50
1972-73	v Pakistan	3	242	1	60.50	5	24.20
1972-73	in West Indies	5	342	1	48.85	4	56.50
1973-74	v New Zealand	3	110	—	36.67	5	30.40
1973-74	in New Zealand	3	449	2	89.80	3	47.00
1974-75	v England	6	608	2	55.27	—	—
1975	in England	4	106	—	21.20	0	—
1975-76	v West Indies†	6	702	3	117.00	3	23.00
1976-77	v Pakistan†	3	343	1	57.16	2	22.50
1976-77	in New Zealand†	2	102	—	34.00	2	38.00
1976-77	v England†	1	42	—	21.00	1	29.00
1977	in England†	5	371	1	41.22	0	—
1979-80	v West Indies†	3	270	1	45.00	1	28.00
1979-80	v England†	3	317	1	79.25	4	16.50
1979-80	in Pakistan†	3	381	1	76.20	3	24.66
1980	in England†	1	106	—	53.00	0	—
1980-81	v New Zealand†	3	180	—	36.00	2	21.00
1980-81	v India†	3	368	1	73.60	1	27.00
1981-82	v Pakistan†	3	251	1	50.20	2	11.50
1981-82	v West Indies†	3	86	—	14.33	0	—
1981-82	in New Zealand†	3	235	1	78.33	1	33.00
1982-83	v England†	5	389	2	48.62	1	44.00
1982-83	in Sri Lanka†	1	66	—	66.00	0	—
1983-84	v Pakistan	5	364	2	72.80	0	—
Totals		87	7,110	24	53.86	47	40.70

Career runs: 24,535 *Average:* 52.20
Highest Test and career score: 247* v New Zealand, Wellington, 1973-74
Career wickets: 291 *Average:* 29.95
Best Test bowling: 5-61 v Pakistan, Sydney, 1972-73
Best career bowling: 7-40, Somerset v Yorkshire, Leeds, 1969

*Not out †Captain

CHAPPELL
Ian Michael b 1943-

It must have been particularly galling for such a competitive cricketer as Ian Chappell that in his first match as captain of Australia, at Sydney in 1971, he had to concede The Ashes. After that, this aggressive strokemaker, excellent slip and useful change spinner showed that captaincy was another of his talents.

A grandson of Vic Richardson who captained Australia in the 1930s, he played in his first Test against Pakistan at Melbourne in 1964-65. His next Test appearance was against England in the following year, on his home ground at Adelaide. The scorecard shows that he achieved little with bat or ball, but early in the match he held a magnificent slip catch from Geoff Boycott which helped set

Australia on the road to victory and the retention of the Ashes.

In South Africa in 1966-67, he did not fulfil initial promise as a batsman, and his bowling was little used. But his batting made a considerable impact in England in 1968. He had played for Ramsbottom in the Lancashire League in 1963 and his technique proved more effective on English pitches than that of the other young Australian batsmen.

Back in Australia in 1968-69, he surpassed all his previous achievements by making 548 runs at an average of 68.50 in the Test series against West Indies. In the first Test he scored 117 and in the second 165. It was his dismissal for 96 in the last innings of the remarkable fourth Test at Adelaide that precipitated Australia's collapse when they were within sight of victory and gave them only a hard-earned draw.

He continued to score prolifi-

CHAPPELL, Ian Michael

Teams: South Australia, Lancashire (1 match), and Australia

Test series	Tests	Runs	100s	Average
1964-65 v Pakistan	1	11	—	11.00
1965-66 v England	2	36	—	18.00
1966-67 in South Africa	5	196	—	21.77
1967-68 v India	4	212	1	30.28
1968 in England	5	348	—	43.50
1968-69 v West Indies	5	548	2	68.50
1969-70 in India	5	324	1	46.28
1969-70 in South Africa	4	92	—	11.50
1970-71 v England‡	6	452	2	37.66
1972 in England†	5	334	1	33.40
1972-73 v Pakistan†	3	341	1	68.20
1972-73 in West Indies†	5	542	2	77.42
1973-74 v New Zealand†	3	127	—	31.75
1973-74 in New Zealand†	3	359	2	59.83
1974-75 v England†	6	387	—	35.18
1975 in England†	4	429	1	71.50
1975-76 v West Indies	6	449	1	44.90
1979-80 v West Indies	1	6	—	3.00
1979-80 v England	2	152	—	50.66
Totals	75	5,345	14	42.42

Career runs: 19,680 Average: 48.35
Highest Test score: 196 v Pakistan, Adelaide, 1972-73
Highest career score: 209, Australians v Barbados, Bridgetown, 1972-73
Career wickets: 176 Average: 37.57
Test wickets: 20 Average: 65.80

†Captain ‡Captain in 1 Test

cally for his country even after passing the captaincy on to his brother, Greg, after winning the series and retaining the Ashes in England in 1975. Turning to business activities, which included television and newspaper journalism, he was one of the central

Ian Chappell in an unusual role as a bowler on the tour of England in 1968.

figures in the setting up of Kerry Packer's World Series in Australia.

When WSC ended and harmony returned to cricket, Chappell, who had returned after retirement to play for Packer, continued for a while and in 1979-80 was recalled for three Tests, but he retired again at the end of the season.

BELOW LEFT Chappell turns to leg at the Oval in 1968.
BELOW RIGHT A typical fine slip catch to dismiss Boycott.

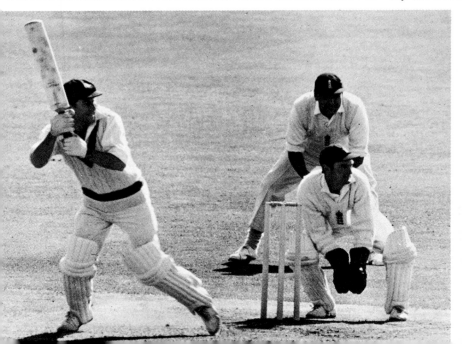

COMPTON
Denis Charles Scott
b 1918-

Whether on the cricket pitch or the football field, Denis Compton was a popular and colourful sporting hero in the Britain of the 1940s. A natural at both games, he thrilled the crowds with his buccaneering spirit and his unorthodox, at times cheeky, play. Few sportsmen have captured, and held, the public imagination as Compton did. And if, perhaps, the statistics do not quite show him as the great all-rounder he undoubtedly was, the vivid memories he left with cricket and soccer fans of the immediate post-war years will long remain as tribute to the wonderful entertainment he provided in that age of austerity.

Compton's place among the greatest batsmen in the history of cricket cannot be disputed. If World War II had not taken six years out of his career at a time when he would have been at his peak, if he had not been handicapped by injury for over half his playing career, and if he had been more conscious of feats and figures, his record would have been even more outstanding than it was.

But it is for the gaiety and personality of his batting that he is remembered even more than for its quality. He had the gift of communicating to the spectator all his own feelings about the bowling, whether it be confidence or concern. This, with the fluency and apparent unorthodoxy of his stroke-play, made his batting fascinating to watch.

Technically he was thoroughly sound, and the strokes that he improvized with what many thought to be a flouting of the textbook in fact had a sound basis. He is associated in cricketers' minds with the sweep, which brought him many runs in safety but is often fraught with peril when imitated by others. But there were few other strokes that he did not play. His delayed drive square on the offside was a feature of his batting, as was the way in which he would step backward and hit the turning off-break to the offside against the spin. And he was deadly in the placing of his masterfully executed on-drive.

In the field he became less mobile after sustaining a serious knee injury, though he was capable of spectacular catches. As a bowler he could bowl orthodox left-arm spin but he had more success with the chinaman and googly. He suffered from the usual inaccuracy that afflicts this type of bowling, but when he found a length he was capable of bothering the best batsmen.

Few English batsmen have risen to the top at an earlier age than Compton. When he was just 18 in 1936 he played his first match for Middlesex, against Sussex, batting No. 11 in the Whitsun match at Lord's. Within a month he had made the first of his 123 first-class hundreds, and by the end of the season there were many who thought that he should have gone to Australia with G. O. Allen's MCC side. He played in his first Test against New Zealand in the following year and in all the subsequent home Tests up to the outbreak of war, making 102 in his first innings against Australia, at Trent Bridge in 1938.

Towards the end of the war he played some first-class cricket in India and returned in excellent form for the 1946 season. In Australia that winter he made a hundred in each innings of the Adelaide Test, and back in England in 1947 he embarked on his golden year and his memorable record-breaking partnerships with Bill Edrich.

When he had made a hundred,

he often considered that enough, unless the requirements of the side made it important for him to go on. In that season, with Middlesex challenging successfully for the championship, he went on often. His record of 3,816 runs and 18 hundreds in the season is unlikely ever to be beaten, especially now that the amount of first-class cricket being played in England is decreasing.

However, in the last match of 1947 his knee let him down and he was seldom free of pain or discomfort afterwards. Yet in 1948 he played what many regard as his greatest innings—145 not out against Australia at Old Trafford, overcoming Lindwall at his most hostile and after being knocked out and retiring hurt early in his innings. He went to South Africa in 1948-49 and made his famous 300 in three hours at Benoni, easily the fastest 300 ever made. But though in the following season he reached the peak of his football career, he missed most of that cricket season through an operation which removed a fragment of bone from his knee. Characteristically he returned with a century against Surrey in August, but the knee continued to trouble him. In 1954 he was still able to play an astonishing innings of 278 in 4 hours 50 minutes against Pakistan at Nottingham, but in November 1955 he had to have his kneecap removed. Again he returned with a hundred—against Somerset—and when fit enough to play in the last Test against Australia in 1956 he made a brilliant 94.

After the 1957 season he retired, making 143 and 48 in his last match for Middlesex. He became a regular commentator on Test matches for BBC television.

Compton's career as a footballer has been somewhat unjustly obscured by his prowess on the cricket field. He was a very good outside-left indeed, powerful, dangerous, quick, unorthodox, with a superb left foot, and also a useful header of the ball. He played eleven times for England during the war, and was thoroughly established in a brilliant forward-line with Stanley Matthews, Raich Carter, Tommy Lawton and Jimmy Hagan, before he was posted to India, with the Army, in 1944.

On his return, he had put on more weight than he was ever fully able to shed, though he won a 'Victory' international cap against Scotland at Hampden Park in 1946. Four years later, after missing a good deal of football through the demands of cricket tours, he played, with his brother Leslie, in Arsenal's cup winning team against Liverpool. It was from his corner that Leslie headed the equalizing goal against Chelsea at Tottenham in the semi-final, and he himself had scored with a tremendous left-footed drive against Burnley in an earlier round.

Compton joined Arsenal, like Leslie, from the Hampstead amateur club in 1935. By the time war broke out, he had already played 22 First Division matches for Arsenal, his league debut being in September 1936 against Derby County. In season 1942-43 he was a regular member of the powerful Arsenal team that won the League South and the League South Cup.

As a footballer, his confidence was limitless. He would casually bounce the ball on his head, before hooking it into the goalmouth, and he was an unflurried taker of penalty kicks, even in the most tense situations. There is little doubt that, had it not been for the war, he would have won numerous full caps for England.

COMPTON Denis Charles Scott

Teams: Middlesex and England

Test series		Tests	Runs	100s	Average
1937	v New Zealand	1	65	—	65.00
1938	v Australia	4	214	1	42.80
1939	v West Indies	3	189	1	63.00
1946	v India	3	146	—	73.00
1946-47	in Australia	5	459	2	51.00
1946-47	in New Zealand	1	38	—	38.00
1947	v South Africa	5	753	4	94.12
1948	v Australia	5	562	2	62.44
1948-49	in South Africa	5	406	1	50.75
1949	v New Zealand	4	300	2	50.00
1950	v West Indies	1	55	—	27.50
1950-51	in Australia	4	53	—	7.57
1950-51	in New Zealand	2	107	—	35.66
1951	v South Africa	4	312	1	52.00
1952	v India	2	59	—	29.50
1953	v Australia	5	234	—	33.42
1953-54	in West Indies	5	348	1	49.71
1954	v Pakistan	4	453	1	90.60
1954-55	in Australia	4	191	—	38.20
1955	v South Africa	5	492	1	54.66
1956	v Australia	1	129	1	129.00
1956-57	in South Africa	5	242	—	24.20
Totals		**78**	**5,807**	**17**	**50.06**

Career runs: 38,942 *Average:* 51.85
Highest Test score: 278 v Pakistan, Trent Bridge, 1954
Highest career score: 300, MCC v North-Eastern Transvaal, Benoni, 1948-49
Career wickets: 622 *Average:* 32.27
Test wickets: 25 *Average:* 56.40
Best Test bowling: 5-70 v South Africa, Cape Town, 1948-49
Best career bowling: 7-36, MCC v Auckland, Auckland, 1946-47

COMPTON Denis Charles Scott

Honours: League Championship medal 1948;
FA Cup winners medal 1950

Club	Season	League Mtchs	Gls
Arsenal	1936-37	14	4
	1937-38	7	1
	1938-39	1	
	1946-47	1	1
	1947-48	14	6
	1948-49	6	2
	1949-50	11	1
Totals		**54**	**15**

COWDREY
Michael Colin b 1932-

No player in the world spent longer at the top in post-war cricket than England's Colin Cowdrey, whose Test career began in Australia in 1954-55 when he was 21. His 114 Tests place him way at the head of the list of most capped cricketers, and he would have undoubtedly played more had not a ruptured achilles tendon in May 1969 put him out of action. He scored more Test runs, 7,624, than any other Englishman (since passed by Boycott), always in a manner of characteristic composure and elegance.

A gifted games player, Cowdrey reached the final of the Amateur Rackets Championship as an Oxford undergraduate and, while convalescing in 1969, proved himself a good enough golfer to win an important professional-amateur tournament at Turnberry with British Ryder Cup Player Brian Huggett. Always heavily built, even as a prodigiously successful schoolboy cricketer, he had wonderfully quick reactions for someone of his size and he was one of the world's best slip catchers.

He first played for Kent in 1950, and was only 18 when he made an impressive 106 for the Gentlemen against a strong Players side at Scarborough. Two fifties for the Gentlemen against the Australians at Lord's in 1953 confirmed his swift advance towards the England team. In 1954, when he was captain of Oxford, he was 12th man in the last Test against Pakistan at the Oval, and was a somewhat unexpected selection for the MCC tour of Australia and New Zealand.

The tour began tragically for him, for, on arrival in Perth, he learnt of the sudden death of his father, who had been a great inspiration to his cricket. However, it was Cowdrey's stand with Peter May, the first of many, that turned the second Test and the series in England's favour, and his remarkable innings of 102—out of a total of only 191—that in the third Test started England on the way to success. He returned to England as a Test player who had succeeded in the highest company and had an immense future.

Yet within a few weeks, a touch of controversy had entered his career, as he was rejected by the RAF because of a foot condition. And through the subsequent years, he tended to be underestimated in his own country, perhaps because it was felt that sometimes he did not make the most of his talent. Abroad he was a greatly respected figure among the cricket public. He toured Australia five times, and visited the other major cricket playing countries at least once. His comfortable, easy-going appearance led some at home to the conclusion that he was too gentle for

captaincy, and his apparent reluctance at times to play strokes made him the target for criticism by people who felt that with his gifts he need not restrict himself.

The truth, perhaps, is that his method of batting, and his reliance on timing rather than on power, was better suited to the harder pitches and faster outfields abroad than to the many pitches in England on which the ball 'stops' and has to be assaulted with vigour if it is to reach the boundary.

English cricket history of the 1950s and 1960s is, however, packed with Cowdrey's achievements. At times he was converted into an opening batsman and at times he became captain. If he were unable to play, his batting and his slip-catching were sorely missed.

In his early days, England were strong in bowling but not in late-order batting, and the innings would often thrive or fall with May and Cowdrey. It was their historic stand of 411 at Edgbaston in 1957 that had a decisive effect on the series with West Indies, and Cowdrey, 150 at Edgbaston, followed with 152 in the next Test at Lord's. As an opening batsman in the West Indies in 1960, he met the West Indian fast bowlers with courage and success and, when Peter May was taken ill, assumed the captaincy that he had first taken over when May was ill in 1959.

In Australia in 1962-63, Cowdrey made his highest score—307 against South Australia in Adelaide. Later in 1963, in the Lord's Test against West Indies, his arm

OPPOSITE ABOVE Colin Cowdrey's typical weighty off-drive, a shot which brought him many of his 40,000 runs in first-class cricket.

BELOW Cowdrey hooks on his first tour of Australia, which was a personal triumph, especially the century which helped to win the third Test at Melbourne.

COWDREY Michael Colin

Teams: Oxford University. Kent and England

Test series	Tests	Runs	100s	Average
1954-55 in Australia	5	319	1	35.44
1954-55 in New Zealand	2	64	–	32.00
1955 v South Africa	1	51	–	25.50
1956 v Australia	5	244	–	30.50
1956-57 in South Africa	5	331	1	33.10
1957 v West Indies	5	435	2	72.50
1958 v New Zealand	4	241	–	60.25
1958-59 in Australia	5	391	1	43.44
1958-59 in New Zealand	2	20	–	10.00
1959 v India[2]	5	344	1	57.33
1959-60 in West Indies[2]	5	491	2	54.55
1960 v South Africa†	5	312	1	34.66
1961 v Australia[2]	4	168	–	21.00
1962 v Pakistan[1]	4	409	2	81.80
1962-63 in Australia	5	394	1	43.77
1962-63 in New Zealand	3	292	1	146.00
1963 v West Indies	2	39	–	13.00
1963-64 in India	3	309	2	103.00
1964 v Australia	3	188	–	47.00
1965 v New Zealand	3	221	1	73.66
1965 v South Africa	3	327	1	65.40
1965-66 in Australia	4	267	1	53.40
1965-66 in New Zealand	3	196	–	49.00
1966 v West Indies[3]	4	252	–	31.50
1967 v Pakistan	2	41	–	13.66
1967-68 in West Indies†	5	534	2	66.75
1968 v Australia†	4	215	1	35.83
1968-69 in Pakistan†	3	133	1	33.25
1970-71 in Australia	3	82	–	20.50
1970-71 in New Zealand	1	99	–	49.50
1971 v Pakistan	1	50	–	25.50
1974-75 in Australia	5	165	–	18.33
Totals	**114**	**7,624**	**22**	**44.06**

Career runs: 42,719 *Average:* 42.89
Highest Test score: 182 v Pakistan, Oval, 1962
Highest career score: 307, MCC v South Australia, Adelaide, 1962-63

†Captain   [1]Captain in 1 Test   [2]Captain in 2 Tests   [3]Captain in 3 Tests

OPPOSITE CENTRE AND BELOW A sequence of Cowdrey at slip snapping up Kanhai off d'Oliveira in the first Test at the Queen's Park Oval, Port-of-Spain, Trinidad, in 1967-68. ABOVE A sweep to the leg-side boundary for four more runs.

was broken by a short ball from Wes Hall. At the end of a dramatic match he had to come in for the last two balls to earn England a draw—which he did, fortunately as the non-striker.

Cowdrey's next innings was eight months later when, having flown out as a reinforcement to the MCC team depleted by illness, he made a hundred in a Test match in Calcutta. Later that year he was dropped from the fourth Test against Australia but was recalled to the team to make 93 not out in the last.

In 1966, Cowdrey became captain again in place of M. J. K. Smith. But after England had been beaten at Leeds he was replaced by Brian Close. He took over again when Close, having been recently censured for unfair play, was not acceptable to the MCC Committee when the party was chosen for the tour of West Indies in 1968.

This proved to be one of Cowdrey's best tours, for his captaincy was happy and successful, and his 534 runs in the Test series played a big part in the final victory. As captain against Australia that summer he made a hundred in his 100th Test match. In 1974-75 he was surprisingly recalled to Test cricket after four years—a sixth trip to Australia. He responded with skill and character against the alarming pace of Lillee and Thomson and, although retiring in 1975, he remained on stand-by duty for his beloved Kent.

DAVIDSON
Alan Keith b 1929-

Alan Davidson became Australia's leading bowler after the retirement of Lindwall, Miller, and Johnston, and he was one of the main reasons for the success of the far from powerful side captained by Richie Benaud between 1958-59 and 1962-63. Such a fine left-arm fast-medium bowler was he that the attempts to convert him into a slow left-arm spinner, when he first went to England in 1953, seem bizarre in retrospect.

'Davo', as he was known, also developed into a great all-rounder. Six feet tall with unusually broad shoulders, he was a powerful left-handed batsman and a brilliantly athletic fielder in any position. But it was his bowling that possessed the greatest quality. From a run of little over 15 yards, and from over the wicket, he moved the ball off the pitch in either direction and had a devastating late swing with the new ball. Tom Graveney is not the only famous batsman to have been bowled or lbw playing no stroke to a ball from Davidson which he had thought was slanting safely away outside his off-stump.

Davidson first played for New South Wales in 1949-50, when the leading Australian players were away in South Africa. He was such a highly promising fast-medium bowler that he went to New Zealand with a representative side at the end of that season.

The first of his three tours of England, in 1953, emphasized his

ABOVE *Alan Davidson during his Test-winning innings in 1961.* LEFT *The action which provided the swing to confuse batsmen.*

DAVIDSON Alan Keith

Teams: New South Wales and Australia

Test series		Tests	Runs	Average	Wkts	Average
1953	in England	5	182	22.75	8	26.50
1954-55	v England	3	71	14.20	3	73.33
1956	in England	2	8	8.00	2	28.00
1956-57	in Pakistan	1	40	20.00	2	7.50
1956-57	in India	1	16	16.00	1	42.00
1957-58	in South Africa	5	127	21.16	25	17.00
1958-59	v England	5	180	36.00	24	19.00
1959-60	in Pakistan	3	90	45.00	12	24.83
1959-60	in India	5	93	18.60	29	15.17
1960-61	v West Indies	4	212	30.28	33	18.54
1961	in England	5	151	30.20	23	24.86
1962-63	v England	5	158	22.57	24	20.00
Totals		44	1,328	24.59	186	20.53

Career runs: 6,804 *Average:* 32.86
Highest Test score: 80 v West Indies, Brisbane, 1960-61
Highest career score: 129, Australians v Western Province, Cape Town, 1957-58
Career wickets: 672 *Average:* 20.90
Best Test bowling: 7-93 v India, Kanpur, 1959-60
Best career bowling: 7-31, New South Wales v Western Australia, Perth, 1961-62

promise, and he played in all five Tests, though with Lindwall, Miller, Johnston, and Archer in the side he was an auxiliary bowler rarely in the front line. He was used experimentally in a slower role after Johnston had been injured in a preliminary match at the start of the tour.

In 1956, on his second tour of England, he was dogged by injury and it was not until the visit to South Africa in 1957-58 that he began to reach his full stature as a Test player. Top of the tour bowling averages with 15.11 and third in the batting with 54.20, he took 25 wickets in the series. A year later in Melbourne he bowled a historic over at the start of the second Test against England—he had Richardson caught at the wicket, bowled Watson with a swinging full toss, and had Graveney lbw the next ball.

His highest Test score—80—was made in 1960-61 against the West Indies at Brisbane, in the famous tied Test—a match to which he made a massive contribution. Having scored 44 in the first innings and taken 11 wickets in the two West Indian innings, he was run out when Australia needed only another seven runs to win. He and Benaud added 134 for the seventh wicket.

His best-remembered innings in England is probably his 77 not out at Old Trafford later in 1961. He was Australia's main bowler on that tour and took 23 Test wickets, but it was his innings in the fourth Test that did more than anything to decide the series and keep the Ashes for Australia. Soon after the start on the last morning Australia were 157 runs ahead with only one second innings wicket left, after four days play in which England had always seemed to be just on top. But Davidson was still there. He hit David Allen, who had taken three wickets in 15 balls that morning, for 20 runs in one over. The last wicket stand of 98 with Graham McKenzie gave England too much to do—Australia won the match, the only one in the series that produced a result.

DEXTER
Edward Ralph b 1935-

Capable of reaching great heights in almost anything he attempted, Ted Dexter, known throughout the cricketing world as 'Lord Ted', was one of the most dashing batsmen and most gifted all-round cricketers to play for England in modern times. His fielding could be brilliant either near or away from the wicket, and his belligerent aspect as he walked to the wicket was a familiar sight. Yet a restless temperament and an apparent lack of concentration sometimes stopped him giving full vent to his talents, and he would exasperate the spectator by getting out needlessly through overconfidence and excessive contempt for the bowling.

From his early days at Radley College and Cambridge, he was also a fine golfer, a tremendous hitter of the ball for whom great things were forecast. These predictions were strengthened in 1969 when, after his retirement from first-class cricket, he was runnerup in the Oxford and Cambridge Golfing Society's President's Putter. As a batsman, too, Dexter was a tremendously hard driver, an especially strong and courageous player of fast bowling. Though he scored a number of centuries, he is best remembered by many people for his innings of 70 in 81 minutes in the Lord's Test of 1963 against the West Indian fast bowlers Wes Hall and Charlie Griffith, then in their menacing prime. And few Australians will ever forget his innings of 93 in the second Test of the 1962-63 series when he set England on the road to victory. In the first Test, he scored 70 and 99.

Dexter captained Cambridge in 1958 and two years later took over the captaincy of Sussex. He had matured early, and at 25 was already established in the front rank of English cricketers. While still at Cambridge, he had given an outstanding bowling performance in the 1957 Gentlemen v Players match. On a wet pitch, he took 5-8 in the Players' first innings and 3-47 in their second with his lively fast-medium bowling. As a bowler, he tended to fall between two stools because of the inability of his captains and himself to decide whether he should be used as a stock bowler or as a striking force. But he had moments of inspiration, and his ability to swing the ball a lot could make him devastating in typically English conditions. This was best illustrated in the Edgbaston Test of 1963 when he took five West Indies first innings wickets for 45. And if Freddy Trueman had not bowled out the West Indies in the second innings, Dexter might well have done so.

Having played in his first Test against the New Zealand tourists in 1958, Dexter was sent out to Australia during the 1958-59 MCC tour when Willie Watson and Ramon Subba Row were injured. He played in two Tests there, and on the New Zealand section of the tour made his maiden Test century, scoring 141 in the first Test, at Christchurch. A year later, after a modest home season, he was selected for the tour of the West Indies. It was a much-criticized selection, but he proved one of the successes of the tour, playing the

Ted Dexter off-drives. He always preferred to get on to the front foot and attack the faster bowling.

For once Ted Dexter's power driving lets him down as he holes out in the deep off Pakistan's leg spinner Intikhab Alam.

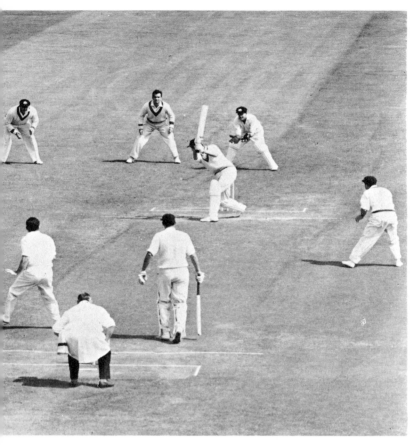

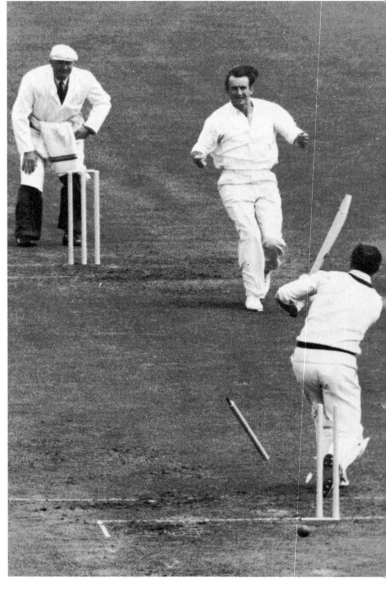

fast bowling with great zest, and topped the Test batting averages.

In a series in which bumpers were hurled at batsmen on both sides in liberal quantities, Dexter was at his most prolific. Batting at number six, he made a punishing 136 not out in the first innings of the series, and he never looked back.

His competitive temperament relished the confrontation with physical danger presented by the pace of the West Indies attack and he never flinched. He was batting at number three when he made his second century of the series at Georgetown. There, in company with Raman Subba Row, he ensured that England could not lose the match. It was this series that above all established Dexter, whose class was never in doubt, as a batsman capable of big Test innings.

In the first Test of the 1961 series against Australia, he earned England a draw with a second innings of 180. And in the decisive Test of the series at Old Trafford, he played a spectacular innings of 76 in 84 minutes which at one time put England in the position of needing only 106 runs from their last nine wickets. But with Dexter's dismissal, they collapsed.

Dexter became captain of England when he took the MCC side to India and Pakistan in 1961-62. In the home series against Pakistan the following summer, he was captain in the first two Tests, but Colin Cowdrey was preferred for the captaincy in the third. However, when Cowdrey was unfit, Dexter was appointed captain for the fourth Test and subsequently led England in Australia and New Zealand in 1962-63. He remained captain until he stood for Parliament in October 1964, and had to delay his acceptance of the invitation to tour South Africa. When he did eventually go, it was as vice-captain to Mike Smith. He did not captain England again and slipped out of regular first-class cricket, preferring to play on Sundays for the International Cavaliers.

When his county's batting was depleted by injury in 1968, Dexter returned to play for Sussex and made an immediate impact, scoring 203 against Kent at Hastings in his first innings. He was then selected for the last two Tests against the Australians.

He scored only 97 runs in his four innings, but the excitement his return caused further illustrated the great loss English cricket suffered when 'Lord Ted' retired from the first-class game. Cricket, especially in the 1960s, could ill-afford to lose one of its most dynamic characters.

He joined a Sunday newspaper as a working journalist, also commentating incisively on television. He joined the editorial board of a new cricket monthly magazine, where he wrote regular articles on the theory of batting. With another ex-England captain, Bob Willis, he instigated an organised search for a new English fast bowler. He played golf as an amateur at a high competitive level. One always felt that whatever task Ted Dexter put his mind to he would perform it with flair and imagination.

ABOVE LEFT Dexter drives Ken Mackay through the covers in the first Test at Edgbaston in 1961. In the second innings he made a glorious 180, hitting 31 boundaries, mostly with powerful drives.

ABOVE Dexter as a bowler was a useful medium-pacer who thought hard about the craft and took occasional vital wickets. Here he bowls Australian captain Benaud in the Test match at Old Trafford in 1961.

DEXTER Edward Ralph

Teams: Cambridge University, Sussex, and England

Test series		Tests	Runs	100s	Average
1958	v New Zealand	1	52	—	52.00
1958-59	in Australia	2	18	—	4.50
1958-59	in New Zealand	2	142	1	71.00
1959	v India	2	58	—	19.33
1959-60	in West Indies	5	526	2	65.75
1960	v South Africa	5	241	—	26.77
1961	v Australia	5	378	1	42.00
1961-62	in Pakistan	3*	303	1	101.00
1961-62	in India	5*	409	1	58.42
1962	v Pakistan	5†	446	1	89.20
1962-63	in Australia	5*	481	—	48.10
1962-63	in New Zealand	3*	84	—	28.00
1963	v West Indies	5*	340	—	34.00
1964	v Australia	5*	384	1	48.00
1964-65	in South Africa	5	344	1	57.33
1965	v New Zealand	2	199	—	99.50
1968	v Australia	2	97	—	24.25
Totals		62	4,502	9	47.89

Career runs: 21,150 *Average:* 40.75
Highest Test and career score: 205 v Pakistan, Karachi, 1961-62
Career wickets: 419 *Average:* 29.92
Best career bowling: 7-24, Sussex v Middlesex, Hove, 1960

EDRICH
John Hugh b 1937-

Tenacious, courageous and totally phlegmatic, John Edrich's left-handed batting served England loyally over 13 years and 77 Tests. He had a particular liking for Australian bowling, making seven centuries and scoring over 2,000 runs in his 32 Tests against them.

A left-handed opening batsman who could bat number three with equal success, he tended to restrict himself to a few highly profitable strokes until he was thoroughly established. He missed little on or outside his legs, and off either back or front foot he scored many runs square of cover-point. Small and sturdily built, he was no classical stylist, but he worked out a method of batting that was safer than it often looked and that, with his great resolution, served him and his side well. And however vulnerable his small frame may have made him look against fast bowling, he met the best in the world successfully. In fact, any lack of success was usually on slow pitches, such as those in Pakistan, where he sometimes got himself out trying to shake off the shackles that spinners can cast on the batsmen in those conditions.

A cousin of the former England and Middlesex batsman Bill Edrich, John left Norfolk for London some 20 years after his famed relation. But rather than go to Middlesex, he chose Surrey, where he had a better chance of standing on his own feet. After two years' national service, he played once in the championship in 1958, and then in 1959, his first full season, he made 1,799 runs, including a century in each innings of the second championship match of his career. This, moreover, was the first time he had opened an innings.

But then a broken finger slowed up his development, and it was 1963 before he played in his first Test, against West Indies. He went to India with M. J. K. Smith's MCC team that winter, but was one of many taken ill there, and it was not until his innings of 120 against Australia in the second Test at Lord's in 1964 that he established himself as a Test batsman. Yet despite this fine innings he was dropped for the final Test of the series and then left out of the MCC side that went to South Africa in 1964-65. But in 1965 he hit back with astonishing success.

From early June he played successive innings of 139 against the New Zealanders; 121 not out v Oxford University; 205 not out v Gloucestershire; 55 v Kent; 96 v Essex; 188 by Northamptonshire; 92 and 105 v Yorkshire—on a bad pitch at Bradford; and 310 not out in the Leeds Test against New Zealand. At this time he was using the pulled drive with great effect and was a prodigious hitter of sixes.

But then the run ended. In the first Test against South Africa, at Lord's, he was hit on the head by a ball bowled by Peter Pollock, and it was some time before he was fully fit. The valuable innings he played in Australia that winter, 109 in the second Test, 103 in the third, and 85 in the fifth—all at number three—were compiled in the more patient, controlled method with which he was remarkably consistent thereafter.

ABOVE LEFT John Edrich drives in the air over mid-on. ABOVE Edrich was often thought to be vulnerable outside off stump, but made 5,000 Test runs.

In 1969 when England lost, for various reasons, the bulk of her experienced batting—Ken Barrington, Colin Milburn, Colin Cowdrey, and Tom Graveney—there was still Edrich. He illustrated his pre-eminence by finishing the season far ahead of the field on top of the first-class averages, having made 2,238 runs at an average of 69.93.

After a fine tour of Australia in 1970-71, he lost some consistency, and his Test place, and his future seemed to lie in a new role as Surrey's captain. But England could not manage without his resolution and he returned in 1974. He scored regularly again against Australia and captained his country in the fourth Test of 1975. His 175 at Lord's was his seventh against Australia, and he was unlucky to miss another in the final Test, when he was bowled by Lillee for 96. A year later, when 39, he was called up again, and batted resolutely against the fierce West Indies pace attack, bowing out courageously at Manchester when he and Brian Close, 45, faced an outbreak of bouncers.

In the relative tranquillity of county cricket, he became the 18th batsman to score 100 centuries when he made 101 not out against Derbyshire at The Oval. Later the same month he scored two centuries in the match against Kent.

In 1977 he was awarded the MBE, and he retired from first-class cricket a year later.

EDRICH John Hugh

Teams: Surrey and England

Test series		Tests	Runs	100s	Average
1963	v West Indies	3	103	—	17.16
1963-64	in India	2	76	—	38.00
1964	v Australia	3	161	1	40.25
1965	v New Zealand	1	310	1	—
1965	v South Africa	1	7	—	7.00
1965-66	in Australia	5	375	2	46.87
1965-66	in New Zealand	3	40	—	13.33
1966	v West Indies	1	35	—	35.00
1967	v India	2	35	—	11.66
1967-68	in West Indies	5	340	1	42.50
1968	v Australia	5	554	1	61.55
1968-69	in Pakistan	3	130	—	32.50
1969	v West Indies	3	169	—	33.80
1969	v New Zealand	3	376	2	75.20
1970-71	in Australia	6	648	2	72.00
1970-71	in New Zealand	2	39	—	9.75
1971	v Pakistan	3	87	—	17.40
1971	v India	3	180	—	30.00
1972	v Australia	5	218	—	21.80
1974	v India	3	203	1	101.50
1974	v Pakistan	3	144	—	36.00
1974-75	in Australia†	4	260	—	43.33
1974-75	in New Zealand	2	75	—	37.50
1975	v Australia	4	428	1	53.50
1976	v West Indies	2	145	—	48.33
Totals		77	5,138	12	43.54

Career runs: 39,790 *Average:* 45.47
Highest Test and career score: 310* v New Zealand, Leeds, 1965

*Not out   †Captain in one Test

EDRICH
William b 1916 – d 1986

In 1934 a young cricketer made his debut for Norfolk in the Minor Counties Championship. Thirty-five years later, in 1969, he was back playing for them. During that 35 years, though, Bill Edrich had gained fame as one half of the Compton-Edrich partnership that devastated bowling for Middlesex and England immediately after World War II.

Born at Lingwood in Norfolk, Edrich was also a good footballer, playing briefly for Tottenham Hotspur. But it was as a professional cricketer that he established himself at an early age. Qualifying for Middlesex in the 1937 season, he came on the county scene as his illustrious predecessor, Patsy Hendren, was in his last season and as another future giant, Denis Compton, was just starting out.

Though lacking the genius or the range of Compton, Edrich had other qualities—courage, fearlessness, resolution in adversity—that imprinted themselves on the imagination of the cricket public. And, unlike Compton, who had moments of vulnerability early in an innings, Edrich seemed merely to carry on where he had left off in the previous one. He was an especially fine player on bad pitches. Sturdily built, he was short of inches and yet when a fast bowler was imperilling the batsmen's existence, he seemed to relish it. A brave hooker and a quick cutter, he was particularly adept at the pulled drive. It was not a classic or attractive method, but allied to his pugnacious temperament it was good to watch and few would dispute its effectiveness.

In only his second full season for Middlesex, he joined the select group of batsmen who have made 1,000 runs before the end of May, and he played in four Tests against Bradman's 1938 Australians. But he met with little success, and

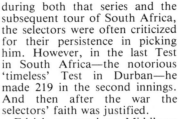

EDRICH William John

Teams: Middlesex and England

Test series		Tests	Runs	100s	Average	Wkts	Average
1938	v Australia	4	67	—	11.16	4	34.75
1938-39	in South Africa	5	240	1	40.00	2	77.00
1946	v India	1	—	—	—	4	17.00
1946-47	in Australia	5	462	1	46.20	9	53.66
1946-47	in New Zealand	1	42	—	42.00	1	35.00
1947	v South Africa	4	552	2	110.40	16	23.12
1948	v Australia	5	319	1	31.90	3	79.33
1949	v New Zealand	4	324	1	54.00	2	48.50
1950	v West Indies	2	94	—	23.50	0	—
1953	v Australia	3	156	—	39.00	—	—
1954	v Pakistan	1	4	—	4.00	—	—
1954-55	in Australia	4	180	—	22.50	0	—
Totals		39	2,440	6	40.00	41	41.29

Career runs: 36,965 *Average:* 42.39
Highest Test score: 219 v South Africa, Durban, 1938-39
Highest career score: 267*, Middlesex v Northamptonshire, Northampton, 1947
Career wickets: 479 *Average:* 33.31
Best Test bowling: 4-68 v India, Oval, 1946
Best career bowling: 7-48, Middlesex v Worcestershire, Worcester, 1946

*Not out

BELOW LEFT Bill Edrich and his Middlesex and England partner Compton.

BELOW Edrich pulls another four against South Africa in the glorious year of 1947.

during both that series and the subsequent tour of South Africa, the selectors were often criticized for their persistence in picking him. However, in the last Test in South Africa—the notorious 'timeless' Test in Durban—he made 219 in the second innings. And then after the war the selectors' faith was justified.

Edrich returned to Middlesex after distinguished service in the RAF in which he won the DFC as a bomber pilot. He played only once against India in 1946, but was one of the successes of the 1946-47 tour of Australia, when his courageous displays against the fast bowlers left him bruised but not bewildered. After which he turned amateur.

His partnerships with Compton in 1947, for Middlesex in their championship-winning year and for England against South Africa, are a legend. Among the most remarkable were an unbroken stand of 287 in 2¾ hours against Surrey at the Oval, another stand of 277 in 130 minutes at Leicester, and 370 in the Lord's Test. At Leicester they opened the second innings with 66 runs needed in 25 minutes and they made them with seven minutes to spare. In that season Edrich made 3,539 runs, an aggregate exceeded in cricket history only by Denis Compton (in that same year).

Edrich did not often approach the golden form in later seasons and was not chosen to go to Australia in 1950-51. But four years later, with England short of opening batsmen, he was picked as a tough, seasoned warrior who would not be overcome by the big occasion. As such, he did a useful job, although he never recaptured the fluency of former days.

In his heyday Edrich had been a fast bowler, who from a few yards run and with a slinging action worked up surprising pace and took some useful wickets. In later years, he acquired a happy touch as joint-captain of Middlesex, with Compton, for two seasons and as captain from 1953 to 1957.

GARNER
Joel b 1952-

Garner was born in Christchurch, Barbados, in 1952 and made his first-class debut for Barbados in the 1975-76 season.

The following season he appeared for the West Indies in all five Tests against the touring Pakistanis, and took 25 wickets at 27.52, including four in each innings, at Georgetown. He has been a regular for the West Indies ever since.

Garner stands 6ft 8in, and is one of the tallest cricketers of all time, known in the game as 'Big Bird'. His height is a powerful weapon in his fast bowling. Approaching the wicket with relatively few paces he uncoils his frame to its full height, and the batsman finds a very steep bounce from the resulting fast delivery. He also swings and cuts the ball, and is a very difficult bowler to score from.

He played part-time for Somerset in 1977 and 1978, before joining the county full-time in 1979. With his West Indian colleague Richards already in the side, and Botham emerging as a world-class player, he helped Somerset enjoy the most successful period in its history, particularly in limited overs games.

He played only two Test matches in his second series, against Australia, in 1977-78—after this all the Packer players, Garner included, withdrew because of a dispute between captain Lloyd and the West Indian Board over team selection. Garner was one of the most successful bowlers in World Series Cricket.

Big Bird made his first major impression on the British public in the World Cup final at Lord's in 1979. A match which despite the West Indians' large score of 286 was still very much in the balance with England 183 for 3, was virtually settled in one over from Garner in which Gooch, Gower and Larkins were all clean bowled. Garner's final 11 balls brought him 5 for 4 and the match was won.

Garner over the next few years was frequently the bowling hero of one-day Somerset victories. In the 1979 Gillette Cup final, Garner's 6 for 28 against Northamptonshire decided the match, and in 1983 his 2 for 15 in 9 overs against Kent was nearly as crucial in winning the NatWest Trophy. In 1981 and 1982 Somerset won the Benson and Hedges Cup. In the Lord's finals Garner's 5 for 14 against Surrey and 3 for 13 against Nottinghamshire were the outstanding bowling performances of the match.

In 1979-80 Garner took 14 wickets in each of the three-match Test series in Australia and New Zealand, including his best Test bowling, 6 for 56 against New Zealand at Auckland. He followed

this in England in 1980 by taking 26 wickets at only 14.61 each, heading the averages for both the Test and tour, in which he took 49 wickets, average 13.93.

The most wickets Garner has in a series to date is the 31 which he captured against Australia in 1983-84, when twice he took six wickets in an innings. He has consistently done well against what might be regarded as the stronger countries, England and Australia, and in the West Indies' 5-0 beating of England in 1984, he took another 29 wickets. In both these series he was the leading West Indian wicket-taker.

In the series against Australia in 1984-85 Big Bird passed 200 Test wickets at little over 20 each, an excellent record. He was awarded the MBE in 1985.

GARNER Joel

Teams: Barbados, Somerset, South Australia and West Indies

Test series	Tests	Wkts	Average
1976-77 v Pakistan	5	25	27.52
1977-78 v Australia	2	13	15.00
1979-80 in Australia	3	14	21.50
1979-80 in New Zealand	3	14	16.78
1980 in England	5	26	14.61
1980-81 in Pakistan	3	10	19.20
1980-81 v England	4	10	30.30
1981-82 in Australia	3	12	24.91
1982-83 v India	4	7	43.00
1983-84 v Australia	5	31	18.03
1984 in England	5	29	18.62
1984-85 in Australia	5	19	29.78
1984-85 v New Zealand	4	10	30.20
Totals	51	220	21.78

Test runs: 609 *Average:* 12.95
Career wickets: 731 *Average:* 18.47
Best Test bowling: 6-56 v New Zealand, Auckland, 1979-80
Best career bowling: 8-31 v Glamorgan, Cardiff, 1977

Career figures correct to end of 1985 season

GAVASKAR
Sunil Manohar b 1949-

Sunny Gavaskar is a model opening batsman. He is as near free from error as possible in defence, yet can score quickly when required, he can handle both fast and slow bowling, he has limitless patience and can build a big innings, and he has the cricketing temperament and sense of theatre to produce his best performances on the biggest stages and in the most tense situations.

These qualities have enabled him to score more Test runs and more Test centuries than any other player: a performance the more meritorious when it is considered that he has been forced to score these runs against the strongest Test attacks.

Gavaskar was born in 1949 in Bombay, the nephew of Madhav Mantri, the Bombay and Indian wicket-keeper. He is now the brother-in-law of Gundappa Viswanath, who made a record 87 consecutive Test appearances, and also captained India.

He played with distinction through schools and University cricket and made his first-class debut for Vazir Sultan Colts in 1966-67. The following year he played for Bombay, and in 1970-71 was selected for the tour to the West Indies.

His Test debut series was sensational. Missing the first Test, his scores in the other four were 65, 67 not out, 116, 64 not out, 1, 117 not out, 124 and 220. Total 774, average 154.80. He thus made a

century in each innings of a Test in his fourth Test (his third and fourth Test centuries). His aggregate 774 is the highest ever made by a batsman in his first Test series. And he made the 220 while suffering from tooth-ache.

Naturally his next appearance, in the series in England in 1971, was eagerly awaited, but he disappointed on his first experience of English conditions. The most famous incident concerning him was when he was knocked over by John Snow, attempting to run him out on a quick single. Snow was omitted from the next Test as a disciplinary measure.

Gavaskar's next two series were also against England, and he again failed to reproduce his initial form. However, India did win the first three series in which Gavaskar played. It as not until 1976 that his form reappeared. In New Zealand in season 1975-76 he scored 266 in five innings, then went to the West Indies, the scene of his first triumphs, and made 390 in seven innings, including two more centuries. In 1976-77 he scored 259 at home to New Zealand in six innings, then when England arrived he hit 38 and 71 in the first Test. Gavaskar thus made 1,024 Test runs in a calendar year, the first Indian to pass 1,000 in a year. He did so again in 1978 and 1979.

In 1978-79 against Pakistan in Karachi he scored a century in each innings of a Test for the second time and passed the record Test aggregate for an Indian, previously held by Polly Umrigar. Later in the season, against the West Indies in Calcutta, he became the only player to score

two separate centuries in a Test on three occasions, making 107 and 182 not out. He also passed 4,000 runs. In this series he made a double century and three centuries against the West Indies for the second time. Between the tour of Pakistan and the visit of the West Indies, Gavaskar replaced Bedi as captain of India.

What some think is his greatest Test innings came in England in 1979, when India made Venkataraghavan the tour captain. At the Oval in the final Test India were set 438 to win and tie the series. They drew at 429 for 8, Gavaskar having made 221, then his highest Test score, in a matchless display of concentration and brilliant technique.

When Australia and Pakistan visited India in 1979-80 Gavaskar was reinstated as captain, and averaged over 50 in each series. However, he resigned the captaincy for the last Test against Pakistan in favour of Viswanath, on the grounds that he was unavailable to tour the West Indies (the tour was subsequently cancelled). The Cricket Board took a poor view of this, believing that Gavaskar was declining the tour in order to play for Somerset, for whom he made 15 appearances in 1980. Later in 1980 the Board asked Gavaskar and Viswanath for explaniations of the fact that their wives stayed in the same hotels during the 1979 tour of England. This appeared to be an indication of the Board's displeasure with Gavaskar and his brother-in-law.

However, he was captain again for the tour of Australia and New Zealand in 1980-81, and was the centre of a storm at Melbourne, when, after being out lbw to Lillee, he remonstrated vehemently and then asked his partner Chauhan to leave the field with him. The manager met them at the gate

and persuaded Chauhan to return, or India would have forfeited a match they eventually won.

In the third Test against Pakistan at Faisalabad in 1982-83 Gavaskar became the first Indian to carry his bat through a completed Test innings with 127 not out in a total of 286. But the series was lost badly, and Kapil Dev was captain when the Indians toured the West Indies in 1982-83, and when they won the World Cup in England in 1983.

Gavaskar made two centuries in a series for the first time in five years when the West Indies visited India in 1983-84. In the third Test at Ahmedabad, when Gavaskar reached 83 he passed Geoff Boycott's record of 8,114 runs in Tests.

In the sixth Test he batted at number four for the first time for India (but went in with the score 0 for 2!). He then made his highest Test score, 236 not out, his 30th Test century (passing Donald Bradman's world record). He also registered, with Shastri, his 48th century stand in Test cricket, passing another Boycott record.

In 1984-85 Gavaskar was captain again in Pakistan, and also against England, when England came back to win the series after being behind. Gavaskar had a poor series, and there was speculation, when Kapil Dev was dropped for the third Test, of rivalry between India's two stars, or at least of the factions behind them.

At the end of this series Gavaskar had been a Test cricketer for 14 years, had played in 106 Tests and scored 8,654 runs at an average of over 50.

Gavaskar is only 5ft 5in and a batsman who scores with impeccable timing and neat placing rather than strength. He keeps a perfectly straight bat, and is an example for those who advocate a correct technique as the surest way to the top.

GAVASKAR Sunil Manohar

Teams: Bombay, Somerset and India

Test series	Tests	Runs	100s	Average
1970-71 in West Indies	4	774	4	154.80
1971 in England	3	144	–	24.00
1972-73 v England	5	224	–	24.88
1974 in England	3	217	1	36.16
1974-75 v West Indies	2	108	–	27.00
1975-76 in New Zealand	3	266	1	66.50
1975-76 in West Indies	4	390	2	55.71
1976-77 v New Zealand	3	259	1	43.16
1976-77 v England	5	394	1	39.40
1977-78 in Australia	5	450	3	50.00
1978-79 in Pakistan	3	447	2	89.40
1978-79 v West Indies†	6	732	4	91.50
1979 in England	4	542	1	77.42
1979-80 v Australia†	6	425	2	53.12
1979-80 v Pakistan‡	6	529	1	52.90
1979-80 v England	1	73	–	36.50
1980-81 in Australia†	3	118	–	23.60
1980-81 in New Zealand†	3	126	–	25.20
1981-82 v England†	6	500	1	62.50
1982 in England†	3	74	–	24.66
1982-83 v Sri Lanka†	1	159	1	159.00
1982-83 v Pakistan†	6	434	1	48.22
1982-83 in West Indies	5	240	1	30.00
1983-84 in Pakistan	3	264	1	66.00
1983-84 v West Indies	6	505	2	50.50
1984-85 in Pakistan†	2	120	–	40.00
1984-85 v England†	5	140	–	17.50
Totals	106	8,654	30	50.60

Career runs: 23,539 *Average:* 51.39
Highest Test score: 236* v West Indies, Madras, 1983-84
Highest career score: 340, Bombay v Bengal, Bombay, 1981-82

*Not out †Captain ‡Captain in first five Tests only
Career figures correct to end of 1985 season

GIBBS
Lancelot Richard b 1934-

At Melbourne Ian Redpath played Lance Gibbs into the hands of Holding and a new page was written into the history of cricket. It was the West Indian off-spinner's 308th Test victim and it broke Fred Trueman's record.

Trueman had often stated that whoever beat his achievement would be 'bloody tired'. Indeed that Test, Gibbs' 79th, proved to be his last—after an international career which began in the 1957-58 series against Pakistan.

He made his first-class debut even earlier, against MCC in 1953-54—a match in which Willie Watson and Tom Graveney shared a partnership of 402. He was to gain his revenge over England many times in the next twenty years. Beginning his cricket career as a leg-spinner, his long fingers and strong wrists, allied to nagging accuracy and variation of pace, transformed him into an off-break bowler of genuine world-class.

He did the hat-trick against Australia at Adelaide in 1960-61 following three wickets in four balls in the preceding Test. In his next series he achieved his personal best in Test cricket, 8 for 38, mesmerizing the Indian batsmen during 53.3 overs, 37 of which were maidens.

Turning to county cricket relatively late in his career—he joined Warwickshire in 1967—he settled slowly to the day-to-day routine. But his 8 for 37 in 1970 was the best first-class return of that season, and the following year, his last for the county, his figures indicated total adjustment.

With Caribbean suppleness and athleticism he became a tremendous fielder, particularly in the gully where his catching was faultless. His batting, however, provided more occasions of high humour than high totals and he never made a first-class fifty.

With Test matches becoming more frequent, Gibbs' record was passed by Lillee and others, but he remains the slowest bowler to pass 300 Test wickets.

ABOVE Gibbs with the special trophy presented to him in Australia when he became the holder of the record number of Test wickets.
RIGHT The action that kept Lance Gibbs in top-class cricket for more than 20 years as a genuine spinner.

GIBBS Lancelot Richard

Teams: Guyana, Warwickshire, South Australia and West Indies

Test series	Tests	Wkts	Average
1957-58 v Pakistan	4	17	23.05
1958-59 in India	1	0	—
1958-59 in Pakistan	3	8	22.25
1960-61 in Australia	3	19	20.78
1961-62 v India	5	24	20.41
1963 in England	5	26	21.30
1964-65 v Australia	5	18	30.83
1966 in England	5	21	24.76
1966-67 in India	3	18	22.05
1967-68 v England	5	20	30.50
1968-69 in Australia	5	24	38.45
1968-69 in New Zealand	3	8	45.25
1969 in England	3	6	52.83
1970-71 v India	1	0	—
1971-72 v New Zealand	2	3	89.00
1972-73 v Australia	5	26	26.76
1973 in England	3	9	25.22
1973-74 v England	5	18	36.72
1974-75 in India	5	21	21.61
1974-75 in Pakistan	2	7	30.00
1975-76 in Australia	6	16	40.75
Totals	79	309	29.09

Career wickets: 1,024 *Average:* 27.22
Best Test Bowling: 8-38 v India, Bridgetown, 1961-62
Best career bowling: 8-37, Warwickshire v Glamorgan, Birmingham, 1970
Highest Test score: 25 v India, Georgetown, 1970-71
Highest career score: 43, West Indians v Combined XI, Hobart, 1960-61

GOWER
David Ivon b 1957-

David Gower has been described as the most accomplished English batsman of his generation, and his languid, graceful style has been likened to that of another great left-hander born in Kent, Frank Woolley. He is not a technician, and relies on the sureness of his eye and perfect timing. When these are slightly awry he can look amateur-ish, failing to move his feet and groping outside the off stump like a beginner. He had a spell like this which stretched from the tour of India in 1984-85 to the beginning of the 1985 season in England. Then the touch returned, and against the Australians Gower once again looked like the supremely gifted player disdain-fully flicking the fast bowlers to the boundary.

Gower was born in Tunbridge Wells on April Fool's day, 1957, and spent his early years in Tanganyika, where his father served in the Colonial Office. He returned for school in Kent and Leicestershire before developing his cricket talent at King's School, Canterbury, and being recom-mended to Leicestershire. He made his first-class debut for the county in 1975, when only 18, and averaged 13.00 in three games. But Leicestershire won the Champion-ship for the first time in their 96 years' history and Wisden de-scribed Gower as 'an exciting pros-pect', perhaps on the strength of a couple of John Player League in-nings. He toured South Africa with English Schools and West Indies with England Young Cricketers, but drifted into a cricket career partly through being bored with his law studies.

He struggled to score runs in 1977 but was picked for the Pru-dential Trophy matches against Pakistan in 1978, and made 114 not out at the Oval. It earned him a Test place at Edgbaston, where he hit his first ball for four and went on to 58. Later that season he made his first Test century, at the Oval against New Zealand. His average after his first two series was 54.75.

In 1978-79 he made his first century against Australia at Perth, and when India visited England in 1979 he hit 200 not out in the first Test at Edgbaston, for six years his highest Test score. Another 82 at Lord's meant his Test average was now 60, but then came two suc-cessive ducks and one of his lean periods. This culminated in his being dropped after the first Test against the West Indies in 1980. He toured the West Indies the follow-ing winter, however, and in an otherwise disappointing series came back to form with 154 not out in Kingston.

When Willis withdrew from the match against Pakistan at Lord's in 1982 with a stiff neck, Gower captained England for the first time.

He was still not fulfilling his potential when he toured Aus-tralia in 1982-83, but in the World Series Cup, a bonanza of one day matches which followed the Test series, made three centuries against New Zealand. Having made over 1,000 runs in five Tests and 10 WSC matches, he was named Benson and Hedges Inter-national Cricketer of the Year, winning a £13,000 Japanese car. More valuable runs came in the New Zealand tour to England in 1983, when he scored two cen-turies in a series for the first time.

This feat was repeated in Paki-stan in 1983-84, when he again took over the England captaincy when Willis was forced to return home early. This time Gower kept the captaincy.

He perhaps regretted his respon-sibilities in his first full series, when West Indies beat England 5-0 in 1984, the worst defeat to be inflicted on England. However, he kept the job, despite being unable to defeat Sri Lanka. Gower's first victory as captain came in India in 1984-85, after seven defeats and three draws in his first ten Tests as captain. England fought back to take that series 2-1, but Gower's form as a batsman had declined to such an extent that his last 18 in-nings had produced less than 400 runs at an average of less than 25. When the Australians arrived in 1985 both his captaincy and his Test place were seriously threatened.

The turning point for Gower came in the third Texaco Trophy match at Lord's. Australia had already won the Trophy with two wins, Gower's contributions being

3 and 0. At Lord's he took a diffi-cult skier of a catch which seemed to release his tension, and then made a fluent 102 to help win the match. Gower's return to form was just in time to retain his place. In the third Test at Trent Bridge he made his first Test century as England captain, 166. In the fifth Test at Edgbaston, a ground he likes, he played one of his greatest innings, and his highest Test score to date, 215, and in the sixth Test he made sure the Ashes returned to England with 157. He scored 732 runs in the series, average 81.33,

ABOVE David Gower nose to nose with Australian premier Bob Hawke at the World Series Cup, Melbourne, 1983.
OPPOSITE Gower hits to mid-wicket against New Zealand in the fourth Test at Trent Bridge in 1983.

and was thoroughly reinstated.

Perhaps, however, as with Woolley, it is not by the figures that he will eventually be judged. When in form, he bats with an ele-gance that suggests cricket is an art-form rather than a game.

GOWER David Ivon				
Teams: Leicestershire and England				
Test series	**Tests**	**Runs**	**100s**	**Average**
1978 v Pakistan	3	153	—	51.00
1978 v New Zealand	3	285	1	57.00
1978-79 in Australia	6	420	1	42.00
1979 v India	4	289	1	71.25
1979-80 in Australia	3	152	—	30.40
1979-80 in India	1	16	—	16.00
1980 v West Indies	1	21	—	10.50
1980 v Australia	1	80	—	40.00
1980-81 in West Indies	4	376	1	53.71
1981 v Australia	5	250	—	25.00
1981-82 in India	6	375	—	44.37
1981-82 in Sri Lanka	1	131	—	131.00
1982 v India	3	152	—	38.00
1982 v Pakistan‡	3	197	—	36.16
1982-83 in Australia	5	441	1	44.10
1983 v New Zealand	4	404	2	57.71
1983-84 in New Zealand	3	69	—	17.25
1983-84 in Pakistan§	3	449	2	112.25
1984 v West Indies†	5	171	—	19.00
1984 v Sri Lanka†	1	55	—	55.00
1984-85 in India†	5	167	—	27.83
1985 v Australia†	6	732	3	81.33
Totals	76	5,385	12	45.63

Career runs: 15,590 *Average:* 40.59
Highest Test and career score: 215 v Australia, Edgbaston, 1985

†Captain ‡Captain in one Test only §Captain in two Tests only
Career figures correct to end of 1985 season

GRACE
William Gilbert
b 1848-d 1915

No cricketer before or since has dominated the world of cricket as W. G. Grace did for nearly 40 years from the middle of the 1860s. In fact, he was said to be the most easily recognized figure in England along with the Prime Minister, William Ewart Gladstone. Tall, heavily built, and, from an early age, heavily bearded, W.G. (or 'The Doctor' as he was later called) was not only an all-round cricketer of great skill whose achievements in an unusually long career broke most of the records of the day but was also a man of formidable and striking personality who in his own time became a legend of dictatorial 'gamesmanship' blended with gruff kindliness.

A precocious boy in the 1860s, he played for the Gentlemen in the big match of the year when only just 17, and he linked the 'disorganized' cricket of those early years with the relatively modern times at the turn of the century of Fry, Ranji, Test matches, and the county championship. He retained his form so well that in 1895 he enjoyed one of his best seasons, becoming the first batsman ever to make 1,000 runs in May, a few weeks short of his 47th birthday.

W.G.'s cricket background is well recorded. He was born the fourth of five sons to Dr Henry Grace and his wife Martha who lived near Bristol. His father was an enthusiastic cricketer but a hard-working doctor, and it was the redoubtable Mrs Grace who was the inspiration of the boys' cricket. Her enthusiasm and her considerable knowledge of the game were passed on in long hours in the family garden to the three youngest brothers of the five.

The third son of the five, Edward, was the first to win fame. Later he became generally known

as 'The Coroner', because of his chosen occupation, and if there had been no W.G., he would have been the leading all-round cricketer of his time. He opened the innings with W.G. in the first Test match played in England in 1880. Their younger brother G.F., who died a fortnight later aged 30, was also in the side.

A tall, strong youth, W.G. made his first appearance in the top class in 1865 when he opened the innings for the Gentlemen at Lord's, making 34 in the second innings, and that same year he took seven wickets at the Oval for the Gentlemen. For some time previously, the Gentlemen and Players fixture had been so one-sided that on some occasions professionals were loaned to the Gentlemen to balance the match. But with the coming of W.G. it all changed. It was 20 years before the Players won again at Lord's, and in the next 50 matches played between the sides on various grounds after W.G.'s arrival, they won only 7 while the Gentlemen won 31. W.G. was always at his best in this fixture, making 15 of his 126 centuries for the Gentlemen as well as taking 271 wickets for them with his rather roundarm, cleverly varied slow bowling. However, as W.G. did not qualify as a doctor until he was 31, there is little doubt that he received some money through his cricket and was not an amateur in the purest sense of the term.

As a batsman, he was entirely sound both in judgement of length and in execution of stroke. He was equally proficient off back foot and front, and was a masterly player of fast bowling, which on some of the rough pitches of the day could terrorize many able batsmen. And his record of 126 centuries stood until 1925 when Jack Hobbs passed it.

W.G.'s pre-eminence in the 1870s, soon after he and his

The Spy cartoon of the most famous cricketer in the world.

GRACE William Gilbert

Teams: Gloucestershire, London County, and England

Test series		Tests	Runs	100s	Average	Wkts	Average
1880	v Australia	1	161	1	161.00	3	22.66
1882	v Australia	1	36	—	18.00	—	—
1884	v Australia	3	72	—	18.00	3	12.66
1886	v Australia	3	200	1	50.00	1	22.00
1888	v Australia	3*	73	—	18.25	—	—
1890	v Australia	2*	91	—	30.33	2	6.00
1891-92 in Australia		3*	164	—	32.80	0	—
1893	v Australia	2*	153	—	51.00	—	—
1896	v Australia	3*	119	—	19.83	0	—
1899	v Australia	1*	29	—	14.50	0	—
Totals		22	1,098	2	32.29	9	26.22

Career runs: 54,904 *Average:* 39.52
Highest Test score: 170 v Australia, Oval, 1886
Highest career score: 344, MCC v Kent, Canterbury, 1876
Career wickets: 2,876 *Average:* 17.92
Best Test bowling: 2-12 v Australia, Lord's, 1890
Best career bowling: 10-49, MCC v Oxford University, Oxford, 1886

*Captain (in two Tests in 1888)
Note: Grace's career figures are in dispute. According to the Association of Cricket Statisticians, he scored 54,211 runs (average 39.45), took 2,808 wickets (average 18.15) and made 124 centuries (not 126 as mentioned in the text).

family had played a big part in founding the Gloucestershire County Cricket Club, is evident from the fact that in 1871, one of his great years, he made 2,736 runs, an unheard of number, and averaged 78. The next highest average was the 34 of a very fine batsman, Richard Daft. In another season, 1876, he was almost as successful. Within eight days in August he made 344 against Kent, 177 against Nottinghamshire, and 318 not out against Yorkshire. A month later, he played what must have been one of his most remarkable innings—400 not out against '22 of Grimsby', a side composed of 22 players, all in the field on an outfield reported as being slow.

In 1872, Grace went on a tour to Canada and took a side to Australia in 1873-74. Yet surprisingly, perhaps, he was to go to Australia only once more, 18 years later. Meanwhile he captained Gloucestershire as he was to do for the first 29 years of their history, and played for England from the first home Test, in which he made 152. In 1886, he made 170 against Australia at the Oval, a score not exceeded in a Test match in England for 35 years. In 1888, he captained England for the first time and remained captain in England, and on the 1891-92 tour of Australia, until after the first Test of 1899, when he was replaced by A. C. MacLaren. By then, though, he was nearly 51 and finding his immobility in the field a

tiresome handicap.

His record against Australia was good without ever being as exceptional as that in other cricket, but his best days were probably before Test cricket started. The glorious year of 1895, however, revealed him, to the general amazement, almost as all-conquering as ever. His 1,000 runs in May were in fact made in 22 days from the 9th to the 30th, and later that year he made his 100th century in an innings of 288 against Somerset. Against Kent at Gravesend, he was on the field throughout the three days, scoring 257 and 73 not out. It was little wonder that a shilling testimonial for W.G. that year produced £9,000.

In 1899 there was a sad episode —the doctor's break with Gloucestershire. Enthusiasts in London started the London County Club to play near the Crystal Palace and W.G. accepted their invitation to become manager. He intended apparently to continue playing for Gloucestershire as well, but the Gloucestershire committee disapproved, and consequently he played solely for London County until 1904 when the venture died for financial reasons. He was still good enough to make 166 on the day after his 56th birthday and to score 150 runs and take 6 wickets against his native Gloucestershire. And it was while he was at the Crystal Palace with London County that W.G., an ardent

bowls enthusiast as well, formed the London County Bowling Club and played an important part in the formation of the English Bowling Association in 1903.

After 1904 his first-class cricket was played mainly for MCC and the Gentlemen, for whom he made 74 at the age of 58. He would doubtless have gone on making runs but for his cumbersomeness in the field. Yet in spite of this, his zest for cricket seems to have remained undulled and he made 69 not out for Eltham against Grove Park in July 1914—in his last match, 10 days before the outbreak of World War I. The next year he died, and was mourned far outside the world of cricket, for he had been a truly national figure.

LEFT W. G.'s fame as a national figure is reflected in a Punch *cartoon on the weather in 1898. The caption reads: 'Ninety in the shade—not out': and umpire* Punch *is saying to W. G. Sol: 'By jove, old man, you've "beaten the record" this* time *and no mistake!'*

ABOVE LEFT W. G. Grace with his younger brother G. F. and the Surrey bowler James Southerton in 1873. Another brother, E. M., was in the same England team, in 1880.

ABOVE RIGHT W. G. takes an interest in the Worcester Park beagles.

ABOVE W. G. posing near the end of a career which made him the most famous Englishman.

GREENIDGE
Cuthbert Gordon b 1951-

Gordon Greenidge was born (as Cuthbert Gordon Lavine) in Barbados, but with his parents he came to live in Berkshire, England, when he was 14 years old. Two years later he played cricket for England Schoolboys, and the following season he joined Hampshire, making his first-class debut in 1970. His opening partner was Barry Richards, the best possible model for a developing batsman. Greenidge developed a hard-hitting aggressive style—indeed in his early days he was accused of attempting to hit the ball too hard. He remains an opening batsman intent on dominating the attack from the start, rather than on building an innings with patience, and there are few batsmen better at reducing a bowling side to despair.

Greenidge was asked about his willingness to play for England in 1972, but preferred to await a summons from the West Indies. It came in 1974-75 and Greenidge went on the tour of India, making his Test debut in the same match as Viv Richards. Greenidge might have equalled Rowe's feat of a century in each innings on his Test debut with any luck: in his first Test he scored 93 run out and 107.

In his sixth Test, on the tour of Australia in 1975-76, he made a pair, and was dropped after scoring 11 runs in four innings. Fortunes changed in England in 1976, however. At Old Trafford in the third Test he made a century in each innings, 134 and 101. His 134 was made out of West Indies all out total of 211, or 63.5 per cent of the runs, the largest percentage in a Test since the very first in 1877. He followed up his two centuries with another in his next Test innings, 115 at Headingley. Although Richards scored more runs in the 1976 Test series, Greenidge scored most runs on the tour: 1,952, average 55.77.

It was not until the West Indies returned to England in 1980 that Greenidge's triumphant Test progress received its next set-back, when he could score only 120 runs in six innings.

Meanwhile, Greenidge had been scoring heavily in one-day limited-overs matches, which were ideal for his brand of bludgeoning batsmanship. At the end of the 1970s he held the record score in all three English domestic competitions: 173 not out v Minor Counties South at Amersham in 1973 (Benson and Hedges Cup), 177 v Glamorgan at Southampton in 1975 (Gillette Cup) and 163 not out v Warwickshire at Birmingham in 1979 (John Player League). In the first match, his unbroken second wicket stand with David Turner of 285 was the record partnership in all one-day competitions.

Greenidge's highest score, 273 not out against the Pakistanis at Eastbourne in 1974, was made in only 4¼ hours and included 13 sixes and 31 fours.

Between 1982-83 in India and 1984 in England Greenidge had a purple patch in Tests, during which he scored 1,769 runs, including six centuries, and averaged over 70. In England in 1984 he was outstanding at Lord's, when West Indies were set to score 342 to win on the last day. They were led to victory by Greenidge, who made 214 not out. In this innings Greenidge passed 4,000 runs in Test cricket. Later, in the fourth Test at Old Trafford, Greenidge made 223, his highest score in Test cricket.

Greenidge is an excellent slip fielder and occasional offbreak bowler. He is the only member of the outstanding West Indian side of the 1980s whose home is basically in England, and once or twice has looked a little remote from his team-mates. He was awarded the MBE in 1985.

Greenidge drives during his 223 at Old Trafford in 1984.

GREENIDGE Cuthbert Gordon (born C. G. Lavine)

Teams: Hampshire, Barbados and West Indies

Test series	Tests	Runs	100s	Average
1974-75 in India	5	371	1	41.22
1975-76 in Australia	2	11	—	2.75
1976 in England	5	592	3	65.77
1976-77 v Pakistan	5	536	1	53.60
1977-78 v Australia	2	131	—	65.50
1979-80 in Australia	3	173	—	34.60
1979-80 in New Zealand	3	274	—	45.60
1980 in England	5	124	—	20.66
1980-81 v England	4	223	—	44.60
1981-82 v Australia	2	134	—	33.50
1982-83 v India	5	393	1	78.60
1983-84 in India	6	411	1	51.37
1983-84 v Australia	5	393	2	78.60
1984 in England	5	572	2	81.71
1984-85 in Australia	5	214	—	26.75
1984-85 v New Zealand	4	264	1	52.80
Totals	66	4,816	12	49.14

Career runs: 28,461 *Average:* 44.75
Highest Test score: 223 v England, Old Trafford, 1984
Highest career score: 273*, D. H. Robins' XI v Pakistanis, Eastbourne, 1974

*Not out

GREIG
Anthony William b 1946-

In 1977 Tony Greig was captain of England in the Centenary Test in Melbourne, having led England in a highly successful tour of India. Then Kerry Packer and World Series Cricket burst upon the scene, and it transpired that Greig was one of the chief organizers of and spokesmen for this 'private' set-up which was effectively challenging established cricket.

Greig was never forgiven by the establishment, and within a couple of years his first-class career had ended. Since then he has been largely ignored by cricket writers, as if he were being written out of history, Russian-style. He was, however, one of the best of England's captains, and an excellent Test all-rounder. A hard-hitting middle order batsman, a nagging medium-pace bowler, a brilliant fielder and inspiring captain, he often produced his best performances when they were most needed.

Greig was born in Queenstown, South Africa in 1946, his Scottish father having gone to South Africa with the RAF during the Second World War to train pilots, and having stayed. Greig made his first-class debut for Border in 1965-66.

Greig joined Sussex in 1966, and made his county debut in May 1967 against Lancashire at Hove. Already standing an impressive 6ft 8in, slim and blond, the 20-year-old Greig saved Sussex with 156 in his first match and it was clear a new star had arrived. He scored 1,299 runs and took 67 wickets in his first season.

In 1970 Greig played for the England XI against the Rest of the World in the series arranged, ironically, after the cancellation of the tour by South Africa.

He made his Test debut in 1972 against Australia, and was top-scorer in both innings with 57 and 62, and took five wickets in an England victory. In the following winter he toured India, where he was a very popular figure, and in the fifth Test made his first Test century, 148, and shared in a record fifth-wicket stand for England of 254 with Fletcher.

He had an extremely successful tour of West Indies in 1973-74, where his competitiveness got him into trouble in the first Test at Port-of-Spain. On the last ball of the second day Julien played the ball back down the pitch and Greig, seeing Kallicharran out of his ground, threw down the wicket and Kallicharran, who was only making his way back to the pavilion, was given out. It took an off-the-field agreement between captains, umpires and officials to reinstate Kallicharran and possibly prevent uproar the following day. Apart from two centuries Greig played a major part in England making a draw of this series when

in the final Test he changed his bowling style from medium swing and seam to off-breaks. He took 8 for 86 and 5 for 70, the best figures of an England bowler against West Indies. Strangely, he could never repeat his success as an off-spinner.

When Lillee and Thomson established a superiority over England in the 1974-75 series in Australia, Greig did not flinch against their awesome and dangerous speed, and his innings of 110 at Brisbane was a brave knock which held England together.

In 1975 Greig became England captain when Denness stood down after the first Test against Australia. In 1976 the West Indies were the visitors, and Greig made a combative but unconsidered remark about making them grovel—in the event the West Indian fast bowlers were merciless in inflicting a 3-0 defeat.

Greig's style of inspirational leadership was welding a more successful England side, however, and the tour of India in 1976-77 was a triumph—India lost the first three Tests to a touring side for the first time ever. On the way back there was the Centenary Test in Melbourne, where although England lost, there were indications of a revival in fortunes against the oldest enemy.

Then Greig's role in World Series Cricket became known. The immediate result was the loss of the England captaincy to Brearley, his vice-captain in India, and it was Brearley who beat Australia 3-0 in 1977 and began a legend for astute captaincy which might have

been Greig's. Greig played in the 1977 series, his last.

On 26 September 1977 WSC and three players, of whom Greig was one, took the ICC and TCCB to the High Court, seeking to have new TCCB rules (to prevent counties employing any Packer players for two years) declared void as a restraint of trade. Greig's side won the case.

However, Greig decided to make his life in Australia. He gave up the first-class game and became managing director of an insurance company set up by Kerry Packer, and one of the cricket presenters on Channel 9 television.

Throughout his career Greig fought against the handicap of epilepsy. For a while he was England's shining knight. During the Packer affair he was articulate, polite and reasonable in his assertions that all was for the best so far as the welfare of cricketers was concerned, a claim that, now the dust has settled, bears examination. He deserves to be remembered not as one who vaguely besmirched the name of cricket, as some traditionalists would like, but as one of England's best captains and all-rounders.

GREIG Anthony William

Teams: Border, Sussex, Eastern Province and England

Test series		Tests	Runs	100s	Average	Wkts	Average
1972	v Australia	5	288	—	37.25	10	39.80
1972-73	in India	5	382	1	63.66	11	22.45
1972-73	in Pakistan	3	261	—	52.20	6	42.50
1973	v New Zealand	3	216	1	43.20	8	23.12
1973	v West Indies	3	122	—	24.40	7	56.00
1973-74	in West Indies	5	430	2	47.77	24	22.62
1974	v India	3	159	1	79.50	6	29.83
1974	v Pakistan	3	90	—	22.50	8	27.75
1974-75	in Australia	6	446	1	40.54	17	40.05
1974-75	in New Zealand	2	51	—	51.00	12	14.66
1975	v Australia‡	4	284	—	35.50	8	35.25
1976	v West Indies†	5	243	—	30.37	5	67.20
1976-77	in India†	5	342	1	42.75	10	33.20
1976-77	in Australia†	1	59	—	29.50	2	33.00
1977	v Australia	5	226	—	32.28	7	28.00
Totals		58	3,599	8	40.43	141	32.20

Career runs: 16,660 *Average:* 31.19
Highest Test score: 148 v India, Bombay, 1972-73
148 v West Indies, Bridgetown, 1973-74
Highest career score: 226 v Warwickshire, Hastings, 1975
Career wickets: 856 *Average:* 28.85
Best Test bowling: 8-86 v West Indies, Port-of-Spain, 1973-74
Best career bowling: 8-25 v Gloucestershire, Hove, 1967

†Captain ‡Captain in last 3 matches only

GROUP
Arthur Theodore Wallace
b 1927-d 1968

Between 1957 and 1965 Wally Grout kept wicket for Australia in 51 Test matches, the last of them less than three years before his much lamented death through heart failure. Short and sturdily built, he was very much a player for the big occasion and very few chances escaped him in a Test match. His bag of 187 victims, 163 caught and 24 stumped, in 51 Tests was an astonishing one, exceeded only by Evans before him, although with more Tests played recently others including Marsh, Knott and Murray, have passed him.

Though he first played for Queensland in 1946-47, he was second string to Don Tallon and did not win a regular place in the State side until Tallon's retirement following the 1953 tour of England. Gil Langley succeeded Tallon as the Australian wicket-keeper though, and it was not until the tour of South Africa in 1957-58 that Grout, then 30, played in his first Test. Once in the side, he was not to be dislodged, even though throughout his Test career Australia had an outstanding second wicket-keeper in Barry Jarman, who was a better

batsman. Grout's own batting, however, was far from negligible and he could be difficult to dislodge in a crisis. He made 74 against England at Melbourne in 1958-59 but his most important innings was probably his 37 at Leeds in 1964. His ninth wicket stand of 89 with Peter Burge gave Australia a first innings lead that enabled them to retrieve a losing position and to win the only finished Test of the series.

In his first Test he held six catches in an innings, four of them off Alan Davidson, who provided him with many chances in the early years of his Test career. This number has since been exceeded in Test cricket only by Bob Taylor and Wasim Bari. However, his feat of taking eight catches in an innings for Queensland against Western Australia in 1959-60 is still without parallel.

Grout is especially remembered in England for a characteristically quick and fair act during the first Test of 1964 at Trent Bridge. One of the England opening batsmen, Titmus, had collided with the bowler, Hawke, and had been knocked over. The ball was thrown to Grout, who could have broken the wicket and run Titmus out at leisure, but having seen what had happened, he sportingly allowed the batsman to rise and regain his crease.

LEFT Wally Grout attempts to run out the West Indian fast bowler Wesley Hall. Grout did not play his first Test until he was 30, when he went on the tour of South Africa in 1957-58, but was Australia's first choice until the 1965-66 season.

ABOVE Grout ended with 187 Test victims in 51 Tests, a figure at that time second only to Godfrey Evans' 219 in 91 Tests. He was one of the most popular of cricketers, and the world of cricket was saddened when he died soon after his retirement.

GROUT Arthur Theodore Wallace

Teams: Queensland and Australia

Test series	Tests	Runs	Average	Catches	Stumpings
1957-58 in South Africa	5	93	18.60	16	3
1958-59 v England	5	119	19.83	17	3
1959-60 in Pakistan	3	98	49.00	8	4
1959-60 in India	4	147	36.75	14	2
1960-61 v West Indies	5	72	8.00	20	3
1961 in England	5	47	7.83	20	1
1962-63 v England	2	17	—	7	2
1963-64 v South Africa	5	84	10.50	13	1
1964 in England	5	84	16.80	10	0
1964-65 in India	1	12	6.00	4	0
1964-65 in Pakistan	1	0	0.00	5	0
1964-65 in West Indies	5	83	13.83	14	4
1965-66 v England	5	34	6.80	15	1
Totals	51	890	15.08	163	24

Career runs: 5,168 *Average:* 22.56
Highest Test score: 74 v England, Melbourne, 1958-59
Highest career score: 119, Queensland v South Australia, Brisbane, 1960-61
Career dismissals: 587, *Catches:* 473, *Stumpings:* 114
Best Test wicketkeeping: 8 dismissals (6 ct 2 st) in match, v Pakistan, Lahore, 1959-60
8 dismissals (all ct) in match, v England, Lord's 1961
Best career wicketkeeping: 8 dismissals (all ct) in innings, Queensland v Western Australia, Brisbane, 1959-60

HADLEE
Richard John b 1951-

When Richard Hadlee performed the double of 1,000 runs and 100 wickets in the 1984 English season, a feat which had not been performed since the number of county championship games were reduced from 28 to 24 in 1969, he confirmed that he was not only the best bowler to come from New Zealand but was one of the world's great all-rounders.

Hadlee was born in Christchurch, New Zealand, in 1951 into a cricketing family. Father Walter captained New Zealand and became a leading figure in the New Zealand Cricket Council, while of Richard's four cricketing brothers Dayle and Barry also played for Canterbury, Dayle also going on to play for New Zealand.

Richard made his debut for Canterbury in 1971-72 as a fast right-arm bowler and an aggressive left-hand batsman. The season after his debut he was chosen to play in the first Test against Pakistan—his older brother, already a Test player, replaced him for the rest of the series.

Both brothers came to England in 1973, and both played in the first Test at Trent Bridge, but Richard performed disappointingly and only Dayle retained his place for the other two Tests.

For a while this was to be the pattern for Richard Hadlee—in and out of the Test side, performing adequately but not brilliantly. The breakthrough came in the third Test against India at Wellington in the 1975-76 season. With India one up in the series, Hadlee, as fourth seam bowler, saved the rubber with 4 for 35 and 7 for 23, the best innings and match figures by any New Zealand bowler in Tests until then. From then onwards he was an automatic selection, and one of the new ball bowlers.

In 1977-78 Hadlee had another big success at Wellington, where New Zealand beat England for the first time. He took 4 for 74 in the first innings, and with England needing only 137 to win in the second took 6 for 26 to shoot them out for only 64.

In 1978 Hadlee made his second tour of England, a much more successful one than his first. He headed the tourists' bowling averages for both Tests and first-class matches with 13 wickets, av. 20.76, and 41, av. 17.41, respectively. In this season he joined Nottinghamshire.

He made his first Test hundred in 1979-80 against the West Indies at Christchurch, scoring 103 against Roberts, Holding, Garner and Croft. New Zealand won this series, their first home rubber victory after 50 years. In the first Test at Dunedin, Hadlee took 5 for 34 and 6 for 68, and scored 51 and a vital 17 in the second innings when New Zealand just managed to make the 104 required to win by one wicket from a leg-bye.

Hadlee began a revival in the fortunes of Nottinghamshire. In 1981 they won the Championship for the first time since 1929 and Hadlee was top of the English bowling averages with 105 wickets at 14.89—the only bowler to take 100 wickets in the season. In 1982 he also topped the bowling averages with 61 at 14.57.

In 1983 New Zealand registered their first Test victory in England. It was their 29th attempt, and came in the second Test at Headingley. Strangely Hadlee did not take a wicket in this match (he had 21 in the other three) but he scored 75 and was at the crease when the 5-wicket win was achieved.

There was so much euphoria over this win in New Zealand that, back home, Hadlee succumbed to the pressure of demands on his time and suffered something of a mental breakdown. He was given a quick course in motivation by a psychologist and 1984 proved a marvellous season for him.

The cricketer's double of 1,000 runs and 100 wickets in a season, once common among the top all-rounders, had become more difficult with the introduction of a growing one-day match programme in the 1960s. Fred Titmus was the last to achieve it in 1967, but in 1969 when the Championship season was reduced by four games, it had become very difficult and had not been performed. Hadlee deliberately set out to perform the double, and achieved it: 117 wickets at 14.05 (easily top of the averages) and 1,179 runs, av. 51.26 (15th in the averages). Hadlee made his first double century (210 not out v Middlesex) that season.

Hadlee is a genuine fast bowler who gets lift and movement from a comparatively short run and a model sideways-on action. As a lower order batsman, few hit the ball as hard, but he is no slogger and frequently scores his runs when they are most needed.

HADLEE Richard John

Teams: Canterbury, Nottinghamshire, Tasmania, and New Zealand

Test series	Tests	Runs	100s	Average	Wkts	Average
1972-73 v Pakistan	1	46	—	46.00	2	56.00
1973 in England	1	4	—	4.00	1	143.00
1973-74 in Australia	3	68	—	11.33	7	36.42
1973-74 v Australia	2	37	—	12.33	10	22.50
1975-76 v India	2	45	—	22.50	12	16.41
1976-77 in Pakistan	3	214	—	53.50	10	44.80
1976-77 in India	3	60	—	10.00	13	33.61
1976-77 v Australia	2	143	—	35.75	6	59.00
1977-78 v England	3	80		16.00	15	24.72
1978 in England	3	32	—	5.33	13	20.76
1978-79 v Pakistan	2	115	—	28.75	18	23.00
1979-80 v West Indies	3	178	1	44.50	19	19.00
1980-81 in Australia	3	98	—	24.50	19	19.15
1980-81 v India	3	29	—	7.25	10	28.80
1981-82 v Australia	3	92	—	23.00	14	16.14
1982-83 v Sri Lanka	2	59	—	29.50	10	14.10
1983 in England	4	301	—	50.16	21	26.61
1983-84 v England	3	144	—	36.00	12	19.33
1983-84 in Sri Lanka	3	75	—	18.75	23	10.00
1984-85 v Pakistan	3	131	—	32.75	16	19.12
1984-85 in West Indies	4	137	—	22.83	15	27.26
Totals	57	2,088	1	24.85	266	23.83

Career runs: 8,737 *Average:* 29.12
Highest Test score: 103 v West Indies, Christchurch, 1979-80
Highest career score: 210* v Middlesex, Lord's, 1984
Career wickets: 1,092 *Average:* 18.70
Best Test bowling: 7-23 v India, Wellington, 1975-76
Best career bowling: 8-41, Nottinghamshire v Lancashire, Trent Bridge, 1985

*Not out

HALL
Wesley Winfield b 1937-

When tall, gangling Wes Hall first went to England with John Goddard's West Indies team in 1957, he was not particularly successful, taking only 27 wickets and not playing in a Test match. But he was then only 19, and had a superb action for a fast bowler. Within two years he had profited from the experience gained in England and was quickly becoming the best fast bowler in the world, a position which he maintained for much of the early 1960s. His run, like that of other fast bowlers, could be criticized as over-long and contributing to a slow over-rate, but his fluent, lissom action, his accelerating run-up to the wicket, his strength, stamina, and speed made him exciting to watch.

Born in Bridgetown, Barbados —much later he moved to Trinidad as a coach—Wes Hall first played as a batsman-wicketkeeper. But by the time he went to England his potential as a fast bowler was widely acknowledged and his batting consisted mostly of a few whirlwind minutes later in the innings.

In 1958-59 he established himself by taking 46 Test wickets during the tour of India and Pakistan, including a hat-trick at Lahore. He followed with 22 wickets against Peter May's

England team in the West Indies and 21 against Australia in the famous series of 1960-61. For a while he played for Queensland in the Sheffield Shield as well as in the Lancashire League for Accrington, and he reached the peak of his fame in England in 1963 with the controversial Charlie Griffith as his partner.

While Hall's action was a joy to watch, Griffith's at times seemed to many people to be outside the law and it is a strange thought that Hall, undoubtedly the finer bowler of the two, does not appear in *Wisden* as a Cricketer of the Year. Griffith was honoured in 1963 when he took 32 wickets, twice as many as Hall, though clearly he could scarcely have achieved so much without his great partner. And it may be significant that when Hall and Griffith returned to England in 1966 on another successful tour and Griffith's

RIGHT Wesley Hall stood 6 ft 2 in, brought the ball down from a great height and bowled at a tremendous speed off a very long run.
BELOW Hall after delivery. During the 1960s his Test partnership with Charlie Griffith formed the most feared spearhead in the world. Where Griffith was regarded as an awkward bowler, Hall was more classical, his run-up and action foreshadowing that of Holding in its length, athleticism and grace.

action was closely watched, Hall took more wickets. By then, however, he was beginning to show signs of decline. These became more evident during MCC's tour of the West Indies in 1968, and he played in only two Tests on the tour of Australia a year later.

One of Hall's most remarkable bowling performances was at Lord's in 1963 on the last day of a memorable second Test. He bowled throughout the 3 hours 20 minutes play possible, taking 4-93, and when play finished, England, with their last batsmen in, still needed six runs for victory. In this match, as at other times, he

bowled short, and there were moments when his onslaught with Griffith on lively pitches was not pleasant to watch and considerably less fun to face.

But he was an immensely like-able personality with something of the clown about him. This was especially so in his batting, though some of his performances were of widely contrasting styles. In 1963 he made a spectacular 102 not out against Cambridge University in 65 minutes. But in 1968 in Trinidad, he batted throughout the last two hours with Gary Sobers to save the first Test against England and he revealed for once a stalwart defence.

HALL Wesley Winfield			
Teams: Barbados, Queensland, and West Indies			
Test series	**Tests**	**Wkts**	**Average**
1958-59 in India	5	30	17.66
1958-59 in Pakistan	3	16	17.93
1959-60 v England	5	22	30.86
1960-61 in Australia	5	21	29.33
1961-62 v India	5	27	15.74
1963 in England	5	16	33.37
1964-65 v Australia	5	16	28.37
1966 in England	5	18	30.83
1966-67 in India	3	8	33.25
1967-68 v England	4	9	39.22
1968-69 in Australia	2	8	40.62
1968-69 in New Zealand	1	1	42.00
Totals	48	192	26.38

Career wickets: 546 *Average:* 26.14
Best Test bowling: 7-69 v England, Kingston, 1959-60
Best career bowling: 7-51, West Indians v Glamorgan, Swansea, 1963
Highest Test score: 50* v India, Port of Spain, 1961-62
　　　　　　　　　50 v Australia, Brisbane, 1960-61
Highest career score: 102*, West Indians v Cambridge University, Cambridge, 1963

HAMMOND
Walter Reginald
b 1903-d 1965

Walter Hammond ranks as one of the greatest cricketers in the history of the game. Mostly thought of as a batsman, he was, however, also a lively and intelligent fast-medium bowler, who took 83 Test wickets, and one of the greatest slip-fielders of his time.

Hammond's first-class career for Gloucestershire and England fell almost entirely between the two world wars. It followed an unusual course, for his first reputation was as a hitter, albeit a polished one. But it was soon clear he was more than that, and he went on the MCC tour of 1925-26 to the West Indies. He became ill and did not play again until 1927.

Few players have returned to the game after illness so sensationally. He made 1,000 runs in May and 2,969 in the season, averaging nearly 70. In one famous innings at Old Trafford, he scored 187 in three hours off bowling that included the great Australian speed merchant McDonald and which was to win Lancashire the championship that year. This was in the second innings; in the first he had made 99. In 1927-28 he toured South Africa where he played in the first of his 85 Tests.

BELOW LEFT Wally Hammond drives to the off. Hammond's off-driving was regarded as the best in the world—a shot of great power and majesty.

BELOW RIGHT Hammond's batting prowess sometimes obscures the fact that he was an all-rounder, a brilliant slip fielder and taker of 83 Test wickets.

ABOVE Nobody has scored more runs at a higher average than Walter Hammond, and his Test aggregate of 7,249 remained a record for over 20 years.

Hammond was now a batsman of impressive command, a superbly balanced athlete, quick and powerful at the crease, with a classical off-drive. The adventure of his youth had been curbed and he had a more considered approach to batting that was in contrast to that of a few years before. He seldom hooked now.

In 1928-29, when he was still only 25, he turned on the Australians, who had been spared a first meeting with him in 1926 by his illness. In the series he made 905 runs, an aggregate exceeded only by Don Bradman's 974 in 1930. Twice he passed 200, and in the fourth Test at Adelaide, which England won by 12 runs, he made 119 not out and 177.

His feats in the next 10 years were sometimes overshadowed by those of his great contemporary, Bradman, but they nevertheless included many superb innings. Of his 22 Test hundreds, 9 were against Australia, 6 against South Africa, and 4 against New Zealand. One of the latter—his 336 not out at Auckland in only 5¼ hours—remained the highest innings in Test cricket until Len Hutton's 364 at the Oval in 1938.

He went through a relatively unsuccessful period in Test cricket in the early 1930s, but he was back at his best in 1936, scoring 167 and 217 against India. And with G. O. Allen's team in Australia in 1936-37 he made 231 not out at Sydney. In 1938 he turned amateur and was appointed captain of England in that summer's series against Australia. He made 240 in the Lord's Test and led England to the victory that squared the series at the Oval, though he himself scored only 59 of England's mammoth 903-7. He led MCC in

South Africa in 1938-39 and made three centuries, including 140 in the last innings of the famous timeless Test at Durban when England made 654-5 and the match was left unfinished after 10 days.

After service in the RAF, much of it in South Africa, Hammond returned to Gloucestershire for the 1946 season, and at the age of 43 headed the first-class averages with 84.90. He was the obvious choice for the captaincy in Australia that winter, but his talents at last failed him. Nor, as a rather aloof and silent, unbending figure, was he a successful captain of a side of much younger men, and apart from the odd match for Gloucestershire he did not play again. He went to live in South Africa, and remained cut off from English cricket until, a few months before his death, he became a frequent and welcome visitor to the headquarters of M. J. K. Smith's MCC team when they were playing in Durban in the 1964-65 season.

Some of the many records Walter Hammond set up are still standing 20 years after his death: his tally of 78 catches in the 1928 season and his 10 in a match—two more than any other fielder. His record of 7,249 runs in Tests stood for almost 25 years until finally beaten by Colin Cowdrey, a player of similar grace and power in the making of strokes. Among English batsmen, only Hobbs and Boycott have made more runs against Australia, and only Hobbs and Hendren have made more first-class hundreds. But it was the manner in which most of them were made, even more than the runs themselves, for which Hammond is remembered.

HARVEY
Robert Neil b 1928-

Until his retirement in 1963, Neil Harvey was the outstanding batsman produced by Australia since World War II. A quick-footed left-hander, he was superbly equipped with strokes and possessed an ever-present urge to attack. He was also a fielder of the highest class, whether in the slips or moving like lightning in the covers—a not unexpected accomplishment of one who was also a successful baseball player.

One of the qualities that lifted

him above the other leading Australian batsmen of his time was his skill on bad pitches. This was especially apparent in England in the 1950s, and he was the most formidable adversary of the strong England bowling of those years. Harvey's playing career covered 17 years from 1946 to 1963, a long span for an Australian. However, he started unusually young. He was just 18 when he first played for Victoria—he was to move to New South Wales 12 years later in 1958—and he was only 19 when he went to England with Sir Donald Bradman's great 1948 side. Though he had played in the last two Test matches against India in

---

HAMMOND Walter Reginald

Teams: Gloucestershire and England

Test series		Tests	Runs	100s	Average	Wkts	Average
1927-28	in South Africa	5	321	—	40.12	15	26.60
1928	v West Indies	3	111	—	37.00	3	34.33
1928-29	in Australia	5	905	4	113.12	5	57.40
1929	v South Africa	4	352	2	58.66	1	95.00
1930	v Australia	5	306	1	34.00	5	60.40
1930-31	in South Africa	5	517	1	64.62	9	26.66
1931	v New Zealand	3	169	1	56.33	2	34.00
1932	v India	1	47	—	23.50	3	8.00
1932-33	in Australia	5	440	2	55.00	9	32.33
1932-33	in New Zealand	2	563	2	563.00	0	—
1933	v West Indies	3	74	—	24.66	0	—
1934	v Australia	5	162	—	20.25	5	72.80
1934-35	in West Indies	4	175	—	25.00	0	—
1935	v South Africa	5	389	—	64.83	6	24.33
1936	v India	2	389	2	194.50	1	94.00
1936-37	in Australia	5	468	1	58.50	12	25.08
1937	v New Zealand	3	204	1	51.00	4	25.25
1938	v Australia	4†	403	1	67.16	0	—
1938-39	in South Africa	5†	609	3	87.00	3	53.66
1939	v West Indies	3†	279	1	55.80	—	—
1946	v India	3†	119	—	39.66	0	—
1946-47	in Australia	4†	168	—	21.00	—	—
1946-47	in New Zealand	1†	79	—	79.00	—	—
Totals		**85**	**7,249**	**22**	**58.45**	**83**	**37.80**

Career runs: 50,551 *Average:* 56.10
Highest Test and career score: 336* v New Zealand, Auckland, 1932-33
Career wickets: 732 *Average:* 30.58
Best Test bowling: 5-36 v South Africa, Johannesburg, 1927-28
Best career bowling: 9-23, Gloucestershire v Worcestershire, Cheltenham, 1928

*Not out †Captain

Neil Harvey plays a typically aggressive on-drive. He was one of the best left-handed batsmen to emerge after World War II, and he forced his way into the great Australian Test side which toured England and won the Test series in 1948.

RIGHT Harvey in a rare moment of trouble as the ball comes on too fast for his attempted hook. FAR RIGHT A characteristically wristy shot through the covers from Harvey. He was himself a brilliant fielder at cover-point, and also an occasional keeper.

the previous home season and had made 153 in the last, at Melbourne, in just over four hours with scarcely a mistake, he was inevitably looked on by many people in England as a hope for the future who would probably not find a place in this strong team of established players.

He did not play in the first three Tests, but he did in the fourth, and he joined the select band of Australians who have made a hundred in their first Test against England. It was, moreover, a brilliantly fluent innings of 112 made in just over three hours. This was the historic Test in which Australia scored 404-3 to win on the last day, and the young Harvey was at the crease with Bradman when the winning run was scored.

For the next 15 years Harvey was the mainstay of Australian batting, scoring more runs in Test matches than any other Australian except Bradman (Chappell, later, also passed his total). In South Africa in 1949-50 he made 660 runs (average 132) in the Test matches, including four centuries, and broke all records for an Australian batsman in South Africa. It was here that his fine technique on bad pitches became evident, for in the third Test at Durban he played a remarkable innings of 151 not out on a crumbling pitch and won the match for Australia after they had been bowled out for 75 in the first innings and had been 59 for three in the second.

Three seasons later he scored 834 runs in the home series against South Africa, averaging 92.66. When he went to England in 1953 on the second of his four tours, he made 10 hundreds and scored over 2,000 runs. Only Bradman and McCabe had scored more than 2,000 runs in an English season previously.

In the next two series against England, in 1954-55 and 1956, his reputation continued to grow. He made 162 at Brisbane when Australia won their only victory against Len Hutton's team, and he played a masterly innings of 92 not out, exactly half the total, when Australia were going down to defeat before Tyson and Statham in the second Test. On the wet and often unpredictable pitches in England in 1956, his average of 19 may seem disastrous compared with the 90 of Peter May for England, but Australia had the worst of the pitches and were up against better bowling, and Harvey played two or three highly skilled innings in testing conditions.

He was less successful in South Africa in 1957-58 than on his first visit. But in 1958-59 he played a vital innings of 167 in a total of 308 which helped Australia to beat England in the second Test. And on his last visit to England, in 1961, he began with a hundred at Edgbaston in the first Test. In the second Test, at Lord's, he captained Australia for the only time, Richie Benaud being unable to play, and won a fine victory by five wickets. At Leeds, where Australia lost on a bad pitch, he was top scorer each time with 73 and 53.

Against Ted Dexter's England team in 1962-63, he was not at his best, and his 154 in the fourth Test, the last of his 21 Test hundreds, owed something to early dropped catches. However, he was still a force in Sheffield Shield cricket and made a characteristically vigorous 231 not out, the highest score of his career, in 5 hours for New South Wales against South Australia. At the end of the season, though, he announced his retirement, and in 1964 was awarded the MBE.

One of the most important parts of Harvey's make-up throughout his long career was the temperament that left him unruffled in the most unnerving situations. There is no stronger evidence of his flair for rising to the occasion than his record in his early days when, though lacking experience of the top class of cricket, he had a better record in it than he did in domestic cricket in Australia. Of his first 31 first-class hundreds, no less than 11 were in Test matches and only four were in the Sheffield Shield.

HARVEY Robert Neil

Teams: Victoria, New South Wales, and Australia

Test series		Tests	Runs	100s	Average
1947-48	v India	2	166	1	83.00
1948	in England	2	133	1	66.50
1949-50	in South Africa	5	660	4	132.00
1950-51	v England	5	362	—	40.22
1951-52	v West Indies	5	261	—	26.10
1952-53	v South Africa	5	834	4	92.66
1953	in England	5	346	1	34.60
1954-55	v England	5	354	1	44.25
1954-55	in West Indies	5	650	3	108.33
1956	in England	5	197	—	19.70
1956-57	in Pakistan	1	6	—	3.00
1956-57	in India	3	253	1	63.25
1957-58	in South Africa	4	131	—	21.83
1958-59	v England	5	291	1	48.50
1959-60	in Pakistan	3	273	—	54.60
1959-60	in India	5	356	2	50.85
1960-61	v West Indies	4	143	—	17.87
1961	in England	5†	338	1	42.25
1962-63	v England	5	395	1	39.50
Totals		79	6,149	21	48.41

Career runs: 21,699 *Average:* 50.93
Highest Test score: 205 v South Africa, Melbourne, 1952-53
Highest career score: 231*, New South Wales v South Australia, Sydney, 1962-63

*Not out †Captain in one Test

HOBBS
Sir John Berry
b 1882-d 1963

A complete batsman, classical in method, calm in temperament, and supremely efficient in execution, Jack Hobbs was the greatest batsman of his generation. He was known to his friends until his death as 'the Master', and roughly from the retirement of W. G. Grace to the hey-day of Don Bradman he was without doubt the world's most accomplished batsman. He made more hundreds —197—in first-class cricket than any other batsman, and it is a tribute to his skill that he made 98 of them after he reached 40, when most batsmen, certainly today, would have been considered past

their best—and ready to retire.

Hobbs went to Surrey and the Oval from Cambridge, and so followed in the path of Tom Hayward who, from 1905 until World War I, was to be his opening partner for Surrey and a strong influence upon him. He had to qualify by residence, but made an immediate impact when he began to play for the county in 1905. He was already 22, by which age both Grace and Bradman in their respective eras were breaking records.

'W. G.' did in fact captain the Gentlemen of England in the first match Hobbs played for Surrey and in which he made 88. Only two weeks later, in his first championship match, against Essex, he scored 155 and was given his county cap.

Hobbs' career for Surrey was to

last for 30 historic years until 1934, and it was only four years before his retirement that he ceased to play for England. And even after his death in 1963, many of his records stood. As well as the 197 centuries, his aggregate of 61,237 runs was still the highest ever made, and his 316 not out against Middlesex in 1926 was the highest innings ever played at Lord's. His 266 not out at Scarborough in 1925 was the highest in the long history of the Gentlemen and Players match, and no one equalled his 16 centuries in the fixture.

During his career, he had four opening partners with whom he was especially successful—Hayward and Andy Sandham for Surrey, and Wilfred Rhodes and Herbert Sutcliffe for England. His 352 with Hayward against Warwickshire at the Oval in 1909 was

their highest partnership together, and in 1907 they had shared in no less than four opening stands of over 100 within a week against Cambridge University and Middlesex, a feat without parallel.

The best remembered stand between Hobbs and Rhodes was their 323 at Melbourne against Australia in 1911-12, which, in the mid-1980s, was still the highest ever made for the first wicket for England against Australia.

After World War I, Sandham succeeded Hayward, and with him Hobbs made 428 against Oxford University at the Oval in 1926. Altogether they shared in 63 stands of over 100. But it is probably Hobbs' opening partnerships with the Yorkshireman Herbert Sutcliffe that are best remembered. In 1924-25 they had three consecutive opening stands in Test matches of 157, 110, and 283. Seven times they exceeded 200 together, and on 26 occasions (15 in Test matches) they passed 100.

The partnership of Hobbs and Sutcliffe was remarkable for their understanding of each other's running and their joint mastery of difficult pitches, such as that at the Oval in 1926 when England won back the Ashes last held before the war. At the start of the second innings they had to bat on a drying pitch, but they made 172 together, Hobbs, 100, coming through the worst of the difficulties and steering England to ultimate victory. In Melbourne three years later, another superb stand of 105 turned a possible defeat into victory in equally difficult conditions.

Hobbs' method had no outstanding idiosyncrasy. It was simple, graceful, and correct, based on a fine eye, a supreme judgement of length, the gift of timing, and an ability always to be in the right position. Like all the great players he was very effective off the back foot, and without appearing to bludgeon the bowler, he would dictate to him and maintain a steady flow of scoring strokes. Slim and of medium height, he was also a brilliant fielder in the covers and in his early days a useful swing bowler. In South Africa in 1909-10 he opened the bowling in three Tests.

Those who saw Hobbs on either side of World War I have said that maturity, while increasing his command, had taken away a little of the dashing side of his batting. But in the 1920s he stood supreme on all pitches and against all types

LEFT Hobbs was known as 'The Master', and was one of the most popular of players, not only for his skill but also for his gentlemanliness and courtesy. Although nobody before or since has scored more first-class runs, Hobbs probably could have scored more. He was not interested in records and frequently got himself out after scoring 100.

ABOVE Hobbs scores the 100th run of his 126th century at Taunton in 1925 to equal the record of W. G. Grace.

BELOW Hobbs, perfectly balanced, sweeps high to leg. Artistry was the keynote of his style.

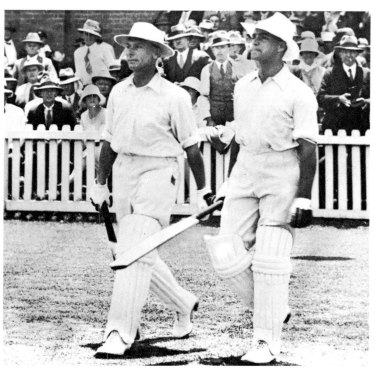

ABOVE Hobbs (left) with his famous opening partner Herbert Sutcliffe, frequently heroes for England.

BELOW The first picture taken of Hobbs bowling, against Oxford University in 1920. He was a useful medium-pacer.

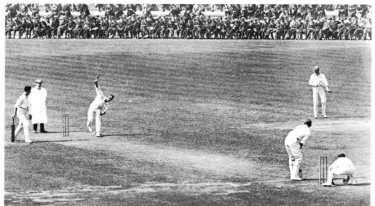

of bowling, and when he was taken ill with appendicitis during the 1921 series against Australia, it was akin to a national disaster. He was amazingly consistent, never appearing to be out of form. In 1923 he passed 100 hundreds and advanced on W.G.'s record 126 amid a fervour of excitement. Each time he failed to make a hundred, he was said to have 'failed again'. He reached 125 with 12 hundreds in the early part of 1925, and was in tremendous form even for him, but the tension built up, and from July 25th to August 15th he and the cricket public waited. Eventually at Taunton against Somerset the 126th 100 was made, and in the second innings the 127th. He went on to make 16 in the season, a record that stood until Denis Compton beat it in 1947.

He went to Australia on five MCC tours and to South Africa twice, before World War I. Just as he had overlapped the Grace era in

his youth, so he overlapped the Bradman era in 1930 when he played in his last series, at the age of 47. He started well with 78 and 74 in the first Test, which England won by 93 runs, but did not pass 50 again. The last of his 61 Tests was the one at the Oval in which England made 405 in the first innings, Hobbs 47, and were beaten eventually by an innings.

In his last season, 1934, he played in only a few matches. He was in his 52nd year and entitled to treat gently what had been a sound but never a robust physique. The fluency of the strokes might have faded a little but the technique was still superb, and when asked by George Duckworth to play in his benefit match at Old Trafford, he went out and scored 116 and 51 not out. With Sandham once again, he put on 184. Lancashire were champions that year, and Hobbs' century was the only one scored against them in the championship.

HOBBS John Berry

Teams: Surrey and England

Test series		Tests	Runs	100s	Average
1907-08	v Australia	4	302	–	43.14
1909	v Australia	3	132	–	26.40
1909-10	in South Africa	5	539	1	67.37
1911-12	in Australia	5	662	3	82.75
1912	v Australia	3	224	1	56.00
1912	v South Africa	3	163	–	40.75
1913-14	in South Africa	5	443	–	63.28
1920-21	in Australia	5	505	2	50.50
1921	v Australia	1	–	–	–
1924	v South Africa	4	355	1	71.00
1924-25	in Australia	5	573	3	63.66
1926	v Australia	5	486	2	81.00
1928	v West Indies	2	212	1	106.00
1928-29	in Australia	5	451	1	50.11
1929	v South Africa	1	62	–	31.00
1930	v Australia	5	301	–	33.44
Totals		**61**	**5,410**	**15**	**56.94**

Career runs: 61,237 *Average:* 50.65
Highest Test score: 211 v South Africa, Lord's, 1924
Highest career score: 316*, Surrey v Middlesex, Lord's, 1926

*Not out
Note: Hobbs' career figures are in dispute. According to the Association of Cricket Statisticians, he scored 61,760 runs (average 50.66) and made 199 centuries, not 197 as stated in the text.

HOLDING
Michael Anthony b 1954-

Michael Holding running up to bowl is one of the most infuriating or most beautiful sights in cricket, according to taste. Infuriating because he has just about the longest run in modern cricket, which coupled with the languid air he affects between deliveries makes an over by him last for at least five minutes. He is one of the worst offenders in the appalling over rate bowled by the West Indians in the late 1970s and 1980s.

His run-up is, however, also a demonstration of grace and athleticism. Tall and slim, Holding, who was a track athlete, approaches the wicket with a feline lissomness that makes him appear to be barely touching the ground, and indeed, at least one umpire has said that he cannot hear him coming. If he releases the ball with a perfect, smooth action at one end of the pitch, the effect at the other end is one of destruction and mayhem in more senses than one.

Holding was born in 1954 at Half Way Tree, Kingston, Jamaica, and he was 19 years old when he made his first-class debut, for Jamaica against Guyana in the Shell Shield.

In 1975-76 he made his Test debut in Australia, but was unimpressive in a series Australia won 5-1. He was much more dangerous back home in the West Indies when India visited, particularly after India had scored 406 for 4 in the fourth innings of the third Test to win by six wickets. In the fourth and final Test Holding, supported by the other quick bowlers, let loose a barrage of bouncers at the Indian batsmen. Three of them were badly injured in the first innings and could take no further part in the match, Gaekwad being sent to hospital after being struck on the ear and Viswanath having his finger broken, both from Holding deliveries. Bedi declared with only six wickets down as a protest, and West Indies duly won when five players were declared 'absent hurt' in the Indian second innings. India were beaten while losing only 11 wickets in the match, seven to Holding.

There was more intimidation in England in 1976 at Old Trafford. England recalled the 45-year-old Brian Close as opener, and he and Edrich were subjected to a terrifying attack of short-pitched bowling, again led by Holding. In the fifth Test at the Oval Holding bowled beautifully on a pitch unhelpful to pace. In a high-scoring match, with a double-century on each side, England used nine bowlers and West Indies eight. Holding, with 8 for 92 and 6 for 57 took exactly half the wickets which fell. He was the first West Indian to take more than 12 wickets in a Test match. He headed both the tourists' Test and tour averages: 28 at 12.71 and 55 at 14.38 respectively.

Holding was a natural for World Series Cricket and its aggressive playing and selling policy, and his was among the four West Indian names in the first list to be announced by Kerry Packer.

Back in Test cricket in Australia and New Zealand in 1979-80, he was less successful than before. He was also at the centre of the display of bad sportsmanship shown by the West Indies in New Zealand, when they considered terminating the tour. Having grown used to Packer razzmatazz and money, the West Indians were taken aback to find themselves treated as ordinary cricketers, and surprised to find that the New Zealanders were not willing to be push-overs before the cricketing 'elite'. When umpiring decisions began to go against them they perpetrated some hooligan-like behaviour. In the first Test, when Holding was refused an appeal for caught behind, he went down to the batsman's end and kicked the stumps from the ground.

Holding recovered some of his form against England in 1980 and was back to something like his best when England returned to the West Indies in 1980-81. One over bowled to Botham was described by Botham as the over he wanted to forget. Dropped, nearly killed, then caught behind from one he did not see, Botham described it as one of the best overs he ever faced.

In 1981 Holding joined Lancashire, but played in only seven matches. Later, in 1982-83 he played seven matches for Tasmania. In 1983 he joined Derbyshire, but played in only six matches.

In 1981-82 Holding destroyed Australia. Two years later he collected 30 wickets in a series in India. In England, in 1984, he played in four of the Tests in the series West Indies won 5-0. In the 1980s West Indies frequently played four fast bowlers, and Holding did not always open the attack. He also experimented with a shorter run. Whenever he comes on, however, and from whatever length run, he remains an awe-inspiring sight as he runs in to bowl.

OPPOSITE Dust flies as Holding bowls at the Oval in 1976 against England, when he took 14 wickets in the match.
BELOW Holding claims the wicket of Brian Rose, caught behind by David Murray at Trinidad in 1980-81.

HOLDING Michael Anthony			
Teams: Jamaica, Lancashire, Derbyshire, Tasmania and West Indies			
Test series	Tests	Wkts	Average
1975-76 in Australia	5	10	53.40
1975-76 v India	4	19	19.89
1976 in England	4	28	12.71
1979-80 in Australia	3	14	22.78
1979-80 in New Zealand	3	7	33.77
1980 in England	5	20	31.60
1980-81 v England	4	17	18.52
1981-82 in Australia	3	24	14.33
1982-83 v India	5	12	41.83
1983-84 in India	6	30	22.10
1983-84 v Australia	3	13	18.84
1984 in England	4	15	21.53
1984-85 in Australia	3	15	16.60
1984-85 in New Zealand	3	9	24.22
Totals	55	233	23.23

Test runs: 786 *Average:* 12.88
Career wickets: 527 *Average:* 23.41
Best Test and career bowling: 8-92 v England, Oval, 1976

HUTTON
Sir Leonard b 1916-

Len Hutton won recognition as one of the greatest batsmen in cricket history through many prodigious feats, one of the earliest being his 364 in the Oval Test of 1938. Made when he was only 22, it was the longest as well as the highest Test innings at that time and it remains the highest innings played in the long England v Australia series. Yet probably his most remarkable feat was in resuming his career for Yorkshire and England with no loss of skill after World War II when, as a result of an accident in an Army gymnasium, his left arm was shorter and less strong than his right.

Hutton is also remembered as the first professional in modern times to captain England, which he did with much success for three years from 1952. He was captain when England regained the Ashes in 1953 and when they retained them on the triumphant tour of 1954-55 by beating Australia 3-1. A profound thinker on the game, he liked to be captain and to be able to put his theories into practice. But the off-the-field commitments of an England captain took more out of this quiet, reserved man and dedicated professional than was fully realized at the time. And at the height of his success as a Test captain—he had never been appointed captain of Yorkshire —he dropped out of first-class cricket in 1955, partly because he was not at his fittest but mostly because he had had enough. He was still only 38 and though on his recent tour of Australia he had not made as many runs as usual, there was no reason to think that his powers were in decline.

However, an interrupted season for Yorkshire in 1955 was his last, and the next year he was knighted for his services to cricket. Since then, he has lived away from his native Yorkshire, near London, absorbed in business interests, though his elder son, Richard, followed him into the Yorkshire and England sides, as an all-rounder.

Len Hutton's influence on the English cricket of his time was often described as dour and defensive. But though he was a tough, practical captain against Australia, the patience he showed in his batting often tended to obscure its great quality. When he really unloosed his superb strokes, it was a sight not to be forgotten, and his 37 in 24 minutes one morning in a Sydney Test is regarded as a great innings in cameo form.

But it was as a technician that he was pre-eminent. No sensible critic would have tried to compare him with his great contemporary Denis Compton, for they were entirely different in approach and

execution. But he was a marvellously correct batsman, stylish if not spectacular, and always in the right position, even though he seldom used his feet to move out to the pitch of the ball. Colin Cowdrey, whose first Test matches were played under Hutton's leadership, once said that he was the most complete batsman he had ever seen.

Hutton's early years with the Yorkshire second XI left little doubt that another England batsman had been found, though few perhaps guessed that in a country where batsmen mature late his impact would be so swift. Born in Pudsey, the home of Herbert Sutcliffe, he came, at an early age, under the eye of another great Yorkshireman, George Hirst, the county coach. He was also a useful leg-break bowler then, and throughout his career he was a competent fielder, mostly near the bat.

He played in his first first-class match for Yorkshire at Cambridge in 1934 and failed to score, as he was to do in his first Test only three years later. Of medium height, he was not strongly built, and in his first two seasons Yorkshire used him sparingly, but awarded him his county cap in the third when he made 1,000 runs for the first time. In later years, he made more than 2,000 runs in a season 10 times and in 1949 scored 3,429 runs, a seasonal aggregate bettered only by Denis Compton, Bill Edrich, and Tom Hayward.

By 1937 Hutton was scoring 10 centuries in the season, but in his first Test against New Zealand that year he made 0 and 1. In his second though he made the first of 19 Test hundreds.

He began the 1938 series against Australia with another 100 and an opening stand of 219 with Charles Barnett. He finished it with his record-breaking 364 made in 13 hours 20 minutes. In the last season before the war, he made 196 against West Indies at Lord's and, in the last pre-war Test, 73 and 165 not out at the Oval. He was the young master with a magnificent future to come.

The injury to his arm occurred early in the war, and subsequently he had three seasons of local and services cricket in which to overcome his disability before first-class cricket began again in 1946. In 1945 he opened in services matches with Cyril Washbrook, with whom he was to share a famous Test partnership, and with Compton and Bill Edrich in their prime there was apparently no shortage of English batting in the post-war years. But Compton was soon affected by his knee injury

RIGHT Hutton hitting the ball high to leg at the Oval against South Africa in 1947. Despite an injury during the war which led to his left arm being shortened, he became the first professional to captain England.

and Australia had formidable bowling sides in those years. Therefore many of Hutton's most important innings before the advent of May and Cowdrey were played sustaining an uncertain England batting side. Once, at Lord's in 1948, he batted so unimpressively that he was dropped for the next Test; a strange decision in retrospect, for he played Lindwall and Miller at their fastest supremely well. This was especially so in 1950-51 when he averaged 88.83, 50 more than the next batsman.

In South Africa in 1948-49 he batted with Washbrook all through a day's play in Johannesburg and they scored 359 for the first wicket. In 1951 he made his 100th hundred, at the Oval against Surrey, and the next year he captained England against India.

At Lord's in 1953, he made 145

HUTTON Sir Leonard

Teams: Yorkshire and England

Test series		Tests	Runs	100s	Average
1937	v New Zealand	3	129	1	25.40
1938	v Australia	3	473	2	118.25
1938-39	in South Africa	4	265	—	44.16
1939	v West Indies	3	480	2	96.00
1946	v India	3	123	—	30.75
1946-47	in Australia	5	417	1	52.12
1947	v South Africa	5	344	1	43.00
1947-48	in West Indies	2	171	—	42.75
1948	v Australia	4	342	—	42.75
1948-59	in South Africa	5	577	2	64.11
1949	v New Zealand	4	469	2	78.16
1950	v West Indies	3	333	1	66.60
1950-51	in Australia	5	533	1	88.83
1950-51	in New Zealand	2	114	—	38.00
1951	v South Africa	5	378	1	54.00
1952	v India	4*	399	2	79.80
1953	v Australia	5*	443	1	55.37
1953-54	in West Indies	5*	677	2	96.71
1954	v Pakistan	2*	19	—	6.33
1954-55	in Australia	5*	220	—	24.44
1954-55	in New Zealand	2*	67	—	22.33
Totals		79	6,971	19	56.67

Career runs: 40,140 *Average:* 55.51
Highest Test and career score: 364, England v Australia, Oval, 1938

*Captain

against Australia and that winter became the first professional to take an MCC side overseas. In the West Indies, England lost the first two Tests but won the third and fifth in which the captain made 169 and 205 respectively. He missed part of the first series against Pakistan in 1954, returning to lead England in the Test they lost at the Oval. But his mind was on the tour of Australia, and though he averaged only 24 in the 1954-55 series, he led England shrewdly and effectively to one of their most decisive victories against Australia.

For Hutton it was the fulfillment of burning ambition to redress the lack of success on his two previous tours. As a batsman his only real innings of the series came appropriately enough in the Fourth Test, which England won to retain The Ashes.

In reply to Australia's score in the first innings of 323, Hutton

carefully showed the way with a painstaking 80. It took four and a half hours and it was his only fifty of the series. But it guided England to a first innings lead after which came Tyson and Statham at their best and eventual victory.

His form in the tour matches was as impeccable as ever—he made over a thousand runs in Australia—but after the two Tests against New Zealand on the way back to England, he left international cricket, and he announced his retirement from the game after injuries had restricted his appearances for Yorkshire in 1955. England did not lose a Test series under his command—a record which pays tribute to his leadership.

After retiring he continued to be involved in the game from the Press box and became a Test selector, his deep appreciation of the game finding a new and most successful outlet.

ABOVE LEFT Hutton plays the ball to leg during his record-breaking 364 in the Oval Test of 1938. The innings lasted 13 hours and 20 minutes, the longest then played in a Test.
LEFT Bradman congratulating Hutton when Hutton had passed Bradman's existing record Test score, 334 made at Headingley in 1930. Joe Hardstaff is the other batsman, and Leslie O'B. Fleetwood-Smith is the bowler at the far end. His analysis in the England innings was 1 for 298, another record.
RIGHT Lindsay Hassett shakes hands with Hutton after England had regained the Ashes at the Oval in 1953.

ILLINGWORTH
Raymond b 1932-

When Yorkshire released Ray Illingworth in 1968, it looked very much as though a promising, but never fulfilled, career was about to go into decline, and his position in international cricket was no brighter. Although having played 30 times for England over 11 seasons he had never succeeded in becoming established.

But on joining Leicestershire as their captain, he achieved a remarkable renaissance that embraced the captaincy of his country and a doubling of the length of his international career.

Within months of his move, injury to Colin Cowdrey gave Illingworth the England captaincy. When his predecessor was fit, Illingworth remained first choice and provided perfect justification when his side regained the Ashes in 1970-71 and retained them in 1972. He captained England 31 times until Mike Denness was chosen to succeed him after England had been beaten in 1973 by West Indies—although he had chosen to miss the 1972-73 series in India and Pakistan.

Illingworth epitomized the philosophy of the professional. A remarkably shrewd leader, he earned the unyielding respect of his team, although at times his single-mindedness forfeited good will. At Sydney in 1970-71, he led his side from the field in protest against some loutishness in the crowd.

In characteristic Yorkshire style he symbolized keen competition.

He was a creator of runs rather than a trail-blazer and he would have been even more productive if he had batted higher in the order. He began his bowling career as a medium-pacer, before settling into a vein of genuine off-spin with grudging accuracy. By the end of his career he had scored more than 24,000 first-class runs and taken more than 2,000 wickets—testimony enough to the totality of his all-round talents.

But even more than this, his successful, practical brand of captaincy set him apart. With Leicestershire he produced results which must have made every Yorkshire official wince. Despite the orthodoxy of his own game, he made an enormous impact, particularly tactically, on one-day cricket. He led Leicestershire to wins in the Benson & Hedges Cup in 1972 and 1975 and they were beaten finalists in 1974. That year they also became champions of the John Player League. But Illingworth's greatest triumph in county cricket came a year later when he led Leicestershire to their first County Championship.

Illingworth was awarded the CBE in 1973. In 1979 he retired from first-class cricket and returned to Yorkshire as manager. In 1982, in the midst of the troubles which beset the county club, he took over as captain, and continued playing to the 1983 season, when he retired again.

ABOVE RIGHT Illingworth the all-rounder as a useful batsman. RIGHT His more usual role as off-spinner. He was also one of England's most successful captains, winning the Ashes.

ILLINGWORTH Raymond

Teams: Yorkshire, Leicestershire and England

Test series		Tests	Runs	100s	Average	Wkts	Average
1958	v New Zealand	1	3	—	—	3	19.66
1959	v India	2	118	—	59.00	4	31.00
1959-60	in West Indies	5	92	—	13.14	4	95.75
1960	v South Africa	4	81	—	20.25	6	24.33
1961	v Australia	2	28	—	9.33	3	42.00
1962	v Pakistan	1	2	—	—	1	81.00
1962-63	in Australia	2	57	—	19.00	1	131.00
1962-63	in New Zealand	3	68	—	22.66	5	14.60
1965	v New Zealand	1	—	—	—	4	17.50
1966	v West Indies	2	7	—	2.33	4	41.25
1967	v India	3	28	—	9.33	20	13.30
1967	v Pakistan	1	13	—	6.50	3	19.33
1968	v Australia	3	51	—	12.75	13	22.39
1969	v West Indies†	3	163	1	40.75	5	43.60
1969	v New Zealand†	3	90	—	22.50	10	15.40
1970-71	in Australia†	6	333	—	37.00	10	34.90
1970-71	in New Zealand†	2	58	—	19.33	—	—
1971	v Pakistan†	3	67	—	16.75	6	27.00
1971	v India†	3	175	1	35.00	7	28.85
1972	v Australia†	5	194	—	32.33	7	28.14
1973	v New Zealand†	3	101	—	20.20	—	—
1973	v West Indies†	3	107	—	21.40	6	51.83
Totals		61	1,836	2	23.24	122	31.20

Career runs: 24,134 *Average:* 28.06
Highest Test score: 113 v West Indies, Lord's, 1969
Highest career score: 162, Yorkshire v Indians, Sheffield, 1959
Career wickets: 2,072 *Average:* 20.28
Best Test bowling: 6-29 v India, Lord's, 1967
Best career bowling: 9-42, Yorkshire v Worcestershire, Worcester, 1957

†Captain

IMRAN KHAN
Niazi b 1952-

Imran Khan, from a privileged background in Lahore, found cricket boring as a child. Yet his family was so prolific in producing cricketers, that had he been a race-horse he would be said to have a Derby-winning pedigree. No fewer than eight first cousins played first-class cricket, and two of them, Majid Khan and Javed Burki, captained Pakistan. Imran eventually became the third member of the family to captain his country.

Developing his cricket as a teen-ager, he made his first-class debut for Lahore as a medium-fast bowler and opening batsman in 1969, aged 16½. He was still at school. The chairman of selectors was his uncle, the captain his cousin. It was not an impressive debut, but he was carefully nursed and impressed the selectors enough to get a place on the tour to England in 1971. He played in the first Test at Edgbaston, still only 18½, and still at school. It was the match in which Pakistan scored 608 for 7 declared: Imran was run out for 5. He bowled 28 overs for only 55 runs, but did not get a wicket, and did not play in the remaining Tests.

However, before this Test he had agreed terms to play for Worcestershire, and made his debut for them in 1971. He continued his studies at Worcester Royal Grammar School and later Oxford University, for whom he won blues in 1973 to 1975. He joined the Pakistan tourists in 1974 after coming down from Oxford and played in three Tests, again very disappointingly. Back in Pakistan in 1975-76 he played for Pakistan International Airways, remaining with that side till 1980-81.

At the end of 1976 he left Worcestershire in some acrimony. He was bored with life in the county—the county thought this insufficient grounds for leaving and tried to block his registration for another county, at first successfully. Sussex employed a lawyer to argue and win the case for Imran to join them towards the end of the 1977 season.

In 1976-77 Imran was given his third chance to establish a Test place when picked to play against New Zealand. Before the second Test there was a revolt of players against the Board of Cricket Control over selectorial muddles and pay. When a new team was picked for the forthcoming tour of Australia and West Indies there was a national outcry. Eventually the players won the day.

Imran's form improved considerably on the tours of Australia and West Indies, and he gained a yard or so of pace to become a genuine fast bowler. He was a natural selection for the Rest of the World side in Kerry

Packer's WSC set-up. He played well, but his brushes with authority and his Packer venture earned him for a while an unjustified reputation as a trouble-maker and 'mercenary'.

He played regularly for Pakistan in 1981-82, becoming his country's leading Test wicket-taker, overtaking Fazal Mahmoud. But 1981-82 brought more internal strife in Pakistan cricket, with the result that Imran, together with seven other leading players, was dropped from the first two Tests against Sri Lanka. Finally, the argument was resolved, and Imran in the third Test achieved his best bowling performance of 8 for 58.

After the 'troubles', Pakistan sought a new captain for the tour to England in 1982. Imran, partly because the objectors to him were fewest, was chosen, and captaincy seemed to inspire him. From then on he has been one of cricket's greatest all-rounders.

Pakistan narrowly lost that series 2-1, although Imran was voted Man of the Series. Against Australia in 1982-83 he won 3-0. He then enjoyed a magnificent series against India, winning 3-0,

Imran Khan leaps into his delivery stride for Pakistan against Australia in 1981-82.

averaging over 60 with the bat and taking 40 wickets at less than 14 each. At Faisalabad, he became the second player (after Botham) to score a century and take ten wickets in a Test. In this season of 1982-83, Imran scored 717 Test runs (av. 65.18) and took 88 wickets (av. 14.03). He experi-

enced a shin injury the following season which prevented him playing in the series against India and England, although on the tour to Australia he played in the final two Tests as captain and batsman only, being unable to bowl—a great compliment to a man who is one of the best fast bowlers in the world.

IMRAN KHAN Niazi

Teams: Lahore, Worcestershire, Oxford University, PIA, Sussex, and Pakistan

Test series		Tests	Runs	100s	Average	Wkts	Average
1971	in England	1	5	—	5.00	0	—
1974	in England	3	92	—	18.40	5	51.60
1976-77	v New Zealand	3	105	—	35.00	14	30.07
1976-77	in Australia	3	86	—	17.20	18	28.83
1976-77	in West Indies	5	215	—	21.50	25	31.60
1978-79	v India	3	104	—	52.00	14	32.50
1978-79	in New Zealand	2	63	—	31.50	10	25.50
1978-79	in Australia	2	90	—	22.50	7	40.71
1979-80	in India	5	154	—	22.00	19	19.21
1979-80	v Australia	2	65	—	32.50	6	24.00
1980-81	v West Indies	4	204	1	29.14	10	23.60
1981-82	in Australia	3	108	—	26.00	16	19.50
1981-82	v Sri Lanka	1	39	—	39.00	14	8.28
1982	in England†	3	212	—	53.00	21	18.53
1982-83	v Australia†	3	64	—	64.00	13	13.15
1982-83	v India†	6	247	1	61.75	40	13.95
1983-84	in Australia†	2	170	—	56.66	—	—
Totals		51	2,023	2	31.12	232	22.91

Career runs: 14,464 *Average:* 35.80
Highest Test score: 123 v West Indies, Lahore, 1980-81
Highest career score: 170, Oxford University v Northants, Oxford, 1974
Career wickets: 1,074 *Average:* 21.95
Best Test and career bowling: 8-58, Pakistan v Sri Lanka, Faisalabad, 1981-82

†Captain

KALLICHARRAN
Alvin Isaac b 1949-

Alvin Kallicharran typifies the quality of West Indian batsmanship. Hawk-eyed, quick on his feet and a breathtaking stroke maker, the diminutive man from Berbice in Guyana has made an enormous impact on Test cricket.

The most startling exhibition of his class came in his demolition of Dennis Lillee in the World Cup preliminary match at The Oval when he repeatedly and unrelentingly hoisted Australia's paceman to the leg-side boundary. But with consistent and equally entertaining batsmanship he has shown his pedigree in the day-to-day demands of county cricket as well as in the international arena.

His entry into Test cricket was spectacular—two thrilling centuries in his first two matches against New Zealand, in 1971-72, just before he added his talents to Warwickshire's mighty batting line-up. In his next Test series, against Australia, his 91 at Port-of-Spain almost brought a spectacular West Indian victory.

His liking for that particular ground brought him a remarkable 158 against England after he had survived the controversial 'run-out' attempt by Tony Greig. By his 23rd Test he had reached centuries against all Test playing countries. Probably his best innings came in India in 1974-75. At Bangalore on a viciously turning wicket, his left-

handed technique continually withstood the sharply turning off-spin of Venkataraghavan; he was last out for 124, including 64 of the last 77 scored by the West Indies as wickets tumbled around him. After 35 Tests his consistent run-getting had brought him an average of over 50.

Against Pakistan he had a quiet series, his best score being a laboured 72 at Georgetown, but he became the centre of attention in July 1977 when, having been among the many West Indian Packer signatories, he withdrew, wishing to preserve his career with Warwickshire, Guyana and West Indies.

In the following season he returned to the headlines, not only for his 127 in the opening Test against Australia, in Trinidad (his ninth Test century), but for his appointment as West Indies captain when Clive Lloyd resigned before the third Test in protest at the non-selection of two Packer players.

Under his leadership, West Indies lost by three wickets at Georgetown, but he made 92 in the next Test, which was easily won, and chalked up an unusual record in becoming the first batsman to make seven scores in the nineties.

In the final Test he made another hundred, a model innings in that the first fifty was made with

the utmost care in 2½ hours, and the balance at a much more commanding rate. It undoubtedly saved his side, for they were still struggling with nine wickets down when the notorious crowd revolt six overs from the end caused an abandonment which saved West Indies from defeat.

Kallicharran, having lost the West Indian captaincy on Lloyd's return from World Series Cricket, had two poor series against Eng-

Kallicharran hoisting Lillee to the boundary in his famous World Cup innings.

land and Pakistan and was dropped, whereupon he accepted an offer from Transvaal to become the first West Indian to play in the Currie Cup. He was immediately successful, but playing in South Africa earned him a life ban from Test matches by the West Indies.

This merely inspired Kalli to brilliance for Warwickshire, and in 1982 he was the only batsman to pass 2,000 runs and become one of Wisden's Cricketers of the Year.

He remains one of the most consistent batsmen in county cricket, and will score many more runs wherever he plays.

KALLICHARRAN Alvin Isaac

Teams: Guyana, Warwickshire, Queensland, Transvaal, and West Indies

Test series	Tests	Runs	100s	Average
1971-72 v New Zealand	2	219	2	109.50
1972-73 v Australia	5	294	—	36.75
1973 in England	3	212	—	42.40
1973-74 v England	5	397	2	56.71
1974-75 in India	5	454	1	56.75
1974-75 in Pakistan	2	251	1	125.50
1975-76 in Australia	6	421	1	38.27
1975-76 v India	4	237	1	47.40
1976 in England	3	180	—	36.00
1976-77 v Pakistan	5	258	—	32.25
1977-78 v Australia‡	5	408	2	51.00
1978-79 in India†	6	538	1	59.77
1979-80 in Australia	3	202	1	50.50
1979-80 in New Zealand	3	146	—	24.33
1980 in England	5	102	—	17.00
1980-81 in Pakistan	4	80	—	16.00
Totals	66	4,399	12	44.43

Career runs: 29,771 *Average:* 44.97
Highest Test score: 187 v India, Bombay, 1978-79
Highest career score: 243* v Glamorgan, Edgbaston, 1983

*Not out †Captain ‡Captain in 3 Tests   Career figures correct to end of 1985 season

KAPIL DEV
Ramlal Nikhanj b 1959-

In an era of record-breaking all-rounders, Kapil Dev has been at the forefront, following hard behind Ian Botham in the achievement of 2,000 Test runs and 200 wickets. He has been invaluable to India, who without him would hardly at times have had a Test-class opening bowler.

Kapil Dev has many similarities to Botham, in that neither are out-and-out fast bowlers yet both have frequently opened the bowling for their countries, neither is a rustic slogger yet nobody hits the ball harder or scores faster, both are attacking players who seem to make things happen on the field, neither has escaped controversy over his methods and effectiveness, and both are larger-than-life charismatic figures. Botham, however, in the middle 1980s has affected long streaky blond hair and the demeanour of a film star, while Kapil Dev is very dark and prefers a military bearing.

Kapil Dev was born in Chandigarh, India, in 1959. His parents moved there from near Rawalpindi on Partition, otherwise Kapil Dev would be a Pakistan player. The family business is building and timber contracting, and like Imran Khan, the great Pakistani all-rounder, Kapil comes from a comfortable background and does not play cricket from necessity. Chandigarh is the capital of both Punjab and Haryana, and Kapil, a Punjabi, made his first-class debut for Haryana in 1975-76. It was against Punjab, and he took 6 for 39 in the first innings.

Two years later he made his Test debut against Pakistan. It was not a successful series either for him or India, but both did better later in the season back in India against the West Indies. India won the series, and Kapil Dev did very well with the bat, hitting 126 not out at Delhi. Typically it took only 124 balls, and he reached his century with a six.

He was soon performing excellently with the ball, and had a brilliant season in 1979-80. He took 28 wickets against Australia and 32 against Pakistan, including 4 for 90 and 7 for 56 at Madras. As he also scored 84 he just failed to be the first to score a century and take 10 wickets in a match, a feat Botham performed exactly one month later. However in the calendar year of 1979 he took 74 Test wickets, a record, although such are the demands on Test players nowadays that he actually played 17 Tests.

In the sixth Test against Pakistan he took his 100th Test wicket when claiming Taslim Arif, in the record time of 1 year 105 days (beating Botham's record). At 21 years 25 days he was the youngest bowler to reach this target (beating Graham Mckenzie's record). Two

days later, he reached 1,000 Test runs, again being the youngest (beating Javed Miandad). Naturally he was the youngest player ever to achieve the 1,000 runs/100 wickets double in Tests.

He slowed down after this, being disappointing in 1980-81 in Australia and New Zealand. In 1981 he joined Northamptonshire, playing only three Championship matches that year. In the winter he regained a little Test form with 22 wickets against the English tourists and 318 runs, including 116 off 84 balls at Kanpur, his second Test century.

In 1982-83 Kapil Dev succeeded Gavaskar as captain of India, and in the first Test at Kingston scored his 2,000th Test run. In the second Test, at Port-of-Spain, he took his 200th Test wicket, the youngest player to do so. He was the fourth player to complete the 'double double' in Tests, after Benaud, Sobers and Botham. Kapil Dev was the youngest at 24 years 67 days, although he had played in 50 Tests already, while Botham reached the milestone in 42 Tests. To celebrate his achievement, he made 100 not out in the second innings (95 balls, 3 sixes, 13 fours).

Then came one of the most surprising of India's successes—the World Cup victory in 1983. On the way Kapil Dev played an outrageous innings against Zimbabwe at Tunbridge Wells, going in at 9 for 4, which soon became 17 for 5. In three hours he hoisted India to 266 for 8, smashing 6 sixes and 17 fours in 175 not out, a World Cup record. If it is ever beaten it is safe to say that it will not be by a batsman coming in at number six.

India beat Australia, England and, in the final, West Indies, to record their deserved victory, and captain Kapil was a hero.

He retained the captaincy in 1983-84, bowling well against the West Indies, particularly at Ahmedabad, where he took 9 for 83, his best career bowling, in the second innings. But for the tour to Pakistan in 1984-85 Gavaskar was captain again. There is a natural rivalry between these two Indian stars which seems at times to divide officials and selectors.

When England toured India in 1984-85, England got back into the

series by capturing the last Indian wickets quickly in the second Test. Kapil Dev was criticized for his carefree batting—he stayed only six balls, hitting Pocock for six and being caught in the deep next ball. Gavaskar was not pleased and Kapil Dev was dropped for the next Test. He returned in the Test which followed, and, as if to make a point, hit his first ball high for four, going on to 53.

Such is Kapil Dev's play—unrepentant, attacking and exciting. He is undoubtedly an entertainer, and also one of the most successful of cricketers.

KAPIL DEV Ramlal Nikhanj

Teams: Haryana, Northamptonshire and India

Test series	Tests	Runs	100s	Average	Wkts	Average
1978-79 in Pakistan	3	159	—	31.80	7	60.85
1978-79 v West Indies	6	329	1	65.80	17	33.00
1979 in England	4	45	—	7.50	16	30.93
1979-80 v Australia	6	212	—	35.33	28	22.32
1979-80 v Pakistan	6	278	—	30.88	32	17.68
1979-80 v England	1	45	—	45.00	3	28.33
1980-81 in Australia	3	55	—	9.16	14	23.78
1980-81 in New Zealand	3	27	—	5.40	8	31.87
1981-82 v England	6	318	1	53.00	22	37.95
1982 in England	3	292	—	73.00	10	43.90
1982-83 v Sri Lanka	1	61	—	30.50	8	25.87
1982-83 in Pakistan	6	178	—	22.25	24	33.50
1982-83 in West Indies†	5	254	1	42.33	19	22.78
1983-84 v Pakistan†	3	46	—	11.54	12	18.75
1983-84 v West Indies†	6	184	—	16.72	27	19.88
1984-85 in Pakistan	2	52	—	26.00	1	126.00
1984-85 v England	4	253	—	42.16	10	43.60
Totals	68	2,788	3	30.30	258	28.70

Career runs: 6,933 *Average:* 30.95
Highest Test score: 126* v West Indies, Delhi, 1978-79
Highest career score: 193, Haryana v Punjab, Chandigarh, 1979-80
Career wickets: 552 *Average:* 26.69
Best Test and career bowling: 9-83 v West Indies, Ahmedabad, 1983-84

*Not out †Captain

KNOTT
Alan Philip Eric b 1946-

At the Oval in 1976, Alan Knott broke the world record for number of Test victims—a statistic alone that proved the class of the latest in a long line of great wicket-keepers from Kent.

What it did not emphasise, however, was the effervescent character of a man who always inspired his team-mates with his exuberance and enthusiasm. Nor did it pay any heed to the character of a player who also won Test matches with his batting skills.

Alan Knott made his entrance into county and Test cricket as though he had come to stay. He made his first-class debut in 1964 and earned his county cap a year later and in 1965 he was voted England's Best Young Cricketer of the year.

In 1967 he arrived on the Test scene with thirteen victims from his two matches against Pakistan. Though still understudy to Jim Parks at the start of the following winter's West Indies tour, he replaced the Sussex wicket-keeper after three drawn Tests. England won the fourth Test on a generous Sobers declaration but only after Knott, 69 not out, had helped Cowdrey to rectify their first innings. Even more vital was his 73 not out which saved the match and the rubber in the fifth Test.

Now established, his work behind the stumps became an inspiration for every bowler.

Neat and lithe, with the sharp-featured profile that earned him the nick-name of 'Mr. Punch', he developed even further agility by continual exercise. On more than one tour, his liking for early morning calisthenics earned him a room on his own. On the field, his wheeling and stretching between deliveries became a trademark.

An integral part of his county's successes, particularly in one-day cricket, his uninhibited strokeplay had brought him five Test centuries. Despite the barrage of bumpers in Australia in 1974-75, his 106 not out at Adelaide made him only the second wicket-keeper —his Kent predecessor Les Ames was the other—to reach three figures for England against Australia.

It was his batting, too, which showed his character in 1976. After an indifferent start to the series against the West Indies, with the bat and behind the stumps, his place became threatened. He responded defiantly by making 116 at Headingley and as England set off for a winter in India and Australia he remained very much the number one wicket-keeper.

It was not until the following spring that his triumphant, record-breaking career was threatened with interruption. One of the English Packer signatories, he was chosen for the Tests against Australia, and continued to justify his inclusion with 12 catches, some of them brilliant, and an important 135 in the Nottingham Test, his finest Test innings which served to inspire Boycott, who was deeply bogged down in his comeback innings. Knott's strokes were as cheeky and inventive as ever, and brought him a five and 18 fours. His final score beat Les Ames's record for a wicket-keeper in England-Australia Tests, and the stand with Boycott of 215 equalled the England sixth-wicket record against Australia set up in 1939 by Hutton and Hardstaff.

In 1977-78 he missed the England tour of Pakistan and New Zealand and played instead for Kerry Packer in Australia, thus ending a run of 65 consecutive Tests for England, a record later equalled by Botham. Returning to England, tired after years of continuous cricket, Knott decided not to play for Kent in the following season.

He returned to the Kent side after the Establishment peace with Packer, and regained his Test place in 1980 and 1981, when he

became the first wicket-keeper to record 100 victims against Australia. But he had expressed an unwillingness to tour regularly, which made his Test place insecure, and when he joined the South African 'rebels' in 1981-82 he effectively lost it for good. His total of 269 Test victims stands second to that of Rodney Marsh, but could well have been more. He retired at the end of the 1985 season, the third of three great Kent wicket-keepers—Ames and Evans were the others—to serve England almost continuously for 50 years.

TOP Alan Knott stumps Lawrence Rowe of the West Indies at the Oval in 1976 to claim his 220th Test victim and pass the record of an earlier Kent wicket-keeper Godfrey Evans. ABOVE Knott breaks the wicket again, this time to run out New Zealand's captain Bev Congdon at Trent Bridge in 1973. OPPOSITE Knott was famous for the care with which he looked after his health and fitness with diet and exercise, and his agility and exuberance were evident on the field.

KNOTT Alan Philip Eric

Teams: Kent, Tasmania (2 matches), and England

Test series		Tests	Runs	100s	Average	Ct	St
1967	v Pakistan	2	28	—	14.00	12	1
1967-68	in West Indies	2	149	—	149.00	4	0
1968	v Australia	5	116	—	16.57	11	4
1968-69	in Pakistan	3	180	—	60.00	6	0
1969	v West Indies	3	139	—	27.80	10	1
1969	v New Zealand	3	54	—	13.50	9	2
1970-71	in Australia	6	222	—	31.71	21	3
1970-71	in New Zealand	1	197	1	98.50	—	—
1971	v Pakistan	3	137	1	45.66	10	1
1971	v India	3	223	—	44.60	10	1
1972	v Australia	5	229	—	28.62	17	—
1972-73	in India	5	168	—	21.00	11	1
1972-73	in Pakistan	3	199	—	49.75	4	—
1973	v New Zealand	3	72	—	14.40	12	—
1973	v West Indies	3	35	—	8.75	7	—
1973-74	in West Indies	5	365	—	45.62	4	—
1974	v India	3	26	—	13.00	15	1
1974	v Pakistan	3	132	—	33.00	7	—
1974-75	in Australia	6	364	1	36.40	22	1
1974-75	in New Zealand	2	29	—	—	3	—
1975	v Australia	4	261	—	37.28	4	—
1976	v West Indies	5	270	1	30.00	5	1
1976-77	in India	5	268	—	38.28	13	2
1976-77	in Australia	1	57	—	28.50	4	—
1977	v Australia	5	255	1	36.42	12	—
1980	v West Indies	4	36	—	5.14	11	—
1981	v Australia	2	178	—	59.33	6	—
Totals		**95**	**4,389**	**5**	**32.75**	**250**	**19**

Career runs: 18,105 *Average:* 29.63
Highest Test score: 135 v Australia, Nottingham, 1977
Highest career score: 156, MCC v South Zone, Bangalore, 1972-73
Career dismissals 1,344 *Catches* 1,211 *Stumpings* 133
Best Test wicketkeeping: 7 dismissals (all ct.) in match v Pakistan, Nottingham, 1967
Best career wicketkeeping: 8 dismissals (6 ct. 2 st.) in match Kent v Middlesex, Gravesend, 1966

LAKER
James b 1922–d 1986

Jim Laker will always be remembered for one of the most extraordinary feats in cricket history—his 19 wickets for 90 runs for England against Australia at Old Trafford in 1956. No one else in the history of the first-class game had ever taken more than 17 wickets in a match. Yet Laker, with his offspin, took 19 in a Test match against Australia and, inexplicably, while another highly skilled spin bowler, Tony Lock, perhaps the most prolific wicket-taker of the time, was taking only one at the other end. Just three weeks before, Lock himself had taken 16 wickets for Surrey against Kent at Blackheath, including all 10 in the second innings. Laker's feat in the Old Trafford Test was spread over four days in a rain-interrupted match. The pitch took spin from an early stage, but it was

not as lethal as many to be met around the country at that period.

Tall and strong, Laker had a lively, high action, great powers of spin, and immaculate control of the variations of length, pace and flight with which he plagued batsmen. In England he mostly pushed the ball through at a pace that kept the batsmen from moving out to him but still allowed the ball to turn. On the harder pitches in Australia, South Africa, and the West Indies, where he had a good but less spectacular record, he would flight it more, yet with equal control. Laker began to bowl off-breaks at 17 just before World War II, having been a batsman and fast bowler at school. Before Yorkshire could become interested in him, the war broke out, but while serving in the RAOC in the Middle East he showed high promise in the good-class cricket played in Cairo. Stationed in London on his return home, he was soon introduced to Surrey who, after a time, con-

vinced him that his future lay in cricket rather than in the banking career on which he had started. Whether Yorkshire would have given permission for Surrey to engage him had they seen more of him will never be known, but in 1946 the memories of his schooldays were over seven years old and they let him go. Within two years of his first-class debut, he was playing for England.

In his first full season of 1947, he finished seventh in the first-class averages with 79 wickets, and that winter went to the West Indies with G. O. Allen's MCC team, playing in his first Test in Barbados and taking 7-103 in the first innings. Back in England, he played in three Tests against Australia, making 63 in a total cf 165 in the first. As a batsman, he was a hearty swinger of the bat at around No. 9 with an effective slash that earned him many runs on the off-side.

The Australians of 1948 played him with a confidence their successors seldom emulated, and after they had made their 404-3 in the last innings at Leeds, Laker, who had had several chances dropped off him but was still really learning the offspinner's trade, was one of those dropped. For a while his career marked time, but he burst into the record books in

the Test trial at Bradford in 1950, when on a drying pitch he took eight 'Rest' wickets for two runs, completely ruining the match as a trial. However, the selectors were still not convinced that he was a valuable bowler on good pitches as well, and he was not a regular choice for England, though his 10-119 against South Africa at the Oval in 1951 had much to do with England's victory there.

In 1952 Surrey's seven-year run of championship successes began, with Laker playing an important part, and in 1953 he and Lock bowled out Australia at the Oval when the Ashes were recovered after 19 years. But there still remained a tendency to identify him too closely with the helpful pitches in vogue at the time, especially at the Oval, and another great bowler, Bob Appleyard, was preferred on Len Hutton's successful tour of Australia in 1954-55.

Laker's greatest triumphs, however, were to come in 1956 when he took 46 wickets in the series against Australia at an average of 9.60 and at Old Trafford accomplished a feat that will almost certainly never be equalled, especially not in a Test match. In addition to his overall bag of 19 wickets, he became the first player to take 10 wickets in a Test innings, and only the fourth player to take 10 wickets in an innings more than once—he had accom-

plished the feat earlier in the season with 10-88 for Surrey, also against the Australians.

Sadly, his later years with Surrey were marred by disagreements, and after his retirement in 1959—when he was only 37 and still a great bowler—he wrote a controversial book which caused the MCC to withdraw his honorary membership and Surrey his pavilion privileges. Happily, these were restored within a few years and the incident has been long forgotten.

Laker returned to first-class

cricket for a time in the early 1960s, playing in a number of matches, mostly at home, for Essex. The pitches by now possessed more grass and had changed in character, but though he rarely had figures to compare with those of earlier years he was still a model bowler for young cricketers to watch and he was seldom played with comfort. When he finally left the first-class scene, he maintained his association with cricket, becoming a successful television commentator and writer.

LAKER James Charles			
Teams: Surrey, Essex, and England			
Test series	**Tests**	**Wkts**	**Average**
1947-48 in West Indies	4	18	30.33
1948 v Australia	3	9	52.44
1949 v New Zealand	1	4	22.25
1950 v West Indies	1	1	86.00
1951 v South Africa	2	14	14.85
1952 v India	4	8	23.62
1953 v Australia	3	9	23.55
1953-54 in West Indies	4	14	33.50
1954 v Pakistan	1	2	19.50
1955 v South Africa	1	7	12.00
1956 v Australia	5	46	9.60
1956-57 in South Africa	5	11	29.45
1957 v West Indies	4	18	24.88
1958 v New Zealand	4	17	10.17
1958-59 in Australia	4	15	21.20
Totals	46	193	21.24

Career wickets: 1,944 *Average:* 18.41
Best Test and career bowling: 10-53 v Australia, Old Trafford, 1956
Highest Test score: 63 v Australia, Trent Bridge, 1948
Highest career score: 113, Surrey v Gloucestershire, Oval, 1954

OPPOSITE Two views of Jim Laker's bowling action, from side on and from the batsman's viewpoint.
LEFT Laker was also a useful tail-ender, with a century to his credit.
ABOVE Laker's record haul of 19 wickets in a Test match seems the most difficult cricket record to beat. Miller walks after being bowled for 0.
RIGHT Ken Mackay is caught in the leg trap by Alan Oakman, also for 0, and Laker is on his way to all ten.

LARWOOD
Harold b 1904-

Many people well placed to judge believe that Harold Larwood was the fastest and best fast bowler in cricket history. It was, therefore, all the sadder that his career should have declined among the bitterness of the bodyline controversy in which he was one of the two central figures and which left unpleasant memories of what, in most ways, was a glorious record.

Fair haired and of only medium height, he did not at first sight possess all the fast bowler's requirements, certainly not in 1925 when he first appeared for Nottinghamshire as a slim 20-year-old from one of the mining villages with which that county abounds. But his run-up, relatively short, yet beautifully balanced and accelerating gradually, at once attracted attention, and his marvellously supple, easy, textbook action left no doubt of his quality. In the following year, he was playing for England against Australia.

Although his pace was exceptional, it was the accuracy derived from his perfect action that made him so deadly and, in time, the ideal instrument of Jardine's bodyline policy in Australia in 1932-33.

Larwood's Test career before that series had not been outstanding. On A. P. F. Chapman's tour of 1928-29, he was never fully fit and at home in 1930 he was thwarted by a combination of Don Bradman and mild pitches. His most successful Test to date had been the first Test of 1928-29 at Brisbane when he took 6-32 and 2-30 and scored 70 and 37. As a batsman at around No. 9 for England, he hit the ball hard and had a sound basic technique.

Before the 1932-33 tour, he had taken only 45 Test wickets. But under the captaincy of A. W. Carr, he had been a great force for Notts, playing a big part in their championship win of 1929. Eight times in all he took 100 wickets in a season, with a best performance of

LARWOOD Harold

Teams: Nottinghamshire and England

Test series		Tests	Wkts	Avge
1926	v Australia	2	9	28.00
1928	v West Indies	2	6	19.00
1928-29	in Australia	5	18	40.22
1929	v South Africa	3	8	23.25
1930	v Australia	3	4	73.00
1931	v New Zealand	1	—	—
1932-33	in Australia	5	33	19.51
Totals		21	78	28.35

Career wickets: 1,427 *Average:* 17.51
Best Test bowling: 6-32 v Australia, Brisbane, 1928-29
Best career bowling: 9-41, Nottinghamshire v Kent, Trent Bridge, 1931
Highest Test score: 98 v Australia, Sydney, 1932-33
Highest career score: 102*, Nottinghamshire v Sussex, Trent Bridge, 1931

*Not out

9-41 against Kent at Trent Bridge in 1931.

In Australia on that unhappy tour, he bowled superbly to his orders. Though it was the short ball, fast and accurate, that undermined the batsmen, he could put in a devastating yorker at will. In addition, he was helped by the fact that there were other fine fast bowlers in the side—G. O. Allen, who did not bowl bodyline, and Bill Voce, Larwood's partner from Notts. In the first Test, Larwood took five wickets in each innings and thereafter he was the spearhead of England's attack, taking 33 wickets in all. And in the last Test, at Sydney, which was to be the last of his career, he went in as nightwatchman and made 98 in two and a quarter hours.

His departure from Test cricket was not entirely due to the aftermath of bodyline and the reluctance of selectors to open old wounds, but to an injury to his left foot. It had been under great pressure, not only through the ordinary demands of fast bowling but through those extra times he thumped the ball in short of a length. He played on for Notts until 1938, but latterly was merely a fast-medium bowler operating off a short run. His name at that time inevitably had unpleasant associations in Australia, but after World War II he, his wife, and five daughters emigrated there. His part in the 1932-33 series had been forgiven and forgotten, and he became a much respected Australian citizen.

LILLEE
Dennis Keith b 1949-

Dennis Lillee took more Test wickets than any bowler before him, and for a decade was one of the most feared fast bowlers ever to play cricket. In the traditions of fast bowlers he was also a fiery character whose antics did not endear him to cricket lovers.

Born in 1949 in Subiaco, Western Australia, he made his state debut in 1969-70 and it was only a season later that he made his first appearance in Tests.

As England reeled under the pace and aggression of Dennis Lillee's bowling in the 1972 Test series, they might have recalled the old proverb about biting the hand that fed you.

Lillee himself points to a season spent in the Lancashire League as one of the significant developments in a career which progressed from sheer pace to the ability to move the ball without any appreciable loss of speed. The result was shown in a magnificent series for Lillee in which he took 31 wickets, the most by any Australian in England.

Sadly, it seemed, the effort had taken its toll. After playing against the Pakistanis the following winter, he broke down on the tour of West Indies in the early part of 1973, an already suspect back weakening under the strain of genuine fast bowling. But he made a remarkable recovery, and was back at his very best for England's tour in 1974-75.

Lillee's own competitive instincts and loyalty to his side had been largely to blame for the breakdown in Jamaica. The previous month in the third and final Test against Pakistan, he was feeling the injury. But with Pakistan only needing 159 to win in the last innings, he willingly lent his frame to the cause. He bowled throughout that innings—a spell of eleven overs one evening and twelve the following day—and played a vital part in a famous Australian victory. He bowled at a reduced speed and wore a sleeveless sweater throughout his stint, but he removed three front-line batsmen, Nasim, Zaheer and Mushtaq.

Lillee first appeared for his state, Western Australia, at the age of 19, finding the life in his home strip at Perth very suitable for the pace of his bowling. His speed attracted the selectors who were looking for support for Graham McKenzie. Lillee was chosen for the 'B' tour to New Zealand at the end of the 1969-70 season, and responded with 18 first-class wickets which cost him only 18 runs each.

The following year, as Australia

ABOVE AND OPPOSITE The bowling actions of two great fast men—Larwood and Lillee.

sought to counter in a series against England which John Snow was winning with pace, he was called into the full national side for the fifth Test. Though England batted well, he took 5 for 84 in the first innings, doing the statutory job of a good quick bowler by briskly polishing off the tail.

He kept his place and though the 1971 tour by the South Africans was cancelled, Lillee opened the Australian attack against a World XI and in the second representative game he really came of age. The World XI were shot out for 59 and in 57 balls Lillee captured 8 for 29, including Gary Sobers for a duck.

Despite problems with his back early on the tour, he carried the same form into the Tests in England the following summer. He bowled a lengthy 59 overs in the first Test at Old Trafford for match figures of 8 for 106, including an impressive 6 for 66 in the second innings.

His hostility proved a potent weapon for Ian Chappell, and throughout the series he was rarely mastered. The three principle batsmen in the 1970-71 series, Boycott, Edrich and Luckhurst, averaged 93.85, 72.00 and 56.87 respectively. In 1972 their returns were 18.00, 21.80 and 24.00 for which much of the credit belonged to Lillee.

After his back troubles, he

LILLEE Dennis Keith

Teams: Western Australia and Australia

Test series		Tests	Wkts	Average
1970-71	v England	2	8	24.87
1972	in England	5	31	17.87
1972-73	v Pakistan	3	12	29.41
1972-73	in West Indies	1	—	—
1974-75	v England	6	25	23.84
1975	in England	4	21	21.90
1975-76	v West Indies	5	27	26.37
1976-77	v Pakistan	3	21	25.71
1976-77	in New Zealand	2	15	20.80
1976-77	v England	1	11	15.00
1979-80	v West Indies	3	12	30.41
1979-80	v England	3	23	16.86
1979-80	in Pakistan	3	3	101.00
1980	in England	1	5	19.20
1980-81	v New Zealand	3	16	15.31
1980-81	v India	3	21	21.52
1981	in England	6	39	22.30
1981-82	v Pakistan	3	15	22.13
1981-82	v West Indies	3	16	19.81
1981-82	in New Zealand	3	7	26.14
1982-83	v England	1	4	46.25
1982-83	in Sri Lanka	1	3	35.66
1983-84	v Pakistan	5	20	31.90
Totals		70	355	23.92

Career wickets: 845 *Average:* 22.86
Best Test bowling: 7-83 v West Indies, Melbourne, 1981-82
Best career bowling: 8-29, Australia v Rest of the World, Perth, 1971-72
Highest Test and career score: 73* v England, Lord's, 1975
Test runs: 905 *Average* 13.71

*Not out

returned and together with Jeff Thomson he dominated the 1974-75 series. He sustained his hostility in England in 1975 and, again with Thomson, destroyed West Indies in the following series

—superb bowling uninterrupted by any recurrence of his back trouble.

His 11 for 165 effectively saved the Centenary Test for Australia, and after missing the 1977 tour of

England, he became one of the main drawcards in Packer cricket.

Returning to Test cricket after the World Series, Lillee earned his wickets with control and swing rather than sheer speed, although he was never short of being genuinely fast. He often reserved his better performances for matches against England. In the 1979-80 series he took 23 wickets in only three Tests.

His belligerent behaviour, which had already earned him comment, seemed to reach new extremes in this series. He barely concealed his contempt for Brearley, the England captain, whom he regarded as an 'Establishment' figure, and in the first Test he had Brearley caught behind to claim his 100th Test wicket against England. Previously he had begun to bat with an aluminium bat and had scored three runs from four balls with it before Brearley objected and the umpires asked Lillee to change it. Lillee threw a tantrum and the bat to square leg and held up the game for ten minutes with his antics.

In 1981, in England, Lillee took 39 wickets in the series, but this was Botham's series, when England won at Headingley after following on—later it was disclosed that Lillee had backed England at 500-1, another action which offended the purists.

Lillee's worst behaviour occurred the following winter, however, when Pakistan toured Australia. On the fourth day of the first Test, he impeded Javed Miandad, the Pakistani captain, and then kicked him. This disgraceful behaviour earned Lillee suspension from two one-day matches.

It is a pity Lillee showed so little regard for the traditions of cricket, because he was a magnificent bowler, with a beautiful action and all the attributes a fast bowler needed, including courage, which he showed most notably in overcoming his back injuries.

In the first Test against West Indies at Melbourne in 1981-82 Lillee produced his best Test figures of 7 for 83. When Gomes was caught he took his 310th Test wicket, beating the previous highest aggregate of Lance Gibbs.

Lillee, battling again against injury, took only seven wickets in 1982-83, but finished his career with a flourish against his old 'enemy' Pakistan in 1983-84. He announced his retirement during the final Test, in which he took eight wickets, including one from his last ball.

In all, Lillee took 355 Test wickets, 167 of which were English, which is the most any bowler has taken against another country.

Dennis Lillee was a bowler of great courage who continued at the top level of international cricket when back injuries might have finished him. Even when appealing he was 'trying'.

LINDWALL
Raymond Russell b 1921-

Ray Lindwall burst upon the cricket world after World War II as a great fast bowler and the more lethal, and more orthodox, in the redoubtable partnership of Lindwall and Miller that made Sir Donald Bradman's unbeaten Australians of 1948 such a devastating attacking force. Of medium height but strongly built, he recalled to many the great English fast bowler Harold Larwood, who also had an easy, perfectly balanced, accelerating run-up and a model action.

Lindwall possessed all the great fast bowler's arts—accuracy, genuine pace achieved without undue effort, subtle variations of pace, and the ability to swing the ball. At first the movement was mainly away from the bat, but while playing in the Lancashire League he developed the inswinger because slip catches off outswingers bowled by someone of his pace were not readily taken. So considerable was his ability to move the ball in the air that he remained an effective bowler long after the sharp edge had gone off his pace, and his Test career continued until he was 38. When experiments were being made in England in 1953 with a smaller ball, he swung it about so absurdly in the nets at Lord's that the project was probably dropped. He was probably at his best in the heavier atmosphere of England, though the first of his three tours there was easily his most successful.

A promising rugby league player before the war, he used his speed and sure-handling to good effect in the field, often making catches of seemingly impossible chances. Such a catch was the one he took to dismiss Peter May at Headingley in 1956. Fielding at square leg, he took the ball only inches from the ground. As a vigorous batsman, he made two Test centuries, one against England at Melbourne in 1946-47, the other in Barbados against West Indies six years later.

The lack of first-class cricket in the war years meant that when Lindwall played in his first Test against England, at Brisbane in 1946, he was merely a name to most people outside Australia. He had had little of the build-up that would have attended a fast bowler of his class in ordinary times. Yet at 25 he was already a mature cricketer and the best fast bowler in the world, waiting only for the opportunity to prove it by performance in the highest class.

He had come under the eye of Bill O'Reilly, then captain of the St George club in Sydney, at an early age, and played for New South Wales in 1941. For some years thereafter he was on war service in New Guinea and the Solomon Islands, and it was not until 1945-46 that he returned to interstate cricket, with success.

Lindwall bowling on his last tour of England in 1956, when he played in four Tests. The non-striking batsman is Hampshire's Roy Marshall.

Towards the end of the season he toured New Zealand, and the following season began his long confrontation with English batsmen, quietly at first, for he developed chicken-pox during the first Test and did not play in the second. But in the third, batting at No. 9, he shared in a stand of 154 in 87 minutes with Don Tallon in the second innings, making 100 himself in under two hours. In the fourth Test he took six wickets and in the fifth nine, including 7-63 in the first innings.

In 1948 Lindwall was helped by the fact that a new ball was available after only 55 overs, in contrast to 85 today, and he swept aside almost all opposition, taking 86 wickets on the tour and 27 in the Test series.

His accuracy is reflected by the fact that half of his 86 victims were bowled. With Keith Miller and Bill Johnston also at the peak of their powers, the England batsmen had an unhappy summer that reached its gloomiest point for them when they were bowled out for 52 and 188 at the Oval, Lindwall taking 6-20 and 3-50.

In a weaker Australian side that lost the Ashes in 1953, he was little less successful himself, taking 26 Test wickets at 18 apiece. Miller came next with 10 wickets.

The first signs that England batsmen were beginning to find him less of a problem came in Australia in 1954-55, when Len Hutton's team held the Ashes and Lindwall took only 14 wickets at 27 apiece. But his 3-27 and 2-50 had helped to win the first Test. In 1956 in England, he took only seven Test wickets, and it seemed, as Australia went home in disarray

RIGHT Ray Lindwall was no rabbit with the bat and in 61 Tests accumulated over 1,500 runs, including two centuries, one in the West Indies.

after that tour, that Lindwall, then 35, must be one of those who had played his last Test. But he was recalled for the fourth Test of the 1958-59 series, taking three wickets in that match and four in the fifth Test.

His return was the more popular for allowing Test crowds another look at a perfect action at a time when some doubtful ones were in vogue. A year later, crowds in Pakistan and India had the same opportunity, for Lindwall was a member of Richie Benaud's side there, and he took the last 9 of his 228 Test wickets. He retired on returning home, and in 1965 he was awarded the MBE.

LINDWALL Raymond Russell			
Teams: New South Wales, Queensland, and Australia			
Test series	**Tests**	**Wkts**	**Average**
1945-46 in New Zealand	1	2	14.50
1946-47 v England	4	18	20.38
1947-48 v India	5	18	16.88
1948 in England	5	27	19.62
1949-50 in South Africa	4	12	20.66
1950-51 v England	5	15	22.93
1951-52 v West Indies	5	21	23.04
1952-53 v South Africa	4	19	20.15
1953 in England	5	26	18.84
1954-55 v England	4	14	27.21
1954-55 in West Indies	5	20	32.15
1956 in England	4	7	34.00
1956-57 in Pakistan	1	1	64.00
1956-57 in India	3†	12	16.58
1958-59 v England	2	7	29.85
1959-60 in Pakistan	2	3	40.66
1959-60 in India	2	6	37.00
Totals	61	228	23.03

Career wickets: 794 *Average:* 21.35
Best Test bowling: 7-38 v India, Adelaide, 1947-48
Best career bowling: 7-20, Australians v Minor Counties, Stoke-on-Trent, 1953
Highest Test score: 118 v West Indies, Bridgetown, 1954-55
Highest career score: 134*, New South Wales v Queensland, Sydney, 1945-46

*Not out †Captain in one Test

LLOYD
Clive Hubert b 1944-

When Clive Lloyd announced his retirement from Test cricket in 1985, the cricket world was inclined to believe him, although he had been 'retiring' from Test cricket for some years. Perhaps the main reason for this belief was that Lloyd was now over 40, having been born in Georgetown, British Guiana (as Guyana was then) in 1944. He is a cousin of Lance Gibbs, the former Test wicket record-holder.

Lloyd made his debut for British Guiana in 1963-64. Three years later he won his first cap for West Indies, and a couple of summers later began his long association with Lancashire. He succeeded Rohan Kanhai as captain of West Indies in 1974-75 and remained captain for over 10 years, a period in which West Indies came to dominate world cricket. Lloyd gradually began to be seen as a father figure guiding and controlling the energies of a battery of fast bowlers and some extravagant batsmen. Small wonder that at his retirement from the Test scene an era seemed to pass.

Lloyd in his early days was best known for his superb fielding at cover point and his immensely powerful hitting. In the field, with his heavy spectacles, his short hair or white sun hat, slightly round shoulders, and his gangling, loose walk he was instantly recognisable even when just prowling with intent. When the ball came his way he would swoop like a great cat and woe betide the batsman out of his ground as Lloyd's long arm reached for the ball. His reach was just as evident as a batsman. When he was attacking there seemed to be no place a bowler could send the ball where Lloyd's heavy bat could not reach it and send it lazily sailing over the ropes. In later years problems with his knees impaired his mobility slightly, but he retained a safe pair of hands and the knack of scoring a big innings when it was most needed.

Lloyd's entry into county cricket in England came via the Lancashire League club of Haslingden, which must have helped mould his philosophy that attack is the best form of defence. Although he made two hundreds against Cowdrey's England in 1967-68, his impetuosity did not always bring results at the start of his Test career.

But the responsibilities of succeeding Rohan Kanhai as captain in India in 1974 provided a great stimulus. In his first match as captain, he made 163 at Bangalore. With the series delicately balanced he responded with his highest-ever score, 242 not out at Bombay, which won the match and the series.

After helping the West Indies to their World Cup triumph in 1975, he underwent the ordeal of a 5-1 series defeat in Australia in 1975-76 —a shattering blow to his morale and a question mark against his future as a captain. But he retained the leadership and put his side back on the rails with a series victory over India. That recovery became

Clive Lloyd in typical powerful form, off-driving against Pakistan in a World Cup match in 1979. Twice his batting helped West Indies win the World Cup.

LLOYD Clive Hubert

Teams: Guyana, Lancashire, and West Indies

Test series	Tests	Runs	100s	Average
1966-67 in India	3	227	—	56.75
1967-68 v England	5	369	2	52.71
1968-69 in Australia	4	315	1	39.37
1968-69 in New Zealand	3	65	—	13.00
1969 in England	3	183	—	30.50
1970-71 v India	5	295	—	29.50
1971-72 v New Zealand	2	66	—	22.00
1972-73 v Australia	3	297	1	59.40
1973 in England	3	318	1	63.60
1973-74 v England	5	147	—	24.50
1974-75 in India†	5	636	2	79.50
1974-75 in Pakistan†	2	164	—	54.66
1975-76 in Australia†	6	469	2	46.90
1975-76 in India†	4	283	1	47.16
1976 in England†	5	296	—	32.88
1976-77 v Pakistan†	5	336	1	42.00
1977-78 v Australia‡	2	128	—	64.00
1979-80 in Australia†	2	201	1	67.00
1979-80 in New Zealand†	3	103	—	17.16
1980 in England†	4	169	1	42.25
1980-81 in Pakistan†	4	106	—	21.20
1980-81 v England†	4	383	1	76.66
1981-82 in Australia†	3	275	—	55.00
1982-83 v India†	5	407	2	67.83
1983-84 in India†	6	496	2	82.66
1983-84 v Australia†	4	170	—	42.50
1984 in England†	5	255	—	51.00
1984-85 in Australia†	5	356	1	50.85
Totals	**110**	**7,515**	**19**	**46.67**

Career runs: 30,885 *Average:* 49.25
Highest Test and career score: 242* v India, Bombay, 1974-75
Test wickets: 10 *Average:* 62.20

*Not out †Captain ‡Captain in first 2 Tests
Career figures correct to end of 1985 season

Two views of Clive Lloyd proving that, even in Test cricket, attack is often the best form of defence.

complete when Lloyd's side devastated England in 1976.

One of Lloyd's fastest innings came in 1976 at Swansea, when, playing for the West Indians against Glamorgan, he scored 201 not out, his double century coming in 120 minutes, equalling a record set by G. L. Jessop in 1903.

Like most of the top West Indians, Lloyd joined Packer's World Series Cricket in 1977, and he resigned as captain of West Indies after the second Test against Australia in 1977-78 after disagreements with the selectors over the Packer issue.

He returned to the Test scene in 1979-80, in Australia, where he missed the first Test but gained revenge for his 1975-76 defeat by leading the West Indies to two overwhelming victories in the last two Tests.

Lloyd had built up a big reputation in limited-overs cricket, for which his skills were ideally suited,

and he helped Lancashire to many titles in the 1970s, in particular with innings of 66, 126 and 73 not out which helped them win three Gillette Cup finals.

The World Cup became the perfect stage for Lloyd. In the first ever final at Lord's in 1975 he hit a magnificent 102 to lead West Indies to victory and in 1979 he was captain again as his side retained the trophy. He was hampered by an injury when the Indians shocked the West Indies in the 1983 final.

From the late 1970s Lloyd's West Indians were almost unbeatable in Tests. Although the side's main strength was in its endless fast bowling, Lloyd contributed his share to the batting. With the emergence of Richards, Greenidge, Rowe, Haynes, Gomes and the rest, he dropped down the order, but was always ready to contribute a telling innings when it was required, which was surprisingly often. Indeed, in his last seven Test series, Lloyd's average only once dropped below 50.

Lloyd is often cited as a great ambassador for West Indian

cricket, a man who always kept calm and exuded an air of confidence no matter what situation the game was in. He always backed his players and clearly had their respect.

It might be that the only valid criticism of him arises from this same loyalty which he and his players offered each other. Occasionally West Indian players have behaved less than perfectly in Tests, and umpires have been brushed and stumps kicked. Lloyd was not, perhaps, as willing to condemn such practices as he might have been. And, with his overwhelming superiority in fast bowling during most of his tenure as captain, he did not go out of his way to be fair to the spectator regarding over rates, nor to batsman and spectator alike in curbing excessive intimidatory bowling. The bowling endured by Edrich and Close of England in the Old Trafford Test in 1976 was excessively dangerous, and night-watchman Pocock, so poor a batsman that he became only the second Englishman to get a 'pair' in successive Tests, had to face vicious bouncers

at the Oval in 1984 from Marshall, who had already put an England opener in hospital, without any intervention by Lloyd.

The strength of Lloyd's West Indian side was at its highest when he stepped down from the Test arena. In 1983-84 in the West Indies, Australia were beaten 3-0, after having much the worst of two draws. In none of the five Tests did West Indies lose a second-innings wicket. In 1984 England were beaten 5-0. Then Australia were beaten again 3-1, West Indies losing the final Test of Lloyd's career. There was much abuse given and taken by both sides in this series, another indication that Lloyd's supremely successful side could not always win gracefully.

Lloyd played in 110 Tests, second only to Cowdrey at the time of his retirement. With 7,515 runs he was fifth in the all-time list. He was captain in 74 Tests, a record, and won 36, almost as many as any two other Test captains. But his success remains secondary to his style—it is the prowling fieldsman and the majestic driver that will be remembered.

McKENZIE
Graham Douglas b 1941-

Though fast bowlers are wont to leap from obscurity into world fame more quickly than other cricketers, few have been more completely unknown than Graham McKenzie when he went on his first tour to England in 1961. He had played two matches for Western Australia at the end of the 1959-60 season, but he took 4-41 in the state match against the West Indians at the start of the next season and did so well in the Sheffield Shield that he was picked for the tour. Yet up to the time of departure, the Australian captain, Richie Benaud, had not seen him.

In England he proved to have been an inspired selection. He became Alan Davidson's partner in the opening attack, took 5-37 in the second innings of the Lord's Test, and played a big part with the bat in the two Tests that Australia won. At Lord's, he shared in stands that added 102 vital runs for the last two wickets and at Old Trafford he made 32 in a famous last wicket stand of 98 with Davidson. In later years, his batting did not develop as seemed likely then, and his record as a bowler in Test matches was nearly always better than that in minor matches.

McKenzie's great ability lay in the fact that he bowled so well on good pitches. A powerfully built 6-footer, he had a short, relaxed run-up and a beautiful action. From this action he derived the ability to thump the ball into an unhelpful pitch, so producing an extra high bounce. He was not especially accurate, but he could produce the ball to undo the best of batsmen.

Gentle, quietly spoken, almost dreamy, McKenzie had none of the fast bowler's traditional belligerence, but from his first tour at the age of 19 it seemed probable that he would break all Australian records for the number of wickets taken in Tests. His career, however, was not quite one of uninterrupted success. In 1965-66 the selectors dropped him from the team chosen to play in the fourth Test in Adelaide, but his replacement broke down before the match and he was recalled. His 6-48 in the first innings gave England a disastrous start from which they never quite recovered.

On joining Leicestershire in 1969 he had no immediate success. And though he did unexpectedly well for a fast bowler in India later that year, taking 26 wickets, he took only one in three Tests in South Africa. Blessed with exceptional soundness of limb and muscle through the years, he may not have been at his fittest in South Africa, and a minor technical flaw had crept into his action.

He played in only three Tests against Ray Illingworth's tour team, though he continued to be a force under Illingworth's leadership in county cricket for Leicestershire until 1975.

McKENZIE Graham Douglas

Teams: Western Australia, Leicestershire, and Australia

Test series		Tests	Wkts	Avge
1961	in England	3	11	29.36
1962-63	v England	5	20	30.95
1963-64	v South Africa	5	16	43.06
1964	in England	5	29	22.55
1964-65	in India	3	13	16.46
1964-65	in Pakistan	1	8	16.27
1964-65	v Pakistan	1	7	20.00
1964-65	in West Indies	5	17	39.82
1965-66	v England	4	16	29.18
1966-67	in South Africa	5	24	26.00
1967-68	v India	2	13	24.00
1968	in England	5	13	45.76
1968-69	v West Indies	5	30	25.26
1969-70	in India	5	21	21.00
1969-70	in South Africa	3	1	333.00
1970-71	v England	3	7	50.14
Totals		60	246	29.78

Career wickets: 1,219 *Average:* 26.96
Career runs: 5,662 *Average:* 15.64
Best Test and career bowling: 8-71 v West Indies, Melbourne, 1968-69
Highest Test and career score: 76 v South Africa, Sydney, 1963-64

ABOVE A young McKenzie bowling at Lord's in 1961. RIGHT Back again for the Rest of the World nine years later.

MARSH
Rodney William b 1947-

Rodney Marsh did not become the most successful wicket-keeper in Test cricket by supreme natural talent. When he was chosen to play for Australia against England in 1970-71 he was not a popular choice, other keepers, particularly Brian Taber and John Maclean, appearing to have better claims. Marsh earned preference because of his batting, but he fumbled so often in his early Tests that he earned the nickname 'Old Irongloves'. By the end of his career his wicket-keeping was so outstanding that his batting was merely a bonus.

Born in Armadale, West Australia, Marsh learned his cricket as a boy with his elder brother Graham, who became a successful professional golfer. He made his first-class debut for Western Australia in the 1968-69 season against the visiting West Indians as a number five batsman and made a second innings 104. Next season he took over as the state wicket-keeper. In this season Dennis Lillee made his debut for the state and the pair were to become a deadly partnership over the next dozen years. Marsh became particularly adept at keeping to fast bowlers, standing well back and commanding a wide arc between himself and first slip, who was allowed to stand wider than usual. Lillee made his Test debut in the same series as Marsh. When Lillee retired in 1983-84 with a record 355 Test wickets, Marsh had kept wicket in every Test except one (against Sri Lanka) in which Lillee had played and the legend 'c Marsh b Lillee' had appeared 95 times in Test score-cards, a record.

Marsh's wicket-keeping had improved considerably by his second Test series, in England in 1972, when he claimed 23 Test victims, and incidentally averaged 34.57 with the bat. Back home in Australia he made his first Test 100, against Pakistan at Adelaide, becoming the first Australian wicket-keeper to score a century. There was no doubt that his Test place was secure.

The Centenary Test at Melbourne in 1976-77 was a high spot in Marsh's triumphant progress. He passed Grout's Australian record of 187 Test victims and made the third and last of his Test centuries, 110 not out in the second innings. He became the first Australian keeper to score 100 in the Ashes series. He also made a sporting gesture when indicating that he had not caught Randall cleanly, thus returning some sporting dignity to an Australian side under criticism for purposeful dangerous bowling and 'sledging'

Rodney Marsh owed his original selection for Australia to his aggressive left-hand batting.

A brilliant dive in front of slip to catch Knott off Thomson at Melbourne in 1974, a typical Marsh effort.

—making derogatory remarks to the batsmen.

As a batsman, Marsh was a burly and pugnacious left-hander, who hit the ball very hard, particularly in front of the wicket, and he was not afraid to hit the ball in the air. Strangely, after the peak of his Centenary 100, his Test batting declined dramatically—he scored 2,230 runs in his first 47 Tests, and only 1,403 in his last 49.

After the series in England in 1977 he played for World Series Cricket, but resumed his Test career in 1979-80 against the West Indies and England when both toured Australia.

Marsh began passing some of his last milestones during the tour of England in 1981. In the first Test at Trent Bridge he became the first wicket-keeper to take 100 wickets in the Ashes series when he caught Woolmer. This catch also passed Alan Knott's then record of 244 Test catches. In the third Test at Headingley he passed Knott's record aggregate of Test wickets,

reaching 264—the vital wicket was, appropriately, 'c Marsh b Lillee'. This was Botham's famous match, in which Marsh and Lillee offended purists by a sporting wager on England at 500-1, which hit the jackpot. In the last Test Marsh passed 3,000 Test runs, the second wicket-keeper (Knott was first) to pass this total.

Marsh particularly enjoyed playing well against England, and in 1982-83, during the series against the old enemy, he took 28 catches, another world record.

During the last Test match against Pakistan in 1983-84 Lillee and Greg Chappell announced their retirements from Test cricket, and shortly afterwards Marsh did the same. Their retirements ended an era in Australian Test cricket. The three had played no fewer than 63 Tests together. All three ended with world records, and it was a nice coincidence that the record haul of wickets of both Lillee and Marsh ended at 355. Marsh's will probably prove the more difficult total to pass in the future. He was awarded the MBE for services to cricket: his 96 Test appearances are an Australian record.

MARSH Rodney William

Teams: Western Australia and Australia

Test series		Tests	Runs	100s	Average	Ct	St
1970-71	v England	6	215	—	23.12	11	3
1972	in England	5	242	—	34.57	21	2
1972-73	v Pakistan	3	210	1	42.00	16	—
1972-73	in West Indies	5	297	—	49.50	17	—
1973-74	v New Zealand	3	148	1	49.33	16	1
1973-74	in New Zealand	3	173	—	28.83	13	—
1974-75	v England	6	313	—	34.77	18	1
1975	in England	4	133	—	26.60	14	1
1975-76	v West Indies	6	236	—	28.50	26	—
1976-77	v Pakistan	3	119	—	23.80	11	—
1976-77	in New Zealand	2	6	—	3.00	13	—
1976-77	v England	1	138	1	138.00	5	—
1977	in England	5	166	—	20.75	9	—
1979-80	v West Indies	3	57	—	11.40	11	1
1979-80	v England	3	70	—	17.50	11	—
1979-80	in Pakistan	3	106	—	21.20	4	1
1980	in England	1	16	—	—	1	—
1980-81	v New Zealand	3	100	—	25.00	10	—
1980-81	v India	3	83	—	16.60	15	1
1981	in England	6	216	—	19.63	23	—
1981-82	v Pakistan	3	142	—	28.40	11	—
1981-82	v West Indies	3	117	—	23.40	10	—
1981-82	in New Zealand	3	59	—	19.66	5	—
1982-83	in Pakistan	3	72	—	12.00	3	1
1982-83	v England	5	124	—	17.71	28	—
1983-84	v Pakistan	5	75	—	18.75	21	—
Totals		96	3,633	3	26.51	343	12

Career runs: 11,067 *Average:* 31.35
Career dismissals: 868 *Catches* 802 *Stumpings* 66
Best Test wicketkeeping: 8 dismissals (all caught) in match, v West Indies, Melbourne, 1975-76 and v New Zealand, Christchurch, 1976-77

MAY
Peter Barker Howard
b 1929-

For a period in the 1950s, Peter May was regarded as the best batsman in the world. And to many he has, more than 20 years after his retirement, no superiors in England among post-war batsmen. His Test career spanned less than 10 years, yet in that time, as well as his feats as a batsman, he captained England a record 41 times.

Fine though his record is, however, it conceals two all-important facts. One is that during his career for Surrey, whom he captained for four years—twice to the championship—he was batting on pitches at the Oval that were far from ideal. In fact, the great Surrey bowlers of the day—Bedser, Loader, Laker, and Lock—reaped hundreds of wickets there. The second is that in Test matches, as well as batting on frequently imperfect wickets, he was continually under pressure, sustaining England batting that had no established opening partnership and had the obdurate but relatively unproductive Trevor Bailey at No. 6 with little afterwards. For years he can seldom have gone to the crease without feeling that a crisis was on, and that if he failed the side failed. Such pressure, along with that of work, a period of ill-health, and the burden of captaincy, was probably a contributory factor to his early retirement in 1961 at 31.

Tall, elegant, and powerful, Peter May had an almost orthodox method, played very straight, and had all the strokes except perhaps the hook, which he did not often seem to need to play. He combined, as few others have, the grace, strength, and classic mould of the old-fashioned amateur with the professional competitiveness now needed in the highest class.

He was already a batsman of limitless potential when he came under the eye of former England and Leicestershire player George Geary, then coach at Charterhouse. At both Charterhouse and Cambridge, May's talents developed on good pitches, and he played his first match for Surrey in 1950. A year later he was playing for England against South Africa at Leeds and it was a sign of the concentration and phlegmatic temperament he was to show so often later that he made 138 in that first Test.

After playing against India in 1952, he became the first target of the Australian bowlers in 1953. Ray Lindwall bowled superbly to him at the Oval in the Surrey match, and when he was out cheaply in the first Test the England selectors dropped him until the vital fifth Test. He returned then to play two important innings and was soon acknowledged as the batsman who would take over the mantles of Hutton and Compton.

He was vice-captain to Len Hutton on the triumphant tour of Australia in 1954-55, and it was his 104 at Sydney in the second Test that turned the series towards England after they had lost the first Test and been 74 runs behind in the first innings of the second. On returning to England May found himself appointed captain, Hutton being ill, and he led England 35 times in succession, beginning with the magnificent series of 1955 against South Africa. He himself scored a brilliant hundred at Lord's and another at Old Trafford, averaging 72 in the series.

The next year he had an even more remarkable record in a low-scoring series against Australia, averaging 90 and sharing a memorable fourth wicket partnership of 187 with the veteran Cyril Washbrook at Leeds after England had lost three wickets for 17.

May was then at his peak of brilliance, and his failure in the Test series in South Africa in 1956-57 has never been satisfactorily explained. He played as well as ever in other matches but fell to brilliant catches and the like in the Tests. But at home in 1957 he soon showed this was merely a fleeting failure, for when England began their second innings in the first Test at Edgbaston 288 behind West Indies, May batted for nearly 10 hours, making 285 not out and sharing in a record fourth-wicket stand of 411 with Colin Cowdrey. The baffling Sonny Ramadhin was never the same again, and England went on to win the series easily.

Early in 1958, May played two of his best innings for Surrey—174 against Lancashire at Old Trafford and 165 against the New Zealanders at the Oval when the next highest score in the match was 25. But that winter in Australia he led an ageing side, and though he still batted well himself they were well beaten by Richie Benaud's more aggressive Australians.

In 1959, May suffered a painful illness midway through the season. He was struck down again during the tour of West Indies that winter, and missed the 1960 season, but returned to play against Australia in 1961 before retiring. Throughout his career he had played as an amateur, and his services to cricket did not stop with his wonderful record on the field. Since retiring, he has served as a Test selector, becoming Chairman of selectors in 1982, and on innumerable committees for Surrey and MCC.

MAY Peter Barker Howard

Teams: Cambridge University, Surrey, and England

Test series		Tests	Runs	100s	Average
1951	v South Africa	2	171	1	57.00
1952	v India	4	206	–	34.33
1953	v Australia	2	85	–	28.33
1953-54	in West Indies	5	414	1	46.00
1954	v Pakistan	4	120	–	24.00
1954-55	in Australia	5	351	1	39.00
1954-55	in New Zealand	2	71	–	23.66
1955	v South Africa	5†	582	2	72.75
1956	v Australia	5†	453	1	90.60
1956-57	in South Africa	5†	153	–	15.30
1957	v West Indies	5†	489	2	97.80
1958	v New Zealand	5†	337	2	67.40
1958-59	in Australia	5†	405	1	40.50
1958-59	in New Zealand	2†	195	1	195.00
1959	v India	3†	150	1	50.00
1959-60	in West Indies	3†	83	–	16.60
1961	v Australia	4‡	272	–	38.85
Totals		66	4,537	13	46.77

Career runs: 27,592 Average: 51.00
Highest Test and career score: 285* v West Indies, Edgbaston, 1957

*Not out †Captain ‡Captain in 3 Tests

MILLER
Keith Ross b 1919-

Perhaps the most exciting personality on the cricket scene in the years following World War II, Keith Miller moved into the press box when his playing days ended and continued his lively association with the game.

As a player, he was unpredictable in everything he did, and the public loved him for it. At times, he looked the greatest fast bowler the game has seen, yet it is well known that bowling was often irksome to him. He was much happier hitting the ball to all corners of the ground. But if the runs were too easy to obtain, he would not be averse to throwing his wicket away. His off-the-field life was equally unexpected. Full of fun and often a practical joker, he had moments of extreme seriousness. And his love of classical music contrasted sharply with his fondness of gambling.

Standing 6 ft. 1 in. tall, lithe, handsome, and debonair, Miller gave the appearance of the perfect athlete, and he became a hero to young and old, male and female. Born in Melbourne while Keith Smith and Ross Smith were making the first flight from England to Australia, he was given the Christian names of the two airmen, and though it is difficult to know whether or not he gained inspiration from the names, he developed the same adventurous spirit.

Early ideas of becoming a jockey had to go by the board when Miller grew more than a foot soon after his 16th birthday. Even when small, he had shown promise as a cricketer, but with increased build came more power, and he developed quickly, especially as a free-hitting batsman. He first played for Victoria in 1937-38, soon making his mark. But the war intervened, and he went to England where he served as a night fighter pilot. It was then that he suffered the back injury that at times handicapped him as a player. Not that he ever let that be an excuse for a poor performance: indeed he would never admit he was in difficulty.

It was in England that Miller blossomed as an all-rounder, and his bowling in the 'victory' Tests for Australia against England was a foretaste of what was to come. Also that season, 1945, he hit himself into the headlines with an innings of 185 in 165 minutes for a Dominions' XI against England at Lord's. It included seven sixes, one of them among the biggest hits ever seen on the ground.

His reputation established, Miller returned to Australia and transferred from Victoria to New South Wales, becoming an automatic Test choice and developing with his great friend Ray Lindwall, a fearsome fast bowling combina-

tion that kept Australia on top of the cricket world for seven years. Rarely did he fail with both bat and ball, and his all-round skill brought him 2,958 runs and 170 wickets in 55 Tests. Not that he concerned himself with figures. They were incidental in the course of thoroughly enjoying himself and communicating that enjoyment to others.

Fast bowling brought him the majority of his wickets, and there were times when his fierce pace, vicious bumper, and ability to make the ball kick from a length made him almost unplayable. Not that he was an out-and-out pace man. Few who saw his bowling at Lord's in 1956 will ever forget it. Approaching the end of his career, the 36-year-old Miller, bowling medium-pace and moving the ball either way, took 5-72 and 5-80. On other occasions, he turned to off-breaks, and in fact his best Test bowling performance, 7-60, came with spin on a sticky pitch in the first Test against England at Brisbane in 1946-47. Yet even when apparently bowling at his fastest and best, Miller would show the refusal to conform that was so characteristic of him by suddenly slipping in a leg-break, googly, off-break, or a round-arm slinging ball. Or he would

RIGHT Power and grace went into a Keith Miller sweep. Miller was an attacking cricketer who, when in the mood, could lay waste the most powerful bowling. BELOW Miller enjoying a cover-drive. The keeper is Sussex skipper S. C. Griffith, later Secretary of the MCC.

MITCHELL
Bruce b 1909-

Opening batsman and anchor of many South African innings for a period of 20 years, Bruce Mitchell first played for his country in England in 1929. He went there at the age of 20, and though he had almost no experience of turf pitches he astonished everyone by his skill on them. Later, he became renowned for his patience and imperturbable temperament. He was often regarded as a dull batsman, but his method was immensely sound and he had an agreeable style.

It is often said, with justice, that predominantly defensive batsmen may save matches but never win them. Mitchell, however, played an all-important part in the victory at Lord's in 1935 that gave South Africa their first win over England in a rubber in England. He batted 5½ hours in the second innings to make 164 not out before South Africa declared at 278-7. His first Test hundred had come against England in Cape Town in 1930-31, when he and I. J. Siedle scored 260 together, still the South African record opening stand over 50 years later.

Mitchell was 38 when he returned to England with Alan Melville's South African side in 1947. His form for the Transvaal had suggested that he had lost little of his old reliability in the war years, and after a slow start he soon made four hundreds in six innings and batted stolidly through the tour to a remarkable climax. At the Oval in the fifth Test, he made 120 in the first innings and then, when South Africa went in needing 451 to win, batted to the end of the match when his side was only 28 short of the target and he himself had made 189 not out. He was off the field for less than 15 minutes in the four days. In all, he made eight hundreds on the tour and averaged 61.

His last series was against England in 1948-49, when he made the last of his eight Test hundreds and missed a ninth by just one run in his final Test.

Bruce Mitchell enjoyed batting at the Oval, where he made his highest score, and where in 1947 he scored centuries in each innings against England, making over 300 for once out.

unexpectedly turn round when walking back to his mark and send down a delivery of rare pace off only a yard-or-so run.

The highlights of Miller's Test batting were three centuries against England and four against West Indies—three of them in the 1954-55 season. When the mood took him, he could annihilate the finest bowling attack with an impressive repertoire of strokes that included powerful drives and the most delicate cutting. He is one of the few cricketers to have scored

ABOVE Keith Miller was a very dangerous fast bowler, off both a long or short run.

a century and taken six wickets in an innings of a single Test. In the fifth Test against West Indies at Kingston in 1954-55, he scored 109 in Australia's first innings after taking six West Indies wickets for 107. Add to this an ability to pick up brilliant catches, especially in the slips, and Miller has claims to rank among the finest all-round cricketers of all time.

MILLER Keith Ross

Teams: Victoria, New South Wales, and Australia

Test series	Tests	Runs	100s	Average	Wkts	Average
1945-46 in New Zealand	1	30	—	30.00	2	3.00
1946-47 v England	5	384	1	76.80	16	20.87
1947-48 v India	5	185	—	37.00	9	24.77
1948 in England	5	184	—	28.26	13	23.15
1949-50 in South Africa	5	246	—	41.00	17	22.94
1950-51 v England	5	350	1	43.75	17	17.70
1951-52 v West Indies	5	362	1	40.22	20	19.90
1952-53 v South Africa	4	153	—	25.50	13	18.53
1953 in England	5	223	1	24.77	10	30.30
1954-55 v England	4	167	—	23.85	10	24.30
1954-55 in West Indies	5	439	3	73.16	20	32.00
1956 in England	5	203	—	22.55	21	22.23
1956-57 in Pakistan	1	32	—	16.00	2	29.00
Totals	55	2,958	7	36.97	170	22.97

Career runs: 14,183 *Average:* 48.90
Highest Test score: 147 v West Indies, Kingston, 1954-55
Highest career score: 281*, Australians v Leicestershire, Leicester, 1956
Career wickets: 497 *Average:* 22.30
Best Test bowling: 7-60 v England, Brisbane, 1946-47
Best career bowling: 7-12, New South Wales v South Australia, Sydney, 1955-56

*Not out

MITCHELL Bruce

Teams: Transvaal and South Africa

Test series	Tests	Runs	100s	Average
1929 in England	5	251	—	31.37
1930-31 v England	5	455	1	50.55
1931-32 in Australia	5	322	—	32.20
1931-32 in New Zealand	2	166	1	55.33
1935 in England	5	488	2	69.71
1935-36 v Australia	5	251	—	31.37
1938-39 v England	5	466	1	58.25
1947 in England	5	597	2	66.33
1948-49 v England	5	475	1	52.77
Totals	42	3,471	8	48.88

Career runs: 11,395 *Average:* 45.39
Highest Test score: 189* v England, Oval, 1947
Highest career score: 195, South Africans v Surrey, Oval, 1935

*Not out

MORRIS
Arthur Robert b 1922-

Arthur Morris could be called 'The Quiet Australian'. A pleasant, modest, and kind man, he was liked wherever he went as well as being regarded as perhaps the best left-handed opening batsman the game has known. In keeping with his manner, Morris was more of a gentle persuader of runs rather than an aggressive acquirer. So successful were his methods that in 24 matches against England he scored 2,080 runs, including eight centuries, and averaged just over 50. A player of complete calm with a sound defence and neat style, he excelled in placing his strokes wide of fieldsmen, and often he would upset bowlers by walking down the pitch and putting them off their length.

His consistency meant that England, in the early days of Morris at least, rarely managed the good start that usually gives a side encouragement. Not that Morris began his Test career auspiciously. He scored just 2 and 5 in his first two games, but the selectors persisted with him, and in the third Test, at Melbourne, England had a sample of his skill when he scored 155 in the second innings. This was followed by 122 and 124 not out at Adelaide, the first time an Australian had hit a century in each innings of a Test in his own country. In the same game, Denis Compton also scored a hundred in each innings. Morris finished the series with an average of 71.85.

He did even better on his first tour of England in 1948 and headed the Test averages, above Bradman and Barnes, with 87.00. He hit 196 at the Oval, 182 at Headingley, and 105 at Lord's. At Headingley, he and Bradman put on 301 for that second wicket and helped Australia to a remarkable victory by seven wickets when set to get 404 in 345 minutes on the last day.

An aggressive shot by Arthur Morris has backward short leg defending himself and even the wicket-keeper taking evasive action.

Morris was unable to maintain such a high level in his next three series against England, although he did score 206, the highest of his career, in the fourth Test at Adelaide in 1950-51. In that series and the next, 1953, Morris so often fell victim of Alec Bedser that he became known as 'Bedser's Bunny'. Against all countries, Morris played in 46 Tests and averaged 46.48. His career average in first-class games was over 55 and included 46 hundreds.

Morris began his cricketing days at school as a slow left-arm bowler and a No. 11 batsman. He was still regarded only as a bowler in his high school days, but gradually his batting improved, and when 16 he hit a century against Sydney University. That led to his being tried as an opening batsman, and he stayed in that position.

While still a schoolboy, Morris was asked to play for New South Wales Second XI against the Victorian Second XI, and was only 19 when he shook the cricket world by scoring a century in each

Morris hits a cover-drive. He averaged 87 in Tests in England in 1948.

innings of his first Sheffield Shield match, 148 and 111 against Queensland at Sydney in December 1940. During the war years Morris played little cricket, being stationed for most of the time in New Guinea, and it was not until the 1946-47 MCC visit that he returned to cricket full-time. He gave up the game seriously at the all too early age of 33.

MORRIS Arthur Robert				
Teams: New South Wales and Australia				
Test series	Tests	Runs	100s	Average
1946-47 v England	5	503	3	71.85
1947-48 v India	4	209	1	52.25
1948 in England	5	696	3	87.00
1949-50 in South Africa	5	422	2	52.75
1950-51 v England	5	321	1	35.66
1951-52 v West Indies	4*	186	—	23.25
1952-53 v South Africa	5	370	—	41.11
1953 in England	5	337	—	33.70
1954-55 v England	4*	223	1	31.85
1954-55 in West Indies	4	266	1	44.33
Totals	46	3,533	12	46.48

Career runs: 12,614 *Average:* 53.67
Highest Test score: 206 v England, Adelaide, 1950-51
Highest career score: 290, Australians v Gloucestershire, Bristol, 1948

*Captain in one Test

POLLOCK
Peter Maclean b 1941-

Far from being overshadowed by the brilliance of his younger brother Graeme, Peter Pollock established himself as a vital member of the South African team as a deadly fast bowler. Standing just over 6 ft. 2 in. tall and well built, he made good use of his physique for both speed and stamina. At one time he relied on sheer pace with plenty of bouncers to unsettle batsmen, but with experience came variation. His extremely long run-up usually meant he took a long time to deliver an over, but he found that he lost effectiveness when he tried to take fewer paces.

At school Peter Pollock used to open both batting and bowling, but his coach George Cox advised him to concentrate on bowling. He was only 17 when he made his first-class debut, and in 1961 he toured England with the Fezelas, a team that included most of South Africa's best young talent. Making excellent progress with Eastern Province, he began his Test career against New Zealand at Durban in 1961-62 with outstanding success. In the first innings he took 3-61 and followed with 6-38 in the second. The 1963-64 tour of Australia showed him to be a top-class bowler. He began with 6-95 in the first Test at Brisbane, claimed 5-83 at Sydney, and altogether took 25 wickets in the

series, heading the South African bowling averages. He followed with 15 wickets in New Zealand at the end of the tour of Australia, including 6-47 at Wellington, so that in eight successive Tests he captured 40 wickets.

He did not have a good series against Mike Smith's Englishmen in 1964-65, but he came back well during the short tour of England in 1965, taking 20 wickets in three Tests for 366 runs. He fell away again against Australia in 1966-67, but on the next Australian visit in 1970 he was well to the fore, his 15 wickets for 258 runs including 5-39 at Johannesburg and 4-20 at Cape Town. And during the 1970 England v Rest of the World series, he was reporting the matches when he was unexpectedly called upon to replace Graham McKenzie in the third match at Edgbaston.

ABOVE *Peter Pollock sends one down against Hampshire in 1965. Pollock took more Test wickets for South Africa than any bowler except Hugh Tayfield.*
LEFT *Pollock in action for the Rest of the World against England in 1970, when he replaced Graham McKenzie.*

POLLOCK Peter MacLean

Teams: Eastern Province and South Africa

Test series	Tests	Wkts	Avge
1961-62 v New Zealand	3	17	17.58
1963-64 in Australia	5	25	28.40
1963-64 in New Zealand	3	15	17.20
1964-65 v England	5	12	37.08
1965 in England	3	20	18.30
1966-67 v Australia	5	12	39.16
1969-70 v Australia	4	15	17.20
Totals	28	116	24.18

Career wickets: 485 *Average:* 21.89
Best Test bowling: 6-38 v New Zealand, Durban, 1961-62
Best career bowling: 7-19, Eastern Province v Western Province, Port Elizabeth, 1962-63
Highest Test score: 75* v Australia, Cape Town, 1966-67
Highest career score: 79, Eastern Province v Transvaal, Johannesburg, 1962-63

*Not out

POLLOCK
Robert Graeme b 1944-

The opportunity came in the summer of 1970 to compare the merits of Graeme Pollock and Gary Sobers, two of the best left-handed batsmen cricket has known. They played in the same Rest of the World side against England, but unfortunately for those who claimed that Pollock was every bit as good as the great West Indian, he failed to show his best form.

Despite that, however, Pollock is acknowledged to be a master of his art, and those who see him play a big innings are enthralled. He makes batting look so easy that most of his partners and opponents suffer badly when in contact with him. At times he hardly seems to put any power behind a stroke, yet the ball races over the turf and defies all efforts to cut it off before the boundary. His off-side shots in particular are played in a lazy, almost contemptuous manner, and his placing in the arc from third man to long off has rarely been bettered. When he decides to put the full strength of his 6ft 2½in frame behind a drive, a six is almost inevitable. With Pollock, timing is everything and he is a real joy to the eye. A noticeable point about him is that he appears to have no nerves and all his play shows a lack of tension.

Pollock was born in Durban, and his father, a Scot, was a keen cricketer who kept wicket for Orange Free State. An exceptional schoolboy player, he hit a century and took 10 wickets in one match when only nine, and like his father, he did everything with his right hand except bat. Until the age of 12 he bowled fast like his brother Peter, but he was then persuaded to try leg-breaks instead. After spending four years in the Grey High School XI, starting at 13 and finishing as captain, he moved to Eastern Province and, at the age of 16 years 335 days, became the youngest player to hit a century in the Currie Cup competition.

He owed a lot to the coaching of George Cox, the Sussex batsman, and when visiting England with his parents in 1961 he played six innings for the county's second XI. Continuing his remarkable progress in South Africa, he became the youngest South African to hit a double century when he scored 209 not out against Richie Benaud's Cavaliers side at Port Elizabeth. He was then 19 years 20 days old, and he was just 20 when he was appointed captain of Eastern Province.

Graeme Pollock made his Test debut in Australia in 1963-64 and

An aggressive Pollock in full flow against Australia in the 1969-70 series in which he made 517 runs, including his best ever score of 274.

quickly made himself a personality with a brilliant 127 not out in the second important match of the tour, against a Combined XI at Perth, his century taking no more than 85 minutes. His first two Tests were far from distinguished, but a change came in the third at Sydney where he made 122, the second 50 of his century coming in 17 scoring strokes. The next Test brought a real triumph, for with Eddie Barlow he added 341 for the third wicket, the highest stand in South African Test history. Barlow made 201 and Pollock 175, a great innings for a 19-year-old.

When England visited South Africa in 1964-65 Pollock was again slow to get started, but in his last seven innings he scored over 50 five times, with the highlight his 137 and 77 not out in the fifth Test on his own ground at Port Elizabeth. The following English summer, 1965, Pollock toured England and scored 291 runs in the three Tests, including 125 at Trent Bridge. When he had scored 28 in that innings he became, at little more than 21, the youngest batsman to reach 1,000 runs in Test cricket. Between the first and second Test, Pollock made 203 not out at Canterbury, an innings that contained 5 sixes and reminded Kent followers of their own great left-hander, Frank Woolley.

Pollock has taken a real toll of Australian bowling, especially in his own country. In 1966-67 he hit 90 in the first Test and helped South Africa gain their first home victory over their opponents in 64 years. That was followed by a tremendous 209 at Cape Town, although it still failed to save South Africa from defeat. He maintained his form with 67 not

A subdued Pollock playing for the Rest of the World in 1970, a disappointing series for him.

out in the third Test at Durban and 105 in the final match at Port Elizabeth, so playing a vital part in South Africa's winning the series 3-1.

When Australia next visited South Africa in 1970, Pollock scored 517 runs in seven innings, with his magnificent 274 at Durban the highest score ever made for South Africa in a Test match. Later that year he visited England again, to represent the Rest of the World, but his only worthwhile innings was 114 in the final game at the Oval.

POLLOCK Robert Graeme

Teams: Eastern Province, Transvaal, and South Africa

Test series	Tests	Runs	100s	Avge
1963-64 in Australia	5	399	2	57.00
1963-64 in New Zealand	1	53	—	26.50
1964-65 v England	5	459	1	57.37
1965 in England	3	291	1	48.50
1966-67 v Australia	5	537	2	76.51
1969-70 v Australia	4	517	1	73.85
Total	**23**	**2,256**	**7**	**60.97**

Career runs: 19,813 *Average:* 54.58
Highest Test and career score:
274 v Australia, Durban, 1969-70

Career figures correct to end of 1985 season

PROCTER
Michael John b 1946-

Mike Procter was most famous for his unique bowling action. He was frequently described as 'bowling off the wrong foot', but this is more or less impossible. In fact, he brought his arm over and released the ball just a little earlier in the delivery stride than most bowlers. This made him look awkward, but, whether it was despite the awkwardness or because of it, he was extremely effective. He was a right-arm fast bowler (who, when he had knee problems, successfully switched to off-breaks) and, judging by his only two Test series, played in his early twenties, he would have been one of Test cricket's most successful bowlers had he not been South African and prohibited from international competition. As his batting developed until he was one of the world's best middle-order hard-hitting batsmen, he became an all-rounder to rival any in the game. Indeed, for a while, until challenged by the younger generation of Botham, Kapil Dev, Imran and Hadlee, he was, without doubt, on his own as the world's best all-rounder.

Procter was born in 1946 in Durban into a cricketing family, his father playing for Eastern Province and his brother for Natal. He came to England and made his first-class debut for Gloucestershire in 1965 (a season in which the South Africans toured England). The following winter he made his debut for Natal.

In 1966-67 he made his Test debut in the third Test against the touring Australians at Durban, his home town. He took 3 for 27 and 4 for 71 (his first victim being Bobby Simpson) as South Africa took a lead in the series that they were to keep. Procter went on to take 15 wickets in the final three Tests.

The England tour to South Africa in 1968-69 was cancelled over the Basil d'Oliveira affair, and Procter's only other chance to play Test cricket came in 1969-70, when once again Australia were visitors. It was a remarkable series in which Bill Lawry's side were beaten in all four Tests, once by an innings, twice by over 300 runs, and once by a mere 170 runs. Procter was South Africa's most destructive bowler, taking at least two wickets in each innings, and ending with 6 for 73 in the last innings played against South Africa in a Test.

In 1970 Procter played for the Rest of the World against England in all five matches of the series which replaced the South African tour, scoring 292 runs, average 48.66, and taking 15 wickets, average 23.93.

Between November 1970 and March 1971, Procter joined two distinguished batsmen, D. G. Bradman and C. B. Fry, in the

Procter's bowling action, often described as 'off the wrong foot', in 1979.

record books, becoming the third to score a century in six successive innings. All were for Rhodesia, the last, 254 against Western Province, being his highest score in first-class cricket.

His best season as a batsman in England was 1971, when he hit 1,786 runs, average 45.79. It was one of nine occasions in which he scored 1,000 runs in a season. In 1972-73 he achieved his best bowling figures, 9 for 71 for Rhodesia against Transvaal. He was around this time at the peak of his powers as both batsman and fast bowler. His particular odd bowling action, already mentioned, in which he bowled chest on to the batsman, required great strength. He was just about the fastest bowler in the world and generated a lot of movement off the pitch.

All this came to an end in 1975 when an injury to his knee caused

him to have an operation and miss the beginning of the 1976 season. It was then that he began bowling off-breaks while waiting for his knee to heal. That he came back to good effect is shown by the fact that his most successful bowling season for Gloucestershire was 1977, with 109 wickets, average 18.04.

Procter was a Gloucestershire player for 17 seasons, and was captain from 1977 to 1981. His highest score for them was made in 1978, 203 against Essex at

Gloucester. He added astute captaincy to his other talents, and frequently produced a captain's performance when it was most needed, particularly in limited-overs games. In 1973 he made 101 in the semi-final and 94 in the final when Gloucestershire won the Gillette Cup, and he captained the side when they won the Benson and Hedges Cup in 1977.

Had a World XI been picked around the mid-1970s, Procter would have had claims to the captaincy.

PROCTER Michael John

Teams: Gloucestershire, Natal, Western Province, Rhodesia and South Africa

Test series	Tests	Runs	Average	Wkts	Average
1966-67 v Australia	3	17	5.66	15	17.53
1969-70 v Australia	4	209	34.83	26	13.57
Totals	7	226	25.11	41	15.02

Career runs: 21,904 *Average:* 36.14
Highest Test score: 48 v Australia, Cape Town, 1969-70
Highest career score: 254, Rhodesia v Western Province, Salisbury, 1970-71
Career wickets: 1,407 *Average:* 19.36
Best Test bowling: 6-73 v Australia, Port Elizabeth, 1969-70
Best career bowling: 9-71, Rhodesia v Transvaal, Bulawayo, 1972-73

REID
John Richard b 1928-

New Zealand's outstanding cricketer in the 1950s and early 1960s, John Reid was worthy of a place among the leading all-rounders of his time. His 58 consecutive Test appearances were a record, and, in what was perhaps the highlight of his career, he had the distinction of leading his country to her first ever Test victory, against West Indies in 1956. It was just his third Test as captain.

More than any place else, Reid demonstrated his all-round ability most consistently in South Africa. On his first tour there, in 1953-54, he became the first cricketer to score 1,000 runs and take 50 wickets in a South African season, and in 1961-62 his tour aggregate of 1,915 runs eclipsed Denis Compton's 13-year-old record. Also on that second tour he headed both the Test and tour batting and the tour bowling averages, as well as being the leading fielder with 22 catches. His seven centuries included 203 against Western Province and 142 in the fourth Test, and his 4-44 off 45 overs following a hard-hit 69 played a vital part in New Zealand's fifth-Test victory that squared the series.

Outstanding at both cricket and rugby as a Wellington schoolboy, Reid made his first-class debut in 1947, and in 1949, at 20, went to England with Walter Hadlee's side, soon establishing himself as its leading all-rounder. His batting

Considered by many to be New Zealand's best-ever all-rounder when he retired, he was also his country's most successful captain. John Reid had scored more runs and taken more wickets than any other New Zealander.

was solid and included Test innings of 50 and 93, his bowling at times was as fast as that of anyone in English cricket, and he proved a capable wicket-keeper in the fourth Test at the Oval. He returned to England in 1952 for three seasons with Heywood in the Central Lancashire League, and it was while playing there that he changed to bowling off-cutters. His immaculate length and control proved their worth in South Africa in 1953-54, and two years later in India and Pakistan he headed the Test bowling averages in both series as well as scoring 1,032 runs on the tour.

It was on his first South African tour that Reid discovered the value of playing off the back foot rather than the front, and subsequently adapted his technique so that he rarely went forward except to drive. The change, however, did not restrict his natural desire to attack, and many bowlers suffered from his powerful driving and savage hooking. One attack to wilt before a Reid onslaught was that of Northern Districts in a 1962-63 Plunket Shield match with Wellington. His 296 included a record number of sixes for an innings—15. Not so productive but equally attacking had been his innings of 84 that started New Zealand on the way to victory over West Indies at Auckland in 1956.

He was an automatic choice as New Zealand's captain from that success until his retirement following the 1965 tour of India, Pakistan, and England. There were times when he alone seemed to hold the New Zealand side together, and he often went in to bat knowing that so much depended on him. Consequently his performances at times suffered. Had he been a member of an established side, though, his record may well have been even greater.

REID John Richard

Teams: Wellington, Otago, and New Zealand

Test series		Tests	Runs	100s	Average	Wkts	Average
1949	in England	2	173	—	43.25	0	—
1950-51	v England	2	72	—	24.00	0	—
1951-52	v West Indies	2	9	—	3.00	0	—
1952-53	v South Africa	2	17	—	5.66	2	56.00
1953-54	in South Africa	5	263	1	29.22	12	32.00
1954-55	v England	2	106	—	26.50	4	19.00
1955-56	in Pakistan	3	133	—	22.16	7	31.57
1955-56	in India	5	493	2	70.42	6	45.16
1955-56	v West Indies	4†	203	—	25.37	7	36.85
1958	in England	5*	147	—	16.33	6	31.16
1958-59	v England	2*	44	—	14.66	3	17.66
1961-62	in South Africa	5*	546	1	60.66	11	19.72
1962-63	v England	3*	263	1	52.60	2	85.50
1963-64	v South Africa	3*	88	—	14.66	12	23.16
1964-65	v Pakistan	3*	229	—	38.16	4	35.50
1964-65	in India	4*	198	—	28.28	3	59.33
1964-65	in Pakistan	3*	296	1	59.20	5	27.00
1965	in England	3*	148	—	24.66	1	54.00
Totals		58	3,428	6	33.28	85	33.35

Career runs: 16,128 *Average:* 41.35
Highest Test score: 142 v South Africa, Johannesburg, 1961-62
Highest career score: 296, Wellington v Northern Districts, Wellington, 1962-63
Career wickets: 466 *Average:* 22.60
Best Test bowling: 6-60 v South Africa, Dunedin, 1963-64
Best career bowling: 7-20, Otago v Central Districts, Dunedin, 1956-57

*Captain   †Captain in 3 Tests

RICHARDS
Barry Anderson b 1945-

Barry Richards was something of a throwback in cricket. The modern theory that batsmen, especially those going in first, cannot score quickly against present-day bowling and scientific field-placing had no place in his make-up. He believed that the aim of a batsman was to dominate an attack from first to last, and because of this outlook he was one of the most attractive and successful batsmen in the game.

After making an early impact in his home town of Durban, Richards captained the South African schools side that visited England in 1963 and made his first-class debut for Natal in 1964-65. Along with Mike Procter, also from Natal, he played for Gloucestershire's Second XI in 1965—they could not appear in the County Championship because of the qualification rules. They did appear together, though, for the first eleven against the South Africans. Richards later returned to England to play for Hampshire.

In his first season for Hampshire, Richards hit 2,039 runs in the Championship, and finished second to Geoff Boycott in the overall averages, with 2,395 runs at an average of 47.90, his five centuries including 206 against Nottinghamshire at Portsmouth. The following season, despite injuries, he averaged 57.60 for 1,440 runs, and in 1970 scored 1,667 runs (averaging 53.77). In 1970-71 he went to Australia where, playing for south Australia, he scored 224 against MCC followed a little later by 356 in the Sheffield Shield match against Western Australia and 146 in the second game with MCC. During his innings of 356, made against Lillee, McKenzie and Lock, he scored 325 not out on the first day, and thought this was his greatest innings. He also broke Don Bradman's South Australian record of 1,448 in a season.

Richards had a brilliant first Test series, scoring 508 runs in seven innings against Australia in South Africa in early 1970, hitting 140 in his second Test at Durban and 126 in the fourth at Port Elizabeth. He also played in all five matches for the Rest of the World against England in 1970, but was not at his best and his highest score was only 64. Ideally suited to the one-day quick-fire cricket, Richards had many excellent performances in the Gillette Cup and John Player League.

Personal disappointment in South Africa's exclusion from Test cricket did not affect his performances either for Hampshire or for Natal, for whom he assumed the extra responsibility of captaincy with considerable success.

RIGHT AND BELOW Barry Richards in action. One of the most attacking of opening batsmen, he was for a spell the best batsman in the world.

An unashamed 'mercenary', he was highly successful in World Series Cricket and played for a while in Holland.

Richards' figures do no justice to his skill, as he frequently got himself out when passing 50 or 100, and his mastery was such that he sometimes got himself out from boredom when he might have made a big score. Some judges regard him as the best batsman to appear since the war.

RICHARDS Barry Anderson

Teams: Natal, Gloucestershire (1 match), Hampshire, South Australia, Transvaal, and South Africa

Test series	Tests	Runs	100s	Avge
1969-70 v Australia	4	508	2	72.57

Career runs: 28,358 *Average:* 54.74
Highest Test score: 140 v Australia, Durban, 1969-70
Highest career score: 356, South Australia v Western Australia, Perth, 1970-71

RICHARDS
Isaac Vivian Alexander
b 1952-

The year of 1976 belonged to Vivian Richards. His total of 1,710 runs in Test matches established a new record over twelve calendar months. Moreover, he dominated the series against England—amassing 829 runs despite missing one game through illness.

Born in St. John's, in Antigua, he began his first-class career playing for the Combined Islands in the Shell Shield. But his development into a formidable player stemmed from joining Somerset in 1974. There he won a Gold Award in his first one-day game and picked up his first Championship century in only his third match.

He began in characteristic West Indian vein—with a vast repertoire of exuberant shots tarnished by the occasional throwing away of his wicket.

Nevertheless his achievements earned him a place on the tour to India and Pakistan, and a place in the team following Rowe's eye problems. After a disappointing debut, he announced himself with a masterful 192 not out in his second Test. It was the first indication of his ability to play the really long innings.

He played his part in West Indies World Cup triumph without showing in a dominant role—his fielding in the final when he ran out three Australians emphasized his value to the side.

As with his colleagues, form in Australia in the 1975-76 series proved elusive. But he fired warning shots in his last three innings—101, 50 and 98—in the makeshift role of opener.

India felt the backlash. Richards, now batting at number three, made hundreds in each of the first three Tests, the third a magnificent 177. A mere 64 in the last Test seemed a failure in comparison.

Not yet 25, he extended his domination in England. He began in comprehensive vein with a masterful 232 at Nottingham, and he sustained his assault through until the Oval. There he played with such untiring brilliance that he threatened Sobers' record 365; it came as a total surprise when he was bowled playing a loose shot at Tony Greig for 291.

That was his seventh Test century of 1976—a year of unparalleled run-scoring. Vivian Richards, the pride of Antigua, had becoming the pride of cricket.

Richards was being freely described as the best batsman in the world, a title which took a knock on the tour to Pakistan in 1976-77, when he averaged a mere 28.55. The 1977 season in England restored his reputation, as he became the only batsman to pass 2,000 runs, finishing effectively second in the averages.

There followed the WSC interlude, when Richards, like most of the prominent West Indians, signed for Kerry Packer. Richards proved to be the outstanding run-getter in World Series Cricket.

A great one-day player, and a man who loves to do well at Lord's, Richards found the 1979 World Cup final against England was the ideal stage for his batting act. He was Man of the Match for a superb 138 not out, which ended with a six behind square leg from the last ball, a good length delivery on off stump from Hendrick.

In 1979-80, when West Indies and England were both in Australia after the Packer peace, Richards played four Test innings against the home country and scored 140, 96, 76 and 74 as West Indies won the series 2-0.

With the West Indians touring England again in 1980, Richards reserved his best performance again for Lord's, delighting his London supporters with an innings of 145. With Lloyd injured and unable to play in the fifth Test at Headingley, Richards captained the West Indies. As Botham captained England, both Test captains were Somerset players.

Richards' liking for Lord's meant victories for Somerset in the one-day competitions—four times in five years a Richards innings helped take a trophy to Somerset. In 1979 he scored 117 as Somerset

beat Northants in the Gillette Cup, in 1981 and 1982 innings of 132 not out and 51 not out ensured Benson and Hedges Cup victories over Surrey and Nottinghamshire respectively, and in 1983 an innings of 51 helped defeat Kent in what was now the NatWest Trophy.

In 1980-81, when England visited the West Indies, Richards made successive centuries in the Test series, following 182 not out at Bridgetown with 114 at St John's in his native Antigua. He was less dominating than usual in the following Test series, although he retained a knack of scoring at least one century a series to demonstrate his mastery.

In 1984-85 Clive Lloyd finally

OPPOSITE Vivian Richards was a claimant for the title of world's leading batsman, especially around 1976 in England, when he scored 829 runs in only four Tests and averaged over 118. He made 1,710 in the year.

ABOVE Richards bowling in the Prudential Trophy match against England at Headingley in 1980, when he dismissed Gooch. He is a regular one-day bowler for West Indies and is rarely expensive.

gave up the captaincy of West Indies and Richards, for long the Crown Prince, finally took over as skipper against New Zealand. Richards made a century in the third Test to put West Indies one up in the series. The fourth and final Test, however, suggested that Richards would continue the policy of Lloyd in using his fast bowlers in as intimidatory a manner as the umpires would allow. On a shower-freshened pitch, Marshall and Garner were allowed to bowl three or four bouncers an over at the New Zealand middle order, during which onslaught the tourist's leading batsman, Coney, suffered a broken arm. Before the match

Richards, commenting on criticism of just such tactics, had said that West Indies, having withstood hostile fast bowling in the past, had to use the weapon now that it was theirs.

Back in the more tranquil role of Somerset's run-getter in England in 1985, Richards finished top of the averages, as he had in 1983. He hit nine centuries including his highest score to date, 322 against Warwickshire at Taunton. The innings took just under five hours, and he became the first West Indian to score 300 runs in a day. Richards was still only 33 years old and could look forward to a great many more runs in all levels of cricket.

RICHARDS Isaac Vivian Alexander

Teams: Leeward Islands, Somerset, Queensland, and West Indies

Test series	Tests	Runs	100s	Average
1974-75 in India	5	353	1	50.42
1974-75 in Pakistan	2	17	—	5.66
1975-76 in Australia	6	426	1	38.72
1975-76 v India	4	556	3	92.66
1976 in England	4	829	3	118.42
1976-77 v Pakistan	5	257	—	28.55
1977-78 v Australia	2	62	—	31.00
1979-80 in Australia	3	386	1	128.66
1980 in England‡	5	379	1	63.16
1980-81 in Pakistan	4	364	1	72.80
1980-81 v England	4	340	2	85.00
1981-82 in Australia	3	160	—	26.66
1982-83 v India	5	282	1	47.33
1983-84 in India	6	306	1	34.00
1983-84 v Australia	5	270	1	54.00
1984 in England	5	250	1	41.66
1984-85 in Australia	5	342	1	42.75
1984-85 v New Zealand†	4	310	1	62.00
Totals	77	5,889	19	54.02

Career runs: 26,841 *Average:* 50.26
Highest Test score: 291 v England, Oval, 1976
Highest career score: 322 v Warwickshire, Taunton, 1985
Test wickets: 19 *Average:* 53.94

†Captain ‡Captain in last Test only   Career figures correct to end of 1985 season

ROBERTS
Anderson Montgomery Everton b 1951-

Andy Roberts, the tall, wiry and unemotional West Indian fast bowler, reached his 100th Test wicket in only his 19th Test—and in a shorter span, 2 years and 142 days, than any other player before him in the history of the game.

He achieved that milestone by having David Steel caught behind the wicket in the fourth Test against England in 1976—a series in which his 28 wickets (av. 19.17) reflected magnificent hostility on pitches which generally had little pace in them.

Roberts, from Antigua where he joined forces with Vivian Richards, had made his Test debut against Mike Denness' side in West Indies in 1974-75—playing in just one match, even though the England players described him as the fastest of the West Indian bowlers.

wickets in the five-match series.

Despite the disappointment of the 1975-76 tour to Australia, Roberts form was one of West Indies' saving graces. He topped the averages for the series and at Perth achieved his best Test figures of 7 for 54.

Roberts was slightly less impressive against Pakistan the following season, and in 1977-78 played only two Tests against Australia before the Packer players withdrew. He performed well in WSC matches and resumed his Test career in 1979-80.

In the 1980s Roberts had to share his Test wickets with a whole battery of West Indian pacemen, and his aggregates began to suffer. However, there was a fine flourish late in his career when he took 24 wickets in the 1982-83 series against India, and in the following season he went to India to take five more wickets which took him past the 200 mark. Having left Hampshire in 1978, he joined Leicestershire in 1981 and bowled well for them for four seasons.

ROBERTS Anderson Montgomery Everton

Teams: Leeward Islands, Hampshire, New South Wales, Leicestershire, and West Indies

Test series	Tests	Wkts	Average
1973-74 v England	1	3	41.33
1974-75 in India	5	32	18.28
1974-75 in Pakistan	2	12	26.83
1975-76 in Australia	5	22	26.36
1975-76 v India	2	6	29.33
1976 in England	5	28	19.17
1976-77 v Pakistan	5	19	40.15
1977-78 v Australia	2	12	17.58
1979-80 in Australia	3	11	26.90
1979-80 in New Zealand	2	3	65.33
1980 in England	3	11	23.81
1980-81 v England	3	8	31.38
1981-82 in Australia	2	6	29.66
1982-83 v India	5	24	22.70
1983-84 in India	2	5	29.60
Totals	47	202	25.61

Career wickets: 889 *Average:* 20.40
Best Test bowling: 7-54 v Australia, Perth, 1975-76
Best career bowling: 8-47, Hants v Glamorgan, Cardiff, 1974
Highest Test score: 68 v India, Calcutta, 1983-84
Highest career score: 89, Leicestershire v Glamorgan, 1984

Career figures correct to end of 1985 season

That series followed a season of tremendous promise for Roberts with Hampshire 2nd XI where he had gone on trial. Spotted in a London cricket school where he had been sent with Richards by benefactors in Antigua, Roberts' impact in England was enormous.

Hampshire engaged him for the 1974 season, at the expense of the New Zealand left-arm spinner David O'Sullivan who had been a key bowler in Hampshire's championship win in 1973. But the county had taken no gamble; Roberts topped the first-class bowling averages with 119 wickets (av. 13.62), and sustained his pace throughout the season.

Moreover, he took his good form with him to India where he clinched his regular place in the West Indian attack by taking 32

Roberts is a useful tail-ender but here is beaten by Willis.

SIMPSON
Robert Baddeley b 1936-

Few comebacks in sport can match that of Bobby Simpson for sheer unlikeliness. In his 42nd year and retired from the first-class game for 10 years, he answered Australia's call late in 1977 when almost an entire Test team had signed themselves out of Test cricket in joining Kerry Packer's World Series organisation. Having continued to play grade cricket in Sydney with much success during the intervening years, he was able to rebridge the gap to senior cricket with relative ease, batting now in the middle order, not as an opener, where his name was made in the late 1950s and early 1960s.

In the series against the visiting Indian side Simpson had scores of 89, 176, 100 and 51, finishing top of the batting for either side with 539 runs in 10 innings. In addition, although slightly more fallible as a slips fielder than in the days when he held almost everything within even the barest reach, he took six more catches to take him past Ian Chappell's then Australian Test record of 103.

Simpson's mature leadership was just what Australian cricket needed in its hour of crisis, as was the closely-fought series, won 3-2 by the home side. Then came a sterner test.

Australia's young side looked to be headed for overwhelming defeat in West Indies early in 1978 —and so it turned out, until the Caribbean Packer players withdrew their considerable services. Each of the first two Tests was over in three days, Simpson having failed as did many of his batsmen. Then came a gallant victory at Georgetown, further defeat in the fourth Test, and gross injustice at Kingston when a crowd disturbance cost Australia victory. It was not a five-nil whitewash after all.

Simpson the 'old man' could hardly have been visualised when the 16-year-old was chosen to make his debut for New South Wales in 1952-53, and he took some time to prove his true worth.

His native State was very strong in those years, and it took a move to Perth to bring his talents to full blossom. In the 1959-60 season he scored 902 runs in six Sheffield Shield innings for Western Australia at an average of 300.66 before touring New Zealand with an Australian 'B' team. Soon he was in the Test side, and becoming an indispensable part of it.

Not that his first Test century came immediately. He was in his 52nd innings for his country, and captain, when he at last reached three figures. It was at Old Trafford in 1964, and he was at the crease for 12¾ hours for a mammoth 311 as Australia shut out England with a total of 656 for 8 declared and retained the Ashes. He was no stranger to triple-

centuries, having made 359 against Queensland the preceding season.

Correct in method, with model patience and his own 'sway back' method of dealing with fast bouncers, Simpson made up for the years when certain critics and sections of the public had doubted his class. In the 4,131 runs he made in the 52 Test matches in the early part of his career were scores of 225 against England, 153 against South Africa, 201 against West Indies, two centuries in a match against Pakistan and two in the 1967-68 series against India which marked his supposed farewell to Test cricket. His opening partnership with tall Victorian left-hander Bill Lawry ranks with that of Woodfull and Ponsford or of Hobbs and Sutcliffe: a record 244 against England at Adelaide in 1965-66, a record 382 against West Indies a year earlier. Opening bowlers and others were relieved when he retired at 32, leaving Australia's first-wicket armoury that much more vulnerable.

As a batsman, he never allowed his solidity to slow the scoring rate for long since he was always looking for the quick single. As an immaculate slip fieldsman and a sometimes destructive legspin/ googly bowler, he occasionally looked the complete cricketer. His captaincy, in the modern tradition, never took on a spectacular glow; like his batting, it was sound. He was also considered the man for the job a record (for Australia) number of times, passing Ian Chappell's 30 Tests as captain. During his comeback, Simpson also passed 20,000 runs in first-class cricket, only the third

Australian to achieve this feat.

Simpson might be described as a 'method' cricketer. He worked on his slip fielding just as thoughtfully as on his batting. He moved economically to pick up catches off fast and spin bowlers alike, often clasping the ball to his chest when it was the safest albeit most painful way of making certain.

His sense of the properness of things led him to be outspoken during the 1965 series in West Indies when he felt that suspect bowling actions were left unchecked and that too many bouncers were being allowed. The sense of outrage was reversed when his book, *Captain's Story*, was published in 1966 and had to be

withdrawn owing to some of his comments concerning Ian Meckiff, the Australian fast bowler who was no-balled in a Test match for throwing. A sizable libel settlement was made out of court.

All this came to pass after his world record in 1964, not realised until almost a decade later: he scored 1,381 runs in 14 Tests within the calendar year. That was the kind of run-accumulator he was. That was the kind of dependability Australia missed after his first retirement. In 1977 the veteran donned his armour again, and if he lost five and won only four, his courage was noted and the old adage 'They never come back' took another shake.

SIMPSON Robert Baddeley

Teams: New South Wales, Western Australia and Australia

Test series	Tests	Runs	100s	Average
1957-58 in South Africa	5	136	—	22.66
1958-59 v England	1	0	—	0.00
1960-61 v West Indies	5	445	—	49.44
1961 in England	5	191	—	23.87
1962-63 v England	5	401	—	44.55
1963-64 v South Africa†	5	361	—	40.11
1964 in England†	5	458	1	76.33
1964-65 in India†	3	292	—	48.66
1964-65 v Pakistan†	1	268	2	134.00
1964-65 v Pakistan†	1	48	—	24.00
1964-65 in West Indies†	5	399	1	49.87
1965-66 v England†	3	355	1	88.75
1966-67 in South Africa†	5	483	1	48.30
1967-68 v India†	3	294	2	58.80
1977-78 v India†	5	539	2	53.90
1977-78 in West Indies†	5	199	—	22.11
Totals	62	4,869	10	46.81

Career runs: 21,029 *Average:* 56.22
Highest Test score: 311 v England, Old Trafford, 1964
Highest career score: 359, New South Wales v Queensland, Brisbane, 1963-64

†Captain. (Captain in 4 Tests v South Africa in 1963-64, and in 2 Tests v India in 1967-68.)

SNOW
John Augustine b 1941-

John Snow finished the 1976 English season in trouble again. This time the charges against him involved illegal advertising on his cricket clothing; nor had he won any friends in high places with his critical and appropriately titled autobiography, *Cricket Rebel*.

But he was coming to the end of a career that had been as successful as it had been controversial. Though he continually flaunted authority—he was once suspended from the England side after an incident with the Indian opener Gavaskar—he became a fast bowler of the highest class with more than 200 Test wickets.

His hostility in Australia in 1970-71, when he took 31 wickets, was largely instrumental in the regaining of the Ashes. When he was surprisingly omitted four years later Australia's relief was immense.

John Snow was always a man for the big occasion—often operating at less than full pace in the county arena and retiring into himself, and into his poetry, until he was stimulated by a new challenge.

His father, a vicar in Sussex and keenly interested in cricket, gave Snow his first lessons on the vicarage lawn, and at Christ's Hospital school, where he stayed nine years, he began as a batsman. In later years, however, he developed as a fast bowler. He began at Sussex in 1961, but not until 1964 did he gain a regular place in the side, being awarded his county cap that summer. The next year, when he took over 100 wickets, his form was good enough to attract the attention of the Test selectors, and he began his Test career with one match against New Zealand and one against South Africa.

In 1966 he captured 126 wickets and began to establish himself as an England bowler. His best bowling and best batting figures up to 1971 came in that year, and he was chosen for three games against West Indies, taking 12 wickets. His most memorable feat, though, was with the bat, for at the Oval he scored 59 not out and with Ken Higgs took part in a last-wicket stand of 128. At this stage of his career, he had not yet developed his real menace, but it burst forth in the West Indies in 1967-68, when he took 7-49 at Kingston, 5-86 at Bridgetown, and 6-60 at Georgetown, altogether capturing 27 wickets for 504 runs in the series.

In the home series with Australia in 1968 he took 17 wickets, and England, appreciating the Australians' discomfort against true fast bowling, looked to him as their main shock bowler in the 1970-71 series. If that edge was slightly blunted in the 1972 series, he still finished with 24 wickets and though the arm was slightly lower, he was still playing for England in 1976.

Those Test appearances proved to be his last, but his tally of 202 wickets in 49 matches put him among the elite of bowlers who have taken 200 wickets in Test cricket. Snow had often toiled without a truly hostile partner at the other end, and had often shouldered the attack alone.

By 1977, when he was approaching 36, he had slipped well down the bowling averages, and many saw his point in accepting an offer to play World Series cricket while he still had something to offer, particularly in Australia, where his feats were well remembered.

Complex and often misunderstood, early in 1978, Sussex cancelled Snow's contract, marking the end of a stormy first-class career. He later played one-day cricket for Warwickshire, often opening the batting.

SNOW John Augustine			
Teams: Sussex and England			
Test series	**Tests**	**Wkts**	**Average**
1965 v New Zealand	1	4	20.00
1965 v South Africa	1	4	36.50
1966 v West Indies	3	12	37.58
1967 v India	3	10	26.40
1967 v Pakistan	1	3	42.00
1967-68 in West Indies	4	27	18.66
1968 v Australia	5	17	29.88
1968-69 in Pakistan	2	4	21.25
1969 v West Indies	3	15	27.06
1969 v New Zealand	2	3	51.33
1970-71 in Australia	6	31	22.83
1971 v India	2	6	28.16
1972 v Australia	5	24	23.12
1973 v New Zealand	3	13	24.61
1973 v West Indies	1	3	44.33
1975 v Australia	4	11	32.27
1976 v West Indies	3	15	28.20
Totals	49	202	26.66

Career wickets: 1,174 *Average:* 22.72
Career runs: 4,832 *Average:* 14.17
Best Test bowling: 7-40 v Australia, Sydney, 1970-71
Best career bowling: 8-87, Sussex v Middlesex, Lord's, 1975
Highest Test and career score: 73 v India, Lord's, 1971

ABOVE Snow on the receiving end for once—the bowler Australia's 'Froggy' Thomson. LEFT Snow's action with which he generated much pace and considerable lift.

OPPOSITE The effort which John Snow put into his bowling is evident in this photo. His best series was against Australia in 1970-71 when he did most to regain the Ashes.

SOBERS
Sir Garfield St Aubrun
b 1936-

A number of cricketers could claim the title of 'the best all-rounder the game has known', but few could have such a strong claim as the West Indian left-hander Gary Sobers. He could hold his place in any side on either his batting or bowling alone. But to these must be added amazing reflexes in the field that enabled him to bring off brilliant catches close to the wicket. Nor was he merely a fine player. He was an astute captain and one of the game's true characters.

Nobody seeing Sobers going out to bat could fail to be filled with expectation—the familiar walk with shoulders slightly stooping, quick strides peculiarly his own; the air of a man eager to get on with the slaughter of bowlers. Rarely was the spectator disappointed. There have been others more elegant in style, but hardly anyone has hit the ball with such power and certainly while obviously enjoying every moment of

his stay at the crease. Glamorgan's Malcolm Nash knows to what extent a bowler can suffer at Sobers' hands. At Swansea in August 1968 playing against Nottinghamshire, he had the mortifying experience of being struck for six off every delivery of a 6-ball over. Never before had a bowler been subjected to such treatment. That particular innings—76 not out in 35 minutes—contained seven sixes and six fours, and it showed the extent to which Sobers could pulverize an attack.

Another world record to his credit is his 365 not out against Pakistan in the third Test at Kingston in 1957-58. As he amassed the highest score in Test history, Sobers shared a second-wicket stand of 446 with Conrad Hunte, the highest partnership ever for West Indies.

When Sobers set himself for a big hit, he put everything behind it. His lithe body wound up and then uncoiled like a compressed spring released; the ball came off the bat with terrific velocity, and many a fieldsman has had bruised hands trying to stop it. His driving on either side of the wicket was equally skilful, his hooks and pulls

were thunderous, and his cutting could be at times vicious, at other times delicate. He was, in effect, the complete batsman, for although he believed and proved that aggression pays, he could also defend as well as most.

As a left-arm bowler, Sobers was three men in one. Opening the attack off a medium-length lolloping run-up he could be fast. His action was well nigh perfect, with a beautiful, classical side-on delivery, and his ability to make the ball swing in late or run away to the slips after pitching made him a real menace, especially while the shine was on the ball. Later in an innings he often switched to slow bowling. If the pitch was helpful, he bowled orthodox spinners; on other occasions he tried off-breaks and googlies from the back of the hand. As a result of his many talents, he was always in the game, and it was not very often that he failed to make an impression in one form or other.

From the moment he entered the first-class arena as a 16-year-old in June 1953, Gary Sobers made his mark. His figures of 22-5-50-4 and 67-35-92-3 for Barbados against that year's Indians were highly

commendable, and a year later he was in the Test side against England at Kingston. He claimed 4-75 with his slow spinners in the England innings of 414. His batting was developing all the time, too, and early in 1955 he opened the innings against Australia in the fourth Test at Bridgetown. Ray Lindwall and Keith Miller were hit for 43 in 15 minutes.

Touring England in 1957 he scored 1,664 runs in first-class matches, including 219 not out against his future county Nottinghamshire, but his Test record was only modest. It was against Pakistan back home that winter that he came into his own with a vengeance, his maiden Test century being the treble hundred at Kingston that beat Len Hutton's 20-year-old Test record by one

BELOW The exciting Sobers in action against India.
OPPOSITE LEFT Sobers hooks against England.
OPPOSITE RIGHT Sobers the bowler gets one past Underwood.
OPPOSITE BELOW Sobers the fielder takes a return catch.

run. In the next game, at Georgetown, he scored 125 and 109 not out, and there was little doubt that Sobers the international batsman had arrived. Realizing his attraction as a crowd-pleaser, Radcliffe, the Central Lancashire League club, signed him as a professional, and it was with them that he developed his new skill—the art of fast bowling.

But when he went with the West Indian side to India and Pakistan in 1958-59 he found the pitches unsympathetic to speed and so changed his style once more— this time trying off-breaks and 'chinamen'. Meanwhile his batting thrived in the conditions, and in successive innings in the first three Tests he made 25, 142 not out, 4, 198, and 106 not out. This meant he had scored six centuries in six successive Test matches.

Against the England touring side of 1959-60 he hit 154 for Barbados, and a few days later

scored 226 in the first Test, sharing a stand of 399 with Frank Worrell (197 not out). It began at 4.50 p.m. on the Friday and ended at 11.40 a.m. on the Tuesday—a total of 9½ hours—and was the best fourth-wicket stand for the West Indies. In that series he also made 147 at Kingston and 145 at Georgetown, scoring 709 runs and averaging 101.28. In Australia in 1960-61 he played a notable part in the tie at Brisbane, scoring 132, and later, at Sydney, made 168. South Australia were so impressed that they persuaded him to sign for them, and he stayed there for three seasons, the state finishing third, second, and first respectively while he was there. In 1962-63, he created an Australian record by becoming the first to get 1,000 runs and 50 wickets in a season.

Many other notable performances with bat and ball followed, and he gained fresh fame when he took over the leadership of West

Indies in 1965. He had another spell in English league cricket, with Norton in the North Staffordshire League, and in late 1967 joined Nottinghamshire. Taking over the captaincy in 1968 he helped them jump from 15th to 4th place that season, and in 1970 his genius was further rewarded when he was appointed captain of the Rest of

the World team that played England. Injury interrupted his run of success and he missed the 1973 series against Australia. But later that year he returned against England, and became the first batsman to score over 8,000 Test runs. He retired in 1974 and was knighted for his services to the game.

SOBERS Sir Garfield St Aubrun

Teams: Barbados, South Australia, Nottinghamshire and West Indies

Test series	Tests	Runs	100s	Average	Wkts	Average
1953-54 v England	1	40	—	40.00	4	20.25
1954-55 v Australia	4	231	—	38.50	6	35.50
1955-56 in New Zealand	4	81	—	16.20	2	24.50
1957 in England	5	320	—	32.00	5	71.00
1957-58 v Pakistan	5	824	3	137.33	4	94.25
1958-59 in India	5	557	3	92.83	10	29.20
1958-59 in Pakistan	3	160	—	32.00	0	—
1959-60 v England	5	709	3	101.28	9	39.44
1960-61 in Australia	5	430	2	43.00	15	39.20
1961-62 v India	5	424	2	70.66	23	20.56
1963 in England	5	322	1	40.25	20	28.55
1964-65 v Australia†	5	352	—	39.11	12	41.00
1966 in England†	5	722	3	103.14	20	27.25
1966-67 in India†	3	342	—	114.00	14	25.00
1967-68 v England†	5	545	2	90.83	13	39.07
1968-69 in Australia†	5	497	2	49.70	18	40.72
1968-69 in New Zealand†	3	70	—	14.00	7	43.00
1969 in England†	3	150	—	30.00	11	28.90
1970-71 v India†	5	597	3	74.62	12	33.50
1971-72 v New Zealand†	5	253	1	36.14	10	33.20
1973 in England	3	306	1	76.50	6	28.16
1973-74 v England	4	100	—	20.00	14	30.07
Totals	93	8,032	26	57.78	235	34.03

Career runs: 28,315 Average: 54.87
Highest Test and career score: 365* v Pakistan, Kingston, 1957-58
Career wickets: 1,043 Average: 27.74
Best Test bowling: 6-73 v Australia, Brisbane, 1968-69
Best career bowling: 9-49, West Indians v Kent, Canterbury, 1966

*Not out †Captain

STATHAM
John Brian b 1930-

Known by his cricketing friends as 'George', England and Lancashire opening bowler Brian Statham could be considered the ideal professional. During a career lasting 19 years, he was a highly popular player both on and off the field, everyone admired the level-headed manner in which he took adversity as well as adulation. Most fast bowlers possess a volatile nature that sometimes gets them into trouble, but there was never the slightest suggestion of Statham giving offence. In this way, he contrasted markedly with his England partner Fred Trueman. The Yorkshireman was all fire and brimstone, the Lancastrian more phlegmatic.

Not that batsmen could ever regard him with anything but the greatest respect, for he was a formidable opponent. At times, the critics would say he was too accurate, meaning that batsmen, even if they found him difficult to score off, knew what to expect. Against that, however, it was claimed that his very accuracy meant that batsmen took more risks than they normally would have done at the other end. Time and time again he would see the ball beat the bat without reward. Other men would have found this galling, but Statham took it all in his stride.

He possessed the philosophical approach to the vagaries of fortune experienced by all bowlers. But he never weakened his resolve to keep plugging away, always aiming at the stumps. Few bowlers have attained such accuracy at such a biting pace, but Statham had his own dictum and his own motivation—"If they miss, I hit," he would explain with a wry smile, and the number of defeated batsmen who went back to the pavilion 'b Statham' accounted for a high proportion of his victims.

After doing his National Service in the RAF, Statham joined Stockport in the Central Lancashire League. He did nothing exceptional there, but his potential was recognized and MCC suggested Statham contact his county club, who offered him a trial. Taken on in May 1950, he came under the guidance of Harry Makepeace, the Lancashire coach, and made such rapid progress that within two months he was making his championship debut against Kent at Old Trafford—on June 17, his 20th birthday. A few weeks later he gained a regular place in the county side. Though he was somewhat raw and his action looked ungainly, there was no denying the speed he possessed, and he had several successes, notably at Bath where in one spell he took 5 Somerset wickets for 5 runs. His remarkably quick advance was far from over, and before the summer

ended he had been awarded his county cap. Then that winter, together with his team-mate Roy Tattersall, he was called upon to reinforce the injury-hit MCC team in Australia. He did not play in any Tests there, but made his England debut against New Zealand at Christchurch.

Lancashire were naturally delighted with his progress, and in his second season he made his mark with 97 wickets at 15.11 apiece. Slim and wiry, Statham was known for a time as 'The Whippet', but gradually he filled out and developed powerful shoulders, which gave him added pace. As a left-handed batsman, he often provided amusing entertainment for the crowd—but not always for his opponents, who found he sometimes stayed at the crease longer than expected. He was also a fine outfield with a sure pair of hands that rarely missed a catch, and an accurate thrower.

From the time he made his Test debut, Brian Statham was usually an automatic choice for England, featuring in the strong sides that won and retained the Ashes in the 1950s. His partnerships with Frank Tyson and Trueman often found him playing a supporting role, but neither would deny the large part he played in their own successes. With just a little bit of luck, however, he himself could easily have been the more successful partner. After 1963, it seemed that Statham's Test career was over, but he came back for one match against South Africa at the Oval in 1965 and with 5-40 and 2-105 completed 250 Test wickets. Among those were his 7-39 against South Africa at Lord's in 1955 and

STATHAM John Brian

Teams: Lancashire and England

Test series		Tests	Wkts	Average
1950-51	in New Zealand	1	1	47.00
1951	v South Africa	2	4	19.50
1951-52	in India	5	8	36.62
1953	v Australia	1	2	44.00
1953-54	in West Indies	4	16	28.75
1954	v Pakistan	4	11	19.36
1954-55	in Australia	5	18	27.72
1954-55	in New Zealand	2	12	7.58
1955	v South Africa	4	17	21.35
1956	v Australia	3	7	26.28
1956-57	in South Africa	4	14	24.92
1957	v West Indies	3	13	33.30
1958	v New Zealand	2	7	18.57
1958-59	in Australia	4	12	23.83
1959	v India	3	17	13.11
1959-60	in West Indies	3	10	28.60
1960	v South Africa	5	27	18.18
1961	v Australia	4	17	29.47
1962	v Pakistan	3	16	17.37
1962-63	in Australia	5	13	44.61
1963	v West Indies	2	3	81.00
1965	v South Africa	1	7	20.71
Totals		**70**	**252**	**24.84**

Career wickets: 2,260 *Average:* 16.36
Best Test bowling: 7-39 v South Africa, Lord's, 1955
Best career bowling: 8-34, Lancashire v Warwickshire, Coventry, 1957
Career runs: 5,424 *Average:* 10.80
Highest Test score: 38 v India, Lord's, 1959
Highest career score: 62, Lancashire v Leicestershire, Old Trafford, 1955

7-57 against Australia at Melbourne in 1958-59.

Outside Test cricket, he topped 100 wickets in 13 seasons, 10 in succession from 1957 to 1966, and his triumphs included three hat-tricks—against Sussex at Old Trafford in 1956, for MCC against Transvaal at Johannesburg in 1956-57, and against Leicestershire at Old Trafford in 1958. At Coventry in 1957 he took 15 wickets (8-34 and 7-55) in the match with Warwickshire, and another 15 (7-71 and 8-37) came against Leicestershire in 1964.

Statham's benefit in 1961 showed the esteem in which the public held him, for it brought him over £13,000. In 1965, he took over the captaincy of Lancashire and in the New Year's Honours List of 1966 was awarded the CBE. The next season, however, he relinquished the county leadership, and in 1968 retired.

OPPOSITE Statham gets South Africa's Bland lbw at the Oval in 1965
ABOVE AND RIGHT Batting left-handed and bowling right.

THOMSON
Jeffrey Robert b 1950-

There has always been a charisma about genuine fast bowlers, but Jeff Thomson superseded most when it came to commercial appeal. One only had to judge by the hum of real interest when he began his gentle approach to the wicket before the acceleration and powerful body-thrust of his last three urgent strides.

The sort of appeal which earned him a multi-thousand dollar radio contract in Brisbane stemmed largely from the fact that he was no conventional performer. As a teenager he lounged around the beaches of his Sydney home and only at the age of 20 did he resume playing cricket. Two years later he had earned a place in the New South Wales side, and one barren appearance for his country.

A season missed through injury appeared to condemn Thomson to the ranks of the also-rans until he earned a recall against England in 1974-75; with Lillee at the other end, the fearsome force generated by his unorthodox action tore England's batting apart. At Brisbane, later to become his home ground as he switched his state allegiances to Queensland, his 6 for 46 was shatteringly decisive. He finished the series with 33 wickets, despite missing the last Test through an arm injury.

When he came to England for the 1975 World Cup and subsequent Test series, he took time to overcome a tendency to bowl no-balls. His best remembered World Cup performance came with the bat when his helter-skelter last wicket stand with Dennis Lillee almost provided the final with a last dramatic twist.

But his bowling in the first Test had more than sufficient renown; he returned 5 for 38 in the second innings. On the lifeless wicket at

the Oval he alone achieved honours and gave another five-wicket performance. His threatening speed again spearheaded Australia's attack in the subsequent series against the West Indies. His 29 wickets took his total to 78 in just 16 Tests. However, a serious injury to his shoulder during 1976 left his future in doubt.

Remarkably, he came back. Passing a fitness test, he embarked on the 1977 tour of England, where he led the attack in a difficult series. His 23 wickets (av. 25.34) were outstanding and occasionally he bowled with the old fire. He was popular with the establishment when he tore up his World Series contract, seeing greater rewards in staying with Queensland and in Test cricket. Compensation came in his appointment as vice-captain to Simpson for the tour of West Indies, where his 20 wickets took his total to 123 in Tests. When Jeff Thomson finally joined Packer in 1978 he disappointed some of cricket's traditionalists who had regarded him as an ally.

Although a 'guest' fast bowler for Middlesex in 1981, Thomson found his Test place in the 1980s was challenged by such as Alderman and Hogg, but he continued accumulating wickets and was very successful in 1982-83 when he took 22 English wickets at only 18.68 each. He also figured in another celebrated but unsuccessful last wicket stand when he and Border added 70 in the fourth Test, but fell four runs short of the target.

Thomson made his third visit to England in 1985 when more likely choices chose instead to tour South Africa. In the first Test Thomson took his total of Test victims to 199, only to have Border drop a sitter which would have given him a coveted 200. It seemed that he would not get another chance, but he was recalled for the fifth Test and Gooch obligingly snicked him to the keeper.

OPPOSITE Jeff Thomson in mid-air after delivery. LEFT BELOW Thomson enjoyed causing trouble with the bat in last-wicket stands.

ABOVE Thomson always has a capacity to work up the crowd, either for him or against. Here he conducts barracking arising from his repeated no-balling.

THOMSON Jeffrey Robert

Teams: New South Wales, Queensland, Middlesex, and Australia

Test series	Tests	Wkts	Average
1972-73 v Pakistan	1	—	—
1974-75 v England	5	33	17.93
1975 in England	4	16	28.56
1975-76 v West Indies	6	29	28.65
1976-77 v Pakistan	1	2	17.00
1977 in England	5	23	25.34
1977-78 v India	5	22	23.45
1977-78 in West Indies	5	20	28.85
1979-80 v West Indies	1	4	23.25
1979-80 v England	1	3	33.33
1981-82 v Pakistan	3	5	43.80
1981-82 v West Indies	2	9	35.22
1981-82 in New Zealand	3	6	32.00
1982-83 in Pakistan	3	3	98.33
1982-83 v England	4	22	18.68
1985 in England	2	3	91.66
Totals	51	200	28.00

Career wickets: 633 *Average:* 26.03
Best Test bowling: 6-46 v England, Brisbane, 1974-75
Best career bowling: 7-27, Queensland v Western Australia, 1984-85
Highest Test score: 49 v England, Birmingham, 1975
Highest career score: 61, Queensland v Victoria, Brisbane, 1974-75

Career figures correct to end of 1985 season

TRUEMAN
Frederick Sewards
b 1931-

Characters in cricket, and no doubt in other walks of life, are often not appreciated until they have retired or at least reached a seniority that gives their peculiar individuality a loveable quality. In the young it would be merely bumptiousness. Thus it was some time before Fred Trueman, 'Fiery Fred' to many, was fully appreciated in all quarters. For most of a first-class career that lasted from 1949 to 1968, however, he was seen by the public as a rugged personality epitomizing the down-to-earth Yorkshireman. For almost as long, his sayings, most of them impromptu and born of a quick wit and unfettered tongue, were a legend in the cricket world. One of the most polite and most well known is that when he was asked if he thought any other bowler would ever take 300 wickets in Test cricket. 'Aye', he said, 'but whoever does will be bloody tired.'

When he first played for Yorkshire, Trueman already had the makings of a fine, almost classical fast bowler's method. The gently curving run-up was on the long side, but the acceleration was right and all that was needed was greater control. He had a natural movement away from the bat, which at the pace he could obviously work up would make him a menace to the best batsmen. But there was a wildness about him, perhaps stemming partly from his not looking at the batsman in the delivery stride, and this temporarily delayed his development. Soon, however, when not much over 20, he was routing the Indians of 1952 and being recognized as one of the world's most formidable fast bowlers.

He was especially welcome in England, where there had been no bowlers of genuine pace since the war until he and Brian Statham appeared, shortly to be followed by Frank Tyson. Nevertheless, throughout Fred Trueman's career there was plenty of competition, and his progress was not unopposed. In a less prosperous period in English cricket, he might have played many more than 67 Test matches. He was not picked to go to Australia in 1954, when Tyson, Statham, and Peter Loader were preferred, but the quality of his bowling became more and more appreciated, especially his ability to move the ball in the air and off the pitch at a high speed. Though he himself was often quoted as claiming to be 'the fastest bloody bowler in the world' and as issuing blood-curdling threats to unwary batsmen, he soon realized that pace alone was not everything. Thus he remained a very good bowler until well into his late 30s.

Nor was bowling his whole

cricket life. He was renowned as a mighty hitter, showing no respect whatsoever for the textbook dictum that the right hand should play an unobtrusive part in most strokes. But he could also turn successfully to defence if the situation demanded. He was a brilliant close fielder and, unusually, could throw almost equally well with either arm.

The son of a miner, Trueman

worked briefly as one before, at 18, making his first appearances for Yorkshire. His immense promise was obvious, but he was brought along gradually during the next few years, two of which were spent doing national service in the RAF. He was in some ways lucky to play his first Tests in 1952 against Indian batsmen unused to fast bowlers on lively pitches, and in four Tests he took 29 wickets at

13.31 apiece, including 8-31 at Old Trafford. The next year, however, he played only once against Australia. That winter he went to the West Indies with Len Hutton's team, but in the turbulent atmosphere of cricket there, his brash, forthright manner frequently had him in trouble, and though he took 134 wickets at home in 1954 the selectors did not call on him for Australia. The Ashes were won

without him. He was not fit in 1956, and he was again left out of a touring side, this time to South Africa.

At this stage he had had several successful but, at the highest level, disappointing seasons. He had now, however, gained experience, and from about 1957 to 1963 was at his peak. In 1960 he had his best home season, taking 175 wickets, and it was not until 1967 that he

took fewer than 100 again. In all he took 100 wickets in a season 12 times, and among bowlers of comparable pace only Brian Statham, 13 times, has done it more often. In his later years, a touch of prudence made his batting more productive overall, and his three first-class hundreds were made between 1963 and 1965.

Valuable though he was to Yorkshire, it was in Test matches

that the real class of his bowling was shown by his ability to surprise the world's best players. Between 1958 and 1964 he missed only odd matches for England. In 1960 in the West Indies he took 21 Test wickets and kept clear of the controversy that had surrounded him on the previous tour. At home that year he took 25 wickets against South Africa and in 1961 20 more against Australia, including 5-58 and 6-30 at Leeds, where he made the most of a poor pitch and enabled England to win by eight wickets.

At Lord's in 1962 he took 6-31 when Pakistan were bowled out for 100 on the first day and in the series added 22 Test wickets to the growing list. Against Frank Worrell's triumphant West Indians of 1963 he took 11 wickets in the famous Lord's Test, followed by 12 at Edgbaston. His 7-44 in the last innings there brought England their only win and was a model of how conditions allowing the ball

to move in the air and off the seam should be exploited. In that series his tally of wickets was 34—against the next most successful English bowler's bag of 15.

In the previous Australian season of 1962-63, with Ted Dexter's MCC side, he had refuted the theory that fast bowlers over 30 are past their best in Australia and had taken 20 wickets. But that was his last official tour. In the 1964 series against Australia he was still the major wicket-taker with 17, but he was dropped for the fourth Test and there were suggestions that his Test career might be over. At this point he was easily the biggest wicket-taker in Test history, and there was widespread hope that he would have a chance to reach 300. He was then on 297. Recalled for the final Test at the Oval, he was for a long time far from dangerous, but eventually, coming on for another spell, he dismissed Redpath and McKenzie with successive balls and soon afterwards made Neil Hawke the 300th victim amid universal jubilation.

The end of his Test career was not delayed for long. He played in only the first two of the six Tests against New Zealand and South Africa in 1965, and after three more seasons liberally sprinkled with bursts of characteristic brilliance, he retired from Yorkshire cricket too. He might almost have stage-managed his farewell season. Yorkshire won their third successive championship and, with Trueman at the helm, inflicted the first defeat on the 1968 Australians. It was Yorkshire's first defeat of an Australian side since 1902, and Trueman took 6 wickets in the match for 83 runs. Trueman was Yorkshire to the core which made incongruous a brief return in one-day matches for Derbyshire.

OPPOSITE TOP All eyes on Colin Cowdrey as he takes the catch from Neil Hawke that gave Fred Trueman (left) his 300th wicket in Test cricket. Trueman had been recalled to the Test team for the fifth Test against Australia at the Oval, having missed the previous game.
OPPOSITE BELOW The England team surround Trueman to offer congratulations on his feat. When he retired he had taken 307 Test wickets, a total since passed as Tests become more frequent.
LEFT Trueman enjoyed batting and occasionally scored valuable tail-end runs.
LEFT BELOW The bowling action which with his outspokenness earned him the nickname 'Fiery'.

TRUEMAN Frederick Sewards

Teams: Yorkshire and England

Test series		Tests	Wkts	Average
1952	v India	4	29	13.31
1953	v Australia	1	4	22.50
1953-54	in West Indies	3	9	46.66
1955	v South Africa	1	2	56.00
1956	v Australia	2	9	20.44
1957	v West Indies	5	22	20.68
1958	v New Zealand	5	15	17.06
1958-59	in Australia	3	9	30.66
1958-59	in New Zealand	2	5	21.00
1959	v India	5	24	16.70
1959-60	in West Indies	5	21	26.14
1960	v South Africa	5	25	20.32
1961	v Australia	4	20	26.45
1962	v Pakistan	4	22	19.95
1962-63	in Australia	5	20	26.05
1962-63	in New Zealand	2	14	11.71
1963	v West Indies	5	34	17.47
1964	v Australia	4	17	23.47
1965	v New Zealand	2	6	39.50
Totals		67	307	21.57

Career wickets: 2,304 *Average:* 18.29
Best Test bowling: 8-31 v India, Old Trafford, 1952
Best career bowling: 8-28, Yorkshire v Kent, Dover, 1954
Career runs: 9,321 *Average:* 15.56
Highest Test score: 39* v New Zealand, Oval, 1958
Highest career score: 104, Yorkshire v Northamptonshire, Northampton, 1963

*Not out

TURNER
Glenn Maitland b 1947-

New Zealand have never been as strong in cricket as they are in the 1980s, but in their previous 50 years of Test status they have often produced a world-class player. Among the batsmen Martin Donnelly and Bert Sutcliffe were outstanding in the 1940s and 1950s, and in the 1970s Glenn Turner was among the best batsmen in the world. Sadly, although he captained New Zealand, his relations with the authorities were not of the best, and his Test career was less than it might have been.

Turner was born in Dunedin in 1947 and developed his skills as an opening batsman, particularly his defensive skills, which early in his career were legendary (he once scored only three runs in a pre-lunch session). He made his debut for Otago in 1964-65, while still at school.

He decided to come to England and took a menial job to save his fare. He was recommended to Warwickshire by Billy Ibadulla, the Warwickshire batsman who had been coaching in Dunedin and who played for Otago in Turner's first seasons. However, Warwickshire had their quota of overseas players and Turner joined Worcestershire instead, ironically saving some of his greatest innings for matches with Warwickshire.

Turner was a slight, trim batsman, scornfully described early in his career as 'not having the strength to hit the ball off the square', but having joined Worcestershire in 1967 and quickly established a place in the side, he dramatically transformed his style, becoming a forcing batsman who favoured the drive. He held the bat with his hands high on the handle, and the left, top hand (he is a right-hander) around the back of the handle, a method which is sometimes said to prohibit a full swing, but which keeps the bat straight.

In 1968-69 Turner made his debut for New Zealand against the West Indies, and the following summer played for the New Zealand tourists in England. At Lord's he carried his bat through the second innings, with 43 out of 131, the youngest batsman to perform this feat in Tests. In 1970 Turner was playing so well for Worcestershire that he set a new county record with ten centuries.

In 1971-72 Turner had an extraordinary series in the West Indies. In the first Test at Kingston he again carried his bat through a Test innings, this time making 223 not out of a total of 386, the highest score by a batsman achieving this feat in a Test match. In the fourth Test in Guyana he scored 259, the highest Test score by a New Zealander, and put on 387 for the first wicket with T. W. Jarvis, the record first-wicket partnership in first-class cricket by New Zea-

Turner being congratulated on 31 May 1973 on scoring his 1,000th run of the season.

landers. Strangely he had made the same score, 259, in the previous match against Guyana.

Turner had one of his best seasons in 1973, when again he joined the New Zealand tourists in England. He reached 1,018 runs by 31 May, the last of seven batsmen ever to achieve 1,000 runs by the end of May. Turner made his best aggregate this season —2,416 runs, average 67.11.

In 1973-74 New Zealand registered their first Test match win over Australia at Christchurch. Turner scored 101 and 110 not out and became the first New Zealander to score a century in each innings of a Test. He achieved this feat six times in all in first-class cricket.

Turner succeeded as New Zea-

land captain for the visit of India in 1974-75, and retained the captaincy until 1976-77. He then confirmed his independent streak by withdrawing from Test cricket in order to concentrate on his benefit with Worcestershire in 1978, a decision many found hard to understand, including the New Zealand authorities. Turner became a Test match commentator.

In 1979, when he scored 109 against Lancashire at Southport, he became the first batsman to score a century against all seventeen English first-class counties. Another interesting record came in 1981 when he scored 141 of Worcestershire's 169 against Glamorgan—83.4 per cent of the total.

It seemed that given the opportunity Turner could perform almost any feat he wanted. In 1982 he played his highest innings. The opportunity came against Warwickshire (naturally) when Turner had 99 first-class centuries. He became the 19th player to reach 100 100s by hitting 128 before lunch, the fifth century before lunch in his career (he added a sixth later in the season). When Worcestershire declared Turner had 311 not out, no higher score having been made in England for 33 years. Had Worcestershire continued batting Turner would no doubt have passed the record score made in one day (345 by Macartney in 1921).

Turner captained Worcestershire in 1981 and 1982. He made a record 72 centuries for the county, and was their highest scorer in all four major competitions. He was the first batsman to pass 6,000 runs in the John Player League. From being a defensive batsman, he had become a complete batsman, capable of scoring as fast as anybody when it was needed.

When Sri Lanka played their first Tests against New Zealand in 1982-83 Turner returned to the Test arena after six years, but was not impressive. Perhaps he needed more of a challenge.

TURNER Glenn Maitland

Teams: Otago, Worcestershire, Northern Districts, and New Zealand

Test series	Tests	Runs	100s	Average
1968-69 v West Indies	3	183	—	30.50
1969 in England	2	126	—	42.00
1969-70 in India	3	105	—	21.00
1969-70 in Pakistan	1	136	1	68.00
1970-71 v England	2	160	—	53.33
1971-72 in West Indies	5	672	2	96.00
1972-73 v Pakistan	3	235	—	47.00
1973 in England	3	116	—	23.20
1973-74 in Australia	2	60	—	20.00
1973-74 v Australia	3	403	2	80.60
1974-75 v England	2	108	—	36.00
1975-76 v India†	3	217	1	54.25
1976-77 in Pakistan†	2	60	—	15.00
1976-77 in India†	3	261	1	43.50
1976-77 v Australia†	2	78	—	19.50
1982-83 v Sri Lanka	2	71	—	23.66
Totals	41	2,991	7	44.67

Career runs: 34,346 *Average:* 49.70
Highest Test score: 259 v West Indies, Georgetown, 1971-72
Highest career score: 311* v Warwickshire, Worcester, 1982

*Not out †Captain

UNDERWOOD
Derek Leslie b 1945-

Quiet and undemonstrative, with a shuffling, unathletic gait, Derek Underwood does not, at first sight, look the type of cricketer to break records and upset traditions. But he has enjoyed a career probably unique among English bowlers. Most bowlers, particularly those relying on length and accuracy, need many years to learn their job. Underwood appeared unheralded in first-class cricket in 1963 aged 17, and that season took 101 wickets.

Underwood's method is unusual too. His slow-medium pace is faster than that of the normal left-arm spinner. And he does not attempt to spin the ball prodigiously, relying instead on numerous subtle variations that can surprise batsmen on the best of pitches. On bad pitches he can be next to unplayable, so quickly can he make the ball turn or lift.

After his remarkable first season, when he became the youngest bowler ever to take 100 wickets, he took 9-28 the next year against Sussex at Hastings, and 9-37 against Essex on another rough pitch, at Westcliff in 1966, when he played in his first Test matches. His debut was against West Indies at Trent Bridge, where he did not take a wicket but bowled 43 overs for 86 runs in the second innings and batted with unexpected obstinacy to share in a last-wick stand of 65 with Basil D'Oliveira.

His first official tour, with the Under-25 side to Pakistan in 1966-67, was also not especially successful, and the tendency grew to regard him as a very good bowler in English conditions but ineffective on hard pitches overseas. He was not taken to the West Indies on the full tour a year later, but went with a Commonwealth side to Pakistan and to Ceylon, where, after rain, he had the astonishing figures of 8-10 and 7-33 against the Ceylon President's XI in Colombo.

Underwood's greatest triumph was to follow in 1968, in the last Test against Australia at the Oval. In the first innings he bowled 54.3 overs with customary steadiness and took 2-89, but on the last day there was a thunderstorm, and when play became possible again only 75 minutes remained. If the pitch became difficult as it dried, Underwood was clearly the match-winner. Forty minutes passed before it did and then, after a wicket fell to D'Oliveira, Underwood took the last wickets in 27 balls to win the match with six minutes to spare, level the series, and finish with 7-50 himself.

In the three-match series against New Zealand in 1969, he was in devastating form, taking 24 wickets at 9 apiece, but there were still those who doubted his effec-tiveness in Australia. Nonetheless he played an important part in the recovery of the Ashes in 1970-71, containing the Australian batsmen while the fast bowlers recovered, and taking 16 wickets. At times the selectors overlooked him. In 1972 he was omitted until the fourth Test at Headingly where, on a pitch ideally suited to his style, he returned match figures of 10 for 82. The match caused much controversy. A freak storm and subsequent strong sunshine led to a fungus removing the grass from the pitch, which took spin from the start. The Australians were never persuaded that the pitch was not prepared especially for 'Deadly' Derek.

Another memorable performance came against Pakistan in 1974, when, on a rain-affected pitch, he took 5 for 20 and 8 for 51 at Lord's in a match where rain was the eventual victor.

That winter he bowled steadily in Australia, coming into his own in the fifth Test, at Adelaide, when he had a damp patch to bowl into on the opening day. He did not allow his prey to escape, and finished with 7 for 113. Once more he shone as an 'umbrella bowler' —always there in case of rain.

Against the all-conquering West Indians of 1976 he took most wickets for England in the series—17—and a few months later, in the successful England tour of India, his 29 Test wickets topped even anything the Indian spinners could achieve.

Underwood was one of the English players who signed for World Series Cricket in 1977. A modest, unassuming man, he said he did it for security for his wife and daughters. In the event he probably suffered more than anybody from the WSC interlude, as, with 265 Test wickets, he would no doubt have been the bowler to overhaul Gibbs' record aggregate of Test wickets.

After Packer, Underwood became the 'token' WSC player in England's touring party to Australia in 1979-80, when he took 13 wickets. He seemed unsure of an automatic Test place, however, despite taking his haul of wickets to 297, and in 1981-82 decided to accept an invitation to the 'rebel' tour of South Africa, and was banned from Tests for three years. He was still bowling well enough in 1985, when the ban was lifted, to merit consideration, but the selectors chose to ignore him.

He continued to bowl immaculately for Kent, especially in limited-overs matches (Underwood's career began the same season as the Gillette Cup). In 1985, when he was again Kent's leading wicket-taker, only Edmonds bowled more first-class overs than Underwood's 807. Perhaps his greatest pleasure came in 1984, however, when in his 22nd season he scored his maiden century, 111 against Sussex at Hastings.

UNDERWOOD Derek Leslie			
Teams: Kent and England			
Test series	Tests	Wkts	Average
1966 v West Indies	2	1	172.00
1967 v Pakistan	2	8	16.12
1968 v Australia	4	20	15.10
1968-69 in Pakistan	3	8	25.50
1969 v West Indies	2	6	16.83
1969 v New Zealand	3	24	9.16
1970-71 in Australia	5	16	32.50
1970-71 in New Zealand	2	17	12.05
1971 v Pakistan	1	0	—
1971 v India	1	4	30.25
1972 v Australia	2	16	16.62
1972-73 in India	4	15	30.47
1972-73 in Pakistan	2	3	71.66
1973 v New Zealand	1	0	—
1973 v West Indies	3	8	41.25
1973-74 in West Indies	4	5	62.80
1974 v India	3	4	36.50
1974 v Pakistan	3	17	12.82
1974-75 in Australia	5	17	35.00
1974-75 in New Zealand	2	7	17.14
1975 v Australia	4	6	44.33
1976 v West Indies	5	17	37.11
1976-77 in India	5	29	17.55
1976-77 in Australia	1	4	13.50
1977 v Australia	5	13	27.84
1979-80 in Australia	3	13	31.07
1979-80 in India	1	0	—
1980 v West Indies	1	1	108.00
1981-82 in India	6	10	43.80
1981-82 in Sri Lanka	1	8	11.87
Totals	86	297	25.83

Career wickets: 2,368 *Average:* 19.98
Best Test bowling: 8-51 v Pakistan, Lord's, 1974
Best career bowling: 9-28, Kent v Sussex, Hastings, 1964
Highest Test score: 45* v Australia, Leeds, 1968
Highest career score: 111 v Sussex, Hastings, 1984

*Not out
Career figures correct to end of 1985 season

Derek Underwood comes round the wicket. He was that rarity— a top-class spinner from his first county match.

WALCOTT
Clyde Leopold b 1926-

The largest and most powerful of the 'Three Ws', Clyde Walcott wrote his name in the record books even more often than Sir Frank Worrell and Everton Weekes. By 1971, only three men—Herbert Sutcliffe, George Headley, and Clyde Walcott—had twice scored a hundred in each innings of a Test match, but only Walcott did it twice in the same series. His scores for West Indies against Australia in the Caribbean in 1954-55 were 108 and 39, 126 and 110, 8 and 73, 15 and 83, and 155 and 110. His 827 runs in that series had been exceeded only by Don Bradman, Walter Hammond, and Neil Harvey, and his five separate hundreds were the most ever made in a series. Yet they were made for the losing side, for Australia, captained by Ian Johnson, won the series 3-0.

This season was the highlight of a career that began, in common with those of Weekes and Worrell, in the war years. Strictly in terms of class, Walcott was perhaps a shade below them, lacking the compact soundness and lightning feet of Weekes and the elegance of Worrell. But he was a tremendous striker of the ball, a driver and hooker of immense power.

He was only 16 when he first played for Barbados and barely 20 when cricket lovers the world over were noting with awe the names of two young men, Worrell and Walcott. Playing for Barbados against Trinidad at Port of Spain, they put on 574 in an unbroken stand for the fourth wicket, the highest partnership on record for any wicket. A year later the Indians Hazare and Gul Mahomed beat it by three runs, but nobody has approached it since.

The first of Walcott's 44 Test matches were played against England early in 1948. In his first Test he opened the innings, which may surprise those who remember him farther down the order at the height of his career, but he achieved little in that series and kept his place mainly because of his wicket-keeping. He kept wicket again in England in 1950, at 6 ft. 2 in. breaking all conventions for wicket-keepers, only this time he made a lot of runs, including 168 not out in the Lord's Test, the first ever won by West Indies in England.

He had a poor tour of Australia in 1951-52, when he was no longer keeping wicket, and played the fast bowling of Lindwall and Miller indifferently. But when Len Hutton's England team arrived in the West Indies early in 1954, he entered on his most prolific period. In the series he made 698 runs, averaging 87, and his 220 in the second Test at Barbados was made in 6½ hours out of a total of only 383. By now he was earning a

reputation as a prop in a crisis, and it was his 116 in the second innings of the last Test that stood for some time between England and the victory that enabled them to draw the series.

His great series against Australia followed a year later, and his reputation was at its highest when he went to England in 1957. He started well with 117 and 49 against MCC, 115 against Notts, and 90 in the first innings of the first Test at Edgbaston, but a leg injury suffered there handicapped him thereafter and he made few runs. When England went to the West Indies in 1960 he was captaining British Guiana, as he was to do for some years more, but he played in only two Tests, and they were his last. He remained, however, an important figure in West Indies cricket, was awarded the OBE in 1965 for his services to it, and beginning in England in 1969, he has several times acted as a popular manager of West Indian touring teams.

TOP Clyde Walcott may not have been quite the batting artist that Weekes and Worrell were, but few batsmen could hit the ball with such immense power. His hooks, drives and cuts flashed to the boundary.

ABOVE Walcott misses a chance in the slips from David Sheppard. Earlier in his career Walcott had held his place in the Test side as a wicket-keeper despite his height—at 6 ft 2 in he is tall for a Test keeper.

WALCOTT Clyde Leopold

Teams: Barbados, British Guiana, and West Indies

Test series	Tests	Runs	100s	Average
1947-48 v England	4	133	—	22.16
1948-49 in India	5	452	2	64.57
1950 in England	4	229	1	45.80
1951-52 in Australia	3	87	—	14.50
1951-52 in New Zealand	2	199	1	66.33
1952-53 v India	5	457	2	76.16
1953-54 v England	5	698	3	87.25
1954-55 v Australia	5	827	5	82.70
1957 in England	5	247	—	27.44
1957-58 v Pakistan	4	385	1	96.25
1959-60 v England	2	84	—	28.00
Totals	44	3,798	15	56.68

Career runs: 11,820 *Average:* 56.55
Highest Test score: 220 v England, Bridgetown, 1953-54
Highest career score: 314*, Barbados v Trinidad, Port of Spain, 1945-46

*Not out

WEEKES
Everton de Courcy
b 1925-

Everton Weekes, smaller in stature than the other two of the famous 'Three Ws' who dominated West Indies cricket in the years after World War II, was the most brilliant on his day—and his day was a frequent occurrence. In New Zealand in 1955-56, he made five successive hundreds, by 1985 a feat only three batsmen had surpassed. And by then, no one had beaten or even equalled his feat of making five hundreds in successive Test innings, one against England in 1947-48 and four against India a year later in India. He was heading for a sixth when he was run out for 90 in the next innings.

Wonderfully quick into position, Weekes at times recalled Don Bradman in his range of ruthless, devastating strokes, which were played off front foot and back with flawless judgement and impeccable timing. He first played for Barbados in 1944, but his entry into Test cricket early in 1948 was disappointing for a batsman who already had a high reputation. However, in the last of the four Tests against England he made 141, an innings that is said to have been only just in time to save him from being left out of the team to go to India later that year. The sequel to it in India was remarkable. He averaged 111 in the Test series, in which he made 779 runs, and 90 in all first-class matches.

When he arrived in England in 1950, he had already acquired a big reputation, and it was soon being lifted even higher. An innings of 232 against Surrey was followed by 304 not out at Cambridge in five hours 25 minutes. Earlier in the match, Dewes and Sheppard had made 343 for the University's first wicket. He was kept within bounds for a month, and then made 279 against Notts, followed a fortnight later by 246 not out against Hampshire and 200 not out against Leicestershire. Not until he scored 129 in the classical partnership of 283 with Frank Worrell in the Trent Bridge Test did he make a hundred without turning it into a double hundred.

Like the other batsmen, he failed in Australia in 1951-52, but in the Caribbean and in league cricket in England he was a tremendous force. In 1952-53 he averaged 102 in the five-match series against India. A leg injury handicapped him against Len Hutton's England team a year later, but he still averaged nearly 70 and made 206 in the fourth Test in Trinidad. He was outshone by Clyde Walcott when the Australians visited the West Indies early in 1955, but made 139 and 87 not out in Port of Spain. His triumphant tour of New Zealand with a mainly young side followed, and in 10 innings he made six hundreds and averaged 104. Weekes was only 32 when West Indies went to England in 1957, and he seemed good for many more runs and records. But he was dogged by sinus trouble and injury, and it was not until the last match of the tour that he made his only hundred. Nevertheless, an innings of 90 with a broken finger in the Lord's Test was up to his very best form.

Back in the Caribbean he had a successful series against Pakistan, but during it he announced his retirement from Test cricket. When Peter May's England side arrived in 1959-60, they met Weekes as captain and coach of Barbados, whom he led to victory against them—without batting, but with some flighted leg-breaks with which he took four useful wickets for 38 in MCC's second innings!

LEFT Everton Weekes goes down on one knee to force the ball to leg. He possessed a wide range of strokes and could score all round the wicket.

ABOVE Weekes forces the ball past point from off the back foot. He holds a record of scoring centuries in five successive Test innings.

WEEKES Everton de Courcy

Teams: Barbados and West Indies

Test series		Tests	Runs	100s	Average
1947-48	v England	4	293	1	48.83
1948-49	in India	5	779	4	111.28
1950	in England	4	338	1	56.33
1951-52	in Australia	5	245	—	24.50
1951-52	in New Zealand	2	60	—	20.00
1952-53	v India	5	716	3	102.28
1953-54	v England	4	487	1	69.57
1954-55	v Australia	5	469	1	58.62
1955-56	in New Zealand	4	418	3	83.60
1957	in England	5	195	—	19.50
1957-58	v Pakistan	5	455	1	65.00
Totals		**48**	**4,455**	**15**	**58.61**

Career runs: 12,010 *Average:* 52.90
Highest Test score: 207 v India, Port of Spain, 1952-53
Highest career score: 304*, West Indians v Cambridge University, Cambridge, 1950

*Not out

WILLIS
Robert George Dylan
b 1949-

From disillusioned fast bowler who left his county for another, through being an old crock and a write-off (more than once) to being hero and England captain—that was the ups-and-downs career of Bob Willis.

The high promise shown by the 21-year-old when, as a near-unknown, he was flown out as a reinforcement to the 1970-71 MCC team in Australia, threatened to remain unrealised in the years that followed. Beset by damaged knees and assorted strains, he seemed destined to join the ranks of cricketers, especially fast bowlers, who have had everything to offer at top level except physical reliability.

However, out of the gloom came spectacular revival. First, after pain-killing treatment had proved to be nothing more than a mortgage on time, he had surgery to the ailing joints. This was followed by a punishing training schedule in a quest for peak fitness and finally, and of most interest, Willis undertook experiments in hypnosis that concentrated his mind and dispelled self-doubt. He emerged as England's bowling spearhead, hurtling in off 22 rapid running paces and delivering with a virile, ungainly action anything from an inswinging yorker to a scorching bouncer that only a leaping wicket-keeper could stop.

In the last four Tests against Australia, in 1970-71, his first Test appearances, he took 12 wickets and some superb catches close to the wicket. But the meteoric rise was halted in 1971 when he became dissatisfied at his prospects with Surrey, the county club which had nurtured him through his teens. Jackman and Arnold were established new-ball bowlers, and the young Test player could not even point to a county cap. He moved, therefore, to Warwickshire, and soon made his mark.

In 1972 he helped his new club to their first County Championship since 1951, taking 8 for 44, including the hat-trick, against Derbyshire in the final home match. He received his county cap.

Spasmodic appearances for England followed. Then came the sensational tour of Australia, when it was claimed in some quarters that Willis and Peter Lever set the pattern for the series by bowling an excessive number of bouncers in the opening Test at Brisbane. Lillee and Thomson won that bumper war hands-down for Australia, and the series with it. Willis was forced to return home early. Operations were carried out to remove a cartilage from his right knee and inflamed tissue from beneath both kneecaps. Surviving the passing crisis of a blood clot, he emerged from hospital a pathetic sight—a fast-bowling giant with little real hope of attaining top speed again. Once more, however, his determination was to carry him through.

In the comeback season of 1976 he played only four championship matches with Warwickshire, but forced his way back into the England side for the last two Tests against the all-conquering West Indians.

In India, the graveyard of so many fast bowlers, Willis overcame a chest infection at the start and took a creditable 20 wickets in the five Tests, including 5 for 27 at Calcutta and 6 for 53 at Bangalore.

In the Jubilee Test against the Australians at Lord's in 1977 he floored the visitors with 7 for 78; at Trent Bridge he took 5 for 88 in the second innings; and in the rain-spoilt last Test at the Oval he pounded in for 29½ overs to take 5 for 102 to finish with 27 wickets in the series, the most by any England bowler of real speed in a home series against Australia.

An uncompromising streak was evident during the Pakistanis' tour of 1978, when in the second innings of the first Test, with England well on top, he struck nightwatchman Iqbal Qasim in the mouth with a bouncer and attracted much criticism from the traditionalists. In the Centenary Test in Melbourne in 1977 he had broken McCosker's jaw with a bumper.

In 1980-81 he was forced to leave the tour of the West Indies when he broke down before the first Test. The replacement flown out was that same Robin Jackman

Bob Willis went on bowling long after injuries suggested he should stop, and he wound up with the England captaincy.

ABOVE Greg Chappell tumbles after a bouncer from Willis whistled past his head.

ABOVE RIGHT Well over a third of Willis' first-class wickets came in Test matches.

whom Willis had been unable to replace at Surrey. Willis entered a Birmingham hospital for yet another knee operation.

Astonishingly he was ready for the Australians in 1981 and enjoyed his best-ever series. The highlight was that never-to-be-forgotten Test at Headingley, when after England, one down in the series, had followed on, Botham played his astonishing innings (Willis helped him add 37 for the last wicket—more than the eventual margin of victory) and paved the way for a final morning in which Australia had to be bowled out for 130 runs if England were to snatch a sensational win. It is history now that Australia, at one stage 56 for 1, ran into an inspired Willis, who knocked them over one by one to finish with 8 for 43 and a famous victory.

The following winter Willis toured India and Sri Lanka under Fletcher, who, perhaps because he showed dissent over an umpiring decision, was not considered thereafter. Willis found himself the new England captain.

His first opponents as captain

were India and Pakistan in 1982. Willis took 25 wickets during the summer, and both series were won —the only match lost was when Willis was absent. He was forced to suffer defeat in Australia but the following summer against New Zealand acquired his cheapest Test wickets, 20 at only 13.65.

In 1984 Willis relinquished the captaincy to David Gower for the series against West Indies. He played in three Tests but his six wickets were very expensive and it was clear that age as well as injury had now caught up with him. It was time to retire.

As well as his 325 Test wickets, Willis holds a curious record—the most Test not-outs (55). One last-wicket stand has already been mentioned, but perhaps his best was that of 117 unbeaten with Peter Willey against the West Indies at the Oval which saved the match. Willis's 24 not out was not his highest, however—he got 28 not out against Pakistan in 1982.

Willis captained Warwickshire from 1980 and in 1982 was awarded the MBE for services to cricket.

WILLIS Robert George Dylan

Teams: Surrey, Warwickshire, and England

Test series		Tests	Wkts	Average
1970-71	in Australia	4	12	27.41
1970-71	in New Zealand	1	2	34.50
1973	v West Indies	1	4	29.50
1973-74	in West Indies	3	5	51.00
1974	v India	1	5	19.40
1974	v Pakistan	1	2	64.50
1974-75	in Australia	5	17	30.70
1976	v West Indies	2	9	26.00
1976-77	in India	5	20	16.75
1976-77	in Australia	1	2	62.00
1977	v Australia	5	27	19.77
1977-78	in Pakistan	3	7	27.14
1977-78	in New Zealand	3	14	18.21
1978	v Pakistan	3	13	17.92
1978	v New Zealand	3	12	19.08
1978-79	in Australia	6	20	23.05
1979	v India	3	10	29.80
1979-80	in Australia	3	3	74.66
1980	v West Indies	4	14	29.07
1981	v Australia	6	29	22.96
1981-82	in India	5	12	31.75
1981-82	in Sri Lnka	1	3	23.33
1982	v India†	3	15	22.00
1982	v Pakistan†	2	10	22.20
1982-83	in Australia†	5	18	27.00
1983	v New Zealand†	4	20	13.65
1983-84	in New Zealand†	3	12	25.50
1983-84	in Pakistan†	1	2	23.00
1984	v West Indies	3	6	61.16
Totals		90	325	25.20

Career wickets: 899 *Average:* 24.99
Best Test bowling: 8-43 v Australia, Headingley, 1981
Best career bowling: 8-32, Warwickshire v Gloucestershire, Bristol, 1977
Test runs: 840 *Average:* 11.50
Highest Test score: 28* v Pakistan, Edgbaston, 1982
Highest career score: 72, Warwickshire v Indians, Edgbaston, 1982

*Not out †Captain

WORRELL
Sir Frank b 1924-d 1967

Famous as one of the 'Three Ws' of West Indian cricket, Frank Worrell was no less prolific than Everton Weekes and Clyde Walcott and was more elegant than either of them. But he became more than just a highly successful batsman. He captained West Indies on that tour of Australia in 1960-61 which, though West Indies lost, captured the imagination of the cricketing world, and he knitted together the different factions of West Indian cricket as never before.

He was captain again on that other triumphant venture to England in 1963, after which he retired. In 1964 he was knighted for his services to cricket, and, an immensely respected figure, he continued to work for cricket and for West Indies in a wider field until his sadly premature death of leukaemia in 1967 at the age of 42. The distinction he won in the last few years of his life was gained by courage, breadth of vision, dignity, and a capacity for leadership, and he was accorded the then unique tribute for a cricketer of a memorial service in Westminster Abbey.

As a cricketer, Worrell was a batsman of sound and orthodox method, wonderfully quick into position. Slim and a little above medium height, he was a fine driver and an especially skilful exponent of the late cut. If Walcott reflected power and Weekes quickfooted pugnacity, Worrell batted with the balanced grace of the artist.

He was also a left-arm bowler who, in the West Indies hey-day of the early 1960s, played a valuable part in the attack at a lively fast-medium pace. But in his early days in Barbados he was a slow left-arm bowler, and it was mainly in this role that he first played for Barbados in 1942.

It did not take him long to display his batting talents, though,

and as early as 1943-44, when only 19, he was making 308 not out against Trinidad at Bridgetown, sharing with John Goddard in an unbroken stand of 502—then the world's best for the fourth wicket. Though twice exceeded in the next few years, once by Worrell himself with Walcott, it was still, in 1985, the sixth highest stand ever recorded for all wickets. His unbroken 574 with Walcott, to which he contributed 255 not out, was made two years later against Trinidad at Port of Spain and was the world's best ever fourth wicket stand and was still, in 1985, only three runs away from the record for all wickets.

By the time Gubby Allen's MCC team arrived in 1947-48, Worrell had moved to Jamaica, for whom he played thereafter. His first Test was the one in Trinidad, and he made 97 in his first Test innings. In his second Test, he scored 131 not out, the first of his nine Test hundreds.

Already recognized as a batsman of the highest class when he went to England in 1950, Worrell made six hundreds there, two of them in the Tests, in which he averaged 89. His innings of 261—made in 5 hours 35 minutes—in the third Test at Trent Bridge is still cited as one of the classic innings seen on the ground.

The next few years were relatively lean ones, though of the West Indies side to Australia in 1951-52 Worrell was one of the few to reproduce something like his best form. He took 6-38 at Adelaide in the Test West Indies won, and made 108 at Melbourne in the next Test, which they only just lost. He was unfit for much of Len Hutton's tour of West Indies in 1953-54, though he made 167 in the Trinidad Test. With a highest score of 61 he had a modest series against Australia a year later, but in England in 1957 he lost none of the lofty reputation earned seven years before. He headed the overall averages, carried his bat through the innings at Trent Bridge, where his 191 not out did much to save the match, and

ABOVE Godfrey Evans claps but Alec Bedser perhaps had not the energy at Trent Bridge in 1950. Frank Worrell raises his bat to acknowledge the applause from all round the ground as he reaches 200.

BELOW His batting tended to dominate his career, but he was an invaluable left-arm medium-pace bowler. With the ball too, Trent Bridge was a happy ground. In 1957 he took 7 for 70 against England.

headed the bowling averages.

After his rescuing act with the bat in that third Test, he almost repeated the feat with the ball in the next match of the series. A wonderfully sustained spell of 38.2 overs at Headingley brought him 7 for 70 and restricted England's first innings to 279. It was all in vain, as West Indies slumped to the second of their three innings defeats of that series. In all matches, Worrell had a marvellous tour, making nearly 1,500 runs in the summer at an average of over fifty, and taking his share of wickets at a reasonable cost.

Since 1948 Worrell had played successfully in the Lancashire League and had studied at Manchester University. Now he took the course in sociology that was to lead to his appointment as Warden of the University College of the West Indies. In time, he also became a senator in Parliament, but before that he embarked on the final triumphant stage of his playing career.

He had a good series against England in 1960, though his 197 not out in the first Test at Bridgetown in a stand of 399 with Gary Sobers was a marathon and rather untypical affair of 11 hours 20 minutes. Later that year he was made captain of the West Indies team for the tour of Australia, which ended with a ticker-tape drive through Melbourne. He was still a valuable batsman and bowler, though others such as his successor Gary Sobers were now commanding the scene as batsmen. But he had become almost a father figure who welded together with tremendous effectiveness the great talents of such players as Hall, Kanhai, Sobers, Hunte, Gibbs, Nurse, and the turbulent Griffith. Though they lost narrowly in Australia, West Indies won conclusively in England in 1963. Frank Worrell ended his long Test career at the Oval, acclaimed by a cricketing world that within four years was to be saddened by his untimely death.

WORRELL Sir Frank Mortimer Maglinne

Teams: Barbados, Jamaica, and West Indies

Test series		Tests	Runs	100s	Average	Wkts	Average
1947-48	v England	3	294	1	147.00	1	156.00
1950	in England	4	539	2	89.83	6	30.33
1951-52	in Australia	5	337	1	33.70	17	19.35
1951-52	in New Zealand	2	233	1	116.50	2	40.50
1952-53	v India	5	398	1	49.75	7	37.57
1953-54	v England	4	334	1	47.71	2	96.50
1954-55	v Australia	4	206	—	25.75	3	103.66
1957	in England	5	350	1	38.88	10	34.30
1959-60	v England	4	320	1	64.00	6	38.83
1960-61	in Australia	5†	375	—	37.50	10	35.70
1961-62	v India	5†	332	—	88.00	2	60.50
1963	in England	5†	142	—	20.28	3	34.66
Totals		51	3,860	9	49.48	69	38.72

Career runs: 15,025 *Average:* 54.24
Highest Test score: 261 v England, Trent Bridge, 1950
Highest career score: 308*, Barbados v Trinidad, Bridgetown, 1943-44
Career wickets: 349 *Average:* 28.98
Best Test and career bowling: 7-70 v England, Trent Bridge, 1957

*Not out   †Captain

ZAHEER ABBAS
Syed b 1947-

In his second Test match, and his first against England, Syed Zaheer Abbas, unknown and bespectacled, struck 274—an astounding innings of concentrated stroke-play of more than nine hours.

A salesman with Pakistan International Airways, Zaheer had come to England fully intending to retire from the game if he did not succeed. Boosted by his outstanding start to that series, he developed into one of the world's most graceful batsmen and revealed his ability to play long innings. In 1974 he batted serenely to another double century against the England attack—this time 240 at the Oval.

But, in between these prolific bursts, he showed a vulnerability at the start of an innings. In eight Tests between his first two series against England he scored only 229 runs. Settling on Gloucestershire for his home in county cricket he took time to adjust; the frequency with which he was dismissed for low scores often suggested carelessness, but his class eventually won through.

In 1976 he outstripped all other batsmen in English domestic cricket. He compiled 2,554 runs in just 39 innings (av. 75.11). He gathered eleven centuries, plus three more in one-day cricket—six more than any other player.

Against Surrey on the Oval wicket, which he has come to love, he slaughtered the home attack for 216 not out and 156 not out, while he hit Kent for 230 not out and 104 not out at Canterbury.

Zaheer continued to have extremes of form and the knack of scoring in huge pairs. He has made a century in each innings of a match on eight occasions, a record. More remarkable is that four of these 16 centuries were double centuries, and twelve of them were not out. He is certainly a century maker. In 1983 he became the 20th batsman to reach 100 centuries—typically the 100th was a double century, 215 against India at Lahore.

After his initial flourish Zaheer reserved his best Test performances for matches with India—his best aggregate for a series was 650 in 1982-83. In three series against them he has averaged over 100.

In 1983-84 Zaheer assumed the captaincy of Pakistan in the absence of Imran Khan.

Zaheer has performed extremely well in one-day international cricket, only four players—Richards, Haynes, Greenidge and Border—having scored more runs to the end of 1985, and only the first two, with eight, having scored more than Zaheer's seven centuries.

A diffident man for whom cricket is the abiding passion of his life, there were rumours in 1985 that he contemplated retiring.

Zaheer hits another boundary on his way to 240 against England at the Oval in 1974.

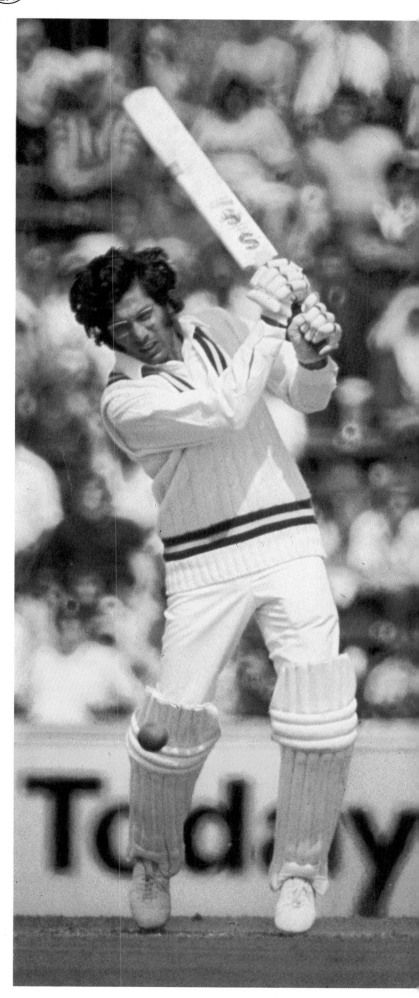

ZAHEER ABBAS Syed

Teams: Karachi, PWD, PIA, Gloucestershire, Sind, Dawood Club, Pakistan

Test series	Tests	Runs	100s	Average
1969-70 v New Zealand	1	39	—	19.50
1971 in England	3	386	1	96.50
1972-73 in Australia	3	144	—	24.00
1972-73 in New Zealand	3	35	—	7.00
1972-73 v England	2	50	—	25.00
1974 in England	3	324	1	54.00
1974-75 v West Indies	2	71	—	17.75
1976-77 v New Zealand	3	60	—	12.00
1976-77 in Australia	3	343	1	57.16
1976-77 in West Indies	3	131	—	21.83
1978-79 v India	3	583	2	194.33
1978-79 in New Zealand	2	177	1	59.00
1978-79 in Australia	2	117	—	29.25
1979-80 in India	5	157	—	19.62
1979-80 v Australia	2	45	—	22.50
1980-81 v West Indies	3	57	—	14.25
1981-82 in Australia	2	170	—	56.66
1981-82 v Sri Lanka	1	134	1	134.00
1982 in England	3	131	—	26.20
1982-83 v Australia	3	269	1	89.66
1982-83 v India	6	650	3	130.00
1983-84 in India†	3	156	—	52.00
1983-84 in Australia‡	5	323	—	40.37
1983-84 v England†	3	195	—	48.75
1984-85 v India†	2	194	1	194.00
1984-85 v New Zealand†	3	93	—	18.60
1984-85 in New Zealand	2	24	—	6.00
Totals	76	5,058	12	45.16

Career runs: 34,285 *Average:* 52.18
Highest Test and career score: 274 v England, Edgbaston, 1971

†Captain ‡Captain in first 3 Tests
Career figures correct to end of 1985 season

Vivian Richards scored 829 runs in four Tests in England in 1976.

PART IV

THE RECORDS

FIRST-CLASS RECORDS

Note: There are now two schools of thought concerning the records of first-class cricketers. One is that of the Association of Cricket Statisticians, the other might be called 'traditional'.

In 1976 the Association published a list of first-class matches, from which players' records are compiled. This list included some matches previously overlooked, and *vice versa*. Acceptance of the Association's list meant that some figures for long held 'sacred' were wrong.

The two instances which traditionalists are most unwilling to accept concern W. G. Grace's career records (the Association found that some of his figures were deliberately 'fiddled' to give him records) and the centuries of J. B. Hobbs, which the Association state to number 199, instead of the long-held record of 197, because they consider two made on a tour of India and Ceylon in 1931-32 to be first-class.

The records which follow give the traditional Wisden figures, with footnotes where appropriate for the two instances given above.

An asterisk (*) indicates 'not out', or in a partnership, 'unfinished'.

HIGHEST TEAM TOTALS

1,107	Victoria v New South Wales, Melbourne, 1926-27
1,059	Victoria v Tasmania, Melbourne, 1922-23
951-7 dec	Sind v Baluchistan, Karachi, 1973-74
918	New South Wales v South Australia, Sydney, 1900-01
912-8 dec	Holkar v Mysore, Indore, 1945-46
910-6 dec	Railways v Dera Ismail Khan, Lahore, 1964-65
903-7 dec	England v Australia, Oval, 1938
887	Yorkshire v Warwickshire, Edgbaston, 1896
849	England v West Indies, Kingston, 1929-30

HIGHEST INDIVIDUAL INNINGS

499	Hanif Mohammad, Karachi v Bahawalpur, Karachi, 1958-59
452*	D. G. Bradman, New South Wales v Queensland, Sydney, 1929-30
443*	B. B. Nimbalkar, Maharashtra v Kathiawar, Poona, 1948-49
437	W. H. Ponsford, Victoria v Queensland, Melbourne, 1927-28
429	W. H. Ponsford, Victoria v Tasmania, Melbourne, 1922-23
428	Aftan Baloch, Sind v Baluchistan, Karachi, 1973-74
424	A. C. MacLaren, Lancashire v Somerset, Taunton, 1895
385	B. Sutcliffe, Otago v Canterbury, Christchurch, 1952-53

HIGHEST AGGREGATE RUNS

	I	NO	Runs	HS	100s	Av
J. B. Hobbs	1,315	106	61,237	316*	197†	50.65
F. E. Woolley	1,532	85	58,969	305*	145	40.75
E. H. Hendren	1,300	166	57,611	301*	170	50.80
C. P. Mead	1,340	185	55,061	280*	153	47.67
W. G. Grace	1,493	105	54,896	344	126	39.55
W. R. Hammond	1,005	104	50,551	336*	167	56.10
H. Sutcliffe	1,088	123	50,138	313	149	51.95
T. W. Graveney	1,223	159	47,793	258	122	44.91
G. Boycott	994	161	47,434	261*	149	56.94
T. W. Hayward	1,138	96	43,551	315*	104	41.79
M. C. Cowdrey	1,130	134	42,719	307	107	42.89
A. Sandham	1,000	79	41,284	325	107	44.82
D. L. Amiss	1,048	117	40,673	262*	96	43.68
L. Hutton	814	91	40,140	364	129	55.51
M. J. K. Smith	1,091	139	39,832	204	66	41.84
W. Rhodes	1,528	237	39,802	267*	58	30.83
J. H. Edrich	979	104	39,790	310*	103	45.47
R. E. S. Wyatt	1,141	157	39,405	232	85	40.04
D. C. S. Compton	839	88	38,942	300	123	51.85
E. Tyldesley	961	106	38,874	256*	102	45.46
J. T. Tyldesley	994	62	37,897	295*	86	40.60
J. W. Hearne	1,025	116	37,252	285*	96	40.98
L. E. G. Ames	951	95	37,248	295	102	43.51
D. Kenyon	1,159	59	37,002	259	74	33.63
W. J. Edrich	964	92	36,965	267*	86	42.39
J. M. Parks	1,227	172	36,673	205*	51	34.76
D. Denton	1,163	70	36,479	221	69	33.37
G. H. Hirst	1,215	151	36,323	341	60	34.13
A. Jones	1,168	72	36,049	204*	56	32.89
Wm. Quaife	1,023	186	36,012	255*	72	35.38
R. E. Marshall	1,053	59	35,725	228*	68	35.95

†According to the Association of Cricket Statisticians, Hobbs made 199 centuries.

HIGHEST BATTING AVERAGES
Minimum 10,000 runs

	I	NO	Runs	HS	100s	Av
D. G. Bradman	338	43	28,067	452*	117	95.14
W. H. Ponsford	235	23	13,819	437	47	65.18
W. M. Woodfull	245	39	13,388	284	49	64.99
A. L. Hassett	322	32	16,890	232	59	58.24
V. S. Hazare	366	46	18,569	316*	59	58.02
A. F. Kippax	254	33	12,747	315*	43	57.67
G. Boycott	994	161	47,434	261*	149	56.94
C. L. Walcott	238	29	11,820	314*	40	56.55
K. S. Ranjitsinhji	500	62	24,692	285*	72	56.37
R. B. Simpson	436	62	21,029	359	60	56.22
W. R. Hammond	1,005	104	50,551	336*	167	56.10
L. Hutton	814	91	40,140	364	129	55.51
E. D. Weekes	241	24	12,010	304*	36	55.34
G. S. Sobers	609	93	28,315	365*	86	54.87
B. A. Richards	576	58	28,358	356	80	54.74
R. G. Pollock	414	51	19,813	274	60	54.58
F. M. M. Worrell	326	49	15,025	308*	39	54.24
R. W. Cowper	228	31	10,595	307	26	53.78
A. R. Morris	250	15	12,614	290	46	53.67
Javed Miandad	505	82	22,534	311	63	53.27
Hanif Mohammad	371	45	17,059	499	55	52.32
P. R. Umrigar	350	41	16,155	252*	49	52.28
G. S. Chappell	542	72	24,535	247*	74	52.20
Zaheer Abbas	746	89	34,285	274	107	52.18

HIGHEST PARTNERSHIPS

577	V. S. Hazare (288), Gul Mahomed (319), fourth wicket, Baroda v Holkar, Baroda, 1946-47
574*	F. M. M. Worrell (255*), C. L. Walcott (314*), fourth wicket, Barbados v Trinidad, Port-of-Spain, 1945-46
561	Waheed Mirza (324), Mansoor Akhtar (224*), first wicket, Karachi Whites v Quetta, Karachi, 1976-77
555	P. Holmes (224*), H. Sutcliffe (313), first wicket, Yorkshire v Essex, Leyton, 1932
554	J. T. Brown (300), J. Tunnicliffe (243), first wicket, Yorkshire v Derbyshire, Chesterfield, 1898
502*	F. M. M. Worrell (308*), J. D. C. Goddard (218*), fourth wicket, Barbados v Trinidad, Bridgetown, 1943-44
490	E. H. Bowley (283), J. G. Langridge (159), first wicket, Sussex v Middlesex, Hove, 1933
487*	G. A. Headley (344*), C. C. Passailaigue (261*), sixth wicket, Jamaica v Lord Tennyson's XI, Kingston, 1931-32
470	A. I. Kallicharran (230*), G. W. Humpage (254), fourth wicket, Warwickshire v Lancashire, Southport, 1982
465*	J. A. Jameson (240*), R. B. Kanhai (213*), second wicket, Warwickshire v Gloucestershire, Edgbaston, 1974
456	W. H. Ponsford (248), E. R. Mayne (209), first wicket, Victoria v Queensland, Melbourne, 1923-24
456	Khalid Irtiza (290), Aslam Ali (236), third wicket, United Bank v Multan, Karachi, 1975-76
455	B. B. Nimbalkar (443*), K. V. Bhandarkar (205), second wicket, Maharashtra v Kathiawar, Poona, 1948-49
451	D. G. Bradman (244), W. H. Ponsford (266), second wicket, Australia v England, the Oval, 1934
451*	S. Desai (218*), R. M. H. Binny (211*), first wicket, Karnataka v Kerala, Chikmagalur, 1977-78
451	Mudassar Nazar (231), Javed Miandad (280*), third wicket, Pakistan v India, Hyderabad, 1982-83

BEST 10-WICKET ANALYSES

10-10	H. Verity, Yorkshire v Nottinghamshire, Headingley, 1932
10-18	G. Geary, Leicestershire v Glamorgan, Pontypridd, 1929
10-20	P. Chatterjee, Bengal v Assam, Jorhat, 1956-57
10-26	A. E. E. Vogler, Eastern Province v Griqualand West, Johannesburg, 1906-07
10-28	A. E. Moss, Canterbury v Wellington, Christchurch, 1889-90
10-28	W. P. Howell, Australians v Surrey, Oval, 1899
10-30	C. Blythe, Kent v Northamptonshire, Northampton, 1907
10-32	H. Pickett, Essex v Leicestershire, Leyton, 1895
10-35	A. Drake, Yorkshire v Somerset, Weston-super-Mare, 1914
10-36	F. Hinds, A. B. St. Hill's XI v Trinidad, Port-of-Spain, 1900-01
10-36	H. Verity, Yorkshire v Warwickshire, Headingley, 1931
10-36	T. W. Wall, South Australia v New South Wales, Sydney, 1932-33

MOST WICKETS IN A SEASON

	Season	O	R	W	Av
A. P. Freeman	1928	1,976.1	5,489	304	18.05
A. P. Freeman	1933	2,039	4,549	298	15.26
T. Richardson	1895‡	1,690.1	4,170	290	14.37
C. T. B. Turner	1888†	2,427.2	3,307	283	11.68
A. P. Freeman	1931	1,618	4,307	276	15.60
A. P. Freeman	1930	1,914.3	4,632	275	16.84
T. Richardson	1897‡	1,603.4	3,945	273	14.45
A. P. Freeman	1929	1,670.5	4,879	267	18.27
W. Rhodes	1900	1,553	3,606	261	13.81
J. T. Hearne	1896	2,003.1	3,670	257	14.28
A. P. Freeman	1932	1,565.5	4,149	253	16.39
W. Rhodes	1901	1,565	3,797	251	15.12

†4-ball overs   ‡5-ball overs

MOST WICKETS IN A MATCH

19-90	J. C. Laker, England v Australia, Old Trafford, 1956
17-48	C. Blythe, Kent v Northamptonshire, Northampton, 1907
17-50	C. T. B. Turner, Australians v England XI, Hastings, 1888
17-54	W. P. Howell, Australians v Western Province, Cape Town, 1902-03
17-56	C. W. L. Parker, Gloucestershire v Essex, Gloucester, 1925
17-67	A. P. Freeman, Kent v Sussex, Hove, 1922
17-89	W. G. Grace, Gloucestershire v Nottinghamshire, Cheltenham, 1877
17-89	F. C. L. Matthews, Nottinghamshire v Northamptonshire, Trent Bridge, 1923
17-91	H. Dean, Lancashire v Yorkshire, Liverpool, 1913
17-91	H. Verity, Yorkshire v Essex, Leyton, 1933
17-92	A. P. Freeman, Kent v Warwickshire, Folkestone, 1932
17-103	W. Mycroft, Derbyshire v Hampshire, Southampton, 1876
17-106	G. R. Cox, Sussex v Warwickshire, Horsham, 1926
17-106	T. W. Goddard, Gloucestershire v Kent, Bristol, 1939
17-119	W. Mead, Essex v Hampshire, Southampton, 1895
17-137	W. Brearley, Lancashire v Somerset, Old Trafford, 1905
17-159	S. F. Barnes, England v South Africa, Johannesburg, 1913-14
17-201	G. Giffen, South Australia v Victoria, Adelaide, 1885-86
17-212	J. C. Clay, Glamorgan v Worcestershire, Swansea, 1937

MOST WICKETS IN A CAREER

	Career	W	R	Av
W. Rhodes	1898-1930	4,187	69,993	16.71
A. P. Freeman	1914-36	3,776	69,577	18.42
C. W. L. Parker	1903-35	3,278	63,821	19.46
J. T. Hearne	1888-1923	3,061	54,342	17.75
T. W. Goddard	1922-52	2,979	59,116	19.84
W. G. Grace*	1865-1908	2,876	51,545	17.92
A. S. Kennedy	1907-36	2,874	61,044	21.24
D. Shackleton	1948-69	2,857	53,303	18.65
G. A. R. Lock	1946-71	2,844	54,710	19.23
F. J. Titmus	1949-82	2,830	63,313	22.37
M. W. Tate	1912-37	2,784	50,567	18.16
G. H. Hirst	1891-1929	2,739	51,300	18.72
C. Blythe	1899-1914	2,506	42,136	16.81

*According to the Association of Cricket Statisticians, Grace took 2,808 wickets, average 18.15.

BELOW LEFT Jack Hobbs, who scored more runs in first-class cricket than anybody else.

BELOW Wilfred Rhodes took most first-class wickets and also scored nearly 40,000 runs.

BEST AVERAGES OF BOWLERS WITH 1,500 WICKETS

	Career	W	R	Av
A. Shaw	1864-97	2,021	24,496	12.12
T. Emmett	1866-88	1,582	21,147	13.36
G. A. Lohmann	1884-98	1,805	25,110	13.91
J. Southerton	1854-79	1,680	24,257	14.43
H. Verity	1930-39	1,956	29,146	14.90
W. Attewell	1881-1900	1,932	29,745	15.39
A. W. Mold	1889-1901	1,673	26,012	15.54
J. Briggs	1879-1900	2,221	35,390	15.93
S. Haigh	1895-1913	2,012	32,091	15.94
R. Peel	1882-99	1,754	28,446	16.21
J. B. Statham	1950-68	2,260	36,995	16.36
W. Rhodes	1898-1930	4,187	69,993	16.71
W. E. Bowes	1928-47	1,639	27,470	16.76
C. Blythe	1899-1914	2,506	42,136	16.81

ALL-ROUND RECORDS

20,000 Runs and 2,000 Wickets in a Career

	R	Av	W	Av	doubles
W. E. Astill	22,726	22.54	2,431	23.76	9
T. E. Bailey	28,642	33.42	2,082	23.13	8
W. G. Grace*	54,896	39.55	2,876	17.99	8
G. H. Hirst	36,323	34.13	2,739	18.72	14
R. Illingworth	24,134	28.06	2,072	20.28	6
W. Rhodes	39,802	30.83	4,187	16.71	16
M. W. Tate	21,717	25.01	2,784	18.16	8
F. J. Titmus	21,588	23.11	2,830	22.37	8
F. E. Woolley	58,969	40.75	2,068	19.85	8

* According to the Association of Cricket Statisticians, Grace scored 54,211 runs, av 39.45, and took 2,808 wickets, av 18.15

2,000 Runs and 200 Wickets in a Season
G. H. Hirst   2,385 runs   208 wickets   1906

3,000 Runs and 100 Wickets in a Season
J. H. Parks   3,003 runs   101 wickets   1937

2,000 Runs and 100 Wickets in a Season

	Season	R	W
W. G. Grace*	1873	2,139	106
W. G. Grace	1876	2,622	129
C. L. Townsend	1899	2,440	101
G. L. Jessop	1900	2,210	104
G. H. Hirst	1904	2,501	132
G. H. Hirst	1905	2,266	110
W. Rhodes	1909	2,094	141
W. Rhodes	1911	2,261	117
F. A. Tarrant	1911	2,030	111
J. W. Hearne	1913	2,036	124
J. W. Hearne	1914	2,116	123
F. E. Woolley	1914	2,272	125
J. W. Hearne	1920	2,148	142
V. W. C. Jupp	1921	2,169	121
F. E. Woolley	1921	2,101	167
F. E. Woolley	1922	2,022	163
F. E. Woolley	1923	2,091	101
L. F. Townsend	1933	2,268	100
D. E. Davies	1937	2,012	103
James Langridge	1937	2,082	101
T. E. Bailey	1959	2,011	100

* Grace's figures, according to the Association of Cricket Statisticians, were 'fiddled' in this season to give him the record. In fact, he scored 1,805 runs and took 75 wickets.

1,000 Runs and 200 Wickets in a Season

	Season	R	W
A. E. Trott	1899	1,175	239
A. E. Trott	1900	1,337	211
A. S. Kennedy	1922	1,129	205
M. W. Tate	1923	1,168	219
M. W. Tate	1924	1,419	205
M. W. Tate	1925	1,290	228

MOST WICKET-KEEPING DISMISSALS IN A CAREER

	ct	st	Total
R. W. Taylor	1,471	175	1,646
J. T. Murray	1,270	257	1,527
H. Strudwick	1,215	253	1,468
A. P. E. Knott	1,211	133	1,344
F. H. Huish	952	376	1,328
D. Hunter	955	372	1,327
B. Taylor	1,082	212	1,294
H. R. Butt	971	291	1,262
J. H. Board	852	354	1,206
H. Elliott	904	302	1,206
J. M. Parks	1,089	93	1,182
R. Booth	946	176	1,122
L. E. G. Ames	698	415	1,113
G. Duckworth	751	339	1,090
H. W. Stephenson	752	332	1,084

Frank Woolley, second to Hobbs in the matter of runs scored in a career, also captured over 2,000 wickets.

TEST CRICKET RECORDS

HIGHEST TEAM TOTALS

903-7	England v Australia, the Oval, 1938
849	England v West Indies, Kingston, 1929-30
790-3 dec	West Indies v Pakistan, Kingston, 1957-58
758-8 dec	Australia v West Indies, Kingston, 1954-55
729-6 dec	Australia v England, Lord's, 1930
701	Australia v England, the Oval, 1934
695	Australia v England, the Oval, 1930
687-8 dec	West Indies v England, Oval, 1976
681-8 dec	West Indies v England, Port of Spain, 1953-54
674	Australia v India, Adelaide, 1947-48
668	Australia v West Indies, Bridgetown, 1954-55

Highest totals for other countries

657-8 dec	Pakistan v West Indies, Bridgetown, 1957-58
644-7 dec	India v West Indies, Kanpur, 1978-79
622-9 dec	South Africa v Australia, Durban, 1969-70
551-9 dec	New Zealand v England, Lord's, 1973
491-7 dec	Sri Lanka v England, Lord's, 1984

LOWEST TEAM TOTALS

26	New Zealand v England, Auckland, 1954-55
30	South Africa v England, Port Elizabeth, 1895-96
30	South Africa v England, Edgbaston, 1924
35	South Africa v England, Cape Town, 1898-99
36	Australia v England, Edgbaston, 1902
36	South Africa v Australia, Melbourne, 1931-32
42	Australia v England, Sydney, 1887-88
42	New Zealand v Australia, Wellington, 1945-46
42	India v England, Lord's, 1974
43	South Africa v England, Cape Town, 1888-89
44	Australia v England, the Oval, 1896
45	England v Australia, Sydney, 1886-87
45	South Africa v Australia, Melbourne, 1931-32

Lowest totals for other countries

62	Pakistan v Australia, Perth, 1981-82
76	West Indies v Pakistan, Dacca, 1958-59
93	Sri Lanka v New Zealand, Wellington, 1982-83

HIGHEST INDIVIDUAL INNINGS

365*	G. S. Sobers, West Indies v Pakistan, Kingston, 1957-58
364	L. Hutton, England v Australia, the Oval, 1938
337	Hanif Mohammad, Pakistan v West Indies, Bridgetown, 1957-58
336*	W. R. Hammond, England v New Zealand, Auckland, 1932-33
334	D. G. Bradman, Australia v England, Headingley, 1930
325	A. Sandham, England v West Indies, Kingston, 1929-30
311	R. B. Simpson, Australia v England, Old Trafford, 1964
310*	J. H. Edrich, England v New Zealand, Headingley, 1965
307	R. M. Cowper, Australia v England, Melbourne, 1965-66
304	D. G. Bradman, Australia v England, Headingley, 1934
302	L. G. Rowe, West Indies v England, Bridgetown, 1973-74

Highest for other countries

274	R. G. Pollock, South Africa v Australia, Durban, 1969-70
259	G. M. Turner, New Zealand v West Indies, Georgetown, 1971-72
236*	S. M. Gavaskar, India v West Indies, Madras, 1983-84
190	S. Wettimuny, Sri Lanka v England, Lord's, 1984

HIGHEST AGGREGATE RUNS

	M	I	NO	Runs	HS	100s	Av
S. M. Gavaskar	106	185	14	8,654	236*	30	50.60
G. Boycott	108	193	23	8,114	246*	22	47.72
G. S. Sobers	93	160	21	8,032	365*	26	57.78
M. C. Cowdrey	114	188	15	7,624	182	22	44.06
C. H. Lloyd	110	175	14	7,515	242*	19	46.67
W. R. Hammond	85	140	16	7,249	336*	22	58.45
G. S. Chappell	87	151	19	7,110	247*	24	53.86
D. G. Bradman	52	80	10	6,996	334	29	99.94
L. Hutton	79	138	15	6,971	364	19	56.67
K. F. Barrington	82	131	15	6,806	256	20	58.67
R. B. Kanhai	79	137	6	6,227	256	15	47.53
R. N. Harvey	79	137	10	6,149	205	21	48.41
G. R. Viswanath	91	155	10	6,080	222	14	41.93

HIGHEST BATTING AVERAGES
Minimum 20 innings

	M	I	NO	Runs	HS	100s	Av
D. G. Bradman	52	80	10	6,996	334	29	99.94
R. G. Pollock	23	41	4	2,256	274	7	60.97
G. A. Headley	22	40	4	2,190	270*	10	60.83
H. Sutcliffe	54	84	9	4,555	194	16	60.73
E. Paynter	20	31	5	1,540	243	4	59.23
K. F. Barrington	82	131	15	6,806	256	20	58.67
E. D. Weekes	48	81	5	4,455	207	15	58.61
W. R. Hammond	85	140	16	7,249	336*	22	58.45
G. S. Sobers	93	160	21	8,032	365*	26	57.78
J. B. Hobbs	61	102	7	5,410	211	15	56.94
C. L. Walcott	44	74	7	3,798	220	15	56.68
L. Hutton	79	138	15	6,971	364	19	56.67
E. Tyldesley	14	20	2	990	122	3	55.00
Javed Miandad	68	108	16	5,044	280*	13	54.92
C. A. Davis	15	29	5	1,301	183	4	54.20
I. V. A. Richards	77	116	7	5,889	291	19	54.02

HIGHEST WICKET PARTNERSHIPS

1st	413	V. Mankad (231) and P. Roy (173), India v New Zealand, Madras, 1955-56
2nd	451	W. H. Ponsford (266) and D. G. Bradman (244), Australia v England, the Oval, 1934
3rd	451	Mudassar Nazar (231) and Javed Miandad (280*), Pakistan v India, Hyderabad, 1982-83
4th	411	P. B. H. May (285*) and M. C. Cowdrey (154), England v West Indies, Edgbaston, 1957
5th	405	S. G. Barnes (234) and D. G. Bradman (234), Australia v England, Sydney, 1946-47
6th	346	J. H. W. Fingleton (136) and D. G. Bradman (270), Australia v England, Melbourne, 1936-37
7th	347	D. St. E. Atkinson (219) and C. C. Depeiza (122), West Indies v Australia, Bridgetown, 1954-55
8th	246	L. E. G. Ames (137) and G. O. Allen (122), England v New Zealand, Lord's, 1931
9th	190	Asif Iqbal (146) and Intikhab Alam (51), Pakistan v England, the Oval, 1967
10th	151	B. F. Hastings (110) and R. O. Collinge (68*), New Zealand v Pakistan, Auckland, 1972-73

MOST CENTURIES

Total	Player	Against							
		E	A	SA	WI	NZ	I	P	SL
30	S. M. Gavaskar (India)	4	5	—	13	2	—	5	1
29	D. G. Bradman (Australia)	19	—	4	2	0	4	—	—
26	G. S. Sobers (West Indies)	10	4	0	—	1	8	3	—
24	G. S. Chappell (Australia)	9	—	0	5	3	1	6	0
22	W. R. Hammond (England)	—	9	6	1	4	2	—	—
22	M. C. Cowdrey (England)	—	5	3	6	2	3	3	—
22	G. Boycott (England)	—	7	1	5	2	4	3	0
21	R. N. Harvey (Australia)	6	—	8	3	0	4	0	—
20	K. F. Barrington (England)	—	5	2	3	3	3	4	—

A dash indicates the batsman did not play against that country.

MOST RUNS IN A SERIES

	M	I	NO	Runs	HS	100s	Av
D. G. Bradman, Aus v Eng 1930	5	7	0	974	334	4	139.14
W. R. Hammond, Eng v Aus 1928-29	5	9	1	905	251	4	113.12
R. N. Harvey, Aus v SA 1952-53	5	9	0	834	205	4	92.66
I. V. A. Richards, WI v Eng 1976	4	7	0	829	291	3	118.42
C. L. Walcott, WI v Aus 1954-55	5	10	0	827	155	5	82.70
G. S. Sobers, WI v Pak 1957-58	5	8	2	824	365*	3	137.33
D. G. Bradman, Aus v Eng 1936-37	5	9	0	810	270	3	90.00
D. G. Bradman, Aus v SA 1931-32	5	5	1	806	299*	4	201.50
E. D. Weekes, WI v Ind 1948-49	5	7	0	779	194	4	111.28
S. M. Gavaskar, Ind v WI 1970-71	4	8	3	774	220	4	154.80
Mudassar Nazar, Pak v Ind 1982-83	6	8	2	761	231	4	126.83

MOST WICKETS IN A MATCH

19-90	J. C. Laker, England v Australia, Old Trafford, 1956
17-159	S. F. Barnes, England v South Africa, Johannesburg, 1913-14
16-137	R. A. L. Massie, Australia v England, Lord's, 1972
15-28	J. Briggs, England v South Africa, Cape Town, 1888-89
15-45	G. A. Lohmann, England v South Africa, Port Elizabeth, 1895-96
15-99	C. Blythe, England v South Africa, Headingley, 1907
15-104	H. Verity, England v Australia, Lord's, 1934
15-124	W. Rhodes, England v Australia, Melbourne, 1903-04

MOST WICKETS IN AN INNINGS

10-53	J. C. Laker, England v Australia, Old Trafford, 1956
9-28	G. A. Lohmann, England v South Africa, Johannesburg, 1895-96
9-37	J. C. Laker, England v Australia, Old Trafford, 1956
9-69	J. M. Patel, India v Australia, Kanpur, 1959-60
9-83	Kapil Dev, India v West Indies, Ahmedabad, 1983-84
9-86	Sarfraz Nawaz, Pakistan v Australia, Melbourne, 1978-79
9-95	J. M. Noreiga, West Indies v India, Port-of-Spain, 1970-71
9-102	S. P. Gupte, India v West Indies, Kanpur, 1958-59
9-103	S. F. Barnes, England v South Africa, Johannesburg, 1913-14
9-113	H. J. Tayfield, South Africa v England, Johannesburg, 1956-57
9-121	A. A. Mailey, Australia v England, Melbourne, 1920-21

MOST WICKETS IN A SERIES

	T	R	W	Av	Teams
S. F. Barnes	4	536	49	10.93	England v South Africa, 1913-14
J. C. Laker	5	442	46	9.60	England v Australia, 1956
C. V. Grimmett	5	642	44	14.59	Australia v South Africa, 1935-36
T. M. Alderman	6	893	42	21.26	Australia v England, 1981
R. M. Hogg	6	527	41	12.85	Australia v England, 1978-79
Imran Khan	6	558	40	13.95	Pakistan v India, 1982-83
A. V. Bedser	5	682	39	17.48	England v Australia, 1953
D. K. Lillee	6	870	39	22.30	Australia v England, 1981
M. W. Tate	5	881	38	23.18	England v Australia, 1924-25
M. J. Whitty	5	632	37	17.08	Australia v South Africa, 1910-11
H. J. Tayfield	5	638	37	17.18	South Africa v England, 1956-57

MOST WICKETS IN A CAREER

	M	R	W	Av
D. K. Lillee	70	8,493	355	23.92
I. T. Botham	79	9,046	343	26.37
R. G. D. Willis	90	8,190	325	25.20
L. R. Gibbs	79	8,989	309	29.09
F. S. Trueman	67	6,625	307	21.57
D. L. Underwood	86	7,674	297	25.83
R. J. Hadlee	57	6,341	266	23.83
B. S. Bedi	67	7,637	266	28.71
Kapil Dev	68	7,406	258	28.70
J. B. Statham	70	6,261	252	24.84
R. Benaud	63	6,704	248	27.03
G. D. McKenzie	60	7,328	246	29.78
B. S. Chandrasekhar	58	7,199	242	29.74

BEST TEST AVERAGES OF BOWLERS WITH 100 WICKETS

	M	R	W	Av
G. A. Lohmann	18	1,205	112	10.75
S. F. Barnes	27	3,106	189	16.43
C. T. B. Turner	17	1,670	101	16.53
R. Peel	20	1,715	102	16.81
J. Briggs	33	2,094	118	17.74
C. Blythe	19	1,863	100	18.63
J. H. Wardle	28	2,080	102	20.39
A. K. Davidson	44	3,819	186	20.53
N. A. T. Adcock	26	2,195	104	21.10
J. C. Laker	46	4,101	193	21.24
F. S. Trueman	67	6,625	307	21.57
H. Trumble	32	3,072	141	21.78
J. Garner	51	4,792	220	21.78

TEST ALL-ROUNDER RECORDS

Century and 10 Wickets
I. T. Botham 114, 6-58, 7-48, England v India, Bombay, 1979-80
Imran Khan 117, 6-98, 5-82, Pakistan v India, Faisalabad, 1982-83

2,000 Runs and 200 Wickets

	M	R	Av	Wkts	Av
R. Benaud	63	2,201	24.45	248	27.03
I. T. Botham	79	4,409	36.13	343	26.37
R. J. Hadlee	57	2,088	24.85	266	23.83
Imran Khan	51	2,023	31.12	232	22.91
Kapil Dev	68	2,788	30.30	258	28.70
G. S. Sobers	93	8,032	57.78	235	34.03

MOST WICKET-KEEPING DISMISSALS IN A CAREER

	M	Ct	St	Total
R. W. Marsh	96	343	12	355
A. P. E. Knott	95	250	19	269
Wasim Bari	81	201	27	228
T. G. Evans	91	173	46	219
D. L. Murray	62	181	8	189
A. T. W. Grout	51	163	24	187
S. M. H. Kirmani	78	145	34	179
R. W. Taylor	57	167	7	174
J. H. B. Waite	50	124	17	141
W. A. Oldfield	54	78	52	130

MOST WICKET-KEEPING DISMISSALS IN A SERIES

28	(all ct)	R. W. Marsh, Australia v England, 1982-83
26	(all ct)	R. W. Marsh, Australia v West Indies, 1975-76
26	(23 ct, 3 st)	J. H. B. Waite, South Africa v New Zealand, 1961-62
24	(21 ct, 3 st)	A. P. E. Knott, England v Australia, 1970-71
24	(all ct)	D. T. Lindsay, South Africa v Australia, 1966-67
24	(22 ct, 2 st)	D. L. Murray, West Indies v England, 1963
23	(22 ct, 1 st)	F. C. M. Alexander, West Indies v England, 1959-60
23	(21 ct, 2 st)	A. E. Dick, New Zealand v South Africa, 1961-62
23	(20 ct, 3 st)	A. T. W. Grout, Australia v West Indies, 1960-61
23	(22 ct, 1 st)	A. P. E. Knott, England v Australia, 1974-75
23	(21 ct, 2 st)	R. W. Marsh, Australia v England, 1972
23	(all ct)	R. W. Marsh, Australia v England, 1981
23	(16 ct, 7 st)	J. H. B. Waite, South Africa v New Zealand, 1953-54

MOST CATCHES IN A CAREER
Excluding Wicket-keepers

122	G. S. Chappell	87 matches
120	M. C. Cowdrey	114 matches
110	R. B. Simpson	62 matches
110	W. R. Hammond	85 matches
109	G. S. Sobers	93 matches
105	I. M. Chappell	75 matches

SUMMARY OF MATCH RESULTS

England

Against	W	L	D	Total
Australia	86	96	75	257
South Africa	46	18	38	102
West Indies	21	30	34	85
New Zealand	30	3	27	60
India	30	9	33	72
Pakistan	13	3	23	39
Sri Lanka	1	0	1	2
Totals	**227**	**159**	**231**	**617**

Australia

Against	W	L	D	Total
England	96	86	75	257
South Africa	29	11	13	53
West Indies (1 tie)	27	19	15	62
New Zealand	8	2	5	15
India	20	8	11	39
Pakistan	11	8	9	28
Sri Lanka	1	0	0	1
Totals (1 tie)	**192**	**134**	**128**	**455**

South Africa

Against	W	L	D	Total
England	18	46	38	102
Australia	11	29	13	53
New Zealand	9	2	6	17
Totals	**38**	**77**	**57**	**172**

West Indies

Against	W	L	D	Total
England	30	21	34	85
Australia (1 tie)	19	27	15	62
New Zealand	7	3	11	21
India	22	5	27	54
Pakistan	7	4	8	19
Totals (1 tie)	**85**	**60**	**95**	**241**

New Zealand

Against	W	L	D	Total
England	3	30	27	60
Australia	2	8	5	15
South Africa	2	9	6	17
West Indies	3	7	11	21
India	4	10	11	25
Pakistan	3	10	14	27
Sri Lanka	4	0	1	5
Totals	**21**	**74**	**75**	**170**

India

Against	W	L	D	Total
England	9	30	33	72
Australia	8	20	11	39
West Indies	5	22	27	54
New Zealand	10	4	11	25
Pakistan	4	6	25	35
Sri Lanka	0	0	1	1
Totals	**36**	**82**	**108**	**226**

Pakistan

Against	W	L	D	Total
England	3	13	23	39
Australia	8	11	9	28
West Indies	4	7	8	19
New Zealand	10	3	14	27
India	6	4	25	35
Sri Lanka	2	0	1	3
Totals	**33**	**38**	**80**	**151**

Sri Lanka

Against	W	L	D	Total
England	0	1	1	2
Australia	0	1	0	1
New Zealand	0	4	1	5
India	0	0	1	1
Pakistan	0	2	1	3
Totals	**0**	**8**	**4**	**12**

ENGLAND v AUSTRALIA

TESTS: 257
Won by England: 86
Won by Australia: 96
Drawn: 75

Highest score by England:
903 for 7 dec, the Oval, 1938

Highest score by Australia:
729 for 6 dec, Lord's, 1930

Lowest score by England:
45, Sydney, 1886-87

Lowest score by Australia:
36, Edgbaston, 1902

Highest individual innings:
England: 364, L. Hutton, the Oval, 1938
Australia: 334, D. G. Bradman, Headingley, 1930

Most wickets in a match:
England: 19-90, J. C. Laker, Old Trafford, 1956
Australia: 16-137, R. A. L. Massie, Lord's, 1972

Record Wicket Partnerships
FOR ENGLAND

1st	323	J. B. Hobbs, W. Rhodes, Melbourne, 1911-12
2nd	382	L. Hutton, M. Leyland, the Oval, 1938
3rd	262	W. R. Hammond, D. R. Jardine, Adelaide, 1928-29
4th	222	W. R. Hammond, E. Paynter, Lord's, 1938
5th	206	E. Paynter, D. C. S. Compton, Trent Bridge, 1938
6th	215	L. Hutton, J. Hardstaff, the Oval, 1938
	215	G. Boycott, A. P. E. Knott, Trent Bridge, 1977
7th	143	F. E. Woolley, J. Vine, Sydney, 1911-12
8th	124	E. H. Hendren, H. Larwood, Brisbane, 1928-29
9th	151	W. H. Scotton, W. W. Read, the Oval, 1884
10th	130	R. E. Foster, W. Rhodes, Sydney, 1903-04

FOR AUSTRALIA

1st	244	R. B. Simpson, W. M. Lawry, Adelaide, 1965-66
2nd	451	W. H. Ponsford, D. G. Bradman, the Oval, 1934
3rd	276	D. G. Bradman, A. L. Hassett, Brisbane, 1946-47
4th	388	W. H. Ponsford, D. G. Bradman, Headingley, 1934
5th	405	S. G. Barnes, D. G. Bradman, Sydney, 1946-47
6th	346	J. H. Fingleton, D. G. Bradman, Melbourne, 1936-37

7th	165	C. Hill, H. Trumble, Melbourne, 1897-98
8th	243	R. J. Hartigan, C. Hill, Adelaide, 1907-08
9th	154	S. E. Gregory, J. McC. Blackham, Sydney, 1894-95
10th	127	J. M. Taylor, A. A. Mailey, Sydney, 1924-25

ENGLAND v SOUTH AFRICA

TESTS: 102
Won by England: 46
Won by South Africa: 18
Drawn: 38

Highest score by England:
654 for 5, Durban, 1938-39

Highest score by South Africa:
538, Headingley, 1951

Lowest score by England:
76, Headingley, 1907

Lowest score by South Africa:
30, Edgbaston, 1924
30, Port Elizabeth, 1895-96

Highest individual innings:
England: 243, E. Paynter, Durban, 1938-39
South Africa: 236, E. A. B. Rowan, Headingley, 1951

Most wickets in a match:
England: 17-159, S. F. Barnes, Johannesburg, 1913-14
South Africa: 13-192, H. J. Tayfield, Johannesburg, 1956-57

Record Wicket Partnerships
FOR ENGLAND

1st	359	L. Hutton, C. Washbrook, Johannesburg, 1948-49
2nd	280	P. A. Gibb, W. J. Edrich, Durban, 1938-39
3rd	370	W. J. Edrich, D. C. S. Compton, Lord's, 1947
4th	197	W. R. Hammond, L. E. G. Ames, Cape Town, 1938-39
5th	237	D. C. S. Compton, N. W. D. Yardley, Trent Bridge, 1947
6th	206*	K. F. Barrington, J. M. Parks, Durban, 1964-65
7th	115	M. C. Bird, J. W. H. T. Douglas, Durban, 1913-14
8th	154	C. W. Wright, H. R. Bromley-Davenport, Johannesburg, 1895-96
9th	71	H. Wood, J. T. Hearne, Cape Town, 1891-92
10th	92	A. C. Russell, A. E. R. Gilligan, Durban, 1922-23

FOR SOUTH AFRICA

1st	260	I. J. Siedle, B. Mitchell, Cape Town, 1930-31
2nd	198	E. A. B. Rowan, C. B. van Ryneveld, Headingley, 1951
3rd	319	A. Melville, A. D. Nourse, Trent Bridge, 1947
4th	214	H. W. Taylor, H. G. Deane, the Oval, 1929
5th	157	A. J. Pithey, H. J. B. Waite, Johannesburg, 1964-65
6th	171	J. H. B. Waite, P. L. Winslow, Old Trafford, 1955
7th	123	H. G. Deane, E. P. Nupen, Durban, 1927-28
8th	109*	B. Mitchell, L. Tuckett, the Oval, 1947
9th	137	E. L. Dalton, A. B. C. Langton, the Oval, 1935
10th	103	H. G. Owen-Smith, A. J. Bell, Headingley, 1929

ENGLAND v WEST INDIES

TESTS: 85
Won by England: 21
Won by West Indies: 30
Drawn: 34

Highest score by England:
849, Kingston, 1929-30

Highest score by West Indies:
687 for 8 dec, the Oval, 1976

Lowest score by England:
71, Old Trafford, 1976

Lowest score by West Indies:
86, the Oval, 1957

Highest individual innings:
England: 325, A. Sandham, Kingston, 1929-30
West Indies: 302, L. G. Rowe, Bridgetown, 1973-74

Most wickets in a match:
England: 13-156, A. W. Greig, Port-of-Spain, 1973-74
West Indies: 14-149, M. A. Holding, the Oval, 1976

Record Wicket Partnerships
FOR ENGLAND

1st	212	C. Washbrook, R. T. Simpson, Trent Bridge, 1950
2nd	266	P. E. Richardson, T. W. Graveney, Trent Bridge, 1957
3rd	264	L. Hutton, W. R. Hammond, the Oval, 1939
4th	411	P. B. H. May, M. C. Cowdrey, Edgbaston, 1957
5th	130*	C. Milburn, T. W. Graveney, Lord's, 1966
6th	163	A. W. Greig, A. P. E. Knott, Bridgetown, 1973-74
7th	197	M. J. K. Smith, J. M. Parks, Port-of-Spain, 1959-60
8th	217	T. W. Graveney, J. T. Murray, the Oval, 1966
9th	109	G. A. R. Lock, P. I. Pocock, Georgetown, 1967-68
10th	128	K. Higgs, J. A. Snow, the Oval, 1966

FOR WEST INDIES

1st	206	R. C. Fredericks, L. G. Rowe, Kingston, 1973-74
2nd	287*	C. G. Greenidge, H. A. Gomes, Lord's, 1984
3rd	338	E. D. Weekes, F. M. M. Worrell, Port-of-Spain, 1953-54
4th	399	G. S. Sobers, F. M. M. Worrell, Bridgetown, 1959-60
5th	265	S. M. Nurse, G. S. Sobers, Headingley, 1966
6th	274*	G. S. Sobers, D. A. J. Holford, Lord's, 1966
7th	155*†	G. S. Sobers, B. D. Julien, Lord's, 1973
8th	99	C. A. McWatt, J. K. Holt, Georgetown, 1953-54
9th	150	E. A. E. Baptiste, M. A. Holding, Edgbaston, 1984
10th	67*	M. A. Holding, C. E. H. Croft, St John's, 1980-81

†231 were added for this wicket: K. D. Boyce added 76 with Julien after Sobers retired hurt.

ENGLAND v NEW ZEALAND

TESTS: 60
Won by England: 30
Won by New Zealand: 3
Drawn: 27

Highest score by England:
593 for 6 dec, Auckland, 1974-75

Highest score by New Zealand:
551 for 9 dec, Lord's, 1973

Lowest score by England:
64, Wellington, 1977-78

Lowest score by New Zealand:
26, Auckland, 1954-55

Highest individual innings:
England: 336*, W. R. Hammond, Auckland, 1932-33
New Zealand: 206, M. P. Donnelly, Lord's, 1949

Most wickets in a match:
England: 12-97, D. L. Underwood, Christchurch, 1970-71
12-101, D. L. Underwood, the Oval, 1969
New Zealand: 10-100, R. J. Hadlee, Wellington, 1977-78
10-140, J. Cowie, Old Trafford, 1937
10-144, B. L. Cairns, Headingley, 1983

Record Wicket Partnerships
FOR ENGLAND

1st	223	G. Fowler, C. J. Tavare, the Oval, 1983
2nd	369	J. H. Edrich, K. F. Barrington, Headingley, 1965
3rd	245	W. R. Hammond, J. Hardstaff, Lord's, 1937
4th	266	M. H. Denness, K. W. R. Fletcher, Auckland, 1974-75
5th	242	W. R. Hammond, L. E. G. Ames, Christchurch, 1932-33
6th	240	P. H. Parfitt, B. R. Knight, Auckland, 1962-63
7th	149	A. P. E. Knott, P. Lever, Auckland, 1970-71
8th	246	L. E. G. Ames, G. O. Allen, Lord's, 1931
9th	163*	M. C. Cowdrey, A. C. Smith, Wellington, 1962-63
10th	59	A. P. E. Knott, N. Gifford, Trent Bridge, 1973

FOR NEW ZEALAND

1st	276	C. S. Dempster, J. E. Mills, Wellington, 1929-30
2nd	131	B. Sutcliffe, J. R. Reid, Christchurch, 1950-51
3rd	190	B. E. Congdon, B. F. Hastings, Lord's, 1973
4th	154	J. G. Wright, J. J. Crowe, Auckland, 1983-84
5th	177	B. E. Congdon, V. Pollard, Trent Bridge, 1973
6th	117	M. G. Burgess, V. Pollard, Lord's, 1973
7th	104	B. Sutcliffe, V. Pollard, Edgbaston, 1965
8th	104	A. W. Roberts, D. A. R. Moloney, Lord's, 1937
9th	118	J. V. Coney, B. L. Cairns, Wellington, 1983-84
10th	57	F. L. H. Mooney, J. Cowie, Headingley, 1949

ENGLAND v INDIA

TESTS: 72
Won by England: 30
Won by India: 9
Drawn: 33

Highest score by England:
652 for 7 dec, Madras, 1984-85

Highest score by India:
510, Headingley, 1967

Lowest score by England:
101, the Oval, 1971

Lowest score by India:
42, Lord's, 1974

Highest individual innings:
England: 246*, G. Boycott, Headingley, 1967
India: 222, G. R. Viswanath, Madras, 1981-82

Most wickets in a match:
England: 13-106, I. T. Botham, Bombay, 1979-80
India: 12-108, V. Mankad, Madras, 1951-52
12-181, L. Sivaramakrishnan, Bombay, 1984-85

TOP LEFT Hedley Verity. TOP RIGHT 'Tich' Freeman. ABOVE Herbert Sutcliffe and Eddie Paynter.

Record Wicket Partnerships
FOR ENGLAND

1st	159	P. E. Richardson, G. Pullar, Bombay, 1961-62
2nd	241	G. Fowler, M. W. Gatting, Madras, 1984-85
3rd	169	R. Subba Row, M. J. K. Smith, the Oval, 1959
4th	266	W. R. Hammond, T. S. Worthington, the Oval, 1936
5th	254	K. W. R. Fletcher, A. W. Greig, Bombay, 1972-73
6th	171	I. T. Botham, R. W. Taylor, Bombay, 1979-80
7th	125	D. W. Randall, P. H. Edmonds, Lord's, 1982
8th	168	R. Illingworth, P. Lever, Old Trafford, 1971
9th	83	K. W. R. Fletcher, N. Gifford, Madras, 1972-73
10th	70	P. J. W. Allott, R. D. G. Willis, Lord's, 1982

FOR INDIA

1st	213	S. M. Gavaskar, C. P. S. Chauhan, the Oval, 1979
2nd	192	F. M. Engineer, A. L. Wadekar, Bombay, 1972-73
3rd	316†	G. R. Viswanath, Yashpal Sharma, Madras, 1981-82
4th	222	V. S. Hazare, V. L. Manjreker, Headingley, 1952
5th	214	M. Azharuddin, R. J. Shastri, Calcutta, 1984-85
6th	130	S. M. H. Kirmani, Kapil Dev, the Oval, 1982
7th	235	R. J. Shastri, S. M. H. Kirmani, Bombay, 1984-85
8th	128	R. J. Shastri, S. M. H. Kirmani, Delhi, 1981-82
9th	104	R. J. Shastri, Madan Lal, Delhi, 1981-82
10th	51	R. G. Nadkarni, B. S. Chandrasekhar, Calcutta, 1963-64
	51	N. S. Yadav, L. Sivaramakrishnan, New Delhi, 1984-85

†415 were added for this wicket: D. B. Vengsarkar added 99 with Viswanath before he retired hurt.

ENGLAND v PAKISTAN

TESTS: 39
Won by England: 13
Won by Pakistan: 3
Drawn: 23

Highest score by England:
558 for 6 dec, Trent Bridge, 1954

Highest score by Pakistan:
608 for 7 dec, Edgbaston, 1971

Lowest score by England:
130, the Oval, 1954

Lowest score by Pakistan:
87, Lord's, 1954

Highest individual innings:
England: 278, D. C. S. Compton, Trent Bridge, 1954
Pakistan: 274, Zaheer Abbas, Edgbaston, 1971

Most wickets in a match:
England: 13-71, D. L. Underwood, Lord's, 1974
Pakistan: 12-99, Fazal Mahmood, the Oval, 1954

Record Wicket Partnerships
FOR ENGLAND

1st	198	G. Pullar, R. W. Barber, Dacca, 1961-62
2nd	248	M. C. Cowdrey, E. R. Dexter, the Oval, 1962
3rd	201	K. F. Barrington, T. W. Graveney, Lord's, 1967
4th	188	E. R. Dexter, P. H. Parfitt, Karachi, 1961-62
5th	192	D. C. S. Compton, T. E. Bailey, Trent Bridge, 1954
6th	153*	P. H. Parfitt, D. A. Allen, Edgbaston, 1962
7th	167	D. I. Gower, V. J. Marks, Faisalabad, 1983-84
8th	99	P. H. Parfitt, D. A. Allen, Headingley, 1962
9th	76	T. W. Graveney, F. S. Trueman, Lord's, 1962
10th	79	R. W. Taylor, R. G. D. Willis, Edgbaston, 1982

FOR PAKISTAN

1st	173	Mohsin Khan, Shoaib Mohammad, Lahore, 1983-84
2nd	291	Zaheer Abbas, Mushtaq Mohammad, Edgbaston, 1971
3rd	180	Mudassar Nazar, Haroon Rashid, Lahore, 1977-78
4th	153	Javed Burki, Mushtaq Mohammad, Lahore, 1961-62
	153	Mohsin Khan, Zaheer Abbas, Lord's, 1982
5th	197	Javed Burki, Nasim-ul-Ghani, Lord's, 1962
6th	145	Mushtaq Mohammad, Intikhab Alam, Hyderabad, 1972-73
7th	75	Salim Malik, Abdul Qadir, Karachi, 1983-84
8th	130	Hanif Mohammad, Asif Iqbal, Lord's, 1967
9th	190	Asif Iqbal, Intikhab Alam, the Oval, 1967
10th	62	Sarfraz Nawaz, Asif Masood, Headingley, 1974

ENGLAND v SRI LANKA

TESTS: 2
Won by England: 1
Won by Sri Lanka: 0
Drawn: 1

Highest score by England:
370, Lord's, 1984

Highest score by Sri Lanka:
491 for 7 dec, Lord's, 1984

Lowest score by England:
223, Colombo, 1981-82

Highest individual innings:
England: 107, A. J. Lamb, Lord's, 1984
Sri Lanka: 190, S. Wettimuny, Lord's, 1984

Lowest score by Sri Lanka:
175, Colombo, 1981-82

Most wickets in a match:
England: 8-95, D. L. Underwood, Colombo, 1981-82
Sri Lanka: 5-103, A. L. F. De Mel, Colombo, 1981-82

AUSTRALIA v SOUTH AFRICA

TESTS: 53
Won by Australia: 29
Won by South Africa: 11
Drawn: 13

Highest score by Australia:
578, Melbourne, 1910-11

Highest score by South Africa:
622 for 9 dec, Durban, 1969-70

Lowest score by Australia:
75, Durban, 1949-50

Lowest score by South Africa:
36, Melbourne, 1931-32

Highest individual innings:
Australia: 299*, D. G. Bradman, Adelaide, 1931-32
South Africa: 274, R. G. Pollock, Durban, 1969-70

Most wickets in a match:
Australia: 14-199, C. V. Grimmett, Adelaide, 1931-32
South Africa: 13-165, A. J. Tayfield, Melbourne, 1952-53

Record Wicket Partnerships
FOR AUSTRALIA

1st	233	J. H. Fingleton, W. A. Brown, Cape Town, 1935-36
2nd	275	C. C. McDonald, A. L. Hassett, Adelaide, 1952-53
3rd	242	C. Kelleway, W. Bardsley, Lord's, 1912
4th	168	R. N. Harvey, K. R. Miller, Sydney, 1952-53
5th	143	W. W. Armstrong, V. T. Trumper, Melbourne, 1910-11
6th	107	C. Kelleway, V. S. Ransford, Melbourne, 1910-11
7th	160	R. Benaud, G. D. McKenzie, Sydney, 1963-64
8th	83	A. G. Chipperfield, C. V. Grimmett, Durban, 1935-36
9th	78	D. G. Bradman, W. J. O'Reilly, Adelaide, 1931-32
	78	K. D. Mackay, I. Meckiff, Johannesburg, 1957-58
10th	82	V. S. Ransford, W. J. Whitty, Melbourne, 1910-11

FOR SOUTH AFRICA

1st	176	D. J. McGlew, T. L. Goddard, Johannesburg, 1957-58
2nd	173	L. J. Tancred, C. B. Llewellyn, Johannesburg, 1902-03
3rd	341	E. J. Barlow, R. G. Pollock, Adelaide, 1963-64
4th	206	C. N. Frank, A. W. Nourse, Johannesburg, 1921-22
5th	129	J. H. B. Waite, W. R. Endean, Johannesburg, 1957-58
6th	200	R. G. Pollock, H. R. Lance, Durban, 1969-70
7th	221	D. T. Lindsay, P. L. van der Merwe, Johannesburg, 1966-67
8th	124	A. W. Nourse, E. A. Halliwell, Johannesburg, 1902-03
9th	85	R. G. Pollock, P. M. Pollock, Cape Town, 1966-67
10th	53	L. A. Stricker, S. J. Pegler, Adelaide, 1910-11

AUSTRALIA v WEST INDIES

TESTS: 62
Won by Australia: 27
Won by West Indies: 19
Tied: 1
Drawn: 15

Highest score by Australia:
758 for 8 dec, Kingston, 1954-55

Highest score by West Indies:
616, Adelaide, 1968-69

Lowest score by Australia:
76, Perth, 1984-85

Lowest score by West Indies:
78, Sydney, 1951-52

Highest individual innings:
Australia: 242, K. D. Walters, Sydney, 1968-69
West Indies: 219, D. S. Atkinson, Bridgetown, 1954-55

Most wickets in a match:
Australia: 11-79, H. Ironmonger, Melbourne, 1930-31
11-181, G. F. Lawson, Adelaide, 1984-85
11-183, C. V. Grimmett, Adelaide, 1930-31
11-222, A. K. Davidson, Brisbane, 1960-61
West Indies: 11-107, M. A. Holding, Melbourne, 1981-82

Record Wicket Partnerships
FOR AUSTRALIA

1st	382	W. M. Lawry, R. B. Simpson, Bridgetown, 1964-65
2nd	298	W. M. Lawry, I. M. Chappell, Melbourne, 1968-69
3rd	295	C. C. McDonald, R. N. Harvey, Kingston, 1954-55
4th	336	W. M. Lawry, K. D. Walters, Sydney, 1968-69
5th	220	K. R. Miller, R. G. Archer, Kingston, 1954-55
6th	206	K. R. Miller, R. G. Archer, Bridgetown, 1954-55
7th	134	A. K. Davidson, R. Benaud, Brisbane, 1960-61
8th	137	R. Benaud, I. W. Johnson, Kingston, 1954-55
9th	97	K. D. Mackay, J. W. Martin, Melbourne, 1960-61
10th	97	T. G. Hogan, R. M. Hogg, Georgetown, 1983-84

FOR WEST INDIES

1st	250*	C. G. Greenidge, D. L. Haynes, Georgetown, 1983-84
2nd	165	M. C. Carew, R. B. Kanhai, Brisbane, 1968-69
3rd	308	R. B. Richardson, I. V. A. Richards, St John's, 1983-84
4th	198	L. G. Rowe, A. I. Kallicharran, Brisbane, 1975-76
5th	210	R. B. Kanhai, M. L. C. Foster, Kingston, 1972-73
6th	165	R. B. Kanhai, D. L. Murray, Bridgetown, 1972-73
7th	347	D. St. E. Atkinson, C. C. Depeiza, Bridgetown, 1954-55
8th	82	H. A. Gomes, A. M. E. Roberts, Adelaide, 1981-82
9th	122	D. A. J. Holford, J. L. Hendricks, Adelaide, 1968-69
10th	56	J. Garner, C. E. H. Croft, Brisbane, 1979-80

AUSTRALIA v NEW ZEALAND

TESTS: 15
Won by Australia: 8
Won by New Zealand: 2
Drawn: 5

Highest score by Australia:
552, Christchurch, 1976-77

Highest score by New Zealand:
484, Wellington, 1973-74

Lowest score by Australia:
162, Sydney, 1973-74

Lowest score by New Zealand:
42, Wellington, 1945-46

Highest individual innings:
Australia: 250, K. D. Walters, Christchurch, 1976-77
New Zealand: 161, B. A. Edgar, Auckland, 1981-82

Most wickets in a match:
Australia: 11-123, D. K. Lillee, Auckland, 1976-77
New Zealand: 9-146, R. J. Hadlee, Melbourne, 1980-81
9-166, R. O. Collinge, Auckland, 1973-74

Record Wicket Partnerships
FOR AUSTRALIA

1st	106	G. M. Wood, B. M. Laird, Auckland, 1981-82
2nd	141	I. R. Redpath, I. M. Chappell, Wellington, 1973-74
3rd	264	I. M. Chappell, G. S. Chappell, Wellington, 1973-74
4th	106	I. R. Redpath, I. C. Davis, Christchurch, 1973-74
5th	93	G. S. Chappell, K. D. Walters, Christchurch, 1976-77
6th	92	G. S. Chappell, R. W. Marsh, Christchurch, 1981-82
7th	217	K. D. Walters, G. J. Gilmour, Christchurch, 1976-77
8th	93	G. J. Gilmour, K. J. O'Keefe, Auckland, 1976-77
9th	57	R. W. Marsh, L. S. Pascoe, Perth, 1980-81
10th	60	K. D. Walters, J. D. Higgs, Melbourne, 1980-81

FOR NEW ZEALAND

1st	107	G. M. Turner, J. M. Parker, Auckland, 1973-74
2nd	108	G. M. Turner, J. F. M. Morrison, Wellington, 1973-74
3rd	125	G. P. Howarth, J. M. Parker, Melbourne, 1980-81
4th	229	B. E. Congdon, B. F. Hastings, Wellington, 1973-74
5th	88	J. V. Coney, M. G. Burgess, Perth, 1980-81
6th	105	M. G. Burgess, R. J. Hadlee, Auckland, 1976-77
7th	66	K. J. Wadsworth, D. R. Hadlee, Adelaide, 1973-74
8th	53	B. A. Edgar, R. J. Hadlee, Brisbane, 1980-81
9th	73	H. J. Howarth, D. R. Hadlee, Christchurch, 1976-77
10th	47	H. J. Howarth, M. G. Webb, Wellington, 1973-74

AUSTRALIA v INDIA

TESTS: 39
Won by Australia: 20
Won by India: 8
Drawn: 11

Highest score by Australia:
674, Adelaide, 1947-48

Highest score by India:
510 for 7 dec, Delhi, 1979-80

Lowest score by Australia:
83, Melbourne, 1980-81

Lowest score by India:
58, Brisbane, 1959-60

Highest individual innings:
Australia: 213, K. J. Hughes, Adelaide, 1980-81
India: 174, S. M. Patil, Adelaide, 1980-81

Most wickets in a match:
Australia: 12-124, A. K. Davidson, Kanpur, 1959-60
India: 14-124, J. M. Patel, Kanpur, 1959-60

Record Wicket Partnerships
FOR AUSTRALIA

1st	191	R. B. Simpson, W. M. Lawry, Melbourne, 1967-68
2nd	236	S. G. Barnes, D. G. Bradman, Adelaide, 1947-48
3rd	222	A. R. Border, K. J. Hughes, Madras, 1979-80
4th	159	R. N. Harvey, S. J. E. Loxton, Melbourne, 1947-48
5th	223*	A. R. Morris, D. G. Bradman, Melbourne, 1947-48
6th	151	T. R. Veivers, B. N. Jarman, Bombay, 1964-65
7th	64	T. R. Veivers, J. W. Martin, Madras, 1964-65
8th	73	T. R. Veivers, G. D. McKenzie, Madras, 1964-65
9th	87	I. W. Johnson, W. P. A. Crawford, Madras, 1956-57
10th	52	K. J. Wright, J. D. Higgs, Delhi, 1979-80

FOR INDIA

1st	192	S. M. Gavaskar, C. P. S. Chauhan, Bombay, 1979-80
2nd	193	S. M. Gavaskar, M. Amarnath, Perth, 1977-78
3rd	159	S. M. Gavaskar, G. R. Viswanath, Delhi, 1979-80
4th	159	D. B. Vengsarkar, G. R. Viswanath, Bangalore, 1979-80
5th	109	A. A. Baig, R. B. Kenny, Bombay, 1959-60
6th	188	V. S. Hazare, D. G. Phadkar, Adelaide, 1947-48
7th	132	V. S. Hazare, H. R. Adhikari, Adelaide, 1947-48
8th	127	S. M. H. Kirmani, K. D. Ghavri, Bombay, 1979-80
9th	57	S. M. H. Kirmani, K. D. Ghavri, Sydney, 1980-81
10th	39	C. G. Bordes, B. S. Chandrasekhar, Calcutta, 1964-65

AUSTRALIA v PAKISTAN

TESTS: 28
Won by Australia: 11
Won by Pakistan: 8
Drawn: 9

Highest score by Australia:
617, Faisalabad, 1979-80

Highest score by Pakistan:
624, Adelaide, 1983-84

Lowest score by Australia:
80, Karachi, 1956-57

Lowest score by Pakistan:
62, Perth, 1981-82

Highest individual innings:
Australia: 268, G. N. Yallop, Melbourne, 1983-84
Pakistan: 210*, Taslim Arif, Faisalabad, 1979-80

Most wickets in a match:
Australia: 11-118, C. G. Rackemann, Perth, 1983-84
Pakistan: 13-114, Fazal Mahmood, Karachi, 1956-57

Record Wicket Partnerships
FOR AUSTRALIA

1st	134	I. C. Davis, A. Turner, Melbourne, 1976-77
2nd	259	W. B. Phillips, G. N. Yallop, Perth, 1983-84
3rd	203	G. N. Yallop, K. J. Hughes, Melbourne, 1983-84
4th	217	G. S. Chappell, G. N. Yallop, Faisalabad, 1979-80
5th	171	G. S. Chappell, G. J. Cosier, Melbourne, 1976-77
	171	A. R. Border, G. S. Chappell, Brisbane, 1983-84
6th	139	R. M. Cowper, T. R. Veivers, Melbourne, 1964-65
7th	185	G. N. Yallop, G. R. J. Matthews, Melbourne, 1983-84
8th	117	G. J. Cosier, K. J. O'Keefe, Melbourne, 1976-77
9th	83	J. R. Watkins, R. A. L. Massie, Sydney, 1972-73
10th	52	D. K. Lillee, M. H. N. Walker, Sydney, 1976-77
	52	G. F. Lawson, T. M. Alderman, Lahore, 1982-83

FOR PAKISTAN

1st	249	Khalid Ibadulla, Abdul Kadir, Karachi, 1964-65
2nd	233	Mohsin Khan, Qasim Omar, Adelaide, 1983-84
3rd	223*	Taslin Arif, Javed Miandad, Faisalabad, 1979-80
4th	155	Mansoor Akhtar, Zaheer Abbas, Faisalabad, 1982-83
5th	186	Javed Miandad, Salim Malik, Adelaide, 1983-84
6th	115	Asif Iqbal, Javed Miandad, Sydney, 1976-77
7th	104	Intikhab Alam, Wasim Bari, Adelaide, 1972-73
8th	111	Majid Khan, Imran Khan, Lahore, 1979-80
9th	56	Intikhab Alam, Afaq Hussain, Melbourne, 1964-65
10th	87	Asif Iqbal, Iqbal Qasim, Adelaide, 1976-77

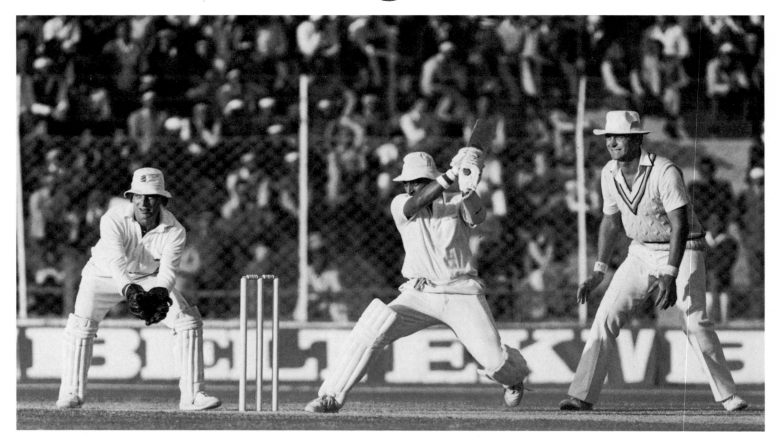

TOP Sunil Gavaskar, top Test run-getter and century-maker.   *ABOVE Ian Botham, top Test all-rounder.*

AUSTRALIA v SRI LANKA

TESTS: 1
Won by Australia: 1

Highest score by Australia:
514 for 4 dec, Kandy, 1982-83

Highest score by Sri Lanka:
271, Kandy, 1982-83

Highest individual innings:
Australia: 143*, D. W. Hookes, Kandy, 1982-83
Sri Lanka: 96, S. Wettimuny, Kandy, 1982-83

Most wickets in a match:
Australia: 7-166, B. Yardley, Kandy, 1982-83
Sri Lanka: 2-113, A. L. F. De Mel, Kandy, 1982-83

SOUTH AFRICA v NEW ZEALAND

TESTS: 17
Won by South Africa: 9
Won by New Zealand: 2
Drawn: 6

Highest score by South Africa:
524 for 8 dec, Wellington, 1952-53

Highest score by New Zealand:
505, Cape Town, 1953-54

Lowest score by South Africa:
148, Johannesburg, 1953-54

Lowest score by New Zealand:
79, Johannesburg, 1953-54

Highest individual innings:
South Africa: 255*, D. J. McGlew, Wellington, 1952-53
New Zealand: 142, J. R. Reid, Johannesburg, 1961-62

Most wickets in a match:
South Africa: 11-196, S. F. Burke, Cape Town, 1961-62
New Zealand: 8-180, J. C. Alabaster, Cape Town, 1961-62

Record Wicket Partnerships
FOR SOUTH AFRICA

1st	196	J. A. J. Christy, B. Mitchell, Christchurch, 1931-32
2nd	76	J. A. J. Christy, H. B. Cameron, Wellington, 1931-32
3rd	112	D. J. McGlew, R. A. McLean, Johannesburg, 1961-62
4th	135	K. J. Funston, R. A. McLean, Durban, 1953-54
5th	130	W. R. Endean, J. E. Cheetham, Auckland, 1952-53
6th	83	K. C. Bland, D. T. Lindsay, Auckland, 1963-64
7th	246	D. J. McGlew, A. R. A. Murray, Wellington, 1952-53
8th	95	J. E. Cheetham, H. J. Tayfield, Cape Town, 1953-54
9th	60	P. M. Pollock, N. A. T. Adcock, Port Elizabeth, 1961-62
10th	47	D. J. McGlew, H. D. Broomfield, Port Elizabeth, 1961-62

FOR NEW ZEALAND

1st	126	G. O. Rabone, M. E. Chapple, Cape Town, 1953-54
2nd	51	W. P. Bradburn, B. W. Sinclair, Dunedin, 1963-64
3rd	94	M. B. Poore, B. Sutcliffe, Cape Town, 1953-54
4th	171	B. W. Sinclair, S. N. McGregor, Auckland, 1963-64
5th	174	J. R. Reid, J. E. F. Beck, Cape Town, 1953-54
6th	100	H. G. Vivian, F. T. Badcock, Wellington, 1931-32
7th	84	J. R. Reid, G. A. Bartlett, Johannesburg, 1961-62
8th	73	P. G. Z. Harris, G. A. Bartlett, Durban, 1961-62
9th	69	C. F. W. Allcott, I. B. Cromb, Wellington, 1931-32
10th	49*	A. E. Dick, F. J. Cameron, Cape Town, 1961-62

WEST INDIES v NEW ZEALAND

TESTS: 21
Won by West Indies: 7
Won by New Zealand: 3
Drawn: 11

Highest score by West Indies:
564 for 8, Bridgetown, 1971-72

Highest score by New Zealand:
543 for 3 dec, Georgetown, 1971-72

Lowest score by West Indies:
77, Auckland, 1955-56

Lowest score by New Zealand:
74, Dunedin, 1975-76

Highest individual innings:
West Indies: 258, S. M. Nurse, Christchurch, 1968-69
New Zealand: 259, G. M. Turner, Georgetown, 1971-72

Most wickets in a match:
West Indies: 11-120, M. D. Marshall, Bridgetown, 1984-85
New Zealand: 11-102, R. J. Hadlee, Dunedin, 1979-80

Record Wicket Partnerships
FOR WEST INDIES

1st	225	C. G. Greenidge, D. L. Haynes, Christchurch, 1979-80
2nd	269	R. C. Fredericks, L. G. Rowe, Kingston, 1971-72
3rd	185	C. G. Greenidge, R. B. Richardson, Port-of-Spain, 1984-85
4th	162	E. D. Weekes, O. G. Smith, Dunedin, 1955-56
	162	C. G. Greenidge, A. I. Kallicharran, Christchurch, 1979-80
5th	189	F. M. M. Worrell, C. L. Walcott, Auckland, 1951-52
6th	254	C. A. Davis, G. S. Sobers, Bridgetown, 1971-72
7th	143	D. St. E. Atkinson, J. D. C. Goddard, Christchurch, 1955-56
8th	84	I. V. A. Richards, M. D. Marshall, Bridgetown, 1984-85
9th	70	I. V. A. Richards, J. Garner, Bridgetown, 1984-85
10th	31	T. M. Findlay, G. C. Shillingford, Bridgetown, 1971-72

FOR NEW ZEALAND

1st	387	G. M. Turner, T. W. Jarvis, Georgetown, 1971-72
2nd	210	G. P. Howarth, J. J. Crowe, Kingston, 1984-85
3rd	75	B. E. Congdon, B. F. Hastings, Christchurch, 1968-69
4th	175	B. E. Congdon, B. F. Hastings, Bridgetown, 1971-72
5th	142	M. D. Crowe, J. V. Coney, Georgetown, 1984-85
6th	220	G. M. Turner, K. J. Wadsworth, Kingston, 1971-72
7th	98	J. V. Coney, R. J. Hadlee, Christchurch, 1979-80
8th	136	B. E. Congdon, R. S. Cunis, Port-of-Spain, 1971-72
9th	62*	V. Pollard, R. S. Cunis, Auckland, 1968-69
10th	41	B. E. Congdon, J. C. Alabaster, Port-of-Spain, 1971-72

WEST INDIES v INDIA

TESTS: 54
Won by West Indies: 22
Won by India: 5
Drawn: 27

Highest score by West Indies:
644 for 8 dec, Delhi, 1958-59

Highest score by India:
644 for 7 dec, Kanpur, 1978-79

Lowest score by West Indies:
151, Madras, 1978-79

Lowest score by India:
90, Calcutta, 1983-84

Highest individual innings:
West Indies: 256, R. B. Kanhai, Calcutta, 1958-59
India: 236*, S. M. Gavaskar, Madras, 1983-84

Most wickets in a match:
West Indies: 12-121, A. M. E. Roberts, Madras, 1974-75
India: 11-235, B. S. Chandrasekhar, Bombay, 1966-67

Record Wicket Partnerships
FOR WEST INDIES

1st	296	C. G. Greenidge, D. L. Haynes, Antigua, 1982-83
2nd	255	E. D. A. McMorris, R. B. Kanhai, Kingston, 1961-62
3rd	220	I. V. A. Richards, A. I. Kallicharran, Bridgetown, 1975-76
4th	267	C. L. Walcott, G. E. Gomez, Delhi, 1948-49
5th	219	E. D. Weekes, B. H. Pairaudeau, Port-of-Spain, 1952-53
6th	250	C. H. Lloyd, D. L. Murray, Bombay, 1974-75
7th	130	C. G. Greenidge, M. D. Marshall, Kanpur, 1983-84
8th	124	I. V. A. Richards, K. D. Boyce, Delhi, 1974-75
9th	161	C. H. Lloyd, A. M. E. Roberts, Calcutta, 1983-84
10th	98*	F. M. M. Worrell, W. W. Hall, Port-of-Spain, 1961-62

FOR INDIA

1st	153	S. M. Gavaskar, C. P. S. Chauhan, Bombay, 1978-79
2nd	344*	S. M. Gavaskar, D. B. Vengsarkar, Calcutta, 1978-79
3rd	159	M. Amarnath, G. R. Viswanath, Port-of-Spain, 1975-76
4th	172	G. R. Viswanath, A. D. Gaekwad, Kanpur, 1978-79
5th	204	S. M. Gavaskar, B. P. Patel, Port-of-Spain, 1975-76
6th	170	S. M. Gavaskar, R. J. Shastri, Madras, 1983-84
7th	186	D. N. Sardesai, E. D. Solkar, Bridgetown, 1970-71
8th	107	Yashpal Sharma, B. S. Sandhu, Kingston, 1982-83
9th	143*	S. M. Gavaskar, S. M. H. Kirmani, Madras, 1983-84
10th	62	D. N. Sardesai, B. S. Bedi, Bridgetown, 1970-71

WEST INDIES v PAKISTAN

TESTS: 19
Won by West Indies: 7
Won by Pakistan: 4
Drawn: 8

Highest score by West Indies:
790 for 3 dec, Kingston, 1957-58

Highest score by Pakistan:
657 for 8 dec, Bridgetown, 1957-58

Lowest score by West Indies:
76, Dacca, 1958-59

Lowest score by Pakistan:
104, Lahore, 1958-59

Highest individual innings:
West Indies: 365*, G. S. Sobers, Kingston, 1957-58
Pakistan: 337, Hanif Mohammad, Bridgetown, 1957-58

Most wickets in a match:
West Indies: 9-95, C. E. H. Croft, Port-of-Spain, 1976-77
9-187, A. M. E. Roberts, Lahore, 1974-75
Pakistan: 12-100, Fazal Mahmood, Dacca, 1958-59

Record Wicket Partnerships
FOR WEST INDIES
1st	182	R. C. Fredericks, C. G. Greenidge, Kingston, 1976-77
2nd	446	C. C. Hunte, G. S. Sobers, Kingston, 1957-58
3rd	162	R. B. Kanhai, G. S. Sobers, Lahore, 1958-59
4th	188*	G. S. Sobers, C. L. Walcott, Kingston, 1957-58
5th	185	E. D. Weekes, O. G. Smith, Bridgetown, 1957-58
6th	151	C. H. Lloyd, D. L. Murray, Bridgetown, 1976-77
7th	70	C. H. Lloyd, J. Garner, Bridgetown, 1976-77
8th	50	B. D. Julien, V. A. Holder, Karachi, 1974-75
9th	46	J. Garner, C. E. H. Croft, Port-of-Spain, 1976-77
10th	44	R. Nanan, S. T. Clarke, Faisalabad, 1980-81

FOR PAKISTAN
1st	159†	Majid Khan, Zaheer Abbas, Georgetown, 1976-77
2nd	178	Hanif Mohammad, Saeed Ahmed, Karachi, 1958-59
3rd	169	Saeed Ahmed, Wazir Mohammad, Port-of-Spain, 1957-58
4th	154	Wazir Mohammad, Hanif Mohammad, Port-of-Spain, 1957-58
5th	87	Mushtaq Mohammad, Asif Iqbal, Kingston, 1976-77
6th	166	Wazir Mohammad, A. H. Kardar, Kingston, 1957-58
7th	128	Wasim Raja, Wasim Bari, Karachi, 1974-75
8th	73	Imran Khan, Sarfraz Nawaz, Port-of-Spain, 1976-77
9th	73	Wasim Raja, Sarfraz Nawaz, Bridgetown, 1976-77
10th	133	Wasim Raja, Wasim Bari, Bridgetown, 1976-77

†219 were added for this wicket: Sadiq Mohammad added 60 with Majid Khan before he retired hurt.

NEW ZEALAND v INDIA

TESTS: 25
Won by New Zealand: 4
Won by India: 10
Drawn: 11

Highest score by New Zealand:
502, Christchurch, 1967-68

Highest score by India:
537 for 3 dec, Madras, 1955-56

Lowest score by New Zealand:
100, Wellington, 1980-81

Lowest score by India:
81, Wellington, 1975-76

Highest individual innings:
New Zealand: 239, G. T. Dowling, Christchurch, 1967-68
India: 231, V. Mankad, Madras, 1955-56

Most wickets in a match:
New Zealand: 11-58, R. J. Hadlee, Wellington, 1975-76
India: 12-152, S. Venkataraghavan, Delhi, 1964-65

Record Wicket Partnerships
FOR NEW ZEALAND
1st	126	B. A. G. Murray, G. T. Dowling, Christchurch, 1967-68
2nd	155	G. T. Dowling, B. E. Congdon, Dunedin, 1967-68
3rd	222*	B. Sutcliffe, J. R. Reid, Delhi, 1955-56
4th	103	G. T. Dowling, M. G. Burgess, Christchurch, 1967-68
5th	119	G. T. Dowling, K. Thomson, Christchurch, 1967-68
6th	87	J. W. Guy, A. R. MacGibbon, Hyderabad, 1955-56
7th	163	B. Sutcliffe, B. R. Taylor, Calcutta, 1964-65
8th	81	V. Pollard, G. E. Vivian, Calcutta, 1964-65
9th	69	M. G. Burgess, J. C. Alabaster, Dunedin, 1967-68
10th	61	J. T. Ward, R. O. Collinge, Madras, 1964-65

FOR INDIA
1st	413	V. Mankad, P. Roy, Madras, 1955-56
2nd	204	S. M. Gavaskar, S. Amarnath, Auckland, 1975-76
3rd	238	P. R. Umrigar, V. L. Manjrekar, Hyderabad, 1955-56
4th	171	P. R. Umrigar, A. G. Kripal Singh, Hyderabad, 1955-56
5th	127	V. L. Manjrekar, G. S. Ramchand, Delhi, 1955-56
6th	193*	D. N. Sardesai, Hanumant Singh, Bombay, 1964-65
7th	116	B. P. Patel, S. M. H. Kirmani, Wellington, 1975-76
8th	143	R. G. Nadkarni, F. M. Engineer, Madras, 1964-65
9th	105	S. M. H. Kirmani, B. S. Bedi, Bombay, 1976-77
	105	S. M. H. Kirmani, N. S. Yadav, Auckland, 1980-81
10th	57	R. B. Desai, B. S. Bedi, Dunedin, 1967-68

West Indian Test players congratulate Michael Holding after a wicket. In the 1970s the West Indians became the most powerful Test side with their strength based on fast bowling.

NEW ZEALAND v PAKISTAN

TESTS: 27
Won by New Zealand: 3
Won by Pakistan: 10
Drawn: 14

Highest score by New Zealand:
492, Wellington, 1984-85

Highest score by Pakistan:
565 for 9 dec, Karachi, 1976-77

Lowest score by New Zealand:
70, Dacca, 1955-56

Lowest score by Pakistan:
114, Lahore, 1969-70

Highest individual innings:
New Zealand: 158*, J. F. Reid,
Auckland, 1984-85
Pakistan: 209, Imtiaz Ahmed,
Lahore, 1955-56

Most wickets in a match:
New Zealand: 9-70, F. J.
Cameron, Auckland, 1964-65
Pakistan: 11-79, Zulfiqar
Ahmed, Karachi, 1955-56
11-130, Intikhab Alam, Dunedin,
1972-73

Record Wicket Partnerships
FOR NEW ZEALAND

1st	159	R. E. Redmond, G. M. Turner, Auckland, 1972-73
2nd	195	J. G. Wright, G. P. Howarth, Napier, 1978-79
3rd	178	B. W. Sinclair, J. R. Reid, Lahore, 1964-65
4th	128	B. F. Hastings, M. G. Burgess, Wellington, 1972-73
5th	183	M. G. Burgess, R. W. Anderson, Lahore, 1976-77
6th	145	J. F. Reid, R. J. Hadlee, Wellington, 1984-85
7th	186	W. K. Lees, R. J. Hadlee, Karachi, 1976-77
8th	100	B. W. Yuile, D. R. Hadlee, Karachi, 1969-70
9th	96	M. G. Burgess, R. S. Cunis, Dacca, 1969-70
10th	151	B. F. Hastings, R. O. Collinge, Auckland, 1972-73

FOR PAKISTAN

1st	147	Sadiq Mohammad, Majid Khan, Karachi, 1976-77
2nd	114	Mohammad Ilyas, Saeed Ahmed, Rawalpindi, 1964-65
3rd	212	Mudassar Nazar, Javed Miandad, Hyderabad, 1984-85
4th	350	Mushtaq Mohammad, Asif Iqbal, Dunedin, 1972-73
5th	281	Javed Miandad, Asif Iqbal, Lahore, 1976-77
6th	217	Hanif Mohammad, Majid Khan, Lahore, 1964-65
7th	308	Waqar Hassan, Imtiaz Ahmed, Lahore, 1955-56
8th	89	Anil Dalpat, Iqbal Qasim, Karachi, 1984-85
9th	52	Intikhab Alam, Arif Butt, Auckland, 1964-65
10th	65	Salah-ud-Din, Mohammad Farooq, Rawalpindi, 1964-65

NEW ZEALAND v SRI LANKA

TESTS: 5
Won by New Zealand: 4
Won by Sri Lanka: 0
Drawn: 1

Highest score by New Zealand:
459, Colombo, 1983-84

Highest score by Sri Lanka:
289 for 9 dec, Colombo, 1983-84

Lowest score by New Zealand:
198, Colombo, 1983-84

Lowest score by Sri Lanka:
93, Wellington, 1982-83

Highest individual innings:
New Zealand: 180, J. F. Reid,
Colombo, 1983-84
Sri Lanka: 108, R. L. Dias,
Colombo, 1983-84

Most wickets in a match:
New Zealand: 10-102, R. J.
Hadlee, Colombo, 1983-84
Sri Lanka: 8-159, V. B. John,
Colombo, 1983-84

INDIA v SRI LANKA

TESTS: 1
Drawn: 1

Highest score by India:
566 for 6 dec, Madras, 1982-83

Highest score by Sri Lanka:
394, Madras, 1982-83

Highest individual innings:
India: 155, S. M. Gavaskar,
Madras, 1982-83
Sri Lanka: 105†, L. R. D.
Mendis, Madras, 1982-83

Most wickets in a match:
India: 8-205, Kapil Dev, Madras,
1982-83
8-232, D. R. Doshi, Madras,
1982-83
Sri Lanka: 7-201, A. L. F. De
Mel, Madras, 1982-83

†Mendis scored 105 in each
innings.

INDIA v PAKISTAN

TESTS: 35
Won by India: 4
Won by Pakistan: 6
Drawn: 25

Highest score by India:
539 for 9 dec, Madras, 1960-61

Highest score by Pakistan:
674 for 6, Faisalabad, 1984-85

Lowest score by India:
106, Lucknow, 1952-53

Lowest score by Pakistan:
150, Delhi, 1952-53

Highest individual innings:
India: 201, A. D. Gaekwad,
Jullunder, 1983-84
Pakistan: 280*, Javed Miandad,
Hyderabad, 1982-83

Most wickets in a match:
India: 13-131, V. Mankad, Delhi,
1952-53
Pakistan: 12-94, Fazal
Mahmood, Lucknow, 1952-53

Record Wicket Partnerships
FOR INDIA

1st	192	S. M. Gavaskar, C. P. S. Chauhan, Lahore, 1978-79
2nd	125	S. M. Gavaskar, M. Amarnath, Hyderabad, 1982-83
3rd	190	M. Amarnath, Yashpal Sharma, Lahore, 1982-83
4th	183	V. S. Hazare, P. R. Umrigar, Bombay, 1952-53
5th	200	S. M. Patil, R. J. Shastri, Faisalabad, 1984-85
6th	121	A. D. Gaekwad, R. M. H. Binny, Jullunder, 1983-84
7th	155	R. M. H. Binny, Madan Lal, Bangalore, 1983-84
8th	122	S. M. H. Kirmani, Madan Lal, Faisalabad, 1982-83
9th	149	P. G. Joshi, R. B. Desai, Bombay, 1960-61
10th	109	H. R. Adhikari, Ghulam Ahmed, Delhi, 1952-53

FOR PAKISTAN

1st	162	Hanif Mohammad, Imtiaz Ahmed, Madras, 1960-61
2nd	250	Mudassar Nazar, Qasim Omar, Faisalabad, 1984-85
3rd	451	Mudassar Nazar, Javed Miandad, Hyderabad, 1982-83
4th	287	Javed Miandad, Zaheer Abbas, Faisalabad, 1982-83
5th	213	Zaheer Abbas, Mudassar Nazar, Karachi, 1982-83
6th	207	Salim Malik, Imran Khan, Faisalabad, 1982-83
7th	142	Zaheer Abbas, Ashraf Ali, Lahore, 1984-85
8th	95	Wasim Raja, Tahir Naqqash, Jullunder, 1983-84
9th	60	Wasim Bari, Iqbal Qasim, Bangalore, 1979-80
10th	104	Zulfiqar Ahmed, Amir Elahi, Madras, 1952-53

PAKISTAN v SRI LANKA

TESTS: 3
Won by Pakistan: 2
Won by Sri Lanka: 0
Drawn: 1

Highest score by Pakistan:
500 for 7 dec, Lahore, 1981-82

Highest score by Sri Lanka:
454, Faisalabad, 1981-82

Lowest score by Pakistan:
270, Faisalabad, 1981-82

Lowest score by Sri Lanka:
149, Karachi, 1981-82

Highest individual innings:
Pakistan: 153, Haroon Rashid,
Karachi, 1981-82
Sri Lanka: 157, S. Wettimuny,
Faisalabad, 1981-82

Most wickets in a match:
Pakistan: 14-116, Imran Khan,
Lahore, 1981-82
Sri Lanka: 9-162, D. S. de Silva,
Faisalabad, 1981-82

Record Wicket Partnerships for Sri Lanka

1st	77	S. Wettimuny, H. M. Goonatillake, v Pakistan, Faisalabad, 1981-82
2nd	217	S. Wettimuny, R. L. Dias, v Pakistan, Faisalabad, 1981-82
3rd	159†	S. Wettimuny, R. L. Dias, v New Zealand, Colombo, 1983-84
4th	148	S. Wettimuny, A. Ranatunga, v England, Lord's, 1984
5th	150	S. Wettimuny, L. R. D. Mendis, v England, Lord's, 1984
6th	109‡	R. S. Madugalle, A. Ranatunga, v New Zealand, Colombo, 1983-84
7th	77	A. N. Ranasinghe, D. S. de Silva, v India, Madras, 1982-83
8th	61	R. S. Madugalle, D. S. de Silva, v Pakistan, Faisalabad, 1981-82
9th	42	J. R. Ratnayeke, A. L. F. De Mel, v India, Madras, 1982-83
10th	60	V. B. John, A. M. J. G. Amerasinghe, v New Zealand, Kandy, 1983-84

†163 runs were added for this wicket: S. Wettimuny retired hurt.
‡119 runs were added for this wicket: R. S. Madugalle retired hurt.

ONE-DAY INTERNATIONALS

SUMMARY OF MATCH RESULTS

	Matches	Won	Lost	Tied	No Result
England	109	56	49	—	4
Australia	136	61	67	1	7
India	75	30	43	—	2
New Zealand	89	42	41	—	6
Pakistan	85	32	49	—	4
Sri Lanka	45	10	33	—	2
West Indies	107	83	22	1	1
Canada	3	—	3	—	—
East Africa	3	—	3	—	—
Zimbabwe	6	1	5	—	—

HIGHEST TEAM TOTALS

60 overs
338-5   Pakistan v Sri Lanka, Swansea, 1983
334-4   England v India, Lord's, 1975
333-9   England v Sri Lanka, Taunton, 1983
330-6   Pakistan v Sri Lanka, Trent Bridge, 1975
328-5   Australia v Sri Lanka, the Oval, 1975
322-6   England v New Zealand, the Oval, 1983
320-9   Australia v India, Trent Bridge, 1983
55 overs
320-8   England v Australia, Edgbaston, 1980
50 overs
323-2   Australia v Sri Lanka, Adelaide, 1984-85
313-9   West Indies v Australia, St John's, 1977-78
309-6   West Indies v Sri Lanka, Perth, 1984-85
304-5   New Zealand v Sri Lanka, Auckland, 1982-83
302-8   Australia v New Zealand, Melbourne, 1982-83
45 overs
333-8   West Indies v India, Jamshedpur, 1983-84
40 overs
263-2   Pakistan v India, Multan, 1982-83
Highest total batting second
297-6 (48.5 overs)   New Zealand v England, Adelaide, 1982-83

HIGHEST INDIVIDUAL INNINGS

189*   I. V. A. Richards, West Indies v England, Old Trafford, 1984
175*   Kapil Dev, India v Zimbabwe, Tunbridge Wells, 1983
171*   G. M. Turner, New Zealand v East Africa, Edgbaston, 1975
158   D. I. Gower, England v New Zealand, Brisbane, 1982-83
153*   I. V. A. Richards, West Indies v Australia, Melbourne, 1979-80
149   I. V. A. Richards, West Indies v India, Jamshedpur, 1983-84
148   D. L. Haynes, West Indies v Australia, St John's, 1977-78
145*   D. L. Haynes, West Indies v New Zealand, Berbice, 1984-85
140   G. M. Turner, New Zealand v Sri Lanka, Auckland, 1982-83

HIGHEST CAREER AGGREGATES

4,071	I. V. A. Richards	2,329	G. S. Chappell
3,348	D. L. Haynes	2,155	Javed Miandad
2,912	C. G. Greenidge	2,129	G. M. Wood
2,898	A. R. Border		
2,464	Zaheer Abbas		
2,427	D. I. Gower		

MOST CENTURIES

8	I. V. A. Richards, D. L. Haynes	6	C. G. Greenidge
7	Zaheer Abbas, D. I. Gower		

HIGHEST WICKET PARTNERSHIPS

1st	188	K. Srikkanth, R. J. Shastri, India v England, Cuttack, 1984-85
2nd	221	C. G. Greenidge, I. V. A. Richards, West Indies v India, Jamshedpur, 1983-84
3rd	224*	D. M. Jones, A. R. Border, Australia v Sri Lanka, Adelaide, 1984-85
4th	157*	R. B. Kerr, D. M. Jones, Australia v England, Melbourne, 1984-85
5th	152	I. V. A. Richards, C. H. Lloyd, West Indies v Sri Lanka, Brisbane, 1984-85
6th	144	Imran Khan, Shahid Mahboob, Pakistan v Sri Lanka, Headingley, 1983
7th	108	Ramiz Raja, Anil Dalpat, Pakistan v New Zealand, Christchurch, 1984-85
8th	68	B. E. Congdon, B. L. Cairns, New Zealand v England, Scarborough, 1978
9th	126*	Kapil Dev, S. M. H. Kirmani, India v Zimbabwe, Tunbridge Wells, 1983
10th	106*	I. V. A. Richards, M. A. Holding, West Indies v England, Old Trafford, 1984

MOST WICKETS IN AN INNINGS

7-51   W. W. Davis, West Indies v Australia, Headingley, 1983
6-14   G. J. Gilmour, Australia v England, Headingley, 1975
6-14   Imran Khan, Pakistan v India, Sharjah, 1984-85
6-15   C. E. H. Croft, West Indies v England, Arnos Vale, 1980-81
6-39   K. H. MacLeay, Australia v India, Trent Bridge, 1983

MOST WICKETS IN A CAREER

122	M. A. Holding	103	D. K. Lillee	100	R. J. Hadlee
116	J. Garner	100	I. T. Botham		

MOST WICKET-KEEPING DISMISSALS IN AN INNINGS

5	(all ct)	R. W. Marsh, Australia v England, Headingley, 1981
5	(all ct)	R. G. de Alwis, Sri Lanka v Australia, Colombo, 1982-83
5	(all ct)	S. M. H. Kirmani, India v Zimbabwe, Leicester, 1983
5	(3 ct, 2 st)	S. Viswanath, India v England, Sydney, 1984-85

MOST WICKET-KEEPING DISMISSALS IN A CAREER

123	(119 ct, 4 st)	R. W. Marsh	62	(52 ct, 10 st) Wasim Bari
93	(85 ct, 8 st)	P. J. L. Dujon		

Vivian Richards has scored most runs, most centuries and made the highest score in one-day internationals.

DOMESTIC COMPETITIONS

THE COUNTY CHAMPIONSHIP ENGLAND

Year	County	Year	County	Year	County
1864	Surrey	1900	Yorkshire	1951	Warwickshire
1865	Nottinghamshire	1901	Yorkshire	1952	Surrey
1866	Middlesex	1902	Yorkshire	1953	Surrey
1867	Yorkshire	1903	Middlesex	1954	Surrey
1868	Nottinghamshire	1904	Lancashire	1955	Surrey
1869	Nottinghamshire Yorkshire	1905	Yorkshire	1956	Surrey
		1906	Kent	1957	Surrey
1870	Yorkshire	1907	Nottinghamshire	1958	Surrey
1871	Nottinghamshire	1908	Yorkshire	1959	Yorkshire
1872	Nottinghamshire	1909	Kent	1960	Yorkshire
1873	Gloucestershire Nottinghamshire	1910	Kent	1961	Hampshire
		1911	Warwickshire	1962	Yorkshire
1874	Gloucestershire	1912	Yorkshire	1963	Yorkshire
1875	Nottinghamshire	1913	Kent	1964	Worcestershire
1876	Gloucestershire	1914	Surrey	1965	Worcestershire
1877	Gloucestershire	1919	Yorkshire	1966	Yorkshire
1878	Undecided	1920	Middlesex	1967	Yorkshire
1879	Nottinghamshire Lancashire	1921	Middlesex	1968	Yorkshire
		1922	Yorkshire	1969	Glamorgan
1880	Nottinghamshire	1923	Yorkshire	1970	Kent
1881	Lancashire	1924	Yorkshire	1971	Surrey
1882	Nottinghamshire Lancashire	1925	Yorkshire	1972	Warwickshire
		1926	Lancashire	1973	Hampshire
1883	Nottinghamshire	1927	Lancashire	1974	Worcestershire
1884	Nottinghamshire	1928	Lancashire	1975	Leicestershire
1885	Nottinghamshire	1929	Nottinghamshire	1976	Middlesex
1886	Nottinghamshire	1930	Lancashire	1977	Middlesex Kent
1887	Surrey	1931	Yorkshire		
1888	Surrey	1932	Yorkshire	1978	Kent
1889	Surrey Lancashire Nottinghamshire	1933	Yorkshire	1979	Essex
		1934	Lancashire	1980	Middlesex
		1935	Yorkshire	1981	Nottinghamshire
1890	Surrey	1936	Derbyshire	1982	Middlesex
1891	Surrey	1937	Yorkshire	1983	Essex
1892	Surrey	1938	Yorkshire	1984	Essex
1893	Yorkshire	1939	Yorkshire	1985	Middlesex
1894	Surrey	1946	Yorkshire		
1895	Surrey	1947	Middlesex		
1896	Yorkshire	1948	Glamorgan		
1897	Lancashire	1949	Middlesex Yorkshire		
1898	Yorkshire				
1899	Surrey	1950	Lancashire Surrey		

THE SHEFFIELD SHIELD AUSTRALIA

Year	Team	Year	Team
1892-93	Victoria	1938-39	South Australia
1893-94	South Australia	1939-40	New South Wales
1894-95	Victoria	1940-46	No competition
1895-96	New South Wales	1946-47	Victoria
1896-97	New South Wales	1947-48	Western Australia
1897-98	Victoria	1948-49	New South Wales
1898-99	Victoria	1949-50	New South Wales
1899-1900	New South Wales	1950-51	Victoria
1900-01	Victoria	1951-52	New South Wales
1901-02	New South Wales	1952-53	South Australia
1902-03	New South Wales	1953-54	New South Wales
1903-04	New South Wales	1954-55	New South Wales
1904-05	New South Wales	1955-56	New South Wales
1905-06	New South Wales	1956-57	New South Wales
1906-07	New South Wales	1957-58	New South Wales
1907-08	Victoria	1958-59	New South Wales
1908-09	New South Wales	1959-60	New South Wales
1909-10	South Australia	1960-61	New South Wales
1910-11	New South Wales	1961-62	New South Wales
1911-12	New South Wales	1962-63	Victoria
1912-13	South Australia	1963-64	South Australia
1913-14	New South Wales	1964-65	New South Wales
1914-15	Victoria	1965-66	New South Wales
1915-19	No competition	1966-67	Victoria
1919-20	New South Wales	1967-68	Western Australia
1920-21	New South Wales	1968-69	South Australia
1921-22	Victoria	1969-70	Victoria
1922-23	New South Wales	1970-71	South Australia
1923-24	Victoria	1971-72	Western Australia
1924-25	Victoria	1972-73	Western Australia
1925-26	New South Wales	1973-74	Victoria
1926-27	South Australia	1974-75	Western Australia
1927-28	Victoria	1975-76	South Australia
1928-29	New South Wales	1976-77	Western Australia
1929-30	Victoria	1977-78	Western Australia
1930-31	Victoria	1978-79	Victoria
1931-32	New South Wales	1979-80	Victoria
1932-33	New South Wales	1980-81	Western Australia
1933-34	Victoria	1981-82	South Australia
1934-35	Victoria	1982-83	New South Wales
1935-36	South Australia	1983-84	Western Australia
1936-37	Victoria	1984-85	New South Wales
1937-38	New South Wales		

THE SHELL SHIELD WEST INDIES

Year	Team	Year	Team
1965-66	Barbados	1975-76	Barbados, Trinidad
1966-67	Barbados	1976-77	Barbados
1968-69	Jamaica	1977-78	Barbados
1969-70	Trinidad	1978-79	Barbados
1970-71	Trinidad	1979-80	Barbados
1971-72	Barbados	1980-81	Combined Islands
1972-73	Guyana	1981-82	Barbados
1973-74	Barbados	1982-83	Guyana
1974-75	Guyana	1983-84	Barbados
		1984-85	Trinidad and Tobago

LEFT Graham Gooch hooking. The England opening batsman is one reason Essex won three Championships in six years.

RIGHT Warwickshire's Gifford bowled by Wayne Daniel at Edgbaston, and Middlesex are the 1985 County Champions.

THE CURRIE CUP
SOUTH AFRICA

1889-90	Transvaal	1952-53	Western Province
1890-91	Kimberley	1954-55	Natal
1892-93	Western Province	1955-56	Western Province
1893-94	Western Province	1958-59	Transvaal
1894-95	Transvaal	1959-60	Natal
1896-97	Western Province	1960-61	Natal
1897-98	Western Province	1962-63	Natal
1902-03	Transvaal	1963-64	Natal
1903-04	Transvaal	1965-66	Natal, Transvaal
1904-05	Transvaal	1966-67	Natal
1906-07	Transvaal	1967-68	Natal
1908-09	Western Province	1968-69	Transvaal
1910-11	Natal	1969-70	Transvaal,
1912-13	Natal		Western Province
1920-21	Western Province	1970-71	Transvaal
1921-22	Natal, Transvaal,	1971-72	Transvaal
	Western Province	1972-73	Transvaal
1923-24	Transvaal	1973-74	Natal
1925-26	Transvaal	1974-75	Western Province
1926-27	Transvaal	1975-76	Natal
1929-30	Transvaal	1976-77	Natal
1931-32	Western Province	1977-78	Western Province
1933-34	Natal	1978-79	Transvaal
1934-35	Transvaal	1979-80	Transvaal
1936-37	Natal	1980-81	Natal
1937-38	Natal, Transvaal	1981-82	Western Province
1946-47	Natal	1982-83	Transvaal
1947-48	Natal	1983-84	Transvaal
1950-51	Transvaal	1984-85	Transvaal
1951-52	Natal		

THE RANJI TROPHY
INDIA

1934-35	Bombay	1951-52	Bombay	1968-69	Bombay
1935-36	Bombay	1952-53	Holkar	1969-70	Bombay
1936-37	Nawanagar	1953-54	Bombay	1970-71	Bombay
1937-38	Hyderabad	1954-55	Madras	1971-72	Bombay
1938-39	Bengal	1955-56	Bombay	1972-73	Bombay
1939-40	Maharashta	1956-57	Bombay	1973-74	Karnataka
1940-41	Maharashta	1957-58	Baroda	1974-75	Bombay
1941-42	Bombay	1958-59	Bombay	1975-76	Bombay
1942-43	Baroda	1959-60	Bombay	1976-77	Bombay
1943-44	Western India	1960-61	Bombay	1977-78	Karnataka
1944-45	Bombay	1961-62	Bombay	1978-79	Delhi
1945-46	Holkar	1962-63	Bombay	1979-80	Delhi
1946-47	Baroda	1963-64	Bombay	1980-81	Bombay
1947-48	Holkar	1964-65	Bombay	1981-82	Delhi
1948-49	Bombay	1965-66	Bombay	1982-83	Karnataka
1949-50	Baroda	1966-67	Bombay	1983-84	Bombay
1950-51	Holkar	1967-68	Bombay	1984-85	Bombay

THE QAID-I-AZAM TROPHY
PAKISTAN

1953-54	Bahawalpur	1974-75	Punjab A
1954-55	Karachi	1975-76	National Bank
1956-57	Punjab	1976-77	United Bank
1957-58	Bahawalpur	1977-78	Habib Bank
1958-59	Karachi	1978-79	National Bank
1959-60	Karachi	1979-80	PIA
1961-62	Karachi Blues	1980-81	United Bank
1962-63	Karachi A	1981-82	National Bank
1963-64	Karachi Blues	1982-83	United Bank
1964-66*	Karachi Blues	1983-84	National Bank
1966-68*	Karachi	1984-85	United Bank
1968-69	Lahore		
1969-70	PIA		
1970-71	Karachi Blues		
1972-73	Railways		
1973-74	Railways		

*Spread over two seasons.

THE PLUNKET SHIELD/SHELL
SERIES, NEW ZEALAND

The Plunket Shield was initially run on a challenge system.
WINNERS

Canterbury	1906-07 to December 1907
Auckland	December 1907 to February 1911
Canterbury	February 1911 to February 1912
Auckland	February 1912 to January 1913
Canterbury	January 1913 to December 1918
Wellington	December 1918 to January 1919
Canterbury	January 1919 to January 1920
Auckland	January 1920 to January 1921
Wellington	January 1921

It was then decided on a league basis.
WINNERS

1921-22	Auckland	1951-52	Canterbury
1922-23	Canterbury	1952-53	Otago
1923-24	Wellington	1953-54	Central Districts
1924-25	Otago	1954-55	Wellington
1925-26	Wellington	1955-56	Canterbury
1926-27	Auckland	1956-57	Wellington
1927-28	Wellington	1957-58	Otago
1928-29	Auckland	1958-59	Auckland
1929-30	Wellington	1959-60	Canterbury
1930-31	Canterbury	1960-61	Wellington
1931-32	Wellington	1961-62	Wellington
1932-33	Otago	1962-63	Northern Districts
1933-34	Auckland	1963-64	Auckland
1934-35	Canterbury	1964-65	Canterbury
1935-36	Wellington	1965-66	Wellington
1936-37	Auckland	1966-67	Central Districts
1937-38	Auckland	1967-68	Central Districts
1938-39	Auckland	1968-69	Auckland
1939-40	Auckland	1969-70	Otago
1945-46	Canterbury	1970-71	Central Districts
1946-47	Auckland	1971-72	Otago
1947-48	Otago	1972-73	Wellington
1948-49	Canterbury	1973-74	Wellington
1949-50	Wellington	1974-75	Otago
1950-51	Otago		

The Plunket Shield was then superseded by the Shell Cup and the Shell Trophy.
CUP WINNERS

1975-76	Canterbury	1977-78	Canterbury
1976-77	Northern Districts	1978-79	Otago

The Shell Cup was then transferred to one-day competition.
SHELL TROPHY WINNERS

1975-76	Canterbury	1980-81	Auckland
1976-77	Otago	1981-82	Wellington
1977-78	Auckland	1982-83	Wellington
1978-79	Otago	1983-84	Canterbury
1979-80	Northern Districts	1984-85	Wellington

INDEX OF PLAYERS

Figures in **bold type** refer to a player's main entry; figures in *italic type* refer to a caption reference

ACKNOWLEDGEMENTS
Some parts of this book are taken from earlier Marshall Cavendish publications. Part 1, The History of
Cricket, is an updated and enlarged version of chapters from *The Story of Cricket* by Robin Marlar (1979).
Some of the material in the Test Match Cricket and The World Cup sections in Part II and the whole or parts
of some biographies in Part III are from *The Illustrated History of Test Cricket*, edited by Martin Tyler and
David Frith with statistics by Irving Rosenwater (reprinted 1979), some of which was first published in the
partwork *The Game*.

Picture credits: Africamera 136TR, 136/37, 137TL, 138; Associated Press 72T, 136TL & BL, 137BR, 140C,
151B, 155T, 159T & B, 160T, 162, 166T & B, 167T, 219BR; Australian News & Information Bureau 137CR;
Barnaby's Picture Library 206; Bridgeman Art Library 10, 14/15, 22/23, 26/27, 30, 31; Colorsport 32/33,
54, 59T, 213B, 214L, 241T, 286, 294, 295R; Patrick Eagar 4, 6, 16, 40, 43, 44, 45, 47T, 49, 51, 52, 53, 56, 58,
60B, 60/61, 62, 63, 78BL, 79T, 78/79, 79BR, 80T & B, 81BL & BR, 82B, 83T & B, 84T & B, 85T & B, 86T &
B, 87, 88, 89, 90, 91, 92, 93B, 106, 107B, 108T, 109, 110T & B, 111, 112, 115, 116T, C & B, 117T, 118, 119,
120B, 122B, 123B, 124TL, TR & B, 125T & B, 126, 126/27, 128, 129, 130/31, 132T, 132/33, 133, 134, 142T &
B, 144/45, 145T & B, 146T & B, 147, 148, 153, 154, 155B, 156, 156/57, 158, 161, 164R, 167B, 168T & B, 171,
172/73, 174B, 177T & CR, 178T, 178/79, 179TL & BR, 180T & B, 181, 182/83, 184, 185, 186, 187, 188T & B,
189L & R, 190, 191, 192, 193, 194, 195, 196, 204R, 205, 207L & R, 210, 211, 212, 217, 218, 229, 230, 232, 233,
236, 237, 239, 246, 247, 250B, 251, 252T & B, 253, 254, 255T, 259, 260, 262, 263L & R, 265, 266, 271T, 273,
275L & R, 277, 278T, 279, 280L & R, 281, 282, 288/89, 289B, 290, 291, 295L, 297, 298, 310T & B, 312, 315,
316, 317; Mary Evans' Picture Library 17, 67B, 94, 234; Sue Gooders 235BL; Ray Green 174TL & TR,
285TR; Herald-Sun 139; G.G.R. Hofmeister 272B; Indian Express Newspapers 164L; Indian High
Commission 61T & B, 121T, 170; Ken Kelly 29, 107T, 108B, 123T, 132B, 143, 149R, 169, 174C, 175T,
177BL, 214R, 231R, 250T, 255B, 276, 278B, 287T; The Mansell Collection 11L & R, 18/19, 24L & R, 25,
28/29, 34T & B, 37L, 94 inset L, R & B; Marylebone Cricket Club 7, 47BL, 64 (Chris Benfield), 68B, 94 inset
C; Melbourne Herald 238R; News Ltd of Australia 117B, 231BL; New Zealand Airlines 60T; New Zealand
High Commission 113RC, 150; Nottinghamshire Cricket Club 36, 198, 199TL, TR, BL & BR, 200L, C & R,
201L & R, 202L, TR & BR, 203TL, R & C, 204L, 301L & R, 302, 307TL, TR & B; The Photo Source/Central
Press 72B, 73T, 76B, 77, 97C, 98/99T, 100B, 103B, 105, 122T, 131B, 141BL, 160B, 219T & BL, 220TL, TR,
BL & BC, 221T, 222C & B, 224L & R, 225L & R, 226 L & R, 228T, BL & BR, 240R, 241BR, 242, 245TL & BL,
248T & B, 249T & B, 256BL & BR, 257L, 261R, 267, 269B, 270T, 272T, 274L, 283TL, TR & B, 284, 285TL,
288T & B, 292B, 296T; The Photo Source/Fox Photos 73B, 74T, 75B, 102BR, 140T, 208T, 245TR, 268T,
292T; The Photo Source/Keystone 76T, 82T, 113T, 137TR, 177BR, 209L & R, 216T, 221B, 296B;
Popperfoto 103T, 220BR, 240L, 258, 261L, 268B; Press Association 46L, 70B, 95B, 102BL, 113LC & B,
149L, 222T, 238L, 244, 245BR, 269T, 293L; Radio Times Hulton Picture Library 37R, 46R, 60C, 64/65, 65T
& CL, 66T & B, 67T, 68T & C, 69T & B, 71T, C & B, 95T, 98/99B, 120T, 135, 235TL, TR & BR, 243R; Ann
Ronan Picture Library 12, 38; Sport & General Press Agency 47BR, 48, 78T, 93T, 96, 96/97 inset, 96/97,
100T, 104T & B, 114T & B, 121B, 141T, 213R, 215T, 223T, 227L & R, 241BL, 243L, 256T, 257TR & BR,
264L & R, 270B, 271B, 274R, 285B, 293R; Sportography 130B; Syndication International 102T, 175B, 208B,
287B; Topix 97B, 215B, 216B; Transworld (Gerry Cranham) 223B; Roy Ullyet 75T; U.P.I. 74B, 81T, 140BL,
141BR, 151T, 152, 163T & B, 165, 176T & B, 179TR & CR.